FROM JOSHUA TO CAIAPHAS

FROM JOSHUA TO CAIAPHAS

High Priests after the Exile

James C. VanderKam

Fortress Press
Minneapolis, U.S.A.

Van Gorcum
Assen, the Netherlands

FROM JOSHUA TO CAIAPHAS
High Priests after the Exile

Cover image: © The Israel Museum, Jerusalem. Inscribed pomegranate, Ivory, Jerusalem, 8th cent. B.C.E. Used by permission of The Israel Museum, Jerusalem.
Cover: Ann Delgehausen
Typesetting and book design: HK Scriptorium

Library of Congress Cataloging-in-Publication Data

VanderKam, James C.
    From Joshua to Caiaphas : high priests after the Exile / James VanderKam.
        p. cm.
    Includes bibliographical references (p.) and index.
    ISBN 0-8006-2617-6 (alk. paper)
    1. Jewish high priests—History. 2. Jews—History—586 B.C.-70 A.D. I. Title.
BM651.V36 2004
296.4'95—dc22

                                                                    2004011406

ISBN 0-8006-2617-6 (Fortress Press)
ISBN 90 232 4074 X (Van Gorcum)

The paper used in this publication meets the minimum requirements of American National Standard for Information Sciences—Permanence of Paper for Printed Library Materials, ANSI Z329.48-1984.
Manufactured in the U.S.A.
08   07   06   05   04   1   2   3   4   5   6   7   8   9   10

Contents

Preface

The plan to write a history of the Second-Temple Jewish high priests took shape in the 1980s. Reading the literature from and about that period discloses that the high priests were prominent actors in events—think of the Hasmoneans like Jonathan and Simon, for example. Modern scholars often write that the high priests were not only the religious leaders of the Jewish nation but were also its civil heads. With the disappearance of rulers from David's line after Zerubbabel, we are told, a political vacuum resulted, and the high priests came naturally to fill the void. There were exceptions (for example, when Nehemiah was governor), but, in time, the high priests became the heads of state.

It was surprising to discover that, though the high priests were undoubtedly central figures in Second-Temple times, the full list of them has rarely if ever been the subject of a comprehensive history. There are, of course, studies of individual high priests or of several of them, but no one, to my knowledge, has surveyed the information about all fifty-one of them. The distinguished historian of the Seleucid Empire, Edwyn Bevan, may seem to be an exception. He wrote a short book entitled *Jerusalem under the High Priests*, but, as the subtitle says, it consists of *Five Lectures on the Period between Nehemiah and the New Testament*.[1] These lectures he considered introductory in nature and directed to a wider audience,[2] and in them he has little to say about the high priests. The title of his book defines a historical period, not the content. Some standard handbooks offer information about many of the high priests; an example is Emil Schürer's invaluable *The History of the Jewish People in the Age of Jesus Christ*. The chronological limits of Schürer's coverage were, however, from 175 BCE to 135 CE; as a result, he did not deal with the high priests from the first three and one-half centuries of the Second-Temple era. Similarly, Joachim Jeremias's *Jerusalem in the Time of Jesus* includes much helpful infor-

---

1. Edwyn Robert Bevan, *Jerusalem under the High Priests: Five Lectures on the Period between Nehemiah and the New Testament* (London: Arnold, 1904; reprinted 1952).

2. Ibid., iv.

mation about high priests but only from the general time in which he was most interested.

Failure to treat the subject of the Second-Temple high priests could at one time have been attributed to the general neglect of the so-called intertestamental period, but the situation has not changed even with the tremendous surge of interest in early Judaism during the last half century. In view of this fact and the relative importance of the subject, it seemed appropriate to write such a history.

Work on the project began in the late 1980s, with the first results being a series of articles on smaller topics (see the bibliography). Although a considerable amount of progress was made during that period, circumstances were soon to dictate that the project be shelved from 1991 until 2002. With all the turmoil surrounding the glacial pace at which the Dead Sea Scrolls were being published and my appointment to the editorial team, work on the nonbiblical texts from Qumran for publication in the Discoveries in the Judaean Desert series had to take priority.

It was not possible to return to the history of the high priests until the spring term of 2002, when I offered a doctoral seminar on the subject—an occasion that jump-started the delayed research and allowed me to revisit what I had done about a decade earlier. It also provided the opportunity to update, revise, and present my findings and to receive suggestions and critiques from a talented group of younger scholars.

Researching and writing the history has surfaced a host of challenging problems. Foremost has been the key question in any historical work—the nature and extent of the sources. The character of the surviving material may, in fact, supply the reason why scholars have not written a history of these high priests. Of course, no ancient writer composed what would qualify as a work of scientific historiography today, and therefore one has no choice but to make do with what is available, realizing that the texts were probably not written to answer our sorts of questions. While that is a general problem for historians, the range and difficulty of the sources available for the Second-Temple high priests are daunting indeed. There are texts in the Hebrew Bible (narratives and lists in Ezra and Nehemiah, prophecies in Haggai and Zechariah), novel-like books such as Judith, documentary papyri from Elephantine, the *Letter of Aristeas*, the Wisdom of Jesus Son of Sirach, the books of Maccabees, fragmentary scrolls from Qumran, the New Testament Gospels and Acts, rabbinic works (Mishnah, talmuds, Tosefta), inscriptions and citations from ancient authors, not to mention archeological data such as bullae and coins. But most of all there is Josephus, who alone covers, in a fashion, the entire period insofar as his limited sources and his purposes permitted. The Flavian historian is both fascinating and frustrating, but without his writings it would not be possible even to attempt the history contained in these pages. Josephus wrote a lot, and there is an immense amount of secondary literature on him and his histories, *The Jewish War* and *Jewish Antiquities*. His major biases are familiar, but how far they affected his treatment, especially of the pre-Herodian period, is debatable. Nevertheless, for better or for worse, Josephus is a huge part of this history. Shaye Cohen once referred to Schürer's *The History of the Jewish People in the Age of Jesus Christ* and some more recent histories as "paraphrases of Josephus with footnotes."[3] I hope not to have written another of those paraphrases, but it is difficult to be entirely innocent of doing so when working with this period.

To deal adequately with the complexities of the sources would require at least a book of its own. In the present work, I have not entered into extended analyses of the nature of the individual sources, although the issue surfaces regularly. Often, as it turns out, we lack an adequate basis for determining the historical reliability of what we are told. Yet, much can still be said about the period. I have endeavored to be fair and sensitive to the character of the texts and artifacts—to evaluate them for what they seem to be—and have tried not to dismiss too quickly the claims made about high priests in texts that appear to be nonhistorical in genre. Historical facts can turn up in strange places. It would be wonderful if all assertions in the sources could be assessed against another source or two, but for sizable stretches of our period we lack information altogether, and for much of it we have only Josephus's writings. Then, too, having more than one source does not necessarily solve our problems. When *War* and *Antiquities* disagree, the more likely claim may not be obvious. Even familiar sources, ones that have been endlessly researched such as the Gospels, may leave one puzzled. An example is the expression "the high priesthood of Annas and Caiaphas," in Luke 3:2. What can this mean when other texts give us no reason to think individuals shared the office?

The primary purpose of this history of the high priests in the Second-Temple age has been to gather and assess all of the available information about each one of them, from Joshua in the late sixth century BCE to Phannias during the Jewish revolt against Rome (66–70 CE). A secondary aim has been to investigate the status of these high-ranking officials—specifically whether they also wielded civic authority. Since we are dealing with a span of some six centuries when circumstances changed many times, distinctions must be

---

3. "The Political and Social History of the Jews in Greco-Roman Antiquity: The State of the Question," in *Early Judaism and Its Modern Interpreters,* ed. Robert Kraft and George W. E. Nickelsburg, *The Bible and Its Modern Interpreters* (Atlanta: Scholars; Philadelphia: Fortress Press, 1986), 41.

made. In some periods, we have evidence for the presence of both high priests and governors (or the like); for others, we do not. We can summarize the results as follows.

1. *Persian period (538 or 516–15 to 330 BCE)*: At several points, the sources name high priests and governors who served at the same time (other than the first term of Nehemiah, we do not know how long any of these officials held office):

   • Joshua and Zerubbabel
   • Joakim
   • Eliashib and Nehemiah
   • Joiada
   • Johanan and Bigvai/Bagohi
   • Jaddua and Hezekiah (?)

   So, for these centuries (or rather, parts of them), it is likely the high priest, whatever the extent of his responsibilities, did not exercise supreme political control. The case of Jaddua is more complicated, but Hezekiah (known from coins) may have been the governor during some of his high priesthood.

2. *Early Hellenistic period (330–152 BCE)*: For these years, we have no firm evidence of a Jewish or foreign governor alongside the high priest. The few surviving texts regarding the third century picture the high priest in contact with foreign monarchs; he conducts affairs of state besides carrying out his cultic functions. Unfortunately, our evidence for the period is such that caution is strongly advisable. It is difficult to know, for instance, what value to attribute to claims about the Areus (a Spartan king)-Onias (a high priest) correspondence. We may safely say that there is no indication of an office of governor in Jerusalem and some evidence, however shaky, for high priests who ruled the state.

3. *The Hasmonean period (152–37 BCE)*: When the Hasmonean family assumed the high priesthood, the offices of high priest and head of state were undoubtedly unified in one person. This was the case from Jonathan's appointment (152 BCE) until the death of Alexander Jannaeus (76 BCE). For most of the reign of Salome Alexandra (76–67 BCE), the offices were separated: she was the queen and her son Hyrcanus II was the high priest. Late in her reign, the two crowns were reunited when Hyrcanus became king. His brother Aristobulus II soon took both offices from him (in 67 BCE), only to lose them when Pompey captured

Jerusalem and Rome imposed a new order (63 BCE). The great general reinstated Hyrcanus in the high priesthood; the latter also ruled in various civil capacities, including that of ethnarch, in the following twenty-four years despite the growing power of the Antipatrids. From 40 to 37 BCE, Antigonus was both high priest and king, but after his execution no one ever again combined the two offices.

4. *The Herodian period (37 BCE to 70 CE)*: During this time, a series of rulers, whether from the family of Herod or other Roman officials (prefects, procurators, and legates), ruled the state and appointed high priests who, while at times influential in political affairs, held no governmental office.

This is the picture that, in my estimation, emerges from the sources. Deborah Rooke, in her recent book, *Zadok's Heirs: The Role and Development of the High Priesthood in Ancient Israel*, has reached rather different conclusions.[4] For her, the postexilic high priests were more insignificant figures who did not rule the Jewish state. She thinks the situation changed in 175 BCE, when high priests assumed governmental responsibilities, but even the Hasmoneans, she argues, regarded themselves as rulers first and high priests second—a surprising inference, judging, for example, from their coins, which consistently list the high priesthood first. I do believe she has raised important questions regarding the common view of high priests as rulers throughout long stretches of the Second-Temple period but finally think she has overstated her case and misconstrued some of the evidence.

It is worth emphasizing what this book is and is not. It is a history of the Second-Temple *high* priests; it is not a history of the *priesthood*. As a result, there is no discussion of thorny issues such as the origin of the Aaronides. Also, I do not examine First-Temple phenomena (Rooke, for one, analyzes the evidence about the leading priests in Solomon's temple). The book is not primarily a history of the Second-Temple period, although the history regularly impinges on the narrative and provides the organizing principle of the presentation.

Because the history covers so much, it would be naive to claim I have read everything. But a concerted effort was made to include as much as was feasible and useful. The manuscript was completed in mid-2003. For that reason it was not possible to incorporate publications that came to my attention later. I regret that I could not use Helen K. Bond, *Caiaphas: Friend of Rome and Judge of Jesus?* (Louisville: Westminster John Knox, 2004). Also, Miriam Pucci Ben

---

4. Deborah W. Rooke, *Zadok's Heirs: The Role and Development of the High Priesthood in Ancient Israel,* OTM (Oxford: Oxford Univ. Press, 2000).

Zeev, Jewish Rights in the Roman World: The Greek and Roman Documents Quoted by Josephus Flavius (TSAJ 74; Tübingen: Mohr/Siebeck, 1998) came to my attention too late to include. The views defended in the book, however, agree with those she put forth in a series of articles which are treated. Unfortunately, it was also not possible to incorporate Christopher J. Seeman's impressive analysis of Hasmonean Judea's relations with Rome ("Rome and Judaea in Transition"[Ph.D. diss., University of California, Berkeley, 2002]).

I have received generous amounts of help in writing the book. Besides the inspiration of teachers such as Frank Moore Cross who has articulated his own views about the early Second-Temple high priests, others have also contributed in various ways. In particular, I wish to thank the students who have aided in moving the work along and in tracking down sources and secondary material. The participants in the seminar mentioned above were: Amy Donaldson, Brian Gregg, Paul Kim, Tae Hun (Taylor) Kim, Brad Milunski, Sam Thomas, and Steve Schweitzer. Each one was a helpful reader and critic. Alas, calmer judgment prevailed so that their ideas for catchy titles for the book had to be rejected. Paul Kim and Sam Thomas continued to help with the project after the seminar was completed. In more recent times other graduate assistants have contributed their skills. Angela Kim proofread the text and also compiled the bibliography. Alison Schofield offered insightful comments on the manuscript and helped in investigating some questions concerning Zadokites; and Ardea Russo has carefully worked through the entire set of galleys. Amy Donaldson and Alison Schofield also labored diligently and mightily in preparing the indexes and reading the proofs. To all of these young scholars I offer hearty thanks.

The staff at Fortress Press has furnished valued services. Special mention goes to Marshall D. Johnson who years ago offered a contract for publication of the book; to K.C. Hanson who worked meticulously through the manuscript; and to James Korsmo who has handled the final stages of corrections and revisions.

Finally, it is a truly pleasant duty to thank the National Endowment for the Humanities for the support it offered at an early stage in the project. An NEH Fellowship for the academic year 1989-90 freed the time to make major strides in advancing the research. The NEH, which has provided noble support for work on many projects such as the official publications of the Dead Sea Scrolls, has been crucial in making this book possible. I am once more profoundly grateful for the Endowment's support.

Abbreviations

Ancient

1QHᵃ	*Hodayotᵃ* (Hymn Scroll)
1QpHab	*Pesher Habakkuk*
4Q163	Isaiah Pesherᶜ (4QpIsaᶜ)
4Q167	Hosea Pesherᵇ (4QpHosᵇ)
4Q169	Nahum Pesher (4QpNah)
4Q171	Psalms Pesherᵃ (4QPsᵃ)
4Q175	4QTestimonia (4QTest)
4Q177	4QCatenaᵃ
4Q243	4Qpseudo-Danielᵃ ar
4Q244	4Qpseudo-Danielᵇ ar
4Q245	4Qpseudo-Danielᶜ ar (4QpsDanᶜ ar)
4Q266-73	Damascus Document (4QDamascus Documentᵃ⁻ʰ)
4Q331	4Q papHistorical Text C
4Q348	4QDeed B heb?
4Q448	4QApocryphal Psalm and Prayer
4Q468e	4QHistorical Text F
4Q523	4QJonathan
4QMMT	4QHalakhic Letter (4Q394-399)
4QpHosᵇ	Hosea Pesherᵇ (4Q167)
4QpIsaᶜ	Isaiah Pesherᶜ (4Q163)
4QpNah	Nahum Pesher (4Q169)
4QpPsᵃ	4QPsalms Pesherᵃ (4Q171)
4QpsDanᶜ ar	4Qpseudo-Danielᶜ ar (4Q245)
4QTest	4Q175 (4QTestimonia)
11Q19	Temple Scroll (11QTᵃ)
11QTᵃ	Temple Scroll (11Q19)
Ag. Ap.	Josephus, *Against Apion*
Ant.	Josephus, *The Jewish Antiquities*
b.	Babylonian Talmud (*Bavli*)
b.	ben or bar (son of)

B. Bat.	*Baba Batra*
BCE	before the Common Era
Bek.	*Bekhorot*
Ber.	*Berakhot*
ca.	*circa*
CD	*Damascus Document* from the Cairo Genizah
CE	Common Era
Gen. Rab.	*Genesis Rabbah*
Giṭ.	*Giṭṭin*
Heb.	Hebrew
Hor.	*Horayot*
J.W.	Josephus, *The Jewish War*
Ker.	*Kerithot*
Ketub.	*Ketubbot*
Lam. Rab.	*Lamentations Rabbah*
LXX	Septuagint
m.	*Mishnah*
Ma'aś. Š.	*Ma'aśer Šeni*
Meg.	*Megillah*
Menaḥ.	*Menaḥoth*
MS, MSS	manuscript(s)
MT	Masoretic text
Nid.	*Niddah*
Pesaḥ.	*Pesaḥim*
Qidd.	*Qiddušin*
R.	Rabbi
Sanh.	*Sanhedrin*
Sheqal.	*Sheqalim*
Spec. Laws	Philo, *The Special Laws*
Sukk.	*Sukkah*
t.	Tosefta
Tg. Onq.	*Targum Onqelos*
Tg. Ps.-J.	*Targum Pseudo-Jonathan*
T. Levi	*Testament of Levi*
T. Reu.	*Testament of Reuben*
TS	Temple Scroll (11Q19 or 11QT[a])
T. Sim.	*Testament of Simeon*
y.	Jerusalem Talmud *(Yerushalmi)*
Yad.	*Yadayim*
Yebam.	*Yebamot*

Modern

AASOR	Annual of the American Schools of Oriental Research
AB	Anchor Bible
ABD	*Anchor Bible Dictionary,* ed. David Noel Freedman, 6 vols., 1992
ABR	*Australian Biblical Review*
ABRL	Anchor Bible Reference Library
AGJU	Arbeiten zur Geschichte des antiken Judentums und des Urchristentums
AGRL	Aspects of Greek and Roman Life
AIPHOS	*Annuaire de l'Institut de philologie et d'histoire orientales et slaves*
AJSR	*Association for Jewish Studies Review*
AJBA	*Australian Journal of Biblical Archaeology*
AnBib	Analecta biblica
ANET	*Ancient Near Eastern Texts Relating to the Old Testament,* 3rd ed., ed. James B. Pritchard, 1969
AP	document numbers from *Aramaic Papyri of the Fifth Century B.C.,* ed. A. E. Cowley, 1923
APOT	*Apocrypha and Pseudepigrapha of the Old Testament in English,* ed. R. H. Charles, 2 vols., 1913
ASOR	American Schools of Oriental Research
ATD	Das Alte Testament Deutsch
AUSS	*Andrews University Seminary Studies*
BA	*Biblical Archaeologist* (continued as *Near Eastern Archaeology)*
BAG	Walter Bauer, William F. Arndt, and F. Wilbur Gingrich, *Greek-English Lexicon of the New Testament and Other Early Christian Literature,* 1957
BAR	*Biblical Archaeology Review*
BASOR	*Bulletin of the American Schools of Oriental Research*
BDB	Francis Brown, S. R. Driver, and Charles A. Briggs, *A Hebrew and English Lexicon of the Old Testament,* 1907
BDF	Friedrich Blass, Albert Debrunner, and Robert W. Funk, *A Greek Grammar of the New Testament and Other Early Christian Literature,* 1961
BHT	Beiträge zur historischen Theologie
Bib	*Biblica*

BibIntSer	Biblical Interpretation Series
BJRL	*Bulletin of the John Rylands University Library of Manchester*
BJS	Brown Judaic Studies
BJSUCSD	Biblical and Judaic Studies from the University of California, San Diego
BM	*Bet Miqra*
BRS	Biblical Resource Series
BSJS	Brill's Series in Jewish Studies
BTT	Blackwell's Theological Texts
BZNW	Beihefte zur Zeitschrift für die neutestamentliche Wissenschaft
CBQ	*Catholic Biblical Quarterly*
CBQMS	Catholic Biblical Quarterly Monograph Series
CHJ	*The Cambridge History of Judaism,* ed. W. D. Davies and Louis Finkelstein, 1984–
CP	*Classical Philology*
CRINT	Compendia rerum iudaicarum ad Novum Testamentum
CSCT	Columbia Studies in the Classical Tradition
DJD	Discoveries in the Judaean Desert
DSD	*Dead Sea Discoveries*
DTTBY	*A Dictionary of the Targumim, the Talmud Babli and Yerushalmi, and the Midrashic Literature,* ed. Marcus Jastrow, 2 vols., 1903
EAEHL	*Encyclopedia of Archaeological Excavations in the Holy Land,* ed. Michael Avi-Yonah and Ephraim Stern, 4 vols., 1975
EBib	*Études bibliques*
EDSS	*Encyclopedia of the Dead Sea Scrolls,* ed. Lawrence H. Schiffman and James C. VanderKam, 2 vols., 2000
ErIsr	*Eretz-Israel*
ET	English translation
ETL	*Ephemerides theologicae lovanienses*
FB	Forschung zur Bibel
FRLANT	Forschungen zur Religion und Literatur des Alten und Neuen Testaments
GPT	Growing Points in Theology
HALOT	*The Hebrew and Aramaic Lexicon of the Old Testament,* ed. Ludwig Köhler, Walter Baumgartner, and J. J. Stamm, 4 vols., 1994–99
HAT	Handbuch zum Alten Testament
HCS	Hellenistic Culture and Society

HCOT	Historical Commentary on the Old Testament
Heb.	Hebrew
Hen	Henoch
HeyJ	*Heythrop Journal*
HKAT	Handkommentar zum Alten Testament
HRCS	Edwin Hatch and Henry A. Redpath, *Concordance to the Septuagint and Other Greek Versions of the Old Testament*, 2 vols., 1897; Supplement, 1906; reprinted 3 vols. in 2, 1983
HSCP	*Harvard Studies in Classical Philology*
HSM	Harvard Semitic Monographs
HSS	Harvard Semitic Series
HTR	*Harvard Theological Review*
HUCA	*Hebrew Union College Annual*
IAA Reports	Israel Antiquities Authority Reports
ICC	International Critical Commentary
IDB	*Interpreter's Dictionary of the Bible*, ed. George A. Buttrick, 4 vols., 1962
IDBSup	*Interpreter's Dictionary of the Bible, Supplementary Volume*, ed. Keith Crim, 1976
IEJ	*Israel Exploration Journal*
IES	Israel Exploration Society
Int	*Interpretation*
JBL	*Journal of Biblical Literature*
JCMAMW	Jews, Christians, and Muslims from the Ancient to the Modern World
JDS	Judean Desert Studies
JJS	*Journal of Jewish Studies*
JNES	*Journal of Near Eastern Studies*
JQR	*Jewish Quarterly Review*
JSHRZ	Jüdische Schriften aus hellenistisch-römischer Zeit
JSJ	*Journal for the Study of Judaism*
JSJSup	Journal for the Study of Judaism Supplements
JSNTSup	Journal for the Study of the New Testament Supplement Series
JSOT	*Journal for the Study of the Old Testament*
JSOTSup	Journal for the Study of the Old Testament Supplement Series
JSP	*Journal for the Study of the Pseudepigrapha*
JSPSup	Journal for the Study of the Pseudepigrapha Supplement Series

JSS	*Journal of Semitic Studies*
JTS	*Journal of Theological Studies*
LCL	Loeb Classical Library
LSJ	Henry George Liddell, Robert Scott, and Henry Stuart Jones, *A Greek-English Lexicon,* 9th ed. with revised supplement, 1996
MGWJ	*Monatschrift für Geschichte und Wissenschaft des Judentums*
NCB	New Century Bible
NEA	*Near Eastern Archaeology* (formerly *Biblical Archaeologist*)
NEAEHL	*New Encyclopedia of Archaeological Excavations in the Holy Land,* ed. Ephraim Stern, 4 vols., 1993
NICOT	New International Commentary on the Old Testament
NovTSup	Novum Testamentum Supplements
NRSV	New Revised Standard Version of the Bible
NTS	*New Testament Studies*
OTL	Old Testament Library
OTM	Oxford Theological Monographs
OTP	*Old Testament Pseudepigrapha,* ed. James H. Charlesworth, 2 vols., 1983–85
PAAJR	*Proceedings of the American Academy of Jewish Research*
PEQ	*Palestine Exploration Quarterly*
PW	*Paulys Realencyclopädie der classischen Altertumswissenschaft,* ed. August Friedrich von Pauly, new edition, ed. Georg Wissowa, 49 vols., 1980
Qad	*Qadmoniot*
RB	*Revue biblique*
REJ	*Revue des études juives*
RevQ	*Revue de Qumran*
SAOC	Studies in Ancient Oriental Civilizations
SBL	Society of Biblical Literature
SBLDS	Society of Biblical Literature Dissertation Series
SBLEJL	Society of Biblical Literature Early Judaism and Its Literature
SBLSBS	Society of Biblical Literature Sources for Biblical Studies
SBLSCS	Society of Biblical Literature Septuagint and Cognate Studies Series
SBLTT	Society of Biblical Literature Texts and Translations
SBT	Studies in Biblical Theology
SC	Sources chrétiennes
S.E.	Seleucid Era

SFSHJ	South Florida Studies in the History of Judaism
SFSMD	Studi Francisci Scholten Memoriae Dicata
SHAW	Sitzungsberichte der heidelberger Akademie der Wissenschaften, Philosophisch-historische Klasse
SJLA	Studies in Judaism in Late Antiquity
SOTSMS	Society for Old Testament Studies Monograph Series
SPNT	Studies on Personalities of the New Testament
SSN	Studia semitica neerlandica
ST	*Studia theologica*
STDJ	Studies on the Texts of the Desert of Judah
StPB	Studia Post-Biblica
SVTP	Studia in Veteris Testamenti pseudepigrapha
TAD	document numbers from *Textbook of Aramaic Documents,* ed. Bezalel Porten and Ada Yardeni, 1986–
TDNT	*Theological Dictionary of the New Testament,* ed. Gerhard Kittel and Gerhard Friedrich, trans. G. W. Bromiley, 10 vols., 1964–76
TDOT	*Theological Dictionary of the Old Testament,* ed. Johannes G. Botterweck and Helmer Ringgren, trans. J. T. Willis, G. W. Bromiley, and D. Green, 13 vols., 1974–
TGUOS	Transactions of the Glasgow University Oriental Society
TLZ	*Theologische Literaturzeitung*
TOTC	Tyndale Old Testament Commentaries
TSAJ	Texte und Studien zum antiken Judentum
TynBul	*Tyndale Bulletin*
VT	*Vetus Testamentum*
VTSup	Vetus Testamentum Supplements
WBC	Word Biblical Commentary
WD	Wadi Daliyeh
WDSP	document numbers from Wadi Daliyeh Samaria Papyri
WUNT	Wissenschaftliche Untersuchungen zum Neuen Testament
WWSS	Word and World Supplement Series
ZAW	*Zeitschrift für die alttestamentliche Wissenschaft*
ZDPV	*Zeitschrift des deutschen Palästina-Vereins*
ZNW	*Zeitschrift für die neutestamentliche Wissenschaft*

1

Beginnings

Biblical records trace the origins of the postexilic Jewish high priesthood to Joshua (or Jeshua), a returnee from Babylonian exile and a descendant of the last high priest of the First Temple. The first task facing Joshua and other leaders upon arriving at Jerusalem was to build a temple where sacrificial worship of Israel's God could resume. In this chapter, we will review the evidence for the first high priest, Joshua, and the temple at which perhaps he and certainly his descendants served.

Cyrus's Proclamation and the Jewish Response

All sources trace the beginnings of the Second Temple to the early part of the Persian period in Jewish history. The biblical histories attribute the inception of the movement that produced the new temple to a proclamation issued by King Cyrus in the first year of his rule over Babylon (539–538 BCE; see 2 Chr 36:22; Ezra 1:1; 5:13; compare 6:3). Even before that year, the anonymous prophet whom scholars call the Second Isaiah had quoted the word of the Lord "who says of Cyrus, 'He is my shepherd, and he shall carry out all my purpose'; and who says of Jerusalem, 'It shall be rebuilt,' and of the temple, 'Your foundation shall be laid'" (44:28). This Cyrus of prophecy, in his first year, "sent a herald throughout all his kingdom and also declared in a written edict" (2 Chr 36:22; Ezra 1:1):

> Thus says King Cyrus of Persia: The LORD, the God of heaven, has given me all the kingdoms of the earth, and he has charged me to build him a house at Jerusalem, which is in Judah. Whoever is among

1

you of all his people, may [+ the Lord (2 Chr 36:23)] his God be with him! Let him go up [2 Chr 36:23 ends] to Jerusalem in Judah, and rebuild the house of the Lord, the God of Israel—he is the God who is in Jerusalem; and let all survivors, in whatever place they reside, be assisted by the people of their place with silver and gold, with goods and with animals, besides freewill offerings for the house of God in Jerusalem. (Ezra 1:2-4)

Although for a long time scholars questioned the authenticity of Cyrus's proclamation, the tide turned in favor of its validity particularly with E. J. Bickerman's vigorous and learned demonstration that it was compatible with what is known from elsewhere about such edicts.[1] One of the major contributions that he made to the debate was to clarify the relationship between Ezra 1:2-4 and 6:3-5. The differences between these two versions of what Cyrus had ordered on behalf of the Jewish people had led noted experts such as Roland de Vaux to argue that the Aramaic document in Ezra 6:3-5 was authentic but that the Hebrew text in 1:2-4 was not.[2] As Bickerman showed, however, the two differ because they are two distinct kinds of documents. They "are not two variants of the same record but two independent records concerning the same case."[3] The document in Ezra 1 is a "royal proclamation addressed to the Jews and published by heralds everywhere and in many languages, including Hebrew."[4] The text that is quoted in Ezra 6 within a document emanating from Darius's court is a "memorandum to the royal treasurer, in Aramaic, which was not made public at the time."[5] The latter was found filed away in Ecbatana some twenty years later when questions were raised about the legality of the Jewish temple-building enterprise (Ezra 6:2).

The proclamation in Ezra 1, which has also been defended as authentic by L. Hensley after a thorough examination of Persian epistolary style,[6] has often

---

1. "The Edict of Cyrus in Ezra 1," *JBL* 65 (1946): 249–75 (= his *Studies in Jewish and Christian History*, Part I [Leiden: Brill, 1976], 72–108 [references below are to this edition]). See also Jacob Liver, *Chapters in the History of the Priests and Levites: Studies on the Lists in Chronicles, Ezra, and Nehemiah,* Publications of the Perry Foundation for Biblical Research in the Hebrew University of Jerusalem (Jerusalem: Magnes, 1968 [Hebrew]), 77–81.

2. "Les décrets de Cyrus et de Darius sur la reconstruction du Temple," *RB* 46 (1937): 29–57.

3. "The Edict of Cyrus in Ezra 1," 73.

4. Ibid., 76.

5. Ibid. See also M. A. Dandamaev, *A Political History of the Achaemenid Empire* (Leiden: Brill, 1989), 63.

6. "The Official Persian Documents in the Book of Ezra" (Ph.D. diss., University of Liverpool, 1977), 211–16.

been treated as an illustration of the general policy that Cyrus pursued in connection with peoples who fell under his control. The famous Cyrus Cylinder describes the benevolent attitude of the great king toward those who were conquered and displaced. After he highlights the anger of Marduk at Nabonidus's neglect of his cult and his own peaceful entry into Babylon, Cyrus begins to speak in the first person about his piety toward Marduk and his care for the people of the god. Then follows his version of what he did for those whom he ruled:

> All the kings of the entire world from the Upper to the Lower Seas, those who are seated in throne rooms, (those who) live in other [types of buildings as well as] all the kings of the West land living in tents, brought their heavy tributes and kissed my feet in Babylon. (As to the region) from . . . as far as Ashur and Susa, Agade, Eshnunna, the towns Zamban, Me-turnu, Der as well as the region of the Gutians, I returned to (these) sacred cities on the other side of the Tigris, the sanctuaries of which have been ruins for a long time, the images which (used) to live therein and established for them permanent sanctuaries. I (also) gathered all their (former) inhabitants and returned (to them) their habitations. Furthermore, I resettled upon the command of Marduk, the great lord, all the gods of Sumer and Akkad whom Nabonidus has brought into Babylon to the anger of the lord of the gods, unharmed in their (former) chapels, the places which make them happy.[7]

Cyrus's mention of restored cultic paraphernalia, sanctuaries, and inhabitants closely resembles his order that Jewish exiles return to their land and city with the vessels of the First Temple (Ezra 1:7-11) and that they construct a new sanctuary.

Amélie Kuhrt has voiced several cautions about drawing direct parallels between the contents of the Cyrus Cylinder and the proclamation about the Jews.[8] She observes that the text, which may not articulate a general policy, relates especially to Marduk, Babylon, and its residents, that peoples and objects are returned to the gods' original cities, and that most of the locales listed are near or in Babylon.[9] She maintains that the document was composed to serve as a building text of the kind that was "generally placed as foundation

7. Translation of A. Leo Oppenheim in *ANET,* 316.
8. "The Cyrus Cylinder and Achaemenid Imperial Policy," *JSOT* 25 (1983): 83–97.
9. Ibid., 87–88.

deposits underneath or in the walls of buildings the construction or restoration of which they served to commemorate."[10] In fact, the Cyrus Cylinder is in several respects similar to what King Ashurbanipal of Assyria, who is mentioned in a new fragment from the end of the Cylinder, had written when he rebuilt Babylon and reinstated the cult of Marduk.[11] In this particular text, Cyrus, the Persian monarch, would appear to be following an older tradition and issuing the requisite propaganda to legitimate his acquisition of Babylon.[12] Concerning what relevance the text may have for Cyrus's treatment of the Jews, Kuhrt writes:

> What has emerged, however, rather tentatively is that Cyrus followed a policy similar to that of some earlier Assyrian rulers, whereby cities occupying a key-position in troublesome areas or areas where there was likely to be international conflict had their privileges and/ or exempt status reinstated and guaranteed by the central government. . . . With such a hypothesis in mind, one could envisage the Old Persian rulers encouraging the rebuilding of Jerusalem as part of a policy to establish support near a frontier in a sensitive zone (if one thinks of its proximity to Egypt) and bordering an area inhabited by the Arab tribes, a population group that had already presented problems of political control to imperial structures.[13]

Although she terms all of this highly speculative, it may be said that what is reported in Ezra 1:2-4 (and 6:3-5) is at least analogous to what Cyrus did in the region of Babylon, regardless of whether it was a general, empire-wide policy.[14]

The forms of Cyrus's communications respecting the Jews and the contents of these documents mirror what is known of official imperial style and Cyrus's policy toward other groups. These documents indicate that he specified three actions:

1. The temple was to be built in Jerusalem (2 Chr 36:23; Ezra 1:2; 6:3). Since the royal treasury was to bear the cost, the king specifies both the dimen-

---

10. Ibid., 88.

11. Ibid., 92.

12. Ibid., 93.

13. Ibid., 94.

14. See also Peter R. Ackroyd, *Exile and Restoration: A Study of Hebrew Thought of the Sixth Century B.C.* OTL (Philadelphia: Westminster, 1968), 140–41; J. Maxwell Miller and John H. Hayes, *A History of Ancient Israel and Judah* (Philadelphia: Westminster, 1986), 440–43; Peter Ross Bedford, *Temple Restoration in Early Achaemenid Judah*, JSJSup 65 (Leiden: Brill, 2001), 132–57.

sions (which are peculiar and presumably have been corrupted in the process of textual transmission)[15] and the building materials to be used (Ezra 6:3-4).
2. The exiles were permitted to return to Jerusalem, and they were entitled to the support of those living in the places of their exile (perhaps even non-Jews were included).[16]
3. The temple vessels, which had been taken by the Babylonians from the First Temple (2 Kgs 24:13; 25:14-15; 2 Chr 36:10, 18; Jer 28:3; Ezra 5:14), were retrieved and given to "Sheshbazzar the prince of Judah" (Ezra 1:8; see 1:7-11; 5:14-15; 6:5).

Cyrus's decree paved the way for rebuilding the temple, but it did not guarantee that the goal would be accomplished. All seems promising from Ezra 1 and 2 Chr 36:22-23—a note so positive that the latter work ends with it; nevertheless, the process of effecting the auspicious plan may have proved more difficult than was first envisaged. It should be recalled that the first Jerusalem temple was built with a massive expenditure of Solomon's royal revenues and with a huge labor pool over a seven-year period (1 Kings 5–7). The returning exiles may have had neither; their numbers were certainly limited, and there is no indication that they ever received imperial funds for their project. Moreover, clearing the temple site of its ruins, preparing the various levels of the foundations, and actually constructing the edifice were immense tasks. According to the book of Ezra, which is the primary narrative source for the period in question, Sheshbazzar transported the temple vessels "when the exiles were brought up from Babylonia to Jerusalem" (1:11). The first chapter of Ezra ends with this notice, and nothing more is said about Sheshbazzar or his accomplishments until later in the book. In Ezra 5, Tattenai, the governor of the province Beyond the River,[17] and his colleagues, after they inspected the building operation in Jerusalem in 520 BCE, requested that a search be made in the royal archives to check whether Cyrus had indeed authorized construction of this temple (5:3-17). In the letter that these officials sent to King Darius, they reported what the Jews had told them about the history of the rebuilding effort. The Jewish elders had mentioned Cyrus's decree and added:

15. Joseph Blenkinsopp, *Ezra-Nehemiah: A Commentary,* OTL (Philadelphia: Westminster, 1988), 125.
16. So Bickerman, "The Edict of Cyrus in Ezra 1," 86–91; see Kurt Galling, "Die Proklamation des Kyros in Esra 1," in idem, *Studien zur Geschichte Israels im persischen Zeitalter* (Tübingen: Mohr/Siebeck, 1964), 75–76.
17. For his appearance with this title in an extrabiblical document, see A. T. Olmstead, "Tattenai, Governor of 'Across the River,'" *JNES* 3 (1944): 46.

and they [the temple vessels] were delivered to a man named Shesh-bazzar, whom he [Cyrus] had made governor [פֶּחָה]; He said to him, "Take these vessels; go and put them in the temple in Jerusalem, and let the house of God be rebuilt on its site." Then this Sheshbazzar came and laid the foundations [יְהַב אֻשַּׁיָּא; compare 6:3] of the house of God in Jerusalem; and from that time until now it has been under construction, and it is not yet finished. (Ezra 5:14b-16)

Search was made, the Jewish claims were confirmed, and Darius ordered that the project be completed (Ezra 6:1-12).[18]

Sheshbazzar has been the subject of a long scholarly controversy. Who was he, and what did he accomplish, if anything? He is mentioned only in Ezra 1:8, 11; 5:14, 16; in none of these passages does one learn anything about his family connections. One reads only of his titles—"prince of Judah" (1:8) and "governor" (5:14)—and of his involvement with the return of the temple vessels (1:7-11) and with laying the foundation of the Second Temple (5:16). Because he does what Zerubbabel is later said to have done—laying the temple foundations (Hag 2:18; Zech 4:9)—and holds the same office (Hag 1:1, 14, and so forth), some have thought that he and Zerubbabel were the same man under two different names (compare 1 Esd 6:18 and Josephus, *Ant.* 11.1, 3 [§13], who practically identifies them because he has Cyrus writing about Zerubbabel)[19] or that they were different individuals who were confused by the editor of Ezra.[20] Neither of these extreme options commends itself, since neither of them accords with the evidence in the book of Ezra.

Eduard Meyer noted that in the Greek spellings of the name *Sheshbazzar,* the first element is regularly σαν-, not σεσ- (1 Esd 2:8, 11; 6:17, 19; Josephus, *Ant.* 11.4, 4 [§93]; 11.4, 6 [§101]; the LXX of Ezra-Nehemiah has σασ- or σαβ-).[21] He suggested that the original spelling was שנבצר, which may reflect the Babylonian name *sin-bal-uṣur* = "Sin protect the son" (for the element

18. Note that the document was found in Ecbatana in the province of Media. Cyrus spent some time there in 538 BCE when his wife, a Median princess, died and was buried in this city. For his stay in Ecbatana, see A. T. Olmstead, *History of the Persian Empire* (Chicago: Univ. of Chicago Press, 1948), 57–58.

19. For example, Heinrich Graetz, *History of the Jews,* vol. 1: *From the Earliest Period to the Death of Simon the Maccabee (135 B.C.E.)* (Philadelphia: Jewish Publication Society, 1891), 351–52.

20. Wilhelm Rudolph, *Esra und Nehemia samt 3. Esra,* HAT 20 (Tübingen: Mohr/Siebeck, 1949), 18, 62.

21. *Die Entstehung des Judentums: Eine historische Untersuchung* (Halle: Niemeyer, 1896), 76–77.

-*bal*-, see the spelling in the Lucianic manuscripts of LXX Ezra-Nehemiah). Meyer also accepted the proposal that this שנבצר was the son of the deported Judean king Jehoiachin, whose name appears in 1 Chr 3:18 as *Shenazzar*. If we make this identification, then the mystery about Sheshbazzar disappears: he was the son of the last true king of Judah—that is, the one through whom the royal line was traced (Zedekiah, Jehoiachin's uncle, was a Babylonian appointee, and his sons were executed [2 Kgs 25:7])—and thus a surviving member of David's line. Consequently, he would have been a natural candidate to lead the Judean exiles back to their homeland.

Although the identification of Sheshbazzar with Shenazzar has enjoyed impressive support (with most experts assuming that the underlying Babylonian name was *sin-ab-uṣur*), it has more recently encountered strong opposition. P.-R. Berger has argued that the identification ought not to be accepted because the letters שש in Hebrew transcribe the name of the sun god Shamash[22] (the spelling *shassu* is attested).[23] Hence, *Sheshbazzar* means: Shamash protect the father; and this is a different name than the one in 1 Chr 3:18. On this view, the identity of Sheshbazzar remains a mystery.

It is not so clear, however, that Berger has refuted a connection between Sheshbazzar and Shenazzar. The main objection is that he has not convincingly explained the consistent early Greek reproductions of *Sheshbazzar* as σαναβασσαρος, which more closely resembles the spelling in 1 Chr 3:18 (LXX σανεσαρ).[24] If the spelling in 1 Esdras is more original, it would enhance the argument for identifying the two. In addition, the next man to hold the office of governor in Judea—Zerubbabel—was certainly a member of the same royal line as Shenazzar (see 1 Chr 3:18-19; Shenazzar was his uncle). Sara Japhet, who has noted these previous points, has also observed that among the leaders named in Ezra-Nehemiah, Sheshbazzar alone appears without a patronym. She suspects that the author omitted it deliberately in order not to call attention to his Davidic connections. This would be in harmony with his tendency not to stress leaders and titles.[25] Thus, despite a recent inclination to

---

22. "Zu den Namen ששבצר und שנאצר (Esr 1 8.11 5 14.16 bzw. 1 Chr 3 18)," *ZAW* 83 (1971): 98–100.

23. For a West Semitic example, see Paul Eugène Dion, "ששבצר und סנורי," *ZAW* 95 (1983): 111–12.

24. Jacob Liver (*The House of David from the Fall of the Kingdom of Judah to the Fall of the Second Commonwealth and After* [Jerusalem: Magnes, 1959], 10–11 [Hebrew]) also emphasizes the information that may be derived from the Greek transcriptions and concludes that, despite all the variations, the names שנאצר and ששבצר are identical.

25. Sara Japhet, "Sheshbazzar and Zerubbabel against the Background of the Historical and Religious Tendencies of Ezra-Nehemiah," *ZAW* 94 (1982): 94–96.

reject the identification of Sheshbazzar and Shenazzar,[26] it remains a serious
and attractive possibility.

If one accepts the thesis that Sheshbazzar was a prince from the Davidic
line, then the first group of returnees (whatever its size) was accompanied by
a member of the old royal family, and Persian authorities entrusted him with
the vessels for the temple that Cyrus had ordered to be built. Regardless who
Sheshbazzar was,[27] he is said to have laid the foundations of the temple (Ezra
5:16), but nothing more is credited to his leadership. Here another problem
arises with this intriguing character: as noted above, both he and Zerubbabel,
the next governor, are said to have laid the temple foundations. Since this
seems to be an act that can be performed just once for a building (there is no
record of an intervening destruction), there seems to be a contradiction in the
biblical sources.[28] This is the conflict that has elicited the creative attempts of
those scholars who have proposed that the two names belonged to one man or
that the editor confused the two. It is worth recalling, however, that the writer
very clearly separates the two in his presentation in Ezra 1–6 (especially in
chaps. 5–6).

There is a possibility that the book of Ezra, whether in source material or
in passages from the editor's hand, does not attribute the same accomplishment to the two men whom it calls governors. According to the Aramaic text of
the letter from Tattenai and his associates (Ezra 5:6-17), the Jewish elders told
them, "[t]hen this Sheshbazzar came and laid the foundations of the house of
God in Jerusalem" (v. 16a). The Aramaic term rendered "foundations" is אֻשַּׁיָּא;
it is related to Akkadian *uššu* and Sumerian *uš* and is used three times in Ezra:
twice in connection with Sheshbazzar's work on the temple (Ezra 5:16; 6:3
[where it is often emended (for example, in the RSV) to אִשּׁוֹהִי "burnt offerings"
with 1 Esd 6:24]); and once for the walls of Jerusalem (Ezra 4:12). The term has
been the subject of several studies, though their implications seem not always

---

26. For example, Ackroyd, *Exile and Restoration*, 143; idem, "The Jewish Community in
Palestine in the Persian Period," *Introduction: The Persian Period, CHJ* 1, ed. W. D. Davies and L.
Finkelstein (Cambridge: Cambridge Univ. Press, 1984), 138; Geo Widengren, "The Persian
Period," in *Israelite and Judaean History,* ed. J. H. Hayes and J. M. Miller, OTL (Philadelphia:
Westminster, 1977), 520; Blenkinsopp, *Ezra-Nehemiah*, 79; H. G. M. Williamson, *Ezra,
Nehemiah*, WBC 16 (Waco: Word, 1985), 5, 17.

27. Paolo Sacchi, who thinks Sheshbazzar was indeed Shenazzar, believes he was a vassal
king in Judah when Cyrus conquered Babylon (*The History of the Second Temple Period*, JSOT-
Sup 285 [Sheffield: Sheffield Academic, 2000], 60–61). There seems to be no basis in any text for
his conclusion.

28. Loring W. Batten, *A Critical and Exegetical Commentary on the Books of Ezra and
Nehemiah*, ICC (Edinburgh: T. & T. Clark, 1913), 138; Japhet, "Sheshbazzar and Zerubbabel,"
91–94.

to have been noted by scholars. The Akkadian word refers to the lowest part of a foundation,[29] the subfoundation as it were.[30] If Sheshbazzar laid this part of the foundation, then the upper part of the foundation would remain to be set at a later time. This latter accomplishment could be the one credited to Zerubbabel and his contemporaries; for their labors, the more general word יסד is used (Ezra 3:6, 10, 11; compare v. 12 [all in Hebrew]). Yet, even if we accept this distinction, we are left with other problems. Ezra 3:10-11 implies that Zerubbabel, Joshua, and others laid the foundation in the second year of the initial return (ca. 537 BCE), while Zech 4:9 places Zerubbabel's work in the second year of Darius (ca. 520 BCE) and Hag 2:15 seems to be saying that nothing had been done to reconstruct the temple before this date.[31]

Consequently, the picture that emerges for the beginning of the Second Temple is confusing. Yet, it may be permissible to say that Sheshbazzar, possibly a Davidic prince, was commissioned by Cyrus to build a temple. He laid the lowest part of the foundations in preparation for building a new sanctuary on its original site. He and those with him succeeded in fulfilling this part of the assignment but apparently accomplished no more. It was from their limited but essential beginnings that Zerubbabel and others resumed the task at some later point, whether shortly after Sheshbazzar's work, eighteen years later, or both. Since there is such a dearth of information regarding the Sheshbazzar episode, little more can be said about it. It is not known why the work progressed only so far, but practical matters such as finances and the extent of the full rebuilding may have been decisive factors in retarding the work. In this connection, it is helpful to adduce a parallel from the time of Alexander the Great. After he had conquered Babylon, he ordered that the temple of Marduk be rebuilt. One would think that with the virtually limitless resources at the disposal of the great conqueror, the work would have proceeded apace, but the opposite happened. Construction advanced so slowly while Alexander was away on his eastern campaigns that he decided to put his soldiers to work on

---

29. C. G. Tuland, "ʾUŠŠAYAʾ and ʾUŠŠARNAʾ: A Clarification of Terms, Date, and Text," *JNES* 17 (1958): 270–71. Compare Ackroyd ("The Jewish Community in Palestine in the Persian Period," 139), who notes the results emerging from studies of the term but apparently thinks the meaning is unclear and the problem unsolved. For the term in later Hebrew and Aramaic, see *DTTBY*, 35; *HALOT* 5.1826–27.

30. See Sidney Smith ("Foundations: Ezra iv, 12; v, 16; vi, 3," in *Essays in Honour of the Very Rev. Dr. J. H. Hertz*, ed. I. Epstein, E. Levine, and C. Roth [London: Goldston, 1942], 386–89), who maintains that the term could also be used for the fill placed within the *uššu* and that bringing such fill is the meaning of the verb מסובלין in Ezra 6:3.

31. For a survey of views on this complicated problem, see Bedford, *Temple Restoration*, 94–102.

the project. Just the clearing of the site of Esagila is mentioned in sources as continuing from Alexander's time to 294 BCE.[32] In other words, the temple of Jerusalem was not the only ancient sanctuary whose rebuilding fell behind schedule; even the availability of imperial resources (if in fact they were available) was no guarantee that prompt success would be realized.

The book of Ezra dates these small beginnings in Jerusalem to 538–37 BCE. Although it mentions that priests and Levites responded to Cyrus's proclamation and that the temple vessels were given to Sheshbazzar—thus establishing a link with the First Temple[33]—it says nothing about a high priest at this stage of the restoration. Temple rebuilding had begun, but the first mention of the high-priestly title and high-priestly actions[34] comes only with the second stage in the return to Zion.

The Four Leaders and the Rebuilt Temple

Although the book of Ezra provides the only narrative account of Cyrus's proclamation and the Jewish response to it, the situation changes for the next episodes in the restoration. Ezra remains a key source, but there are others to consult. 1 Esdras builds upon Ezra and may contain some more original readings, although it adds some clearly fictitious elements such as the so-called Joust of the Pages (3:1—5:6). Josephus's account in *Antiquities* follows 1 Esdras throughout. For a short time in the period that will be under consideration in this section, the prophetic books of Haggai and Zechariah offer great chronological precision and also intriguing interpretations of the roles played or to be played by Zerubbabel, the governor, and Joshua, the high priest. It is often claimed that there are marked differences between the presentations in Ezra and the prophetic books and even between the prophetic

---

32. For references, see Susan B. Downey, *Mesopotamian Religious Architecture: Alexander through the Parthians* (Princeton: Princeton Univ. Press, 1988), 7–10.

33. Compare Peter R. Ackroyd, "The Temple Vessels—A Continuity Theme," in *Studies in the Religion of Ancient Israel,* VTSup 23 (Leiden: Brill, 1972), 172–80.

34. Ezra 2:63 uses the phrase "until there should be a priest to consult Urim and Thummim." These articles are associated with the high priest (Exod 28:30), so that one could infer that a high priest was to be involved in the decision mentioned here. In fact, 1 Esd 5:40 reads the word *high priest* in this passage. It may be, however, that the expression in Ezra 2:63 is only a "proverbial" way of saying that a divine decision would be needed and thus we need not assume the presence of a high priest here (so Blenkinsopp, *Ezra-Nehemiah,* 93; compare Deborah W. Rooke, *Zadok's Heirs: The Role and Development of the High Priesthood in Ancient Israel,* OTM [Oxford: Oxford Univ. Press, 2000], 157–58).

works themselves. For this reason, the procedure here will be to examine the evidence of each work separately, with the narratives of Ezra receiving attention first and then the prophecies of Haggai and Zechariah.

The Book of Ezra

The first chapters of Ezra give one the impression that the events of Ezra 2:1—4:5 followed immediately upon those of chapter 1. The first chapter ends with a notice about the return associated with Sheshbazzar in 538 BCE. Chapter 2 then offers a lengthy list of returnees who should be, one would think, those who accompanied Sheshbazzar, though he is not listed among the leaders in Ezra 2:2. No regnal year is given in Ezra 2:1—4:5, but 3:1 mentions the seventh month and 3:8 refers to "the second year after their arrival at the house of God at Jerusalem, in the second month." Only in Ezra 4 does the writer mention kings; there, he notes that local opposition frustrated the work of the returned exiles "throughout the reign of King Cyrus of Persia and until the reign of King Darius of Persia" (4:5). Ezra 4:24 states that work on the Lord's house stopped as a result of these enemies until the second year of Darius when the noteworthy events of 5:1—6:13 took place.

While the author of Ezra implies that Ezra 1 and 2:1—4:5 relate to the same short time span, this is not actually stated in the text. Sheshbazzar is never brought into direct contact with the events and people of the following chapters. He is not among the leaders named in Ezra 2, but it is not impossible that he appears in the list under the title "the governor" (הַתִּרְשָׁתָא) in 2:63 (= Neh 7:65). This official renders a decision regarding priests whose registration could not be found among the genealogies (he disqualified them from service). Unfortunately, the governor's name is not given, so that his identity remains uncertain (1 Esd 5:40 reads "Nehemiah and Attharias," but the latter word appears to be a transcription of הַתִּרְשָׁתָא, while the name Nehemiah is inserted here because he is called the הַתִּרְשָׁתָא in Neh 8:9; 10:2).[35]

Some chronological uncertainty is likely to remain regarding this phase in the restoration because the book of Ezra uses two different dating systems: by the year of the kings' reigns and by the year of the return. So, according to the writer, during the reign of Cyrus there was a return of exiles under the leadership of the eleven or twelve men listed in Ezra 2:2 and Neh 7:7. The year is not specified, and, despite the context in Ezra, the return is not explicitly con-

---

35. Batten, *Ezra and Nehemiah*, 94; Zipora Talshir, *1 Esdras: From Origin to Translation*, SBLSCS 47 (Atlanta: SBL, 1999), 151.

nected with that of Sheshbazzar. Zerubbabel and Joshua/Jeshua are the first two leaders to be named. Then, in a still (or also) unnamed year, "Jeshua son of Jozadak, with his fellow priests, and Zerubbabel son of Shealtiel with his kin set out to build the altar of the God of Israel, to offer burnt offerings on it, as prescribed in the law of Moses the man of God" (Ezra 3:2). The text mentions the seventh month as the time when the altar construction occurred (3:1). It has been suggested that this date is not original to the context in Ezra 3 but that it has rather been drawn from Neh 7:72, where it refers to the seventh month in Artaxerxes' twentieth year. On this theory, the date belongs to the list in Nehemiah 7, and the author of Ezra 2, in copying the list, also borrowed the date, though it was intended for a much later year.[36] It seems unlikely, however, that the form of the list in Nehemiah is the earlier one; the Nehemiah Memoirs identify it as an old list. As Nehemiah considers how to repopulate Jerusalem after he had finished the city wall ("The city was wide and large, but the people within it were few and no houses had been built" [Neh 7:4]), he has an inspired idea: "Then my God put it into my mind to assemble the nobles and the officials and the people to be enrolled by genealogy. And I found the book of the genealogy of those who were the first to come back, and I found the following written in it" (Neh 7:5; the list of names follows). Thus, the context in Nehemiah favors the view that it was cited from an older document, and nothing in the form of the list in Ezra 2 and Nehemiah 7 gives any indication that the original context is other than the one in Ezra 2.[37] This entails that the date in Ezra 3:1, which is part of the document with the list of names, refers to some year in Cyrus's reign—or at any rate that is what the editor wishes for the reader to conclude.[38]

At this point, the book of Ezra divides the work on the temple site by Zerubbabel and Joshua into two stages. The first phase involved building the altar in the seventh month of an unspecified year in Cyrus's reign. The group accomplished its task, and, as it was the seventh month, they celebrated the

---

36. Williamson (*Ezra, Nehemiah*, 29–30) holds this view and surveys the arguments used to support it. It is difficult to understand why scholars who ascribe priority to Nehemiah's list think the date in the seventh month in Ezra's version (3:1) is, to use Williamson's words, "left completely in the air" (29). As a matter of fact, it is an integral part of Ezra 3:1-7, all of which centers on the seventh month. See Blenkinsopp, *Ezra-Nehemiah*, 43–44, for a refutation of the theory advanced by Williamson.

37. James VanderKam, "Ezra-Nehemiah or Ezra and Nehemiah?" in *Priests, Prophets, and Scribes: Essays on the Formation and Heritage of Second Temple Judaism in Honour of Joseph Blenkinsopp*, ed. E. Ulrich, J. Wright, R. Carroll, and P. R. Davies, JSOTSup 149 (Sheffield: Sheffield Academic, 1992), 67–69.

38. Liver (*The House of David*, 81–85) argues strongly against the idea that Zerubbabel and Joshua returned at the beginning of Darius's reign.

festival of booths and offered on the new altar the sacrifices prescribed in the law for each day (Ezra 3:4). One learns (3:6) that offerings actually had begun on the first day of the seventh month (the festival of booths begins on the fifteenth), but "the foundation of the temple of the LORD was not yet laid" (3:6). At this point, the returnees also began making provision for the temple structure. They imitated Solomon, the builder of the First Temple, by paying Sidonians and Tyrians "to bring cedar trees from Lebanon to the sea, to Joppa, according to the grant that they had from King Cyrus of Persia" (Ezra 3:7; compare 1 Kgs 5:1-12).[39]

What appears to be a continuation of this work is introduced directly afterward in Ezra 3: "In the second year after their arrival at the house of God at Jerusalem [compare Ezra 2:68: "as soon as they came to the house of the LORD in Jerusalem"], in the second month, Zerubbabel son of Shealtiel and Jeshua son of Jozadak made a beginning, together with the rest of their people, the priests and the Levites and all who had come to Jerusalem from the captivity. They appointed the Levites, from twenty years old and upward, to have the oversight of the work on the house of the LORD. And Jeshua with his sons and his kin, and Kadmiel and his sons, Binnui and Hodaviah along with the sons of Henadad, the Levites, their sons and kin, together took charge of the workers in the house of God" (Ezra 3:8-9). After these preparations, the builders finally laid the temple foundation (3:10; compare v. 11). Not surprisingly, it occasioned a great celebration (3:10-13). For chronological reasons, it is worth noting that at this time there were still reportedly some Judeans who had seen the First Temple, which had been destroyed in 587 BCE, some fifty years earlier.

The building activities caught the attention of the "adversaries of Judah and Benjamin" (Ezra 4:1) who came to Zerubbabel and the other leaders and offered to help with the great project on the grounds that they worshiped the same God (v. 2). "But Zerubbabel, Jeshua, and the rest of the heads of families in Israel said to them, 'You shall have no part with us in building a house to our God; but we alone will build to the LORD, the God of Israel, as King Cyrus of Persia has commanded us'" (Ezra 4:3; note the continuing association of their project with Cyrus). Difficulties then developed with the result that "the people of the land" (v. 4) hindered the building "throughout the reign of King Cyrus of Persia and until the reign of King Darius of Persia" (v. 5). According to 4:24, the work actually stopped until Darius's second year (which is obviously, judging by the context in Ezra, not identical with the second year of the returnees' arrival at Jerusalem).

---

39. Compare Williamson, *Ezra, Nehemiah*, 47.

Stage two of the project is set in Darius's second year, that is, either in 521 or 520 BCE. Ezra 5:1-2, Haggai, and Zechariah 1–8 associate Zerubbabel, Joshua, and the two prophets themselves with this date and with the inception of an effort that, according to Ezra 6:15, led to the completion of the temple in the sixth year of Darius, on the third day of the twelfth month. In the presentation in Ezra 5–6—chapters that devote much space to correspondence with Darius about the temple—there is no conflict with the previous accounts in the book. In them, Zerubbabel and Joshua are again building the temple, not laying its lower foundations (Ezra 5:2; compare 5:3, which mentions building and finishing the structure; 5:4, 8, 9, 11, 16; 6:7, 8, 14).[40]

A number of points in Ezra 1–6 raise the issue of the historical reliability of this material; or, better, they lead one to reflect on the literary character of these chapters. There is no doubting some chronological confusion in Ezra 4:6-24 if the editor placed this section here because he thought that was its sequential place. The arrangement appears thematic, not chronological. Perhaps such influences were at work elsewhere in these chapters, so that we should be hesitant about drawing historical conclusions from them. We should also grant that Ezra 1–6 is written to express a distinctive message— the restoration resulted from the returnees, not people of the land, and it bore the blessing of Persia because God so moved Cyrus and Darius.[41] Yet, with all this in mind, we may still accept as possible and perhaps even likely the picture of an initial but short-lived attempt at temple construction under Sheshbazzar and a later (whenever that may have been) resumption of work under the leadership of Zerubbabel, Joshua, and the prophets Haggai and Zechariah.[42]

---

40. References to the second year of the return and to the second year of Darius could, of course, have been triggers for confusion in the tradition about the dates for the work of Zerubbabel and Joshua. However, it may be the case, as Baruch Halpern has proposed, that the editor of Ezra has attempted to give a false impression of continuity from the time of Cyrus to that of Darius. He did not want the reader to know that the project ordered by Cyrus had failed and so fashioned a sequence such that the work started during his reign but was frustrated by the adversaries of Ezra 4, only to be completed in Darius's time. He accomplished this by blending two chronologies—one dating by regnal year, the other by the year of the return. Halpern thinks that Zerubbabel returned only in the time of Darius. See his "A Historiographic Commentary on Ezra 1–6: Achronological Narrative and Dual Chronology in Israelite Historiography," in *The Hebrew Bible and Its Interpreters,* ed. W. H. Propp, B. Halpern, and D. N. Freedman, BJSUCSD 1 (Winona Lake, Ind.: Eisenbrauns, 1990), 81–142, esp. 108–11.

41. See the convenient summary in Jonathan E. Dyck, *The Theocratic Ideology of the Chronicler,* BibIntSer 33 (Leiden: Brill, 1998), 84–90.

42. This is the picture accepted by a number of historians of ancient Israel, despite differences in details. See, for example, Martin Noth, *The History of Israel,* 2nd ed., trans. P. R. Ackroyd (New York: Harper & Row, 1960), 306–15; John Bright, *A History of Israel,* 3rd ed. (Philadelphia:

Problems arise at this point, not because of internal conflicts in the book of Ezra, but because the books of Haggai and Zechariah date the foundation of the temple to the second year of Darius (520 BCE). The relevant evidence in these two prophetic books should now be considered.

Haggai and Zechariah

The dates that are offered in Ezra 4:24—6:15 (Haggai and Zechariah are mentioned in 5:1; 6:14) and those found in the two prophetic books document the fact that they are talking about the same episode in the rebuilding of the temple. Each of Haggai's few oracles is dated to the second year of Darius (= Ezra 4:24): Hag 1:1 dates his first oracle to the sixth month, the first day (= 6/1), with a response on 6/24 (1:15); 2:1 locates another oracle on 7/21; and 2:10 (compare v. 18) and 2:20 place two oracles on 9/24. Zechariah's prophecies begin in Darius's second year (Zech 1:1—the eighth month of his second year, thus approximately one month before Haggai's last recorded prophecy; Zech 1:17 gives 11/24 of the same year), but they continue beyond this year to the fourth year of his reign (Zech 7:1 mentions 9/4 in his fourth year). Ezra, Haggai,[43] and Zechariah agree, then, in situating vigorous activity having to do with the Second Temple in Darius's second year. A few lines in Haggai and one passage in Zechariah, however, complicate matters.

Laying the foundations: According to Hag 1:4, the Lord castigates the people for living in their "paneled [?] houses, while this house [the temple] lies in ruins [חרב]." The implication often drawn from this statement is that the adjective חרב refers, not to a building that is in the process of reconstruction, but to one that has been destroyed with only the debris remaining from it.[44]

Westminster, 1981), 364–72; Miller and Hayes, *A History of Ancient Israel and Judah*, 443–48. Siegfried Herrmann, however, concludes there was a single building program near the beginning of Darius's reign (*A History of Israel in Old Testament Times*, trans. J. Bowden, 2nd ed. [Philadelphia: Fortress Press, 1981], 298–305).

43. In connection with Haggai, Carol L. Meyers and Eric M. Meyers (*Haggai, Zechariah 1–8*, AB 25B [Garden City, N.Y.: Doubleday, 1987], 20) suggest that concern about the approaching end of Jeremiah's seventy-year prophecy stimulated work on the temple. They also observe that dating by the year of the Persian monarch in the two prophetic books indicates their acceptance "of the legitimacy of the Persian rule over Yehud" (5–6). Compare this with Japhet's understanding of the world view of Ezra-Nehemiah in her "Sheshbazzar and Zerubbabel," passim.

44. See, for example, Kurt Galling, "Serubbabel und der Hohepriester beim Wiederaufbau des Tempels in Jerusalem," in his *Studien zur Geschichte Israels im persischen Zeitalter* (Tübingen: Mohr/Siebeck, 1964), 127–34.

Taken in this sense, Haggai's statement about the condition of the temple in the sixth month of Darius's second year would conflict with information in Ezra, which pictures work on the temple as continuing—or rather stopping and starting—from the time of Cyrus to Darius's second year (and beyond).

A second passage that implies a conflict with Ezra's portrait of continuity is Hag 2:15: "But now, consider what will come to pass from this day [9/24 in Darius's second year; 2:10] on. Before a stone was placed upon a stone in the LORD's temple, . . ." One is left with the impression that prior to this date nothing had been done to rebuild the temple itself. The same point is made more emphatically in Hag 2:18: "Consider from this day on, from the twenty-fourth day of the ninth month. Since the day that the foundation of the LORD's temple was laid [יסד], consider . . ." The prophecy of Zechariah reinforces Haggai's words because in it, too, one reads about Zerubbabel's work of laying the temple foundations (יסדו in Zech 4:9) no earlier than Darius's second year. It would be reasonable to connect these givens about the second year of Darius with the events related in Ezra 3, where Zerubbabel lays the temple foundation (Ezra 3:8-10) and there is disappointment among some who were able to compare the character of the Second Temple with that of the first (Ezra 3:12-13 and Hag 2:1-9). The problem is that Ezra by implication assigns these events to the time of Cyrus (between 538 and 530 BCE), while the prophetic works place them in the second year of Darius (520 BCE). The situation seems to be that Ezra has separated by some years events that, according to Haggai and Zechariah, all belonged in the same year—the year 520 BCE.

The words חרב *and* יסד: There have been various attempts to interpret and relate the data in Ezra 3–6 and the two prophetic books. One approach involves trying to discern the precise meaning in context of the words חרב (Hag 1:4) and יסד (for example, Hag 2:18; Zech 4:9).

Francis I. Andersen has thoroughly investigated the use of these two terms in the Hebrew Bible.[45] The value of his work lies primarily in documenting the fairly considerable range of meanings that they have. He does make some claims that are not substantiated; for example, on the basis of 2 Chr 8:16, he holds that "the day of foundation is the day of completion, since the building is only really established when it is securely finished."[46] But in a more helpful way, he points to passages such as 2 Chr 24:27. It refers to the *repairs* on the temple during the reign of King Joash (24:12 uses the verb "restore" [חדש] for the process) as the "founding" (יסד) of the temple. In other words, in the context of work on a building, the root יסד need not refer only to laying the foun-

---

45. "Who Built the Second Temple?" *ABR* 6 (1958): 1–35.
46. Ibid., 19.

dations;[47] repairs to an existing structure were made in Joash's time. The verb also need not refer to something that occurs only at one temporal point. As Gelston notes: "it may have a more general meaning—'repair, restore, rebuild', with the emphasis on the idea of firmness and durability."[48] If we apply this information to the problem at hand, it becomes apparent that both what Zerubbabel accomplished during the reign of Cyrus according to Ezra 3 and what occurred in 520 BCE according to the prophets could be encompassed in the one word יסד.

Andersen has also subjected the various uses of חרב to careful analysis.[49] The basic sense of the word has to do with dryness. From this fundamental meaning, derivative nuances developed. It came to be employed to describe the state of cities and nations after warfare had devastated them: "Such ravaged places then come to resemble the desert, not primarily in dryness but in being uninhabited"[50] (see Isa 34:10; Jer 26:9; Ezek 12:20; Zeph 3:6). In Nehemiah, it is used of the city Jerusalem (2:3, 17), which, as one learns later, is in need of repopulation (11:1-2; compare Jer 33:10, 12; Ezek 36:35, 38). Haggai 1:4 and 9 are the only two passages in which חרב refers to a building. In light of the uses of the word elsewhere, Andersen concludes about these verses: "Haggai's complaint is not that the house of God is not in existence, but that it is deserted. It is not that the people are building their own homes and not building the temple, it is that they sit in their houses when they should be in church."[51] While it is not impossible that Haggai is referring to the condition of the building itself, the comparison in Haggai 1 is with houses that have roofs (1:4; NRSV translates ספונים as "paneled"; literally it means "covered" and is understood as "roofed" in 1 Esd 6:4).[52] Also, there are a few indications in the text that at this time the building was at least partially constructed: there is a high priest, sacrifices are offered, priestly teachings are given, and work is proceeding on the temple (see also Hag 2:3).[53]

47. Ibid., 18; see also A. Gelston, "The Foundations of the Second Temple," *VT* 16 (1966): 235.

48. Gelston, "The Foundations of the Second Temple," 235; see Andersen, "Who Built the Second Temple?" 20–21. Rudolf Mosis ("יסד," in *TDOT* 6.115–16), while mentioning 2 Chr 24:27 (and 2 Chr 31:7), says that the usages of the verb with regard to the Second Temple (in the piel, pual, and hophal) refer to the beginning of the building process. "This usage is clearly distinct from that of the qal and niphal, which refer to the construction of the entire building" (116).

49. Andersen, "Who Built the Second Temple?" 22–26. See also Otto Kaiser, "חרב," in *TDOT* 5.150–54. Kaiser distinguishes two semantic fields—dry, be desolate—for the term.

50. Andersen, "Who Built the Second Temple?" 23–24.

51. Ibid., 25; see also Meyers and Meyers, *Haggai, Zechariah 1–8*, 24, 32.

52. See Anderson, "Who Built the Second Temple?" 25–26.

53. Ibid., 26.

As a result, it is within the realm of possibility that the two stages of rebuilding in Ezra 3–6 and Haggai's and Zechariah's descriptions of conditions and events in 520 BCE are compatible with one another. At some unspecified point in Cyrus's reign, Zerubbabel and Joshua led the returnees in the process of building an altar and beginning to construct the superstructure on the lower foundations laid by Sheshbazzar and his fellows. Their work was, however, soon halted, only to be resumed in 520 BCE, at which time it remained far from complete and use of the sanctuary area was slight. Under those depressing conditions, the prophets exhorted their contemporaries, especially Zerubbabel and Joshua, to finish the work of reconstructing the house of the Lord.[54] According to the combined evidence of Ezra and Haggai, they then completed the great task in approximately four and one-half years.

1. Joshua/Jeshua, the First High Priest[55]

The first high priest of the Second-Temple era figures in several biblical sources.

In Ezra

All sources name Joshua/Jeshua the son of Jehozadak as the first high priest of the Second Temple. The genealogy of Levi found in 1 Chr 5:27-41 (English 6:1-15) provides the names of individuals who are often thought to have been the high priests (chief priests) of the First Temple, though this does not seem to be the case for all of them.[56] It concludes with the names *Seraiah*, whom 2 Kings 25:18 and Jer 52:24 call כהן הראש and whom Nebuchadnezzar executed, and his son *Jehozadak* who "went into exile when the LORD sent Judah and Jerusalem into exile by the hand of Nebuchadnezzar" (1 Chr 6:15). As the execution of Seraiah occurred after the First Temple had been burnt to the ground (2 Kings 25:9; Jer 52:13), it follows that Jehozadak never actually officiated as high priest in the First Temple before his deportation. Josephus calls

---

54. For Hag 2:15, 18 as denoting "refounding," see Meyers and Meyers, *Haggai, Zechariah 1–8*, 59–60, 63–64.

55. The number given to each high priest in the heading corresponds to the List of High Priests, pp. 491–92.

56. See Yehoshua M. Grintz, "Chapters in the History of the High Priesthood," *Zion* 23 (1958): 124–40 (Hebrew). The list traces the line that runs from Levi through Zadok and beyond and thus includes the Zadokite genealogy.

him a high priest, nevertheless (*Ant.* 10.8, 5 [§150]) and adds a detail found in no biblical source, namely, that at a later time Nebuchadnezzar "released the high priest from confinement" (10.8, 7 [§154]).

Ezra and Haggai refer to Joshua/Jeshua as the son of this Jehozadak. He thus stands in the Zadokite line as the direct descendant of the last high/chief priests of the First Temple. In this sense, he parallels Zerubbabel, the scion of the royal house of David. In the immediate postexilic period, the two families holding the top political and hierocratic positions were the ones who controlled them in the time of the First Temple. The relations between them were drastically changed, however, as Zerubbabel was not a king but only a governor; their relationship is the subject of several passages in the prophecy of Zechariah (see below).

Joshua appears first in Ezra 2:2 (= Neh 7:7; 12:1; compare 12:7; and 1 Esd 5:5, 8) as one of those who returned from the Babylonian exile—as one of the "people of the province who came from those captive exiles" (Ezra 2:1). Because his name is given already in Ezra 2:2, before the long list of the returnees in verses 3-63, he appears to have been one of the leaders of the group, with Zerubbabel and nine or ten (so Neh 7:7) others.[57] It should be recalled that this return is not dated to a particular year in the book of Ezra; it is simply placed in the time of Cyrus, judging by the context (see the discussion above). Ezra 3:2 first identifies Joshua more fully as the son of Jozadak (a shortened form of Jehozadak) and mentions him and his priestly fellows. This is worth noting, since in the book of Ezra Joshua is never called *the high priest*. We know of his priestly status only from his patronym and from his association with other priests.[58]

Joshua, his priestly colleagues, Zerubbabel, and his associates are said to have built the altar of the God of Israel (Ezra 3:2 = 1 Esd 5:48). They "set up the altar on its foundation" and offered the morning and evening burnt offerings upon it (v. 3 = 1 Esd 5:50). These actions are dated to the seventh month (Ezra 3:1, 4 = 1 Esd 5:47, 51); we also learn that beginning with "the first day of the seventh month they began to offer burnt offerings to the LORD" prior to the time when the foundations of the temple itself were laid (Ezra 3:6 = 1 Esd

---

57. According to Rooke (*Zadok's Heirs*, 155–56), the fact that Joshua's name appears after that of Zerubbabel in four of five cases in Ezra (3:2 is the exception) and is never used without Zerubbabel, though Zerubbabel is mentioned without Joshua, shows somehow that Joshua lacked authority. She makes a similarly baseless claim for references in Haggai.

58. On avoidance of titles as part of a larger tendency in Ezra, see Japhet, "Sheshbazzar and Zerubbabel," 73–76, 82–89. As Liver adds, we would not know that Sheshbazzar and Zerubbabel were from the line of David apart from the genealogy in 1 Chronicles 3 (*The House of David*, 72 n. 1).

5:53). Altar construction apparently inspired a certain momentum toward building the temple in line with King Cyrus's grant (Ezra 3:7 = 1 Esd 5:54-55; see Ezra 1:3-4 = 1 Esd 2:2-3). As Solomon had for the First Temple, so now the returnees enlisted the help of the Sidonians and Tyrians for cedar trees (Ezra 3:7 = 1 Esd 5:55). Zerubbabel, Joshua, and the others then, in the second year of their arrival in Jerusalem, "made a beginning" (Ezra 3:8 = 1 Esd 5:56). The temple-building effort was placed under priestly supervision: the Levites had control of the "work on the house of the Lord" (Ezra 3:8), while Joshua and others "took charge of the workers in the house of God" (v. 9). The foundations were laid on an occasion accompanied by celebration and poignant reminders of what once had been (3:10-13).

Joshua does not reappear until Ezra 5, which is set in the second year of King Darius (4:24). Here, too, he is paired with Zerubbabel (5:2) in another attempt to bring the sanctuary construction to a conclusion after the delay which is described in Ezra 4. At this point, they had the added support of the prophets Haggai and Zechariah (Ezra 5:1 = 1 Esd 6:1-2). This is the last time that Joshua is mentioned in connection with the project; rather remarkably, in the account about the end of the task, neither he nor Zerubbabel is named as a participant, nor do they figure in the dedication of the temple that took place at that time (Ezra 6:15-22 = 1 Esd 7:4-15). In fact, the only other passage in which Joshua's name surfaces in Ezra is 10:18 (= 1 Esd 9:19), where it is reported that among his descendants were some who married foreign women and thus aroused the ire of Ezra. They agreed to expel these wives and offered a sacrifice because of their guilt in the matter.

In sum, Joshua's lineage, high standing, and leading role in rebuilding the temple emerge clearly from the book of Ezra. Yet, in the book he is never called *high priest*, and he never engages in any explicitly cultic act. The sacrifices offered on the new altar in Ezra 3:4-6 no doubt involved his ministrations, but the text does not specify what he did. It is evident from the dates in the book that he returned to Jerusalem from the Babylonian captivity (into which his father had been led) at some unidentified time in Cyrus's reign (between 538 and 530 BCE) and that he was still active in the year 520 BCE.[59] Some attempts have been made to calculate his age on the basis of the meager biblical evidence. If his grandfather Seraiah was executed in 587 BCE while serving as high priest, his son Jehozadak may not yet have been very old at the time. Thus, it is possible that Joshua was born in Babylon. Frank Moore Cross suggests that he was born in about 570 BCE.[60] This would make him about

---

59. But note the comments above regarding problems with the dates in this part of Ezra.
60. "A Reconstruction of the Judean Restoration," *Int* 29 (1975): 203; so also Meyers and Meyers, *Haggai, Zechariah 1–8*, 16.

thirty-two years of age when the first return took place and about fifty when the successful effort to rebuild the temple began in 520 BCE. Needless to say, these suggestions are highly speculative; we do not know his age at any of the times mentioned in the Bible, nor do we learn how long he served as high priest.

In Haggai

As noted above, the same Joshua is mentioned five times in the small prophetic book of Haggai. It adds little to what is said about the man in Ezra apart from the fact that it always identifies him not only by name and patronym but also by title.[61] In Haggai, for the first time one learns that Joshua was the high priest (הכהן הגדול: Hag 1:1, 12, 14; 2:2, 4).[62] His title appears to be related to the expression in Lev 21:10: הכהן הגדול מאחיו ("the priest who is exalted above his fellows"), and this may be the earliest instance of the usage in biblical literature. It is perhaps worth noting that Joshua is always mentioned second after Zerubbabel and that he is not included with the Davidic heir in the enthusiastic oracle that closes the book (Hag 2:20-23). After the overthrow of kingdoms, it is Zerubbabel who will be made "like a signet ring; for I have chosen you, says the LORD of hosts."[63] Joshua is not part of this eschatological political scenario, but in the book of Zechariah he assumes a more commanding position in pictures of the future.[64]

---

61. Rooke, who argues that Joshua was inferior to Zerubbabel, finds evidence for her position in Haggai where Joshua is never mentioned alone or without his title/descent, while Zerubbabel appears at times alone and without his title. For her, this is "something which suggests that he was not as well-known in the community as Zerubbabel, and which would therefore point away from his having any significant authority in civil government over against Zerubbabel" (*Zadok's Heirs*, 130). It even implies "some uncertainty over Joshua's identity and position in the community" and the repetition of the full information about him may have been a way of establishing his position (130). See also p. 32. It is difficult to understand how this follows from the data in the text.

62. For the title, compare Meyers and Meyers, *Haggai, Zechariah 1–8*, 180–82; Rooke, *Zadok's Heirs*, 27–28; Werner Dommershausen, "כהן," in *TDOT* 7.71–72.

63. Rooke is certainly correct to stress that Joshua appears in connection with temple-building and thus within the cultic sphere (*Zadok's Heirs*, 135).

64. See Meyers and Meyers, *Haggai, Zechariah 1–8*, 17: "The eschatological context there allows for the resumption of monarchic authority, with a king as Yahweh's viceroy. The priest at that time would recede in relative power, and hence Joshua's name does not appear. Haggai clearly has a different perspective than does Zechariah, who retains a vision of dyarchy (4:14 and 6:11-14)." Compare also p. 74.

In Zechariah

There are three pericopes within Zechariah 1–8 that deal with the high priest Joshua the son of Jehozadak, all in the night visions of Zech 1:7—6:15: Zech 3:1-10 (a vision with appended oracle[s]); chapter 4 (the vision of the lampstand); and 6:9-15 (an oracle about crowns). Joshua is named in Zech 3:1, 3, 6, 8, 9; and 6:11 (that is, not in chap. 4); his father Jehozadak's name is added in 6:11, and his title (הכהן הגדול) is specified in 3:1, 8. Although the book contains several specific dates, no one of the Joshua sections is tied to a particular time. Zechariah 1:7 says that the word of the Lord came to Zechariah "[o]n the twenty-fourth day of the eleventh month, the month of Shebat, in the second year of Darius." Zechariah 7:1 informs the reader that the Lord's message came to the prophet "[i]n the fourth year of King Darius, . . . on the fourth day of the ninth month which is Chislev." It would be natural to infer from these dates that the intervening visions and oracles belong at one or several points between them, that is, between February 15, 519 and December 7, 518 BCE.[65] Thus, all of them would fall after Haggai's last dated prophecy (December 18, 520) and before completion of the temple (March 10, 515). These appear to be the temporal limits for the visions and oracles, but not all agree that they are presented in their proper chronological order. Benjamin Uffenheimer, for example, maintains that the Zerubbabel passage in Zechariah 4 (vv. 6b-10a, the only place where his name appears in Zechariah) belongs to a time when he still exercised his office as governor, whereas Zechariah 3 and 6:9-15 come from a time after his (supposed) disappearance. On Uffenheimer's reading, the title Branch in Zech 3:8 and 6:12 refers, not to Zerubbabel, but to a future ruler from the line of David.[66] It remains a more widely accepted understanding, however, that Branch refers to Zerubbabel and that the term צמח may actually be a play on his Babylonian name zēr-bābili = "the seed of Babylon."[67]

A fundamental concern that appears to motivate the messages of the three passages about Joshua is to define the nature of his office and the relationship between him or his office and that of the civil ruler. During the centuries when the First Temple stood, the king of course ruled supreme over all, including the highest ranking priests with whom there was an occasional clash (as 2 Chr

---

65. Meyers and Meyers (Haggai, Zechariah 1–8, xlvi) give these precise dates.

66. The Visions of Zechariah: From Prophecy to Apocalyptic (Jerusalem: Kiryat Sepher, 1961 [Hebrew]), 1–7. Compare also Janet E. Tollington, Tradition and Innovation in Haggai and Zechariah 1–8, JSOTSup 150 (Sheffield: JSOT Press, 1993), 172–73 (Branch refers to an unidentified ruler in the new age).

67. So, for example, Hinckley G. Mitchell, A Critical and Exegetical Commentary on Haggai, Zechariah, Malachi, and Jonah, ICC (Edinburgh: T. & T. Clark, 1912), 186–87.

24:17-22 reports [there is no parallel in 2 Kings]). The sources also tell about one period of priestly superiority (2 Kings 12:1-3; 2 Chr 24:1-3). In the first years of the restoration, the situation was dramatically altered: the top political and ecclesiastical offices remained in the hands of the descendants of the preexilic families that had held them, but the roles of those who occupied these positions were different. Zerubbabel was governor, not king; and he ruled at the pleasure of Persian authorities. The high priest appears to have assumed an expanded role under these circumstances; he was certainly no longer a royal official as he had been during the monarchy.[68] He not only had responsibility for supervising construction of the temple (compare Ezra 3:9), but he also undertook some judicial duties that had once been the prerogative of the king (see below). In the existing form of the text, Zechariah endorses expanded high-priestly powers and posits a reduced sphere of authority for the Davidic heir in the present time. In the future, however, someone from David's line named *Branch* would sit upon the throne of his fathers and build the temple of the Lord as Solomon once had.

In his detailed study of Haggai and Zechariah, Wim Beuken argues that it is precisely in the Joshua material in Zechariah that the levitical tradents who reworked the reports about the night visions revised most thoroughly. He thinks that it was not Zechariah himself but (slightly) later traditionists who ascribed to Joshua a role equal to that of the Davidide Zerubbabel.[69] Despite his minute analysis, there seems to be no compelling reason to accept Beuken's thesis. It appears to rest on his more general view that in the immediate postexilic climate, with great excitement about the coming of a Davidic scion, the high priest could not have occupied so elevated a position. Only after Zerubbabel's disappearance, he thinks, did the rank of the high priest rise to the level found in Zechariah 3, 4, and 6. Beuken's conclusion, like that of other scholars, suffers from overestimating Zerubbabel's importance in Zechariah (and in the early period of the restoration).

For the sake of convenience, the three pertinent sections of Zechariah will be treated in their canonical order.

---

68. Compare Aelred Cody, *A History of Old Testament Priesthood*, AnBib 35 (Rome: Pontifical Biblical Institute, 1969), 176.

69. *Haggai–Sacharja 1–8: Studien zur Überlieferungsgeschichte der frühnachexilischen Prophetie*, SSN 10 (Assen: van Gorcum, 1967), 230–317. See also Paul L. Redditt, "Zerubbabel, Joshua, and the Night Visions of Zechariah," *CBQ* 54 (1992): 249–59. He thinks the three passages relevant to Joshua (Zech 4:6b-10a; 6:9-15; 3:1-10) were "added to the night visions and that they transformed those visions from a document addressed to Babylonian Jews summoning them to Judah into a politico-theological treatise for Judah and Jerusalem for the year 520 B.C." (250). Zechariah himself may have been the redactor (257).

Zechariah 3:1-10: The vision of Joshua the high priest:[70] The present arrangement of Zechariah's visions accords a certain prominence to this unit because it (with Zechariah 4) is placed in the center of the eight vision reports in Zech 1:7—6:15 and is distinct from the others in form and content.[71] The setting is the divine courtroom, with 3:1-5 offering brief glimpses of the scene and comments made during the trial of the high priest, and 3:6-10 containing statements from the angel of the Lord to Joshua (vv. 6-7) and to Joshua and his priestly colleagues (vv. 8-10). There has been some debate about which of the sayings or oracles belonged with the vision originally (if any) and which (if any) were added to it. Albert Petitjean and Meyers and Meyers consider verses 8-10 to be a supplementary oracle,[72] but Beuken thinks these verses conclude the vision naturally by affixing to the picture of Joshua's purification a promise of better times to come. For him, verses 6-7 are from a reviser who worked a short time later.[73] David Petersen, however, finds three oracular responses in verses 6-10: verses 6-7, 9, and verse 8 are responses that were not original components with the vision account; verse 10 is a "deuteroprophetic response" that builds upon the oracular responses.[74] Since such divisions of the material are highly speculative and do not appreciably modify the interpretation, they do not affect the following analysis.

> 3:1 Then he showed me the high priest Joshua standing before the angel of the Lord, and Satan [literally: the satan] standing at his right hand to accuse him. 3:2 And the Lord said to Satan, "The Lord rebuke you, O Satan! The Lord who has chosen Jerusalem rebuke you! Is not this man a brand plucked from the fire?" 3:3 Now Joshua was dressed with filthy clothes as he stood before the angel. 3:4 The angel said to those who were standing before him, "Take off his filthy clothes." And to him he said, "See, I have taken your guilt away from you, and I will clothe you with festal apparel." 3:5 And I [or: he] said,

---

70. For a more extensive study of the passage, see VanderKam, "Joshua the High Priest and the Interpretation of Zechariah 3," *CBQ* 53 (1991): 553–70. The following section parallels the presentation in the article.

71. Meyers and Meyers, *Haggai, Zechariah 1–8*, 179, 213–15.

72. Albert Petitjean, *Les oracles du Proto-Zacharie: Un programme de restauration pour la communauté juive après l'exil*, EBib (Paris: Gabalda, 1969), 161; Meyers and Meyers, *Haggai, Zechariah 1–8*, 178.

73. *Haggai–Sacharja 1–8*, 283, 290–300. Note that this conclusion fits with his general view that the earlier form of the material in Zechariah highlights Zerubbabel, not Joshua.

74. David L. Petersen, *Haggai and Zechariah 1–8*, OTL (Philadelphia: Westminster, 1984), 202.

"Let them put a clean turban on his head." So they put a clean turban on his head and clothed him with the apparel; and the angel of the LORD was standing by.

The leading characters in the scene play the parts of accused (Joshua), prosecutor (the satan), and defense attorney (the angel of the Lord). A peculiar feature of the report about the trial is that the satan does not express his accusation(s); presumably he had done so before the action that the prophet reports began. As a result, the first words uttered by any character are the rebuke delivered by the Lord to the satan; the charges made by the prosecutor must be inferred from the rebuke.[75] From it, we may presume that he questioned the fitness of Jerusalem and Joshua (v. 2).

Two statements are made about Joshua: (1) he is "a brand plucked from the fire" (v. 2) and (2) he "was dressed with filthy clothes as he stood before the angel" (v. 3). The former expression probably refers to his stay in Babylon, the land of captivity where Joshua may have been born and from which he had returned.[76] His sojourn in Babylon may have been viewed as a cause of defilement for him—a blemish that had to be effaced before he could serve as high priest in the new temple. Consequently, the metaphor of the "brand plucked from the fire" signifies his return from Babylon and possibly even an improvement in his aristocratic family's status vis-à-vis the ruling power now that Persia rather than Babylon was in control.[77] Petersen has also noted that the image explains the dirty appearance of the high priest at the beginning of the scene.[78]

Joshua's filthy apparel is associated with his guilt (עון); when the former is removed, the latter is as well (v. 4). The soiled clothing on this "brand plucked from the fire" is replaced with "festal apparel" (vv. 4-5). The high priest himself must be in a state of purity before he can be involved in removing the guilt of others.[79] Through this ritual, Joshua is transported from the realm of defile-

---

75. Meyers and Meyers, *Haggai, Zechariah 1–8*, 182, 185; Petersen, *Haggai and Zechariah 1–8*, 191–92.

76. So Uffenheimer, *The Visions of Zechariah*, 97; Petersen, *Haggai and Zechariah 1–8*, 195; Meyers and Meyers, *Haggai, Zechariah 1–8*, 185–88; compare Mitchell, *A Critical and Exegetical Commentary*, 150. For rabbinic treatments of the image, see Y. Greenwald, *The History of the High Priests in its Relation to the General Political and Religious History of the Jewish People from the Earliest Times till the Destruction of the Second Temple* (New York: published privately, 1932) 50 [Hebrew]. Compare also VanderKam, "Joshua the High Priest," 555–56.

77. Meyers and Meyers, *Haggai, Zechariah 1–8*, 187.

78. *Haggai and Zechariah 1–8*, 193.

79. Petersen, *Haggai and Zechariah 1–8*, 195.

ment to that of purity or holiness so that in the new sanctuary he may serve the chosen people in their quest to become pure.[80]

The rich apparel (מחלצות)[81] in which Joshua is arrayed is obviously the splendid clothing of the high priest. The biblical passage that describes these garments in greatest detail is Exodus 28, in which the Lord prescribes the vestments for Aaron. Exodus 28:4 explains: "These are the vestments that they shall make: a breastpiece, an ephod, a robe, a checkered tunic, a turban [מצנפת], and a sash." Zechariah 3 mentions none of these items except the turban (v. 5). Exodus 28:36-38 pictures the turban thus:

> You shall make a rosette of pure gold, and engrave [ופתחת] on it, like the engraving [פתוחי] of a signet, "Holy to the LORD." You shall fasten it on the turban [המצנפת] with a blue cord; it shall be on the front of the turban. It shall be on Aaron's forehead, and Aaron shall take on himself any guilt [עון] incurred in the holy offering that the Israelites consecrate as their sacred donations; it shall always be on his forehead, in order that they may find favor before the LORD. (Compare Lev 8:9; for Aaron and his sons as bearing the iniquity of the temple and priesthood, see Num 18:1)

It is likely that the writer of Zechariah 3 had this passage before him or in his mind when he composed his vision report, as several of the terms in Exodus 28 recur in Zechariah 3: a verbal and nominal form of פתח (3:9), a turban (3:5), and guilt in connection with the chief priest (3:4).

The turban alone is singled out for treatment in the Zechariah passage, and its importance is underscored by the envelope structure of 3:4-5:[82] "I will *clothe* you with *festal apparel*"; "Let them put a *clean turban on his head*" / "they put a *clean turban on his head*"; "and *clothed him with the apparel*." It has been suggested that the word that Zechariah employs for the turban—צניף—is significant; it is related but not identical to the one used in Exodus 28 (מצנפת).

80. Uffenheimer, *The Visions of Zechariah*, 101; on pp. 100–101, he surveys the different views about the nature of Joshua's guilt, which is not further defined in this chapter; see also Meyers and Meyers, *Haggai, Zechariah 1–8*, 189; Rooke, *Zadok's Heirs*, 140.

81. M. Zer-Kavod ("Studies in the Book of Zechariah, 3," in *Biram Volume*, ed. H. Gevaryahu, B. Z. Luria, and J. Mahlman, Publications of the IES 2 [Jerusalem: Kiryat Sefer, 1956], 117–18 [Hebrew]) maintains that מחלצות means "underwear," comparing Judg 14:9 (חליצות; compare the Targum). Thus, once Joshua had been stripped of his soiled garments, he was left naked. New underclothing was then put on him, and the specifically priestly apparel was added to it. It seems more likely, however, that the term is related to a root חלץ, whose Arabic and Akkadian cognates signify "to purify" (so D. W. Thomas, "A Note on *mḥlṣwt* in Zechariah 3:4," *JTS* 33 [1931–32]: 279–80; Meyers and Meyers, *Haggai, Zechariah 1–8*, 190).

82. So Meyers and Meyers, *Haggai, Zechariah 1-8*, 190.

צָנִיף appears rather infrequently in the Hebrew Bible. It is included in Isa 3:18-23 within a list of finery worn by the wealthy ladies of Jerusalem (Isa 3:23; note that in 3:22 the word מַחֲלָצוֹת is used as it is in Zech 3:4; the two passages also share forms of the verb סור [Isa 3:18; Zech 3:4]); and in Isa 62:3, it forms part of the phrase מְלוּכָה [*qere*] צָנִיף = "a royal diadem." Thus, it refers to a costly piece of headgear and possibly has royal connotations.[83] It could be argued that Zechariah chose this particular word as a subtle hint that Joshua would now hold a quasi-royal position (so especially Meyers and Meyers). Moreover, in Sirach, צָנִיף functions as a "special mark of royalty" (see Sir 11:5; 40:4; 47:6).[84] Nevertheless, the word צָנִיף alone does not seem to have stronger royal overtones than מִצְנֶפֶת, which figures in Exodus 28. The latter term, too, has royal associations, as Ezek 21:31 (English 21:26) shows. There, the words מִצְנֶפֶת and עֲטָרָה are parallel to one another: "Remove the turban, take off the crown."[85] The essential point is that Joshua's headpiece suggests royalty, just as Aaron's turban did. There is no change in this regard, only continuity. A new day dawns with Joshua's donning the turban and other finery, but the new day is related to the past. Through his cleansing, the entire system of ritual purification is reestablished by authority of the divine council.[86]

The scene in Zechariah 3 continues as Joshua, now clad in his rich priestly vestments,[87] is addressed by the angel of the Lord regarding the future:

> 3:6 Then the angel of the LORD assured Joshua, saying 3:7 "Thus says the LORD of hosts: If you will walk in my ways and keep my requirements, then you shall rule my house and have charge of my courts, and I will give you the right of access among those who are standing here. 3:8 Now listen, Joshua, high priest, you and your colleagues who sit before you! For they are an omen of things to come: I am going to bring my servant the Branch. 3:9 For on the stone that I have set before Joshua, on a single stone with seven facets [literally: eyes or pairs of eyes], I will engrave its inscription, says the LORD of hosts, and I will remove the guilt of this land in a single day. 3:10 On that

---

83. See Petersen, *Haggai and Zechariah 1–8*, 198; Meyers and Meyers, *Haggai, Zechariah 1–8*, 192. See also Tollington, *Tradition and Innovation*, 159 (in the absence of a monarchy, royal prerogatives passed to the senior priest).

84. Jacob Myers, "Turban," in *IDB* 4.718.

85. Petersen, *Haggai and Zechariah 1–8*, 198.

86. Ibid., 198–201.

87. Beuken alludes to Gen 35:2 and Lev 16:3-4 in which a change of clothing serves as an atoning rite (*Haggai–Sacharja 1–8*, 299). In his opinion, Zechariah is describing the investiture of Joshua; compare Exod 29:6; Lev 8:9; 16:4. In these P passages, clothing Aaron is the final act before his anointing takes place (see also 284).

day, says the LORD of hosts, you shall invite each other to come under your vine and fig tree.

The conditional sentence in verse 7 has been divided in two ways. The NRSV opts for the view that there are two conditions (the two clauses introduced by אִם = if) and two apodoses (the two clauses introduced by וְגַם).[88] The other approach is to take all four of these clauses as protases, with the apodosis coming only with the word וְנָתַתִּי, "and I will give."[89] Either interpretation is grammatically acceptable, and, in the final analysis, the results are nearly the same. The first two items are undoubtedly conditional: "if you will walk in my ways and keep my requirements." The next two are either conditions for something else or are promises that will become reality through fulfilling the first two conditions: "you shall rule my house and have charge of my courts." Only the clause "I will give you the right of access among those who are standing here" is certainly the apodosis. All of these actions—whether conditional or not—are viewed positively by the writer, and each of them is important for understanding the high-priestly roles here envisioned.

1. Walk in my ways: This appears to be a general admonition to follow priestly law and perhaps to administer justice.[90] The phrase is common in the deuteronomistic literature.[91]
2. Keep my requirements: The meaning is cultic, and in Ezekiel such language is used for the work of the Levites (44:8, 14).[92] It appears to include care for the sanctuary itself and may have broader application.
3. Rule [literally: judge] my house: The verb דִּין is not used elsewhere with a building as its object. Its primary sense is juridical, but it can also express the notion of ruling,[93] as the parallel here "have charge of my courts" demonstrates. Although there are verses that speak of Levites as judging (Deut 17:9-11; 21:5; Ezek 44:24 [at the sanctuary]; 2 Chr 19:8, 11), others name this as a royal duty (for example, 2 Sam 15:1-4; 1 Kgs 3:16-28; Jer 21:11-12; 22:1-4). This responsibility is now to be placed on the shoulders

---

88. Meyers and Meyers favor the same understanding (*Haggai, Zechariah 1–8*, 178, 194).

89. So Uffenheimer, *The Visions of Zechariah*, 101; Beuken, *Haggai–Sacharja 1–8*, 290–93; Petersen, *Haggai and Zechariah 1–8*, 206–8.

90. Meyers and Meyers, *Haggai, Zechariah 1–8*, 194–95. They refer to Exod 18:20.

91. Petersen, *Haggai and Zechariah 1–8*, 204.

92. See BDB 1038; Petersen, *Haggai and Zechariah 1–8*, 204; Meyers and Meyers, *Haggai, Zechariah 1–8*, 195.

93. BDB 192; Vinzenz Hamp and G. Johannes Botterweck, "דִּין," in *TDOT* 3.190: "does not denote an exclusive judicial activity but more broadly the administration and management of the temple."

of the high priest Joshua. Consequently, the prophet may here be crediting him with greater authority in a sphere in which the king had predominated.[94]

4. Have charge of my courts: These words express the idea that the high priest is to operate as the chief official in the entire temple area (note the plural *courts*). "Unlike the temple itself, which was off limits to the general public, the temple courtyards were the places where the people interacted with the priesthood and came closest to God's presence. The charge to Joshua concerning the courts apparently represents his responsibility for all the business and activities in connection with the public."[95] So, Joshua is to become the sole ruler of the whole temple compound,[96] with no civil power rivaling his—a condition that was unparalleled in earlier times.[97]

5. The right of access among those who are standing here: The NRSV's translation "right of access" is only one possibility; an alternative and perhaps more likely rendering is "ones who go about those who are standing here."[98] As the entire scene transpires in the divine assembly or courtroom, the angel is promising to Joshua that, if he keeps the conditions stated, he himself (if the first option is taken) will be able to enter that august assembly, or (if the second option is selected) he will be given individuals who have such access. In either way, he will enjoy, directly or indirectly, even greater access to God than the temple afforded. If some of Joshua's duties that were enunciated earlier in the verse articulate an expansion of high-priestly authority into spheres once controlled by the king, this promise of access shows a sacerdotal advance into the traditional territory of the prophets. The promised right of access recalls passages such as 1 Kings 22:19-23 (Micaiah), Isaiah 6, and Jer 23:18, in which a prophet either participates in the deliberations of the divine council or claims to have the ability to witness the proceedings in it.[99]

---

94. Meyers and Meyers, *Haggai, Zechariah 1–8*, 195; compare Petersen, *Haggai and Zechariah 1–8*, 205–6; Christian Jeremias, *Die Nachtgesichte des Sacharja*, FRLANT 117 (Göttingen: Vandenhoeck & Ruprecht, 1977), 214–15.

95. Meyers and Meyers, *Haggai, Zechariah 1–8*, 196.

96. Uffenheimer, *The Visions of Zechariah*, 102.

97. Mitchell, *A Critical and Exegetical Commentary*, 154–55. Rooke disagrees (*Zadok's Heirs*, 144–45), citing priestly authority in the First Temple area, but she does regard the passage as granting "more of a quantitative than a qualitative promotion, extending his area of authority within the cultic sphere but keeping it in that sphere" (145).

98. See the summary in VanderKam, "Joshua the High Priest," 559–60.

99. See Mitchell, *A Critical and Exegetical Commentary*, 154–55; Petersen, *Haggai and Zechariah 1–8*, 207–8; Meyers and Meyers, *Haggai, Zechariah 1–8*, 196–97.

To this point in Zechariah 3, then, the prophetic vision and oracles describe the removal of Joshua's impurity and guilt (thus revivifying the effectiveness of the cult), his investiture with the clean and splendid clothes of the high priests, and the charge to him to follow the Lord's will and to exercise full authority over the deity's house. But more is added. In Zech 3:8-10, the angel continues to address Joshua and to paint a bright and colorful picture of times to come. The high priest and his colleagues (possibly a priestly assembly or group)[100] are exhorted to listen. These colleagues and perhaps Joshua too[101] are called "an omen of things to come" (literally: men of portent). In explanation of this phrase, the commentators regularly point to biblical passages in which prophets are so designated, especially to Isa 8:18: "See, I and the children whom the LORD has given me are signs and portents [מוֹפְתִים] in Israel from the LORD of hosts, who dwells on Mount Zion" (see also Ezek 12:6; 24:24, 27; compare 2 Chr 32:24). As Mitchell wrote about the reference in Zechariah: "the idea seems to be that these men, the priests as a class, are prophetic of good to the community they are serving."[102] The other biblical references give reason for thinking that the priestly office is now to embody something of the old prophetic role in communicating divine messages or teachings to the people.[103]

The following clause in Zech 3:8 contains Zechariah's first reference to someone called "my servant the Branch."[104] Clearly, he belongs to the future of which the priests sitting before Joshua (and perhaps Joshua himself) are portents. Jeremiah employed the same word Branch (צֶמַח) for a Davidic ruler of the future: "The days are surely coming, says the LORD, when I will raise up for David a righteous Branch, and he shall reign as king and deal wisely, and shall execute justice and righteousness in the land. In his days Judah will be

---

100. Albert Petitjean, "La mission de Zorobabel et la reconstruction du Temple: Zach. III, 8-10," *ETL* 42 (1966): 40–41; idem, *Les oracles du Proto-Zacharie*, 164–65 (where he refers to the phrase וְהַכֹּהֵן הַגָּדוֹל מֵאֶחָיו in Lev 21:10).

101. On the text-critical issue here—"they/you are men of good omen"—see Petitjean, *Les oracles du Proto-Zacharie*, 164–65; Meyers and Meyers, *Haggai, Zechariah 1–8*, 199. Petersen thinks that all of the returnees are meant, not just a group of priests (*Haggai and Zechariah 1–8*, 209–10).

102. *A Critical and Exegetical Commentary*, 156.

103. Meyers and Meyers, *Haggai, Zechariah 1–8*, 200; Petitjean ("La mission de Zorobabel," 42–44) surveys different interpretations of the phrase but thinks it must be interpreted in light of v. 9 (see his *Les oracles du Proto-Zacharie*, 168–70). Compare also Beuken, *Haggai–Sacharja 1–8*, 301–2.

104. The Hebrew [צֶמַח] and Greek ['Ανατολήν] texts lack a definite article; "a Branch" or just "Branch" would be a more accurate rendering. For "my servant," see Hag 2:23 where it is used of Zerubbabel.

saved and Israel will live in safety. And this is the name by which he will be called: 'The LORD is our righteousness'" (Jer 23:5-6; virtually the same words appear at 33:14-15; see also Isa 4:2). The majority of commentators see in Zechariah's Branch a reference to Zerubbabel, the heir of David who ruled as governor in Judea. For example, Petitjean[105] thinks that the word stresses the principle of succession and does not suggest a messianic ideology (note also the literal meaning of the Babylonian name Zerubbabel = *zēr bābili* = seed of Babylon). In fact, Petersen understands the oracle in this verse to center on Zerubbabel and to be a corrective to the claims advanced for Joshua in the preceding verse.[106] Yet, as has frequently been observed, there is a future ring to this statement about a Branch: the angel will bring (the participle מביא is used) "my servant the Branch."[107] This future aspect may not be compatible with the situation of Zerubbabel who, according to Ezra 2:2, returned to Jerusalem at the same time as Joshua and who had been in Jerusalem for perhaps nineteen years when Zechariah spoke these words.[108] Uffenheimer, who has examined other biblical uses of the word צמח, contends that it never refers to an individual existing at the present time of the writer but always to an ideal figure of the future.[109] In light of this scriptural usage and the fact that Zerubbabel and Joshua were contemporaries and apparently in office at the time when this passage was written, it seems preferable to see in Zechariah's Branch a ruler who *will* come from David's line (see also Zech 6:12).

Zechariah 3:9 contains the image of a single stone with seven facets or eyes/pairs of eyes. On it, the Lord will etch an inscription whose contents are not cited. The text declares that there is a connection between this imagery and removal of the land's guilt. The identity of the stone has been the subject

---

105. "La mission de Zorobabel," 63–71; *Les oracles du Proto-Zacharie*, 195–205. See also Beuken, *Haggai–Sacharja 1–8*, 288.

106. *Haggai and Zechariah 1–8*, 210–11. This is the opposite of the conclusion reached by Beuken, who thinks that vv. 8-10 are original and that vv. 6-7 were added to exalt Joshua at the expense of Zerubbabel (*Haggai–Sacharja 1–8*, 290–303).

107. See Mitchell, *A Critical and Exegetical Commentary*, 156.

108. Liver connects the Branch references to Zechariah's theological conviction that the present is a time of small things but that God will bring redemption in his good time (*The House of David*, 101–2). Zerubbabel *will be* that Branch; however, when Zechariah utters the prophecy, he does not yet give him the title. We should again recall, however, the problems with the chronology of Ezra 1–6.

109. *The Visions of Zechariah*, 1–7. Uffenheimer moves beyond this observation to the conclusion that Zech 4:6b-10a—the only place in Zechariah where Zerubbabel is named—dates from a time during his governorship and that Zechariah 3 and 6:9-15—the Branch passages—come from a later time after his disappearance. Accepting his thesis about the meaning of צמח does not necessarily entail this further inference.

of lively scholarly debate. There now appear to be two principal options for interpreting the stone and what is on it: (1) the temple-building theory, and (2) the vestments theory.

1. The temple-building theory. This view, which has become the dominant one after publication of Petitjean's article and book, explains the stone within the context of the rites and mythology of royal temple-building, restoration, and dedication in ancient Mesopotamia. That is, Zechariah's stone is an especially significant stone for the physical construction of the temple—perhaps the cornerstone or a stone for a foundation deposit. One piece of information that is often adduced in support of this approach is Zech 4:7, which says of Zerubbabel: "he shall bring out the top [or: first] stone [הָאֶבֶן הָרֹאשָׁה] amid shouts of 'Grace, grace to it!'"[110] This verse is uttered in a setting that connects the governor with construction of the sanctuary (4:6b-10a). Petitjean, who thinks that the oracular material in Zechariah (that is, 1:16-17; 2:10-17; 3:8-10; 4:6b-10a; 6:9-15) once stood together, defends this view at length and uses 4:6b-10a to explicate 3:9. When the two are read together, it is evident that 3:9 deals with the rebuilding of the temple.[111] He notes that in Zech 6:12, the Branch builds the Lord's house, and this verse parallels 3:9 (both use the term Branch; compare the phrases וּמִתַּחְתָּיו יִצְמָח in 6:12 and מֵבִיא in 3:9). For Petitjean, the stone in Zech 3:9 is a foundation stone on which the Lord makes an engraving, just as kings who founded temples in the Assyro-Babylonian period did in order to perpetuate their memory and announce their pious deed to posterity.[112] The rites that accompanied this deed were meant to remove impurity from the sanctuary (compare 3:9), and the laying of this symbolic stone was associated with fertility of the land (see v. 10).[113] The phrase "in that day" (v. 10) refers to the day of founding the temple.[114] As in times past, the Lord's favorable message (for the stone, in this instance) is conveyed through the priests, the repositories of תורות.[115]

Although this theory is appealing, it does encounter sizable difficulties. For example, while there may be some points of contact between Zech 3:9 and 4:6b-10a, the former passage now appears within chapter 3. To reach his conclusion, Petitjean ignores the present context of the verse within the third

---

110. For a summary of the various theories about the stone, see Meyers and Meyers, *Haggai, Zechariah 1–8*, 204–6; Beuken, *Haggai–Sacharja 1–8*, 284–90.

111. "La mission de Zorobabel," 40–51; *Les oracles du Proto-Zacharie*, 173–85.

112. "La mission de Zorobabel," 53; *Les oracles du Proto-Zacharie*, 184–85.

113. "La mission de Zorobabel," 53–55; *Les oracles du Proto-Zacharie*, 184–91.

114. "La mission de Zorobabel," 56–57; *Les oracles du Proto-Zacharie*, 187–89.

115. "La mission de Zorobabel," 60–62; *Les oracles du Proto-Zacharie*, throughout, especially 161–206. For others who have accepted and modified Petitjean's thesis, see VanderKam, "Joshua the High Priest," 564–66.

chapter in favor of a hypothetical original setting amid the various oracles that are now scattered throughout Zechariah 1–8. It would be taxing indeed to infer from Zechariah 3 alone that temple building was under consideration because it is never mentioned. Also, although the passage is supposed to have Zerubbabel in view, the prophet fails to mention him by name until chapter 4. Throughout Zechariah 3, Joshua is the center of interest, not Zerubabbel or even Branch. Dating, too, may be a problem: if Zechariah's vision and oracles of chapter 3 fall within the dates given elsewhere in the book, the founding ceremony may already have taken place by this time (perhaps on 9/24 according to Haggai; Zech 1:7 mentions 11/24). These objections invite one to consider another approach.[116]

2. The vestments theory: The second thesis accords greater weight to the *present* context of Zechariah 3 and thus relates the stone to the high priest's headgear. Mitchell understood the rock to be a precious stone whose "seven eyes" are its seven facets.[117] He pointed to Exodus 28 where fourteen engraved stones for the shoulders of the high priest (v. 9) and breastplate of the ephod (v. 21) are mentioned. Moses is also told to make for Aaron "a rosette [צִיץ] of pure gold, and engrave on it, like the engraving of a signet, 'Holy to the LORD'" (Exod 28:36; v. 37 stipulates that it is to be fastened to the turban). This rosette (or plate), placed on Aaron, allows him to "take on himself any guilt incurred in the holy offering [עֲוֹן הַקֳּדָשִׁים]" (v. 38).[118] The plate of Exodus 28, then, could be what Zechariah has in mind in 3:9 when he alludes to a stone with seven facets. Petersen accepts this position,[119] but his suggestion that the seven facets or eyes of the stone symbolize the seven Hebrew letters (assuming an earlier orthography) in the inscription of Exod 28:36—קֹדֶשׁ לַיהוֹ—is unlikely. In a more helpful way, however, he does stress that there are different leading actors in Exodus 28 and Zechariah 3: in the former, Moses is to make the garments, and Aaron bears the guilt; in Zechariah, the Lord performs all the actions. The new time will be of his doing.[120]

This theory has the advantage of reading Zech 3:9 in the context in which it is placed and of exploiting the verbal similarities with Exodus 28 that were noted. Nevertheless, it too must surmount major obstacles: the rosette of Exodus 28 is not called a stone, and the guilt removed in Exodus 28 is not that of the land but of "the holy offering." Moreover, as Uffenheimer objects, the stone in Zechariah 3 cannot mean the stone of the ephod because only one is

---

116. For these and other objections, see VanderKam, "Joshua the High Priest," 566–67.
117. *A Critical and Exegetical Commentary*, 157.
118. Petersen, *Haggai and Zechariah 1–8*, 158–59.
119. Ibid., 211–12.
120. Ibid., 212; see also Galling, "Serubbabel und der Hohepriester," 146–47.

involved whereas Exodus has multiple stones. For him, the stone is the temple itself and the eyes symbolize the divine providence over all of it.[121]

These objections to the second thesis are significant, but they do not undermine the case for seeing a connection between Zech 3:9 and Exodus 28 and thus between the context in Zechariah 3 and the reference to the stone. The strong relation of language surely connects the two, but another thought should also be considered. In Exodus 28, the apparel of the high priest includes fourteen stones: two are on the shoulder piece of the ephod (v. 12), and the breastpiece, which is also connected to the shoulder piece of the ephod (vv. 25-28), contains twelve stones arranged in four rows (vv. 17, 21). Both groups of stones represent the tribes of Israel. The single stone set before Joshua, which is engraved like the plate on Aaron's turban, is said to have seven עֵינָיִם. A literal translation would yield "seven pairs of eyes" or fourteen altogether, that is, the same number as the stones in Aaron's clothing. This raises the possibility that the one stone with seven sets of eyes is meant to symbolize the full sacred attire of the high priest, not just one item in it. The symbol unifies his apparel, as his apparel signifies the unity of the people (compare v. 10). Also, it may be purely accidental, but the plate of Exod 28:36-38 is to be placed on Aaron's forehead. The words for forehead (מֵצַח) and for Branch (צֶמַח) have the same consonants in a different order and very nearly the same vowels. Perhaps the word מֵצַח in Exodus 28 was another incentive for the author of Zechariah 3 to make use of the epithet צֶמַח for the coming Davidic ruler.[122]

Zechariah 3 concludes with a picture of a purified land that is verdant and the home to a unified society. The new conditions follow upon the cleansing and renewal of the high priest (and his colleagues), which have been described in the preceding verses. Now, the restored community will have the opportunity to engage in the proper worship and service of God who has made these new times possible. In this prophetic chapter, we meet the first postexilic mention of the high-priestly garments that were to catch the fancy of later writers (see Sir 50:5-13; Let. Aris. 96–99; and Josephus Ant. 11.8, 5 [§§331–35]); here they are tied to larger themes essential to the role of the high priest. We also read about the prophet Zechariah's conviction regarding the expanded and crucial place of the high priest in the proper functioning of the temple cult and life before God in the land. Here, Joshua is the primary character, and Zerubbabel the governor is not named.

121. The Visions of Zechariah, 103–6.
122. For a fuller statement of the idea that the "seven pairs of eyes" represent the fourteen stones, see VanderKam, "Joshua the High Priest," 567–70.

Zechariah 4: The vision of the lampstand: There is no need to enter into a protracted analysis of this chapter because not all of it is germane to Zechariah's teachings about the high priesthood. A point of similarity between Zechariah 3 and 4 is that two rulers—a Davidic leader and a high priest—continue to receive attention; they differ in that chapter 3 centered about Joshua while chapter 4 names Zerubbabel alone and has little to say about the high priest, who is present only under the symbol of an olive tree (unless he is meant by the pronoun "you" in v. 7).[123] Virtually all commentators label the oracle addressed to Zerubbabel in Zech 4:6b-7 and the one about him in verses 8-10 an interpolation into the vision of the menorah. These verses are marked off from the surrounding context by the fact that the conversation of verses 2-5 is resumed in verse 10b with the angel's answer to Zechariah's question in verse 5, while the intervening sayings seem to have little connection with it.[124]

The inserted words—if that is what they are—directly address the temple-building project. Several expressions in these verses that have traditionally given difficulty to interpreters have recently been clarified as technical references to the ritual of making a building deposit:[125] הראשה האבן (4:7) (NRSV = "the top stone") appears to be what in Akkadian is called a *libittu maḫritu* = a former brick that was removed from the preceding temple and placed in the new one to express continuity;[126] and הבדיל האבן (v. 10) (NRSV = "the plummet") seems to parallel the Akkadian "tin or metallic tablet, a building deposit" for increasing the value of the temple.[127] Zechariah 4:6b-10a, then,

---

123. This is the view of Galling, who thinks that Joshua doubts the temple will soon be completed—the "great mountain" is the pile of rubble that remains from the First Temple ("Serubbabel und der Hohepriester," 137, 143–44); Petersen ("Zerubbabel and Jerusalem Temple Reconstruction," *CBQ* 36 [1974]: 367, 372; *Haggai and Zechariah 1–8*, 239–40) believes that Joshua is being warned to leave the work of temple building to Zerubbabel and that הגדול הר (= "O great mountain") is possibly a wordplay on הגדול הכהן (= "O high priest"). The suggestion of such a wordplay, though Petersen makes it only tentatively, seems forced. Beuken (*Haggai–Sacharja 1–8*, 266–70) explains the mountain as an image for the opposition that Zerubbabel experienced in the process of rebuilding the sanctuary.

124. For views about the original location of the intervening verses, see Petitjean, *Les oracles du Proto-Zacharie*, 207–13. Beuken (*Haggai–Sacharja 1–8*, 260–64, 270–74), who also sees these verses as later material, finds they are not unified. The form of Zech 4:8, with the introductory formula of divine speech, marks vv. 8-10a as a unit. He regards vv. 6aβ-7 as original to this "Wortsymbolvision," but they belong after v. 10b. Thus, the original form was vv. 1-6aα, 10b, 6aβ-7. This last pair of verses provides the point of the vision. Verses 11-14 are a later explanation of the vision and do not fit it very well.

125. See Petitjean, *Les oracles du Proto-Zacharie*, 215–26.

126. Ibid., 241–51.

127. Ibid., 230–36; Beuken, *Haggai–Sacharja 1–8*, 267, 286–90; Petersen, "Zerubbabel and Jerusalem Temple Reconstruction," 368–70; idem, *Haggai and Zechariah 1–8*, 237–44. Galling

definitely connects Zerubbabel with building the sanctuary; whether another individual is critical of him here is less certain. In addition, the words to Zerubbabel—"Not by might, nor by power, but by my spirit, says the LORD of hosts" (v. 6b)—may convey a rebuke to the Davidic scion for his previous approach to the project.[128]

The central image of the vision is the lampstand that is flanked by (or is below) two olive trees that supply it with oil (Zech 4:2-3). The menorah was, of course, part of the furniture of the tabernacle (Exod 25:31-40), and Solomon's temple had ten of them (1 Kings 7:49; 2 Chr 4:7; Jer 52:19 says that the Babylonians removed them).[129] It served as a symbol of God's presence in the sanctuary[130] or of God's very self,[131] while the two olive trees that stand beside it and supply it with oil are suggestive of fruitfulness and perhaps stability. Olive oil was a staple of the land's economy, and some of it was offered at the temple.[132] Zechariah's vision sets forth numerous complicated details about the structure and functioning of the menorah, but the interpretation offered in Zech 4:10b-14 ignores most of them, including the lampstand itself.[133] The interest here narrows rather to the seven lamps of verse 2 and the two olive trees or branches of verse 3. The lamps are explained as "the eyes of the LORD, which range through the whole earth" (4:10), and the olive trees or branches symbolize "the two anointed ones [literally: sons of oil] who stand by the Lord of the whole earth" (4:14). References to "the Lord," though different terms are used, and "the whole earth" bind the two interpretive verses together and imply a unity of images. The eyes should be taken as denoting the Lord's providential supervision over the earth.[134] The image may have been drawn from the Persian network of the "eyes of the king" who annually "made a careful inspection of each province";[135] it is a favorable image for the people

---

thinks this latter term refers to the *urim* and *tummim* and that in this verse Zerubbabel invests Joshua with the high priesthood ("Serubbabel und der Hohepriester," 145–46).

128. For the רוח here, see Petitjean, *Les oracles du Proto-Zacharie*, 262–63. On this passage, compare also Liver, *The House of David*, 97–99.

129. For extensive discussion of these lampstands and the one in Zechariah 4, see Uffenheimer, *The Visions of Zechariah*, 50–57; Petersen, *Haggai and Zechariah 1–8*, 216–23; and Meyers and Meyers, *Haggai, Zechariah 1–8*, 229–38, 263–65.

130. Meyers and Meyers, *Haggai, Zechariah 1–8*, 229–40, 256, 273–74.

131. Petersen, *Haggai and Zechariah 1–8*, 227–28.

132. Meyers and Meyers, *Haggai, Zechariah 1–8*, 239, 256.

133. See Uffenheimer, who writes about the fragmentary character of the interpretation (*The Visions of Zechariah*, 58–60).

134. Uffenheimer, *The Visions of Zechariah*, 59–61; Beuken, *Haggai–Sacharja 1–8*, 265–68, 288.

135. Olmstead, *History of the Persian Empire*, 59; J. M. Cook, *The Persian Empire* (New York: Shocken, 1983; reprinted Barnes & Noble, 1993), 143; Uffenheimer, *The Visions of Zechariah*, 61.

of the providential God.[136] The two "sons of oil," who are not named but, given the context, are thought to be Joshua and Zerubbabel, are emblematic of the restored priesthood of Zadok and house of David. The notion of "anointed" brings with it a highly suggestive set of associations, but here the term for oil (יִצְהָר) is not the one that is used elsewhere in the Bible in connection with the ceremony of anointing priests and kings (= שֶׁמֶן). The word יִצְהָר appears regularly with terms for wine and grain as the staples of the land; its presence here presumably is meant to arouse thoughts of plenty in the reader's mind.[137]

The fact that the two "sons of oil" are on the same level vis-à-vis the lamp-stand—both stand "by the Lord" or "above the Lord" (the preposition is עַל)—expresses the equality of the two officials. In monarchic times, the image would have been inappropriate, since the king was dominant; but in the new situation, after the return from exile, governor and high priest are equals.[138] Moreover, the imagery of the vision also articulates the thought that they are essential for the proper functioning of the divinely chosen community as it centers about the new temple. The two trees provide the requisite oil, without which the menorah would shed no light.[139] It is also possible that the prophet here borrows the language of the divine council, in that he pictures the two standing as courtiers above the seated Lord.[140] That is, in Zech 3:7, the possibility of access to the divine presence is held out to Joshua, if he is obedient; here it is given to both Zerubbabel and Joshua, the two divinely ordained leaders of the nation. Petersen also maintains that the word "sons" in the phrase "sons of oil" is significant: previously the king was spoken of as God's son; now there are two of them.[141] This seems a rather implausible inference from an

---

136. Petersen, *Haggai and Zechariah 1–8*, 225–27.

137. Ibid., 230–31; Meyers and Meyers, *Haggai, Zechariah 1–8*, 257–59. Beuken (*Haggai–Sacharja 1–8*, 270–74), for whom 4:11-14 are secondary and incompatible with the original vision, finds here an allusion to the anointing of the two to their offices. Since Beuken thinks it would be most unlikely that at a time of heightened expectations connected with the Davidic house there would be talk of anointing the high priest, he assigns this to a later time when Zerubbabel had disappeared. That is, the original form of the text addressed only Zerubbabel. It is not clear, however, that anointing is under consideration here, nor is Beuken's understanding of the early restoration in line with a fairly substantial body of evidence about the respective roles of Joshua and Zerubbabel.

138. Kenneth E. Pomykala, *The Davidic Dynasty Tradition in Early Judaism: Its History and Significance for Messianism*, SBLEJL 7 (Atlanta: Scholars, 1995), 59; Rooke fails to deal with this point (*Zadok's Heirs*, 145–46).

139. Petersen, *Haggai and Zechariah 1–8*, 234.

140. Ibid., 232–33; Meyers and Meyers, *Haggai, Zechariah 1–8*, 276.

141. Petersen, *Haggai and Zechariah 1–8*, 233.

expression in which "sons of" serves the idiomatic function of indicating people who are characterized in some way by the word that follows.[142]

Zechariah 6:9-15: The oracle about crowns: The third and final section in Zechariah that pertains to the high priest Joshua resembles chapter 3 in naming Joshua and mentioning a Branch and chapter 4 in dealing with temple building. It differs in that here Zechariah receives the word of the Lord, not a vision, and a divine command that names specific individuals. It may well be that Heldai, Tobijah, and Jedaiah (6:10), who are said to be from the exile and to "have arrived from Babylon" (v. 10; compare v. 15), are bringing contributions from Jewish people who had not returned to Jerusalem but nevertheless supported the temple-building project.[143] Zechariah is told to convey the precious metals that they brought to the house of Josiah, son of Zephaniah. If this Zephaniah was the same person as the second-ranking priest in the last days of the First Temple (like the high priest Seraiah, he was executed at Riblah [2 Kings 25:18, 21]), then Josiah may have been a prominent citizen of Jerusalem who perhaps had never left the land to go into exile.[144] These identifications are hypothetical in the extreme, but if they are correct the characters in this episode would represent virtually all the recent experiences of the Judean people.

With the metals thus obtained, Zechariah is ordered to fashion crowns (6:11—עֲטָרוֹת). Here, despite frequent attempts to emend to the singular (for example, by NRSV, RSV, *BHS*), the plural form is firmly established as correct by the MT and LXX.[145] One of the crowns is to be placed on the head of Joshua

---

142. Compare Beuken, *Haggai–Sacharja 1–8,* 271.

143. Uffenheimer, *The Visions of Zechariah,* 117; Petersen, *Haggai and Zechariah 1–8,* 274. Meyers and Meyers (*Haggai, Zechariah 1–8,* 338–43) speculate about the identity of the three: Heldai may have been a delegate from the Babylonian Jews, Jedaiah a returnee who now resided in Yehud, and Tobijah a returnee who now lived outside Yehud. For the names and the evidence of the versions, see Petitjean, *Les oracles du Proto-Zacharie,* 271–74. The LXX translates them as nouns here and in v. 14.

144. For this point, see Meyers and Meyers, *Haggai, Zechariah 1–8,* 344–45.

145. Many exegetes have attempted to restore an original form of the oracle in which Zerubbabel alone receives a crown; after his alleged disappearance, the name *Joshua* was substituted for his in v. 11. Compare Sacchi, *The History of the Second Temple Period,* 67–68. For the history of this interpretation, which lacks any textual support (correctly noted by Pomykala, *The Davidic Dynasty Tradition,* 57–58), see Petitjean, *Les oracles du Proto-Zacharie,* 283–84. Petitjean recognizes that עֲטָרוֹת is plural in form but thinks that only one crown is meant (279–81). He sees the placing of a crown on Joshua as symbolic, announcing the arrival and crowning of Zerubbabel, the principal character of the restoration. Petitjean thinks that the scene belongs in a time prior to Zerubbabel's true arrival into his patrimony and that there are different pictures presented in vv. 10-12 and vv. 13-14. In the former (the more ancient of the two), Zerubbabel is

(v. 11; his patronymic and title are added). This is the only biblical passage in which a priest wears an עטרה; otherwise, kings (for example, 2 Sam 12:30) and a few other individuals (in Song 3:1 the word is used for a wedding wreath, and in Esth 8:15 for Mordecai's crown) wore them. This is the second time in Zechariah that the headgear of the high priest Joshua receives attention (for the turban, see 3:5). Meyers and Meyers comment that in both places "a non-priestly or royal term has been applied to the high priest, a usage that must be intentional and fully within the prophet's overall purpose."[146]

As in Zechariah 3, so in 6:9-15 mention of what Joshua wears on his head is accompanied by an oracle about a Branch who is coming. There is great uncertainty about the meaning of the phrase ומתחתיו יצמח, which NRSV renders as "he shall branch out in his place" (v. 12). It clearly derives, like *Branch*, from botanical imagery and may signify deep rootage.[147] It is much clearer, however, that the prophet sees this sprouting of Branch as an event of the future and as connected with temple building. How far it lies in the future is not said, but it need not be distant.[148] In this section, the writer is leaning heavily on Jeremiah 33, from which he seems to borrow his most important terms and ideas.[149] Note in particular these items: (1) עטרת שלום = a crown

---

the central character, and the person and mission of the high priest are defined in terms of the prince. In the latter, the two share a bicephalic authority (286–99). Beuken, too, considers what the present text says to be unacceptable for Zechariah. He rejects the notion of a high priest with a crown on his head immediately after the exile and finds it somewhat more believable that Joshua would have been crowned in a symbolic fashion as a guarantee for the future (*Haggai–Sacharja 1–8*, 275). All of this sounds as if the text is being ignored in favor of what we supposedly know about the situation at the time of Zechariah's prophecy. Uffenheimer (*The Visions of Zechariah*, 118) surveys different proposals about עטרות. Petersen (*Haggai and Zechariah 1–8*, 273) claims that the LXX has a singular form; actually, some LXX manuscripts read a singular, although the best ones have a plural noun.

146. *Haggai, Zechariah 1–8*, 351; compare Petersen, *Haggai and Zechariah 1–8*, 275.

147. So Uffenheimer, *The Visions of Zechariah*, 119. Beuken (*Haggai–Sacharja 1–8*, 276) thinks the expression constitutes a play on the meaning of *Zerubbabel*. A creative if entirely speculative proposal was made by Zer-Kavod ("Studies in the Book of Zechariah, 3," 120–21): a haplography has served to delete a reference to Zerubbabel's death. On his view, the text originally read: הנה איש צמח שמו ומת ומתחתיו יצמח (compare Job 2:10).

148. Beuken, *Haggai–Sacharja 1–8*, 276.

149. In the MT, Jeremiah 33 has twenty-six verses, while the Greek renders only thirteen. Since the shorter LXX version of Jeremiah reflects a shorter Hebrew form of the book that may be the older one (see Emanuel Tov, *Textual Criticism of the Hebrew Bible*, 2nd rev. ed. [Minneapolis: Fortress Press, 2001], 319–27), vv. 14-26 of Jeremiah 33 may indeed come from a time later than Jeremiah himself (although this is not a necessary inference). Beuken, who devotes a section to a comparison between Jer 33:14-22 and Zechariah 3, sees in the Jeremiah passage a subsequent interpretation of Jer 23:5-6; it mirrors the same milieu as the revision that he posits for Zechariah 3, 4, and 6 in the direction of exalting Joshua. A theme that is particularly tied to

of peace (Jer 33:6; the term for *crown* is not in the LXX [40:6] and is not reflected in NRSV); (2) return of exiles (though different words are used for *exile*, שבות in Jeremiah, גולה in Zechariah [see Jer 33:7, 11, 26]); (3) the temple (בית יהוה in Jer 33:11, היכל יהוה in Zech 6:12-14); (4) peace (33:6, 9); (5) the sprouting of a Branch (33:15, where he is identified as Davidic); and (6) two chosen families, royal and priestly, neither of which will ever lack descendants (33:17, 18, 21, 22, 24). In Jeremiah 33, the Davidic ruler sits on a throne (כסא in v. 17) from which he rules as king (v. 21). The priestly family is usually referred to in the plural (for example, "the levitical priests" in 33:18; compare vv. 21, 22), but in verse 18, a single member of it is mentioned in parallel with the single scion of David's line: "the levitical priests shall never lack a man in my presence to offer burnt offerings, to make grain offerings, and to make sacrifices for all time."

As the writer of Zechariah 6 works with this material from Jeremiah 33, he modifies it to address the new situation of his time, when the representative of David's family is reduced in status and the offspring of Zadok's line has risen in standing. In Zechariah, the two chosen lines continue to function, but the representatives of the two are put on equal footing and enjoy harmonious relations. One indication of Joshua's enhanced office is the crown that is placed on his head (6:11);[150] another is the throne on which he sits (v. 13; Jeremiah has a throne only for the Davidic ruler). Zechariah first designates a throne for Branch and, as in Jer 33:17, 21, proclaims that he will sit and rule on this throne. However, he continues by writing in 6:13: והיה כהן על כסאו. NRSV, among other versions, translates as though the reference continues to be Branch's throne: "There shall be a priest by his throne." This rendering is most unlikely to be correct for the Hebrew text; it requires that in one sentence the same phrase (על כסאו) have two meanings (on his throne/by his throne). In a pericope that speaks of crowns and two individuals, the evident intention is that both persons have thrones.[151] The interpretation of the passage that

---

this situation is the paralleling of the levitic and Davidic lines in the sense that neither will ever lack one who is to perform the group's special function (*Haggai-Sacharja 1–8*, 303–9). As a result, the borrowings by Zechariah 6 from Jeremiah 33 listed above would be valid for Jer 33:1-13; those from the second half of the chapter could also be borrowings, but the uncertainty of dating makes this thesis more difficult to establish.

150. Rooke, for whose thesis a crown on Joshua's head is awkward, thinks the crown is a symbol for the temple (*Zadok's Heirs*, 147–49). There seems to be no basis for this inference.

151. See Meyers and Meyers, *Haggai, Zechariah 1–8*, 336, 361. They refer to Eli's sitting upon a כסא as he executed his sacerdotal responsibilities. Petitjean surveys other passages in which, as here, the LXX does not use θρόνος for כסא (*Les oracles du Proto-Zacharie*, 291–93). Rooke does not mention the possibility that Joshua has his own throne in this verse (*Zadok's Heirs*, 149).

places the priest *next to* Branch's throne is influenced by the LXX: the priest will be on his right side (it lacks a reference to a throne). Beuken accepts the Greek reading and notes that היה is strange with על כסאו. The verb would fit better with the reading reflected in the LXX. The throne of the priest is, for Beuken, another manifestation of the revision that took place when Zerubbabel had disappeared and the high priest had assumed greater prominence.[152] Petersen, who accepts the LXX-influenced reading, finds here a borrowing from the language of the royal court or divine council, with an attendant standing above (על) a seated ruler. In that case, Joshua (or whoever "a priest" is) would possess an inferior status relative to the Davidic heir. This supposedly stands in harmony with Zech 4:6b-10, which, according to Petersen, denigrates Joshua in comparison with Zerubbabel.[153]

It seems more plausible, in view of the context, to see in Zechariah 6 two thrones with two occupants—an image that corresponds with the picture elsewhere in the book of a royal and priestly dyarchy. As the prophet says, the two seated figures, far from being rivals, coexist through their "peaceful understanding" (6:13; see Jer 33:6, 9). It is important to notice, however, that Zechariah has more to say about the royal figure than about the priest. In addition to his ruling, he will build[154] the temple and he "shall bear royal honor" (v. 13).

The crowns return in Zech 6:14 where, again, there has been long debate about whether a singular or plural is to be read. The evidence of the MT is mixed: the consonantal text could be vocalized as either singular (הָעֲטֶרֶת) or plural as in the received text (הָעֲטָרֹת). The verb for which it serves as subject is definitely singular in form (תהיה). The person who translated the text into Greek had the same text before him as this consonantal form, but he read the noun as singular and in this way produced a grammatically consistent sentence. Textually, then, it is advisable to accept two singular forms.[155] As one crown has already been placed on Joshua's head in Zech 6:11, there remains only a single crown with which the prophet must deal. The context leads one to think that it is a crown for the future Davidic ruler; however, since he is a figure of days to come, it is deposited in the temple. There it is to be kept in readiness for that time when he will appear in order to construct the Lord's

152. *Haggai-Sacharja 1–8*, 277–78, 281.

153. *Haggai and Zechariah 1–8*, 277; compare Petitjean, *Les oracles du Proto-Zacharie*, 293.

154. The future tense raises the question which sanctuary is intended; see Meyers and Meyers, *Haggai, Zechariah 1–8*, 355–58.

155. So Uffenheimer, *The Visions of Zechariah*, 117–18; Meyers and Meyers, *Haggai, Zechariah 1–8*, 362–63; Petersen (*Haggai and Zechariah 1–8*, 273, 278–79), however, prefers "crowns."

dwelling, helped by those of Judean extraction who live far away and who, like the three men in this section, bring silver and gold from Babylon.[156]

The material surveyed conveys rather clearly that the first high priest of the Second Temple, Joshua/Jeshua, was not only a leader in the return to Zion and the efforts to rebuild the temple but, at least in the estimation of Zechariah, also enjoyed a status that put him on a kind of equal footing with the Davidic heir and governor Zerubbabel. Since Zerubbabel was the civil ruler, Joshua seems not to have exercised such authority outside the sphere of the sanctuary. Yet, the status of this high priest is more elevated vis-à-vis the Davidic leader than had been the case for his predecessors during the time of the First Temple.

---

156. Compare Uffenheimer, *The Visions of Zechariah*, 120; Meyers and Meyers, *Haggai, Zechariah 1–8*, 363.

2

The High Priests of
the Persian Period

The sources for one year (520 BCE) of Joshua's high priesthood are relatively plentiful and varied, though little is said about what he did or the extent of his authority (see chap. 1). For any later years of his tenure (after 520), the biblical books are silent, and for his successors they also offer virtually no information apart from the names of the first five. The relevant names figure in two lists in Nehemiah 12. There, they are not identified explicitly as high priests, but since their names are given in genealogical form and some of them are known from other sources to have been high priests, it is reasonable to assume that Nehemiah 12 is presenting them as such.[1] These meager lists can be supplemented to some extent by the narratives and other allusions in Nehemiah (and in Ezra on some theories) and also from a few of the Elephantine papyri. The most extended and significant source for the period in question is, however, the *Antiquities* of Josephus. His book is the only extant account of Jewish history during the later Persian age. He mentions all of Nehemiah's high priests and adds some extrabiblical stories about two of them in particular. The sources from which he derived his extrabiblical information remain unknown today, and, as will be seen below, this information has been the subject of intense scrutiny and controversy among scholars. All of the pertinent information about the high priests from Joshua's successor Joiakim to Jaddua (a contemporary of Alexander the Great) will be analyzed in this chapter, which, because of the nature of the material, is divided into three parts: the

---

1. See, for example, Benjamin E. Scolnic, *Chronology and Papponymy: A List of the Judean High Priests of the Persian Period,* SFSHJ 206 (Atlanta: Scholars, 1999), 5–6.

evidence about each of the high priests mentioned in the lists of Nehemiah and the narratives of Josephus; the chronology of the high priests together with a discussion of the problem whether the extant lists are complete; and the cultic and political roles of the high priests during the Persian period.

The High Priests

The earliest indications about who served, in all probability, as high priests after Joshua are found in the book of Nehemiah, especially chapter 12. This chapter begins with a list of priests and Levites who immigrated to Jerusalem with Zerubbabel and Joshua. The priests are listed in Neh 12:2-7, the Levites in verses 8-9. With verse 10, there begins a *genealogy* of Jeshua/Joshua: "Jeshua was the father of Joiakim, Joiakim the father of Eliashib, Eliashib the father of[2] Joiada, Joiada the father of Jonathan, and Jonathan the father of Jaddua" (12:10-11). After citing this genealogy that includes six names—three of which have the Yahwistic prefix "Y/Jo"—the compiler records a list of priests who lived at the time of Joshua's son Joiakim (Neh 12:12-21 [note v. 12: "In the days of Joiakim the priests, heads of ancestral houses . . . "]). Nehemiah 12:22-23 adds: "As for the Levites, in the days of Eliashib, Joiada, Johanan, and Jaddua, there were recorded the heads of ancestral houses; also the priests until the reign of Darius the Persian. The Levites, heads of ancestral houses, were recorded in the Book of the Annals until the days of Johanan son of Eliashib" (compare Ezra 10:6). Finally, Neh 12:26 notes with regard to the Levites mentioned in verses 24-25: "These were in the days of Joiakim son of Jeshua son of Jozadak, and in the days of the governor Nehemiah and of the priest Ezra, the scribe."

The flurry of names from Joshua/Jeshua's family in these lists yields these sequences:

12:10-11, 26	12:22	12:23 (Ezra 10:6)
Jeshua		
Joiakim		
Eliashib	Eliashib	Eliashib
Joiada	Joiada	Johanan
Jonathan	Johanan	
Jaddua	Jaddua	

---

2. The word translated "the father of" by the NRSV is not present in the MT and LXX.

These short and seemingly innocuous lists, when compared among themselves and with external data, give rise to a whole series of difficulties that will be treated throughout the present chapter. It is particularly noteworthy that the son of Joiada is named *Jonathan* in the first list but *Johanan* in the second, while in the third Johanan appears as the son, not the grandson (as in list two), of Eliashib. In approaching these problems, it will be helpful first to compile the information available from the various sources for each of the individuals in the lists, aside from Joshua/Jeshua who was the subject of the previous chapter.

2. Joiakim (יויקים)[3]

Joiakim is not named in the Bible outside the lists that have been cited (Neh 12:10, 12, 26; compare 1 Esd 5:5). It may be assumed, though, that he was included among Joshua's sons who, according to Ezra 3:9, helped with the construction of the temple. Josephus (*Ant.* 11.5, 1–5 [§§121–58]) places him in the time of Xerxes (486–465 BCE) and considers him a contemporary of Ezra. In fact, the historian seems to envision a situation in which Joiakim and Ezra were simultaneously operating as high priests but in different places: "Now the high priest [ἀρχιερεύς] at that time was Joakeimos [= Joiakim], the son of Jesus [= Joshua]. And there was also in Babylon a righteous man who enjoyed the good opinion of the masses, called Ezra; he was the chief priest [πρῶτος ἱερεύς] of the people and, being very learned in the laws of Moses, became friendly with King Xerxes" (§121).[4] 1 Esdras 9:39, 40, 49 call Ezra ἀρχιερεύς, the standard term for high priest. It is not only in 1 Esdras and Josephus, however, that he has the rank of a leading priest: his genealogy in Ezra 7:1-5 (1 Esd 8:1-2) could hardly be improved, as it traces his descent through the Zadokite line during the First Temple back to Zadok himself and eventually to Aaron (none of the postexilic high priests is named in this list).[5] Joseph Blenkinsopp

---

3. The number given to each high priest in the heading corresponds to the List of High Priests, pp. 491–92.

4. Translations of *Antiquities* 11 are from Ralph Marcus, *Josephus 6: Jewish Antiquities, Books 9–11,* LCL (Cambridge: Harvard Univ. Press, 1937).

5. See Jacob M. Myers, *I and II Esdras,* AB 42 (Garden City, N.Y.: Doubleday, 1974), 95–96. Nisan Ararat ("Ezra and His Mission in the Biblical and Post-Biblical Sources," *BM* 17 [1972], especially 480–86) argues at length that in fact Ezra was high priest (the title הכהן הראש in Ezra 7:5 refers to him, not to Aaron) and that he assumed office when Nehemiah forced Joiada from the post (Neh 13:28). He maintains in his long essay (pp. 451–92) that there was an original "Comprehensive Book of Chronicles" that included the material in 1–2 Chronicles, the apocryphal book of Ezra (1 Esdras), Nehemiah's memoirs, and Josephus's stories about the high priest Johanan and his brother Jeshua and about the high priest Jaddua and his brother Man-

writes: "Since the author of 1 Esd 9:39-40 describes Ezra as high priest during his mission in Judah, he may be reflecting an early tradition, which survived for centuries, that Ezra replaced or deposed Joiakim."[6] There does, indeed, seem to have been such a tradition, but there is no early evidence that he, in fact, either replaced or deposed him. It seems more likely that what we have here is an early instance of the use of ἀρχιερεύς in the sense of "chief/important priest."

Klaus Koch has, however, maintained that Ezra was, in fact, the high priest.[7] He draws attention to Ezra 8:32-34, where he and his caravan arrive in Jerusalem and on the fourth day deliver their precious cargo of silver, gold, and utensils at the temple. These they "weighed into the hands of the priest Meremoth son of Uriah, and with him was Eleazar son of Phinehas, and with them were the Levites, Jozabad son of Jeshua and Noadiah son of Binnui" (8:33). The oddity that Koch notes here is that while we would expect the high priest to be the one receiving the cultic valuables (compare Num 31:48-54), no one from the lists of high priests in Nehemiah 12 is mentioned. For Koch, the designation הכהן in Chronicles and Nehemiah always designates the high priest (including an otherwise unknown Shelemiah in Neh 13:13). As a consequence, Ezra 8 by calling him הכהן identifies Meremoth as the high priest at the time when Ezra reached Jerusalem.

Ezra himself receives the title הכהן in several passages (Neh 8:9; 12:26); in the book of Ezra, apart from Meremoth, only Ezra is called הכהן (Ezra 10:10, 16-18; 1 Esd 9:39, 40, 49). To this, we may add that Ezra performs high-priestly functions such as his prayer in Ezra 9 (compare Lev 16:21), and his genealogy in Ezra 7:1-5 includes only individuals who served as chief/high priests.

Koch acknowledges that Ezra and Meremoth fail to appear in the lists in Nehemiah 12, but he finds those lists to be incomplete (see below for others

---

asseh (on these stories see below). The editor of the biblical Ezra-Nehemiah later removed all references to Ezra as הכהן הראש except the one in Ezra 7:5, which he mistakenly thought referred to Aaron. He was motivated to excise these references because he was an enthusiastic advocate of the high priests from Joshua's line who held office in his day and did not want to preserve any indication that someone outside this family had held the high priesthood after one of its members, Joiada, had been banished from the office. His case is unconvincing at many points, including the existence of a hypothetical "Comprehensive Book of Chronicles" and his debatable interpretation of Neh 13:28 (that it speaks of Joiada's banishment rather than the removal of his son).

6. Joseph Blenkinsopp, *Ezra-Nehemiah: A Commentary*, OTL (Philadelphia: Westminster, 1988), 338.

7. Klaus Koch, "Ezra and Meremoth: Remarks on the History of the High Priesthood," in *Sha'arei Talmon: Studies in the Bible, Qumran, and the Ancient Near East Presented to Shemaryahu Talmon*, ed. M. Fishbane and E. Tov (Winona Lake, Ind.: Eisenbrauns, 1992), 105–10; see also idem, "Ezra and the Origins of Judaism," *JSS* 19 (1974): 190–93.

who share this view). He thinks there was too long a time gap between Joshua and Eliashib for just one high-priestly reign (that of Joiakim). As a result, he inserts Meremoth and Ezra (Shelemiah should also be added at some point) into the roster of high priests. Meremoth would later have been removed from the post in favor of Ezra.

Meremoth, according to Koch, was from the clan of Hakkoz (Neh 3:4, 21). It was this priestly house that, according to Ezra 2:61-63 and Neh 7:63-65, was among those disqualified from the priesthood when they could not document their genealogy. First Chronicles 24:10, however, shows that the restrictions were removed and the group reinstated. These varying fortunes of the Hakkoz family reveal disputes within the priesthood in Ezra's time. Koch thinks the Chronistic redactor has reduced the family of Joshua/Jeshua in status. They kept the high priesthood until about 500 BCE, when they were replaced. Meremoth and Ezra were high priests during the time that Joshua's family was out of office. After Ezra's tenure, though, the family regained the position from Eliashib through Jaddua.

There are several reasons why this reconstruction should be rejected. First, it is moving beyond the evidence to say that the term הכהן in Chronicles-Ezra-Nehemiah always refers to the high priest (use of it for Shelemiah should give one pause). It is true that in Ezra, no one is called "the high priest," but "the priest" has a more general meaning. Also, the text of Ezra indicates that we should not expect him to hand over the treasures he brought to the high priest. Ezra 8:29 has Ezra himself tell the priests to whom he entrusted them before they left on their journey to Jerusalem : "Guard them and keep them until you weigh them before the chief priests [שרי הכהנים] and the Levites . . . within the chambers of the house of the LORD." They act in harmony with these instructions in Ezra 8:32-34. In other words, we lack any indication that Meremoth and Ezra were high priests.[8]

Returning to Josephus, the historian relates the biblical Ezra story but concludes his account with details unknown from other sources: "And it was his [Ezra's] fate, after being honoured by the people, to die an old man and to be buried with great magnificence in Jerusalem. About the same time also died the high priest Joakeimos, whom his son Eliashib succeeded in the high priest-hood" (*Ant.* 11.5, 5 [§158]). It is likely that Josephus made Joiakim and Ezra contemporaries because of the way in which he read certain biblical details. His source for the Ezra story—1 Esdras—locates it in the reign of Artaxerxes (465–424 BCE), as does Ezra 7, but Nehemiah 12 could be interpreted as if it

---

8. Compare Scolnic, *Chronology and Papponymy*, 203; he thinks there may not have been an unbroken and hereditary succession in the high priesthood in this period and that Joshua may have been the last one to serve until the time of Ezra. This seems highly unlikely as we will see.

synchronized Joiakim and Ezra during an earlier reign: "In the days of Joiakim the priests, heads of ancestral houses, were: of Seraiah, Meraiah; . . . of Ezra, Meshullam" (Neh 12:12-13.) And Neh 12:26 states: "These were in the days of Joiakim son of Jeshua son of Jozadak, and in the days of the governor Nehemiah and of the priest Ezra, the scribe." Thus, it appears that Josephus saw fit to fill the scriptural gap between Ezra 6 and 7, in which one jumps from the reign of Darius I (522–486 BCE) to that of Artaxerxes I (465–424 BCE), by relating the Ezra story to the days of the intervening monarch Xerxes. For this maneuver, he found support in Nehemiah 12, which seems to make Ezra the contemporary of the second high priest Joiakim who very likely served during Xerxes' reign.[9]

This exhausts the information in Nehemiah and in Josephus concerning the second high priest Joiakim, with only Josephus actually giving him the title. Later, however, Joiakim does surface in other texts.[10] The book of Judith reports that the high priest during the great crisis that befell the nation at the time described in the story was Joakim (Jdt 4:6, 8 [Ιωακιμ ὁ ἱερεὺς ὁ μέγας], 14; 15:8), and it is quite possible that the author means by this name the high priest of Nehemiah 12. This inference is likely because the writer of Judith dates the events of the book to a time that agrees roughly with the chronology implied in Ezra and Nehemiah for Joiakim: "For they had only recently returned from exile, and all the people of Judea had just now gathered together, and the sacred vessels and the altar and the temple had been conse-

---

9. For an investigation of Josephus's chronological interests in distinction from the more thematic concern in the book of Ezra, see G. C. Tuland, "Josephus, *Antiquities*, Book XI: Correction or Confirmation of Biblical Post-Exilic Records?" *AUSS* 4 (1966): 176–92.

10. In Bar 1:7, it is said that in Jerusalem "the priest" (τὸν ἱερέα, which may signify "the high priest" as the NRSV renders it) in the fifth year of the exile was a certain Joakim. It is not clear whom the author intends by this name, but the ancestry given for him there shows that, unless the author is skipping over several generations, he was not considered the Joiakim of Nehemiah's list: "the high priest Jehoiakim son of Hilkiah son of Shallum." These names are also associated in 2 Kings where Hilkiah was the priest during Josiah's reform, Shallum was the husband of the prophetess Huldah, and Jehoiakim was one of Josiah's successors (2 Kings 22–23). Carey A. Moore points to 1 Chr 6:13-15 (Hebrew 5:39-41) where Shallum, Hilkiah, Azariah, Seraiah, and Jehozadak are the last high priests before the exile (*Daniel, Esther, and Jeremiah: The Additions*, AB 44 [Garden City, N.Y.: Doubleday, 1977] 271). Shallum's father is identified as Zadok (1 Chr 6:12 [Hebrew 5:38]). See also Odil Hannes Steck, "Das Buch Baruch," in O. H. Steck, R. G. Kratz, and I. Kottsieper, *Das Buch Baruch, Der Brief des Jeremia, Zusätze zu Ester und Daniel*, ATD Apokryphen 5 (Göttingen: Vandenhoeck & Ruprecht, 1998), 30–31. He notes that this Joiakim is pictured as being the leading priest (not necessarily the high priest) in the time between Jozadak and Joshua and that the name has been derived from the tradition. He also raises the possibility that the name reflects that of the high priest reigning when Baruch was written—Alcimus/Jakim.

crated after their profanation" (Jdt 4:3). The book attributes an interesting kind of authority to this Joakim. As Holophernes, the all-conquering general of Nebuchadnezzar, marched against the rebellious Judeans, "[t]he high priest, Joakim, who was in Jerusalem at the time, wrote to the people of Bethulia and Betomesthaim, which faces Esdraelon opposite the plain near Dothan, ordering them to seize the mountain passes, since by them Judea could be invaded; and it would be easy to stop any who tried to enter, for the approach was narrow, wide enough for only two at a time to pass" (Jdt 4:6-7). Judith 4:8 traces this command to "the high priest Joakim and the senate [γερουσία] of the whole people of Israel, in session at Jerusalem."

A high priest with military power and a senate in Jerusalem have struck commentators as clear marks that Judith was written in the Hellenistic period and that it reflects the situation of that time rather than circumstances of the Persian era. Moore notes that no high priest of the pre-Maccabean age exercised such military authority; moreover, the first reference to a senate in Jerusalem is not found until the letter of Antiochus III (223–187 BCE) to Ptolemy (Josephus, *Ant.* 12.3, 3 [§138]).[11] Actually, the situation is not quite so clear. Josephus, as will be explained later in this chapter, does picture Jaddua, the sixth postexilic high priest, as commander of Judean troops, when Alexander the Great unsuccessfully requested military support from him; also, he speaks of the Jewish elders as a power bloc in the controversy at that time about Manasseh's marriage to Nikaso. But, the book of Judith is so filled with inaccuracies and confusions that scholars now regularly dismiss it from the category of historical literature.[12] Thus, its claims ought not to be used to supplement the sparse historical givens in other sources for the tenure of the second postexilic high priest.[13]

3. Eliashib (אלישיב)

Eliashib is mentioned not only in Neh 12:10, 22, but also in 3:1, 20-21, and 13:28. Some claim that the same person appears as well in Ezra 10:6; Neh 12:23; 13:4, 7, but the identity of this Eliashib is disputed. In Neh 3:1, as the report about rebuilding the wall of Jerusalem begins, the text relates: "Then

---

11. Carey A. Moore, *Judith*, AB 40 (Garden City: Doubleday, 1985), 149–52.

12. See, for example, the data in ibid., 46–49.

13. For much later traditions about Joiakim and his authorship of the scroll of Esther (which is set in the time of Xerxes), see Y. Greenwald, *The History of the High Priests in its Relation to the General Political and Religious History of the Jewish People from the Earliest Times till the Destruction of the Second Temple* (New York: published privately, 1932 [Hebrew]), 51.

the high priest [הכהן הגדול] Eliashib set to work with his fellow priests and rebuilt the Sheep Gate. They consecrated it and set up its doors; they consecrated it as far as the Tower of the Hundred and as far as the Tower of Hananel." The stretch of wall in question is a short span on the north side of the city, immediately adjacent to the temple complex.[14] Nehemiah 3:20-21 identifies his house as the point that marked the division between the areas of two working groups (neither of which was his own crew). These references are important from a chronological perspective because they make Eliashib a contemporary of Nehemiah (and thus probably of Ezra, too), on whose project he cooperated. As Nehemiah came to Jerusalem in the twentieth year of Artaxerxes I (= 445 BCE; Neh 1:1; 2:1), Eliashib was the high priest in the year 445 (Josephus places him, with Ezra, in the reign of Xerxes, *Ant.* 11.5, 6–8 [§§159–83]). This date, some seventy-five years after work resumed on the temple in 520 BCE, suggests that the terms of the first three high priests covered a fairly substantial amount of time. The final certain reference to Eliashib may also be significant for dating purposes: "And one of the sons of Jehoiada [= Joiada, see below], son of the high priest Eliashib, was the son-in-law of Sanballat the Horonite; I [Nehemiah] chased him away from me" (Neh 13:28). It is not at all clear from the Hebrew text of this verse who is being called the high priest, Jehoiada or Eliashib. The NRSV punctuates as though Eliashib is the pontiff and is still, therefore, in office (the year is sometime after 433 BCE [Neh 13:6]), but there is no way of telling this for sure from the Hebrew text.[15] So, it is possible that Eliashib's reign continued past the year 433, when Nehemiah returned to the Persian court; but it is equally plausible that by this time his son Joiada had succeeded him in office. The son of Jehoiada who was Sanballat's son-in-law is not named in the text. It is also significant that there is intermarriage between a member of the high-priestly family and the gubernatorial family of Samaria. Both families were presumably part of the local aristocracy.

The passages given above are the secure references to Eliashib, but the same name appears in four other verses (Ezra 10:6; Neh 12:23; 13:4, 7), where the identity of the person called *Eliashib* is disputed. It may be helpful to take the last two passages first. Nehemiah 13:4-9 relates an incident that occurred around the year 433 BCE, since in the middle of the story Nehemiah, who is speaking in the first person, mentions that he was away when this episode began. As he was away in Artaxerxes' thirty-second year (Neh 13:6), the year of

---

14. See the helpful map of Nehemiah's Jerusalem in *IDB* 3.533.

15. So Wilhelm Rudolph, *Esra und Nehemia samt 3. Esra,* HAT 20 (Tübingen: Mohr/ Siebeck, 1949), 209; H. G. M. Williamson, *Ezra, Nehemiah,* WBC 16 (Waco: Word, 1985), 399; and Blenkinsopp, *Ezra-Nehemiah,* 365.

the event would be 433 or a short time later. The passage opens as follows: "Now before this, the priest Eliashib, who was appointed over the chambers of the house of our God, and who was related to Tobiah, prepared for Tobiah a large room where they had previously put the grain offering, the frankincense, the vessels, and the tithes of grain, wine, and oil, which were given by commandment to the Levites, singers, and gatekeepers, and the contributions for the priests" (Neh 13:4-5). When he returned, Nehemiah discovered what Eliashib had done, tossed Tobiah's belongings from the chamber, and restored the area to its former use (13:7-9). Is this Eliashib the high priest? He may seem to be the same man because he is an important figure in the temple—so important that he could displace fundamental elements of the sacrificial cult for the convenience of Tobiah the Ammonite (see Neh 2:10 where Tobiah is pictured as an opponent of Nehemiah). It is a fact, nevertheless, that this Eliashib is styled only "the priest," not "the high priest." It is also possible that by this time Eliashib's son Joiada had become the pontiff (if Neh 13:28 is to be read in that way).[16]

The third disputed reference to an Eliashib is in Ezra 10:6. It has figured very prominently in the study of the postexilic period because it has become part of the seemingly interminable debate about the chronological order of Ezra and Nehemiah. Ezra 10:6 (= 1 Esd 9:1) appears in the context where Ezra is handling the problem of mixed marriages. According to Ezra 10:1, as he "prayed and made confession, weeping and throwing himself down before the house of God, a very great assembly . . . gathered to him out of Israel; the people also wept bitterly." After he had extracted an oath from the leaders to remedy the situation, "Ezra withdrew from before the house of God, and went to the chamber of Jehohanan son of Eliashib" (Ezra 10:6). This Eliashib is often equated with the man who was high priest at Nehemiah's time, and, as Ezra is here said to be associated with his son (or perhaps grandson; see Neh 12:22-23[17]) who became high priest (here he has his own chamber in the temple),

---

16. Williamson surveys the different opinions about the Eliashib in Ezra 10:6 and argues that the phrase "who was appointed over the chambers of the house of our God" is employed to distinguish this Eliashib from the high priest (*Ezra, Nehemiah*, 151–54). Clearly, this would be a peculiar way in which to refer to the man who was in charge of the entire temple complex. Rudolph (*Esra und Nehemia*, 203–4) and Blenkinsopp (*Ezra-Nehemiah*, 353–54) also maintain that he is not the high priest. Jacob Myers, however, identifies the two (*Ezra-Nehemiah*, AB 14 [Garden City, N.Y.: Doubleday, 1965]).

17. Since the J(eh)ohanan of Ezra 10:6 is the son of Eliashib (as in Neh 12:23) but according to Neh 12:22 the high priest Johanan is the grandson of Eliashib, some scholars hold that the word "son" in Ezra 10:6 actually means "grandson"; see, for example, Kurt Galling, *Studien zur Geschichte Israels im persischen Zeitalter* (Tübingen: Mohr/Siebeck, 1964), 160, who cites passages such as Gen 29:5; 31:28, 43; Ruth 4:17; Ezra 5:1 in support of this interpretation. However,

the verse is supposed to prove that Ezra followed Nehemiah chronologically. Yet, neither of the men in this verse is described as high priest. Of course, it should also be remembered that no one is called "high priest" in Ezra (except perhaps Aaron in 7:5, but the title is different there). A second problem is that the order Eliashib-Jehohanan does not fit with the list of high priests in Neh 12:22 where a generation intervenes. It would not be surprising if the Eliashib of Neh 13:4, 7 (see the previous paragraph) and the one of Ezra 10:6 proved to be the same man (a temple chamber is under consideration in both places), but he was not the high priest.

The fourth disputed passage, Neh 12:23, has already been mentioned. In it, the writer reports: "The Levites, heads of ancestral houses, were recorded in the Book of the Annals until the days of Johanan son of Eliashib." The father-son pair here have the same names as those in Ezra 10:6; thus they fit no better with the high-priestly list of Neh 12:22 than do those of Ezra 10:6. And they, too, are not identified as high priests. For these reasons, they should not be considered in a discussion of the high priests. They appear rather to have been members of a ranking priestly family that had some special position with respect to chambers in the temple. In Nehemiah 12, the reader is told that the heads of the levitical houses were recorded until their time (that is, the time of Ezra and Nehemiah). It is worth stressing that not all the lists of Nehemiah 12 are said to have chronicled names until the time of a certain high priest; some of them end with the times of characters such as King Darius (v. 22; on his identity, see below), Nehemiah, and Ezra (v. 26). So, in this case, a list leads down to the time of the prominent priest Johanan, who happened to have the same name as a later high priest but who was not identical with him.[18] It should be added that the name *Eliashib*, like *Johanan*, is more widely attested in Chronicles and Ezra: there are five other people who bear the name *Eliashib*: 1 Chr 3:24 (a descendant of Zerubbabel); 24:12 (a priest in the time of David); Ezra 10:24 (a temple singer with a foreign wife), 27 (a nonpriest with a foreign

---

J. R. Porter has surveyed the evidence from the Bible and the Elephantine Papyri and has concluded: "What may be suggested is that it is invalid to claim that 'son' in this verse has the meaning of 'grandson', if that claim rests on an alleged regular Hebrew idiom" ("Son or Grandson [Ezra X.6]?" *JTS* 17 [1966]: 67 [54–67]). Williamson (*Ezra, Nehemiah*, 153–54) and Blenkinsopp (*Ezra-Nehemiah*, 190) also oppose identifying this Eliashib (and thus Jehohanan) with the high priests of those names.

18. For further discussion of this passage and the other disputed ones and different views about them, see the section below about the chronology of the period and whether the high-priestly lists are complete as given in Nehemiah and Josephus. Compare also Deborah W. Rooke, *Zadok's Heirs: The Role and Development of the High Priesthood in Ancient Israel*, OTM (Oxford: Oxford Univ. Press, 2000), 159–60.

wife), 36 (another layman with a mixed marriage).[19] In these books and in Nehemiah, some nine or ten men have the name *Johanan* and eight the alternate spelling *Jehohanan*.[20]

One final note may be added to this section about the high priest Eliashib. Josephus locates Ezra and Nehemiah in the reign of Xerxes (for Ezra, see above; for Nehemiah, see *Ant.* 11.5, 6 [§159]). He associates Eliashib as well with the reign of this monarch (11.5, 5 [§158]) but extends his term of office into the time of Artaxerxes, in whose reign he places the Esther story (11.6, 1–13 [§§184–296]). He mentions Eliashib's death only after completing his paraphrase of Esther (11.7, 1 [§297]).

4. Joiada (יוידע)

The fourth postexilic high priest fails to appear in any story in the Bible. His name is found only in the lists of Neh 12:10-11, 22 and in Neh 13:28, where he may be designated as high priest at the time when his unnamed son who was married to Sanballat's daughter was driven out by Nehemiah. Although it is not evident from this passage whether Joiada or his father Eliashib is named the high priest, it is absolutely clear that the high-priestly genealogy of Neh 12:10-11, 22 reappears here: Joiada, not Johanan, is the son of Eliashib. This is one more reason for thinking that the Eliashib-Johanan pair (see above) did not belong to the high-priestly line.

It is interesting, from a sociological and political perspective, to see that the governing family of Samaria (on Sanballat and his line, see below) and the leading family of Yehud were joined by marriage. This is not the first case in which a member of the high-priestly family married outside what appear to have been considered acceptable limits;[21] Ezra 10:18 discloses that some of

---

19. See James M. Ward, "Eliashib," in *IDB* 2.87; J. W. Wright, "Eliashib," in *ABD* 2.460–61.

20. See Bruce T. Dahlberg, "Johanan," in *IDB* 2.929–30; idem, "Jehohanan," in *IDB* 2.810–11; Steven L. McKenzie and John M. Berridge, "Johanan," in *ABD* 3.880–82.

21. On the rules regarding high-priestly marriages, see Lev 21:13-15; Ezra 9:2; and Myers, *Ezra-Nehemiah*, 218; Rudolph, *Esra und Nehemia*, 209, who mention Malachi's criticisms in this matter (Mal 2:10-16). Jacob Liver (*Chapters in the History of the Priests and Levites: Studies on the Lists in Chronicles and Ezra and Nehemiah* [Publications of the Perry Foundation for Biblical Research in the Hebrew University of Jerusalem; Jerusalem: Magnes, 1968], 40–42 [Hebrew]) compares the names of the priestly ancestral houses as listed in Neh 10:3-8 (these are the signatories to the covenant made at that time) with those given in Neh 12:1-7, 12-21. The list in Nehemiah 12 has six names that fail to appear in chap. 10. In considering why Joiarib and Jedaiah are in chap. 12 but not in chap. 10, Liver thinks it possible to demonstrate that three or four

Joshua/Jeshua's sons, too, had married "foreign" women. The severe strictures of Ezra and Nehemiah against such marriages were manifestly not shared by at least some aristocratic priests, and, as Neh 13:28 shows, this caused friction between the Jewish governor and the high-priestly family. Marriage practices in the high-priestly family will attract attention again at later times.

Josephus, like the Bible, has virtually nothing to say about Joiada. He writes only: "On the death of the high priest Eliasib his son Jodas [= Joiada] succeeded him in the high priesthood. And, when he also died, Joannes, who was his son, assumed this office" (*Ant.* 11.7, 1 [§297]). In other words, the historian merely reproduces the relevant part of the list in Neh 12:22; he also fails to mention in this context Nehemiah's expulsion of Joiada's son.

5. *Johanan* (יוֹחָנָן)

The name of the fifth postexilic high priest poses a problem. It was noted above that in Neh 12:11, Joiada's son is named *Jonathan*; but the list in Neh 12:22, which does not take a genealogical form (that is, the words "was the father of" [הוֹלִיד] are not used here, as they were in vv. 10-11), calls Joiada's successor *Johanan*. Josephus, too, gives his name as *Johanan* (Ἰωάννης) and says nothing about a Jonathan at this point (*Ant.* 11.7, 1 [§297]). Thus, he reflects the high-priestly list of Neh 12:22, not the form found in verse 11. Although some scholars have urged the seemingly more cautious approach of not changing Jonathan to Johanan,[22] it does, in the final analysis, appear to be simpler to

---

of the six extra names in chap. 12 are related to the family of Jedaiah, who were the most prominent of the priestly families that came from Babylon, and that the high priest belonged to this family. Note that Ezra 2:36-39 includes the house of Jeshua among the sons of Jedaiah. The absence of Jedaiah's family and associated ancestral houses from the list of those who sealed the covenant is unlikely to be accidental. Rather, it is in harmony with the failure of the high priest's name to appear in the same list in chap. 10 and with the system of relations then obtaining between Nehemiah and the high priest Eliashib and his family (see especially Liver, 42).

22. So Williamson, *Ezra, Nehemiah*, 363; and Blenkinsopp, *Ezra-Nehemiah*, 338–39. Both think that the high-priestly lists in Nehemiah are not complete, but these commentators confuse the issue by introducing the Eliashib-Johanan passages that were discussed above. In an earlier essay, H. G. M. Williamson ("The Historical Value of Josephus' *Jewish Antiquities* XI.297–301," *JTS* 28 [1977]: 61–64) had dealt with the issue of the identity of this Johanan and wrote: "it is precarious to start, as many seem to do, by equating the Jonathan of Neh. xii.11 with the Johanan of Neh. xii.22, 23. Rather, we should follow Mowinckel in observing that not only are the names different, but that their positions within the family are different: according to the explicit statements of Neh. xii.10f., Jonathan was the grandson of Eliashib; Johanan, however, is said in verse 23 to be the son of Eliashib, and there are no valid grounds for taking this statement other than at its face value in the first instance" (62). It is peculiar that Williamson, who is concerned here

argue that *Jonathan* in Neh 12:11 is a copyist's mistake for *Johanan*. In Hebrew script, the two names have nearly an identical appearance (יונתן and יוחנן). Once the mistake was made in Neh 12:11, the second instance of *Jonathan* in the same verse would also have been changed to make the genealogical statements there consistent.[23] It is not impossible that Jonathan was the oldest son of Joiada who, for some reason (such as the banishment of Neh 13:28), did not become high priest; but verse 11 lists Joiada's descendants as the very men who appear in the high-priestly list of verse 22. In either case—whether *Jonathan* is a scribal error for *Johanan* or Jonathan was a man who never served as high priest (his place was taken by a brother named *Johanan*) but whose descendants did occupy the post—no one named Jonathan is attested as having been high priest in this period. Conversely, there is relatively plentiful evidence outside the Bible that a man named *Johanan* did serve in this position.

The first piece of extrabiblical evidence comes from the Elephantine Papyri, especially papyrus 30. TAD A4.7 = AP 30 (TAD A4.8 = AP 31 is a copy of it[24]) dates itself to the "20th of Marheshvan the 17th year of Darius the king" (line 30). Factors of history and script indicate that the Darius in question is Darius II Nothus (424–423 to 404 BCE).[25] The twentieth day of the eighth month (= Marheshvan) of his seventeenth year would be November 26, 407 BCE.[26] The text is a letter from "Yedoniah and his colleagues, the priests

---

about starting with assumptions, himself starts with another assumption, namely, that the Eliashib-Johanan of Neh 12:23 are high priests. What is the evidence for that? For a different view, see his *Ezra, Nehemiah*, 153–54. Scolnic (*Chronology and Papponymy*, 4–5) takes another approach that also lacks any basis: he thinks that Johanan was also called Jonathan and that this interchange of names illustrates the flexibility characteristic of such lists.

23. This solution has been adopted by many scholars, among whom are: C. C. Torrey, *Ezra Studies* (reprinted: New York: Ktav, 1970 [originally published in 1910]), 321; H. H. Rowley, "Sanballat and the Samaritan Temple," in idem, *Men of God: Studies in Old Testament History and Prophecy* (London: Nelson, 1963), 248 n. 5; and Rudolph, *Esra und Nehemia*, 190. Rudolph points to the same interchange of names in Neh 12:35 where the MT reads יונתן but a strongly attested Greek reading is Ιωαναν.

24. The TAD abbreviations are the designations for the texts in Bezalel Porten and Ada Yardeni, *Textbook of Aramaic Documents from Ancient Egypt*, 4 vols. (Jerusalem: Hebrew Univ., 1986–99). The AP abbreviations are from A.E. Cowley, *Aramaic Papyri of the Fifth Century B.C.* (Oxford: Clarendon, 1923; reprinted: Osnabrück: Zeller, 1967). TAD A4.8 = AP 31 was copied by the scribe who began writing on line 12 of TAD A4.7 = AP 30 (see Bezalel Porten, *The Elephantine Papyri in English*, Documenta et Monumenta Orientis Antiqui 22 (Leiden: Brill, 1996), 139, 145. It was written on the same date and scroll and offers some fifty stylistic changes.

25. See Cowley, *Aramaic Papyri*, 108–10 and his introductions to documents such as AP 1. All translations from the Elephantine Papyri are from Cowley's edition.

26. So Pierre Grelot, *Documents araméens d'Égypte*, Littératures anciennes du Proche-Orient (Paris: Cerf, 1972), 406. Porten gives Nov. 25, 407 (*The Elephantine Papyri in English*, 139).

who are in Yeb the fortress" (line 1). Its primary concern is with the rebuilding of the temple of Yahu, which had been demolished by local elements in the
month Tammuz of Darius's fourteenth year (lines 4–13), that is, July–August
410 BCE,[27] at a time when the satrap Arsames was away from Egypt. The per-
petrators of this act against the Jewish temple were later punished (lines
16–17). Not long after the time when the temple was leveled, Jedoniah and his
colleagues wrote to influential Jews, seeking their support in convincing officials in Egypt to permit rebuilding of the sanctuary. They wrote in lines 17–19:
"Also before this, at the time when this evil was done to us, we sent a letter to[28]
your lordship [Bigvai, the governor of Yehud; line 1] and to Johanan the high
priest [יהוחנן כהנא רבא] and his colleagues the priests who are in Jerusalem,
and to Ostanes the brother of Anani, and the nobles [חרי] of the Jews. They
have not sent any letter to us." The present letter is addressed to Bigvai (or
Bagohi), the governor, in the hope that he will, on this occasion, respond to
their plea for help. It is not known why the high priest (or the governor) did
not answer the first letter. It has been surmised that Johanan's silence was
caused by his opposition to there being another Jewish temple where a sacrificial cult was conducted.[29] Bigvai's assistance was sought because the authorities had not permitted reconstruction of the building (line 23); the request is
that he write his friends in Egypt about the subject. The writers added: "Also
the whole matter we have set forth in a letter in our name to Delaiah and
Shelemiah the sons of Sanballat governor of Samaria [סנאבלט פחת שמרין]"
(line 29). All the principal characters in this letter, with the exception of Sanballat whose name would have appeared in a lost section in AP 30 line 28, are
also mentioned in the preserved sections of TAD A4.8 = AP 31, a more damaged copy of AP 30 (it has the same dates in lines 4, 19, and 29): Johanan (line
17), Ostanes the brother of Anani (18), Delaiah and Shelemiah (28).

TAD A4.9 = AP 32 (by the scribe who copied TAD A4.8 = AP 31) contains
the brief reply of Bigvai and Delaiah to TAD A4.7 = AP 30. In Cowley's opinion, it is a written note made from an oral reply.[30] These two men instruct the
recipient "to say to Arsames about the altar-house of the God of Heaven,
which was built in the fortress of Yeb formerly, before Cambyses, which

27. Grelot, *Documents araméens*, 406; Porten, *The Elephantine Papyri in English*, 140 n. 15.

28. The preposition is absent from the Aramaic text but is presupposed by the following ול,
and it appears in the parallel in TAD A4.8 = AP 31.17.

29. Bezalel Porten, *Archives from Elephantine: The Life of an Ancient Jewish Military Colony*
(Berkeley: Univ. of California Press, 1968), 291–92; Menahem Mor, "Samaritan History: The Per-
sian, Hellenistic, and Hasmonaean Period," in *The Samaritans,* ed. A. D. Crown (Tübingen:
Mohr/Siebeck, 1989), 4.

30. *Aramaic Papyri*, 122.

Waidrang, that reprobate, destroyed in the 14th year of Darius the king, to rebuild it in its place as it was before, and they may offer the meal-offering [מנחתא] and incense [לבונתא] upon that altar as formerly was done" (lines 2–11). A number of scholars have observed that the reply of Governor Bigvai and Delaiah does not mention the sacrifice of animals in the new sanctuary, although TAD A4.7 = AP 30.21–22 specifically names meal-offering (מנחה), incense (לבו[נ]ה), and burnt offering (עלוה) and implies that they were offered in the temple previously, and 30.25 expresses the wish that they may be offered in the future in the rebuilt temple.[31] TAD A4.10 = AP 33 also relates to this incident. In it, the five writers from Yeb say, perhaps in acknowledging receipt of official permission to rebuild from the satrap:[32] "If your lordship is *favou*rable and the temple of Ya'u the God which *we had (?) be rebuilt (?)* in the fortress of Yeb as it was form*erly built*, and sheep, oxen (and) goats are not offered as burnt-sacrifice [מקלו[33]] there, but incense, meal-offering *and drink-offering only*, and (if) your lordship giv*es* orders *to that effect, then* we will pay to your lordship's house the sum *of . . . and also* a thou*sand* ardabs of barley" (lines 7–14). It appears, then, that with the elimination of animal sacrifice, as proposed by Bigvai and Delaiah, rebuilding was acceptable to the authorities.

The importance of these papyri for the history of the high priesthood is great, indeed. In the first place, TAD A4.7 = AP 30 names the Jerusalem high priest *Johanan* (יהוחנן), gives his Aramaic title (כהנא רבא), and firmly dates one incident in his reign to the year 410 BCE (the date when a letter was sent to him from Yeb). These data are thoroughly compatible with the chronological information in the book of Nehemiah, where Eliashib was high priest in 445 BCE and continued possibly to 433, though by that time Joiada, Johanan's predecessor, may already have been in office (see Neh 13:28). The least one can say is that Joiada had a son of marriageable age by 433. Consequently, it would not be at all surprising to find his successor serving by 410. The reference to Johanan also demonstrates that his name belongs in the high-priestly list, as Neh 12:22 leads one to believe. Second, the fact that the Jews of Elephantine wrote to the high priest in Jerusalem to ask for his support shows the high regard in which this office was held by at least one group in the Diaspora.[34]

---

31. Ibid., 124; Porten, *Archives from Elephantine*, 291–92; idem, *The Elephantine Papyri in English*, 148–49; and Grelot, *Documents araméens*, 416.

32. So Grelot, *Documents araméens*, 417–19.

33. On the term, see Porten, *The Elephantine Papyri in English*, 151 n. 14.

34. Rooke (*Zadok's Heirs*, 182–83) claims that the correspondence proves the provincial governor was "the most important and authoritative figure in the Judaean community." She suspects the appeal to the authorities was a financial one, that the request does not reveal any governing authority on the part of Johanan, and that we see here as in Ezra and Nehemiah a high

That they failed to receive his help may imply his opposition to the temple in Egypt, but there are, naturally, other possible explanations for his not responding. He is said to have with him a group called "his colleagues the priests" (כהניא כנותה, TAD A4.7 = AP 30.18); the same was the case for Jedoniah (line 1). Similar expressions for colleagues are attested for Joshua (Zech 3:8) and Eliashib (Neh 3:1). Third, the Elephantine correspondence supplies names and details about the political situation in Yehud in the last years of the fifth century. The governor of Yehud is named Bigvai/Bagohi, while the governor of Samaria is Sanballat, although his two sons Delaiah and Shelemiah are the ones to whom Jedoniah and his colleagues wrote for support. Possibly they were the active powers in Samaria because their father was rather elderly by this time.[35] This Sanballat is almost certainly the man whom Nehemiah calls "Sanballat the Horonite" (Neh 2:19; 13:28; compare 4:1-2, 7; 6:1-9, 12-14), as the chronology entails. Nehemiah never provides his title, but TAD A4.7 = AP 30.29 does. It is noteworthy that the reply to the request from Elephantine came from both Bigvai and Delaiah. Relations between the two must have been cordial enough to allow mutual responses of this kind. These two leading officials of Samaria and Jerusalem seem not to have been sworn enemies in 410 BCE, the date of their reply. The fact that the governor Bigvai gave a limited favorable response to the letter may also suggest that he took a different approach to the Elephantine temple than did the high priest Johanan, who, as far as the evidence allows us to say, never responded to the letter sent to him (if he ever received it).

The second piece of extrabiblical evidence about a high priest named *Johanan* comes from Josephus. As he reproduces the order of the high priests in Neh 12:22, he puts Johanan after Joiada and adds a full story about the former that is attested in no other extant source. The story runs as follows (*Ant.* 11.7, 1 [§§297–301]).

On the death of the high priest Eliasib his son Jodas succeeded him in the high priesthood. And, when he also died, Joannes, who was his son, assumed this office; it was through him that Bagoses [βαγώσης], the general [στρατηγός] of the second [ἄλλου] Artaxerxes, defiled the sanctuary and imposed tribute on the Jews, so that before offering the daily sacrifices they had to pay from the public treasury fifty

priesthood with authority limited to issues of temple and cult. She may be correct, but at least the letter implies some influence on the part of the high priest, an influence that reached beyond Jerusalem. How his influence compared with that of the governor we are not told.

35. Compare Porten, *The Elephantine Papyri in English*, 144 n. 92.

drachmae for every lamb. The reason for this was the following happening. Joannes had a brother named Jesus, and Bagoses, whose
friend he was, promised to obtain the high priesthood for him. With
this assurance, therefore, Jesus quarreled with Joannes in the temple
and provoked his brother so far that in his anger he killed him. That
Joannes should have committed so impious a deed against his
brother while serving as priest was terrible enough, but the more terrible in that neither among Greeks nor barbarians had so savage and
impious a deed ever been committed. The Deity, however, was not
indifferent to it, and it was for this reason that the people were made
slaves and the temple was defiled by the Persians. Now, when Bagoses,
the general of Artaxerxes, learned that Joannes, the high priest of the
Jews, had murdered his own brother Jesus in the temple, he at once
set upon the Jews and in anger began to say, "You have dared to commit murder in your own temple." But, when he attempted to enter the
temple, they sought to prevent him, whereupon he said to them, "Am
I, then, not purer than he who was slain in the temple?" and, having
spoken these words, he went in to the temple. This, then, being the
pretext which he used, Bagoses made the Jews suffer seven years for
the death of Jesus.

Josephus undoubtedly understood the Joannes of his story to be the high
priest Johanan of Nehemiah's list. Bagoses, however, is more of a problem.
Once the Elephantine Papyri were found, it seemed natural to identify the
man in this story with the Bigvai/Bagohi to whom TAD A4.7 = AP 30 was written and whose response is reflected in TAD A4.9 = AP 32: the name is the
same—a Persian name that appears in Aramaic form as בגוהי and as βαγώσης
in Greek—and they seem to have the same function. The brother Jesus
(Jeshua/Joshua) of this story figures in no other source, although the use of
the name illustrates that it continued to be found within the high-priestly
family. The case for the identity of Bagoses appeared to be solid because the
same cast of characters play roles and the time for the story would fit the
chronology that may be inferred from Nehemiah.

   Williamson has subjected this widely accepted interpretation of Josephus's
story to searching criticism.[36] He shows that the story in Josephus follows a pat-

---

36. "The Historical Value," 49–67. The treatment here of Williamson's arguments is based
on VanderKam, "Jewish High Priests of the Persian Period: Is the List Complete?" in *Priesthood
and Cult in Ancient Israel,* ed. G. Anderson and S. Olyan, JSOTSup 125 (Sheffield: Sheffield Academic, 1991), 81–87.

tern or form attested in many other places in the *Antiquities* in which the historian writes his own introduction (derived from what follows), lists the conclusion or result, connects these statements to the story itself with a proposition in which the word αἰτία (= cause) appears, and then gives the story, which is a close paraphrase of a source. The introduction in this case includes Josephus's words, "it was through him that Bagoses, the general of the second Artaxerxes, defiled the sanctuary" (*Ant.* 11.7, 1 [§297]). As Williamson notes, the word ἄλλου does not quite mean *second* but rather *other, another,* and it is used here to distinguish the present Artaxerxes from the one mentioned previously (Artaxerxes I in the Esther paraphrase). This implies that Josephus, who is here making the identification (the source itself in *Ant.* 11.7, 1 [§§298–301] does not further define which Artaxerxes is meant), knew of only two kings by this name—a fact that leaves open the possibility that the source is talking about either Artaxerxes II or III. Other data in the source itself lead Williamson to place the story in the time of Artaxerxes III (358–338 BCE), much later than the time of the Johanan and Bigvai/Bagohi of the Elephantine correspondence.

Of crucial importance to Williamson's case is the identity of the Bagoses who figures in Josephus's account. There are undeniable differences between the Bigvai/Bagohi of TAD A4.7 = AP 30 and this man: In TAD A4.7 = AP 30, he is the governor of Yehud (פחת יהוד) in the time of Darius, whereas in Josephus he is στρατηγός . . . ἀρταξέρξου (both in Josephus's introduction and in the source itself).

> [I]t seems most unlikely that the Bagoses of our source is the same man as the governor of Judah known from the Elephantine Papyri. On the one hand, there is no reason to suppose that Josephus' source would not have applied to Bagoses the obvious title of governor (σατράπης) had that in fact been his position; on the other hand we know of a Bagoses who precisely fits the description as reconstructed from Josephus' source, namely the Persian general of Artaxerxes III. His role as a military officer fits the title στρατηγός of *Ant.* xi.300, whilst the fact that he is also known to have been involved in civil administration (cf. Diodorus Siculus XVI.l.8) suggests that he could well have imposed a tax on the Jews as recounted in this narrative.[37]

From this sort of evidence he concludes that Josephus's story belongs in the time of Artaxerxes III and that, as a consequence, the high priest Johanan of the story is not the one of Neh 12:22. Williamson, like many others, believes that the high-priestly lists for this period are not complete; apparently a

---

37. "The Historical Value," 58.

Johanan was dropped from the enumeration, thus leaving only the biblical Johanan and Jaddua to fill the long chronological gap between 410 BCE and the time of Alexander the Great.

However appealing it is, there are some fundamental flaws in Williamson's arguments. First, if (as seems likely) it is Josephus who identifies the king as *the other Artaxerxes*, it may indeed imply that he failed to distinguish between the second and third monarch of that name. This, however, says nothing about the source itself. The Artaxerxes for the source in *Ant.* 11.7, 1 (§§298–301) could be either the second or the third, with nothing favoring one or the other. Second, it is amusing to read that "we know of a Bagoses who precisely [!] fits the description as reconstructed from Josephus' source." The man whom he has in mind is described by the first-century BCE historian Diodorus as a general of Artaxerxes III, but nothing that is reported about him by Diodorus, apart from the title, would fit what Josephus says about Bagoses. According to Diodorus, Bagoses or rather Bagoas (always spelled βαγώας by Diodorus) distinguished himself in Artaxerxes' service. When the king invaded Egypt, Bagoas was appointed as one of three Persian generals who were paired with three Greek commanders to lead the monarch's army. Diodorus says that Bagoas was "a man preferred above the others for valour and loyalty" (*Library of History* 16.47, 1).[38] Bagoas and the Sidonian Mentor teamed together on the expedition (the word for their common endeavor is συνεστρατεύετο [16.47, 4]). At this point, Diodorus says of Bagoas that he was one "whom the king trusted most, a man exceptionally daring and impatient of propriety" (16.47, 4). Eventually, with Mentor, he became the greatest power in the empire ("Master of the kingdom" [16.50, 8]). His administrative work to which Williamson appeals is described thus by Diodorus: "he administered all the King's affairs in the upper satrapies" (16.50, 8).[39] Later, Bagoas would poison Artaxerxes, make Arses the next king, poison him, crown Darius, and finally lose his life to Darius's poison (Bagoas had intended to poison him too [17.5, 3–6]).

There is no doubt that this Bagoas was a military man, but beyond that nothing that is known about him reminds us at all of the Bagoses in Josephus's story. One telling problem for Williamson's theory is that we have no evidence that Diodorus's Bagoas was ever in Jerusalem or Yehud or that he took any interest in the affairs of this minor political unit. His administrative duties as reported by Diodorus involved no contact with the people of Yehud and

---

38. Translation of Charles L. Sherman, *Diodorus of Sicily*, vol. 7, LCL (Cambridge: Harvard Univ. Press, 1952).

39. As Sherman observes, "the upper satrapies" are in the interior (*Diodorus Siculus*, 7, 381 n. 1).

certainly no interest in high-priestly politics. It is difficult to believe that this man, who was so close to the center of power or was himself that center, would befriend the brother of the Jewish high priest and *try* to obtain the office for him. The story that Josephus tells is a local account; we certainly do not get the impression that the great Bagoas came from afar to settle the affairs of his friend in Jerusalem. Rather, from *Antiquities* it seems that Bagohi/Bagoses is already there, is well acquainted with the principal characters, and is expected to act when the murder occurs.

Williamson calls attention to the fact that Josephus's Bagoses holds the office of στρατηγός, not governor or satrap. Although that word does have a military meaning (= general), it evolved to cover a broader semantic field. It "became one of the main terms for leading provincial or municipal officials."[40] In the LXX, στρατηγός renders a Hebrew or Aramaic word some twenty-seven times; it translates שׂר (a military title) seven times, סֶרֶן (title of a Philistine ruler) once, סָגָן or Aramaic סְגַן (prefect, ruler) sixteen times, אֲחַשְׁדַּרְפְּנִים (satraps) once (possibly twice), and מֶלֶךְ (king) once.[41] Thus, in nineteen or twenty of twenty-seven instances, στρατηγός renders the title of a civil, not a military, ruler. There are also a number of cases in Josephus's writings where it has a similar sense (*Ant.* 12.3, 3–4 [§§134–47] where there are several examples; 14.10, 22 [§247]; 14.10, 24 [§259]; 20.6, 2 [§131]; *J. W.* 6.5, 3 [§294]).[42] As a consequence, one would not be justified in assuming that στρατηγός has a military sense in Josephus's introduction or in the source; it is a perfectly acceptable term for a civil ruler. And, one must admit that Josephus's Bagoses acts more like a governor than a general.[43]

Williamson, then, is mistaken in claiming that Diodorus's Bagoas "precisely fits" what can be reconstructed from Josephus's source. He fits hardly at all. This means that, in the absence of any contrary evidence, one should take the logical course of identifying the Johanan and Bigvai/Bagohi of TAD A4.7 = AP 30 with the Joannes and Bagoses of Josephus's story.[44] There is no difficulty in imagining that both men continued to hold their offices into the reign of Artaxerxes II (404–358 BCE). It is not unlikely that Johanan had recently come to office in 410 BCE; we would anticipate, then, that he would

---

40. O. Bauernfeind, "στρατεύομαι κτλ.," *TDNT* 7.704. He points out that it acquired a political or administrative meaning because such responsibilities often devolved on military officials.

41. HRCS, 1295.

42. For New Testament examples, see BAGD, 778.

43. Josephus may have thought that the Bagoses of his source was the general of Artaxerxes (the one known to be the third of that name), but this would still not reveal whether the author of his source made the same identification.

44. So also Rooke, *Zadok's Heirs*, 222–25, 235–36.

have remained as high priest well into the fourth century. If we accept this solution, there is no need to invent both another high priest named *Johanan* and a time when Artaxerxes' Bagoas was in Jerusalem and in charge of affairs there.[45]

It is admittedly difficult to come to assured conclusions when working with material such as *Ant.* 11.7, 1 (§§297–301). Josephus himself very likely complicated matters through his imperfect knowledge of the Persian kings and history. But, what his source relates fits well with the sparse data that have survived regarding the end of the fifth and the beginning of the fourth century in Yehud. If, as seems likely, the story reports what actually happened, it shows that the high priesthood had become an object of political intrigue and a prize sought by ambitious men. Competition for the office was so keen in this case that it led to fratricide. The story also shows that the government could act forcefully under such circumstances, although the text says nothing about removal of Johanan from his office. If the fine that Josephus names ("fifty drachmae for every lamb" [§297]) was in fact imposed, it would have had the effect of virtually eliminating offerings of this kind at the temple for the seven years. The Jerusalem temple may for a time, then, have joined the one in Elephantine—if it was ever reconstructed—as a place where only nonanimal sacrifices were offered.[46]

6. Jaddua (ידוע)

Nehemiah 12:11 names Jaddua last in its genealogical line, and 12:22 places him in final position among those for whose days the names of Levites were

---

45. Several scholars have sensed another difficulty that is mentioned by Williamson, namely, that in Josephus's story Bagoses appears to be a Persian (in §297 he defiles the temple, but in §300 the Persians are said to have done this) while the Bigvai/Bagohi of TAD A4.7 = AP 30 is probably a Jew (see Williamson, "The Historical Value," 59 and the references there). In neither case, however, is his nationality known. It is a reasonable inference that the Bagoses of Josephus is Persian, though the text may entail only that he effected Persian orders. The nationality of the man mentioned in TAD A4.7 = AP 30 is part of a larger problem that will be treated in the second part of this chapter.

46. For this point, see the discussion in Marcus, *Josephus* 6, 503–4, where he cites Julius Morgenstern with approval. Morgenstern surmised that the tax "may therefore well have been a superficially diplomatic means by which Bagoas sought to abrogate the offering of animal sacrifices also in the Temple at Jerusalem" ("Supplementary Studies in the Calendars of Ancient Israel," *HUCA* 10 [1935]: 127 n. 206). There is no textual reason to think that the two were related responses on the part of Bagoas, even though the Elephantine compromise and the Jerusalem fine may have had the same effect.

recorded. These are the only biblical references to the man, but, as with his predecessor Johanan, there is extrabiblical evidence about him.[47] Josephus has made him a central actor in a complex drama that included not only Jaddua, but also a Sanballat who built the temple of the Samaritans and Alexander the Great who visited Jerusalem in his time (*Ant.* 11.7, 2–8, 7 [§§302–47]). The story runs as follows.

> When Joannes departed this life, he was succeeded in the high priest-hood by his son Jaddus.[48] He too had a brother, named Manasses, to whom Sanaballetes—he had been sent to Samaria as satrap by Darius the last king, and was of the Cuthaean race from whom the Samaritans also are descended—, knowing that Jerusalem was a famous city and that its kings had given much trouble to the Assyrians and the inhabitants of Coele-Syria, gladly gave him his daughter, called Nikaso, in marriage, for he believed that this alliance by marriage would be a pledge of his securing the goodwill of the entire Jewish nation. (11.7, 2 [§§302–3])

At this point it appears there was no objection to the marriage between the high priest's brother and the daughter of the Samaritan governor.

The local story is then interrupted by a paragraph in which Josephus narrates Alexander's succession to the throne of Macedon, his victory over Darius III (336–330 BCE) at the Granicus, and the continuation of his campaign

---

47. A coin bearing the name Jaddua (ידוע) without adjoined title and dating from the late Persian period has been found and published. A. Spaer ("Jaddua the High Priest?" *Israel Numismatic Journal* 9 [1986–87]: 1–3) published it and dated it to the time of Jaddua I (see below for the theory that there were two high priests named Jaddua in the fourth century BCE). Ya'akov Meshorer has more recently pointed to the difficulty of dating the Aramaic lapidary script in which the name is written and puts it later, at the time of the person he considers Jaddua II (the last high priest of the Persian period). However, discovery of similar coins at Samaria, Gaza, and elsewhere has led him to conclude that the Jaddua coins may have been minted in Samaria, not Jerusalem, and that this Jaddua may have been, not a Jewish high priest, but a Samarian governor (Meshorer, *A Treasury of Jewish Coins from the Persian Period to Bar-Kochba* [Jerusalem: Yitzhak ben-Zvi, 1997 (Hebrew)] 22). Mention should also be made of what Meshorer calls the Yehudah coin—a coin on which are the words יהד and יהודה (*A Treasury of Jewish Coins*, 23). He interprets these, not as the name of the province in both Aramaic and Hebrew, but as the provincial name and the name of an individual who was either governor, high priest, or both. His name, although it is not attested among high priests or governors, should therefore be added to the list. He puts this Yehudah between his Jaddua II and Hezekiah (on him, see below) but recognizes that there is no evidence for an official with this name. One may agree that this would be very weak support for adding a name to either the high-priestly or the gubernatorial list.

48. Josephus therefore, unlike Neh 12:11, considered Johanan, not Jonathan, to be Jaddua's father.

into Pamphylia (11.8, 1 [§§304–5]). When the historian's attention returns to affairs in Jerusalem, he writes:

> Now the elders of Jerusalem, resenting the fact that the brother of the high priest Jaddus was sharing the high priesthood [μετέχειν τῆς ἀρχιερωσύνης] while married to a foreigner, rose up against him, for they considered this marriage to be a stepping-stone for those who might wish to transgress the laws about taking wives and that this would be the beginning of intercourse with foreigners. They believed, moreover, that their former captivity and misfortunes had been caused by some who had erred in marrying and taking wives who were not of their own country. They therefore told Manasses either to divorce his wife or not to approach the altar. And, as the high priest shared the indignation of the people and kept his brother from the altar, Manasses went to his father-in-law Sanaballetes and said that while he loved his daughter Nikaso, nevertheless the priestly office was the highest in the nation and had always belonged to his family, and that therefore he did not wish to be deprived of it on her account. But Sanaballetes promised not only to preserve the priesthood for him but also to procure for him the power and office of high priest and to appoint him governor of all the places over which he ruled, if he were willing to live with his daughter; and he said that he would build a temple similar to that in Jerusalem on Mt. Garizein—this is the highest of the mountains near Samaria—, and undertook to do these things with the consent of King Darius. (11.8, 2 [§§306–11])

Under these conditions Manasseh agreed to remain with Nikaso, whose father Sanballat was by now an elderly man (§311).

While these events were taking place in Samaria and Jerusalem, Alexander and Darius were moving toward their fateful encounter at Issus where the Macedonians, quite contrary to Sanballat's expectations, crushed the Persian forces and became the new masters of the Syro-Palestinian region (11.8, 3 [§313–16]).[49] Alexander's relations with various towns and rulers in the area now become the subject of Josephus's narrative. As the king besieged Tyre,

---

49. On the significance of the phrase "[n]ow about this time" in §313, compare Daniel R. Schwartz, "ΚΑΤΑ ΤΟΥΤΟΝ ΤΟΝ ΚΑΙΡΟΝ: Josephus' Source on Agrippa II," *JQR* 72 (1982): 241–68. He contends that it is a literary marker used more often by Josephus for a specific purpose: "If the passage in question, or the resumption based on the main source immediately thereafter, is introduced by the words 'about this time,' it is probable that it was copied from an auxiliary source" (246). See p. 248 where he refers to the present passage and §§304–5, both of which interrupt Josephus's narrative about the high-priestly family and Sanballat to give "a short summary based upon a Hellenistic history of Alexander."

he dispatched a letter to the high priest of the Jews, requesting him to send him assistance and supply his army with provisions and give him the gifts which they had formerly sent as tribute to Darius, thus choosing the friendship of the Macedonians, for, he said, they would not regret this course. But the high priest replied to the bearers of the letter that he had given his oath to Darius not to take up arms against him, and said that he would never violate this oath so long as Darius remained alive. When Alexander heard this, he was roused to anger, and while deciding not to leave Tyre, which was on the point of being taken, threatened that when he had brought it to terms he would march against the high priest of the Jews and through him teach all men what people it was to whom they must keep their oaths. (11.8, 3 [§§317–19])

While the high priest (note that in this section he is called "the high priest of the Jews"), perhaps not yet sure about the lay of the political landscape, rejected Alexander's demand for help, Sanballat transferred his loyalty from Darius to Alexander and came with eight thousand men to the Macedonian king at Tyre. Alexander gladly received his assistance and lands and did him a favor in turn:

As Alexander received him in a friendly fashion, Sanaballetes now felt confident about his plan and addressed him on that subject, explaining that he had a son-in-law Manasses, who was the brother of Jaddus, the high priest of the Jews, and that there were many others of his countrymen[50] with him who now wished to build a temple in the territory subject to him. It was also an advantage to the king, he said, that the power of the Jews should be divided in two, in order that the nation might not, in the event of revolution, be of one mind and stand together and so give trouble to the kings as it had formerly given to the Assyrian rulers. When, therefore, Alexander gave his consent, Sanaballetes brought all his energy to bear and built the temple and appointed Manasses high priest, considering this to be the greatest distinction which his daughter's descendants could have. But Sanaballetes died after seven months had been spent on the siege of Tyre and two on that of Gaza. (11.8, 4 [§§322–25])

Once he completed this section about Alexander and Sanballat, Josephus reverted to the monarch's relations with the high priest. Following the victory

---

50. That is, Manasseh's countrymen; see §312.

at Gaza, Alexander was eager to punish Jerusalem. Jaddua presumably under-stood by this time that the Macedonians were a force to be taken seriously and not an ephemeral invader. He was terrified and ordered the people to pray and sacrifice so that God would save them from their peril.

> But, when he had gone to sleep after the sacrifice, God spoke oracu-larly [ἐχρημάτισεν] to him in his sleep, telling him to take courage and adorn the city with wreaths and open the gates and go out to meet them, and that the people should be in white garments, and he himself with the priests in the robes prescribed by law, and that they should not look to suffer any harm, for God was watching over them. Thereupon he rose from his sleep, greatly rejoicing to himself, and announced to all the revelation that had been made to him, and, after doing all the things that he had been told to do, awaited the coming of the king. (11.8, 4 [§§327–28])

The story about Alexander's meeting with Jaddua (*Ant.* 11.8, 5 [§§329–39]) is both highly dramatic and sharply disputed. The high priest led his people to a place named Saphein—probably Mount Scopus[51]—and there the encounter occurred. Although the Phoenicians and Chaldeans who were with Alexander and hoping for plunder expected the worst for Jerusalem and the death of the high priest, Alexander surprised all of them.

> For when Alexander while still far off saw the multitude in white gar-ments[,] the priests at their head clothed in linen, and the high priest in a robe of hyacinth-blue and gold, wearing on his head the mitre with the golden plate on it on which was inscribed the name of God, he approached alone and prostrated himself before the Name and first greeted the high priest. Then all the Jews together greeted Alexander with one voice and surrounded him, but the kings of Syria and the others were struck with amazement at his action and sup-posed that the king's mind was deranged. (11.8, 5 [§§331–32])

When asked about his conduct by Parmenion, Alexander explained that he had not actually prostrated himself before the high priest but rather before the God served by the pontiff. He claimed to have seen him dressed in such clothing in a dream while he was still in Macedonia. As the king put it, the high priest "urged me not to hesitate but to cross over confidently, for he himself [God?] would lead my army and give over to me the empire of the Persians" (§334).

---

51. Marcus, *Josephus*, vol. 6, 472–73 n. b.

Alexander himself then

> gave his hand to the high priest and, with the Jews running beside
> him, entered the city. Then he went up to the temple, where he sacri-
> ficed to God under the direction of the high priest, and showed due
> honour to the priests and to the high priest himself. And, when the
> book of Daniel was shown to him, in which he had declared that one
> of the Greeks would destroy the empire of the Persians, he believed
> himself to be the one indicated; and in his joy he dismissed the mul-
> titude for the time being, but on the following day he summoned
> them again and told them to ask for any gifts which they might desire.
> When the high priest asked that they might observe their country's
> laws [τοῖς πατρίοις νόμοις] and in the seventh year be exempt from
> tribute, he granted all this. Then they begged that he would permit
> the Jews in Babylon and Media also to have their own laws, and he
> gladly promised to do as they asked. And, when he said to the people
> that if any wished to join his army while still adhering to the customs
> of their country, he was ready to take them, many eagerly accepted
> service with him. (11.8, 5 [§§336–39])

Josephus completed this section of his narrative by relating an incident that
involved the Samaritans and Alexander. The substance of the report is that
they, upon seeing how Alexander had honored the Jews, decided to present
themselves to him as Jews. They invited him to their city so that he could come
and honor their temple as well. The king postponed his visit, but when they,
too, asked to be exempt from taxes in the seventh year he inquired more
closely about their identity, and they had to admit that they were not Jews. So,
he promised to deal more fully with them when he returned and had more
information. He then led his soldiers and those of Sanballat to Egypt
(§§340–45). The historian closed the eleventh book of *Antiquities* by recording the death of Alexander, the continuing existence of the Samaritan temple
and the territory of the Shechemites as a place to which renegade Jews fled
when expelled from Jerusalem, and the death of Jaddua. Regarding him, Josephus wrote: "Now by that time the high priest Jaddus was also dead, and his
son Onias succeeded to the high priesthood" (11.8, 7 [§347]). Thus, in the
final paragraph of the story, he again mentioned its three major subjects:
Alexander, the Samaritan temple, and Jaddua.

For this story, Josephus is the most ancient source, and none of the incidents in it concerning Jerusalem or Samaria is mentioned by any of the
ancient historians who chronicled this part of Alexander's career. How is it to

be assessed? Does it relate what happened, or is it a kind of fiction, or is it both? There is no avoiding the fact that the complex account contains improbable claims and downright falsehoods. Since it involves Alexander, a figure around whom so many romances arose, it is not surprising that Josephus's story has been dismissed by modern scholars as an unlikely repository of historical information about Alexander and Jerusalem. As Tcherikover put it: "Alexander's visit to Jerusalem is not a historical episode which the Greek writers 'forgot' to relate and which has 'by chance' been preserved in Josephus; it is a historical myth designed to bring the king into direct contact with the Jews, and to speak of both in laudatory terms. Here is material for research worthy not of the historian, but of the student of literature."[52] Although students of such literature would probably share Tcherikover's judgment, most, including Tcherikover himself, have still seen a number of historical facts in it. The question of the historicity of all or part of the story is worth pursuing, because the answer to it bears directly on how one understands the history of the high priesthood at the end of the Persian period. In the following paragraphs, the results of the more important literary analyses will be sketched. Then, in an effort to zero in on the question of historicity, the improbable and false elements of the story will be isolated, the possible historical aspects of it will be enumerated, and finally, an attempt will be made to draw appropriate conclusions from the data.

The most influential literary analysis of Josephus's story was made by Adolf Büchler,[53] who found in *Ant.* 11.7, 2–8, 6 (§§302–45) three distinct units that Josephus has simply juxtaposed (with some additional comments): (1) a Samaritan story that centers about Manasseh, Sanballat, and his relations with Alexander (§§302–3, 306–12, 315, 321–25);[54] (2) a Jewish account that focuses

---

52. Victor Tcherikover, *Hellenistic Civilization and the Jews* (New York: Atheneum, 1970), 45. Erich S. Gruen writes: "The legend of Alexander in Jerusalem can best be understood as one of several comparable fictions that gave voice to Hellenistic Jews seeking to define their place in a world governed by Greek monarchs" (*Heritage and Hellenism: The Reinvention of Jewish Tradition,* Hellenistic Culture and Society 30 [Berkeley: Univ. of California Press, 1998], 194). He later refers to the story about Alexander's visit to Jerusalem as "outright fabrication" (195). See also Marcus, *Josephus* 6, Appendix C, 528–29; Martin Hengel, *Jews, Greeks, and Barbarians: Aspects of the Hellenization of Judaism in the Pre-Christian Period,* trans. J. Bowden (Philadelphia: Fortress Press, 1980), 6–7; and E. J. Bickerman, *The Jews in the Greek Age* (Cambridge: Harvard Univ. Press, 1988), 5, as distinguished examples of the many who reject the historicity of Josephus's story.

53. "La relation de Josèphe concernant Alexandre le grand," *REJ* 36 (1898): 1–26. The article is summarized in the text above without indication of page numbers for each statement.

54. Büchler himself did not list exactly which sections belonged, in his view, to each part, but a reading of his essay suggests that the ones given here are the ones that he intended. The same is the case for the following two strands.

on the high priest Jaddua and his relations with Alexander (§§317–19, 326–39); and (3) a brief description of the expeditions of the Persian and Macedonian armies (§§304–5, 313–14, 316, 320). The first unit never criticizes the Samaritans, has Manasseh as its central character, and accounts for the origins of the Samaritan temple. It is clear that §321 is the sequel of §316 and that the exchange of letters between Alexander and Jaddua is intrusive in the Sanballat story. The juxtaposing of units has produced problems in geography (the story moves from Tyre to Gaza and back to Tyre). Büchler maintained that the details about Darius and Alexander were integral to the Sanballat story and had been combined with it by an editor, even though Sanballat, according to Büchler, belonged to the time of Nehemiah, not that of Darius III and Alexander. The Jaddua story, he thought, was written as a response to the Sanballat narrative; its purpose was to show through contrasts that Alexander had been more favorable to the temple at Jerusalem than to the one on Mount Gerizim. The Samaritan story for him conformed with reality (for example, that Samaria, like the rest of the region, submitted peacefully during the siege at Tyre); the Jewish tale does not fit what is known of Alexander at this time. Thus, the story about Jaddua has no historical value in the material that serves the author's tendentious aim. Büchler also distinguished §§340–45. The anti-Samaritan tone in these paragraphs shows that the author was not Samaritan, and they are not related to the Jaddua story. He read the material against the backdrop of the first century BCE, claiming that the Jaddua source is based upon Caesar's relations with the Jews at that time.

While many scholars accept Büchler's division of sources, it encounters some significant difficulties. The most important is that Josephus's story shows greater unity than he allowed.[55] It seems unlikely that a large part of the narrative stems from a Samaritan source written by an author who wished to extol the royal origin of the temple on Mount Gerizim. There are too many indicators in the supposedly Samaritan paragraphs that the Jews, not the Samaritans, are being praised. Jerusalem is said to be a famous city with which a neighboring ruler would want to ally himself in order to win the favor of its inhabitants (§303). The Jewish authorities disapprove of intermarriage with the Samaritans and want Manasseh to divorce his wife (§306–9). Manasseh himself prefers the Jewish priesthood to Nikaso (§309). Sanballat has to offer a tremendous bribe to convince Manasseh to remain with his daughter; thus, the first Samaritan high priest is a Jerusalem priest who signs on only after

---

55. Two scholars who find unity in the story are Aryeh Kasher, "Alexander of Macedon's Campaign in Palestine," *BM* 20 (1975): 187–208 (Hebrew); Jonathan Goldstein, "Alexander and the Jews," *PAAJR* 59 (1993): 59–101.

receiving the promise of a substantial bonus (§§310–11). The Samaritan temple is to be similar to the one in Jerusalem (§310). Sanballat buys support for his son-in-law among other Jewish practitioners of mixed marriages (§312). Sanballat, unlike the faithful Jaddua, swiftly and cheerfully switches his sworn allegiance from Darius to Alexander when it fits his personal agenda (§§317–21, only the last paragraph of which Büchler assigned to the Samaritan source). Also, according to Sanballat, the power of the Jews is such that it would be advantageous for Alexander to divide them in two (§323). Are these the claims of a Samaritan who is exalting his people and temple? The story, like the remainder of Josephus's tale, looks decidedly pro-Jewish. It is true, as Büchler argued, that the Jaddua story offers numerous contrasts between the high priest and Sanballat, but that was possible because Sanballat is pictured in rather a negative light in the allegedly Samaritan source.[56]

It is also debatable whether one can isolate §§340–45 as an independent unit, since the material in them presupposes both of the other main blocks of the text. The Samaritans act after they see how Alexander has honored the Jews (§340), and they meet Alexander just after he leaves Jerusalem (§342). They then ask for the very tax concession (in the seventh year) that he has made to the Jews (§§343–44). Cross-references to the Sanballat story surface when his troops are mentioned twice (§§342, 345) and Alexander is invited to visit the Samaritan temple.

As a result, it is fair to say that there are definable blocks of material in the story, but that each had a separate author—one Samaritan and two Jewish—with unique agendas seems implausible. Once this conclusion is rejected, Büchler's hypothesis about the historical value of the Samaritan source and the worthlessness of the Jaddua source also is called into serious question.

More recently Cohen has examined the Jaddua section of the story (he accepts Büchler's source division) from a different literary angle.[57] His central thesis, offered with some reservation, is that "the Jaddus-Alexander story is a combination of two sub-stories: the high priest and the Jews greet Alexander the Great (an *adventus* story); the temple and the Jews are rescued from Alexander the Great by a divine manifestation (an *epiphany* story)."[58] He demonstrates very clearly that the *adventus* section has numerous parallels in ancient literature; it is a story of the Jews' surrender to Alexander. The epiphany block

---

56. Although he does not think the story is a unity, Gruen believes the "Samaritan" sections come from Jewish circles hostile to the Samaritans (*Heritage and Hellenism*, 194–95).

57. Shaye J. D. Cohen, "Alexander the Great and Jaddus the High Priest According to Josephus," *AJSR* 7-8 (1982–83): 41–68.

58. Ibid., 44–45. The remainder of the article is summarized without references to page numbers.

recalls others of a soteriological type. The comparison is less successful here, and Cohen has to reconstruct a "more original" form of Josephus's tale because, as it stands, it does not match the pattern particularly well (for example, Alexander's dream has to be moved to the night before his meeting with Jaddua).[59] In this story, Alexander surrenders to the Jews. As both types of story were common, there is no need to posit behind them specific historical events.

Both Büchler and Cohen deny historical value to the Jaddua account. It has been shown above that Büchler's case may not be convincing; Cohen's must be considered a possible inference from typical kinds of tales. In light of this, we ought now to ask what are the specific pieces of evidence that lead many to reject all or part of Josephus's story as unhistorical. Among the unlikely claims made by Josephus, many scholars would include the marriage of Manasseh and Nikaso, because accepting it as factual would entail that twice within a relatively short time a brother of a high priest married a daughter of a man named Sanballat with unfortunate consequences in both cases. According to Neh 13:28, "one of the sons of Jehoiada, son of the high priest Eliashib, was the son-in-law of Sanballat the Horonite; I [= Nehemiah] chased him away from me." As Cowley remarked: "The view that there were two Sanballats, each governor of Samaria and each with a daughter who married a brother of a High Priest at Jerusalem, is a solution too desperate to be entertained."[60] As a result, many have concluded that Josephus's story about the Manasseh-Nikaso marriage is a garbled version of the case in Neh 13:28, which the historian has misplaced by about a century, perhaps because he confused Darius II and Darius III.[61] To this should be added the fact that Samaritan sources offer no trace of Manasseh as the first high priest in the temple on Mount Gerizim.

Second, to judge from Josephus's chronological notices, it took an incredibly short time for Sanballat's men to build a temple. Alexander is supposed to

---

59. See a critical evaluation of this part of Cohen's essay by Tae Hun Kim, "The Dream of Alexander in Josephus *Ant.* 11.325–39," *JSJ* 34 (2003): 425–42.

60. *Aramaic Papyri*, 110. Daniel R. Schwartz is a more recent defender of this position and even thinks, with the added information available today, that we can see how Josephus made his mistake ("On Some Papyri and Josephus' Sources and Chronology for the Persian Period," *JSJ* 21 [1991]: 175–99). The following pages attempt to show that such a conclusion is hardly the most likely implication of the evidence.

61. H. H. Rowley, "Sanballat and the Samaritan Temple," 251–52, 256 (he observed that Josephus had omitted any reference to Sanballat from his version of the Nehemiah story and transferred him to this later setting); Tcherikover, *Hellenistic Civilization and the Jews*, 44, 419 n. 12; Marcus, *Josephus* 6, Appendix B, 507–11; compare also Cowley, *Aramaic Papyri*, 110; F.-M. Abel, "Alexandre le grand en Syrie et en Palestine (suite)," *RB* 44 (1935): 49; R. J. Coggins, *Samaritans and Jews: The Origins of Samaritanism Reconsidered*, GPT (Atlanta: John Knox, 1975), 96; and Williamson, *Ezra, Nehemiah*, 400–401.

have authorized the construction when the governor came to him as he besieged Tyre (§§323–24); Sanballat then went to work with diligence and the project was completed by the time Alexander came to Jerusalem just after the siege of Gaza, since at that time the Samaritans invited him to visit it (§§340–42). The time spent building the temple could not have been longer than approximately nine months, as the sieges of the two cities combined lasted nine months.[62] It is sometimes thought that the inadequate amount of time for building the temple resulted from Josephus's clumsy combination of two sources regarding the Samaritans. As Tcherikover explained the matter:

> Sanballat was the central figure of the first tale, but was unmentioned in the second [that is, the one in which Alexander declines the invitation to visit the Samaritan temple]; Josephus, therefore, had to remove him in the middle of the account in order to explain to his readers why he was missing from the end of the narrative. In the first story Sanballat obtains from Alexander the permit to build the shrine, whereas in the second it has been standing for a long time, and the Samaritans invite Alexander to visit it. When both narratives were combined the result was that the temple appeared to be constructed within a few months.[63]

A third improbable claim is that Alexander, who received Sanballat, his lands, and his eight thousand troops at Tyre and authorized construction of the Samaritan temple, when he is invited to see the shrine is not reminded of his own authorization and, moreover, does not seem to know who the Samaritans are ("he inquired who they were" [§343]).[64]

Another unlikely element in Josephus's story about Alexander is the prominence of dreams. Alexander is supposed to have seen the Jewish high priest in a dream that he experienced in Dium before leaving Macedonia (§§334–35).[65] Jaddua, too, had a dream or rather learned "oracularly . . . in his

---

62. Rowley, "Sanballat and the Samaritan Temple," 259–60; Coggins, *Samaritans and Jews*, 96.

63. *Hellenistic Civilization and the Jews*, 44. See also Büchler, "La relation de Josèphe," 22–23; Arnaldo Momigliano, "Flavius Josephus and Alexander's Visit to Jerusalem," *Athenaeum* 57 (1979): 444. Mor thinks the Samaritans exploited the power vacuum in the area to build the temple, when the Persians had not yet been totally defeated ("Samaritan History," 7).

64. See Tcherikover, *Hellenistic Civilization and the Jews*, 44; Momigliano, "Flavius Josephus and Alexander's Visit to Jerusalem," 444.

65. Diodorus (*Library of History* 17.16, 3-4) mentions that Alexander stayed at Dium, but he reports nothing about a dream on this occasion. Compare Abel, "Alexandre le grand en Syrie et en Palestine," 51.

sleep" (§327) that God would protect his people from harm.[66] When the two men met, Alexander recognized Jaddua from his dream and "prostrated himself [προσεκύνησε] before the Name" (§331). Resort to dreams of these kinds has not inspired confidence in the historicity of Josephus's tale; they are a theme belonging to the genre of soteriological epiphany stories.[67]

To these dubious elements, one should add Josephus's statement that the book of Daniel was shown to Alexander and that the monarch believed he was the conquering Greek foretold in it (§337). The passage in question is Dan 8:21 ("The male goat is the king of Greece, and the great horn between its eyes is the first king"), a part of the book that is commonly dated to about 165 BCE, some 167 years after Alexander's alleged arrival in Jerusalem.[68]

Alongside these claims we may place others that scholars have judged to be outright historical errors. First, Josephus locates Alexander's march on Jerusalem to punish the recalcitrant city in a time after he took Gaza (§325). The sources for this point in his campaign, however, indicate that he moved from Gaza to Pelusium in one week, thus leaving no time for a side trip to Jerusalem.[69] And, of course, no other historical text even mentions Alexander's visit to Jerusalem, whether from Gaza or any other place.

There are several other details in the narrative that scholars have declared to be unhistorical—at least for this point in Alexander's career—in that they presuppose his later status as conqueror of the known world. Among these are the reference to *proskynesis* (§333)—a Persian practice that is not attested at

---

66. For an analysis of this dream report in light of scriptural examples such as 1 Kings 3, see Robert Gnuse, "The Temple Experience of Jaddus in the *Antiquities* of Josephus: A Report of Jewish Dream Incubation," *JQR* 83 (1993): 349–68.

67. Cohen, "Alexander and Jaddus," 49–55, where he cites several parallels but notes (see especially 56–60) that Alexander does not, as other sovereigns in similar situations do, proclaim explicitly the might of God. Regarding Alexander's prostration, compare Tcherikover, *Hellenistic Civilization and the Jews*, 45; and Coggins, *Samaritans and Jews*, 95.

68. This point is made repeatedly in the literature. See, for example, Marcus, *Josephus* 6, 477 n. d. Gruen (*Heritage and Hellenism*, 197) writes about the vision foretelling Alexander's conquests and Daniel's confirmation of it: "One could hardly wish for a better example of Jewish expropriation and transformation of a Hellenistic theme."

69. Büchler, "La relation de Josèphe," 1; Tcherikover, *Hellenistic Civilization and the Jews*, 41, 45. For a response to the objection that Curtius and Arrian do not make Alexander leave Gaza immediately after capturing the city and that, as he attended to affairs there, he could have taken time to go to Jerusalem, see Marcus, *Josephus* 6, Appendix C, 525–26. Gruen adds: "There was certainly no reason for our Greek sources to have suppressed a visit to the holy city. They regularly report Alexander's arrival at key shrines and sacred places, where he honored native gods and performed public acts of sacrifice. Jerusalem would fit nicely into that repeated scenario, and the Alexander historians could hardly have missed or omitted it. The tale is a fiction" (*Heritage and Hellenism*, 195).

this time among the Macedonians and that Alexander later tried to force upon his men in the face of considerable resistance. In addition, Josephus says that Chaldeans followed Alexander as he approached Jerusalem (§330), but he would not have had associates of this nationality before he became ruler of Babylon. Moreover, the high priest's petition to him that he allow the Jews of Babylonia and Media as well to enjoy their own laws (§338) also presupposes that Alexander controlled those two lands, which he had not yet visited, much less conquered.[70]

Any informed reader of Josephus's story about Alexander must grant that it can hardly be considered a scientific historical account of events that happened in 332 BCE. It shows the marks of a good story that got better as it was told and retold. But, there are grounds for thinking that, despite the embellishments that it undoubtedly contains, it rests upon some sort of historical foundation. Then, too, not all of the objections to it stand up to rigid scrutiny.

First, more is known today about the Sanballats of ancient Samaria, and this new knowledge places the marriages of Neh 13:28 and Manasseh with Nikaso in a different light. There is now documentary evidence for more than one Sanballat. Nehemiah's enemy (Neh 2:10, 19; 3:33; 4:1; 6:1, 2, 5, 12, 14; 13:28; TAD A4.7 = AP 30.29) lived in the fifth century and had sons named Delaiah and Shelemiah. A second Sanballat is mentioned twice in the material discovered in the Wadi Daliyeh: in WDSP 11 recto 13 (formerly papyrus 14), after a gap, it is possible to read: ‏]ו בר סנאבלט וחנן סגנא‎ (son of Sanballat, and Hanan the prefect). Since the papyri in this find were written between about 375 and 331 BCE, the reference to a son of Sanballat in all likelihood comes from a time between these two temporal poles. A sealing (WD 22, a bulla) attached to WDSP 16 (formerly papyrus 5) bears the words ‏יהו בן‎ ‏[סנא]בלט פחת שמרין‎ (. . . yahu son of[San]ballat the governor of Samaria).[71]

---

70. Büchler, "La relation de Josèphe," 14; Tcherikover, *Hellenistic Civilization and the Jews,* 45; many others have repeated the same list.

71. Frank Moore Cross has reported these readings and dates in several publications: "Papyri of the Fourth Century B.C. from Dâliyeh: A Preliminary Report on Their Discovery and Significance," in *New Directions in Biblical Archaeology,* ed. D. N. Freedman and J. C. Greenfield (Garden City, N.Y.: Doubleday, 1971), 46–48 (based on a lecture given in 1966); "Aspects of Samaritan and Jewish History in Late Persian and Hellenistic Times," *HTR* 59 (1966): 203–6; and "The Papyri and Their Historical Significance," in *Discoveries in the Wadi Ed-Daliyeh,* ed. P. W. Lapp and N. L. Lapp, AASOR 41 (Cambridge: ASOR, 1974), 18–19 (pl. 61 shows the sealing). The same material is summarized in R. Klein, "Sanballat," in *IDBSup* 782; Cross, "Daliyeh, Wadi ed-," in *ABD* 2.3–4. The official edition of the Wadi Daliyeh texts appeared subsequently: Douglas Marvin Gropp, *Wadi Daliyeh II, The Samaria Papyri from Wadi Daliyeh and Qumran Cave 4 XXVIII Miscellanea, Part II,* consulting ed. J. VanderKam and M. Brady, DJD 28 (Oxford: Clarendon, 2001). The text designations used first above are those of Gropp. In the edition, only a photograph of WDSP 11

A reasonable inference is that there was a Sanballat who governed Samaria in the first half of the fourth century. This, in turn, would imply that Josephus's Sanballat—the one who met Alexander—was a third individual of that name and position. As Cross reconstructs the Samaritan list of governors, there are six names: Sanballat I (of the book of Nehemiah and the Elephantine Papyri), Delaiah, Sanballat II (of the Daliyeh texts), Yeshua (a name reconstructed in the line from WDSP 11 [papyrus 14] that was quoted above), Hananiah (see the same text), and Sanballat III (Josephus's Samaritan governor).[72] There are several uncertainties in this list (for example, that Hanan = Hananiah and that he is the son of Sanballat II), but the existence of three Sanballats in the fifth and fourth centuries is now a likely conclusion.[73] If there were several Sanballats, it reduces the level of suspicion aroused by the two reported marriages between daughters of Sanballats and brothers of high priests. It should be obvious, too, that, apart from the families involved and the position of the husband and wife in them, there are no similarities between the union of Neh 13:28 and the Manasseh-Nikaso marriage. Their dates are far different; in the one, Nehemiah expels the husband and, in the other, Manasseh is enticed to leave by his father-in-law; and in the latter, the elders play a part. Josephus's narrative about the latter marriage should no longer be grouped among the implausible elements in his story.

The impressively short time it took to finish the Samaritan temple remains a serious problem, but at least Josephus's dating of that temple to the very beginning of the Hellenistic period remains a possibility, although the final archeological verdict has not yet been pronounced. Earlier excavations atop Tell er-Ras (on the northern ridge of Mount Gerizim) revealed a structure (called Building A by the archaeologists) that is believed to be the Hadrianic temple mentioned in ancient sources and pictured on some coins. It rests above "a large building complex centered around a half cube [= Building B] sixty-six feet wide, sixty-six feet long, and thirty feet high, constructed of large unhewn stones, laid without cement and without internal structuring . . . . This structure rests on the bedrock of the mountain in the midst of a 135-

---

appears—pl. XI—no transcription. Mary Joan Winn Leith published many of the bullae in *Wadi Daliyeh I: The Wadi Daliyeh Seal Impressions,* DJD 24 (Oxford: Clarendon, 1997) but did not include WD 22 on the grounds that it had been sufficiently published elsewhere (10).

72. See, for example, Cross, "Aspects of Samaritan and Jewish History," 204; "A Reconstruction of the Judean Restoration," *Int* 29 (1975): 188; Gropp, "Sanballat," in *Encyclopedia of the Dead Sea Scrolls,* ed. L. Schiffman and J. VanderKam (Oxford: Oxford Univ. Press, 2000), 823–25. Compare too the survey in Scolnic, *Chronology and Papponymy,* 134–41 (he seems unconvinced about Sanballat II).

73. That there was more than one Sanballat is a thesis that was entertained long before the Daliyeh discovery was made; see Rowley, "Sanballat and the Samaritan Temple," 251–52.

foot-wide, rectilinear courtyard built with walls of unhewn stone. The latest pottery taken from the foundation trenches of the walls is from the third century B.C."[74] In an early report about this find, Robert J. Bull thought the building might be the Samaritan temple mentioned by Josephus but considered this "certainly nothing more than a hypothesis so far."[75] The larger complex, however, came to be identified as the Samaritan temple and the half cube as a massive altar.[76] This conclusion was called into question by the preliminary results of excavations conducted under the direction of I. Magen. From his work, "it became clear that there was no Hellenistic construction phase on the Tell. The Hellenistic pottery sherds that were found there and had been used by archeologists to date Building B, were brought as fill from the Hellenistic city on the main peak, only about twenty metres away."[77] Or, as Magen himself put the matter: "A reexamination of Bull's exacavations shows, however, in the writer's opinion, that there was no Hellenistic temple at Tell er-Ras, and that both building phases belong to the Roman period."[78]

Magen,[79] who has been excavating on Mount Gerizim since 1979, has more recently issued reports on a large site elsewhere on the mountain where first a sacred precinct and later an adjacent city were constructed. These are found at a very high part of the mountain commanding an excellent view of surrounding territory. From the excavated materials, Magen has concluded that this temple was built in the first half of the *fifth* century BCE, that is, approximately in the time of Sanballat I and Nehemiah, not more than a century later in the days of Sanballat III as Josephus reports. He says that the Persian period pottery discovered in the sacred precinct dates from the beginning of the fifth and continues through the fourth century and that the numismatic evidence points to the same time span. Some sixty-eight coins from Persian times extend in date from 480 BCE to the time of Alexander. He found no indication of a break in occupation between the Persian and Hellenistic periods. The earlier stage of the site overlaps with a considerable stretch of the Persian period and the beginning of the Hellenistic age, while a later phase belongs to Seleucid times.

---

74. "Gerizim, Mount," in *IDBSup* 361.

75. "The Excavation of Tell er-Ras on Mt. Gerizim," *BA* 31 (1968): 71.

76. Bull, "Er-Ras, Tell," in *EAEHL* 4.1022.

77. Reinhard Pummer, "Samaritan Material Remains and Archaeology," in *The Samaritans*, ed. A. D. Crown (Tübingen: Mohr/Siebeck, 1989), 168.

78. I. Magen, "Gerizim, Mount," in *NEAEHL* 2.489.

79. An issue of the journal *Qadmoniot* was dedicated to the work on Gerizim (*Qadmoniot* 33 [2000]). The next paragraphs summarize particularly Magen's essay "Mt. Gerizim—Temple City," 74–118, especially 97, 113–18.

Consequently, Magen thinks that Sanballat the Horonite, the first native governor of the area, built the temple. As a high priest for his sanctuary, he was able to attract the grandson of the Jewish high priest Eliashib; to him he gave his daughter in marriage (Neh 13:28). So, Magen joins those scholars who think that Josephus's story about the Manasseh-Nikaso marriage is a badly misdated version of the union that so offended Nehemiah.

Study of the material remains from the site is not complete, but if Magen is correct in his dating of them, then Josephus's account of constructing the Samaritan temple at the time of Alexander is not historically accurate. For the present, we should probably be skeptical of this claim in Josephus, but, conversely, we may hesitate to accept Magen's conclusion, since more work remains to be done and it is not clear from the coins, at least, that he has drawn the correct inference.

It has also been claimed that the two sections of Josephus's story that deal with the Samaritan temple—the episodes involving building it and inviting Alexander to visit it—are contradictory: in the former, Alexander knows Sanballat and the Samaritans who become his allies, while in the latter he is forced to ask who they are. A closer reading of the text, however, should demonstrate that the critics are not being fair to Josephus here. The text says nothing about whether Alexander knows who the Samaritans are. Rather, Alexander inquires about their relationship to the Jews. As they had asked for the same exemption in the seventh year that Alexander had just granted to the Jews, he asks the proper legal question concerning the ethnic identity of this group that lived so close to Jerusalem and followed the same religiously motivated agricultural practice. His query is not motivated by ignorance of who they were but by his knowledge that they, though they were Samaritans, wished to be considered Jews. There is no reason to think that Alexander would have asked or been told about such issues when he met Sanballat at Tyre.

For a long time, students of the text have sought to find a historical kernel for Josephus's account of Alexander's more negative attitude toward the Samaritans (*Ant.* 11.8, 6 [§§340–45]) in the Samaritan revolt against Alexander's prefect in Coele-Syria—Andromachus—whom they burned alive. According to Q. Curtius Rufus, one of the historians of Alexander's campaigns, the Samaritans executed him while Alexander was in Egypt. When the king returned from Egypt, he punished the Samaritan leaders. Christian writers such as Eusebius, Jerome, and Syncellus say that he then made the city a Macedonian military colony.[80] Moreover, Josephus cites Hecateus of Abdera

---

80. For a convenient summary of these sources, see Marcus, *Josephus* 6, Appendix C, 523–25. Compare also Tcherikover, *Hellenistic Civilization and the Jews*, 47–48; and Hengel, *Jews, Greeks and Barbarians*, 8.

to the effect that Alexander gave the Jews the territory of Samaria as a tax-free possession (*Ag. Ap.* 2.43). In recent years, the discoveries in the Wadi Daliyeh have been interpreted as at least partially confirming these reports. As Cross reconstructs the setting for the documents found there:

> The leaders in Samaria who were implicated in the rebellious acts that led to the prefect's death fled Samaria on learning of Alexander's rapid march on the city. Presumably they followed the main road down the Wadi Far'ah into the wilderness, and found temporary refuge in the Wadi Daliyeh cave. A great number fled, whole families, fairly well supplied with food. Their origin and status are well attested by their seals and their legal documents. They were discovered in their hiding place by the Macedonians, either by assiduous search or, more likely, through betrayal by their fellows who remained in Samaria, and mercilessly slaughtered to a man.[81]

All of this, while important for understanding local history (Alexander may have given Samaritan territory to the Jews after he took the city), is not precisely the substance of Josephus's story, which is dated to the time before Alexander left for Egypt. It is a useful reminder, however, that historical fact may be found in unexpected places such as a story attested only in Curtius's history of Alexander and a report given in the chronicles of Christian writers.

A few comments should be added about other improbable features or historical blunders that experts have found in Josephus's story. The reference to Daniel is, of course, too early, but it corresponds with Josephus's procedure elsewhere in connection with Cyrus who saw himself as fulfilling the prophecy of Isaiah (*Ant.* 11.1, 2 [§§5–6]). In other words, the Daniel episode may, indeed, be a touch that Josephus added to the story and may not be part of the source(s) that he used. The Chaldeans who are in Alexander's train are unexpected but probably not impossible; then, too, the term Χαλδαίων may be a scribal error for Χουθαίων (Cutheans = Samaritans).[82] Also, mention of *proskynesis* is not anachronistic: Alexander prostrates himself before a deity in good Greek fashion (§331), and, after the victory at Issus, oriental subjects honored the king in this way.[83]

---

81. "Papyri of the Fourth Century," 58. Compare G. Ernest Wright, *Shechem: Biography of a Biblical City* (New York: McGraw-Hill, 1965), 181; Hengel, *Jews, Greeks, and Barbarians*, 8–9; Bickerman, *The Jews in the Greek Age*, 8–9. Coggins offers some cautions about this hypothetical reconstruction (*Samaritans and Jews*, 107–8).

82. See Marcus, *Josephus* 6, 474 n. a., where he rejects this old emendation and thinks that Josephus is reflecting here the later incident related in 1 Macc 3:41.

83. For prostration before gods, see H. Greeven, "προσκυνέω, προσκυνητής," in *TDNT* 6.759; BAGD 724. For *proskynesis* by orientals before Alexander, see Kasher, "Alexander of

These considerations remove or modify some of the critical objections to Josephus's story (although the Samaritan temple may be problematic), but it remains the case that no historian of Alexander mentions a trip by him to Jerusalem or any relations with the Jews. And, of more immediate concern, it seems unlikely that Alexander, even if he did meet Jaddua, would have bowed before his miter and acceded to his request about the rights of Jews in lands that he had never visited. The account is a literary production, and it is not surprising that there are variations of it in nonhistorical Jewish and Samaritan texts.[84] Yet, there is another side to the story that has been stressed by David Golan: the tale accurately reflects what is known from other sources about Alexander's policies at this stage in his career.[85] His thesis should now be sketched; then conclusions will be drawn from Josephus's account for the history of the high priesthood.

Golan, who refers to Josephus as the first Thucydidean historian among the Jews, thinks that in his upbringing he received information derived from the non-Thucydidean oral-historical tradition of his people. He always considered this tradition factual and employed it as such throughout his writings—both in his biblical paraphrase and elsewhere. This must be remembered in evaluating his story about Alexander and Jaddua. Judging by his policy at this time, it would have been unusual for Alexander not to have met with the leaders in Jerusalem and not to have offered sacrifice at their temple. Arrian says that the conqueror had resolved not to leave a hostile city on his flank as he marched along. He knew the advantages of winning others to his side through diplomacy rather than warfare. Many rulers accepted Alexander's lordship as he moved southward from Issus. Their submission involved various ritual acts, among which his sacrificing in the temple of his new subjects was very important to him. He had sent Menon and six hundred

---

Macedon's Campaign in Israel," 198–99. Presumably there is some exaggeration in Parmenion's assertion that all prostrate themselves before Alexander.

84. A version of the story is found in *b. Yoma* 69a and in a scholion to *Megillat Ta'anit* (for Chislev 21). Marcus (*Josephus* 6, 517–18) gives a translation of the latter (the text from Pseudo-Callisthenes that he gives on 514–15 [Recension C, ii.24] is now thought to have been derived from Josephus; see Momigliano, "Flavius Josephus and Alexander's Visit to Jerusalem," 443). In the rabbinic texts, the high priest is identified as Simeon the Just and the meeting occurs at Antipatris. For the Samaritan version of the story, as it appears in Chronicle II, see C. H. R. Martin, "Alexander and the High Priest," TGUOS 23 (1969–70): 102–14. The Samaritan account has many of the traits found in Josephus's story, but the Samaritans of Shechem replace the inhabitants of Jerusalem and the Samaritan high priest Hezekiah plays the part of Jaddua.

85. "Josephus, Alexander's Visit to Jerusalem, and Modern Historiography," in *Josephus Flavius: Historian of Israel in the Hellenistic-Roman Period,* ed. U. Rappaport (Jerusalem: Yitzhak ben Zvi, 1982), 29–55 (Hebrew).

cavalrymen into the cities of the area to announce the new situation and obtain their pledges of loyalty. They would not have omitted Jerusalem; moreover, the fact that no new leaders were appointed in the city suggests that no need for removing the existing powers was perceived.

As Golan sees the situation, it is likely that, when Alexander laid siege to Tyre and wanted to build a causeway to the island city, he wrote to different peoples in the area for their assistance with the massive project. Jerusalem would have been among them. The high priest, however, may have found the political situation too unclear at this point, since he would have known that Darius was amassing a great army for a decisive battle with the Macedonians. So, he responded evasively and, presenting himself as head of an ancient temple and Darius's sworn ally, hoped to profit from Alexander's strongly religious nature. Although the king was enraged, he may have appreciated the legal aspects of the situation. At any rate, Jerusalem offered no assistance at Tyre. Jaddua knew, however, that he would have to face Alexander eventually, if he, as head of state, were to accept his sovereignty and also hope to retain traditional Jewish rights in the new political structure. Apparently, the representatives of Jerusalem took the initiative and were successful in proving to Alexander that they were not opposing him as Tyre and Gaza had.

Golan argues that the talmudic account, which locates the meeting between Alexander and the high priest near the junction of the Jerusalem road and the way along the sea—close to Ramatayim Sophim—is more likely to be correct and that Josephus confused this Sophim with the one northeast of Jerusalem. The meeting was successful; Alexander, in line with his policy, allowed the Jews to live in accord with their ancestral ways. It is also likely that he hired Jewish mercenaries, as various sources disclose that they were highly prized. Golan thinks that Alexander himself did come to Jerusalem, not after the conquest of Gaza, but during the siege of that city. He would have come with a small contingent and sacrificed in the temple—a fixed part of his practice. The high priest's concern for fellow Jews in yet unconquered lands could have served as an expression of confidence in what Alexander would accomplish; to the king it may have seemed like one of the oracles that he is known to have valued so highly.

An analysis of this kind shows that the form of the story in Josephus, while it rests upon something of a historical foundation, has been shaped by a process of popular telling and retelling. All of this has important implications for how the account is used in reconstructing the history of the high priesthood. It would not be valid, given the nature of the material, simply to accept all of its details about Jaddua as historically reliable. In his meeting with Alexander, as described by Josephus, he has assumed unlikely stature.

After surveying the long story in *Antiquities* and various theories about it, what may be gleaned from it about the high priest? The following assertions about Jaddua are credible.

1. Jaddua was the son of Johanan (not Jonathan) and succeeded him upon his death. In other words, the hereditary principle remained in effect, as it had since the beginning of the Second Temple (note Manasseh's claim that "the priestly office was the highest in the nation and had always belonged to his family" [§309]).

2. Jaddua's brother married into the gubernatorial family of Samaria. There is no reason to see in this a botched version of the marriage mentioned in Neh 13:28; the time, characters, and circumstances are all different. These two cases of intermarriage between the aristocratic families of Jerusalem and Samaria are likely to be historical.

3. Josephus mentions "the elders of Jerusalem" [οἱ δὲ τῶν Ἱεροσολυμιτῶν πρεσβύτεροι (§306)] who have sufficient authority to force Manasseh "either to divorce his wife or not to approach the altar" (§308). To be sure, Jaddua himself sided with the elders and thus lent the power of his office to their cause, but they are pictured as an influential group alongside the high priest. He is the top authority, but they, too, exercise a supervisory role.

4. In explaining the reason for the elders' opposition to Manasseh, Josephus writes that they resented "the fact that the brother of the high priest Jaddus was sharing the high priesthood [μετέχειν τῆς ἀρχιερωσύνης] while married to a foreigner" (§306). It is not clear what "sharing the high priesthood" involved. As far as we know, it would have been unprecedented for there to be a diumvirate in the office; also, Josephus gives no suggestion of this elsewhere in the story. Marcus, while granting that the meaning is unclear, offered two possibilities: (1) "in the general sense that he was a member of the high priest's family, as was the case with the 'high priests' mentioned in the Gospels," and (2) "[p]ossibly . . . Josephus means that Manasses occupied the position of *sagan* . . . ; although this term appears to denote a member of the aristocracy in the Persian period (as in Ezra ix.2), in later rabbinic usage it means an assistant of the high priest, compare Mishnah, *Yoma* vi and Bab. Talmud, *Yoma* 39a."[86] The only hint provided in the context is that Manasseh could approach the altar and that Jaddua kept him from it (§§308–9; two different but apparently synonymous terms for *altar* are used). Drawing near to the altar is, however,

---

86. *Josephus* 6, 463 n. c.

listed as a prerogative of every priest, not just of the highest-ranking clergy. The passage, then, does not clarify the nature of Manasseh's sharing the high priesthood, but it may supply the first indication of an office such as that of *sagan,* which eventually became the second-highest priestly position.[87] Whether he attained that position because he was the high priest's brother is not said.

5. In his letter to the high priest—a believable phenomenon as noted above—Alexander asked him "to send assistance [συμμαχίαν] and supply his army with provisions and give him the gifts which they had formerly sent as tribute to Darius" (§317). It is significant that the king is said to have addressed a request for what appears to be military help to the high priest who is here, it seems, pictured as the chief of Jewish military and diplomatic affairs. No governor is named alongside, above, or below him. There is no way to check the accuracy of Josephus's report at this point, but what it implies is crystal clear. At least according to Josephus, the high priest had by this time become the supreme civil and religious head of the Jewish people, and the only power bloc alongside him is the body of elders.[88] A similar conclusion may be drawn from the sequel in which Jaddua replies to Alexander "that he had given his oath to Darius not to take up arms against him [μὴ βαστάζειν ὅπλα κατ᾽ αὐτοῦ]" (§318). The high priest was a military man who had pledged lifelong loyalty to the Persian king. Naturally, he became the object of Alexander's wrath and later switched his allegiance to the Macedonian side. Jerusalem must have had some sort of military capability in the Persian period (at least for defensive purposes; compare Neh 7:2); the high priest is portrayed as having that force at his disposal.

6. Although the section that deals with the meeting between Jaddua and Alexander is probably the most highly embellished part of the entire narrative, it is noteworthy that the high priest appears as one to whom God speaks. This view of the high priest, whatever one thinks about the particular incident in question, accords with the notion that the role of the prophet had ended and now the deity communicated with the priest (compare Zech 3:7).

---

87. See Joachim Jeremias, *Jerusalem in the Time of Jesus: An Investigation into Economic and Social Conditions during the New Testament Period,* trans. F. H. Cave and C. H. Cave (Philadelphia: Fortress Press, 1969), 160–63. The *sagan* assisted the high priest in his ceremonial tasks and could serve as his substitute if, for some reason, the high priest was disqualified from performing his duties on the Day of Atonement.

88. Rooke (*Zadok's Heirs,* 221) rejects this conclusion because she considers the story of Alexander and Jaddua to be legendary.

7. It is of some interest that Josephus describes the high priest's clothing. His robe was "of hyacinth-blue and gold, wearing on his head the mitre with the golden plate on which was inscribed the name of God" (§331). The biblical description of Aaron's garments divulges that they were made of "gold, blue, purple, and crimson yarns" (Exod 28:5; see 39:1); the ephod, its band, and the breastpiece were also of these colors (Exod 28:6, 8, 15; compare 39:2-3, 5, 8). The robe of the ephod was to be entirely of blue (Exod 28:31; 39:22; Sir 45:10; 50:11), and its pomegranate decorations of "blue, purple, and crimson yarns" (Exod 28:33; 39:24) to which golden bells were attached (28:33-34; 39:25). Exodus 28:36 speaks of the golden plate (with a lace of blue [39:30]); it bears the inscription "Holy to the LORD."[89] The clothing worn by Jaddua on this occasion is the apparel peculiar to the high priest (Exod 28:4) and was to be worn by him, according to P, "only for those rites that it is his duty to perform within [the sanctuary],"[90] though Sir 45:8-15 may suggest that he wore them outside as well (this is the matter discussed in the talmudic story about Simeon the Just and Alexander).

8. The high priest is depicted as representing the interests of the nation and indeed of all Jewish people when he asks that his fellow countrymen and the Jews of Babylon and Media be allowed to live according to the ancestral laws. Even if it seems unlikely that Jaddua would have done this before Alexander had conquered these latter areas, the role that he plays is not unprecedented; the Jews of Yeb (Elephantine) had earlier written to the high priest Johanan to seek his support in their effort to gain permission from Persian authorities to rebuild their temple.

If we may place some confidence in Josephus's story insofar as it represents internal Jewish matters and relations, it shows that the high priest had attained an exalted status by the close of the Persian period. He was head of the cultic, political, and even military affairs of the nation and as such handled relations with the imperial government (but see below for a possible governor at this time). Moreover, he wore splendid vestments and was regarded at least

---

89. See *Ant.* 3.7, 4–6 (§§159–78), where Josephus writes that the gold plate had "graven in sacred characters the name of God." Sirach 45:12 mentions only the word "holiness." Menahem Haran observes: "The Rabbis assumed that the diadem was engraved with the two words קֹדֶשׁ ליהוה (Bab. Tal. Shabbath, 63b *et al.*). But according to the Hellenistic sources it was only the tetragrammaton which was inscribed" (*Temples and Temple-Service in Ancient Israel* [reprinted ed.: Winona Lake, Ind.: Eisenbrauns, 1985], 169 n. 45).

90. Haran, *Temples and Temple-Service*, 211; compare also his discussion of each of the eight items of the high-priestly clothing.

by some as a mouthpiece of God. It should also not escape our notice that Jaddua modeled an approach toward an overwhelming foreign power that Josephus applauded and found woefully lacking in the tragic events of the Jewish Revolt that transpired in his time.[91]

The Chronology of the High Priests and the Completeness of the Lists

As noted at the beginning of this chapter, Nehemiah 12 supplies two lists of the high-priestly line from Joshua through Jaddua. The extant information about each of the five who succeeded Joshua has now been presented. Here, it is necessary to approach another question about the brief list of high priests: Is it complete? Were Joshua, Joiakim, Eliashib, Joiada, Johanan, and Jaddua the only men who occupied the office while Persia ruled Yehud?[92]

In recent years, there has been a lively debate about the chronology of the Jewish high priests who served during the Persian period. Although the topic had often been broached in older studies, the contemporary debate has been stimulated by Frank Moore Cross Jr.'s paper "A Reconstruction of the Judean Restoration."[93] Cross argued that the biblical list of six men who are supposed to have ruled for the two hundred years of Persian dominion is too short and that four names have dropped from the high-priestly genealogy. The trigger for the omission was the widespread practice of papponymy: the repetition caused by naming grandsons after grandfathers led to two cases of haplography and thus the elimination of four names from the list. The following section reexamines the high-priestly chronology in light of Cross's hypothesis and the reactions that it has elicited. First, the evidence will be reviewed; second, theories—especially Cross's—about missing names will be sketched; third, reactions will be assessed; and fourth, a case will be made that the existing six-member list is complete.

The Evidence

According to the surviving biblical evidence, Joshua and five of his descendants served as high priests in the postexilic age until an unspecified time. The

---

91. Clemens Thoma, "The High Priesthood in the Judgment of Josephus," in *Josephus, the Bible, and History,* ed. L. H. Feldman and G. Hata (Leiden: Brill, 1989), 206.

92. The remainder of this section is a slightly revised version of VanderKam, "Jewish High Priests of the Persian Period: Is the List Complete?" 67–91.

93. The essay was published in *JBL* 94 (1975): 4–18 and in *Int* 29 (1975): 187–203.

beginning of the period is known approximately. Ezra 2:2, in its present context, implies that Joshua came from exile during the reign of Cyrus and after his proclamation, that is, between 539–38 and 530 BCE, the year of Cyrus's death. He and others built the altar at that time (Ezra 3:2) and soon thereafter laid the foundations of the Second Temple (3:7-13). Most of the biblical passages that mention Joshua, however, associate him with the second year of Darius (ca. 520 BCE). This is the case for Ezra 4:24—5:2; Hag 1:1, 12, 14-15; 2:1-4; Zech 1:7 and Zech 3.

Eliashib, the third high priest, was, as noted above, a contemporary of Nehemiah; that is, he was serving as high priest in 445 BCE when the latter arrived in Jerusalem and may still have been in office after 433, depending upon the meaning of Neh 13:28. In that text, Nehemiah reports: "And one of the sons of Jehoiada [= Joiada], son of the high priest Eliashib, was the son-in-law of Sanballat the Horonite; I chased him away from me." The wording in the NRSV relates the title "high priest" to Eliashib, but the Hebrew text is ambiguous as to whether it refers to him or Jehoiada. Extrabiblical texts offer relatively fixed chronological points for the last two high priests in the list. TAD A4.7/8 = AP 30//31 places Johanan in office during the fourteenth year of Darius II, that is, about 410 BCE (see A4.7 = 30.4–12); and Josephus (*Ant.* 11.7, 1 [§§297–301]) relates an episode involving this Johanan and dates it during the reign of Artaxerxes, who must be the second of that name (404–358 BCE). Josephus also provides a historical context for Jaddua, the sixth and last high priest in the biblical list: he was a contemporary of Alexander the Great whom he received when the Macedonian king visited Jerusalem in 332 BCE. *Antiquities* 11.8, 7 (§§346–47) may imply that by the time of Alexander's untimely demise in 323 BCE, Jaddua was already dead.

If we combine these chronological markers, the result is a span of slightly more than two hundred years—from the reign of Cyrus (539–538 to 530 BCE) to that of Alexander (336–323 BCE)—in which just six men are supposed to have held the high-priestly office. This would entail an average of 33.3 years or more per reign—a figure that is quite high but comfortably within the range of the possible. The data at hand, however, do not permit one to assign roughly thirty-three years to each man. TAD A4.7/8 = AP 30//31 provides documentary evidence that Johanan, the fifth high priest, was in office in 410 BCE. This date would produce no problem for the preceding period (five high priests in 120+ years), but it implies that, if the list is complete, the tenures of the last two high priests extended some eighty years and perhaps a few more (410–330 BCE and beyond, even if one makes the minimal assumption that Johanan began serving in 410). These numbers would be formidable enough, but, to add to the problem, some scholars have argued that Neh 12:22 dates the beginning of *Jad-*

dua's high priesthood to the reign of Darius II (424–423 to 404 BCE). There one reads: "As for the Levites, in the days of Eliashib, Joiada, Johanan, and Jaddua, there were recorded the heads of ancestral houses; also the priests until[94] the reign of Darius the Persian." In the context of Nehemiah 12, the most likely identification of this monarch is Darius II, though commentators have also defended each of the other two Dariuses.[95] Those who think that Darius the Persian is Darius II then move from this identification to associate the end of the list of high priests in the previous clause (Jaddua) with the reign of this king.[96] If this inference should be correct, then Neh 12:22 would locate the beginning of Jaddua's tenure within the years 424–423 to 404 BCE; and, since his father Johanan was in office in 410 (TAD 4.7/8 = AP 30 // 31), he would have commenced as high priest between 410 and 404. In other words, he would have been high priest for about seventy-five years and possibly more.

Theories about Missing Names

In light of such implausible figures, scholars have for a long time sought to remedy the situation by adding one or more names to the list in order to fill the long stretch of years implied by Nehemiah 12 and Josephus's *Antiquities*. As C. C. Torrey wrote in 1910: "We can by no means be certain that his [Johanan's] term of office immediately preceded that of Jaddua. One or more other incumbents may have intervened between the two."[97] Albright also pro-

---

94. The preposition is על which does not, of course, mean "until." There have been many suggestions for emendation, some of which assume that the preposition is a remnant of a longer reading. Rudolph (*Esra und Nehemia*, 193–94) thought that one should augment it in accord with the phrase in v. 23, reading therefore: על ספר דברי הימים עד. William F. Albright preferred מעל ("The Date and Personality of the Chronicler," *JBL* 40 [1921]: 113); and he has been followed by Myers (*Ezra, Nehemiah*, 195). The LXX has ἐν.

95. Defenders of Darius I (522–486 BCE) include Albright ("The Date and Personality of the Chronicler," 113) and Myers (*Ezra-Nehemiah*, 198–99), but their view depends upon emending על to מעל. Williamson (*Ezra, Nehemiah*, 364–65) believes, with Sigmund Mowinckel (*Studien zu dem Buche Ezra-Nehemia, 1: Die nachchronische Redaktion des Buches. Die Listen* [Oslo: Universitetsforlaget, 1964], 161), that the epithet "the Persian" is used to distinguish this Darius from Darius the Mede in Daniel. Among the advocates of Darius II are Menaham Mor, "The High Priests in Judah in the Persian Period," *BM* 23 (1977): 58–61 (Hebrew); and Rudolph, *Esra und Nehemia*, 193–94 (who emends the text; see the previous footnote); compare Blenkinsopp, *Ezra-Nehemiah*, 340. Torrey (*Ezra Studies*, 249, 320), for one, thought he was Darius III (336–31 BCE).

96. So Mor, "The High Priests," 58–61. Cross (for example, in "A Reconstruction of the Judean Restoration," 189) also accepts this inference.

97. *Ezra Studies*, 320, 263–64. More recently, Williamson (*Ezra, Nehemiah*, 363), Blenkinsopp (*Ezra-Nehemiah*, 338), and Scolnic (*Chronology and Papponymy*, 235–59) have suggested

posed that the list was short and suggested that a second Jaddua should be added. He wrote in support of his conjecture: "There is no difficulty in assuming that the name was repeated, since this becomes the rule in the third century with the Oniads."[98] The time of Johanan and Jaddua is not the only span that has been perceived as too long; some have also sensed that the gap between Joshua (520 BCE is the last known date of his service) and Eliashib (445 and beyond) is rather much for one high priest (Joiakim) to have filled.[99]

Cross has advanced beyond these less specific proposals to a detailed, broader thesis in which he posits exactly which names were omitted and why they are absent from the extant texts. He had adumbrated his position in earlier publications,[100] but in his essay "A Reconstruction of the Judean Restoration," he elaborated it in full form.[101] According to him, two pairs of names were omitted from Nehemiah's list through two haplographies induced by papponymy—a practice that, he argues, was common in the Persian and Hellenistic periods (p. 190). He repeats his earlier conclusion that haplography had occurred at the end of the high-priestly list: the present sequence Johanan-Jaddua is the remnant of an original Johanan-Jaddua-Johanan-Jaddua series (pp. 188–89) that resulted when a copyist's eye jumped from the first to the second instance of Johanan. Josephus's stories about a Johanan who killed his brother Jeshua (*Ant.* 11.7, 1 [§§297–301]) and a Jaddua who greeted Alexander the Great (11.7, 2–8, 7 [§§302–47]) concern the last two men in the reconstructed list. That is, the Johanan of Josephus's account is not the Johanan who is mentioned in the Elephantine Papyri. The Artaxerxes who is mentioned in the Johanan-Jeshua story is Artaxerxes III who reigned from 358–338 BCE, not Artaxerxes II (405–358 BCE; pp. 188–89).

Addition of these two names relieves the problem of the long reigns that one would otherwise have to assume for Johanan and Jaddua. Nevertheless, difficulties remain. Cross calculated that without these two extra names, the current form of the high-priestly list requires an average of 34.3 years per gen-

---

that the list is not complete. Scolnic leaves open the possibility that there was just one Johanan and one Jaddua but that there are gaps in the biblical list or even that no one was serving as high priest at certain times.

98. "The Date and Personality of the Chronicler," 112 n. 18; see also 112, 122.

99. For example, Rudolph, *Esra und Nehemia*, 192, though he recognizes that an unusually long reign would have been possible.

100. See "Papyri of the Fourth Century B.C. from Dâliyeh," 60–63; "The Papyri and Their Historical Implications," 20–22 (he adds another Johanan and Jaddua before the final two names of the list); and "Aspects of Samaritan and Jewish History in Late Persian and Hellenistic Times," 202–5.

101. The page references given in the text are to the essay as it appears in *Int* 29 (1975).

eration.[102] Inserting their names into the roster yields generations averaging 27.5 years, "still suspiciously high" (p. 193). He suspects that, as the average length of a generation between Jozadak (Joshua's father who, Cross suggests, was born ca. 595 BCE) and Johanan (born ca. 445) would still be approximately thirty years, "at least one generation, two high priests' names, have dropped out of the list through a haplography owing to the repetition produced by papponymy" (p. 193). The problem centers about Eliashib. The third postexilic high priest, who was born about 545 BCE on Cross's figures, was still in office when Nehemiah arrived a century later. Moreover, he was spry enough at his advanced age to help construct the city wall (Neh 3:1, 20). As it is unlikely he was capable of this at age one hundred, something must be amiss in the text.

In order to solve this problem, Cross appeals to Ezra 10:6 and Neh 12:23, both of which (as seen above) refer to a J(eh)ohanan who is identified as the son of Eliashib. These same names figure in the list of high priests but as grandfather and grandson. The former text associates this J(eh)ohanan with Ezra. "The key to the solution, however, is in the juxtaposition of the priests Yōhanan son of ʾElyašīb and Yōyadaʿ son of ʾElyašīb. We must reckon with two high priests named ʾElyašīb, and given papponymy, two priests named Yōhanan. Thus, we have the following sequence: (1) ʾElyašīb I father of (2) Yōhanan I contemporary of Ezra, followed by (3) ʾElyašīb II contemporary of Nehemiah and grandfather of (4) Yōhanan II" (pp. 193–94). When Cross's extra priests are added to all the names from the Bible and Josephus (with Jaddua's two successors), the result is a sequence of twelve high priests who average the proper twenty-five years per generation (p. 203; the dates in parentheses are proposed dates of birth; each member of the list is the son of the preceding member except ʾElyašīb I):

1. Yōṣadaq (before 587 BCE)
2. Yēšūaʿ (570)
3. Yōyaqīm (545), the brother of
[3. ʾElyašīb I (545)]
[4. Yōhanan I (520)]
5. ʾElyašīb II (495)
6. Yōyadaʿ I (470)
7. Yōhanan II (445) (of TAD A4.7 // A4.8 = AP 30.18 // 31.17)

8. Yaddūaᶜ II (420)[103]
[9. Yōḥanan III (395)
[10. Yaddūaᶜ III (370)]
11. Onias I (345) = Yōḥanan IV
12. Šimᶜōn I (320)

Cross's hypothesis of two haplographies in the postexilic high-priestly list has transparent advantages. First, it eliminates the need to posit several extraordinarily long reigns by high priests at two points in the genealogy. Second, it incorporates the father-son pair J(eh)ohanan and Eliashib into the high-priestly roster without having recourse to the much-canvassed question whether "son" in this case can mean "grandson."[104] On Cross's view, they are not the grandfather and grandson of the lists in Nehemiah 12 but are two different high priests who bear the same names as the ones given there.

Reactions to Theories of Missing Names

Despite its attractiveness, Cross's theory has encountered significant opposition. Geo Widengren mounted a strong challenge to part of it in the course of treating the age-old problem of the historical order in which Ezra and Nehemiah appeared.[105] Since he places Nehemiah before Ezra, he could not accept Cross's explanation of Ezra 10:6, which has often been regarded as one of the strongest arguments in favor of reversing the biblical order of Ezra and Nehemiah. Widengren's handling of the Ezra-Nehemiah problem is not relevant here, but he does point to some problematic aspects of Cross's arguments. His first criticism is that Cross must resort, in one short list, to two cases of haplography, neither of which has any textual support. Second, the list, even as reconstructed by Cross, does not follow the principle of papponymy: "Of a supposed list of 12 names (in reality 13 names!), 9 names would be illustrations of papponymy. . . . [T]he name of Eliashib disappears

---

103. Cross labels him Yaddūaᶜ II because Yaddūaᶜ is a caritative form of Yōyadaᶜ (hence no. 6 is Yōyadaᶜ I). See p. 189 n. 12, where he also provides the evidence that shows that Onias is a Greek spelling of Ḥōnay, which in turn is "the caritative or diminutive form of Yōḥanan." As a result, no. 11 is Onias I, who would also be Yōḥanan IV.

104. See the survey in Williamson, *Ezra, Nehemiah,* 151–54 (Williamson does not think that "son" here means "grandson"); and Porter, "Son or Grandson (Ezra X.6)?" 54–67.

105. "The Persian Period" in *Israelite and Judaean History,* ed. J. H. Hayes and J. M. Miller, OTL (Philadelphia: Westminster, 1977), 506–9. References to page numbers in the text are to this essay.

from the list with Eliashib II. After him the supposed papponymy has changed
character in so far as we do not find a sequence Eliashib + Johanan but Joiada
+ Johanan" (p. 508). As Widengren notes, Cross identifies as instances of repetition names that are not actually identical; that is, he considers full
theophoric names as equivalents of hypocoristic forms (Joiada/Jehoiada
would thus be the same as Jaddua; Johanan/Jehohanan and Onias would be
another example). Of the names that do in fact occur in the list, "only Joiada,
Johanan, Jaddua, and Onias show a tendency toward papponymy—that is,
granted that we accept the hypocoristica as identical with the complete
names" (p. 508).

As a third objection, Widengren questions the claim that generations
averaged approximately twenty-five years; in the dark days of the sixth century, he writes, perhaps not all priests married and fathered sons by this age.
Happily, even Widengren himself recognizes that this argument has little to
commend it (pp. 508–9). Finally, he isolates a curious feature in Cross's list: he
identifies his hypothetical Eliashib I as the brother, not the son, of his predecessor Joiakim, whereas Neh 12:10 makes him his son. "If Joiakim was born
about 535 BCE, Eliashib could have been born about 500 BCE or some years
earlier. That would give him in 445 an age of fifty-five to sixty years. Such an
age could not possibly have been an obstacle to his participation in the work
on the walls" (p. 509).

Widengren has exposed some important flaws in Cross's proposals as they
relate to the period from the return to about 410 BCE; his criticisms largely
ignore the more problematic time span from about 410–332 (and beyond) for
which Cross can make a more convincing case that names are missing from
the high-priestly list. A critique that resembles Widengren's has been fashioned by Mor.[106] With Widengren, Mor rejects Cross's first reconstructed pair
(Eliashib I and Yohanan I), but unlike Widengren, he also deals with the high-
priestly chronology of the period from 410–332 BCE and accepts Cross's suggestion that two names must be added here. His is a more detailed study than
that of Widengren and deserves careful scrutiny.

As he deals with the high priests and their periods of service in the fifth
and fourth centuries, Mor draws attention to Neh 12:22, a passage noted several times above: "As for the Levites, in the days of Eliashib, Joiada, Johanan,
and Jaddua, there were recorded the heads of ancestral houses; also the priests
until the reign of Darius the Persian." He thinks that proper identification of
this Darius holds the key to determining how far forward in history the high-

---

106. "The High Priests in Judah in the Persian Period"; page references in the text are to
this essay.

priestly list extended. TAD A4.7 = AP 30 allows him to recognize in "Darius the Persian" Darius II, in whose fourteenth year (410 BCE) Johanan was high priest (pp. 57–58). This means that the high-priestly lists in Neh 12:10-11, 22 reach to the time of this king, that is, the end of the fifth century. As a result, Jaddua, the last high priest to be named in Nehemiah 12, began his term of office during Darius II's reign—at some point between 410 and 404 BCE (p. 58).

With this limit in mind, he considers the specifics of Cross's case. First, the additional pair of high priests whom Cross names Eliashib I and Johanan I comes from Ezra 10:6 (erroneously given as 6:6 in the article) and Neh 12:23 (the "J[eh]ohanan son of Eliashib" passages). But, Mor observes that these texts are problematic in themselves, with many scholars accepting the arrangement of Nehemiah 12 in which Johanan is the grandson, not the son, of Eliashib. He also mentions the suggestion of Jacob Liver and Hayim Tadmor[107] that the author of Ezra-Nehemiah anachronistically gave to "the chamber of Jehohanan son of Eliashib" the name that it had in the time when he wrote (p. 59).

Mor repeats Widengren's objections that Cross has made his Eliashib I the brother, not the son, of Joiakim (or at least assigns them to the same generation), and that the list of high priests does not in fact exhibit the principle of papponymy (Joiada's successor should have been named Eliashib, if the principle were operative [pp. 59–60]). A more telling criticism is actually an enlargement of Widengren's objection to the twenty-five-year generation thesis. Mor notes that with Cross's proposed birth dates for the high priests, Jaddua would have been born in about 420 BCE. However, if he began to serve as high priest between 410, when Johanan was still in office, and 404, the date of Darius II's death, then he would have assumed the office at some time when he was between the ages of ten and sixteen years—a most unlikely age for a high priest (p. 60). He makes the point that the generation principle is not particularly helpful in determining how many high priests there were from the return until Jaddua; rather, the salient issue is how long each man held the office (p. 60). There are no data concerning this matter, but the fixed chronological points that are available in the sources can function as guidelines in reconstructing the list. These points are: Joshua returned in 538 BCE; Eliashib was high priest in 445–444, and he was still in office when Nehemiah left in 433–432 (see Neh 13:4-5); when Nehemiah returned one year later (which Mor considers the meaning of "[a]fter some time" in Neh 13:6), Joiada was

---

107. Jacob Liver, "יוחנן," *Encyclopaedia Miqraᶜit* 3.590–91 (Hebrew); Hayim Tadmor, "כרונולוגיה," ibid. 4.307 n. 2 (Hebrew).

high priest (Neh 13:28); Johanan served in 410; and Jaddua's term began between 410 and 404. Mor sees no need to add names to the list for the period between Joshua and Johanan and suggests for the priests named in Nehemiah 12 birthdates that differ somewhat from those proposed by Cross (using the twenty-five-year generation principle, starting in effect with Joshua who would have been born in ca. 570 BCE; Jaddua's birthdate would have been ca. 445). Thus, Joshua would have been about thirty-three years of age when he returned; Eliashib would have been about seventy-five when Nehemiah arrived in Jerusalem and about eighty-eight when Nehemiah departed. Joiada would then have assumed the post at the relatively advanced age of sixty-four; by 410 BCE, his son was high priest. Since Johanan was born in approximately 470 (incorrectly printed as 410 on p. 62), he was about sixty years of age when he received the letter from Elephantine. Jaddua began his term at about thirty-five years of age—a far more likely figure than Cross's proposed ten to sixteen years of age for him (pp. 60–62).

Turning to the high priest Jaddua, Mor argues that Josephus's story about him and his brother Manasseh, who married Nikaso, Sanballat's daughter, is not, as many claim, a reworked version of the incident in Neh 13:28. The two are quite separate. But, if Jaddua became high priest between 410 and 404 BCE and was still in office in 332 when Alexander the Great visited Jerusalem, he served an extraordinarily long term. Consequently, as papponymy was widespread at this time, it is very likely that two names fell from the list through haplography. The repeating names are Johanan-Jaddua-Johanan-Jaddua, with the last two being the ones about whom Josephus tells stories in *Ant.* 11.7, 1— 8, 7 (§§297–347) (Mor, pp. 62–67).

If the proposal of Cross, supported by Mor, that two names have been omitted toward the end of the high-priestly list is correct, then a difficulty (see above) in one of Josephus's stories is solved. Josephus says that when Johanan killed his brother Jeshua, a man named Bagoses was an important official. He calls him the στρατηγός of the other Artaxerxes. No general of Artaxerxes II is known to have had this name, but Artaxerxes III (358–338 BCE) did have such a commander.[108] Thus, if the story is placed in the time of the third Artaxerxes (whom Josephus fused with Artaxerxes II), the name of Bagoses is nicely explained. This, too, would entail, however, that the Johanan of Nehemiah 12 and TAD A4.7 = AP 30 is not the Johanan of Josephus's account.

Several of the objections raised by Widengren and Mor should be retained but in modified form. First, one ought not to insert a pair of names in the list for the fifth century. There is no hint of papponymy at this point in the roster

---

108. See earlier in this chapter for the available information about this man.

(Jeshua, Joiakim, Eliashib, Joiada, Johanan); thus, the alleged trigger for haplography is absent. It is often claimed that a generation lasted twenty-five years in antiquity, but there is rarely much evidence adduced to support the assertion. Moreover, in this case the point is irrelevant. The high-priestly office was held for life, and the practice was that the incumbent was succeeded at death by his *oldest surviving* son—whatever his age might be at that juncture (provided, of course, that it was not too low[109]). In other words, the hypothetical dates of birth for each high priest are not helpful in this discussion. According to the lists in Nehemiah 12, combined with the evidence from TAD A4.7 = AP 30, five high priests served from the return to 410 BCE. Seven Persian monarchs ruled during the same time—a period that includes only the last years of Cyrus, the brief reign of Cambyses, and the exceedingly short reign of Xerxes II in 424. Despite the repetition of names in the royal line, there is no need to interpolate additional ones, just as there is not in the roster of high priests.

Second, Widengren and Mor have pointed out that Cross makes his Eliashib I the brother, not the son, of Joiakim, while Neh 12:10 presents them as father and son. They have not, however, seen what is entailed by this proposal. Cross himself perceives that adding two generations at this point would produce too many extra years, but if papponymy has caused the omission, then two names had to be dropped. So, he adds two names but only one generation and in this way arrives at a twenty-five-year generation for each of the other high priests. Even Cross's numbers, then, make it unlikely that two names have fallen from the list of fifth-century high priests.

Third, Cross finds support for his extra pair of high priests—Eliashib I and Johanan I—in Ezra 10:6 and Neh 12:23, where two priests who are father and son have these names. Since this point has already been treated above, the data need not be repeated here. If this father-son pair is not from the high-priestly line (and nothing in any text suggests it was), then these passages offer no support for adding names to the high-priestly list.

The situation is more difficult for the period from 410–332 BCE (and beyond), since there may indeed appear to be too much time for the reign(s) of one or two high priests. But, a closer look at the evidence indicates that, even for this span of time, the situation is not so improbable as it is often represented. The crucial piece of evidence for those who find a major chronological problem here is Neh 12:22, which has been quoted above. If this passage

---

109. As we will see, Josephus records a case in which a high priest named Simon, who ruled in the early Hellenistic period, died and left an infant son Onias. Rather than passing the office to the child, Simon's brother Eleazar served as high priest (*Ant.* 12.2, 5 [§§43–44]). Later, Eleazar was succeeded by his uncle Manasseh before Onias finally became high priest (12.4, 1 [§§157–58]).

reports that Jaddua was already high priest during the reign of Darius II (thus no later than 404 BCE), then it is almost certain that at least one and perhaps more names have been lost in some way from the list. Nevertheless, it is difficult to see why scholars have derived information of this sort from Neh 12:22. It does not date the end of the *high-priestly* list to the time of Darius the Persian but only a list of priests. And, the problem of what the preposition על before the king's name means remains unsolved. All that Neh 12:22 relates about the high priests from Eliashib to Jaddua is that during their times the heads of ancestral levitical houses were recorded; Darius the Persian is not brought into connection with the high priests who are named at the beginning of the verse. When Jaddua began his high-priestly tenure is never indicated.[110]

The only information about the high priests Johanan and Jaddua—apart from their names—comes from extrabiblical sources, especially Josephus's *Antiquities*. Recently, two kinds of arguments have been fashioned to demonstrate that the existence of a second high priest named Johanan is actually attested for the mid-fourth century. As we saw at the beginning of this chapter, Williamson has argued that a careful reading of one of the extrabiblical sources—Josephus's story about Johanan and his brother Jeshua in *Ant.* 11.7, 1 (§§297–301)—shows that its Johanan and the one in Nehemiah and TAD A4.7 = AP 30 are not the same man and that therefore there was another Johanan who served as high priest in this period. In the discussion above, Williamson's case was found to be unconvincing; the story provides no support for relating Josephus's story to the time of Artaxerxes III and for creating a second Johanan. In light of the existing data, it is more logical to assign the episode to the days of Artaxerxes II, the biblical high priest Johanan, and the governor Bagohi. One implication of this dating is that, at least according to Josephus's source, both Johanan and Bagohi continued in office past the death of Darius II and into the reign of Artaxerxes II. That is, we have in the story one more indication that the accession of Jaddua did not occur in the reign of Darius II.

Cross and others believe that a silver coin confirms his thesis to the extent that it demonstrates the existence of another high priest named Johanan in the mid-fourth century BCE. After publication of Cross's 1975 essay, L. Mildenberg included in his survey of Judean numismatic evidence a small silver coin with a two-word inscription that he read as יחזקיה הפחה, though he considered the

---

110. Another difficulty with the case articulated by Cross is that the understanding of papponymy underlying it may not be accurate. Scolnic has examined various priestly lists and possible instances of papponymy and mentions a number of times in his book that a grandson would usually be named after a grandfather if the grandfather was already deceased. This is not always true in Cross's reconstructed lists (for example, *Chronology and Papponymy*, 119–47).

writing to be careless.[111] Later, Dan Barag restudied the coin "and discovered that left of the owl, from the bottom and working upward, one can clearly read 'Johan[an],' and the word 'ha-kohen' (or priest) appears to the right of the owl from the top downward."[112] The inscription does not add the adjective הגדול to the noun הכהן to produce the full title of the high priest, but Barag thinks that the chief cultic official must be intended: "Except for the legend this coin is exactly similar to one of the types struck by Yehezqiyah the governor. This demonstrates that Johanan was not merely an ordinary priest but was the high priest for he maintained a very important position—his status being equal to that of the governor nominated by the Persians."[113] He also maintains that the mask on the reverse of the coin parallels that on Yehezqiyah's coins. "Yehezqiyah also struck coins with a winged animal and his name (without the title governor) on one side and on the other side a head in a style which can hardly antedate the mid-fourth century. This, therefore, seems to be the date of the coins of Johanan as well."[114] If, then, Johanan was striking coins in the mid-fourth century, it is unlikely that he was the same Johanan as the one named in Neh 12:22 and dated in TAD A4.7 = AP 30 to about 410 BCE.

If we grant that experts have now read the inscription on the coin correctly, the argument for identifying the Johanan of the coin with Cross's

111. "Yehud: A Preliminary Study of the Provincial Coinage of Judaea," in *Greek Numismatics and Archaeology: Essays in Honor of Margaret Thompson*, ed. O. Mørkholm and N. M. Waggoner (Wetteren: NR, 1979), 183–96. The coin in question is no. 17. See also Ya'akov Meshorer, *Ancient Jewish Coinage*, vol. 1: *Persian Period through Hasmonaeans* (Dix Hills, N.Y.: Amphora, 1982), 13, 16 (no. 11, where he writes that "the inscription is blundered"), and pl. 2.11.

112. Dan Barag, "Some Notes on a Silver Coin of Johanan the High Priest," *BA* 48 (1985): 167. See also idem, "A Silver Coin of Yohanan the High Priest and the Coinage of Judea in the Fourth Century B.C.," *Israel Numismatic Journal* 9 (1986–87): 4–21 with pl. 1. In the latter, Barag maintains that, while there is no need to add high priests to Nehemiah's list for the fifth century, the evidence indicates that we should insert an extra Johanan-Jaddua pair in the fourth century. Rooke (*Zadok's Heirs*, 225–33) rightly critiques a number of Barag's conclusions but includes in her criticism that the designation הכהן should not be assumed to mean the high priest. Yet her suggestion (taken from Mildenberg) that the word could mean only that this Johanan was from a priestly family seems implausible. Naturally, the idea of a high priest minting coins would fit uncomfortably with her thesis that the high priests in this period did not possess such authority.

113. "Some Notes on a Silver Coin," 167. Meshorer (*A Treasury of Jewish Coins*, 21–22) agrees with Barag's assessment.

114. "Some Notes on a Silver Coin," 168. For Cross's comments on this coin, see "Samaria and Jerusalem," in *The History of the People of Israel: The Return from the Babylonian Exile—The Period of the Persian Rule*, ed. H. Tadmor (Jerusalem: 'Am 'oved, 1983 [Hebrew]), 88–89, especially p. 274 n. 50. He argues that, as the coins with the Hebrew script are prior to the Tennes revolt of ca. 350 BCE and are almost certainly anterior to Alexander the Great, this Johanan is probably the predecessor of Jaddua, Alexander's contemporary.

reconstructed Johanan is still unconvincing. J. Betlyon has reinvestigated the date of the coin in question and has argued, on the basis of parallels from neighboring mints, that it should be assigned to the years 335–331 BCE.[115] If he is correct, then Johanan could hardly be the high priest whom Cross hypothesizes (though Betlyon thinks he is), since Jaddua was almost certainly the high priest during this short period. It is more likely, if the coin can be dated roughly to these years, that the Johanan who is mentioned on it was Onias I (= Johanan)[116] who, according to Josephus, succeeded Jaddua at some point after Alexander's arrival in 332 BCE and before the young king's death in 323. Consequently, this small silver coin also does not demonstrate the existence of a second high priest named Johanan in the mid-fourth century.

A Case for Retaining the Present Six-Member List

Although Cross and more recently Williamson, in their different ways, have revived the older hypothesis that the list of high priests for the fifth century needs augmenting, their views should be rejected for lack of compelling evidence. Although Joshua is mentioned in 520 BCE and not after this, we now have no way of ascertaining how long he held the high-priestly office. Neither the date of his birth nor the year of his death is ever specified in the sources. It is also not necessary to assume that he was the eldest son of his father; he is named simply as the son of Jozadak and may have been his oldest surviving son. This possibility highlights even more strongly the uncertainty about the chronology of his life. It is possible, however, that he continued as high priest into the first years of the fifth century. Joshua was followed by Joiakim, about whom nothing besides his familial connection is reported. If Joshua's high-priestly tenure extended into the early fifth century, the term of Joiakim could have reached to about 460–450 BCE without any difficulty. The reign of Eliashib included the year 445 and may have lasted until about 433, but the latter date is uncertain. His son Joiada would have served as high priest from approximately 433 BCE until some time before 410 when his son (?) Johanan

---

115. "The Provincial Government of Persian Period Judea and the Yehud Coins," *JBL* 105 (1986): 633–42.

116. This suggestion was made by D. Schwartz, "On Some Papyri and Josephus' Sources and Chronology for the Persian Period," 182 n. 19. The versions of Sir 50:1 demonstrate the equivalence of the two names: where the Hebrew text says that Simeon was the son of יוחנן, the Greek text gives the father's name as Ὀνίου. For the texts, see Francesco Vattioni, *Ecclesiastico: Testo ebraico con apparato critico e versioni greca, latina e siriaca* (Pubblicazioni del Seminario di Semitistica, Testi 1; Naples: Instituto Orientale di Napoli, 1968). On the name, see also Cross, "A Reconstruction of the Judean Restoration," 189 n. 12.

is attested as being in office. The lengths of these men's terms offer no chronological problems. They neither leave room for short reigns nor presuppose
unusually long ones. The span of time that would have to be attributed to their
high priesthoods causes no special difficulties and does not require the addition of completely unattested individuals.

There also may be no need to posit a gap in the roster of high priests for
the fourth century. No text reports when Johanan became high priest. If
Eliashib reigned until 432 BCE and after (which may be what Neh 13:28
implies), then Joiada would not have been in office for a very long time even
if Johanan did not become high priest until close to 410. These circumstances
leave open the possibility that the latter was rather young when he assumed
the position. If one may trust Josephus's story about Johanan and his brother
Jeshua, then he continued to officiate into the reign of Artaxerxes II. But neither Nehemiah nor Josephus relates how long he served. If he had recently
come to the post in 410 BCE, then it is not unlikely that he remained high priest
until about 370 or perhaps even beyond. There is no evidence that contradicts
such an assumption. Johanan's son Jaddua became high priest at an unspecified time (nothing requires that the beginning of his reign be put in the time
of Darius II), and, according to Josephus, he was the high priest who met
Alexander the Great in 332 BCE. If one employs the chronology that is being
suggested here, he would have held the office for some thirty-eight years by
the time the Macedonian army reached Jewish territory. Josephus adds that
by the time the age of the Diadochoi began, Jaddua was dead. Even if he lived
until 323 BCE (the latest possibility, if Josephus is accurate), he would have
been high priest for no more that about forty-seven years—a very long term
but not as long as that of some biblical kings.

One minor objection to a chronology of this kind has been that Jaddua,
at the time of the great battles between Alexander and Darius III, had a brother
Manasseh who was of marriageable age (he married Sanballat's daughter
Nikaso when Darius III still controlled the area [between 336 and 332 BCE])—
something that would be unlikely if Jaddua himself were elderly by then.[117]
When Manasseh was born is not said, nor is the phrase "marriageable age"
very specific for a man. Moreover, it is often overlooked that in the same story,
when Sanballat promised Manasseh a temple, the latter stayed with his father-
in-law, "believing that he would obtain the high priesthood as the gift of Darius, for Sanaballetes, as it happened, was now an old man" (πρεσβύτερον
εἶναι [*Ant.* 11.8, 2 (§311)]). If the elderly Sanballat had a *daughter* of marriageable age during the reign of Darius—and the age of the woman would be

---

117. For example, Cross, "The Papyri and Their Historical Implications," 22.

more important than that of her husband, when, as in this case, children were anticipated—why should the aging Jaddua not have had a brother who met the same criterion? In point of fact, this objection places much weight on Josephan details that may not be able to bear it (that is, the marriage may have occurred before Darius became king), but even the data that he gives do not refute the claim that Jaddua was an elderly man by the year 332 BCE.

We may conclude, therefore, that, though the list of high priests as given in Nehemiah and *Antiquities* is a short one for a period of slightly more than two hundred years, the six men who are said to have held office could have served throughout those two centuries. The list itself presents conditions that would have been conducive to haplography, not because papponymy was practiced in Joshua's line, but because several of the names begin with a Yahwistic prefix (Joiakim, Joiada, Johanan) and others with *yod* (Joshua, Jaddua). Yet, though omissions could have been made by homoioarchton, there is no evidence that they occurred and no convincing reason to posit them. The high priests who reigned during the Persian period had rather long terms of office (Joiada may be an exception), but none of them would have been so long as to become implausible. In other words, it is likely that the extant list of high priests for the Persian period is complete.

The Political Situation in Yehud and the Role of the High Priest

The Bible furnishes very little historical information about the period after the Second Temple was completed. In Ezra 4:6-23—a section that has long been recognized as falling outside the chronological order that is otherwise followed in Ezra—the writer refers to events that occurred during the reigns of Xerxes (486–465 BCE) and Artaxerxes (465–424), and it may now be possible to connect them with developments in the empire at those times. In Ezra 4:6 one reads: "In the reign of Ahasuerus [= Xerxes], in his accession year [486–485 BCE], they wrote an accusation against the inhabitants of Judah and Jerusalem." Who wrote the accusation and what the cause for it may have been are not explained, but the fact that Xerxes himself traveled through the coastal areas on his way to suppress a revolt in Egypt has led some to think that Judean political unrest gave rise to the complaint.[118]

---

118. See A. T. Olmstead, *History of the Persian Empire* (Chicago: Univ. of Chicago Press, 1948), 234–35. Olmstead seems to know more than the text says: "As so often, revolt on the Nile led to Jewish unrest in Jerusalem. Whether the unrest eventuated in open revolt may be doubted; the opportunity was seized by the 'peoples of the land,' now actively hostile to the newly arrived settlers." J. M. Cook has a much more restrained comment on the situation: "Whether Xerxes had

The next verses—Ezra 4:7-23—report about an event or events in the days of Artaxerxes, when Bishlam, Mithredath, Tabeel, and their associates wrote to the king. Other than the notice that a letter was sent, nothing more is said concerning the matter. Ezra 4:8 then moves to what appears to be another set of circumstances—also during Artaxerxes' reign—when Rehum, Shimshai, and sundry other officials from the area of Samaria wrote to him to explain that Jerusalem was a city which had a long record of revolts against authority. They relayed to the king that the city walls were being constructed by Jews who "came up from you to us" (v. 12) and that they posed a danger to the realm. The king, after investigating the records about Jerusalem, ordered that work on the walls stop "and that this city not be rebuilt, until I make a decree" (v. 21). The group who came up is often identified as Ezra's band,[119] but neither Ezra nor his associates are said to have worked on the city walls. It is extraordinarily unlikely that Nehemiah and his fellow travelers are meant, since the same monarch gave them permission to rebuild the city's devastated walls. It is tempting to connect this letter with the time of the Egyptian revolt at the beginning of Artaxerxes' reign or with the revolt of the satrap Megabyzus, which flowed directly from it.[120]

Ezra's arrival in Jerusalem is dated to the seventh year of Artaxerxes, but, as the text does not specify which Artaxerxes is meant, scholars have long debated whether it was Artaxerxes I (hence the arrival date would be 458 BCE) or Artaxerxes II (397). There is no need to enter that discussion here; suffice it to say that no strong evidence opposes and much commends placing this event in the reign of Artaxerxes I. If this dating is correct, then there may be some sort of connection between his mission to Jerusalem by command of the king and Persian efforts to fortify and secure the area, which lay close to Egypt, that perennial trouble spot.[121] Nehemiah's mission, too, may have been a second stage in this official effort. Nehemiah, who reached Jerusalem in the king's twentieth year (445 BCE; see Neh 1:1; 2:1; 5:14), says that, in the monarch's

---

trouble in Judah is not clear" (*The Persian Empire* [New York: Shocken, 1983; reprinted Barnes & Noble, 1993], 100). There is no need to review the elaborate case made by Julius Morgenstern for the "catastrophe of 485 B.C." See his three essays: "Jerusalem—485 B.C.," *HUCA* 27 (1956): 101–79; "Jerusalem—485 B.C. (continued)," *HUCA* 28 (1957): 15–47; and "Jerusalem—485 B.C. (concluded)," *HUCA* 31 (1960): 11–29. For a detailed summary and critique, see Kenneth G. Hoglund, *Achaemenid Imperial Administration in Syria-Palestine and the Missions of Ezra and Nehemiah,* SBLDS 125 (Atlanta: Scholars, 1992), 51–61.

119. See the comments of Blenkinsopp, *Ezra-Nehemiah,* 113–14; Williamson, *Ezra, Nehemiah,* 63.

120. Compare Blenkinsopp, *Ezra-Nehemiah,* 114; Olmstead, *History of the Persian Empire,* 312–14.

121. Hoglund, *Achaemenid Imperial Administration,* chaps. 3–5.

thirty-second year (433), he returned to the king, only to travel once more to Jerusalem after a short stay in the east (Neh 13:6-7). The text does not indicate precisely how long he remained away or how long his second sojourn in Jerusalem lasted.

These and associated events in the time of Ezra and Nehemiah are the only ones recorded in the Bible for the period from about 516–515 BCE, when the Second Temple was completed, to the last third of the fifth century, when Nehemiah was in his second term as governor. Nevertheless, it is possible to reconstruct from the Bible and from some external sources something of the political arrangement that prevailed in Yehud during this period of about one century. Establishing the nature of the government in Jerusalem is important for evaluating the position of the high priest in Jewish society and under Persian rule. In the book of Ezra, two men are designated as political leaders: Sheshbazzar was the "prince of Judah" (הנשיא ליהודה [Ezra 1:8]) and governor (פחה [Ezra 5:14]). The book assigns no title to Zerubbabel, but in Haggai he is called "governor of Judah" (the phrase is פחת יהודה in Hag 1:1, 14; 2:2, 21). After Zerubbabel, the Bible mentions no official with the title of governor until Nehemiah, who also is called הפחה in Neh 5:14 (compare 12:26 and התרשתא [= excellency or the like] in Neh 8:9; 10:2 [Hebrew v. 1]; compare Ezra 2:63 = Neh 7:65, 70). Thus, in about 538, 520 and 445–433 BCE (at least), there was a man in Jerusalem who served as governor. In Neh 5:15, Nehemiah himself observes: "The former governors who were before me laid heavy burdens on the people, and took food and wine from them, besides forty shekels of silver." These words may imply that before Nehemiah there were other governors besides Sheshbazzar and Zerubbabel, neither of whom is associated with oppression in the sources.

Nehemiah's reference to "the former governors who were before me" has enjoyed renewed interest in light of recent archeological finds. Nahman Avigad has assembled evidence from bullae, seals, and coins and has reconstructed from them a fairly complete list of the names of Jewish governors who served during the early Persian period.[122] According to him, the large number of bullae that were discovered suggests that they belonged to an official archive, although the place in which they were found remains unknown.[123] Avigad argued that the bullae date from Persian times in Yehud and does so for at least two reasons. First, the names fit Persian-period Jewish nomenclature. "In any event, it is significant that all the names mentioned on

---

122. *Bullae and Seals from a Post-Exilic Judean Archive*, Qedem 4 (Jerusalem: The Institute of Archaeology, the Hebrew Univ. of Jerusalem, 1976).
123. Ibid., 30.

the bullae have their parallels in the Books of Ezra and Nehemiah, and some of them appear only there."[124] The one likely case for identifying a name on a bulla with a specific biblical character is Shelomith, which, according to 1 Chr 3:19, was the name of Zerubbabel's daughter.[125]

Second, paleographical analysis led Avigad to place the material in the very late sixth century and the early fifth.[126] Herein lies the crux of his argument. The script of the bullae and seals "is the Aramaic lapidary with a strong blend of archaic elements. Except for the *yod*, all these archaic letter-forms went out of general use in the Aramaic script after the sixth century BCE."[127] As he notes, the forms are not characteristic of either the fifth or the seventh century. In order to peg the date more precisely, he resorts to what he calls "historical and regional considerations."[128] Although there is no relevant linguistic evidence from the Babylonian period in Israel, Aramaic came into significant use only after the return from exile. Moreover, the title פחוא points to Persian times. For Avigad, the special conditions following the return account for the nature of the script. "Basically, it is possible that regional differences arise in the rate of development of a script, and its development in a given outlying land would not necessarily be dependent upon the mainstream course."[129] But if, as he thought, the persons who inscribed the bullae were among those who returned with Zerubbabel, why would their script not reflect the stage that it had reached in Babylon by that time? To answer this question, he opted for what he calls a "paradoxical solution":

> What I mean is that much of the archaic quality of the script of the bullae is to be associated with the fact that the Aramaic script in Judah was not local and early, but imported and recent. At the time of the bullae, it had not yet crystallized in its new environment. As we have seen, there is a considerable struggle between Aramaic forms and archaic forms of one and the same letter. It appears that in these cases the archaic forms originated in the local Hebrew script.[130]

He found support for his theory of converging linguistic influences in the fact that the script of these artifacts is Aramaic but their language Hebrew.

---

124. Ibid., 32.

125. Ibid.; Eric M. Meyers, "The Shelomith Seal and the Judean Restoration: Some Additional Considerations," *ErIsr* 18 (1985): 35*–38*.

126. *Bullae and Seals*, 13–25, especially 14–19.

127. Ibid., 17.

128. Ibid.

129. Ibid., 18.

130. Ibid., 18.

On the basis of these data, Avigad concluded that the bullae, the seals associated with them, and some Aramaic jar-impressions are "earlier than Nehemiah and belongs [*sic*] to the period between Zerubbabel (515 BCE) and Nehemiah (445 BCE)."[131] If his proposal is correct, then interesting consequences follow. He understood Neh 5:15 to be referring to Nehemiah's immediate Jewish predecessors in the gubernatorial office and believed that the names on the material remains inform one who these people were. Their names are:

- Elnathan (end of the sixth century)
- Yeho'ezer (early fifth century)
- ʾAhzai[132]

These men preceded Nehemiah; other documents reveal the names of two men who were among his successors: Bagohi (TAD A4.7 = AP 30.1) and Yehezqiyah, who is called "the governor" on some coins. Of special interest also is Avigad's item no. 14, which is a seal inscribed with the words לשלמית: אמת אלנתן פח[וא].[133] As we have seen, according to 1 Chr 3:19, Zerubbabel had a daughter named Shelomith. Avigad interpreted the word אמה (= maidservant) as possibly a parallel to עבד (= servant), which can be used of higher officials in the service of a king. Another possibility is that it refers to a wife-concubine who labored in her husband-master's administration or as a "functionary of the governor," "a woman of high standing."[134] He advanced the opinion that she was in charge of the archive or "rather, she was responsible for the administrative centre of which the archive was part."[135] If this Shelomith is to be identified with Zerubbabel's daughter, then Elnathan would have married into the gubernatorial family and would have become governor in his own right. The situation does, nevertheless, remain somewhat curious if this Shelomith is really from an aristocratic family such as Zerubbabel's.

If Avigad has correctly dated the seals and bullae so that the governors named on them served in the period between Zerubbabel and Nehemiah, then it follows that a fairly complete list of governors is now available for this little-

---

131. Ibid., 32.

132. H. G. M. Williamson agrees with Avigad about Elnathan and adds him to the list of governors ("The Governors of Judah under the Persians," *TynBul* 39 [1988]: 69–72). Regarding the other two, known from finds at Ramat Raḥel, he thinks the date of the material is less certain and thus does not include them.

133. *Bullae and Seals*, 11.

134. Ibid., 13; compare 31–32.

135. Ibid., 31.

known period in Jewish history.[136] It is also noteworthy that no descendant of Zerubbabel appears among these governors, because no one of his male descendants named in the biblical genealogy of the Davidic line figures in the list. Naturally, this has significant ramifications for one's understanding of the political situation in Yehud in the early Second-Temple period.

The genealogy of Zerubbabel is found in 1 Chr 3:19-24, where the MT names Pedaiah as his father and the LXX (with Haggai, Ezra, and Nehemiah) lists Shealtiel. Although several textual problems make the genealogy difficult to analyze, it is possible to obtain from it a reasonable idea of who Zerubbabel's descendants were for the next several generations. A very literal rendering of MT 1 Chr 3:19-20 would yield: "And the son of Zerubbabel Meshullam and Hananiah and Shelomith their sister and Hashubah and Ohel and Berechiah and Hasadiah Jushab-hesed, five." The LXX supports changing the singular "son of" to "sons of"—a reasonable (and thus probably a corrective) reading in view of the fact that more than one son's name follows. The more obvious problem is, however, that the number *five* (also in the LXX) at the end of the passage is not equal to the number of Zerubbabel's sons listed (seven) or of his children (eight). Also, the number is expressed in the form used with feminine, not masculine nouns. Various solutions to the difficulties have been proposed. For example, some have claimed that the number gives the total for the sons whose names follow Shelomith and that these are enumerated separately because they, unlike Meshullam, Hananiah, and Shelomith, were born after the return to Jerusalem.[137] Liver suggested that the passage provides a listing of children by several wives and that the number *five* indicates those who shared a mother.[138] Yet, whatever the correct explanation may be for the number, no one of Zerubbabel's sons is called governor, either in the Bible or in the bullae, seals, and coins that have been uncovered. Only the name Shelomith appears in connection with a governor, as explained above.

First Chronicles 3 next proceeds to name the sons of Zerubbabel's second son Hananiah. Here again, consistency would lead one to read "sons of" instead of the MT's "son of," but even with this change the MT remains puzzling. Literally it says: "And the son of Hananiah Pelatiah and Jeshaiah; the sons of Rephaiah, the sons of Arnan, the sons of Obadiah, the sons of

---

136. See also Ephraim Stern, *Material Culture of the Land of the Bible in the Persian Period 538–332 B.C.* (Warminster: Aris & Phillips, 1982), 202–6, 237. He thinks the material dates to a later time in the Persian period (fifth–fourth centuries).

137. So Wilhelm Rudolph, *Chronikbücher*, HAT 21 (Tübingen: Mohr/Siebeck, 1955), 29; H. G. M. Williamson, *1 and 2 Chronicles*, NCB (Grand Rapids: Eerdmans, 1982), 57.

138. Jacob Liver, *The House of David from the Fall of the Kingdom of Judah to the Fall of the Second Commonwealth and After* (Jerusalem: Magnes, 1959), 12 (Hebrew). He compares vv. 5, 8.

Shecaniah" (v. 21). From this listing, it appears that Hananiah had two sons and that after naming them the Chronicler enumerated families, the sons of various individuals, none of whom seems to have a connection with any preceding name.[139] In those several instances where the MT reads "the sons of," the LXX has "his son" (it is also found after the last name). That is, where MT uses בְּנֵי, LXX presupposes בְּנוֹ. The Greek text could be translated as: "And the sons of Hananiah: Pelatiah and Jeshaiah his son, Rephaiah his son, Arnan his son, Obadiah his son, Shecaniah his son." It would be possible to interpret the verse in two ways: it names the six sons of Hananiah, or it lists the six generations that followed him. However, as Hattush who is mentioned in verse 22 as a grandson of Shecaniah was a contemporary of Ezra (Ezra 8:2, if the same person is meant in both passages), reading the list as a six-generation genealogy would place him in the ninth generation after Zerubbabel and thus would produce too many generations, regardless whether one dates Ezra's return to 458 or 397 BCE. Hence, it seems more likely that verse 21 lists six sons of Hananiah, not six generations that followed him.[140]

One final problem concerns 1 Chr 3:22, which reads literally: "And the sons of Shecaniah Shemaiah and the sons of Shemaiah Hattush and Igal and Bariah and Neariah and Shaphat, six." The number *six* does not correspond with the listed sons of Shecaniah (five), and the plural "sons of" at the beginning would be inaccurate as only one son of Shecaniah is given. Liver followed an older suggestion that the phrase "and the sons of Shemaiah" is an addition—a copyist's error. If it is removed, the verse makes sense: it names the six sons of Shecaniah, the oldest of whom is Shemaiah.[141] Further support for the omission of the offending phrase comes from 1 Esd 8:29 in which, among the sons of David, Hattush is identified as a son of Shecaniah. Here, 1 Esdras appears to offer a text that is superior to the confused listing in Ezra 8:2-3, 5.[142] Apart from the singular "son of" in 1 Chr 3:23 (the LXX again has "sons of"), there are no difficulties in verses 23-24: "The sons of Neariah: Elioenai, Hizkiah, and Azrikam, three. The sons of Elioenai: Hodaviah, Eliashib, Pelaiah, Akkub, Johanan, Delaiah, and Anani, seven."

If the above analysis of Zerubbabel's genealogy in 1 Chr 3:19-24 is accurate, then his line can be traced thus:

---

139. See the comments of Kenneth E. Pomykala, *The Davidic Dynasty Tradition in Early Judaism: Its History and Significance for Messianism*, SBLEJL 7 (Atlanta: Scholars, 1995), 104–7.

140. Sara Japhet, *I and II Chronicles: A Commentary*, OTL (Louisville: Westminster John Knox, 1993), 101. She considers both readings possible and that no conclusive evidence is available for one or the other.

141. Liver, *The House of David*, 14.

142. Ibid.

- Zerubbabel
- Hananiah
- Shecaniah
- Neariah (Hattush is also in this generation)
- Elioenai
- Hodaviah (and Anani)

Liver has used this reconstruction and other biblical and extrabiblical evidence to calculate birth dates for the various individuals in the line. Zerubbabel was, of course, a descendant of the royal line. First Chronicles 3:16-19 reports that Jehoiachin's (the Judean king in 598 BCE) son Pedaiah was the father of Zerubbabel; Haggai and Zechariah, however, refer to Zerubbabel as the son of Shealtiel, who was another of Jehoiachin's sons. Whichever is correct, Zerubbabel is presented as a grandson of King Jehoiachin. Second Kings 24:8 says that Jehoiachin was eighteen years of age when he became king in the seventh year (598–597 BCE) of Nebuchadnezzar. Jehoiachin is mentioned in several Babylonian documents. One of them (no. 28186; see *ANET* 308) mentions the five sons of the king of Judah (who seems to be Jehoiachin, although he himself is called "son of the king of Judah" in the preceding line). From these data, Liver argued in this fashion: The Babylonian document that mentions the five sons of Jehoiachin dates from 592 BCE. By that time, Jehoiachin would have been twenty-three or twenty-four. If he had five sons by this time, the oldest—Shealtiel—would have been born around 596 BCE. Then, using the thesis that a generation consists of twenty-five years, he arrived at about 570 BCE for the birth of Zerubbabel, who was, on his view, Shealtiel's first son. Hananiah would, then, have been born in about 545 BCE and his first son in about 520 but Shecaniah (his sixth son) in about 510. This would mean that Neariah's birth should be placed in 490–485 BCE and his younger brother Hattush at roughly the same time. Consequently, when he reached Jerusalem with Ezra in 458 BCE, he would have been about thirty years of age. Elioenai's birth should be dated to about 460 BCE, Hodaviah's to about 435 and his youngest brother Anani (the last individual in the genealogy) to about 425. Thus, the list in 1 Chronicles 3 would bring the line of David to end of the fifth century.[143]

If one compares this list of Davidides with the names of the governors for the period between Zerubbabel and Nehemiah—as reconstructed by Avigad—there is no overlap at any point. There is no evidence that any of Zerubbabel's descendants ever held the top political office in the province Yehud. The governors came from other families. What motivated the change is not

---

143. Ibid., 17–19.

reported, although modern scholars have taken advantage of the absence of evidence to claim that Zerubbabel had become involved in a revolt against Persian authority and was, as a result, forcibly removed from office or even executed for his efforts. No ancient text even hints at this, though it could have happened. It is interesting that one of the Davidides in the genealogy, Hattush, is said to have come from Babylon with Ezra; hence, at least this member of the family was not in Yehud for some time before 458 BCE and thus not serving as governor there.

Each of the men who held the office of governor after Zerubbabel is called in Hebrew פחה or in Aramaic פחוא. While the word is regularly translated as *governor*, there has been some dispute about precisely what the office involved. Were these men rulers of a separate political unit Yehud or were they subordinate officers to Persian governors who were stationed in Samaria? Discussion of this point regularly begins with the theory of Albrecht Alt that in the period from the exile until Nehemiah (587–445 BCE), Jerusalem and the territory in its immediate environs did not constitute a separate political unit but were under the control of the governor in Samaria. Only with the appointment of Nehemiah to the governorship did Judea become a province on its own. In brief, Alt's argument was that neither Sheshbazzar nor Zerubbabel exercised the authority of a true governor. The former was not able to build the temple, while the report about the investigation conducted by Tattenai (Ezra 5:3— 6:15) fails to mention a governor and thus shows that Zerubbabel had no authority. It is only with Nehemiah that one meets a governor who acts as ruler of a separate political unit. His fortification of Jerusalem—something none of his predecessors had succeeded in doing—was carried out to make it a proper provincial capital. This move evoked the hostility of neighboring peoples, prominent among whom was Sanballat of Samaria who thus stood to lose part of his territory.[144]

Alt's reconstruction has been accepted by many but rejected by others. Morton Smith for one has stressed its thoroughly hypothetical nature and remarked that when Nehemiah refers to his predecessors (Neh 5:15), they must have been "of his own rank—otherwise the point is lost."[145] It is difficult, nevertheless, to accept Smith's way of accounting for the absence of Zerubbabel from the Tattenai pericope:

144. Alt, "Die Rolle Samarias bei der Entstehung des Judentums," in *Festschrift Otto Procksch zum 60. Geburtstag* (Leipzig: Deichert, 1934), 5–28; reprinted in Alt, *Kleine Schriften zur Geschichte des Volkes Israel,* 3rd ed. (Munich: Beck, 1964) 2.316–37.

145. Morton Smith, "Appendix: Alt's Account of the Samaritans," in his *Palestinian Parties and Politics That Shaped the Old Testament* (Lectures on the History of Religions 9 [New York: Columbia Univ. Press, 1971], 196 [193–201]).

The investigation seems to have followed Zerubbabel's disappearance, as well it might, and it might equally well have preceded the appointment of a successor. It may well be that the elders of Jerusalem got permission to go on with the temple because they persuaded the investigating officials that Zerubbabel had been put out of the way on account of his incipient disloyalty. That a successor was appointed is indicated by Malachi 1:8, which is normally understood to refer to the governor of Judah.[146]

In this discussion, much depends on the meaning of two words: מדינה and פחה (or its Aramaic cognate), and Sean McEvenue, for one, has attempted to clarify the issue through an analysis of these terms.[147] He argues that the pre-exilic usage of מדינה for lower level administrative units such as Solomon's districts continues into postexilic texts. It means little more than the word *region*. In Neh 11:1-3, it denotes "confusedly the people and the land, and in this case the land is specifically that land which is outside Jerusalem."[148] But surely, the text does not say this. When it says "[t]hese are the leaders of the province [המדינה] who lived in Jerusalem; but in the towns of Judah all lived on their property in their towns," it shows only that at least some leaders of the province lived in Jerusalem (compare vv. 1-2), not that Jerusalem somehow was not part of the province. Next, McEvenue turns to Ezra 2:1 = Neh 7:6: "These are the people of the province who came up out of the captivity of those exiles whom King Nebuchadnezzar of Babylon had carried into exile; they returned to Jerusalem and Judah, each to his town." He thinks that this list was drawn up "to reassure Tattenai and Darius—to write 'province of Juda' would arouse fears of separatism."[149] Eventually, he arrives at the conclusion that the word "province" (מדינה) is used here because "they are claimants of the land on the basis of Solomonic administrative divisions. Here again the pre-exilic usage of the term is retained."[150] F. Charles Fensham seems to agree with those who say that the province in question here is Babylonia from which the exiles were returning,[151] but Williamson understands "the people of the province" to be a "summary heading supplied to the list somewhat later than the events it describes" and believes it means "of all those who live in the province, these are the ones who returned from exile."[152]

---

146. "Alt's Account," 196.
147. "The Political Structure in Judah from Cyrus to Nehemiah," *CBQ* 43 (1981): 353–64.
148. Ibid., 359.
149. Ibid., 360.
150. Ibid., 360.
151. *The Books of Ezra and Nehemiah,* NICOT (Grand Rapids: Eerdmans, 1982), 48.
152. *Ezra, Nehemiah,* 33.

McEvenue also considers the instances of the word in the Aramaic parts of Ezra (5:8; 6:2 [mistakenly given as 6:20]; and 7:16). In them, the term is used for the provinces of Judah, Media, and Babylon. He admits that the first two lead one to think that מדינא has the specific meaning of province; the third case shows, on his view, that this is false. He understands the rescript of Artaxerxes in Ezra 7 to date from 429 BCE (thus accepting the dubious middle dating of Ezra's mission) and states: "At this point, Babylon was like Jerusalem! It had been razed 60 years earlier, because of the revolt of Belshimanni under Xerxes in 482. Babylon was fully incorporated into Assyria and lost its administrative identity. Here, therefore, *medina* means only region of Babylon."[153] Consequently, in Ezra 5:8, one does not have a reference to a separate "province of Judah" but merely to the "region of Judah."

In his treatment of the noun פחה, McEvenue notes that in Esther it "seems to indicate a governor subject to a satrap, and superior to *sarim*, i.e., feudal lords. In Aramaic texts of Daniel (3:2, 27; 6:8), the same seems to be true. Moreover, in Mal 1:8 the term refers to someone with fearsome authority."[154] In preexilic usage, the word is found in military contexts and "seems to designate a person who marches with the army, whatever the exact nature of his authority may be" (1 Kgs 10:15 = 2 Chr 9:14 is the exception).[155] In the Bible, the term is employed for people who do not enjoy the same status. "It follows that the term is non-technical in Aramaic, and specifically that it can equally well designate a governor (Tattenai) or an official who . . . does not act like a governor (Sheshbazzar)."[156] He does not identify for us the source that tells how Sheshbazzar acted. The title פחה, then, according to McEvenue, offers insufficient evidence for claiming that those to whom it is attributed were governors of separate political units. While this is also the case for Nehemiah, it is what he does that marks him as such a governor.

McEvenue would have been correct if he had said only that the philological evidence is not decisive. But if, as is obviously the case, both מדינה and פחה *can* be used in technical senses, he would have to demonstrate that they are not so employed in Ezra and Nehemiah. That is, to establish his case for their non-technical use in Ezra and Nehemiah, he would have to adduce some evidence that a governor in Samaria had the legal right to exercise authority in Jerusalem. But neither he nor Alt has managed to do this. Moreover, McEvenue confuses the issue by introducing preexilic usage into the discussion. The

---

153. "The Political Structure," 360.
154. Ibid., 362.
155. Ibid., 362.
156. Ibid., 363.

terms are used in Ezra and Nehemiah for rulers who belong within the Persian imperial system; consequently, their meaning should be established within that setting. References to Solomonic administrative districts are quite irrelevant. A general lack of evidence makes any final decision difficult, but the impression received from the biblical accounts and titles is that governors in Jerusalem ruled a political division and that they were not subordinate to a governor in Samaria.

Ephraim Stern has proposed a somewhat different solution. He thinks that after the return from exile and before 515 BCE, there was an attempt to form a separate political unit in Yehud with its own governors. After 515, however, Yehud came under Samarian administration and remained that way until Nehemiah's arrival in 445 BCE. He finds support for his reconstruction in seals that date from the early Persian period and others that come from a time after Nehemiah. For the pre-Nehemiah period, there are uninscribed stamp impressions with Achemenid motifs; but later there appear numerous seal impressions bearing the inscription *Yehud*.[157] There are also small silver coins that bear the name of the province; some of these date to the end of the fifth century.

However one conceives of the development of a political structure in Jerusalem during the Persian period, there appears always (or almost always) to have been a civil ruler. The evidence indicates that at several times there were governors of a separate political entity in Jerusalem. Yet, no one of these governors was a direct descendant of Zerubbabel as his offspring are listed in the Chronicler's genealogy. It is possible that Elnathan, if he belongs in the pre-Nehemiah period, was related to this family through his wife Shelomith. But the era of Davidic rulers seems to have ended. Even if we were to bracket the governors named on the seal impressions from the pre-Nehemiah period, we would have the following list of high priests and governors from other sources:

- Joshua and Zerubbabel
- Joiakim
- Eliashib and Nehemiah
- Joiada and Nehemiah
- Johanan and Bagoas
- Jaddua

---

157. *Material Culture*, 202–6, 237–83; idem, "The Persian Empire and the Political and Social History of Palestine in the Persian Period," in *Introduction; The Persian Period*, ed. W. D. Davies and L. Finkelstein, *CHJ* 1 (Cambridge: Cambridge Univ. Press, 1984), 70–87.

If the gubernatorial names of the seal impressions date from early in the Persian period, presumably one or more would have been in office at the time of Joiakim; if we place them late in the Persian period, probably one or more of them would have ruled at the time of Jaddua (especially the Hezekiah mentioned on some coins), even though Josephus's story about Jaddua does not mention a governor.

The regular presence of a governor in Jerusalem means that the high priest was not the only high-ranking, authoritative official in the city and province. In other words, there appears to have been no political vacuum into which the occupants of this office were drawn. The nature of the high-priestly office and the ancient aura that surrounded it may have added luster to the position, but the existence of a civil ruler in Jerusalem in the years of Persian control meant that the high priest was not the sole ruler politically in Yehud.[158]

158. In this sense, one can agree with Rooke (*Zadok's Heirs*, Part III, 125–239), but that the high priest was subordinate to the governor is not clear. At least we may say that a governor handled political matters and that this seems not to have been the role of the high priest at this time.

3

The High Priests in
the Early Hellenistic Period

The sources of information for the high priests who served from the time of Jaddua's successor Onias I (beginning in approximately the 320s BCE) to the reign of Onias III (before 175 BCE) are perhaps even more exasperating than those for the Persian period. The major source continues to be Josephus's *Antiquities*. In Book 12.1, 1—12.5, 1 (§§1–237), the Flavian historian provides data about the people and events of the first one hundred fifty years or so of the Hellenistic age, but his narrative, far from being continuous, is episodic in the extreme. Apparently, Josephus did not have at his disposal adequate sources for writing a cohesive report about the Judeans during Ptolemaic and early Seleucid times. After he sets the stage by describing the conquest of Jerusalem by Ptolemy I (satrap of Egypt 323–305 BCE and king 305–283)[1] in 12.1, 1—12.2, 1 (§§1–11), he summarizes the *Letter of Aristeas* (12.2, 2–15 [§§11–118]), which is set in the time of Ptolemy II (joint king with his father beginning in 285 BCE and sole king 283–246). A short section (12.3, 1–2 [§§119–28]) about how the Jews "received honour from the kings of Asia when they served with them in war" (12.3, 1 [§119]) consists largely of examples from the much later times of Vespasian, Titus, and Agrippa (§§121–28).

---

1. For the dates cited in this chapter, the sources consulted include especially: Edwyn Bevan, *A History of Egypt under the Ptolemaic Dynasty* (London: Methuen, 1927); E. J. Bickerman, *Chronology of the Ancient World,* 2nd ed., Aspects of Greek and Roman Life (Ithaca, N.Y.: Cornell Univ. Press, 1980); F. W. Walbank, *The Hellenistic World,* rev. ed. (Cambridge: Harvard Univ. Press, 1981); and Peter Green, *Alexander to Actium: The Historical Evolution of the Hellenistic Age,* Hellenistic Culture and Society 1 (Berkeley: Univ. of California Press, 1990).

From this subject, Josephus moves to the reign of the Seleucid monarch Antiochus III (223–187 BCE), his wars that eventually led to his taking possession of Judea, and the documents that he wrote on behalf of the Jews (12.3, 3–4 [§§129–53]). His reign provides the setting for the Tobiad Romance that extends from 12.4, 1 (§154) to 12.4, 11 (§236). By the end of the Romance, Antiochus IV (175–164 BCE) is upon the throne in Antioch, and the events of Maccabean history become the center of attention. Josephus, therefore, in effect used just two stories (the narrative from Aristeas and the Tobiad tale) and a set of official documents (several of which do not belong to this period) to cover a span of approximately one hundred fifty years.

Introductory Matters

There are several reports about high priests and one about a possible high priest in a few sources that are difficult to fit into a chronological sequence. For that reason, they are taken up separately in the next section, and a sketch of the political situation follows. The chronologically ordered survey of the high priests then resumes.

The Evidence from Hecateus of Abdera

The sources that Josephus cites are often difficult to assess, both as to their meaning and their historical value. One of the more important cases is Hecateus of Abdera. Near the beginning of his narrative about the Hellenistic age, Josephus relates that Ptolemy I had taken many captives from Judea; upon bringing them to Egypt, however, he gave them military positions and civic rights (*Ant.* 12.1, 1 [§§7–9]). "But not a few of the other Jews as well came to Egypt of their own accord, for they were attracted by the excellence of the country and Ptolemy's liberality" (§9). This statement recalls another passage in Josephus's *Against Apion* in which he quotes from Hecateus of Abdera's book *On the Jews*. He takes care to show that Hecateus was a prominent man during the reign of Ptolemy I (*Ag. Ap.* 1.184–85) and that, since Hecateus wrote an entire book about them, "[i]t is evident, therefore, that our race was flourishing both under Ptolemy and under Alexander" (§185).[2] This Hecateus had written about Ptolemy I: "Having heard of his kindliness and

---

2. This and other quotations of *Ag. Ap.* are from the translation of H. St. J. Thackeray, *Josephus*, vol. 1, *The Life, Against Apion*, LCL [Cambridge: Harvard Univ. Press, 1926]).

humanity, [many residents of Syria] desired to accompany him to Egypt and to associate themselves with his realm" (§186). Elsewhere, Hecateus is credited with making two statements that impinge on the high priesthood; consequently, it will be useful to consider who he was, the likelihood that he might have written what others attributed to him, and what his sources might have been.[3]

The historical Hecateus of Abdera, who lived in the late fourth through early third centuries BCE, wrote several works: a treatise on the poetry of Homer and Hesiod, a book *On the Hyporboreans*, and another *On the Egyptians*. Diodorus preserves an extract from his *On the Egyptians* (Diodorus, *Library of History* 1.28, 2)[4] in which Hecateus refers to the Jews as emigrants from Egypt, and he also quotes from him another far more extended description of the Jews (40.3, 1–8; compare 40.2). Scholars have discerned a different attitude in the two citations: in the former, the Jews leave Egypt voluntarily, whereas in the latter they are expelled. In spite of this inconsistent portrayal of the issue, the two extracts attributed to Hecateus in Diodorus's *Library of History* are commonly considered authentic.[5]

Other authors relate that Hecateus wrote about Jewish matters. *Letter of Aristeas* 31 reproduces his explanation for why ancient authors had not mentioned the Torah: "Writers therefore and poets and the whole army of historians have been reluctant to refer to the aforementioned books, and to the men past (and present) who featured largely in them, because consideration of them is sacred and hallowed, as Hecataeus of Abdera says."[6] Josephus also claims that Hecateus wrote a book about Abraham (*Ant.* 1.7, 2 [§159]).[7]

---

3. The major study is Bezalel Bar-Kochva, *Pseudo-Hecataeus, "On the Jews": Legitimizing the Jewish Diaspora,* HCS 21 (Berkeley: Univ. of California Press, 1996). As his title suggests, Bar-Kochva considers the work a Jewish forgery, not a composition by Hecateus of Abdera. For another detailed survey, see Gregory L. Sterling, *Historiography and Self-Definition: Josephos, Luke-Acts, and Apologetic Historiography,* NovTSup 64 (Leiden: Brill, 1991), 59–91.

4. Translated by Charles L. Sherman, *Diodorus of Sicily*, vol. 7, LCL (Cambridge: Harvard Univ. Press, 1952).

5. See Carl R. Holladay, *Fragments from Hellenistic Jewish Authors*, vol. 1: *Historians*, SBLTT 20 (Chico, Calif.: Scholars, 1984), 277; Robert Doran, "Pseudo-Hecataeus," in *OTP* 2.907. There is a survey of the differing views on the question in Bar-Kochva, *Pseudo-Hecataeus*, 3–6.

6. Translation of R. J. H. Shutt, "Letter of Aristeas," in *OTP* 2. Josephus, in his paraphrase of the *Letter of Aristeas*, reformulates the passage thus: "For this reason, Hecataeus of Abdera tells us, the poets and historians have made no mention of it or of the men whose lives were governed by it, on the ground that it was sacred and not to be revealed by profane mouths" (*Ant.* 12.2, 4 [§38]).

7. Menahem Stern argues that the book about Abraham "may be assumed, with almost absolute certainty, to be a product of Jewish religious propaganda, since it includes, according to the evidence of Clement of Alexandria, spurious verses of Sophocles that have a militant monotheistic ring" (*Greek and Latin Authors on Jews and Judaism*, vol. 1, *From Herodotus to*

Of more immediate relevance to the subject at hand is the material in *Against Apion* that Josephus credits to Hecateus. The Jewish historian here attempts to prove the antiquity of his people by adducing statements from numerous non-Jewish authors (*Ag. Ap.* 1.69–160). The sixth Greek author to whom he turns is Hecateus, "at once a philosopher and a highly competent man of affairs, who rose to fame under King Alexander, and was afterward associated with Ptolemy, son of Lagus [= Ptolemy I]. He makes no mere passing allusion to us but wrote a book entirely about the Jews, from which I propose briefly to touch on some passages" (*Ag. Ap.* 1.183). He then cites a range of materials from Hecateus in 1.183–204 (note the concluding statement in §205). Among these citations are some claims that will be treated below and also a comment about Alexander's relations with the Jews: "The honour in which he held our nation may be illustrated by the statement of Hecataeus that, in recognition of the consideration and loyalty shown to him by the Jews, he added to their territory the district of Samaria free of tribute" (*Ag. Ap.* 2.4).[8]

Some scholars have doubted that the lengthy excerpts that Josephus claims to draw from Hecateus's *On the Jews* (*Ag. Ap.* 1.183–204) actually derive from the historical Hecateus. Others consider them genuine.[9] It is not unlikely that they come from the hand of a writer such as Hecateus. He himself was in Egypt, and he would have had ample opportunity to meet Jews there and to learn about their customs and history from them.[10] In fact, Josephus quotes him to the effect that he had close contact with a Jew by the name of *Ezechias*

Plutarch [Jerusalem: The Israel Academy of Sciences, 1976], 20). See also Doran, "Pseudo-Hecataeus," 907; Holladay, *Fragments from Hellenistic Jewish Authors*, 279.

8. This, as we saw in the previous chapter, may relate to the episode of Alexander's revenge on the Samaritans who had executed one of his officials. Origen (*Against Celsus* 1.15) knew of the claim that Hecateus had written a book on the Jews in which he praised them highly: "Moreover, a book about the Jews is attributed to Hecataeus the historian, in which the wisdom of the nation is emphasized even more strongly—so much so that Herennius Philo in his treatise about the Jews even doubts in the first place whether it is a genuine work of the historian, and says in the second place that if it is authentic, he had probably been carried away by the Jews' powers of persuasion and accepted their doctrine" (translation of Holladay, *Fragments from Hellenistic Jewish Authors*, 323).

9. See the surveys of opinions in Doran, "Pseudo-Hecataeus," 906–7; Emil Schürer, *The History of the Jewish People in the Age of Jesus Christ 175 B.C.—A.D. 135*, rev. and ed. G. Vermes and F. Millar with M. Black (Edinburgh: T. & T. Clark, 1973–87), 2.671–77; and M. Pucci Ben Zeev, "The Reliability of Josephus Flavius: The Case of Hecataeus' and Manetho's Accounts of Jews and Judaism: Fifteen Years of Contemporary Research (1974–1990)," *JSJ* 24 (1993): 217–24.

10. So Jörg-Dieter Gauger, "Zitate in der jüdischen Apologetik und die Authentizität der Hekataios-Passagen bei Flavius Josephus und in Ps. Aristeas-Brief," *JSJ* 13 (1982): 28–29; compare Sterling, *Historiography and Self-Definition*, 87–91.

(= Hezekiah). In the context, Hecateus is describing those from Syria who were attracted to Ptolemy I and Egypt:

> Among these (he says) was Ezechias [Ἐζεκίας], a chief priest [ἀρχιερεύς] of the Jews, a man of about sixty-six years of age, highly esteemed by his countrymen, intellectual, and moreover an able speaker and unsurpassed as a man of business. Yet (he adds) the total number of Jewish priests who receive a tithe of the revenue and administer public affairs is about fifteen hundred.

Reverting to Ezechias, he says:

> This man, after obtaining this honour and having been closely in touch with us, assembled some of his friends and read to them [a statement showing] all the advantages [of emigration]; for he had in writing the conditions attaching to their settlement and political status. (*Ag. Ap.* 1.187–89)

The Ezechias named and admired by Hecateus has become the subject of much speculation because he is said to be ἀρχιερεύς, although his name fails to appear in any ancient list of the high priests. It would be easy to dismiss Hecateus's claim about the man's title as a misunderstanding by a foreign observer, but some years ago it appeared that scholars had discovered independent evidence confirming at least the existence of this Ezechias, if not his priestly office. A coin found in the excavations at Beth Zur was first read as bearing the names חזקיהו and (ן)יהוחנ. From them, some concluded that Jehohanan was the high priest Onias (*Onias* is a caritative or diminutive form of Yehohanan) and that Hizqiyahu (= Ezechias) was the treasurer.[11] Later, the word read as (ן)יהוחנ was correctly deciphered as יהוד, the name of the province. Even a scholar such as Victor Tcherikover continued, however, to think that this Hezekiah (= Ezechias) was the ἀρχιερεύς mentioned by Hecateus.[12] Numismatists, who have in the interval found other coins with the name יחזקיה on them and some of which also read הפחה, now realize that the Beth Zur coin has nothing to do with Hecateus's priest, Ezechias. Rather, the coins evidence the name of a governor of Yehud who ruled in the late Persian period.[13]

---

11. See Ovid R. Sellers, *The Citadel of Beth Zur* (Philadelphia: Westminster, 1933), 73–74.

12. *Hellenistic Civilization and the Jews* (New York: Atheneum, 1970), 425–26.

13. See the survey in L. Mildenberg, "Yehud: A Preliminary Study of the Provincial Coinage of Judaea," in *Greek Numismatics and Archaeology: Essays in Honor of Margaret Thompson*, ed. O. Mørkholm and N. M. Waggoner (Wetteren, Belgium: NR, 1979), 183–96 with pls. 21–22. The Hezekiah coins were mentioned at the end of chap. 2 above.

It is unlikely that the priest Ezechias was ever high priest in the Jerusalem temple. Josephus, in his citation from Hecateus, does not call him ὁ ἀρχιερεύς but only ἀρχιερεύς. For the sense of the term, scholars have for a long time appealed to later usage in which it is employed for a high-ranking priest, not only for a high priest.[14] If Hecateus was opting for the word in this sense, he would be designating Ezechias only as an important priest. This may be the correct approach, but Gauger has recently suggested another possibility. He finds the usage to which scholars usually appeal to be later. On his view, scholars have overlooked the fact that we do not have a Jew speaking here but a "heathen." At an earlier time (he refers to Herodotus 2.142; Plato, *Laws* 947, and Diodorus 1.73) the term ἀρχιερεύς had, especially in Egypt, the meaning *chief priest* in the sense of a leader of a temple community.[15] Specifically for Ezechias the title ἀρχιερεύς suggests that somewhere in Egypt a perhaps small Jewish cultic community had been formed and the leader of the priests who participated in founding it was designated, following an Egyptian model, as ἀρχιερεύς.[16] His proposal removes the need to appeal to later usage of the word. This Ezechias may, then, have been the cultic head of a small Jewish community that migrated to Egypt.

Bar-Kochva, who has reviewed these matters in considerable detail, has also concluded that this Hezekiah should not be added to the high-priestly list, but he approaches the subject in a different way.[17] After noting the various sources that disclose that Ptolemy I treated the Jews harshly and unjustly (he connects this with events around the battle of Ipsus in 301 BCE), he expresses strong doubt that a Jewish high priest (he insists that that is the meaning of ἀρχιερεύς in the passage) would willingly emigrate to Egypt, bringing other Jews with him. Rather, this "was a forced deportation and not a voluntary emigration. And if this was indeed the case, it should rather be dated to the days of Ipsus [not of Gaza in 312–311, where Hecateus puts it]. The author, then, transformed an exile into an emigration."[18] This and other information suggest that Hecateus of Abdera, active in Ptolemy's court, did not write the

---

14. Compare M. Stern, *Greek and Latin Authors*, 1.40–41; Holladay, *Fragments from Hellenistic Jewish Authors*, 326.

15. "Zitate in der jüdischen Apologetik und die Authentizität der Hekataios-Passagen," 45.

16. Ibid., 46. Benjamin E. Scolnic suggests that Ezechias may have been the Samaritan high priest (Hezekiah is the name of the high priest in the Samaritan version of the story about Alexander the Great) (*Chronology and Papponymy: A List of the Judean High Priests of the Persian Period*, SFSHJ 206 [Atlanta: Scholars, 1999], 263). Josephus cites Hecateus as saying, however, that he was high priest of the Jews, so that for Scolnic's idea to work, we would have to assume that Hecateus or his source confused Jews and Samaritans.

17. *Pseudo-Hecataeus*, 79–91.

18. Ibid., 79.

account of Hezekiah—a story apparently not known to the author of the *Letter of Aristeas* who was eager to use evidence about favorable relations between the Jews and the Ptolemaic government.

Bar-Kochva argues that Josephus was unlikely to have skipped over a high priest, because his list is supposed to be based on excellent records. He also denies that the term ἀρχιερεύς should be understood in light of its later, more general use (it was not so used in Persian and Hellenistic times).[19] The Hezekiah coins do not deal with a priest but with a governor. There are two types among these coins: the earlier ones (about 340–338 BCE) have the name and title (הפחה), while the later ones (from the time of Alexander and his successors) have only the name. That is, he was a governor for a long time, spanning the transition from the Persian to the Hellenistic period. As the Persians did not give the high priesthood and governorship to one person, it is unlikely they did so in this case. Other statements from Hecateus indicate that he had good information about the Jewish high priesthood and was thus not the author of this section about Hezekiah. Bar-Kochva does not think there is reason to doubt that a Jewish governor was exiled to Egypt, but he was not a high priest.[20] All of this is part of Bar-Kochva's larger argument denying that the extracts from Hecateus's *On the Jews* in Josephus's *Against Apion* are authentic.[21]

Even if one does not accept all of Bar-Kochva's arguments about the nature of the passage, the name Ezechias should be removed from consideration as one of the high priests at the Jerusalem temple during the reign of Ptolemy I. He does not appear in the extant lists, and the title applied to him by Hecateus can be explained in a satisfactory way as referring to someone other than the high priest of the temple in Jerusalem. Hecateus does, however,

---

19. Ibid., 84.

20. "This suggests that the author was inspired by the name and personality of that governor, but transformed Hezekiah from governor into High Priest, just as he transformed the forced exile to Egypt into a voluntary migration, the harsh treatment of the local population by Ptolemy into 'philanthropy,' and probably also the time of Ipsus into the time of Gaza" (*Pseudo-Hecataeus*, 89).

21. Bar-Kochva finally determines that the story served as the *origo* component of the ethnography (*Pseudo-Hecataeus*, 219–31) that was written by a Diaspora Jew between 107 and 93 BCE, justifying Jewish residence in Egypt (pp. 232–48). Erich S. Gruen takes the περὶ Ἰουδαίων to be part of the process by later Jews in Egypt to tidy up the ugly facts about Jewish relations with the first Ptolemy (*Heritage and Hellenism: The Reinvention of Jewish Tradition*, HCS 30 [Berkeley: Univ. of California Press, 1998], 202–3). Hugo Willrich had thought the story about Ezechias was a version of Onias IV's move to Egypt in the 160s (*Juden und Griechen vor der makkabäischen Erhebung* [Göttingen: Vandenhoeck & Ruprecht, 1895], 32, 80–82).

provide other information that is directly relevant to the history of the high priesthood. Diodorus, in his *Library of History* 40.3—a passage whose authenticity is widely accepted[22]—writes: "Now that we are about to record the war against the Jews [that is, in Pompey's time], we consider it appropriate to give first a summary account of the establishment of the nation, from its origins, and of the practices observed among them" (40.3, 1).[23] As his notice that concludes this section discloses (40.3, 8), the information is said to come from Hecateus, although the surviving text (from Photius) reads Ἑκαταῖος ὁ Μιλήσιος, a writer who lived around 500 BCE. This attribution is generally believed to be a mistake made by Photius, not by Diodorus.[24] Hecateus of Abdera is more likely to be the author intended, and the passage comes from his *On the Egyptians*.

His account of the Jews, beginning with the exodus, is fascinating throughout, but of primary interest here is his description of the high-priestly office. Hecateus claims that Moses gave the leadership of the nation to the priests:

> He picked out the men of the most refinement and with the greatest ability to lead the entire nation, and appointed them priests; and he ordained that they should occupy themselves with the temple and the honours and sacrifices offered to their god. These same men he appointed to be judges in all major disputes, and entrusted to them the guardianship of the laws and customs. For this reason the Jews never have a king, and authority [προστασίαν] over the people is regularly vested in whichever priest is regarded as superior to his colleagues in wisdom and virtue. They call this man the [the article is not in the text] high priest [ἀρχιερέα], and believe that he acts as messenger [ἄγγελον] to them of God's commandments. It is he, we are told, who in their assemblies and other gatherings announces what is ordained, and the Jews are so docile in such matters that straightway they fall to the ground and do reverence to [προσ-κυνεῖν] the high priest when he expounds the commandments[25] to them. (40.3, 5–6)

---

22. See Sterling, *Historiography and Self-Definition*, 75–78.

23. Translation of Francis R. Walton, *Diodorus of Sicily*, vol. 12, LCL (Cambridge: Harvard Univ. Press, 1967).

24. Ibid., 286–87. Regarding the manuscripts and the emendation, see M. Stern, *Greek and Latin Authors*, 1.34–35.

25. The translation "expounds the commandments" renders the one word ἑρμηνεύοντα.

It takes little effort to uncover flaws in Hecateus's presentation, at least when it is compared with the biblical history of monarchic Israel.[26] His portrait of Judaism may be viewed as an instance of *interpretatio graeca* and as a product of blending three periods of the past: Exodus and wandering, settlement in Canaan, and restoration and beyond.[27] Stern attempts to explain Hecateus's reference to the *selection* of high priests by appealing to his apparent ignorance of the hereditary principle of succession in the high-priestly line and to the fact that there were indeed certain exceptions to this rule.[28] D. Mendels, however, finds expressed here the views of a Jewish priestly group that, at the end of the fourth century BCE, denigrated monarchy—a stance enjoying biblical grounding and one that continued to have support in late Hasmonean times (compare Josephus, *Ant.* 14.3, 2 [§41]).[29] By using the verb δίδοσθαι, Hecateus means "that however the transfer of the function of High-Priest may have taken place, the function is in any case vested in a priest of 'most refinement and ability', hence 'chosen' from among all other priests. Such a view could be expected from those circles which were interested in emphasizing the superiority and sole legitimacy of the High priests as head of the nation."[30]

At a minimum, we may say that Hecateus's source of information saw the Jewish community of Judea as one dominated by priests, at the head of whom stood the high priest, a man of sterling qualities.[31] It may be significant that

---

26. See M. Stern, *Greek and Latin Authors*, 1.31; he notes that Israel's kings are rarely mentioned in Hellenistic literature, while theocracy was thought to be the special Jewish form of government.

27. Bar-Kochva, *Pseudo-Hecataeus*, 26. He shows that, as in other ethnographies, the purpose was to deal with the origins and the customs of a people. Compare Martin Hengel, *Judaism and Hellenism: Studies in Their Encounter in Palestine during the Early Hellenistic Period*, 2 vols., trans. J. Bowden (Philadelphia: Fortress Press, 1974), 1.256.

28. *Greek and Latin Authors*, 1.31. He notes Alon's claim that the succession of the high priests was not completely fixed in the Hellenistic period (Gedalia Alon, *Studies in Jewish History*, 2 vols. [Tel Aviv: Hakkibbutz Hameuchad, 1957], 1.72 [Hebrew]). The surviving lists of high priests hardly support this point. Compare also Bar-Kochva, *Pseudo-Hecataeus*, 33–34.

29. "Hecateus of Abdera and a Jewish 'patrios politeia' of the Persian Period (Diodorus Siculus XL, 3)," *ZAW* 95 (1983): 104–6. The essay has been reprinted in Mendels, *Identity, Religion, and Historiography: Studies in Hellenistic History*, JSPSup 24 (Sheffield: Sheffield Academic, 1998), 334–51.

30. Mendels, "Hecateus of Abdera," 105–6. See also Bar-Kochva, *Pseudo-Hecataeus*, 34, who thinks Hecateus may have misinterpreted some complimentary references to priests and high priests. "In addition, as the position of High Priest was sometimes conferred upon the brother of the legal heir, some process of formal ratification must have existed. This being reported to him, it may have contributed to the misunderstanding. Hecateus may also have had parallels in Plato's *Laws* (759a-b, 947a-b) at the back of his mind." The situation mentioned by Bar-Kochva occurred, however, only when the legal heir was too young to assume office.

31. His phrasing "whichever priest is regarded as superior to his colleagues" reminds one of the description of the high priest in Lev 21:10: "the priest who is exalted above his fellows."

Hecateus says "authority [προστασίαν] over the people" is given to the high priest. As we shall see below when examining the Tobiad Romance, this word, at times at least, seems to refer to a kind of political rule over the populace.[32]

Hecateus continues his description of the high priest by declaring that he "acts as a messenger to them of God's commandments." As commentators have observed, the term ἄγγελος here reminds us of Mal 2:7: "For the lips of a priest should guard knowledge, and people should seek instruction from his mouth, for he is the messenger of the LORD of hosts."[33] This passage from Malachi was exploited by later writers such as the author of the *Book of Jubilees* (see 31:13-17) as if it referred to Levi himself (he is mentioned in v. 4) and thus to the first and leading priest. Hecateus reports the same connection between תורה and priest found in a number of biblical passages (besides Mal 2:7, see Hag 2:10-13; compare Lev 10:10-11; Num 31:21-24; Deut 27:9-10; 31:9-13; 33:10; Ezra 7:10). Hecateus's word πρόσταγμα is the standard Septuagintal equivalent of חק and חקה.[34] He also speaks of various gatherings of the Jews at which the high priest "announces what is ordained." Continuing with the role of the high priest as the one who conveys commands, he remarks on Jewish docility in the presence of the pontiff as he dispenses Torah. The description is not entirely favorable but the words he uses are interesting. According to Hecateus, the Jews prostrate themselves [προσκυνεῖν] before the high priest when he expounds [ἑρμηνεύοντα].[35] Their prostration reminds one of Sir 50:17, part of the paean to the high priest Simon, son of Onias: after the high priest poured the libation of wine at the foot of the altar and the priests shouted and blew on trumpets (vv. 15-16),

> Then all the people together quickly
> fell to the ground on their faces
> to worship [προσκυνῆσαι] their Lord,
> the Almighty, God Most High. (50:17)

---

32. Bar-Kochva (*Pseudo-Hecataeus*, 297–98), however, thinks that in the citation nothing is said about secular duties for the high priest. One could, though, infer this from some comments, such as the one about προστασίαν.

33. See Francis R. Walton, "The Messenger of God in Hecataeus of Abdera," *HTR* 48 (1955): 255–57. Walton notes the fusion of prophetic and priestly aspects in Hecateus's report: "His Moses is in part the ideal Greek *nomothetes*, in part the philosopher, and he appears to have regarded the High Priest essentially as the successor to Moses, both as the highest civil authority and as a mouthpiece for the continuing revelation of God's will" (256). He finds this "telescoping" of the two functions "no doubt in the main untrue to history" (256–57).

34. HRCS, 1219.

35. M. Stern (*Greek and Latin Authors*, 1.31–32) thinks that the liturgy of the Day of Atonement, when the high priest enters the Holy of Holies, may have influenced Hecateus's description.

A few verses later the poet adds:

> Then Simon came down and raised his hands
> over the whole congregation of Israelites,
> to pronounce the blessing of the Lord with his lips,
> and to glory in his name;
> and they bowed down in worship [ἐν προσκυνήσει] a second time,
> to receive the blessing from the Most High. (50:20-21)

The two references to prostration here are to the people's bowing with faces to the ground to the deity, but the distinction between bowing to the Lord and bowing to the high priest may have been lost on an outside observer.

Hecateus, then, proves to be a helpful source for giving us some idea of what, at least for a foreign writer who seems to have tapped into Jewish sources, the high priest did and how he was regarded by some of his contemporaries. He never supplies the name of a high priest, although he does mention Ezechias as a leading priest. If he is to be believed and the text is not a later Jewish forgery, in the time around 300 BCE, the high priest carried out important cultic functions, taught Torah, and enjoyed great prestige; he may also have exercised political functions.[36]

The Political Situation

As for the Persian period, so in the early Hellenistic age little is known about the political administration of Judea. The sources are too sparse to divulge the names of any governors (with the possible exception of Hezekiah), and the specific forms under which the area was administered remain unclear. It is quite possible, however, that coins once more provide valuable and suggestive information. There are now available series of coins that come from Judah during the time of Macedonian occupation and the earliest years of Ptolemaic rule.[37] As Mildenberg sketches the evidence, the coins should be categorized in this way.

---

36. Deborah W. Rooke (*Zadok's Heirs: The Role and Development of the High Priesthood in Ancient Israel* [OTM; Oxford: Oxford Univ. Press, 2000], 246–50) is properly cautious about the historical reliability of the fragment, noting the absence of other sources with which to compare Hecateus's report. As we have seen, we do not entirely lack comparative material, but the question of historicity remains.

37. We should recall the argument in chap. 2 above that the coin bearing the name Yohanan may have been minted by Onias I, the first high priest of the Hellenistic age.

1. A small group of minute Yehud coins with certain figures and bearing the name יחזקיה (see chap. 2 above); this type does not add the title פחה that the late Persian coins attached to Hezekiah. The absence of the title may be interpreted as indicating that Governor Hezekiah was not subject to the Persian satrap in Damascus but to Alexander or someone whom he had appointed. These coins also have on them a lynx protome—an image found on early Ptolemaic minute coins from Judah.[38]

2. A new, well represented series of silver coins, many of which have the portraits of Ptolemy I and his queen Berenike I stamped on them, betray a new situation, since they bear the Hebrew name of the area—יהודה. These coins may be subdivided into different classes.[39]

An important fact about the Judean coins from the Macedonian (ca. 330–312 BCE) and early Ptolemaic (ca. 300–283 BCE) periods is that none of them has the name of a governor stamped on it. Rappaport has concluded from this given that the political situation in Yehud/Yehudah had changed with the arrival of Hellenistic rule. The fact that the late Persian-period coins have the name of the governor on them but the Macedonian-Ptolemaic coins do not means for Rappaport that there was no longer a governor in Judah and that the high priest had, in the absence of such a political leader, become the local minting authority.[40] The data are too meager to confirm his inference, but at least the extant evidence makes it an attractive possibility. If so, the implication would be that the high priests of the very earliest post-Persian decades exercised greater power in the crucial economic sphere of minting

---

38. For these coins, see Yaʿakov Meshorer, *A Treasury of Jewish Coins from the Persian Period to Bar-Kochba* (Jerusalem: Yitzhak ben-Zvi, 1997 [Hebrew]), 23–24.

39. Mildenberg, "Yehud: A Preliminary Study of the Provincial Coinage of Judaea," 188–91. Meshorer (*Treasury*, 26–27) thinks these coins date from the time of Ptolemy II.

40. Uriel Rappaport, "The Coins of Judea at the End of the Persian Rule and the Beginning of the Hellenistic Period," in *Jerusalem in the Second Temple Period: Abraham Schalit Memorial Volume*, ed. O. Oppenheimer, U. Rappaport, and M. Stern (Jerusalem: Yitzhak ben-Zvi, Ministry of Defence, 1980 [Hebrew]), 7–21, especially 10–14. Although he was speaking about bronze coins, his conclusion is more widely applicable: "It appears that the local administrative powers and thus the raising of taxes were given to the high priest. A conclusion that is almost necessary is, then, that the act of minting under consideration was done by his command, if only because no other authority in Yehudah is known to us who was capable of acting in this area on his own. There is reflected here, therefore, a strengthening of the high priest's position—a process that had previously been surmised and that began after the transition from Persian rule to the rule of the Hellenistic states" (13 [author's translation]). For the dating of the coins from the late Persian and earliest Hellenistic years, see Bar-Kochva and Arie Kindler, "The Hezekiah Coins" (Appendix A in Bar-Kochva, *Pseudo-Hecataeus*, 255–70).

coins. Ultimate sovereignty, of course, remained with the foreign overlord, but local control may have rested with the high priests. This situation was short-lived because, especially in the reign of Ptolemy II, centralized control of the currency became more extensive and the local authorities, such as the Jewish high priests, lost the minting authority they may have exercised for a short time.

The High Priests in the Early Hellenistic Period

7. Onias I[41]

The first high priest after Jaddua in the Hellenistic age is mentioned by Josephus in the last paragraph of *Antiquities* 11: "Now by that time [that is, of Alexander's death and the division of the conquests between his successors] the high priest Jaddus was also dead, and his son Onias succeeded to the high priesthood" (11.8, 7 [§347]). Josephus says nothing about the reign of Onias I at this point in his narrative, but he does refer to him one more time near where he begins to paraphrase the *Letter of Aristeas*. He relates that Ptolemy II Philadelphus, at the instigation of his librarian Demetrius of Phalerum, wrote to "the high priest of the Jews" (*Ant.* 12.2, 1 [§16]) for the purpose of having the Jewish books about their laws (see §14) translated into Greek for inclusion in the royal library (note the official language in 12.2, 4 [§39]). The high priest at that time is said to have been a man named Eleazar (12.2, 5 [§40]). As he had said nothing about him before, Josephus felt obliged to explain how he had come to the office: "On the death of the high priest Onias, he was succeeded by his son Simon. . . . But as he, when he died, left an infant son named Onias, his brother Eleazar, of whom we are now writing, took over the high priesthood" (12.2, 5 [§43]).

Although he did not realize it, Josephus probably also referred to Onias I in a later context in the *Antiquities* (12.4, 10 [§§225–27]). There, our historian is writing about another high priest named Onias—Onias III, an early second-century BCE leader. He reports that the Lacedemonian king Areios (= Areus) sent a letter to the high priest Onias. Although the historian dates this correspondence between the Spartan king and the Jewish high priest to the time of Onias III, scholars have objected that this is impossible because there were

---

41. The number given to each high priest in the heading corresponds to the List of High Priests, pp. 491–92.

only two Spartan kings named Areus and neither of them ruled at any time near the period when Onias III was in office. Areus I served as Spartan monarch from 309 to 265 BCE, and Areus II (262–254 BCE) died when a child of eight years.[42] It is highly improbable that the child Areus II during his short reign wrote the letter cited by Josephus; moreover, there may have been no high priest named Onias in office in about 255 BCE. Consequently, if there is any truth to Josephus's claim about the exchange of letters, Areus I would seem the only likely candidate as author of the epistle. This certainly entails that the high priest Onias who received the letter was not Onias III, as Josephus thought. As it was probably also not Onias II, Onias I should have been the addressee (see below).[43]

Versions of the letter may be read in *Ant.* 12.4, 10 (§§226–27) and 1 Macc 12:19-23, Josephus's source for most of the text. The author of 1 Maccabees introduces it in connection with an embassy that Jonathan, the second Maccabean ruler (152–142 BCE), dispatched to Rome (12:1). Besides sending men to Rome, he "also sent letters to the same effect to the Spartans and to other places" (v. 2). The chapter then gives the text of Jonathan's message to the Spartans (vv. 6-18) in which he mentions renewing the bonds between the two peoples (v. 10) that had been established some time ago. "Already in time past a letter was sent to the high priest Onias from Arius, who was king among you, stating that you are our brothers, as the appended copy shows. Onias welcomed the envoy with honour, and received the letter, which contained a clear declaration of alliance and friendship" (vv. 7-8). The earlier letter, which is appended to the later one sent by Jonathan in 1 Maccabees, reads as follows in the two versions.

1 Macc 12:20-23	*Ant.* 12.4, 10 (§§226–27)
King Arius of the Spartans, to the high priest Onias, greeting. It has been found in writing concerning the Spartans and the Jews that they are brothers and are of the family of Abraham. And now that we have learned this, please write us concerning your welfare; we on our part write to you that your livestock and your property belong to us,	Areios, king of the Lacedaemonians, to Onias, greeting. We have come upon [literally: found] a certain document from which we have learned that the Jews and Lacedaemonians are of one race and are related by descent from Abraham. It is right, therefore, that you as our brothers should send to us to make known whatever you may wish. We

---

42. See, for example, Marcus, *Josephus*, 7, 114–15 n. e.

43. So Marcus, *Josephus*, 7, 114–15 n. e; and Burkhart Cardauns, "Juden und Spartaner: Zur hellenistisch-jüdischen Literatur," *Hermes* 95 (1967): 318.

and ours belong to you. We therefore command that our envoys report to you accordingly.

also shall do this, and shall consider what is yours as our own, and what is ours we shall also share with you.

Antiquities adds what seems to be the technically worded ending of an official document: "Demoteles, the courier, is bringing this letter to you. The writing is square. The seal is an eagle holding fast a serpent" (12.4, 10 [§227]).

The authenticity of the letter has often been affirmed and denied.[44] Questions about it may be handled under four headings: (1) the textual evidence, (2) the king and high priest in question, (3) the nature of the text in its existing versions, and (4) the Abraham connection. To some extent these problems are interrelated.

(1) The textual evidence: The version in *Antiquities* begins by naming the Spartan king and the high priest and uses acceptable spellings: βασιλεὺς Λακεδαιμονίων ἍΑρειος Ὀνίᾳ. But 1 Maccabees, which antedates *Antiquities* by about two centuries, is clearly corrupt at this point. The various witnesses to the text of 1 Macc 12:20 offer spellings such as ονιαρος, ον(ε)ιαρης, and *oniarex,* with αρης attested only in Codex Sinaiticus.[45] The spelling in the majority of witnesses may be a combination of Ὀνίᾳ and ἍΑρειος;[46] if so, as Jonathan Goldstein has observed, Onias's name came first in the original form of 1 Maccabees and would not have been repeated after the king's name.[47] Apart from these differences, the contents of the two versions are parallel, although Josephus extensively rephrases the text.[48] The major discrepancy

44. See Cardauns, "Juden und Spartaner," 317–18 n. 1 for scholars on the two sides of the issue, and also the survey in Menaham Stern, "Relations between Sparta and the Jews in the Hellenistic Period," in his *Hasmonaean Judaea in the Hellenistic World: Chapters in Political History* (ed. D. Schwartz; Jerusalem: Zalman Shazar Center for Jewish History, 1995 [Hebrew]), 63-70.

45. For the evidence see Werner Kappler, ed., *Maccabaeorum liber I,* Septuaginta: Vetus Testamentum Graecum Auctoritate Societatis Litterarum Gottingensis editum IX, 1 (Göttingen: Vandenhoeck & Ruprecht, 1936), 125.

46. See, for example, Menahem Stern, *The Documents on the History of the Hasmonaean Revolt* (Tel Aviv: Hakkibbutz Hameuchad, 1965 [Hebrew]), 113; Schürer, *History of the Jewish People,* 1.184–85 n. 33. In 1 Macc 12:7, where Areus should be mentioned, the witnesses have δαρ(ε)ιου for the expected αρειου. It is clear that the royal name caused scribes of 1 Maccabees difficulty, probably because it was unfamiliar.

47. *I Maccabees,* AB 41 (Garden City, N.Y.: Doubleday, 1976), 460.

48. The changes made by Josephus are noted by S. Schüller, "Some Problems Connected with the Supposed Common Ancestry of Jews and Spartans and Their Relations during the Last Three Centuries B.C.," *JSS* 1 (1956): 258. He explains that Josephus's alterations give the letter "a somewhat more Greek touch." Scholars have often noted that the text of the letter in 1 Maccabees has had a tortured history: if authentic, the Spartan letter would have been written in Greek, translated into Hebrew by the author of the original 1 Maccabees, and then retranslated into

comes at the end where Josephus has an additional line about the courier Demoteles and the description of the writing and seal. It has been claimed that Josephus borrowed the name *Demoteles* from Xenophon who writes about a Spartan herald with the same name.[49] As Cardauns has noted, in the same chapter of Xenophon's work *Hellenica,* other points of similarity with Josephus's extra line surface in the words ὁ Πέρσης ὁ φέρων τὰ γράμματα δείξας τὴν βασιλέως σφραγῖδα ἀνέγνω τὰ γεγραμμένα (*Hell.* 7.1, 39). As he sees it, this could be an accidental agreement since the same subjects are being discussed in the same language; but the presence of the Spartan messenger Demoteles in the same chapter makes one wonder whether the writer (or at least the author of the addition in Josephus) could have borrowed from Xenophon.[50] Such parallels, however, could be explained in the opposite way: they may demonstrate that Josephus had a reliable source for his final sentence, a source that expressed Spartan *realia* of the time.

(2) The king and the high priest in question: As indicated above, it seems rather likely, if the Spartan letter is authentic (see below), that the writer and addressee are Areus I of Sparta (309–265 BCE) and Onias I, the successor of Jaddua and first high priest of the Hellenistic age. There should be no disputing that the Areus of the epistle is Areus I to whom Diodorus (*Library of History* 20.29) assigns a reign of forty-four years. As noted above, the only other Areus among Spartan kings was Areus II who, according to Pausanias (*Description of Greece* 3.6, 6) died at the tender age of eight years after a short reign (in 254 BCE). No other Spartan king had a name that would have been easily confusable with *Areus.* The obvious implication is that the king of the letter was Areus I, and this fact sets the chronological limits for the correspondence between 309 and 265 BCE.

There has been far more dispute about the identity of the high priest. Three men named Onias served as high priest: Onias I at the beginning of the Hellenistic age; Onias II at a later point in the third century, although exactly when has also been a matter of debate; and Onias III, whose tenure as high priest ended in 175 BCE. Onias III lived too late to be a serious candidate, although he is the one Josephus thought was the addressee of the letter.[51] Each

Greek to yield the form of the text that we possess. See, for example, Eduard Meyer, *Ursprung und Anfänge des Christentums,* 3 vols. (Stuttgart: Gotta'sche, 1921), 2.30; and Michael S. Ginsburg, "Sparta and Judaea," *CP* 29 (1934): 122.

49. For references, see Marcus, *Josephus* 7, 115 n. i.

50. Cardauns, "Juden und Spartaner," 319.

51. See Marcus, *Josephus* 7, 114–15 n. e. Lester Grabbe incorrectly writes that *Josephus* located the letter in the time of Onias I (*Judaism from Cyrus to Hadrian,* vol. 1: *The Persian and Greek Periods* [Minneapolis: Fortress Press, 1992], 264).

of the other two high priests named Onias has, however, found significant support among scholars, although all are forced to admit that our chronological data for the high-priestly succession in the third century are too limited to permit certainty in the matter.

Onias I: It would be simple to infer from Areus I's dates that the high priest must have been Onias I who was probably in office during at least the early years of the monarch's reign, and this is precisely the conclusion that most scholars have drawn.[52] As the successor of Jaddua who, according to Josephus, was dead by the time Alexander the Great died, Onias I served during the last decades of the fourth century and perhaps into the first decade or two of the third century, that is, during the first years of Areus I as king of Sparta. In fact, if he was the recipient of the letter, we would have evidence that Onias I was high priest until at least 309 BCE and almost certainly for some time after this.

Onias II: It may seem from the little our sources disclose that Onias II would have been in office later than the time of Areus I. Uncertainty arises in this connection from the fact that Josephus may have confused two individuals and thus disturbed the chronology. Onias II was the son of Simon I, Onias I's successor. Nevertheless, he did not assume the office until two older relatives had served terms as high priest: Simon's brother Eleazar, the high priest of the *Letter of Aristeas*, and "his uncle Manasses" (*Ant.* 12.4, 1 [§157]). Elsewhere Josephus indicates that when Simon I died, Onias was too young to become high priest (he refers to him as a νήπιον, "infant," in *Ant.* 12.2, 5 [§44], though the term can refer to someone older than an infant). Eleazar's term in office may not have been long, if youth was the reason why Onias II did not take over even after his death (there are, of course, other possibilities). Josephus then mentions Onias II in connection with a number of political events. For example, when the high priest "did not render on behalf of the people the tribute of twenty talents of silver which his fathers had paid to the kings out of their own revenues, he aroused the anger of King Ptolemy" (*Ant.* 12.4, 1 [§158]). If we consult the context in which this statement occurs, we learn that the Ptolemy here is a contemporary of Antiochus III (223–187 BCE);[53] he would have to be, therefore, Ptolemy III Euergetes (246–221), Ptolemy IV

---

52. See for example, Marcus, *Josephus* 7, 114–15 n. e; Schürer, *History of the Jewish People*, 1.185 n. 33; F.-M. Abel and Jean Starcky, *Les livres des Maccabées*, 3rd ed. (Paris: Cerf, 1961), 183 n. a; John Christopher Dancy, *A Commentary on I Maccabees*, BTT (Oxford: Blackwell, 1954), 166; Bickermann, "Makkabäerbücher," in *PW* 14.786; Cardauns, "Juden und Spartaner," 318; Ginsburg, "Sparta and Judaea," 119; and many others.

53. Compare *Ant.* 12.3, 4 (§153) with 12.4, 1 (§154). But, see the treatment below of the Tobiad Romance for the problems of chronology at this point.

Philopator (221–203), or Ptolemy V Epiphanes (203–181). The short time that their reigns overlapped makes Ptolemy III a less likely candidate for being Josephus's Ptolemy, but each of the other two ruled contemporaneously with Antiochus III for more than fifteen years.

Before dismissing Ptolemy III, however, we should study the case made by M. Stern that he is indeed the king whom Josephus connects with Onias II.[54] He observes that Onias's refusal to pay tribute is associated with the events of the Third Syrian War (246–241 BCE). Moreover, Josephus says that by this time Onias was an elderly man (12.4, 3 [§172]: διὰ τὸ γῆρας = "because of his age"; note τοὺς πρεσβύτας = "old people" in the next sentence). Since Onias was too young to succeed his father when he died and as his uncle Eleazar was high priest early in Ptolemy II Philadelphus's reign,[55] Onias may have become high priest in about 270 BCE—a reasonable date if he were an elderly man by the 240s. Areus's letter cannot be later than 265 BCE (the date of his death after a defeat at the hands of Antigonus). Thus, Onias II could have received the letter which would have been written very late in Areus's reign. Stern adds that there are problems with identifying the high priest of the letter with Onias I: for reasons of form and content, it is difficult to believe that the letter was written in about 300. If it had been, we would have expected the name of the second Spartan king to be mentioned; also, early in Areus I's reign the international relations of the nation were not yet so comprehensive as they were to become toward the end of his years as monarch.[56]

Goldstein also thinks that Onias II is more likely to have been the recipient of the letter. He highlights the fact that only later in his reign did Areus act in the autocratic manner that the letter evidences by its failure to mention the ephors of Sparta. If the king did write to the high priest in his latter years, Onias II is a strong candidate for being the addressee.[57]

It is a pity that Josephus is nearly the only source of information for this point. The chronology of Onias II is intertwined with that of Joseph the Tobiad (Onias's nephew), and it is well known that Josephus's dates for this Joseph cause major chronological problems. Although it is clear from his narrative that Josephus places him in the time of Ptolemy V (203 to 181–180 BCE), many scholars maintain that his rise to prominence occurred during the reign of Ptolemy III (see below for an analysis of the Tobiad Romance and its chronology).

---

54. For this paragraph, see his *The Documents*, 114–15.

55. He infers the latter point from various references in the *Letter of Aristeas*, such as the mention of Demetrius of Phaleron.

56. M. Stern defends the same position in "Relations between Sparta and the Jews," 65–68.

57. *I Maccabees*, 455–56.

Despite the learned apologies for Onias II as recipient of the Spartan letter, he is less likely than Onias I, although uncertainty remains since Josephus's chronology is in places difficult for the time of Onias II. Below, a case will be made that the Tobiad Romance relates events that began during Ptolemy III's reign (246–221 BCE), but there is no evidence that Onias II was in the high-priestly office before the time of the third Ptolemy. Hence, as far as we can now see, he probably served as pontiff at too late a time to be a contemporary of Areus I. This means that the only remaining Onias to whom the Spartan king may have written is Onias I. But, all of these issues would be irrelevant if the letter itself is a forgery and not an authentic Spartan document.

(3) Authenticity: Here, too, opinion is divided. A number of the leading authorities have emphatically denied that the letter from Areus to Onias is authentic. Adolf Büchler wrote that Areus's writing to Onias was without a doubt a forgery.[58]

The specific objections to the authenticity of the Spartan letter may be summarized under several headings.

1. The letter lacks references to two entities that would be expected in a formal letter from Sparta: mention of the second king and the ephors (the five annual leaders of the Spartans). At the beginning of the letter, Areus mentions himself alone. It is for this reason that Bickermann assigns it to the first quarter of the second century when Sparta no longer had ephors.[59]

2. Some experts—such as Bickermann—have found it incredible that a Spartan king living in about 300 BCE (his understanding of the time presupposed by the letter) would have sought out the friendship of an inconsequential barbarian nation[60] or would have claimed common ancestry from the Jewish patriarch Abraham.[61]

3. As noted above, the technical details found at the end of the Josephan version of the letter closely resemble data found elsewhere in Spartan correspondence and may have been lifted from Xenophon.

---

58. *Die Tobiaden und die Oniaden im II. Makkabäerbuche und in der verwandten jüdisch-hellenistischen Litteratur: Untersuchungen zur Geschichte der Juden von 220–160 und zur jüdisch-hellenistischen Litteratur* (Vienna: Hölder, 1899; reprinted: Hildesheim: Olms, 1975), 127–28.

59. "Makkabäerbücher," in *PW* 14.786; see also Dancy, *A Commentary on I Maccabees*, 167.

60. "Makkabäerbücher," in *PW* 14.786. Compare also Cardauns, "Juden und Spartaner," 318, 321.

61. Compare Dancy, *A Commentary on I Maccabees*, 167; and Cardauns, "Juden und Spartaner," 318. The claim of common descent from Abraham is one of the two elements (besides a lack of Greek expressions in the letter) that led M. Stern to consider it inauthentic ("Relations between Sparta and the Jews," 66).

4. The document does not express concrete proposals for an alliance, contrary to what 1 Macc 12:8 asserts.[62]

5. A minor point that is recognized as weak is that the letter has a Hebraic ring to it—something one would not expect in a letter from a Spartan king. Cardauns mentions the following expressions: γράφοντες ἡμῖν περὶ τῆς εἰρήνης ὑμῶν (1 Macc 12:22) and τὰ κτήνη ὑμῶν καὶ ἡ ὕπαρξις ὑμῶν ἡμῖν ἐστιν (v. 23).[63] Furthermore, as Dancy has observed, Sparta was an agricultural community, not one that practiced animal husbandry. Josephus sensed the inappropriateness of the term τὰ κτήνη and dropped it from his version of the letter.[64]

The three last points may be readily dismissed. The third objection is a possibility but, as mentioned earlier, it may point rather to the authenticity of the details, not to borrowing of them by Josephus. The fourth criticism says nothing about the document itself, only about the context and interpretation within which 1 Maccabees places it, and the fifth may be a product of the complicated textual history through which the document passed before achieving the form it has in 1 Maccabees (Greek to Hebrew to Greek). That a Hebraic ring sounds from the text may be explained from the fact that the Greek of 1 Maccabees is a rendering of a Hebrew base. The other two objections are more substantial and should, therefore, be handled at greater length. Both of these points can be countered as part of an argument that the letter may be a genuine missive from Areus I to Onias I at some point in the first third of the third century BCE.

1. The missing ephors and second king: Omission of such items should be telling because they are formal matters that could easily be overlooked by a forger. Stern and Goldstein in particular have tried to cope with this problem. Stern notes that Areus I was not a normal king. He was the first Spartan monarch to mint silver coins bearing his name; moreover, his political and military successes allowed him to drive out Archidamus, the second king. Stern points to Chremonides's Decree, a document resulting from the treaty between Athens and Sparta. The agreement was ratified near the end of Areus's reign, and it emphasizes Areus without mentioning a second king. In the same document, the ephors have a limited role. In other words, failure to mention the ephors and second king would mesh with his autocratic policy. Stern adds that the letter in 1 Maccabees and *Antiquities* is itself unusual, just

---

62. See, for example, Cardauns, "Juden und Spartaner," 318.
63. Ibid.
64. Dancy, *A Commentary on I Maccabees*, 167.

as the king himself was. It does not deal with relations between the king of
Sparta and the overlord of Judah (the Ptolemaic king in this case). It "is a
friendly letter from the king of distant Sparta to the leading personage of
Judah."[65] Goldstein, too, emphasizes that the Areus who comes to expression
in the letter is the Areus known from other sources, a monarch who did indeed
act independently of the ephors. Also, the "period in the second century B.C.E.
during which there were no ephors was probably too short to lead even an
ignorant Jew to omit mention of the ephors in a letter forged in the name of a
third-century king."[66] Here, it is interesting to adduce the view of a historian
of Sparta. W. G. Forrest comments on the order of precedence "King Areus
and the Lacedaemonians" found in the Athenian decree of alliance before the
Chremonidean War. He notes that it was an order "which the coinage had
already established. There is a story, often doubted, of diplomatic contact
between the Spartans and the Jews in Areus' reign. Politically such a rap-
prochement is likely enough (the Jews were with Ptolemy at the time) but a
stronger argument for the truth of the tale is the opening of the letter quoted
in First Maccabees, 'Areus King of the Spartans to. . . .'"[67]

Areus I clearly achieved a lofty status in Greek politics at the time. The
sources, after noting that he was a child when selected as king in 309 BCE, are
silent about him until 281–280 when Sparta led a movement to free Greece
from the control of Antigonus Gonatas of Macedon. There has been some disagreement about what part he may have played in the negotiations that preceded the movement. "All that is known for certain concerns his military role:
he was in command of the war, his attack against the Aetolians ended in an
early defeat, and his forces retreated to the Peloponnese after suffering heavy
losses."[68] Thus, at this time (280 BCE) he was a major force in Greek politics
and was apparently engaged in forming alliances. Areus may have found it easier to assert himself in Sparta because the other royal house produced two of
the most inept or at least most poorly attested monarchs in its history: Archi-

---

65. *The Documents*, 114; compare "Relations between Sparta and the Jews," 65–66.

66. *I Maccabees*, 456. This point is directed against Bickermann, who dated the letter to that
short period precisely because the ephors did not appear in it.

67. W. G. Forrest, *A History of Sparta 950–192 B.C.*, Norton Library (New York: Norton,
1968), 142. See also Schüller, "Some Problems Connected with the Supposed Common Ancestry
of Jews and Spartans," 265–66.

68. Ephraim David, *Sparta between Empire and Revolution (404–243 B.C.): Internal Problems and Their Impact on Contemporary Greek Consciousness,* Monographs in Classical Studies
(New York: Arno, 1981), 126. The present survey of high (low) points in Areus's career is based
on David's analysis on pp. 117–41. The Aetolians who are mentioned in the words quoted above
were allies of Antigonus and the first object of Areus's attack.

damus IV receives no mention in the sources after his defeat at the hands of Demetrius in 294 BCE; and about his successor Eudamidas II they are silent.[69] The next notable set of events in Areus's life occurred in 272 BCE when Pyrrhus, the king of Epirus, attacked Sparta in the hope of putting Areus's longtime rival Cleomynes on the throne (Areus had been chosen over him for the kingship in 309 BCE). Areus and his son Acrotatus were instrumental in thwarting Pyrrhus's plan.

What was perhaps the greatest event in his career also led to his death. His prestige and that of his house grew because of what Areus and Acrotatus had done in 272 BCE, and Cleomynes, who by this time was in exile, was no longer a factor. Areus appears to have introduced customs practiced by other Hellenistic rulers at this time. He minted the first coins in Sparta, and some of them included engravings of his head (with a crown) and his name. Various statues were set up in his honor, and they contained inscriptions that lauded his achievements. Even Ptolemy II of Egypt erected a statue for him in Olympia. In 266 BCE, Areus attained his greatest prominence, when Sparta headed an alliance against Macedonia—an alliance that included a number of Greek cities such as Athens and enjoyed the backing of Ptolemy II. The ties at this time between Sparta and Egypt provide the setting, according to David, for the correspondence with Onias. Since Judah was within the Ptolemaic empire in the third century, an alliance with Egypt may well have had repercussions for Judah. David recognizes that the correspondence between Areus and Onias has been disputed, but concludes: "The tradition on these diplomatic contacts can offer additional evidence of Areus' role as the architect of his country's foreign policy during these years."[70]

Chremonides's Decree (named after the Athenian who proposed it) is often cited as the best evidence for Areus's prominence. The decree is a document that records the agreements between the allies in 266–265 BCE; in effect it started the war against Antigonus. It stresses the union of Athens, Sparta, and Ptolemy against Antigonus. Four times it uses the phrase "the Lacedaemonians and Areus," that is, Areus is the only Spartan named, and no other officials are listed. Nevertheless, it is true that the same document refers to "the Lacedaemonians and the Kings of the Lacedaemonians," and, although the text is damaged in each case, it probably also mentions the ephors with Areus as the objects of praise.[71] Areus led the coalition into battle but met his death outside Corinth in 265 BCE.

---

69. Ibid., 132, 234 n. 58.

70. Ibid., 136.

71. The text of the decree is in Hatto H. Schmitt, ed., *Die Staatsverträge des Altertums*, vol. 3: *Die Verträge der griechisch-römischen Welt von 338 bis 200 v. Chr.* (Munich: Beck, 1969), 476;

Although Areus reached the pinnacle of his influence and fame after 272 BCE, he was evidently a noteworthy king in Greece for some years before this, certainly by 281–280. David thinks that the correspondence with Onias would fit in the latest part of his reign, but, if so, the date would again raise in acute form the problem of a long high-priestly reign. If, as Josephus writes, Onias was in office before 323 BCE (the death of Alexander), by 281 he would have served as high priest for forty-two to forty-three years. If the letter were postponed to the period 272–265 BCE, his tenure would have extended more than fifty years. This is not impossible, but clearly an earlier date would be more plausible.[72] The important conclusion is that, at any of these times, it is conceivable that Areus would have dispatched a document such as the letter in 1 Maccabees and *Antiquities*; it would occasion no surprise if he failed to mention the second king, and it would hardly be shocking if he omitted the ephors.

2. A Spartan king seeking out a barbarian nation and asserting a common ancestry from Abraham: This may be an unlikely set of circumstances, but perhaps the procedure was not so uncommon. We might expect the initiative to lie with the barbarian people, not with the Greeks. However, as Moses Hadas remarks: "It was the Greeks themselves who set up the precedent; their ancient genealogies . . . made a place for the founders of various eastern nations, including Egypt and Persia, and in the historical period they were not above inventing such genealogies when it suited their political ambitions."[73] It would be leaving the realm of what a historian can demonstrate to say, as Bickermann did, that it is *inconceivable* that this would have happened in about 300 BCE.

The more interesting issue here is not so much whether Sparta reached out to the Jews but their supposed common ancestry from Abraham. The

---

an English translation is in Roger S. Bagnall and Peter Derow, *Greek Historical Documents: The Hellenistic Period,* SBLSBS 16 (Chico, Calif.: Scholars, 1981), 39–41. Ginsburg also considers the letter believable within the context of Sparta's role in international relations during Areus's time ("Sparta and Judaea," 119–21). See, too, Schüller, "Some Problems Connected with the Supposed Common Ancestry of Jews and Spartans," 259, 264. After listing six examples of Spartan foreign policy during Areus I's reign pertinent to the topic, Schüller writes: "All these facts may serve as illustrations of the tendency in Spartan foreign policy in Areus's days to establish friendly relations with the different Hellenistic monarchies in the Eastern Mediterranean; closer connections with Judea, moreover, as a form of opposition to Antigonus I and Demetrius I, seem to fit only too well into this general picture" (264).

72. This point has, of course, figured as an argument in favor of identifying the high priest as Onias II.

73. *Hellenistic Culture: Fusion and Diffusion* (Morningside Heights, N.Y.: Columbia Univ. Press, 1959), 84. Hadas thinks that the letter from Areus to Onias is spurious but one that was based on a document that did mention that the Spartans and Jews were related (86–87). For some examples of creative genealogical relations in the Hellenistic period, see F.-M. Abel, *Les livres des Maccabées,* EBib (Paris: Gabalda, 1949), 233.

letter from Areus claims: "It has been found in writing concerning the Spartans and the Jews that they are brothers and are of the family of Abraham" (1 Macc 12:21). The issue is not whether there was such a genealogical relation between the two peoples but whether there is good reason for believing that a Spartan king might make such an assertion in the early third century BCE. On this point, scholars have assembled an intriguing set of texts illustrating such a claim and possibly even revealing why someone first made the association.

At a later time, a similar phenomenon is attested. In *Antiquities* 14, Josephus adduces a series of decrees from various cities recognizing Jewish rights and dealing with other matters. Among them is a decree from the city of Pergamum, generally thought to date from the time of John Hyrcanus I (134–104 BCE).[74] The closing words of the document urge Hyrcanus

> to preserve and increase his friendship with us and always be responsible for some act of good in the knowledge that he will receive a fitting recompense, and also remembering that in the time of Abraham, who was the father of all Hebrews, our ancestors were their friends, as we find in the public records. (§255)

In the last third of the second century BCE, the citizenry of Pergamum, a city located a few miles from the eastern coast of the Aegean Sea, found an ancient point of contact between their ancestors and Abraham. They did not claim that they were actually related through him, only that there was friendship between them at that distant time. In other words, some one hundred fifty years later than the Areus-Onias correspondence, a Greek city claimed a common past with the Jews.

If Areus I did in fact maintain that the Spartans had found written somewhere that the two peoples were related, what might have been his source of information for the assertion? It will be recalled that Hecateus of Abdera, who, according to Plutarch (*Lycurgus* 20.3), visited Sparta at the time of Archidamus, the coruler with Areus I,[75] is credited with writing a book *On Abraham and the Egyptians*.[76] Whether he actually composed a work about Abraham is doubtful, but in one of his genuine compositions, *On the Egyptians*, he wrote

---

74. For the evidence that Hyrcanus I, not Hyrcanus II (the ruler in whose time Josephus sets it), is the one named in the decree, see the notes to *Ant.* 14.10, 22 (§§247–55) in Marcus, *Josephus* 7.

75. Compare Goldstein, *I Maccabees*, 458.

76. See M. Stern, *Greek and Latin Authors*, 1.22. Josephus mentions this work at *Ant.* 1.7, 2 (§159). As noted above, Stern considers the book about Abraham "with almost absolute certainty, to be a product of Jewish religious propaganda" (1.22). Schürer, too, was almost certain about this (*History of the Jewish People*, 1.674).

about a time when a pestilence arose in Egypt. Since the natives believed the cause was the religious practices of foreigners in Egypt, they expelled them.

> At once, therefore, the aliens were driven from the country, and the most outstanding and active among them banded together and, as some say, were cast ashore in Greece and certain other regions; their leaders were notable men, chief among them being Danaus and Cadmus. But the greater number were driven into what is now called Judaea, which is not far distant from Egypt and was at that time utterly uninhabited. [77]

The name Danaus (Δαναός) is particularly interesting because he was regarded as the ancestor of the Danoi who lived in the Peloponnesus and who produced both dynasties of Spartan kings.[78] Hecateus thus paired the ancestors of the Spartans and Jews as two groups who were expelled from Egypt at the same time (the time of Moses) and under the same circumstances. Why would he do this?

It may be that Hecateus's association of the peoples led from Egypt by Danaus and Cadmus on the one hand and Moses on the other arose in some fashion from a reading of Gen 25:2-3, the list of the six sons born to Keturah and Abraham. The lists vary somewhat from version to version, but the second son of the marriage was Jokshan, who became the father of Sheba and Dedan (דדן; Δαιδαν). The name *Dedan* resembles that of Danaus to some extent; moreover the name of his son—Leummim—was translated in *Tg. Onq.* Gen 10:5 as נגון, a term for the islands inhabited by Gentiles descended from Japheth, that is, the Greeks.[79] It is possible that Hecateus had heard of an equation of the names Danaus and Dedan and that he was the source behind Areus's claim that the two peoples shared Abraham as an ancestor.[80]

A plausible case can be created, then, for the conclusion that Areus I sent a letter to Onias I (with Onias II being possible but less likely). If this in fact happened, then we have evidence for what appears to have been a significant event in the high priesthood of a man who is otherwise mentioned only briefly by Josephus and probably also (see the previous chapter) on a coin stamped

---

77. The translation is from M. Stern, *Greek and Latin Authors*, 1.27–28.

78. Goldstein, *I Maccabees*, 458; Ginsburg, "Sparta and Judaea," 120–21.

79. Goldstein, *I Maccabees*, 458.

80. If Hecateus was Areus's source of information about Abraham and the Jews, then there is no need to posit the existence of a Jewish community in Sparta to explain the reference. See Schüller, "Some Problems Connected with the Supposed Common Ancestry of Jews and Spartans," 266–67. See also 2 Macc 5:9 for a later reference to kinship between the Spartans and the Jews.

with the words "Yohanan the priest." That a king of a Hellenistic city-state, and Sparta at that, would write to the Jewish high priest shows that the high priest was considered the leading governmental official in Jerusalem at the time. The high priest was the one with whom a foreign head of state would correspond, and he mentions no other ruler or ruling body.[81]

8. Simon I

Josephus indicates that, at the death of Onias I, the normal course of hereditary succession, which seems to have been followed since the reign of Joshua at the beginning of the Second-Temple period, continued for another generation. The historian mentions the next high priest Simon in his paraphrase of the *Letter of Aristeas*. When Demetrius of Phalerum proposed that the Jewish books regarding their Law be translated into Greek and placed in the king's famous library (*Ant.* 12.2, 1 [§§12–15]), Ptolemy II Philadelphus accepted his librarian's advice and "wrote to the high priest of the Jews [τῷ τῶν Ἰουδαίων ἀρχιερεῖ] that this might be done" (§16). Following Aristeas's successful petition that the king release the Jewish slaves brought to Egypt by his father Ptolemy I (and those who came before and after him), Demetrius prepared a formal document embodying his proposal. It included the words: "If, then, O King, it be your pleasure, write to the high priest of the Jews [the same Greek phrase as above] to send six elders from each tribe who are most versed in their laws, in order that when we have learned from them the clear and consistent meaning of these and obtained an accurate translation, we may have a collection of these books which shall be worthy of their contents and of your design" (12.2, 4 [§39]). In the next paragraph, Josephus finally names the high priest of the Jews. "The king ordered a letter to be written about these matters to Eleazar, the high priest of the Jews, informing him, at the same time, of the release of the Jewish slaves in their country" (12.2, 5 [§40]). It may be that the king also sent one hundred talents to the high priest[82] to cover costs of the sacrificial cult (§41). Aristeas then tells Philocrates, the addressee of his composition, that he will reproduce "the letter written to the high priest Eleazar, who obtained this office in the following way. On the death of the high priest Onias, he was succeeded by his son Simon, who was surnamed the Just because of both his piety toward God and his benevolence

---

81. Rooke fails to deal with the Areus-Onias letter in *Zadok's Heirs*.

82. There is a text-critical problem here: some manuscripts read τῷ ἱερεῖ while others have τῷ ἱερῷ (= to the temple). See Marcus, *Josephus* 7, 22–23.

to his countrymen. But as he, when he died, left an infant son named Onias . . ." (12.2, 5 [§§42–43]). Nothing more is said about this Simon in any other source for the period. However, the simple fact that Josephus calls him "the Just" has spawned a longstanding debate about whether other references to someone styled *Simon the Just* are also to this otherwise obscure high priest of the early Hellenistic period or to some other worthy.[83]

Josephus himself leaves no doubt about his identity: he was the first Simon who succeeded his father Onias (= son of the biblical Jaddua) in the early years of the Ptolemaic period. However, almost all scholars today reject the historian's unambiguous statement and prefer, on the basis of other sources, to identify Simon the Just as Simon II—a high priest who held office about one century later. The dispute centers about the ways in which one evaluates texts for their historical value. In the following paragraphs, the question of the identity of Simon the Just will be addressed. In the first part, the relevant evidence is collected; in the second the standard scholarly handling of these sources—that is, the case formulated by G. F. Moore—is summarized; and in the third an indirect case for considering Simon I to be Simon the Just is advanced.

The sources: The several texts that mention Simon the Just may be divided into two categories: those that imply that he lived very early in the Hellenistic period (some time after 300 BCE), and those that suggest that he lived around the end of the third century (not far from 200 BCE).

1. The sources entailing that a high priest from earlier in the third century BCE was Simon the Just include Josephus and rabbinic texts.

a) Josephus (from 37 to about 100 CE): In *Antiquities,* Josephus mentions this Simon (= Σίμων, the Greek form of Hebrew שמעון) in two places. The first (12.2, 5 [§§43–44]) is set, as we have seen just above, in the context of the story that the historian borrows from the *Letter of Aristeas,* that is, in the time of Ptolemy II Philadelphus (283–246 BCE). The Jewish high priest who plays a most prominent role in that tale is named Eleazar, and Josephus had to explain to his readers how he had obtained the office. Here Josephus mentions him as little more than a name in the priestly genealogy and describes him as exceedingly virtuous but says nothing specific about what he did to merit the epithet ὁ δίκαιος.

---

83. The following treatment of the issue is a revised version of James VanderKam, "Simon the Just: Simon I or Simon II?" in *Pomegranates and Golden Bells: Studies in Biblical, Jewish, and Near Eastern Ritual, Law, and Literature in Honor of Jacob Milgrom,* ed. D. Wright, D. N. Freedman, and A. Hurvitz (Winona Lake, Ind.: Eisenbrauns, 1995), 303–18.

The only other context in which he refers to this Simon is in *Ant.* 12.4, 1 (§§157–58), by which point his narrative has perhaps reached the reign of Ptolemy IV Philopator (221–203 BCE)[84] and Antiochus III (223–187 BCE). The Jewish high priest at the time was another Onias (§156), whose lineage Josephus explains thus: "For, when Eleazar [of the *Letter of Aristeas*] died, his uncle Manasses took over the high priesthood, and after he departed this life, the office came to Onias, who was a son of Simon, called the Just [τοῦ δικαίου κληθέντος]. And Simon was a brother of Eleazar, as I have said before." Here Josephus merely extends the genealogy he had begun in *Ant.* 12.2, 5 (§§43–44) and implies again that Simon the Just had lived earlier in the third century.

b) Two rabbinic texts offer variant but closely related accounts that make Simon the Just a contemporary of Alexander the Great; in fact, the two are said to have met and conversed with one another.

1) Scholion to *Megillat Ta'anit* for Kislev 21:[85]

This is the day when the Cuthim (Samaritans) asked Alexander of Macedon (for permission to destroy) our temple, saying to him, "Give us five *kurs* of land on Mount Moriah." These he gave to them. But when they came, the inhabitants of Jerusalem went out and beat them off with sticks. They then informed Simon the Just of this. He thereupon put on his priestly garments and wrapped himself in his priestly garments [*sic*] and went out, accompanied by the nobles of Jerusalem and a thousand counsellors [*bouleutai*] dressed in white and young priests who made the sacred instruments resound. As they marched through the hills, the Macedonians saw their lighted torches, and when the king asked what this meant, the informers replied, "These are the Jews who have rebelled against you." When they arrived at Antipatris, the sun was shining, and when they came to the first station, the Macedonians asked them, "Who are you?" The Jews replied, "We are the people of Jerusalem, who have come to greet the king." But when Alexander of Macedon saw Simon the Just, he descended from his chariot and prostrated himself before him. Thereupon his men exclaimed, "Do you prostrate yourself before this

---

84. For the textual problem regarding which Ptolemy is intended in §158, see below and the note in Marcus, *Josephus* 7, 82–83 n. c. Some manuscripts identify him as "Ptolemy Euergetes who was the father of Philopator"—that is, Ptolemy III Euergetes (246–221 BCE).

85. The English translation is cited from "Appendix C: Alexander the Great and the Jews" in Marcus, *Josephus*, vol. 6: *Jewish Antiquities Books 9–11*, LCL (Cambridge: Harvard Univ. Press, 1937), 517–18. The text itself may be found in H. Lichtenstein, "Die Fastenrolle: Eine Untersuchung zur jüdisch-hellenistischen Geschichte," *HUCA* 8-9 (1931–32): 339–40.

man who is only a mortal?" And he replied, "I see his image whenever I go to war and am victorious." Then the king asked him, "What do you wish?" The priest replied, "The gentiles have deceived you concerning the temple in which we pray for the welfare of your reign, and you have given it to them." The king then asked, "Who deceived me?" Simon answered, "It was these Cuthim who stand before you." Thereupon Alexander said, "They are herewith given into your hands." The Jews then pierced the heels of the Cuthim and tied them to the tails of their horses and dragged them over thorns and briers until they came to Mount Gerizim. And when they came to Mount Gerizim, they ploughed it under and sowed it with vetch, just as the Cuthim had intended to do to our temple. And the day on which they did this was made a festival.

2) *b. Yoma* 69a: The same story (with minor variations) appears here amid a discussion of whether priestly garments might be worn outside the temple area. The Talmud attaches the account to Tebet 25, the day of Mount Gerizim.[86]

It is the day on which the Cutheans demanded the House of our God from Alexander the Macedonian so as to destroy it, and he had given them the permission, whereupon some people came and informed Simeon the Just. What did the latter do? He put on his priestly garments, robed himself in priestly garments, some of the noblemen of Israel went with him carrying fiery torches in their hands, they walked all night, some walking on one side and others on the other side, until the dawn rose. When the dawn rose he [Alexander] said to them: Who are these [the Samaritans]?[87] They answered: The Jews who rebelled against you. As he reached Antipatris, the sun having shone forth, they met. When he saw Simeon the Just, he descended from his carriage and bowed down before him. They said to him: A great king like yourself should bow down before this Jew? He answered: His image it is which wins for me in all my battles. He said to them: What have you come for? They said: Is it possible that star-worshippers should mislead you to destroy the House wherein prayers are said for you and your kingdom that it be never destroyed!

---

86. The translation is that of L. Jung, *Yoma,* The Babylonian Talmud, ed. I. Epstein, 2/5 (London: Soncino, 1938).

87. The translator's (or editor's) identification of the referent here is obviously wrong as the sequel and parallel show. The king is asking about the identity of the Jewish group who had just arrived, not about the Samaritans.

He said to them: Who are these? They said to him: These are the Cutheans who stand before you. He said: They are delivered into your hand. At once they perforated their heels, tied them to the tails of their horses and dragged them over thorns and thistles, until they came to Mount Gerizim, which they ploughed and planted with vetch, even as they had planned to do with the House of God. And that day they made a festive day.

The story is used to demonstrate that Simon the Just, a high priest, had worn his priestly garments far outside the temple precincts—even as far away as Antipatris.

2. Several other texts are thought to imply that Simon the Just was a high priest from about 200 BCE.

a) Sirach 50:1-21: In these verses, Ben Sira lauds a high priest named Simon for repairing the temple, fortifying the city, and officiating splendidly during a festival. Several key excerpts from the panegyric should be cited.

> The leader of his brothers and
>   the pride of his people
> was the high priest, Simon son of Onias,
> who in his life repaired the house,
>   and in his time fortified the temple.
> He laid the foundations for the high double walls,
>   the high retaining walls for the temple enclosure.
> In his days a water cistern was dug,
>   a reservoir like the sea in circumference.
> He considered how to save his people from ruin,
>   and fortified the city against siege.
> How glorious he was, surrounded by the people,
>   as he came out of the house of the curtain.
> Like the morning star among the clouds,
>   like the full moon at the festal season; . . . (vv. 1-6)

As he describes the liturgical acts that Simon performed, the poet writes with impressive detail, as in verses 14-15:

> Finishing the service at the altars,
>   and arranging the offering to the Most High, the Almighty,
> he held out his hand for the cup
>   and poured a drink-offering of the blood of the grape;
> he poured it out at the foot of the altar,
>   a pleasing odor to the Most High, the king of all.

Or in verses 20-21:

> Then Simon came down and raised his hands
>   over the whole congregation of Israelites,
> to pronounce the blessing of the Lord with his lips,
>   and to glory in his name;
> and they bowed down in worship a second time,
>   to receive the blessing from the Most High.

Commentators have argued from the vivid detail found in the passage that Jesus ben Sira had actually witnessed such a scene; as a result, this Simon was contemporary with ben Sira who lived in the first part of the second century BCE. Also, the repairs that he made are taken to be work necessitated by damage done during the war between Antoichus III and Ptolemy V. It should be noted that the high priest is not called "Simon the Just" in Sirach 50; he is simply Simon son of Onias (for a fuller treatment of this important passage see below).

b) *b. Menaḥ.* 109b contains variant forms of a story about the sons of Simon the Just, one of whom (Onias) founded the temple at Leontopolis in Egypt. The stories figure at the point where *m. Menaḥ.* 13:10, which deals with the validity of sacrifices pledged to be offered at the Leontopolis temple, is under discussion.

Rabbi Meir (second century CE) related a story to the effect that, after Simon the Just had learned of his imminent death and had explained how he had discovered this fact, the following occurred:[88]

> In the hour of his departure [from this life], he said to them, "My son Onias shall assume the office [of high priest] after me." His brother Shime'i, who was two years and a half older than he, was jealous of him and said to him, "Come and I will teach you the order of the Temple service". He thereupon put upon him a gown, girded him with a girdle, placed him near the altar, and said to his brethren the priests, "See what this man promised his beloved [his wife], and has now fulfilled: 'On the day in which I will assume the office of High Priest I will put on your gown and gird myself with your girdle'." At this his brethren the priests sought to kill him. He fled from them but they pursued him. He then went to Alexandria in Egypt, built an altar there, and offered thereon sacrifices in honour of idols.

---

88. The translation is by Eli Cashdan, *Menaḥoth,* The Babylonian Talmud, ed. I. Epstein, 5/2 (London: Soncino, 1948).

In the sequel, Rabbi Judah (ben Ila'i—a contemporary of Meir) counters Meir's version of the story by pointing out that the roles of the two brothers were actually reversed: Shime'i, not Onias, was the victim of the prank. Then, at the point in the story when the priests tried to kill Shime'i, "he explained to them all that had occurred. They thereupon sought to kill Onias; he fled from them but they pursued him. He fled to the King's palace, but they pursued him there; and whoever saw him cried out, There he is, there he is. He thereupon went to Alexandria in Egypt, built an altar there, and offered thereon sacrifices in honour of God" (compare *y. Yoma* 43cd).

c) *m. 'Abot* 1:2 (with 1:3-12): "Simeon the Just was of the remnants of the Great Synagogue. He used to say: By three things is the world sustained: by the Law, by the [Temple-]service, and by deeds of loving-kindness."[89] The next paragraphs list the six successors (the last five of which are pairs) of Simon, ending with Hillel and Shammai who lived in the last years BCE and the first CE. Hence, working from them back through the generations to Simon, we would reach about 200 BCE.

Simon the Just is mentioned in several other texts, in which we read about remarkable events that occurred regularly during his forty-year pontificate but not afterwards. For example: "Throughout the forty years that Simeon the Righteous ministered, the lot ['For the Lord'] would always come up in the right hand; from that time on, it would come up now in the right hand, now in the left" (*b. Yoma* 39a). But, as such passages offer no hint about when this Simon lived, they may be left aside for the purposes of the present discussion.

G. F. Moore's evaluation of the sources: The most influential study regarding the identity of Simon the Just was published by G. F. Moore in 1927.[90] The frequency with which his essay is still cited favorably on the matter shows that his arguments have carried the day. His analysis of the evidence will now be summarized, with page references to his article given in parentheses. Generally stated, his thesis is that the sources that imply that Simon the Just was Simon II who lived in about 200 BCE are historically more weighty than are those that place him at an earlier time and entail that he was Simon I. Moore wrote that he intended "to examine the testimony about Simeon the Righteous as far as possible by itself, . . . and to show that for the supposed Simon I

---

89. The translation is from Herbert Danby, *The Mishnah* (Oxford: Oxford Univ. Press, 1933), 446.

90. "Simeon the Righteous," in *Jewish Studies in Memory of Israel Abrahams,* ed. G. A. Kohut (New York: Jewish Institute of Religion, 1927), 348–64. Similar materials are found in his *Judaism in the First Centuries of the Christian Era,* 2 vols. (New York: Schocken, 1971 [originally published in 1927, 1930]), 1.34–36 with n. 5.

there is no historical evidence, thus eliminating at least one of the disputed elements in the problem of the Great Synagogue." (p. 349).

First, he highlighted the second group of texts given above, which imply a Simon the Just about 200 BCE. The stories about Simon's two sons make him a contemporary of the Onias who founded the Jewish temple at Leontopolis in Egypt. As the foundation of that temple took place in the first half of the second century BCE (so Josephus, *J.W.* 1.1,1 [§§31–33]; 7.10, 2–4 [§§420–36]), the talmudic stories imply that Simon the Just lived in about 200 BCE; he must, therefore, have been Simon II (pp. 350–53).

Moore attached greater weight to the testimony of Jesus ben Sira. The sage, unlike most Jewish writers of the early Hellenistic age, can be dated rather securely because his translator-grandson mentioned in his Prologue the exact year of his arrival in Egypt (the thirty-eighth year of Ptolemy VIII Euergetes II = 132 BCE), some time after which he rendered his grandfather Jesus's book into the Greek language. If the grandson worked in the last third of the second century, it is likely that his grandfather was active in the first third. Hence, the Hebrew form of the book is usually dated to about 190–180 BCE. Ben Sira wrote a poetic panegyric to the high priest Simon in chapter 50, parts of which were cited above. About it, Moore observed: "The impression which this eulogy makes throughout is that the subject of it was a contemporary of the writer, perhaps recently deceased; and this would probably never have been questioned but for the fact that, according to Josephus in the Antiquities, Simeon the Righteous, with whom Sirach's Simeon was rightly identified, lived at the beginning of the preceding century" (p. 353).

In addition to this general impression left by the poem, Moore thought some lines in it offered a specific chronological connection. The poet relates that Simon restored the temple and the fortifications of Jerusalem (Sir 50:2, 4). He became a builder because of the destruction caused by the war between the Seleucid and Ptolemaic forces in about 200 BCE. For this point, Moore was able to adduce as documentary evidence the letter preserved in *Ant.* 12.3, 3 (§§138–44), in which the Seleucid monarch Antiochus III (223–187 BCE) orders that work on the Jerusalem temple and other construction projects in Jerusalem be performed. The king states about the Jewish nation that had helped him: "we have seen fit on our part to requite them for these acts and to restore their city which has been destroyed by the hazards of war" (*Ant.* 12.3, 3 [§139]). Somewhat later (§141), he adds: "And it is my will that these things [the provisions mentioned in the previous paragraph] be made over to them as I have ordered, and that the work on the temple be completed, including the porticoes and any other part that it may be necessary to build." The correspondence between what is said in Sir 50:2, 4 and the letter of Antiochus, a king whose dates are known, demonstrated to Moore's satisfaction that the Simon of Sir 50:1-21 is the high priest who served in about 200 BCE (pp. 354–55).

The third piece of textual evidence is the list of names given in *m. 'Abot* (see above), where a series of teachers form a connected chain of traditionists. They are:

- Simon the Just
- Antigonos of Socho
- Jose ben Joezer and Jose ben Johanan
- Jehoshua ben Perahiah and Nittai the Arbelite
- Jehuda ben Tabbai and Simeon ben Shetah
- Shemaiah and Abtalion
- Hillel and Shammai

It is possible to relate some of these names to fairly specific dates: a tradition associates Jose ben Joezer with the high priest Alcimus (162–159 BCE) who had him put to death (see 1 Macc 7:16).[91] Simeon ben Shetah was a brother-in-law of Alexander Jannaeus (103–76 BCE), while Shemaiah and Abtalion were active in the early years of Herod's reign.[92] The evidence of the list, Moore concluded, implies a date of about 200 BCE for Simon the Just, the first member in it. He did think that one link was missing from the chain but only one. "This chain of seven links is stretched over a period of nearly two centuries; it obviously could not be made to extend to three, as it must if Simeon the Righteous be put in the times of the first Ptolemy" (p. 356).

As a consequence, Moore maintained that identifying Simon II as Simon the Just was supported by three texts, all of which were inconsistent with ascribing the title to the earlier Simon. Nevertheless, there remained several pieces of contrary evidence to which he next turned his attention. The first—the rabbinic narratives about Simon's meeting with Alexander the Great (above)—he could dismiss fairly easily, or rather turn into additional evidence for Simon II as the Just. He recognized, of course, that the stories were variants of the one that Josephus puts forward as a meeting between the high priest Jaddua and Alexander (*Ant.* 11.8, 4–5 [§§321–39]); but he was also favorably inclined toward Zeitlin's proposal that in the original form of the story, which

---

91. For the texts and analysis of them, see Goldstein, *I Maccabees*, 334–35.

92. References made elsewhere to the various names in the list are given in Danby, *Mishnah*, 446–47; and R. Travers Herford, *The Ethics of the Talmud: Sayings of the Fathers* (New York: Schocken, 1962), 22–32.

lies behind the one in *b. Yoma* 69a, the king was not Alexander but Antiochus
III with whom several details in the account fit more closely (pp. 356–58).[93]

He regarded the way in which *m. 'Abot* 1:2 referred to Simon the Just as a
more potent objection to his general thesis. There, he is termed "of the remnants of the Great Synagogue." Since the sources regularly associate the assembly with the time of the restoration to Jerusalem—the age of Ezra, Nehemiah,
and others—the phrase would seem to indicate an earlier date for Simon the
Just. Apparently for Moore, the well-known ignorance manifested in rabbinic
sources about the true length of the Persian period removed any force from
this argument. The mishnaic association of Simon the Just with the Great Synagogue by no means implied that he must have lived well before 200 BCE (pp.
358–59).

What, then, is one to do with Josephus's overt identification of Simon I as
Simon the Just? In order to assess the value of his statement, Moore studied
Josephus's narratives for the postexilic period to the time of Antiochus IV
(175–164 BCE) and found them quite unimpressive as historical sources. Of
them, he said: "The matter of these stories is palpable fiction, even where the
actors are real persons as in the case of the Tobiads. The external history, of
which the author shows a respectable knowledge, is used solely to locate the
stories in time and give them a historical coloring. The succession of high
priests noted in them serves no other purpose" (p. 361). The two references to
Simon I appear in what were for Moore suspicious circumstances: the first figures in Josephus's introduction to his paraphrase of the *Letter of Aristeas*, and
the second in his preamble to the Tobiad Romance. It is unlikely that the historian's high-priestly list for this period is based on archival sources; there are too
many idiosyncrasies in it, such as his earnest report in *Ant.* 12.9, 7 (§§382–89)
about a later Onias who had three sons—two named Onias—all of whom
became high priests. After highlighting some other peculiarities of Josephus's
high-priestly roster, Moore concluded: "This evidence should suffice to prove
that the fact that Josephus (or his source) in the *Antiquities* attaches the epithet Righteous to a Simon, son of an Onias and father of an Onias, high priest
in the time of the first Ptolemy, instead of to the contemporary of Antiochus
the Great to whom it is given by the rabbinical sources, is a mere confusion of
Simons, and that even the existence of this 'Simon I' is problematical" (p. 364).

A review of the literature quickly reveals that Moore's essay, or at least the
kinds of arguments that he marshaled, has proved singularly convincing.
Today, almost all scholars accept the identification of Simon II as Simon the

---

93. Solomon Zeitlin argued the point in "שמעון הצדיק וכנסת הגדולה," *Ner ma'aravi* 2
(1924): 137–42.

Just—whether those scholars are authors of general reference works or of more specialized studies. Some years after Moore's paper was published, Ralph Marcus briefly surveyed the data and arrived at the same conclusion.[94] We find similar arguments developed by authors of major works about Judaism and Jewish literature of the early Hellenistic period or of commentaries on the Wisdom of Jesus Son of Sirach. Noteworthy examples are Tcherikover,[95] the new Schürer,[96] and Skehan and Di Lella.[97]

Simon the Just as Simon I: Even a cursory glance at Moore's essay should show that, despite the general acceptance it has enjoyed, its argumentation is weak and fundamentally flawed at several points. It is true, of course, that no certainty can be attained regarding a historical question of the kind being discussed here; the sources are simply inadequate for that purpose. Nevertheless, it can be shown that, with the extant data, it is more logical to conclude that Simon I was Simon the Just. The point will be made through a source study that gives rise to inferences that are directly opposed to Moore's conclusions.

First, the rabbinic texts in both sections above (Simon the Just as early third century or about 200 BCE) should be eliminated from consideration since they carry no weight as historical sources. Even if we do not summarily dismiss the two versions of the stories about Simon's sons as fiction, both suffer from acute difficulties. The Tannaitic scholars who are said to have

---

94. "Appendix B: The Date of the High Priest Simon the Just (the Righteous)," in *Josephus* 7, 732–36.

95. *Hellenistic Civilization and the Jews*, 80–81 (see 437 n. 112).

96. *History of the Jewish People*, 2.359–60.

97. Patrick W. Skehan and Alexander Di Lella, *The Wisdom of Ben Sira*, AB 39 (Garden City, N.Y.: Doubleday, 1987), 8–9, 550. The same identification is found in numerous other works. As representatives of the consensus note the following: Joachim Jeremias, *Jerusalem in the Time of Jesus: An Investigation into Economic and Social Conditions during the New Testament Period*, trans. F. H. Cave and C. H. Cave (Philadelphia: Fortress Press, 1975), 149 n. 7 ("In this brilliant essay Moore has proved that Simeon the Righteous lived after 200 BC, and that the alleged Simeon I . . . owes his existence to a duplication by Josephus of the same person"); Hengel, *Judaism and Hellenism*, 1.52, 64, 73, 270–72 (with n. 89 [2.180]), etc.; Louis Finkelstein, "The Men of the Great Synagogue (*circa* 400–170 B.C.E.)," in *The Hellenistic Age*, ed. W. D. Davies and L. Finkelstein, *CHJ* 2 (Cambridge: Cambridge Univ. Press, 1990), 229 (n. 2: "conclusive discussion of the date of Simeon the Just by George F. Moore"), and other writers in the same volume; Morton Smith, *Palestinian Parties and Politics That Shaped the Old Testament*, Lectures on the History of Religions 9 (New York: Columbia Univ. Press, 1971), 186; Walter Franklin Smith, "A Study of the Zadokite High Priesthood within the Graeco-Roman Age: From Simeon the Just to the High Priests Appointed by Herod the Great" (Ph.D. diss., Harvard University, 1961), 13–29; and H. L. Strack and G. Stemberger, *Introduction to the Talmud and Midrash*, 2nd ed., trans. and ed. Marcus Bockmuehl (Minneapolis: Fortress Press, 1996), 70. The list could easily be lengthened.

transmitted the story did not agree on the roles of the leading characters in it, and both versions attribute the founding of the temple to the wrong Onias. There were, as nearly as we can tell, two men named Onias whose fathers were named Simon (Simon I and Simon II): both went on to become high priests in the Jerusalem temple, not in the Leontopolitan sanctuary. It is most likely that the Onias who is associated with the Egyptian temple was the son of Onias III (who was Simon II's son). This follows from the testimony of Josephus who relates that this Onias assisted Ptolemy VI Philometor (181–146 BCE) in his struggle with Antiochus IV Epiphanes (*J.W.* 1.1, 1 [§§31–33]; 7.10, 2–3 [§§420–32]). He fled to the Ptolemaic monarch, not as a result of indiscreet clothing, but to escape from Jerusalem after he had expelled the pro-Seleucid sons of Tobias.[98] The talmudic tales were told, as Moore himself recognized, to give a disreputable origin to the temple at Leontopolis. Where, if anywhere (other than the name and rank of the founder), the historical kernel of the story may lie is difficult to ascertain. At least it should not be used as evidence that Simon the Just lived in about 200 BCE.

Similar points should be made about the narratives regarding a meeting between Alexander the Great and Simon the Just. The story has been transferred from the high priest Jaddua to his grandson Simon and clearly serves purposes other than reporting historical fact. As we have seen in the previous chapter, there may actually be some historical foundation to the tale that Josephus transmits about Jaddua and Alexander,[99] but, to note only the obvious, there is virtually no possibility that Alexander met Simon I while he was high priest (for chronological reasons) and none at all that he conversed with Simon II who assumed office about one century after Alexander died. In addition, scholars have often noted that the reference to Antipatris in both versions is anachronistic, since Herod the Great gave this name to the city in honor of his father (*Ant.* 16.5, 2 [§§142–43]).[100] The tale belongs to the huge body of Alexander romances and to the narrower corpus of Jewish anti-Samaritan literature.[101] Even Zeitlin's attempt to rescue something historical from it by

---

98. For references and discussion of the texts, see Schürer, *History of the Jewish People*, 3.47–48, 145–47; John J. Collins, *The Sibylline Oracles of Egyptian Judaism,* SBLDS 13 (Missoula: SBL, 1974), 49–52. This issue will be treated in detail in the section on the high priests who ruled just before the Maccabean revolt.

99. See, for example, David Golan, "Josephus, Alexander's Visit to Jerusalem, and Modern Historiography," in *Josephus Flavius: Historian of Israel in the Hellenistic-Roman Period,* ed. U. Rappaport (Jerusalem: Yitzhak ben-Zvi, 1982), 29–55.

100. For example, Tcherikover, *Hellenistic Civilization and the Jews,* 48. Naturally, the later name of the site could have been added by a copyist or editor to an earlier story.

101. As we saw in chap. 2 above, another version of the story surfaces in Samaritan literature (Chronicle II), where the Samaritans of Shechem replace the inhabitants of Jerusalem and

substituting Antiochus III's name for that of Alexander fails to address the problem with Antipatris and collapses before the fact that the Judeans did not rebel against Antiochus.

Second, Moore's handling of Sir 50:1-21—perhaps his most important evidence—is unconvincing. Of course, as everyone recognizes, the Simon who is there lauded is never called Simon the Just; he is simply Simon son of Onias, a name that would fit either Simon I or Simon II.[102] It is the elaborate nature of the praise given to him that leads scholars to see in him Simon the Just. Perhaps this Simon is Simon the Just, but when did he live? Moore and others have spotted two elements in the passage that make them think this Simon officiated as high priest in about 200 BCE: the detailed, vivid nature of the description suggests that ben Sira was an eyewitness to what he here describes; and the high priest Simon does what Antiochus III ordered in his letter written shortly after 200 BCE.

The argument from specific, vivid detail is a slippery one: how much vividness and specificity are needed to demonstrate that the author actually viewed a scene rather than having simply cribbed it from a source? Some of the phrases in question can be paralleled in ben Sira's other sections about heroes who lived long before 200 BCE. For example, he wrote about Simon: "How glorious he was, surrounded by the people" (Sir 50:5). Ben Sira used the same "how glorious" expression for Joshua (46:2), Solomon (47:14), and Elijah (48:4). In fact, in the case of Elijah, we could argue that the wording is more appropriate for an eyewitness, since he is addressed in the second person ("how glorious you were"), not referred to in the third person as Simon is. The highly detailed poetic words about Simon's officiating at a sacrifice are paralleled by the attention to specifics in passages such as Sir 45:8-13, where Aaron's robe is held before the readers' eyes, and 47:8-10, where David's cultic innovations are enumerated. Just as we ought not to conclude that ben Sira was a contemporary of Aaron, Joshua, David, Solomon, or Elijah from the manner in which they are presented, so we need not conclude that he was a contemporary and eyewitness of this Simon from the way in which he praises him.

Moore and those who agree with him admit that the Simon of Sir 50:1-21 belonged to the past when the author wrote, but they claim to know somehow

---

the Samaritan high priest Hezekiah plays the role of Jaddua. For this text, see C. H. R. Martin, "Alexander and the High Priest," TGUOS 23 (1969–70): 102–14.

102. See, as an example, Hugo Mantel, *Studies in the History of the Sanhedrin*, HSS 17 (Cambridge: Harvard Univ. Press, 1965), 50–51 (although it is not clear from his long n. 278 whether he thinks Simon the Just was Simon I or II).

that he was recently deceased.[103] Several phrases in the poem strongly imply that he was a figure of the past: "in his life," "in his time," and "in his days" (50:1, 3).[104] That much is evident, but what these time indicators leave undefined is how far in the past he belonged. Ben Sira could be describing either his contemporary Simon II or Simon I; the text itself precludes neither. Another piece of information may, however, favor Simon I. Scholars are divided about whether the "Praise of Famous Men" extends from chapter 44 through chapter 49 or from 44 through 50. Thomas R. Lee, reinforcing an older thesis, has maintained that the unit does include chapter 50. He supports his contention from two sides: thematically, chapter 50 is the conclusion of 44–49 in that "fulfilled and embodied in Simon . . . are deeds and characteristics introduced in Sirach's enumeration in 44–49 of Israel's cultic and political heroes";[105] and formally, doxologies at the end of chapters 45 and 50 are appended to sections about the high priests Aaron—Phinehas on the one hand and the high priest Simon on the other (Sir 50:24 [Hebrew, MS B] refers to the covenant with Phinehas).[106] If, then, Sirach 50 belongs to the literary unit and all of the other heroes lauded in it lived in what was the distant past already in ben Sira's time, possibly the same is the case for the Simon of chapter 50. Perhaps he, too, is one of the "famous men, our ancestors in their generations" (44:1).

The second argument offered for believing that ben Sira was praising Simon II (= Simon the Just) is the correspondence between what this Simon did and what Antiochus III commanded should be done for the temple and Jerusalem. It should be recalled that even if one could demonstrate this point, it would not entail that Simon II was Simon the Just. It would mean only that ben Sira was writing about Simon II, his contemporary whom he does not further designate as "the Just." But, here as well, there are problems. For one, Antiochus's letter never mentions a high priest and certainly not Simon.[107] This

---

103. Moore, "Simeon the Righteous," 353; Skehan and Di Lella, The Wisdom of Ben Sira, 9.

104. The Geniza Hebrew text has four references of this kind: בדורו and בימיו (v. 1), בימיו (v. 2), and בדורו (v. 3). M. S. Segal makes the same point, although he too thinks the Simon of chap. 50 is Simon II and refers to the vividness of the praise offered (The Complete Book of Ben Sira, 2nd ed. [Jerusalem: Bialik, 1972 (Hebrew)], 3, 342). All citations of the ancient witnesses to the text of Sirach are from Francesco Vattioni, Ecclesiastico: Testo ebraico con apparato critico e versioni greca, latina e siriaca, Pubblicazioni del Seminario de Semistica (Naples: Instituto Orientale di Napoli, 1968).

105. Studies in the Form of Sirach 44–50, SBLDS 75 (Atlanta: Scholars, 1986), 12 (see 12–18).

106. Ibid., 19–21. It should be noted that Lee thinks the Simon of Sirach 50 is Simon II (for example, p. 10), though he does not formulate an argument for this position.

107. E. J. Bickerman observed that no such official document before the Maccabean era mentions the high priest ("La charte séleucide de Jérusalem," REJ 100 [1935]: 32). If one accepts

may be unimportant, but at least it is true that the king does not order the high priest to carry out the building projects. Second, none of the projects that he names in the letter finds a verbal reflex in Sir 50:1-21. Simon "repaired the house [ὑπέρραψεν οἶκον]" and "fortified the temple [ἐστερέωσεν ναόν]" (v. 1), laid foundations for the retaining walls of the temple compound [ἐθεμελιώθη ὕψος αὐλῆς] (v. 2), constructed a cistern [ἐλατομήθη ἀποδοχεῖον ὑδάτων] (v. 3), and fortified the city against siege [ἐνισχύσας πόλιν ἐν πολιορκήσει] (v. 4). Antiochus wrote that he wished to "restore their city [τὴν πόλιν αὐτῶν ἀναλαβεῖν]" (Josephus, *Ant.* 12.3, 3 [§139]) and to repopulate it after the ravages of the war. He also desired that "the work on the temple be completed, including the porticoes and any other part that it may be necessary to build [τὸ περὶ τὸ ἱερὸν ἀπαρτισθῆναι ἔργον τάς τε στοὰς καὶ εἴ τι ἕτερον οἰκοδομῆσαι δέοι]" (§141). Somewhat later, he refers to "making the restoration of the temple more splendid [ἐπιφανεστέραν γίγνεσθαι τὴν τοῦ ἱεροῦ ἐπισκευὴν δέῃ]" (§141). There are undoubted similarities, but would Antiochus have been interested in fortifying Jerusalem against a siege as Simon is said to have done?

To this should be added that, although Jerusalem had suffered damage in the war between the Ptolemaic and Seleucid armies, the same had probably happened in the time of the first Simon. Josephus mentions that Ptolemy I Soter conquered Jerusalem by taking advantage of the Jews' strategically dubious Sabbath customs and that he ruled it harshly (*Ant.* 12.1, 1 [§§3–7]). Indeed, Judea was, throughout the Hellenistic period, the regular victim of military exercises.[108] The damages suffered in Jerusalem as a result of these conflicts could have been the ones to which the Simon of Sir 50:1-4 directed his attention. Although no text says Simon I did work of this kind, no text says Simon II did either.

There is little point in dwelling on the connection between Simon the Just and the Great Synagogue mentioned in *m. 'Abot* 1. The very existence of this institution is debatable, and the list of traditionists in the passage, especially at its beginning, can hardly sustain a precise historical conclusion.[109]

There is only one source that claims to be a work of history and that provides information about who Simon the Just was. That source is, of course, Josephus's *Antiquities* in which he is explicitly identified as the first Simon and

the argument stated above, the letter of Areus to Onias would be an exception (Bickerman dates it to the second century BCE).

108. M. Smith pointed out that, in the 260 years after Alexander died, some two hundred campaigns across Palestine are attested (*Palestinian Parties and Politics*, 65; he lists all of them in n. 57 [231–32]). Several of these took place in the time of the first Ptolemy.

109. See the comments in Schürer, *History of the Jewish People*, 2.358–59.

grandson of the high priest Jaddua (Neh 12:11, 22) who is supposed to have
met Alexander the Great. Josephus, like all historians, does make mistakes in
his history and bases himself at times on inadequate sources; but, at least his
work packages itself as history, unlike any of the other sources adduced above.
In the case of the high-priestly list, it is possible that he, a priest from a prominent family, had access to documentary evidence. He mentions in *Against
Apion* that "our forefathers took no less, not to say even greater, care than the
nations I have mentioned in the keeping of their records—a task which they
assigned to their chief priests and prophets—and that down to our own times
these records have been, and if I may venture to say so, will continue to be, preserved with scrupulous accuracy" (1.29). [110] He goes on to note the
importance of genealogical purity in the priestly line and hence the need to
have such information in the archives (1.30–35) and concludes with a
statement about high-priestly lists: "But the most convincing proof of our
accuracy in this matter is that our records contain the names of our high
priests, with the succession from father to son for the last two thousand years"
(1.36). In two places (apart from the many individual references in his
narratives), Josephus provides or alludes to rosters of high priests: *Ant.* 10.8, 6
(§§152–53) lists the seventeen high priests of the First Temple, and *Ant.* 20.10,
2 (§§231–34) relates that eighteen served in the First Temple (apparently the
last one—Seraiah—was omitted from the list in Book 10)[111] and that Joshua
and fourteen descendants held the post until the time when Antiochus V
Eupator ended the line (with his appointment of Alcimus in 162 BCE).

We may entertain doubts about what Josephus has written (the reference
to two thousand years makes one uneasy), but it is, at the very least, clear that
he intended to report what happened and that he attempted to base his narrative on records.[112] These facts sharply distinguish Josephus's evidence from
that of the other sources that have played a part in the debate about Simon the
Just. It is a dubious procedure, in drawing a historical conclusion, to favor a
series of legendary (and later) texts along with inferences from a poetic
encomium over the explicit statement of a historical composition. If one were
to do this (and there are probably cases in which it would be defensible), then
there would have to be weighty external data that would tip the scales in the

---

110. The translation is that of H. St. J. Thackeray, *Josephus*, vol. 1: *The Life, Against Apion*,
LCL (Cambridge: Harvard Univ. Press, 1926).

111. So Marcus, *Josephus* 6, 243 n. e (where he suggests it may have been left out because of
its similarity with the preceding name [Azariah]).

112. For a summary of scholarly views regarding Josephus's use of sources, see Per Bilde,
Flavius Josephus between Jerusalem and Rome: His Life, His Works, and Their Importance, JSPSup
2 (Sheffield: JSOT Press, 1988), 189–206.

unexpected direction. An examination of the sources demonstrates, nevertheless, that no data that possess such force exist.

The conclusion that should be drawn from the surviving texts is that there
is only one relevant piece of historical information regarding the identity of
Simon the Just: Josephus gives the epithet to Simon I. There is no *historical* evidence that relates it to Simon II.

Another implication of the preceding analysis is that the high priest
Simon whom ben Sira praises so highly was probably Simon I. The information from that chapter should now be studied, since Sir 50:1-21 is the first text
that pictures for us in some detail what sorts of duties the high priest performed in the Second-Temple period. In this chapter, ben Sira, writing in the
early second century BCE, concludes his Praise of Famous Men with an enthusiastic poem about Simon, who seems to be Simon I (compare vv. 23-24).

In the Greek text (supported by the Syriac), Simon is called ἱερεὺς ὁ
μέγας,[113] a fairly frequent form of the high-priestly title in the Septuagint (see
Josh 20:6 [A]; 2 Kgs 12:10[11]; 22:4, 8; 23:4; 2 Chr 34:9; Neh 3:1; Jdt 4:6, 8, 14;
15:8; Hag 1:1, 12, 14; 2:3[2], 5[4]; Zech 3:1, 9[8]; 6:11; 1 Macc 12:20; 14:20;
15:2). Ben Sira calls him "[t]he leader of his brothers[114] and the pride of his
people" (Sir 50:1).[115] In other words, he outranked the other priests and also
rose above the nation. In Sir 50:1-4, several telling actions are attributed to
Simon, from which much can be learned about the expansion of high-priestly
power in the Second-Temple period. First, he tended to the temple compound:

> . . . Simon son of Onias,
> who in his life repaired the house,
> and in his time fortified the temple.[116]
> He laid the foundations for the high double walls,
> the high retaining walls for the temple enclosure. (vv. 1b-2)

We have seen above that Simon's labors in verses 1b-2 are often compared with
the orders given by Antiochus III for repairs on the temple after hostile armies

---

113. The medieval Hebrew MS B has הכהן alone.

114. "Brothers" is used in several biblical passages for fellow priests; for example, Lev 21:10;
Num 8:26; 18:2, 6; Ezra 3:2.

115. For an explanation of why this line was displaced to 49:15 in the Greek, see Skehan and
Di Lella, *Wisdom of Ben Sira*, 548.

116. The verb ὑπέρραψεν (translated "repaired" above) presupposes a Hebrew form נבדק,
not נפקד as in MS B (S. Schechter and C. Taylor, *The Wisdom of Ben Sira* [Cambridge: Cambridge
Univ. Press, 1899], 63). Forms of both בדק and חזק ("fortified") appear in 2 Chr 34:10 in connection with work on the temple performed in Josiah's time (see Segal, *The Complete Book of Ben
Sira*, 342–43) when repairs were also needed but not because an invading army had damaged the
building.

had battered it. It is doubtful, however, that the same building enterprise is under consideration. Nothing in these verses implies that the work on the temple involved more than renovations and other improvements on an old building.

Sirach 50 also praises Simon for building activities that may have had nothing to do specifically with the temple (vv. 3-4).

> In his days a water cistern was dug,
> a reservoir like the sea in circumference.
> He considered how to save his people from ruin,
> and fortified (ומחזק) the city against siege.[117]

Insuring a supply of water[118] and fortifying the city remind one of what King Hezekiah did in the late eighth century (2 Kgs 20:20). Sirach 48:17 uses similar language to celebrate Hezekiah's efforts. Naturally, the verb חזק also invites comparison with the work of the Judean king. As Lee has shown, all of Simon's accomplishments in verses 1-4 find close parallels in what ben Sira elsewhere says about biblical kings and governors.[119] These verses demonstrate in dramatic form the extent to which the high priest had shouldered the responsibility for security and maintenance once borne by monarchs. Georg Sauer, who notes the connections between chapters 44–49 and chapter 50, writes that the two parts are always tied together and depend on each other. With Moses was Aaron, with David, Solomon. In Ben Sira's time these different tasks were united in Simon, the political power growing together with the priestly. Simon was the guarantor of the external security of the city and its inhabitants in so far as he was in a position to do this. He was especially the guarantor of God's

---

117. MS B has מצר = from an enemy. The Greek presupposes ממצור. See G. H. Box and W. O. E. Oesterley, "Sirach," in *APOT* 1.507–8. Whichever is the preferred reading, the implication would be that Simon was concerned about the defensive readiness of Jerusalem. See also Segal, *The Complete Book of Ben Sira*, 343.

118. In the context, the "reservoir like the sea" does not seem to be the water container in the temple area called the sea.

119. *Studies in the Form of Sirach 44–50*, 18–19. Rooke, who argues that there is no evidence for an expansion of high-priestly power into the civil sphere in the Ptolemaic period, has some difficulty dealing with 50:4 (*Zadok's Heirs*, 263–64). For her, since 50:1-3 deal with the temple, "50:4 need not be taken to indicate large-scale building works undertaken throughout the city, but can be seen instead as a general summary reference to the building works carried out on the Temple, since the geographical position of the Temple mount in Jerusalem meant that fortifying it as described in 50:1a-3 would effectively strengthen the whole city against attack and ruin by turning the mount into a kind of acropolis" (264). We may at least say that if this is what the poet meant, he chose an odd way to phrase it.

presence among the people as he carried out the festal ceremonies and dispensed blessings to those participating in the cult.[120]

The remainder of the poem about Simon falls into two parts. The first (Sir 50:5-11) contains the poet's effusive words of wonder at the glorious appearance of the high priest when he was performing his duties at the temple. The second (vv. 12-21) pictures in poetic language a ceremony that was conducted by Simon and the priests before the congregation.[121]

The moving reactions to Simon's splendor were, it seems, evoked by the clothing worn by the high priest (see v. 11). The author resorts to eleven consecutive "like"-clauses to express how strongly the spectacle of the high priest Simon had moved him:

> How glorious he was, surrounded by the people,
> as he came out of the house of the curtain.
> Like the morning star among the clouds,
> like the full moon at the festal season;
> like the sun shining on the temple of the Most High,
> like the rainbow gleaming in the splendid clouds;
> like roses in the days of first fruits,
> like lilies by a spring of water,
> like a green shoot on Lebanon on a summer day;
> like fire and incense in the censer,
> like a vessel of hammered gold studded with all kinds of precious stones;
> like an olive tree laden with fruit,
> and like a cypress towering in the clouds.
> When he put on his glorious robe
> and clothed himself in perfect splendor,
> when he went up to the holy altar,
> he made the court of the sanctuary glorious. (vv. 5-11)[122]

---

120. *Jesus Sirach / Ben Sira*, ATD Apokryphen 1 (Göttingen: Vandenhoeck & Ruprecht, 2000), 338. Sauer thinks Simon II is under discussion (pp. 338–39).

121. According to Segal, the amount of space devoted to Simon's priestly appearance and duties compared with the number of lines that deal with his political or military roles suggests that the former had greater importance for the author of chap. 50 (*The Complete Book of Ben Sira*, 343).

122. In his comments on this passage, Sauer highlights connections with the creation material in Sirach 43 and writes that the entire creation is present when the high priest appears (*Jesus Sirach / Ben Sira*, 339–40).

In scholarly comment on the passage, the key to interpreting the nature of the occasion depicted has been the meaning of "the house of the curtain" in verse 5. Manuscript B reads בית הפרכת and the Greek οἴκου καταπετάσματος. In biblical Hebrew, הפרכת refers primarily to the veiling curtain that separated the Holy of Holies from the holy place in the tabernacle; it is used once regarding the same object in the temple (2 Chr 3:14).[123] If the meaning in Sir 50:5 corresponds with the dominant scriptural usage, Simon would be emerging from the Holy of Holies,[124] something the high priest did only on the Day of Atonement. The ceremony in verses 12-21, therefore, should reflect at least some of the rituals for Yom Kippur.[125]

The view that Sir 50:12-21 describes rituals for the Day of Atonement has been challenged by F. Ó Fearghail who finds a greater degree of similarity between our passage and the rituals for the daily whole burnt offerings than the rites of Yom Kippur.[126] His proposal has been accepted by Skehan and Di Lella, whereas Lee thinks that 50:5-10 echoes the Day of Atonement and 50:11-19 belongs to the daily offering.[127] As the point is not important for our purposes, it need not be discussed in detail. However, the description in Sir 50:5-21 does not fit the mishnaic evidence for the daily offering very well, while the treatment of Yom Kippur in the Mishnah does at least stress the high priest's costly clothing (*m. Yoma* 3:7; 7:3–5), something that is not the case for the daily offering in *m. Tamid*. Simon himself, whatever the occasion may have been, offers the sacrifice with its libation at the altar; after he completes it, the priests sound trumpets and the people prostrate themselves (compare the

---

123. For the veil, see Carol L. Meyers, "Veil of the Temple," in *ABD* 6.785–86; Menahem Haran, *Temples and Temple-Service in Ancient Israel: An Inquiry into Biblical Cult Phenomena and the Historical Setting of the Priestly School* (Oxford: Clarendon, 1978; reprinted: Winona Lake, Ind.: Eisenbrauns, 1985), 152–53, 161–62.

124. Segal, *The Complete Book of Ben Sira*, 344.

125. Box and Oesterley, "Sirach," 508.

126. "Sir 50, 5-21: Yom Kippur or the Daily Whole-Offering?" *Bib* 59 (1978): 301–16. Ó Fearghail appeals to *m. Tamid* 6:3—7:3, which describes what happens when the high priest himself chooses to present the daily offering; it does mention the פרכת though it hardly seems to be the one for the Holy of Holies, since other priests also go through it and emerge (7:1). Ben Sira says nothing about anyone but Simon coming out of "the house of the curtain." Naturally, the Mishnah mentions the פרכת in connection with Yom Kippur (*m. Yoma* 5:1 refers to two of them, separated by a cubit; they divide the holy place from the Holy of Holies).

127. Skehan and Di Lella, *Wisdom of Ben Sira*, 550–54; Lee, *Studies in the Form of Sirach 44–50*, 216, 219–20 (vv. 20-21 deal with the Yom Kippur blessing, see 223). Segal also thinks the *tamid* is being pictured beginning at v. 14 (*The Complete Book of Ben Sira*, 345); Sauer agrees that the passage deals with the *tamid* offering and that it is too general to allow identification of a particular festival (*Jesus Sirach / ben Sira*, 340).

report of Hecateus noted above). The high priest then blesses the congregation with hands raised, and they again bow down.[128]

Ben Sira concludes the section about Simon, first with a blessing of God and then a prayer that he would give wisdom and peace to his readers (the second person plural is used). Finally, he writes (according to the Hebrew): "May his love abide upon Simeon, and may he keep in him the covenant of Phinehas; may one never be cut off from him; and as for his offspring, (may it be) as the days of heaven" (v. 24, author's translation).

In Sirach 50, we find that, at the time of Simon I, the high priest, heir of the unconditional promise to Phinehas of an eternal priesthood (v. 24 [Hebrew]; see Num 25), performed the scriptural duties of the leading priest. He wore the colorful vestments described in Exodus 28 (vv. 5-11); he participated in sacrifice assisted by the other priests (vv. 12-21); and he blessed the people, presumably with the benediction of Num 6:24-26. But, beyond those ancient duties, he also assumed responsibilities that in earlier times would have been the concern of civil rulers—repairing the temple structure and fortifying the city of Jerusalem. Simon seems to be both civil and religious leader.

9. Eleazar

According to Josephus, when Simon died, his son Onias was too young to become high priest; under the circumstances, Simon's brother Eleazar became the high priest (*Ant.* 12.2, 5 [§44]), the first such case on record. Appointing a brother when no appropriate heir was available among a person's children follows the guidelines in Num 27:8-11, where, if a man had no son, a daughter was to be the first option; however, if he had no daughter (a point irrelevant for priestly succession) the inheritance was to pass to his brothers.[129] This Eleazar might have joined several high priests of the Persian and early Hel-

---

128. Segal (*The Complete Book of Ben Sira*, 347–48) compares *m. Yoma* 6:3 where the people bow upon hearing the tetragrammaton, though he adds that such prostration occurred daily, not only on Yom Kippur.

129. See Daniel Tropper, "The Internal Administration of the Second Temple at Jerusalem" (Ph.D. diss., New York, Yeshiva University, 1970), 27–28. We have no evidence regarding how old a person had to be to qualify as a high priest. There are several scriptural references to Levites having to be twenty years of age and above to perform their duties (for example, Ezra 3:8; 1 Chr 23:24, 27; 2 Chr 31:17), but this is not said of priests. In *b. Ḥul.* 24b, two views are reported: one may perform priestly duties when one produces two hairs, or when one is twenty years (citing Ezra 3:8 among other passages and discussing whether rules for Levites also applied to priests). We will meet this problem again in 35 BCE when Aristobulus III became high priest at age sixteen.

lenistic periods as a faceless name in a list were it not for the fact that he is a principal character in the well-known story about translating the Torah from Hebrew into Greek. The author of the so-called *Letter of Aristeas* reports that Eleazar was the reigning high priest when Ptolemy II Philadelphus (283–246 BCE) wrote requesting a copy of the Jewish laws and scholars capable of rendering the Hebrew texts into Greek. The *Letter of Aristeas* should now be studied and its claims about Eleazar should be assessed.

Aristeas, who identifies himself as a courtier of Ptolemy II, wrote what he calls a *narrative* (διήγησις) for his brother Philocrates regarding his meeting with Eleazar the Jewish high priest (1). The visit took place in the course of Aristeas's participation in a larger royal project. Demetrius of Phalerum, who was the official in charge of the great library at Alexandria, told the king that among the works that he wished to add to the already sizable collection were the laws of the Jews; however, before they could become a usable part of the library, they would have to be translated from the unfamiliar characters and language in which they were extant.[130] Though only a small percentage of the *Letter of Aristeas* actually relates the events that led to the translation, the theme serves as a minimally unifying element in an otherwise extremely discursive text. At the moment when the king agreed to arrange and fund the translation, Aristeas seized the favorable opportunity to ask Philadelphus to free the many Jewish slaves in his realm. As he always does in the *Letter of Aristeas*, the king responded magnanimously by ordering that they be released. He then wrote to the high priest Eleazar, reporting the large-scale emancipation and requesting that Eleazar send six translators from each of the twelve tribes. Demetrius had earlier made such a proposal to the king: "asking him to dispatch men of the most exemplary lives and mature experience, skilled in matters pertaining to their Law, six in number from each tribe, in order that after the examination of the text agreed by the majority, and the achievement of accuracy in the translation, we may produce an outstanding version in a manner worthy both of the contents and of your purpose" (32).[131]

Eleazar responded favorably to the king's request and thanked him for the lavish gifts that he had sent with his messengers. The action of the narrative is then suspended for some time as Aristeas pauses to name the seventy-two translators (47–50) and to dwell on the king's priceless presents for the high priest (51–82). Next he writes that he will recount his journey to Eleazar (Aris-

---

130. For the fictive setting of the *Letter of Aristeas*, see P. M. Fraser, *Ptolemaic Alexandria*, 3 vols. (Oxford: Clarendon, 1972), 2.973 n. 123; he finds internal clues that the *putative* setting is before 270 BCE.

131. Translations of the *Letter of Aristeas* are by R. J. H. Shutt in *OTP* 2.

teas was one of the king's emissaries to the high priest) but must first describe the country of the Jews, especially the temple and its underground water system (83–91). This leads him to picture the priestly labors in the sacred service (92–96), Eleazar's apparel when officiating (96–99), the guard for the temple situated in the adjacent citadel (100–104), the city Jerusalem, and the country in general (105–20). Only after this long excursus does Aristeas return to the translators who were to be sent to Egypt (121–27); he then promptly interrupts his story again with another digression in which Eleazar, responding to questions from Aristeas and Andreas (who delivered the king's letter to the high priest), explains the fundamental provisions and postulates of the Jewish Law (128–71). Finally, the translators actually go to Alexandria laden with gifts and escorted by Aristeas and Andreas (172). When they arrived in the capital city, the king deviated from court protocol by having the translators admitted at once into his presence. He welcomed all seventy-two of them, admired the parchments on which the Law was written, and provided sumptuously for their needs (173–81).

Most of the remaining sections in the *Letter of Aristeas* are devoted to the seven banquets at which Ptolemy Philadelphus asked each of the translators a question and from each of the seventy-two received a profound answer (182–294). The work of translation occupies little space in the book (301–307). In an isolated, luxuriously furnished place, the translators worked at rendering the books of the Torah, compared their results, and agreed upon a common text. Happily, they completed their task in exactly seventy-two days. Their Greek version was read to the Jewish population of Alexandria, who indicated their hearty approval and decreed that it should not be changed, since it was perfect (308–11). Ptolemy, too, heard the Law read and was astonished at its contents. To his query why no historians or poets had alluded to it, Demetrius replied that its sacred character had prevented such attention. He named Theopompus and Theodectus as writers who had intended to use it; both, however, suffered physically for their presumption (312–16). At last, Philadelphus showered the translators with gifts and sent them home with a standing invitation to return and grace his kingdom once more with their presence (317–21).

As the preceding survey shows, Eleazar the high priest figures prominently in the account. We often read his name and/or title, and there are a number of other allusions to him: 1, 3, 11, 32, 33, 35–40 (the letter sent to him), 41–46 (his reply), 51, 81, 83, 96–98 (his vestments), 112, 122–23, 130–69, 172, 173, 175, 177, 320. His title is regularly ὁ ἀρχιερεύς, and he is depicted as honorable, pious, and incredibly learned—in short, an ideal leader. Aristeas says he was a "gentleman, whose integrity and reputation have

won him preeminent honor in the eyes of citizens and others alike, and who
has gained a very great benefit for his own circle and for (fellow) citizens in
other places" (3). The question on which the king wrote to him was religious
in nature, but it is evident that he was, in the view of the author, the supreme
leader among the Jews. So, for example, he was the one whom the king
informed about the emancipation of Jewish slaves in Egypt. There is no hint
in the text that a civil officer ruled alongside Eleazar. After detailing the wonders of Eleazar's vestments—not the first time they have caught the attention
of an author (compare the account of Alexander and Jaddua; Sirach 50)—
Aristeas wrote: "The wearer is considered worthy of such vestments at the services" (98). The high priest was knowledgeable even about the most successful
farming practices (compare 112). The seventy-two translators, each of whom
was highly impressive in his own right, were "worthy of their leader and his
outstanding qualities. It was possible to perceive how inseparable was their
attachment to Eleazar, and his to them" (122–23). The high priest was most
solicitous that the translators be returned to their land (123–27). As he bade
farewell to them and their sizable escort, he "offered sacrifice, selected the
men, and made ready an abundance of gifts for the king" (172). One reason
for the king's unusually prompt and enthusiastic reception of the Judeans was
the status of Eleazar: "he deemed the present arrivals to be deserving of greater
honor, having regard to the preeminence of him who sent them" (175; compare 177). His qualities made him outrank all other rulers whose representatives called on Ptolemy II: "The unprecedented nature of this step [immediate
reception of the translators] was very clear to all, because it was an established
procedure that important bona fide visitors should be granted an audience
with the king only four days after arrival, while representatives of kings or
important cities are rarely admitted to the court within thirty days" (175).[132]
Then, after completion of the translation, the king for a second time sent
lavish gifts to Eleazar: "ten silver-footed couches, with all accessories to go with
them, a cup worth thirty talents, ten robes, purple cloth, a magnificent crown,
one hundred lengths of finest linen, vessels, bowls, and two golden goblets for
a dedication" (320). In short, Eleazar was a worthy counterpart to great
Ptolemy himself; the two communicated as equals.

Perhaps the most extraordinary data about the high priest Eleazar emerge
from the section in which he answers Aristeas's questions about the Law
(128–71). When he was asked why, in the one creation of God, some foods
were considered clean and others not, Eleazar explained:

---

132. This is one of the cases in which the author displays his precise knowledge of Ptolemaic court protocol. See Fraser, *Ptolemaic Alexandria*, 1.698; 2.976 n. 141.

"You observe," he said, "the important matter raised by modes of life and relationships, inasmuch as through bad relationships men become perverted, and are miserable their whole life long; if, however, they mix with wise and prudent companions, they rise above ignorance and achieve progress in life." (130)

That is, regulations about food and contact with persons and objects point to larger issues of human relationships. The high priest expounded the fact that nothing is hidden from God—whether a thought or a deed, "thus indicating the power of God through the entire legislation" (133). Eleazar criticized the polytheism of the nations, especially the Egyptians.

In his wisdom the legislator, in a comprehensive survey of each particular part, and being endowed by God for the knowledge of universal truths, surrounded us with unbroken palisades and iron walls to prevent our mixing with any of the other peoples in any matter, being thus kept pure in body and soul, preserved from false beliefs, and worshiping the only God omnipotent over all creation. (139)

The strict laws of the Jews had a positive rationale:

So to prevent our being perverted by contact with others or by mixing with bad influences, he hedged us in on all sides with strict observances [literally: purities] connected with meat and drink and touch and hearing and sight, after the manner of the Law. In general everything is similarly constituted in regard to natural reasoning, being governed by one supreme power, and in each particular everything has a profound reason for it, both the things from which we abstain in use and those of which we partake. (142–43)

Eleazar scoffed at the idea that Moses had concentrated on trivia: "Do not take the contemptible view that Moses enacted this legislation because of an excessive preoccupation with mice and weasels or suchlike creatures. The fact is that everything has been solemnly set in order for unblemished investigation and amendment of life for the sake of righteousness" (144). The birds used and consumed by the Jews eat "wheat and pulse" (145), while the ones forbidden are carnivorous and given to violence.

By calling them impure, he has thereby indicated that it is the solemn binding duty of those for whom the legislation has been established to practice righteousness and not to lord it over anyone in reliance

upon their own strength, nor to deprive him of anything, but to govern their lives righteously, in the manner of the gentle creatures
among the aforementioned birds which feed on those plants which
grow on the ground and do not exercise a domination leading to the
destruction of their fellow creatures. By means of creatures like this
the legislator has handed down (the lesson) to be noted by men of
wisdom, that they should be righteous, and not achieve anything by
brute force, nor lord it over others in reliance upon their own
strength. (147–48)

Even the cloven hooves of permitted animals are a symbol "of setting apart
each of our actions for good, because the strength of the whole body with its
action rests upon the shoulders and the legs. The symbolism conveyed by
these things compels us to make a distinction in the performance of all our
acts, with righteousness as our aim. This moreover explains why we are distinct from all other men" (150–51). Animals with cloven hooves and rumi-
nants "express, to those who perceive it, the phenomenon of memory" (153).

After explicating related reminders of God throughout the daily exercise
of Judaism, Eleazar concludes:

Our Law forbids harming anyone in thought or in deed. I have therefore given a brief résumé of these matters, indicating further to you
that all the regulations have been made with righteousness in mind,
and that no ordinances have been made in Scripture without purpose
or fancifully, but to the intent that through the whole of our lives we
may also practice justice to all mankind in all our acts, remembering
the all-sovereign God. (168)

The reader may be forgiven for feeling some surprise at Eleazar's manner
of explaining the Law, almost a Philonic allegorical reading of the sacred
text.[133] Although the style of the section in which the high priest treats the Law
remains consistent with what we meet elsewhere in the book, "[t]he whole
passage demonstrates an adherence to allegorical interpretation which is quite
unlike the practice of the author elsewhere, and it seems that it may well have
been borrowed by him wholesale from another work, to embellish his own."[134]
The allegorical method for interpreting passages in the Bible is thought to
have originated among Alexandrian Jews. It had been applied for a long time
to Homeric and Hesiodic texts in an effort to salvage some value from them in

---

133. John M. G. Barclay, *Jews in the Mediterranean Diaspora: From Alexander to Trajan (323
BCE–117 CE)* (Edinburgh: T. & T. Clark, 1996), 146.
134. Fraser, *Ptolemaic Alexandria*, 1.701; 2.980 n. 159.

a new age when advances in knowledge had shown the old works to be incredible on a literal level of meaning. But, if allegory entails abandoning the literal for the sake of a nonliteral reading, it is not fully accurate to call Eleazar's exposition allegorical. That is, there is no indication that he ignored the literal meaning of the laws. Instead, he took the simple sense of the laws as something that both demanded literal obedience and pointed to wider significance.[135]

Does the *Letter of Aristeas* deliver an authentic report about Eleazar, about his splendor and brilliance? Scholars are unanimous in dismissing the account from the realm of historical writing, though many admit that a Greek translation of the Torah must have been made in the third century, possibly during the reign of Ptolemy II Philadelphus, that most splendid of Ptolemaic monarchs.[136] Demetrius, who wrote during the reign of Ptolemy IV Philopator (221–203 BCE), already used a Greek Pentateuch.[137] Nevertheless, the early existence of a Greek translation of part of Scripture does not verify the historicity of the *Letter of Aristeas*, and experts have spotted in the text a number of hints that it was written at a considerably later time than the putative setting of the composition and that it is largely fiction. H. T. Andrews listed the following indications of its nonhistorical character:[138]

1. Demetrius of Phalerum was not the head of the Alexandrian library in the reign of Philadelphus. Hermippus (in Diogenes Laertius 5.78) says that Demetrius was banned at the beginning of Philadelphus's reign for supporting Keraunus, Philadelphus's older brother, in the competition for the throne. Demetrius died a short time later.
2. In 180, Ptolemy mentions that it was the anniversary of his naval victory over Antigonus. If, as seems most likely, the referent is the battle of Andros, Philadelphus is somewhat off target on his dates, since the battle occurred no earlier than the last year of his reign and possibly in the time of his successor.

---

135. See Friedrich Büchsel, "ἀλληγορέω," in *TDNT* 1.261, who makes the same point regarding Philo. Eleazar's speeches in this section and the teachings of the writer elsewhere (for example, in the seventy-two answers of the translators) present the general perspective that, while there is admiration for Greek thought and even some remarkably tolerant language about the beliefs of cultured Greeks, Judaism is still superior and distinctive. See Gruen, *Heritage and Hellenism*, 213–22; Barclay, *Jews in the Mediterranean Diaspora*, 143–50. Their interpretation opposes that of M. Beavis ("Anti-Egyptian Polemic in the Letter of Aristeas 130–165 [The High Priest's Discourse]," *JSJ* 18 [1987]: 145–51) who thinks the author's comments about separateness are directed at lower types of religion, especially Egyptian, not at the religion of sophisticated Greeks.

136. See Schürer, *History of the Jewish People*, 3.679.

137. Holladay, *Fragments from Hellenistic Jewish Authors*, 52–53.

138. "The Letter of Aristeas," in *APOT* 2.83–84. The points that Andrews made are often repeated in the literature.

3. The Greek scholars who are mentioned—Menedemus (201), Theopompus (314), and Theodectus (316)—also do not fit within the alleged time of the action.

4. The *Letter of Aristeas* assumes the existence of the Septuagint before it was made. Thus, for example, its readings, which in places differ from the Hebrew, lie behind the description of the table sent by the king to the high priest.

Bickermann argued that none of these objections has been demonstrated.[139] For example, the dates in the career of Demetrius of Phalerum are not as clear as Andrews and others have suggested. The evidence that he was banned at the beginning of Philadelphus's reign comes from Hermippus, whose authority is no greater than that of his contemporary Aristobulus (an Alexandrian Jewish writer of the mid-second century BCE), who claims that Demetrius was still librarian under Philadelphus.[140] In addition, the problem arising from the king's reference to his sea victory may be solved, according to Bickermann, by positing an error in the text: it originally read *Antiochus*, not *Antigonus*. Ptolemy II did in fact defeat Antiochus I in 280 BCE.[141] Bickermann did agree that the work was a later forgery, but he based his inference on the formulae used in official documents quoted in the *Letter of Aristeas*. These he compared with the extensive evidence that is available for the evolving practices in official Ptolemaic texts. He observed that it was precisely in such incidental features that an author would betray his time; in his paraphrase, Josephus altered a number of the formulae in the *Letter of Aristeas* to wording that was more typical when he wrote.[142]

Although he found no comparative data for two of the documents in the *Letter of Aristeas*,[143] the royal *prostagma* in 22–25 and Philadelphus's letter to Eleazar in 35–40 lend themselves to the kind of analysis Bickermann intended. In the former, the style and content are appropriate, but its opening (τοῦ βασιλέως προστάξαντος) is too concise for Ptolemy II's

---

139. E. J. Bickermann, "Zur Datierung des Pseudo-Aristeas," *ZAW* 29 (1930): 280–98.

140. Nina L. Collins has written an extended defense of Aristeas's claims about Demetrius, basing herself on some chronological notices in patristic literature that are not derived from the *Letter of Aristeas* (*The Library in Alexandria and the Bible in Greek*, VTSup 82 [Leiden: Brill, 2000]). She dates the translation to 281 or 280 BCE (with the former being the date by a Jewish reckoning, the latter by a Greek reckoning) and thinks Ptolemy was the one who wanted it, not the Jews of Alexandria.

141. "Zur Datierung des Pseudo-Aristeas," 281–82.

142. "Zur Datierung des Pseudo-Aristeas," 287.

143. The two are the report in 29–32 and Eleazar's letter to the king in 41–46.

chancery.[144] In the latter, the forger supplies titles that were fitting in letters between rulers (βασιλεὺς Πτολεμαῖος Ἐλεαζάρῳ ἀρχιερεῖ χαίρειν καὶ ἐρρῶσθαι); otherwise, as in private letters, they were avoided. But, the greeting χαίρειν καὶ ἐρρῶσθαι betrays the author as a forger: it is an abbreviation of the normal one that is not attested until 160 BCE, one century after Ptolemy II's reign. The formula in the *Letter of Aristeas* became common in the second and first centuries but disappeared completely in the Roman period, when it was replaced by χαίρειν καὶ ὑγιαίνειν.[145] The evidence of formulae, then, establishes 160 BCE as the earliest and 30 BCE as the latest dates when they were current.

Bickermann next turned to the phrase ἐὰν οὖν φαίνηται in the report from Demetrius of Phalerum (32). It, too, appeared first around 160 BCE, while previously ἐάν σοι φαίνηται was customary in such contexts. The words καλῶς οὖν ποιήσεις (introduced by a participle [39, 46]) demonstrate that the author was familiar with official style in the third and second centuries; the expression largely disappears in the first century.[146] On the basis of these data, we may narrow the date of the book to between 160 and 100 BCE. Two other terms allowed Bickermann to lower the upper limit to 145 BCE: ἀρχισωματοφύλακας (12) and the designation Ἀνδρέαν τῶν σωματοφυλάκων. Moreover, the geographical description of the land in 107 reflects conditions after three Samaritan regions were added to Judea in 145 BCE,[147] while this and other references (13, 22, 117) indicate that the date of composition must have been before 127 BCE when Idumea was Judaized (it is an independent political unit in the book). Hence, he concluded, formulaic and historical criteria require a date for the book between 145 and 127 BCE.[148]

Bickermann's remarkably precise dating is often cited with approval, but Fraser has found it unconvincing. While he accepts the premise of Bickermann's argument, he holds that the data point to an earlier time of writing. For example, regarding ἐὰν οὖν φαίνηται he writes: "Since both ἐὰν φαίνηται and ἐὰν οὖν φαίνηταί σοι occur in iii B.C. it would be rash to maintain that ἐὰν οὖν φαίνηται could not do so."[149] His study of the evidence leads him to

---

144. Compare, however, Moses Hadas, who thought that the decree in 22–25 was strongly similar to Ptolemy II's *prostagma* from the year 262–261 or 261–260 BCE (*Aristeas to Philocrates [Letter of Aristeas]*, Jewish Apocryphal Literature [New York: Harper, 1951], 28–32).

145. "Zur Datierung des Pseudo-Aristeas," 288–89.

146. Ibid., 289–90.

147. Ibid., 290–92.

148. "Zur Datierung des Pseudo-Aristeas," 293–95. He added that the ideal, platonic description of Judea suggests a time before Jewish expansion began in 128 BCE.

149. *Ptolemaic Alexandria*, 2.970.

the time of Philometor, specifically between 164 and 145 BCE, when the Ptolemy pursued a philo-Judaic policy.[150] For him, the statements about geography, rather than arising from a particular historical period, make one wonder whether Aristeas's geography is real.[151] If Fraser is correct, both pillars of Bickermann's argument fall.

Other scholars have found the data more conducive to a time of composition near the beginning of the second century BCE. Schürer noted two points in favor of this earlier date. First, Aristobulus, a Jewish philosopher who was active in about 180–145 BCE, seems to use the *Letter of Aristeas*, since he, too, attributes the initiative for the translation to Demetrius of Phalerum. As the attribution is historically inaccurate, we see here a telltale agreement in error. Second, internal factors point in the same direction. The general political situation of the Jewish population in Judea reflects conditions in pre-Seleucid times (that is, before ca. 200 BCE), when the fortress was in Jewish hands (100–104) and the high priest was "head of the community but is not a worldly ruler in the style of the Hasmoneans."[152]

It is safe to say that at some point in the second century, probably in the earlier part of it, an Alexandrian Jewish author wrote the *Letter of Aristeas* in which he demonstrates an impressive knowledge of Ptolemaic courtly practice.[153] It is transparent that while historical facts underlie parts of the story[154] the work itself belongs to a genre of fiction that pictures an ideal situation.[155] In it, an ideal monarch with unlimited resources corresponds with an ideal high priest of massive wealth and erudition.[156] He, in turn, appoints ideally

---

150. Ibid., 2.971.

151. Ibid.

152. *History of the Jewish People*, 3.680 (for the two arguments, see 680–82). Although he does not argue in detail for it, A. Pelletier also favors a date at the beginning of the second century (*Lettre d'Aristée à Philocrate: Introduction, texte critique, traduction et notes, index complet des mots grecs*, SC 89 [Paris: Cerf, 1962], 57–59). Sidney Jellicoe concludes that it was written before 170 BCE (*The Septuagint and Modern Study* [Oxford: Clarendon, 1968; reprinted: Winona Lake, Ind.: Eisenbrauns, 1993], 48–51; idem, "The Occasion and Purpose of the Letter of Aristeas: a Re-examination," *NTS* 12 [1965–66]: 144–50).

153. Fraser, *Ptolemaic Alexandria*, 1.698–99; Schürer, *History of the Jewish People*, 3.684; Barclay, *Jews in the Mediterranean Diaspora*, 140–41.

154. Jellicoe gives a list of them; it centers around the translation itself (*The Septuagint and Modern Study*, 55–56).

155. Bickermann termed it a utopian writing ("Zur Datierung des Pseudo-Aristeas," 287). Gruen believes a translation was made in Alexandria to meet Jewish needs and that scholars from Palestine were involved (*Heritage and Hellenism*, 206–22). But, he also finds that the "yarn spun by the *Letter of Aristeas*" to be "largely creative fiction" (210).

156. For Gruen, he is clothed "in terms that evoke a cultivated Hellenic aristocrat"; indeed, the author "has the High Priest speak like a Greek philosopher" (*Heritage and Hellenism*, 215).

trained scholars from the ideal number of units in the nation (twelve tribes); they perform in exemplary fashion and produce a perfect translation of the divine legislation.[157] It is not impossible that Eleazar was a truly impressive man, but we have no evidence apart from our text that he was. Perhaps he was a skilled interpreter of the Torah who perceived connections to larger issues in the smaller details of the laws, but again there is no confirmation outside the *Letter of Aristeas.*

What is of interest for our purposes is that an early second-century Jewish writer saw fit to present Eleazar in such glowing terms. He paid careful attention to chronology so that he picked a high priest who was contemporary with Ptolemy II Philadelphus; that high priest corresponded with the great king as an equal, as the form of the prescript in Philadelphus's letter shows.[158] The high priest was without rival as the head of the Jewish state and his influence spread beyond the borders of Judea; the king naturally turned to him when he needed to communicate about the Pentateuch. Our second-century author apparently expected his audience to find it believable, or at least entertainingly plausible, that an otherwise obscure high priest, the uncle of the heir apparent, was a man of extraordinary stature and authority. Here, we find a second indication (with Areus's letter to Onias), also difficult to assess, in which a foreign king corresponds with the Judean high priest. In it, as in Areus's letter, there is no hint of a civil ruler alongside of, above, or below the high priest. We really do not have the historical data to secure this point as factual, but it should be noted.[159]

The Eleazar of history, whatever his character and level of learning may have been, is located by the *Letter of Aristeas* and, following it, by Josephus in the early third century.

10. Manasseh

The high-priestly list employed in Josephus's *Antiquities* contains an anomaly with regard to the process of succession upon the death of Eleazar. It should

---

157. Barclay, *Jews in the Mediterranean Diaspora*, 142.

158. "Bickermann, "Zur Datierung des Pseudo-Aristeas," 287.

159. In line with her thesis, Rooke concludes there is nothing in the *Letter of Aristeas* to alter her understanding of the high priest as an official limited to religious matters. But, this seems a strange inference from this composition in which there is no Jewish civil ruler (unless the high priest was a governor) and in which the Ptolemy, writing as to a head of state, informs the high priest that he has freed Jewish slaves and receives impressive gifts from him (*Zadok's Heirs*, 256–57).

be recalled that when Simon the Just died, his son Onias was considered too young to become high priest (*Ant.* 12.2, 5 [§44]). As a result, Simon's brother Eleazar assumed the office, perhaps as the senior surviving male of the family. It may be that Eleazar's term was a short one because, when he passed away, Simon's son Onias again did not inherit the office. He may still not have been old enough to serve; perhaps a power struggle occurred and he lost out temporarily; or possibly some other hindrance kept him from assuming the office. Josephus's laconic report says less than we would like to know: "For, when Eleazar died, his uncle Manasses took over the high priesthood, and after he departed this life, the office came to Onias, who was a son of Simon, called the Just" (*Ant.* 12.4, 1 [§157]).

Josephus is the only ancient Jewish historian to mention a third-century high priest named Manasseh. In *Ant.* 12.4, 1 (§157) the possessive pronoun αὐτοῦ in the phrase ὁ θεῖος αὐτοῦ Μανασσῆς ("his uncle Manasses") should refer to Eleazar, who is named in the preceding clause. That is, Manasseh was Eleazar's, not Onias's, uncle (see Num 27:9-10). It is possible that Josephus intended to say that Manasseh was Onias's uncle, but his notice a few words later that Eleazar was Simon's brother, without mentioning that Manasseh too was his brother, does not favor this interpretation. *Manasseh*, despite its association with the infamous, long-reigning king of Judah, is a name well attested in the high-priestly family: Jaddua, the sixth high priest of the Second Temple, had a brother Manasses who married Sanballat's daughter Nikaso and became the first high priest of the Samaritan sanctuary (*Ant.* 11.7, 2 [§§302–3]; 8, 2 [§§306–12]). If Manasseh did become high priest because of Onias's tender age, both Eleazar and he probably had fairly short reigns, or at least Eleazar did. It seems quite likely that Manasseh would not have taken the office if Onias had been of sufficient age. However long he reigned, we learn about nothing he did during that time.

11. Onias II

Simon I (the Just) was the son of Onias I and the father of Onias II,[160] who became high priest only after two other relatives held the office, perhaps during his minority. We possess more information about Onias II than we do about some of the other third-century high priests, but, as we might expect, the nature of the data is again problematic. Onias II not only figures in some of Josephus's chronological statements; he also is a major character in a story

---

160. This is the first unmistakable instance of papponymy in the high-priestly list.

that the historian has drawn from a source. That story is the so-called Tobiad Romance (*Ant.* 12.4, 1–11 [§§154–236]), which tells principally about the rise of Joseph, son of Tobias, to great wealth and power in the Ptolemaic Empire through his tax-farming work, that is, the supervision and enforcing of tax collection; his supreme good fortune serves as a background for the adventures of his eighth and most successful son Hyrcanus, who assumed his father's lucrative profession. Since the Tobiads were related by marriage to the high-priestly family, members of both clans appear in the intriguing tale. Büchler, who wrote an extensive study of the story, found in it an account not only about the rise of the Tobiad family to prominence in Jerusalem but also about the decline of high-priestly power.[161]

Josephus lodges the Tobiad Romance after a collection of testimonies to the high regard in which authorities held the Jews. He concludes that section with: "Concerning, then, the friendship of Antiochus the Great [223–187 BCE] for the Jews let the testimony here given suffice" (12.3, 4 [§153]). He then opens a new unit with a brief transitional μετὰ δὲ ταῦτα (12.4, 1 [§154]) and immediately launches into a description of the treaty between Ptolemy and Antiochus along with the marriage of Antiochus's daughter Cleopatra to Ptolemy. After references to tax-farming and Samaritan oppression of the Jews, he remarks:

> and this happened in the high priesthood of Onias. For, when Eleazar died, his uncle Manasses took over the high priesthood, and, after he departed this life, the office came to Onias ['Ονίας τὴν τιμὴν ἐξεδέ-ξατο], who was a son of Simon, called the Just. And Simon was a brother of Eleazar, as I said before. This Onias was small-minded and passionately fond of money [βραχὺς ἦν τὴν διάνοιαν καὶ χρημάτων ἥττων] and since for this reason he did not render on behalf of the people the tribute [τὸν ὑπὲρ τοῦ λαοῦ φόρον] of twenty talents of silver which his fathers had paid to the kings out of their own revenues [ἐκ τῶν ἰδίων], he roused the anger of King Ptolemy.[162] And the king sent an envoy to Jerusalem to denounce Onias for not rendering the tribute [τοὺς φόρους], and threatened that, if he did not receive it, he would parcel out their land and send his soldiers to settle on it. Accordingly, when the Jews heard the king's message, they were

---

161. *Die Tobiaden und die Oniaden*, 2.

162. Several witnesses read after "Ptolemy": τὸν Εὐεργέτην ὃς ἦν πατὴρ τοῦ Φιλοπάτορος. As we will see, it identifies the Ptolemy who is meant here but, in so doing, raises other problems with the story. See below for a discussion of this issue.

dismayed, but Onias was not put out of countenance by any of these threats, so great was his avarice. (12.4, 1 [§§156–59])

This remarkably negative portrait of the high priest Onias II functions in Josephus's narrative to introduce Joseph, son of Tobias, who steps in to save the nation in its time of peril.[163] The danger created by Onias's financial irresponsibility left an opening for the energetic Joseph. As part of his introductory words about this Joseph, Josephus writes that he was "still a young man but because of his dignity and foresight had a reputation for uprightness among the inhabitants of Jerusalem, his father being Tobias [Τωβίου], and his mother a sister of the high priest Onias" (12.4, 2 [§160]). Thus, the early protagonists in the Tobiad Romance are an uncle who is also the Jewish high priest and a nephew who is, at a young age, already highly regarded in the capital and scion of a notable family. The story leaves us in no doubt as to who was the villain and who the hero.

The young Joseph learned from his mother (Onias's sister) about the Judean crisis and arrival of the king's messenger, since he himself had been away at the time in his hometown of Phichola. Although we do not know either why the high priest withheld the tax (other than a reference to his love of money) or how Joseph had achieved personal prominence (perhaps it was due to family connections alone), the young man immediately seized the opportunity and acted with clever decisiveness:

> he went to the city (of Jerusalem) and upbraided Onias for not regarding the safety of his fellow-citizens and for being willing, instead, to place the nation in danger by withholding the money on account of which, Joseph said, he had received the chief magistracy and had obtained the high-priestly office [δι᾽ ἃ καὶ τοῦ λαοῦ τὴν προστασίαν λαβεῖν αὐτὸν ἔλεγε καὶ τῆς ἀρχιερατικῆς τιμῆς ἐπιτυχεῖν]. But, if he was so passionately fond of money that for its sake he could endure to see his country endangered and his fellow-citizens suffer all sorts of things, he advised him to go to the king and request him to remit to him either the whole of the money or a part

---

163. From such statements the perspective from which the story is told emerges clearly. That it criticizes Onias so strongly is an argument against Jonathan Goldstein's theory that Onias's descendant Onias IV authored the Tobiad Romance ("The Tales of the Tobiads," in *Christianity, Judaism, and Other Greco-Roman Cults: Studies for Morton Smith at Sixty*, Part 3: *Judaism Before 70*, ed. J. Neusner, SJLA 12 [Leiden: Brill, 1975], 85–123). For this argument, see John J. Collins, *Between Athens and Jerusalem: Jewish Identity in the Hellenistic Diaspora*, 2nd ed., BRS (Grand Rapids: Eerdmans, 2000), 76.

of it. As Onias, however, answered that he did not desire to hold office [μήτε ἄρχειν ἐθέλειν] and that he was ready to give up the high-priesthood if that were possible [καὶ τὴν ἀρχιερωσύνην δ᾽ εἰ δυνα-τόν ἐστιν, ἑτοίμως ἔχειν ἀποθέσθαι λέγοντος], and would not go to the king, for he was in no way concerned about these matters, Joseph asked him whether he would give him leave to go as an envoy to Ptolemy on behalf of the nation. And, when Onias gave his permission, Joseph went up to the temple and, calling the people together in assembly, exhorted them not to be disturbed or frightened because of his uncle Onias' neglect of them. (12.4, 2 [§§161–64])

Onias granted his permission and thus, as it turned out, launched Joseph on his new career. The latter won the royal envoy's favor by generous treatment, and the official, upon returning to Egypt, "reported to the king the arrogant behaviour of Onias and informed him of the excellence of Joseph" (12.4, 3 [§167]). He added that Joseph himself would be coming to Egypt "to ask that the sins of his people be excused, for he was their protector [αὐτοῦ προστάτην]" (12.4, 3 [§167]).

Like his ancient namesake, this Joseph met the Egyptian sovereign face-to-face, and, as had the pharaoh of Genesis, Ptolemy welcomed Joseph into his chariot.[164] The monarch

> began to complain about the actions of Onias. Then Joseph said, "pardon him because of his age; for surely you are not unaware that old people [τοὺς πρεσβύτας] and infants are likely to have the same level of intelligence. But from us who are young you will obtain everything so as to find no fault." (12.4, 3 [§172])

Joseph's wit earned him royal approval and a daily place at the king's table, much to the chagrin of the "chief men of Syria" (§174) who had earlier mocked Joseph's relative poverty when all of them were traveling to Alexandria to bid for the annual tax-farming rights (§§168–69). As we might expect,

---

164. Commentators have noted various parallels between this latter-day Joseph and his biblical counterpart, both of whom were spectacularly successful in the royal court of Egypt. See, for instance, Willrich, *Juden und Griechen,* 94–95. These similarities some have regarded as significant pointers toward the nonhistorical character of these parts of the story (for example, Dov Gera, "On the Credibility of the History of the Tobiads [Josephus, *Antiquities* 12, 156-222, 228-236]," in *Greece and Rome in Eretz Israel,* ed. A. Kasher, U. Rappaport, and G. Fuks [Jerusalem: Yitzhak ben-Zvi, IES, 1990], 32–33).

Joseph managed to obtain those lucrative rights after an exorbitant bid and clever ploy (12.4, 4 [§§175–79]); and he exercised his virtually unlimited revenue-raising powers to great royal and personal advantage (§§180–85). Josephus relates little more about his career but does record that Joseph carried out his successful labors for twenty-two years (12.4, 6 [§186]; see 12.4, 10 [§224]) and became the father of seven sons by one wife and of an eighth— Hyrcanus—by his niece whom his brother (her father) had substituted for the foreign dancing girl to whom Joseph had taken a fancy while drunk. The brother acted in this fashion to protect Joseph from violating the law prohibiting a Jew from having sexual relations with a foreign woman (§§186–89). Joseph's son Hyrcanus actually becomes the protagonist in the story, as commentators have observed. Like his father, he was audacious, and he proved far more adept than his brothers in carrying on their father's legacy (§§190–95).

The intriguing tales about Hyrcanus's lavish gifts to King Ptolemy on the occasion of his son's birth (12.4, 7–9 [§§196–222]) need not detain us, but the rivalry between Hyrcanus and his brothers became a crucial element in the political climate of Judah in the succeeding decades. These brothers, we learn, had written "to all the friends of the king that they should make an end of him [Hyrcanus]" (12.4, 7 [§202]; compare 12.4, 9 [§218]). He, of course, outsmarted them and even persuaded the king, who had offered him any gift he desired, to intervene:

> But he asked that the king do no more for him than to write to his father and brothers about him. And so the king, after showing him the highest honour and giving him splendid presents, wrote to his father and brothers and to all his governors and administrators, and sent him away. But when Hyrcanus' brothers heard that he had obtained these favours from the king and was returning with great honour, they went out to meet him and do away with him. (§§219–21)

Even Joseph was angry with Hyrcanus for having spent so much of his money on a royal present. A fratricidal war resulted:

> And when Hyrcanus' brothers encountered him in battle, he killed many of the men with them and also two of the brothers themselves, while the rest escaped to their father in Jerusalem. Hyrcanus therefore went to that city, but as no one admitted him, he withdrew in fear to the country across the river Jordan, and there made his home, levying tribute on the barbarians. (§222)

At *Ant.* 12.4, 10 (§§223–24), Josephus or his source supplies chronological data:

> At that time there had begun to reign over Asia Seleucus, surnamed Soter, who was the son of Antiochus the Great.[165] And then also died Hyrcanus' father Joseph, who had been an excellent and high-minded man and had brought the Jewish people from poverty and a state of weakness to more splendid opportunities of life during the twenty-two years when he controlled the taxes of Syria, Phoenicia and Samaria. And death also came to his uncle Onias, who left the high priesthood to his son Simon.

At this point there is an interlude in Josephus's recounting of the Tobiad Romance, while he reproduces the letter that the Spartan king Areus sent to Simon's successor Onias (on this see above, under Onias I). The historian returns to the conflict between Hyrcanus and his half-brothers in 12.4, 11 (§228). Since they were prominent men, their disputes had repercussions far beyond family confines: "Now on the death of Joseph there arose factional strife among the people on account of his sons. For the elder brothers made war on Hyrcanus, who was the youngest of Joseph's children, and the population was divided into two camps. And the majority fought on the side of the elder brothers, as did the high priest Simon because of his kinship with them" (§§228–29). Josephus credits Hyrcanus with a seven-year rule in parts of the Transjordan and with constructing magnificent quarters there. We learn that these seven years transpired during the reign of Seleucus over Asia. After a note (§§234–35) about the accession of Antiochus Epiphanes (in 175 BCE) and the death of Ptolemy Epiphanes (in 181 BCE), Josephus writes: "As for Hyrcanus, seeing how great was the power which Antiochus had, and fearing that he might be captured by him and punished for what he had done to the Arabs, he ended his life by his own hand. And all his property was seized by Antiochus" (12.4, 11 [§236]). With this reminder that Hyrcanus was an enemy of the Seleucid monarch (and presumably a friend of the Egyptian king), the Tobiad Romance ends.

The many details and fascinating characters in the story have been subjected to numerous studies. An obvious question for our purposes has to do with the amount of historical reliability there may be in the text.[166] This issue

---

165. This should be Seleucus IV (187–175 BCE) who was Antiochus the Great's (Antiochus III [223–187 BCE]) son, but Seleucus III (226–223 BCE) was called Soter while Seleucus IV was known as Philopator.

166. Scholars have reached widely divergent conclusions on this point. Goldstein ("The Tales of the Tobiads," 123) ends his essay by writing: "Except for the exaggerated figure for the Ptolemaic revenues, the stories of Joseph and Hyrcanus are entirely true." Gera ("On the Credi-

is tied to that of chronology. When are these events supposed to have happened? If there is an element of historicity in the story, what does it divulge about Judean politics and especially about the roles of the high priest?

1. The historical setting of the Tobiad Romance: Scholars have long realized that, as Josephus presents it, the romance suffers from serious chronological difficulties. Briefly stated, Josephus begins the story around the time when Antiochus III and Ptolemy V Epiphanes made a treaty of friendship that included marriage of Antiochus's daughter Cleopatra to Ptolemy (12.4, 1 [§154]), an event that occurred in about 193 BCE.[167] The historian allotted twenty-two years to Joseph's tax-farming career, which began some time after the marriage, and seven years to his son Hyrcanus, without indicating whether those seven years followed immediately on Joseph's twenty-two. At a minimum, the two careers, if they came end on end, would require twenty-nine years. However, Josephus also relates that Hyrcanus took his own life when Antiochus IV was established on the Seleucid throne. If he means by this the beginning of Antiochus IV's reign in 175 BCE, his chronology is at least eleven years too short to accommodate the number of years for Joseph and Hyrcanus (assuming a twenty-nine-year span for their careers). There is the added problem that if these events occurred in the first decades of the second century, Onias II, whose father was high priest about one century earlier, would be improbably elderly by this point.

2. Furthermore, it is obvious that, at least for Joseph's career and for part of Hyrcanus's as well, Ptolemaic rule of Palestine is presupposed. The elder Tobiad could hardly be Ptolemy's successful tax farmer in the areas of Coele-Syria, Samaria, Judea, and Phoenicia if they were not then included in the

bility of the History of the Tobiads," 21), however, thinks both parts of the story may be classified with the *Letter of Aristeas* as "fictional accounts set in a historic framework." A number of older studies express a similarly negative verdict regarding the tale's historicity (for example, Willrich, *Juden und Griechen*, 91–95; Julius Wellhausen, *Israelitische und jüdische Geschichte,* 2nd ed. [Berlin: Reimer, 1895], 231–32). See also Gruen, *Heritage and Hellenism*, 236–40, although he does speak of a substratum of historical material in the story (99–106).

167. See Marcus, *Josephus* 7, 80 n. c. Some scholars have concluded that Josephus actually does not think of the marriage as occurring in 193 BCE but rather immediately after the beginning of Ptolemy V's reign in 204 BCE—an example is Daniel R. Schwartz, "Josephus' Tobiads: Back to the Second Century?" in *Jews in a Graeco-Roman World,* ed. M. Goodman (Oxford: Clarendon, 1998), 56. It is not at all clear that this is true, because there are general references to a range of times in the context, as a result of which it is not evident at exactly which time Josephus located the event. It must be admitted, though, that if Josephus understood the marriage to have taken place in 204 BCE, the twenty-nine years he attributes to Joseph and Hyrcanus would end just as Antiochus IV took the Seleucid throne—something that happened around the time when Hyrcanus committed suicide.

Egyptian empire. Josephus's chronology, however, would entail that throughout the entire twenty-nine years of Joseph and Hyrcanus, the area was under Seleucid control, since Antiochus III had snatched it from Ptolemy V in 200 BCE, a fact recognized in the peace treaty of 198. In fairness to Josephus, it should be said that he anticipated this objection by reproducing the widely attested tradition—part of the propaganda at the time about who owned Coele-Syria—that the treaty between Antiochus III and Ptolemy V in 193 BCE, which involved a marriage, included a dowry of "Coele-Syria, Samaria, Judaea and Phoenicia. And when the tribute was divided between the two sovereigns [apparently Ptolemy and Cleopatra],[168] the prominent men purchased the right to farm the taxes in their several provinces and, collecting the sum fixed, paid it to the royal pair" (12.4, 1 [§§154–55]). Thus, although the Seleucids had taken Judea, Antiochus III supposedly returned the tax rights to it and other surrounding areas as a nuptial gift. Joseph could, therefore, farm the taxes of these areas for the Ptolemaic king. While a number of ancient sources do mention this agreement about the tribute of the areas in question and later Ptolemaic claims to the territories were based on the alleged agreement, there is no indication it was ever implemented; furthermore, Antiochus III denied the claim.[169] As Tcherikover put it:

> The main point is that the question concerned solely Ptolemy's right to enjoy the revenues and not Antiochus' authority to rule the country, which Josephus specifically negates in his story, when he depicts Ptolemy as ruling the country with unlimited power and threatening to drive the Jews from their land. It is clear that all the events described by Josephus occurred when the country was really subject to Egypt—before 200 B.C.E—since after that year the rule of Coele-Syria passed into Seleucid hands.[170]

Several items in *Antiquities* itself suggest that even if one were to accept the thesis about the dowry, the post-200 BCE setting is incorrect. First, as

---

168. So Marcus, *Josephus* 7, 80 n. g, referring to M. Holleaux, "Sur un passage de Flavius Josèphe (*Ant.* xii.4)," *REJ* 39 (1899): 161–76.

169. See Edwyn R. Bevan, *The House of Seleucus,* 2 vols. (London: Edward Arnold, 1902; reprint: New York: Barnes & Noble, 1966), 2.296 (Appendix D). Bevan notes that Polybius knows of no such arrangement. Compare also Goldstein, "The Tales of the Tobiads," 86. Schwartz ("Josephus' Tobiads," 48–50, 58–59) reviews some older views suggesting that the evidence from Polybius and Livy attests to an "ambiguous" situation regarding Coele-Syria, but the passages from these writers are consistent with the idea that, while Antiochus III and his successors ruled Coele-Syria, Ptolemaic monarchs did not accept the loss of land.

170. *Hellenistic Civilization and the Jews,* 128.

noted earlier, the text at 12.4, 1 (§158) identifies the Ptolemy whom Onias II defied. Marcus's edition of the text reads τὸν βασιλέα Πτολεμαῖον, but the critical apparatus shows that manuscripts PLAW are more specific: τὸν Εὐεργέτην ὃς ἦν πατὴρ τοῦ Φιλοπάτορος. That is, these manuscripts name the Ptolemy as Euergetes the father of Philopator or Ptolemy III Euergetes (246–221 BCE), the father of Ptolemy IV Philopator (221–204 BCE). A few lines later, manuscripts PAW read Εὐεργέτην Πτολεμαῖον where other witnesses have only the second word, not the epithet. Here again, Marcus preferred the shorter reading.[171] Another point is that the story not only presupposes Ptolemaic control of Palestine, but it also uses official Ptolemaic terms for geographical regions, as M. Stern observed.[172] This, too, would place the story in the third century, not in the later period when the Seleucids controlled Palestine. If Euergetes is the Ptolemy who figures in the first part of the story, then Joseph's rise would be dated far earlier than the context in *Antiquities* suggests; a concomitant result would be that Onias II would belong at a considerably earlier time.

An argument against an earlier dating for the story has been the name of the Ptolemy's wife—Cleopatra. The first Cleopatra in Ptolemaic history was the daughter of the Seleucid monarch Antiochus III, whom Ptolemy V wed in 193 BCE. Hence, if Cleopatra was the queen's name, the story could be no earlier than this date. However, the standard reply has been that by the time the story was written the name *Cleopatra* had become so common for Ptolemaic consorts that it was assumed that all of them must have been named Cleopatra. Even Livy makes this mistake.[173]

If we accept the Tobiad Romance as having a substratum of history (to use Gruen's term) beneath some romantic frills,[174] a reasonable chronology can be constructed, although it seems impossible to salvage Josephus's arrange-

---

171. Goldstein argues that the Ptolemy whom Joseph impressed must be Euergetes ("The Tales of the Tobiads," 87–88). He accepts the two longer readings mentioned above and also draws attention to the term εὐεργέτῃ in 12.4, 8 (§206). It is used by Hyrcanus with reference to the Ptolemy of whom he says that he "had been his father's benefactor." This may be another clue that, in the source story, the Ptolemy was Euergetes, but, on Goldstein's chronology, he would be Ptolemy IV, not Ptolemy III. Schwartz considers the readings with the epithet *Euergetes* to be a "learned correction inserted by scribes motivated by arguments similar to those followed by modern sceptics" ("Josephus' Tobiads," 54).

172. "Notes on the Story of Joseph, Son of Tobiah (*Ant.* 12.154ff.)," *Tarbiz* 32 (1962): 38–39 (Hebrew).

173. For example, Goldstein, "The Tales of the Tobiads," 99.

174. For folktale elements, see Susan Niditch, "Father-Son Folktale Patterns and Tyrant Typologies in Josephus' Ant. 12.160-222," *JJS* 32 (1981): 47–55.

ment as it stands. Tcherikover and Goldstein have produced lists of the key dates in the Romance as they place them historically:[175]

Event	Tcherikover	Goldstein
Onias's nonpayment	242–240 BCE	227–224 BCE
Joseph as tax-farmer	230–220	227–224
Hyrcanus in Egypt	205–200	210
Death of Hyrcanus	175–170	170–169

The periods that they posit are roughly the same, although they differ on individual dates within the general limits. It is quite likely that they are correct in placing the beginning of the events in the reign of Ptolemy III. Not only does the occurrence of his epithet in the story indicate as much; what is known of the Tobiad family also points clearly in this direction.

The Tobiads appear in a number of sources that span several centuries in the Second-Temple period. Nehemiah mentions a Tobiah the Ammonite servant (Neh 2:10, 19; 4:3, 7; 6:1, 12, 14, 17-19 [where he is politically and familially related to Judeans]; 13:4-9 [where the priest, not the high priest, Eliashib prepared a chamber in the temple for Tobiah]). His name and place in the temple make one think he was Jewish, despite the gentilic "Ammonite" that Nehemiah gives him.[176] His presence in Ammon favors a genealogical connection between this Tobiah and the Tobiah who is mentioned several times in the Zenon papyri.[177] The Tobiah of the papyri can be dated fairly accurately because he corresponded with officials of Ptolemy II Philadelphus (283–246 BCE) and even sent gifts to the king; also, two of the papyri from Tobiah give the exact date on which they were written—the equivalent of what Tcherikover and Fuks calculate as 12 May 257.[178] A deed of sale (no. 1) in which one of

---

175. Tcherikover, *Hellenistic Civilization and the Jews*, 130; Goldstein, "The Tales of the Tobiads," 101–2.

176. Benjamin Mazar, "The Tobiads," *IEJ* 7 (1957): 143–44. Mazar thinks it likely he was an official, the Persian governor, in Ammon. Mazar mistakenly identifies the priest Eliashib as the high priest of the same name and thus is misled into thinking that he was "not only a ruler in his own country and a 'great man' in Jerusalem but also the head of a party supporting the Zadokite high priest" (145); Rooke makes the same mistake (*Zadok's Heirs*, 260); see chap. 2 above. Mazar's results are regularly repeated in the literature, but Schwartz ("Josephus' Tobiads," 59–60) thinks the discovery of a Tobias in the Zenon papyri is the real reason why scholars have mistakenly rejected Josephus's chronology for the Tobiad story. As we have seen, however, there are other good reasons to alter it; also, a Transjordanian Tobias in contact with the Ptolemaic government in 257 BCE obviously could be Joseph's father.

177. Mazar surveys the more certain and other possible references to Tobiads of the same family over several centuries in "The Tobiads," 137–45, 229–38 (note the list on p. 235).

178. Victor A. Tcherikover and Alexander Fuks, *Corpus Papyrorum Judaicarum*, 3 vols. (Cambridge: Harvard Univ. Press, 1957–63), 1.125–29 (nos. 4–5). The same Tobiah is mentioned

Tobiah's men sold a slave girl is said to have been written ἐν Βίρται τῆς ᾽Αμμανίτιδος, "in the stronghold of Ammanitis."[179] That is, this Tobias too was from Ammon. He was very likely the father of Joseph who is called the son of Tobiah in the Tobiad Romance (for example, *Ant.* 12.4, 2 [§160]). If he was his father, then some point in the reign of Ptolemy III would be a reasonable time for Joseph to attain prominence. Also, the contacts between Tobiah and the Ptolemaic administration form an instructive backdrop for the rise of Joseph.

Scholars who place the earlier phases of the romance in Ptolemy III's reign have at times attempted to uncover a specific historical context that might explain the high priest's refusal to pay the annual tribute that he himself owed to the government. Tcherikover, following others, wrote:

> The year 242 would have been the most suitable for Onias' attempt to break off his connections with Egypt and to go over to Syria.[180] That year Seleucus II Callinicus gathered his scattered forces, which had been defeated by Ptolemy Euergetes at the beginning of the campaign, and took the offensive against Egypt; he was able to beat Ptolemy's forces on several occasions and drive them back on Damascus. These victories may have aroused Onias to hope that Seleucus would be the victor, hence he refused to pay Ptolemy the customary tribute, in the belief that his rule was at an end. However, he encountered resistance from the supporters of Egypt whose most prominent representative was Joseph the son of Tobiah; Seleucus' successes were short-lived and Onias' attempt remained an isolated incident which brought no change in the Jewish political situation.[181]

Goldstein thinks this setting in the Third Syrian War is unlikely. Not only did Ptolemy III retain control of Jerusalem, but the Tobiad Romance presupposes a time of peace, not of war. He thinks Onias's refusal to pay the tribute should

---

in texts 1 and 2. His name is spelled Τουβίας. See pp. 115–16 for a summary of the evidence that the papyri divulge about him.

179. *Corpus Papyrorum Judaicarum*, 1.116, 119–20. Tcherikover and Fuks discuss the various names for the site (116). The first element in one of them, Σωραβιττ—or Σουραβιττ—reflects the Hebrew word צור (fortress), which appears as Τύρον in Josephus, *Ant.* 12.4, 11 (§233).

180. Note the assumption, often met in the literature, that pro-Seleucid/Ptolemaic or anti-Seleucid/Ptolemaic stances dictated actions by Jewish leaders at this time. The story does not say that Onias II tried to shift his loyalty to the Seleucids; it says merely that he did not wish to pay the tribute and did not want to rule.

181. *Hellenistic Civilization and the Jews*, 129. The last statement can hardly be what Tcherikover meant, since he believed that the incident produced a most significant change in the political situation (see p. 132). For this setting see also M. Stern, "Notes," 43.

be placed in the later, inactive years of Ptolemy III.[182] There does not appear to be very strong evidence for determining when this incident may have occurred. While the rivalry between the two Hellenistic monarchies for Syria and Palestine and the presence of differing parties in Judah at the time ought not to be ruled out as a possible explanation for Onias's withholding the money, we should acknowledge that Josephus's source did not connect the incident with this tension.[183]

A good case can be made for placing the beginning of the events included in the Tobiad story during the reign of Ptolemy III, although it is not possible to specify a date within it. We should next treat what the story says about the high priest Onias and about the high priesthood itself. The wording of the account of Onias's action in refusing to pay tribute may reveal some important details about both. Josephus, as we have seen, charges Onias with greed and narrow-mindedness. These personal traits were the cause of his foolish, short-sighted action in not paying what is described as τὸν ὑπὲρ τοῦ λαοῦ φόρον, ὃν τοῖς βασιλεῦσιν οἱ πατέρες αὐτοῦ ἐτέλουν ἐκ τῶν ἰδίων, τάλαντα εἴκοσιν ἀργυρίου (*Ant.* 12.4, 1 [§158]). There are several questions that arise from these words. First, the payment, which was traditional in Onias's high-priestly family, is defined as one "concerning the people." This at first sight sounds like a national tax of some kind and one that the high priests had paid from their private resources. Nevertheless, the size of the tax— twenty silver talents—makes it unlikely that it was a tax on the nation, as Tcherikover has observed.[184] It seems to be a special levy that is further clarified by the prepositional phrase ὑπὲρ τοῦ λαοῦ. Tcherikover raised the possibility that the high priests paid this tax to purchase the office of προστασία.[185]

---

182. "The Tales of the Tobiads," 96.

183. Hengel (*Judaism and Hellenism*, 1.27) rejects Josephus's explanation and says that Onias acted "because of general weariness in face of constant regimentation by the Ptolemaic administration." He also thinks there may have been a connection with Seleucus II's short-lived success toward the close of the Third Syrian War.

184. *Hellenistic Civilization and the Jews*, 459 n. 39.

185. Ibid. One possibility worth considering is that the tribute was a λειτουργία, that is, one of the "public and constitutionally regulated services in the discharge of all kinds of compulsory tasks and the execution of all possible offices" in the Ptolemaic kingdom (Hermann Strathmann, "λειτουργέω," in *TDNT* 4.217). Joseph's own words cited in *Ant.* 12.4, 2 (§161) say the tax was for obtaining Onias's offices. A different approach is advocated by Gera ("On the Credibility of the History of the Tobiads," 34–35): he believes the writer "fabricated the story of the High Priest's refusal to pay taxes in order to allow Joseph to become the leader of the Jews, while the auction of taxes in Alexandria was used by him to make his hero the virtual ruler of the non-Jews of Syria and Phoenicia." The author would not have to invent the high priest's action to produce this effect; indeed, it is difficult to understand how the first part of Gera's sentence arises from any point in the story.

In the context, this makes excellent sense, because this very office may have been transferred to Joseph in the sequel.[186]

The term first occurs in the summary of young Joseph's harsh criticism directed at his uncle Onias: he upbraided him for disregarding "the safety of his fellow-citizens and for being willing, instead, to place the nation in danger by withholding the money on account of which, Joseph said, he had received the chief magistracy [τοῦ λαοῦ τὴν προστασίαν λαβεῖν αὐτόν] and had obtained the high-priestly office" (Ant. 12.4, 2 [§161]). Here, the position called τὴν προστασίαν is qualified directly by the phrase τοῦ λαοῦ, just as the tax was in the passage quoted above. It does seem likely, too, that the text also connects obtaining the high-priestly office with the payment in question.

The office termed ἡ προστασία has engendered a lengthy debate among historians. What could be meant by this position that the high priest is supposed to have held? It should be recalled that Hecateus of Abdera had employed the same word in connection with the Jewish high priest. The Mosaic constitution, he wrote, gave to the high priest "authority over the people [τὴν δὲ τοῦ πλήθους προστασίαν]." Tcherikover maintains that Hecateus is here accurately reflecting historical reality for his time (shortly after 300 BCE) when "the High Priest was the central personality in Judaea and that the historic process of the transfer of the traditional authority from the king to the High Priest, which began in the time of Zerubbabel ben Shealtiel of royal descent, and of Joshua ben Jehozadak the High Priest, had ended with the decisive victory of the High Priest."[187] That is, the προστασία was the political side of the high-priestly authority.

In the story of Joseph the Tobiad, that office seems to be transferred from Onias to his nephew. Onias declared to Joseph that he had no desire to rule (ἄρχειν) and also that he would be willing to abandon the high priesthood, were that possible (Ant. 12.4, 2 [§163]). The high priest's bold statement distinguishes ruling from the high priesthood; in other words, he seems to be saying that he wished to cede the political side of his office and, if it could be arranged, the priestly side as well. Joseph received his permission to serve as an

---

186. Rooke (Zadok's Heirs, 257–58) thinks an official of the Ptolemaic administration would have overseen the finances of the Jerusalem temple. As a matter of fact, we know of no such official from the sources, though Rooke is right to say the high priests were not tax farmers for the Ptolemies. In her study of the Tobiad tale, she fails to deal with the implications of the term προστασία (see 256–62). For the silence of the sources regarding a supreme Ptolemaic administrator in Palestine at this time, see Victor Tcherikover, "Palestine under the Ptolemies (A Contribution to the Study of the Zenon Papyri)," Mizraim 4–5 (1937): 39.

187. Hellenistic Civilization and the Jews, 58–59. Hengel attributes Hecateus's words to his idealistic portrait of the Jews and thinks they have "only limited historical value" (Judaism and Hellenism, 2.22). Compare also Gruen, Heritage and Hellenism, 105 n. 147.

envoy for the nation to represent their cause before Ptolemy, and this was announced to the populace to reassure them. Ptolemy's emissary to Jerusalem,[188] whom Joseph favorably impressed, reported later to the king that Joseph would request forgiveness for the populace "for he was their protector [αὐτοῦ προστάτην]" (§167). Experts such as Marcus have doubted that Ptolemy's official was referring to the office that Joseph had just obtained from Onias.[189] But, Joseph had clearly received something from Onias that involved representing and defending the people before the king, and, furthermore, what he had gained is to be distinguished from the right to the tax-farming monopoly because Joseph purchased that right later under different circumstances. Hence, Tcherikover seems to be incorrect when he asserts that the office of προστάτης included the right to levy taxes;[190] the high priest may have imposed a tax to pay those twenty talents (although this opposes what Josephus says), yet the right to levy taxes apparently did not rest with the high priest alone. It is true that nothing is said of Joseph's paying the twenty talents for the προστασία, but he did make arrangements to provide much more revenue for the royal purse. Whether or not Joseph obtained the προστασία, the high priest did have it according to the story.

There is some reason for thinking that Onias II, for whatever reason, relinquished an aspect of high-priestly power to Joseph and that the word προστασία represents the secular or political side of his authority[191]—something for which he and his ancestors had paid a considerable amount of money to the Ptolemaic government. If so, we have another indication of high-priestly political power, again with no mention of a civil ruler. In this respect, the Tobiad Romance joins the letter from Areus to Onias I and the Letter of Aristeas; unfortunately for our purposes, it also joins them as a source whose historical reliability we cannot gauge.

12. Simon II

A case was made above that the high priest who is called *Simon the Just* in some texts was Simon I, who served early in the third century BCE. The

188. That is, no local Ptolemaic official intervenes; one comes from Alexandria.

189. *Josephus* 7, 88 n. a: he became "merely their spokesman or envoy."

190. *Hellenistic Civilization and the Jews*, 132. For more on the position of προστασία, see the section below on Onias III and his opponent Simon.

191. Klaus-Dietrich Schunck supports this position after briefly surveying some of the other texts treated above in which the high priest deals with foreign rulers ("Hoherpriester und Politiker? Die Stellung der Hohenpriester von Jaddua bis Jonatan zur jüdischen Gemeinde und zum hellenistischen Staat," *VT* 44 [1994]: 500–503).

sources for his reign as high priest and for his character were examined in that section. Josephus makes only a few references to Simon II in the *Antiquities*, and it may be, although this is less likely, that the Simon lauded in Sirach 50 is Simon II.

Near the end of the Tobiad Romance, Josephus writes: "And death also came to his [Hyrcanus's] uncle Onias [= Onias II], who left the high priesthood to his son Simon. When he too died, his son Onias became his successor in office" (*Ant.* 12.4, 10 [§§224–25]). The statement reads like an excerpt from a list, but it does reveal useful information. In reporting that Onias left the high priesthood to his son, Josephus discloses that the hereditary principle once again established itself. Simon's father, Onias, had indeed been the son of Simon I, but two other high priests—Eleazar and Manasseh—held the office before Onias II became the high priest. He, however, passed the office directly to his son.

The historian's next reference to Simon II deals with his political loyalties. Josephus notes that, after the death of the Tobiad Joseph, conflicts broke out among the Judean population "on account of his sons. For the elder brothers made war on Hyrcanus, who was the youngest of Joseph's children, and the population was divided into two camps. The majority fought on the side of the elder brothers, as did the high priest Simon because of his kinship with them. Hyrcanus, therefore, gave up his intention of returning to Jerusalem, and settled in the country across the Jordan" (12.4, 11 [§§228–29]). The division and strife of the Tobiad sons had been mentioned earlier in the Romance (12.4, 9 [§§221–22]), although the factionalism among the populace was not explicit in that paragraph.[192] What is of interest for our purposes here is that the high priest Simon stands on the side of the older brothers—a stance that appears to make him pro-Seleucid, as we will see.[193] Josephus, in accounting for Simon's alliance with the older brothers—brothers who fared so poorly in the Tobiad Romance—claims that he supported them "because of his kinship with them [διὰ τὴν συγγένειαν]" (12.4, 11 [§229]). The motivation ascribed to the high priest is puzzling because he was related to all of Joseph's sons, not just to the older ones. In fact, as Marcus observed, "the statement of the 'Tobiad Romance,' §§187ff., that Hyrcanus was the son of Joseph by a different mother [the daughter of his brother] would only make his relation to the high priestly family closer, since his mother was also related to the high priest. It is just possible,

---

192. Josephus says only that Hyrcanus withdrew after no one would allow him into Jerusalem (*Ant.* 12.4, 9 [§222]), although he seems to have won the skirmish with his brothers.

193. Compare *Ant.* 12.4, 11 (§236) for Hyrcanus's fear of Antiochus IV, and 12.5, 1 (§§237–41) for Antiochus's support of the other Tobiads.

however, that by συγγένειαν Josephus means something like 'common interests.'"[194] This latter suggestion commends itself because it makes better sense of the expression in the context. W. Michaelis has catalogued many instances in which συγγένεια does refer to genealogical relationship, but he notes that it also has a wider range of meanings: "It thus refers to the relationship which exists between men and peoples by descent, . . . or by agreement and compatibility of disposition, . . ."[195] If the broader meaning of συγγένεια is adopted for the present context, the sentence conveys only the general idea that the high priest was of the same mind as the elder Tobiads. It is significant that the views of the nation were split between the Tobiad factions and that the high priest is presented merely as a supporter of one of them.

Apart from the few lines quoted above, Josephus has no more to say about Simon II with the exception of a confusing claim about his sons. When he is writing about the later high priest Jason/Jesus (see below), he explains: "Jesus, however—this was the brother of Onias [= Onias III]—was deprived of the high-priesthood when the king became angry with him and gave it to his younger brother, named Onias; for Simon had three sons, and the high-priesthood came to all three of them as we have shown" (12.5, 1 [§238]). That is, Josephus identifies Simon II's sons as Onias (III), Jesus/Jason, and Onias (= Menelaus). We will deal with this curious section later when discussing the evidence concerning Jason and Menelaus.

A final reference to Simon II is found in 3 Maccabees 2. There, the setting is the time of Ptolemy IV Philopator (221–204 BCE [1:1]) and his great victory over Antiochus III at the battle of Raphia in 217 BCE. Following the success of his troops, the king toured the region and gave gifts to local temples in order to encourage the people living in the area. He included Jerusalem in his itinerary, was greeted by a delegation of the council [τῆς γερουσίας] and elders (τῶν πρεσβυτέρων; 1:8), and offered the appropriate sacrifices at the temple. The splendor of the place and the good order maintained there aroused in the monarch a desire to enter not only the sanctuary but the Holy of Holies itself. The Jews who were with him explained that this was not permitted "because not even members of their own nation were allowed to enter, not even all of the priests, but only the high priest who was pre-eminent over all [τῷ προηγουμένῳ πάντων ἀρχιερεῖ]—and he only once a year" (1:11). They failed to convince the king, who reiterated his intention to enter the forbidden room. Jewish people of all ranks and types took to praying that the supreme God would intervene to prevent the Ptolemy from profaning the holy place.

194. *Josephus* 7, 116–17 n. b.
195. "συγγενής, συγγένεια," in *TDNT* 7.737.

Philopator, however, advanced on the temple to carry out his intention. At this point, we meet Simon II.[196]

> Then the high priest Simon, facing the sanctuary, bending his knees and extending his hands with calm dignity, prayed as follows: "Lord, Lord, king of the heavens, and sovereign of all creation, holy among the holy ones, the only ruler, almighty, give attention to us who are suffering grievously from an impious and profane man, puffed up in his audacity and power. For you, the creator of all things and the governor of all, are a just Ruler, and you judge those who have done anything in insolence and arrogance." (3 Macc 2:1-3)

Simon rehearses three instances of divine punishment for the arrogant in the past (the giants in the flood, the people of Sodom, and the pharaoh of the exodus) and reminds the deity of his promise to hear petitions offered from the sanctuary when the people were in distress (1 Kgs 8:33-34, 48-50).[197] He also asks that the people not be held accountable for any profanation the place should suffer from the king and his men. As commentators have observed, the role of Simon here is balanced later in the book by the priest Eleazar, who offers a prayer, also citing scriptural examples, in another situation of danger, this time for the Jews in Egypt (6:1-15).[198]

Third Maccabees reports that God responded to the high priest's intercessory and mediatorial prayer. Philopator was punished in a way that reminds one, at least superficially,[199] of the fate that later befell the Seleucid

---

196. Although 3 Macc 2:1 is not present in some manuscripts, including it appears to be the preferable reading. Compare C. Emmet, "III Maccabees," in *APOT* 1.164; H. Anderson, "3 Maccabees," in *OTP* 2.518 n. 2 a.

197. Judith H. Newman has studied the prayer in depth, relating it to and contrasting it with other uses of exempla from Scripture and with parallels in Greek traditions (*Praying by the Book: The Scripturalization of Prayer in Second Temple Judaism* [SBLEJL 14; Atlanta: Scholars, 1999], 155–200). The exempla were selected to illustrate the punishment of arrogance, in this case of arrogant individuals who, like Ptolemy, were non-Israelites. Inclusion of the pharaoh was particularly apt. As Newman shows, the exempla are cases of scriptural passages as they had come to be interpreted.

198. See, for example, George W. E. Nickelsburg, *Jewish Literature between the Bible and the Mishnah: A Historical and Literary Introduction* (Philadelphia: Fortress Press, 1981), 171. For the connection between Palestinian and Egyptian Jews that comes to expression in the two parts of 3 Maccabees, see D. Williams, "*3 Maccabees*: A Defense of Diaspora Judaism?" *JSP* 13 (1995): 17–29; Barclay, *Jews in the Mediterranean Diaspora*, 198.

199. Compare Aryeh Kasher, *The Jews in Hellenistic and Roman Egypt: The Struggle for Equal Rights*, TSAJ 7 (Tübingen: Mohr/Siebeck, 1985), 212–13 n. 16.

emissary Heliodorus according to 2 Maccabees 3 (see below). The deity shook Ptolemy until he lay helpless on his side and had to be removed for safety by his friends and bodyguards. Once the ordeal was over, the king was in no mood for conciliation but subjected the Jews of Egypt to trying times—the subject of the remaining chapters in 3 Maccabees.

The intent here is not to suggest that 3 Maccabees is a reliable historical source for events in the third century;[200] rather, it is merely proposed that aspects of the story's framework may reasonably be taken as reflecting what happened then. True, "[o]ur narrative purports to give an historical account of certain incidents in the life of Ptolemy IV Philopator. . . . From the start, however, its rhetorical tone indicates the author's primary interest in drama, pathos and religious propaganda."[201] At least, 3 Maccabees puts the right Ptolemy at the battle of Raphia and the right high priest in Jerusalem, and it accurately reports a few other details.[202] The chronology that the author uses implies that by about 217 BCE—the date of the battle of Raphia—Simon II was the high priest in Jerusalem.[203] This in turn entails that Onias II had died by this time. Here we have another indication, though not a very strong one, that the reign of Ptolemy III Euergetes is the original setting for the Tobiad Romance. We may also add 3 Maccabees to the list of sources that envisage no civil ruler beside the high priest in Jerusalem, since only a council, not a governor, is mentioned.

We should pause briefly here to consider a decree of Antiochus III (223–187 BCE) regarding the Jews. It is a response by the Seleucid king to Jewish assistance to his forces during the Fifth Syrian War (202–195 BCE), when Antiochus finally wrested control of Coele-Syria from Ptolemy V. The decisive battle occurred at Panion in 200 BCE.[204] The royal decree, which takes the form

200. For an excellent overview of the introductory issues relating to 3 Maccabees (for example, date, themes), see Gruen, *Heritage and Hellenism*, 222–36. In "The Third Book of Maccabees as Ideological Document and Historical Source," *Hen* 10 (1988): 143–82, F. Parente provides an extended survey of views about the book and offers his own arguments for two editions, one from ca. 75 BCE (with a positive view of the king) and one from ca. 20–15 BCE after Egypt became a Roman province and Augustus subjected noncitizens to a census (ca. 20–15 BCE).

201. Barclay, *Jews in the Mediterranean Diaspora*, 192.

202. See, for example, Anderson, "3 Maccabees," in *OTP* 2.513; Barclay, *Jews in the Mediterranean Diaspora*, 194. In its description of the battle of Raphia, 3 Maccabees shares a number of elements with Polybius's account. The issues of historicity raised by the larger part of 3 Maccabees that is set in Egypt are not related to the history of the high priests in Jerusalem and are therefore not treated here.

203. One often reads in the literature that Simon II was high priest in the years 219–196 BCE (for example, Skehan and Di Lella, *Wisdom of Ben Sira*, 9, 550), but the basis for this claim is not evident. We know neither when Simon began to reign nor when he died.

204. Josephus offers a brief account of it in *Ant.* 12.3, 3 (§§129–37). See also Green, *Alexan-*

of a letter from the king to Ptolemy, governor of Coele-Syria and Phoenicia, is preserved in *Ant.* 12.3, 4 (§§138–44). The Jews had supported the king during the war, but Jerusalem and its temple (located adjacent to the Ptolemaic fortress) had suffered when he first took the city and when it was later regained by Ptolemaic forces and finally won back by the Seleucid side (202–200 BCE). As the edict must date (if it is genuine) from the 190s BCE, it may belong to the time of Simon II; it is possible, however, that his son Onias III had begun to rule as high priest when it was issued. Although the text does not mention the high priest, it should be treated here because that is precisely the problem. We might expect him to be named in such a document.

> King Antiochus to Ptolemy, greeting. Inasmuch as the Jews, from the very moment when we entered their country, showed their eagerness to serve us and, when we came to their city, gave us a splendid reception and met us with their senate [τῆς γερουσίας] and furnished an abundance of provisions to our soldiers and elephants, and also helped us to expel the Egyptian garrison in the citadel, we have seen fit on our part to requite them for these acts and to restore their city which has been destroyed by the hazards of war, and to repeople it by bringing back to it those who have been dispersed abroad. In the first place we have decided, on account of their piety, to furnish them for their sacrifices an allowance of sacrificial animals, wine, oil and frankincense to the value of twenty thousand pieces of silver, and sacred *artabae* of fine flour in accordance with their native law, and one thousand four hundred and sixty *medimni* of wheat and three hundred and seventy-five *medimni* of salt. And it is my will that these things be made over to them as I have ordered, and that the work on the temple be completed, including the porticoes and any other part that it may be necessary to build. The timber, moreover, shall be brought from Judaea itself and from other nations and Lebanon without the imposition of a toll-charge. The like shall be done with the other materials needed for making the restoration of the temple more splendid. And all the members of the nation shall have a form of government in accordance with the laws of their country, and the senate, the priests, and scribes of the temple and the temple-singers shall be relieved from the poll-tax and the crown-tax and the salt-tax

___

der to Actium, 303–5; Dov Gera, *Judaea and Mediterranean Politics 219 to 161 B.C.E.*, BSJS 8 (Leiden: Brill, 1998), 20–35. Dan 11:13-16 probably describes the war between Ptolemy V and Antiochus III.

which they pay. And, in order that the city may the more quickly be inhabited, I grant both to the present inhabitants and to those who may return before the month of Hyperberetaios exemption from taxes for three years. We shall also relieve them in the future from the third part of their tribute, so that their losses may be made good. And as for those who were carried off from the city and are slaves, we herewith set them free, both them and the children born to them, and order their property to be restored to them.

In *Ant.* 12.3, 4 (§§145–46) Josephus reproduces another proclamation of Antiochus regarding the purity of the temple; in it, he bans foreigners from the temple enclosure and unclean animals from the city.[205]

E. J. Bickerman wrote a widely used study of the first decree of Antiochus.[206] He showed that the version of the document in *Antiquities* stems from a copy of the letter to Ptolemy, not from the letter itself;[207] he also supplied copious references to Hellenistic parallels for the various parts of Antiochus's decree. It was intended to regulate matters for the Jewish *ethnos*, that is, the Jews of Jerusalem and its country. Specifically on the question why the document, which concerns itself so much with temple-related issues, fails to mention the high priest—a point often cited against its genuineness by earlier critics of the document—Bickerman wrote that the Jews constituted an *ethnos*, that is, their government was aristocratic. The chief priest who is generally presented as the prince of the Jews never appears in public acts before the Maccabean period. This is true of the Persian edicts in Ezra (and 1 Esdras) and in Josephus, the only exception being the forged document in *Ant.* 12.2, 8 (§62). As late as 164/63 and even 153/52 the official letters to the Jews do not name the high priest. The earliest public act recognizing him as the leader of the people is Demetrius II's letter to Jonathan and the Jewish people dating to 145/44. As a result it is not surprising that an edict from the year 200 fails to mention the high priest.[208]

---

205. On it, see E. J. Bickerman, "Une proclamation séleucide relative au temple de Jérusalem," *Syria* 25 (1946–48): 67–85. More evidence for its authenticity and the detailed knowledge of Jewish matters it reveals has come with the publication of the Temple Scroll from Qumran.

206. "La charte séleucide de Jérusalem," 4–35. The essay is reprinted with some changes in Bickerman, *Studies in Jewish and Christian History*, 3 vols., AGJU 9 (Leiden: Brill, 1976–86), 2.44–85. The references below are to the reprinted version.

207. "La charte séleucide de Jérusalem," 66–67.

208. "La charte séleucide de Jérusalem," 81–82. He found it amusing (82 n. 190) to read that Willrich considered the absence of the high priest to be proof of the document's inauthenticity. Tcherikover thought that the confirmation of Jewish right to live according to their ancestral

He found the manner in which the decree limited tax privileges to the leading groups, the senate and the priests, to be normal in such texts. The document is genuine because it corresponds perfectly to the sort of edict a Hellenistic king promulgated after annexing a city. In it, Antiochus confirmed the status of the Mosaic Law as the law of the Jewish people in Palestine and the privileged status of the clergy. In comparison with other such edicts, the concessions made by Antiochus III to the Jews were rather "mediocre."[209]

It may be, then, that Antiochus's failure to mention the high priest explicitly (whoever he may have been at this time) ought not to surprise us; it follows the official practice of the time. For this reason, we should not draw large consequences from it regarding the ruling authority in Judea at the time.[210]

13. Onias III (?–175 BCE)

Onias III was the son of Simon II according to the testimony of Josephus: "When he [Simon II] too died, his son Onias became his successor in office" (*Ant.* 12.4, 10 [§225]). Josephus himself has little to say about this high priest,[211] but 2 Maccabees partially fills the gap, and the books of Daniel and 1 Enoch may also disclose information about him. As it turns out, he was the last Oniad high priest to receive the office in hereditary succession.

---

laws meant the Mosaic Law was expanded in the developing oral law. As a result he could write: "The real content of Antiochus' declaration thus lay in his confirmation of the political situation which he found in Judaea and in his acknowledgment of the rule of the High Priest and his assistants over Judaea and Jerusalem" (*Hellenistic Civilization and the Jews*, 84; compare 87–88). Even though the high priest is not mentioned in the decree, scholars have more often drawn conclusions like those of Tcherikover. See, for example, Schunck, "Hoherpriester und Politiker?" 503–4; he thinks the προστασία that the pro-Ptolemaic Joseph and Hyrcanus had acquired now reverted to the high priest who was pro-Seleucid. This seems to go beyond our evidence.

209. "La charte séleucide de Jérusalem," 82–85. For a helpful summary of older views and of Bickerman's contribution to the debate, see Marcus, *Josephus* 7, Appendix D, 743–61 (in the remainder of the appendix, 761–66, he surveys opinions about the other two documents from Antiochus III adduced by Josephus).

210. M. Stern thinks the edict presents the senate as the official leadership of the ethnos, not the high priest (*The Documents on the History of the Hasmonaean Revolt*, 34). As parallels, he refers to 3 Macc 1:8 where Ptolemy IV has contact with the senate and elders and 2 Macc 11:27 where Antiochus IV does the same. He does, however, believe that Simon II headed the Pro-Seleucid faction in Jerusalem during the Fifth Syrian War (36).

211. In the passage, Josephus identifies this Onias (Onias III) as the one to whom the Spartan king Areus sent a letter, but, as we have seen, he has selected the wrong Onias. Goldstein has some highly speculative suggestions for why Josephus considered Onias III the recipient, all relating to his unconvincing theory about Onias IV as the author of the Tobiad Romance ("The Tales of the Tobiads," 119–21).

Second Maccabees, which after chapters 1–2 is an epitome of Jason of Cyrene's five-volume work (see 2:23-32), deals with Onias as part of the background for the "story of Judas Maccabeus and his brothers" (2:19), which, with the related topic of the temple, is the main subject of the book. The material in 2 Macc 3:1—5:10 is, in most cases, our only source of information about Judean history in about 176–169 BCE—years in which momentous events happened in connection with the high-priestly office. As it usually is the only source, one can rarely verify what it says, but there is reason to be confident that the story here rests on a reliable historical foundation, as we shall see. The epitome begins with a picture of an ideal time:

> While the holy city was inhabited in unbroken peace and the laws were strictly observed because of the piety of the high priest Onias and his hatred of wickedness, it came about that the kings themselves honored the place and glorified the temple with the finest presents, even to the extent that King Seleucus of Asia defrayed from his own revenues all the expenses connected with the service of the sacrifices. (2 Macc 3:1-3)

As the sequel makes evident, the king is Seleucus IV (see 4:7), and therefore the time in question is between the years 187 and 175 BCE. That monarch is pictured as continuing the centuries-old practice that the foreign overlord of Judea pay at least a part of the expenses involved in the Jerusalem cult. The book of Ezra (6:8-10; 7:17-23) documents the custom for Persian kings, and the edict of Antiochus III (*Ant.* 3.3, 3 [§§138–44]; see above), Seleucus IV's father, also provides for the needs of the sacrificial system (compare 2 Macc 9:16 where the dying Antiochus IV is said to have vowed he would do the same). By noting the piety of Onias[212] that was accompanied by the king's generosity (he payed for *all* the expenses, despite the financial difficulties the empire was experiencing[213]), the writer sets up a stark contrast with what happened in the sequel as a result of a certain Simon's impiety: "whereas Onias'

---

212. See also 2 Macc 15:12, which describes him as "a noble and good man, of modest bearing and gentle manner, one who spoke fittingly and had been trained from childhood in all that belongs to excellence." In that passage, he (from beyond the grave) and the prophet Jeremiah pray for Judas Maccabeus and Israel (15:12-16).

213. After the battle of Magnesia in 190 BCE, at which the Romans defeated Antiochus III, the victors imposed a war indemnity on the Seleucid realm in the peace of Apamea (Polybius, *Histories* 21.17, 4-5). The Seleucids not only had to pay an annual tribute of one thousand talents (so Diodorus, *Library of History* 29.13) but also lost some provinces that had been sources of revenue. Antiochus III died while attempting to rob a temple (*Library of History* 29.15; 28.3).

piety induced the king himself to make huge contributions to the temple, wicked Simon instigated a royal attempt to violate the deposits there (vv. 5-11)."[214] The descriptions of Onias III in 2 Maccabees could hardly be more different than Josephus's portrait of his "small-minded" grandfather Onias II in the Tobiad Romance.

The idealistic introductory paragraph (2 Macc 3:1-3) stands before the story of a Jewish official named Simon and the attempt by the Seleucid agent Heliodorus to confiscate the funds in the temple. The tale of what happened to Heliodorus, described as one who was in charge of the king's affairs (3:7), has been compared to similar accounts of divinely thwarted attacks on temples.[215] Its details need not detain us, only the information disclosed about the high priest Onias. A conflict arose when Simon, "of the tribe of Benjamin, who had been made captain of the temple [προστάτης τοῦ ἱεροῦ], had a disagreement with the high priest about the administration of the city market" (3:4). There are several important terms in this verse. For one, "the tribe of Benjamin" is surprising, as Simon holds a high position in the temple and should therefore, one would think, be of priestly extraction. The textual witnesses here are divided. The Greek copies attest "the tribe of Benjamin," as does the Syriac. However, a number of Latin manuscripts offer readings such as *Balcea*, *Balgei* (also supported by the Armenian version), *Bargea*, *Balgeus*. It is widely thought that "all reflect the name of the priestly clan Balga (Masoretic spelling: Bilgah) mentioned in Neh 12:5, 18 and 1 Chr 24:14."[216] The commentators

---

214. Jonathan A. Goldstein, *II Maccabees*, AB 41A (Garden City, N.Y.: Doubleday, 1983), 201.

215. See N. Stokholm, "Zur Überlieferung von Heliodor, Katurnaḫḫunte und anderen missglückten Tempelräubern," *ST* 22 (1968): 1–28 (a chart of the parallels is on p. 20); Goldstein, *II Maccabees*, 198; E. J. Bickerman, *The Jews in the Greek Age* (Cambridge: Harvard Univ. Press, 1988), 234–36. Robert Doran notes that the story "has all the earmarks of accounts written in praise of a deity who defends his/her temple or city" and refers to this as a topos or pattern, not a literary form (*Temple Propaganda: The Purpose and Character of 2 Maccabees*, CBQMS 12 [Washington, D.C.: Catholic Biblical Association, 1981], 47).

216. Goldstein, *II Maccabees*, 201. The idea that *Bilgah* is the correct reading was first advanced by D. De Bruyne, "Le texte grec des deux premiers livres des Machabées," *RB* 31 (1922): 46–47 and has been accepted by many since. See Tcherikover, *Hellenistic Civilization and the Jews*, 403–4 (he first thought that *Benjamin* was a mistake for *Minjamin* [2 Chr 31:15; Neh 12:17, and so forth], an attested priestly name); Tropper, "The Internal Administration of the Second Temple at Jerusalem," 211–14; W. F. Smith, "A Study of the Zadokite High Priesthood," 45–63. The priestly course of Bilgah is mentioned in a negative way in *m. Sukkah* 5:8 (referring to the showbread): "[The Course of] Bilgah always divided it to the south, since their ring was immovable and their wall-niche blocked up." As Herbert Danby explains, the passage indicates that the course of Bilgah had lost the normal rights of a priestly course; he quotes *t. Sukkah* 4:28, which explains that "Miriam, the daughter of one among their number, had married a Greek soldier and had denounced the priesthood; or that they had been so dilatory in their duty that the

surmise that a copyist, who assumed that the term "tribe" meant one of the traditional twelve tribes of Israel, was misled to "correct" Bilgah to Benjamin.[217] As a result, Simon may well have been from the priestly clan of Bilgah. The answer to the question about the identity of Simon's family will be important for the high priesthood when Menelaus, Simon's brother, takes over the position a few years later.

Simon's role as captain of the temple (προστάτης τοῦ ἱεροῦ) is also worth noting. Nothing is said in the context to help the reader understand what the position involved. A similar title is, however, familiar from papyri found in Egypt; it is a general term for officials with various kinds of responsibilities, including financial ones.[218] Goldstein, building on the case made by earlier scholars, sees in the term the official called in rabbinic literature the סגן, the priest second in rank only to the high priest.[219] If so, the conflict involved powerful people indeed: the high priest and an officer who was probably familiar with the financial resources of the temple.[220]

Specifically, the dispute concerned "the administration of the city market" (2 Macc 3:4). The exact nature of the conflict is not known, but individuals in charge of the ἀγορονομία are known from other sources. Apparently, the person who held the office was responsible for weights and measures used in the market. "In Greek cities an *agoranomos* supervised and policed the market; he inspected merchandise for quality, controlled the licensing of merchants to

---

Course of Jeshebeab replaced them" (Danby, *The Mishnah*, 181). P. Kehati (*Mishnayot*, vol. 4 *Moed* 2 [Jerusalem: Hekhal Shelomoh, 1991 (Hebrew)], 142–44) adduces the various opinions on the meaning of the Mishnaic passage.

217. Abel, *Les livres des Maccabées*, 316. Solomon Zeitlin, however, supports the Greek reading (*The Second Book of Maccabees* [Jewish Apocryphal Literature; New York: Harper & Brothers, 1954], 118).

218. Bickerman says that the title "correspond exactement à l'ἐπιστάτης τοῦ ἱεροῦ dans l'Égypte ptolémaïque" and that therefore "Simon était commissaire du gouvernement, responsable, à l'égard du fisc, de la gestion des biens du sanctuaire" ("Héliodore au temple de Jérusalem," *AIPHOS* 7 [1939–44]: 7; reprinted in his *Studies in Jewish and Christian History*, 2.161]). Page references below are to the reprinted version.

219. *II Maccabees*, 202–3; compare Abel, *Les livres des Maccabées*, 316–17.

220. Tropper ("Internal Administration," 114–16) speculates that the προστάτης τοῦ ἱεροῦ was the equivalent of the biblical נגיד בית האלהים (for example, Jer 20:1; Neh 11:11; 2 Chr 28:7; 31:13; 35:8), an officer who was "a Temple, not a priestly, administrator. And his participation in the silencing and arrest of Jeremiah would indicate a role relating to Temple security and order" (112). With the development of priestly power, temple administrators became powerful civil rulers as well; hence, Simon was also a high city official who "had grown so powerful in city administration that he was prepared to challenge his superior high priest in matters relating to the economic life of the city" (115). De Bruyne ("Le texte grec," 46) thought that the context "insinue qu'il avait la garde du trésor du temple."

sell their goods in the city marketplace (*agora*), and saw to the legal validity of transactions and to the documents recording them, and might also have had religious duties."[221]

Scholars have debated not only about the immediate clan/tribe from which Simon came but also the wider family connections of this Simon and his brother Menelaus, who later became the high priest. Some distinguished students of the period claim that they were Tobiads (although see the discussion above concerning the word συγγένεια), while others see in them only supporters of the Tobiads, people with the same political loyalties. The evidence is not extensive, but it is suggestive. Josephus, as we have seen, indicates that Simon II sided with the older Tobiad brothers, and from this we may infer that he was pro-Seleucid as they were. Then, writing about a later time when Menelaus had become high priest, the historian says:

> And when the former high priest Jesus [= Jason; see below] arose against Menelaus, who was appointed after him, the populace was divided between the two, the Tobiads being on the side of Menelaus, while the majority of the people supported Jason. . . . Menelaus and the Tobiads withdrew, and going to Antiochus [= Antiochus IV] informed him that they wanted to abandon their country's laws and the way of life prescribed by these, and to follow the king's laws and adopt the Greek way of life. (*Ant.* 12.5, 1 [§§239–40])

In this instance, the Tobiads and Menelaus, the brother of the Simon who opposed Onias III, are in league and seek the support of the Seleucid monarch for their scheme. Does this entail that Menelaus and Simon, opponents of Onias III, were pro-Seleucid while he was pro-Ptolemaic? Other evidence for this position could come from 2 Macc 3:10-11, which reports that Hyrcanus the Tobiad had a large deposit in the temple. As we learned from the Tobiad Romance, Hyrcanus and his half-brothers were enemies, with Hyrcanus apparently remaining pro-Ptolemaic. The fact that he had money in the temple may show a favorable relationship with Onias III.[222]

---

221. Goldstein, *II Maccabees*, 203.

222. See, for example, Tcherikover, *Hellenistic Civilization and the Jews*, 159; Hengel, *Judaism and Hellenism*, 1.272. Presumably, pro-Ptolemaic sentiments would have revived with the weakening of the Seleucids after the battle of Magnesia. Büchler argued that Simon and Menelaus were Tobiads (*Die Tobiaden und die Oniaden*, 38–43). Gera does not find evidence for a pro-Ptolemaic stance in the material about Onias III in 2 Maccabees (*Judaea and Mediterranean Politics*, 105–8), but he, for inadequate reasons, rejects the Ptolemaic proclivities attributed to Hyrcanus in the Tobiad Romance (36–58). Compare also Rooke, *Zadok's Heirs*, 271–73. Schunck ("Hoherpriester und Politiker?" 504–6) thinks that the financial concessions granted by

According to 2 Maccabees, when Simon was frustrated in his dispute with Onias, "he went to Apollonius of Tarsus [or rather: son of Thraseas], who at that time was governor of Coelesyria and Phoenicia" (2 Macc 3:5). Simon told Apollonius "that the treasury in Jerusalem was full of untold sums of money so that the amount of the funds could not be reckoned, and that they did not belong to the account of the sacrifices, but that it was possible for them to fall under the control of the king" (v. 6). The wording of the passage reminds one of the previous notice that Seleucus IV had paid for "all the expenses connected with the service of the sacrifices" (v. 3); Simon seems to be referring to a different sum of money, one not designated for meeting the cost of the offerings in the temple. Bickerman interpreted the passage to mean that Simon claimed improper usage of the royal grant: Simon affirms that the amount left from the royal subvention, intended to pay for sacrifices, was not spent on them, as it should have been.[223] However, it may be that he was referring to other monies on deposit at the temple, that is, monies not consecrated to support of the sacrificial cult and thus accessible to the king.[224] The subject of Simon's report suggests that the issue between him and the high priest, although it concerned the city market, was also related to the temple treasury.[225] Large sums of money will dominate the history of the high priesthood in the ensuing years.

Apollonius dutifully transmitted the report to the king, and the monarch appointed Heliodorus "who was in charge of his affairs" to "effect the removal of the reported wealth" (2 Macc 3:7). As we might expect, when the great official reached Jerusalem he was "kindly welcomed by the high priest of[226] the city" (3:9). As the ranking ruler in Jerusalem, he was the one to greet the representative of Seleucus. In answer to Heliodorus's question whether matters were as Simon said, Onias III replied that there "were some deposits belonging to widows and orphans, and also some money of Hyrcanus, son of Tobias,

---

Antiochus III to the Jews were withdrawn later when the realm came under intense financial pressure from Rome and that Onias III, disappointed by this development, became pro-Ptolemaic. The presence of Hyrcanus's wealth in the temple suggests the same (see 2 Macc 4:1-2).

223. "Héliodore au temple de Jérusalem," 165. See also 166.

224. So Goldstein, *II Maccabees*, 205–6.

225. It seems unlikely that Simon was trying, as Tcherikover claims (*Hellenistic Civilization and the Jews*, 157), to show Onias's pro-Egyptian sympathies by mentioning Hyrcanus's deposit. According to 2 Maccabees, it was not Simon but Onias himself who disclosed that information (see 3:11).

226. There is strong support for the reading "and" here (compare 4:22); see Goldstein, *II Maccabees*, 207; Christian Habicht, *2. Makkabäerbuch*, JSHRZ 1.3 (Gütersloh: Gütersloher, 1979), 211; that is, if "and" is read, the text says that both the high priest *and* the city welcomed Heliodorus.

a man of very prominent position" (vv. 10-11). He gave the total of such deposits as four hundred silver talents and two hundred gold talents.[227] "And he said that it was utterly impossible that wrong should be done to those people who had trusted in the holiness of the place and in the sanctuary and inviolability of the temple that is honored throughout the whole world" (3:12). Heliodorus, however, had his orders and he insisted on doing as the king had directed. A dramatic scene of priestly and lay supplication precedes the account of Heliodorus's attempt to enter the sanctuary and the miraculous, violent way in which he was repulsed by a powerful horse and rider and by two strong men who whipped him repeatedly (3:14-34).[228] In this fashion, the epiphanies promised by the epitomator in 2 Macc 2:21-22 make their first appearance in the narrative.[229]

The section includes an account of Onias's anguish about the threat to the temple (2 Macc 3:16-17)[230] and also about his intercession on behalf of the battered Heliodorus. This high-priestly role in the passage is worth considering in more detail:

> Some of Heliodorus' friends quickly begged Onias to call upon the Most High to grant life to one who was lying quite at his last breath. So the high priest, fearing that the king might get the notion that some foul play had been perpetrated by the Jews with regard to Heliodorus, offered sacrifice for the man's recovery. While the high priest was making an atonement, . . . (3:31-33a)

The high priest, mindful of the poor appearance the event could have in the royal capital, complied with the friends' request. His response took the form of offering a sacrifice, making this one of the few occasions to this point in Second-Temple history when we read about a high priest engaging in such a

---

227. Goldstein (*II Maccabees*, 209), assuming that the ratio of silver talents to gold ones was one to ten, concludes that the money deposited in the temple was 2,400 talents. If one recalls that the annual Seleucid tribute to Rome amounted to 1,000 talents, the value of the Jerusalem funds to the king is obvious.

228. The parallel in the later 4 Macc 4:1-14 says this happened to Apollonius. Compare, too, the story in 3 Macc 1:8—2:24, which was treated above under Simon II (where Ptolemy IV was prevented from entering the Holy of Holies).

229. Doran, *Temple Propaganda*, 52.

230. As Goldstein notes, the changed face of Onias contrasts with the description of Onias II in the Tobiad Romance, where the latter was not discountenanced by the trouble in which he had placed his countrymen (*II Maccabees*, 210).

cultic function. The offering is said to be a sacrifice for Heliodorus's recovery and an atonement (ἱλασμόν). In the LXX, the latter term renders several Hebrew words (אשמה once, חטאת[231] once, כפרים twice, and סליחה once). There appears to be no biblical precedent for the high priest's action, if this was a sin or guilt offering, as these were supposed to be brought by the individual(s) concerned. Goldstein explains the matter in this way:

> We do not know what system of Jewish law Onias followed. According to the rabbinic law a non-Jew could not bring a sin or guilt offering but he could bring a burnt offering *(M. Sheqalim* 1:5), and Onias or Heliodorus' friends could bring a burnt offering on Heliodorus' behalf (cf. Job 1:5). Such a burnt offering could secure atonement (Lev 1:4 . . .).[232]

It is the case, nevertheless, that the text of 2 Maccabees does not use a word for burnt offering. Whatever type it was, the sacrifice offered by the high priest is said to have moved the Lord to save Heliodorus's life (3:33b).

It would be interesting to know what happened in Jerusalem on this occasion and what the circumstances were; whatever took place, Heliodorus's visit to Jerusalem, which apparently secured no new funds for the royal coffers, was not to be the end of the matter.

The sequel shows that Simon, at least, put out the claim that Onias was the one "who had incited [ἐπισεσεικώς] Heliodorus and had been the real cause of the misfortune. He dared to designate as a plotter against the government the man who was the benefactor of the city, the protector of his compatriots, and a zealot [ζηλωτήν] for the laws" (2 Macc 4:1b-2). Simon made the report to Apollonius, governor of Coele-Syria and Phoenicia, and he and Simon worked together, even using violent means, to disrupt Onias's rule. Their collusion left the high priest with no choice, he thought, but to bring the matter to the king's attention (4:3-6). The high priest is here envisioned as the political leader of the nation as well as its cultic head, even though the issue centered on funds held in the temple.[233]

---

231. Abraham Kahana uses this term in his Hebrew translation of 2 Maccabees ("מקבים ב" in הספרים החיצונים, ed. A. Kahana, 2 vols. (reprinted Jerusalem: Maqor, 1970), 2.188.

232. *II Maccabees*, 214.

233. Rooke finds it naïve to see Onias as the lone ruler of his nation in this story and thinks the account implies he did not have responsibility for the financial management of the area (*Zadok's Heirs*, 270–71). "The whole point of the story of Onias is that he was powerless in

An interesting sidelight to 2 Macc 4:1-6 is that Heliodorus soon afterwards (in 175 BCE) is supposed to have assassinated Seleucus IV (so Appian,
Syriaca 45) and attempted to install Seleucus's young son as king under his
control.[234] The narrative in 2 Maccabees may not be unrelated to these events
as we shall see, because the youthful prince was later killed by the man said to
be responsible for the death of Onias III—Andronicus.

There has been some disagreement about what Simon charged Onias with
having done to Heliodorus. The verb in question—ἐπισεσεικώς—could be
translated "mistreated" or "frightened,"[235] in which case the charge would be
that the high priest had in some way harmed the king's messenger and therefore risked reprisal from the imperial government. If one translates as the
NRSV does ("incited"), then a different image is conjured, although nothing
is said about what Onias is supposed to have incited Heliodorus to do. Goldstein understands the verb in this sense and, somehow, takes it to entail that
Simon tried to get Onias in trouble with his fellow Jews.[236] It does seem from
the context that Onias was deeply concerned about the way in which
Heliodorus's experience would be construed in Antioch, not in Jerusalem; the
disturbances credited to Simon would have caused him further worries along
this line. If the high priest did harbor pro-Ptolemaic sympathies, he may have
been all the more eager to deflect royal suspicions from himself.

Although 2 Maccabees does not narrate a journey by Onias, it is said that
he "appealed to the king" (4:5) and, the next time we hear of him, he is in the
area of Antioch where he was murdered (4:33-34). Apparently, while he was

---

political terms to prevent seizure of the Temple funds and so had to be aided by heavenly power;
had he had earthly power in the first place the story would have been meaningless" (271). This
seems a strange conclusion to draw. The story concerns a dispute between two Jewish officials
that, for all we know, could have been settled locally had Simon not involved a high-ranking
Seleucid official in the matter. The claim that the high priest had political authority does not
mean, of course, that he ruled supreme. Obviously, he was subject to the king and his administration. Against them, his power was limited. At least, we may say that Simon seems to have
lacked the authority on his own to confiscate the monies in question. Schunck too thinks that
Onias III here acts as political leader, the head of the senate ("Hoherpriester und Politiker?" 506).

234. See Bevan, *The House of Seleucus*, 2.125–26; Gera, *Judaea and Mediterranean Politics*,
109–13 (he cites all of the evidence, including that of the Seleucid king list).

235. So many commentators (for example, Abel, *Les livres des Maccabées*, 328; Bickerman,
"Héliodore au temple de Jérusalem," 189 [pointing to 2 Macc 3:25 where the same verb occurs];
Zeitlin, *The Second Book of Maccabees*, 131 [although see the n. to v. 1 on p. 129 "egged on"];
Habicht, *2. Makkabäerbuch*, 214–15).

236. *II Maccabees*, 220. He correctly notes that the verb, with an accusative, has this meaning, whereas the meaning "intimidate" is found with the dative. Yet, if it is read as "incited," we
still do not know to what Onias is supposed to have incited Heliodorus.

away, his brother Jason took the opportunity to acquire the high priesthood in an unprecedented manner: he offered a payment of 360 talents of silver and another 80 talents, with yet 150 more talents if he were given the right to "establish by his authority a gymnasium and a body of youth for it, and to enroll the people of Jerusalem as citizens of Antioch" (4:8-9).

For the effective end of Onias's high priesthood, we have the opportunity, rare to this point, of being able to specify the date. Just after writing that Onias appealed to the king, the epitomator says: "When Seleucus died and Antiochus, who was called Epiphanes, succeeded to the kingdom, Jason the brother of Onias obtained the high-priesthood by corruption" (2 Macc 4:7). The transition between the two high priests is thus correlated with the end of one Seleucid reign and the beginning of another. Appian asserts that Heliodorus assassinated Seleucus IV, while the cuneiform Seleucid king list simply mentions his death and the accession of Antiochus, just as 2 Maccabees does. The list says Seleucus ruled for twelve years and that he died in the year 137 (of the Seleucid reckoning), on the tenth day of the month Elul (= the sixth month).[237] This translates into September 2 or 3, 175 BCE.[238] Hence, the end of Onias's actual reign as high priest in Jerusalem occurred probably in the same year. Yet, he did not meet his death until some three years later (for this, see below).[239]

14. Jason (175–172 BCE)

The name by which the new high priest was known is the first non-Semitic one in the male line; the fact that he took a Greek name comports well with what 2 Maccabees discloses about the man who supervised the official entry of Hellenistic institutions into Jerusalem. According to Josephus, his name was Jesus (= Joshua): "Now Jesus changed his name to Jason" (*Ant.* 12.5, 1 [§239]). Jason is also the first high priest of the Second-Temple period for whom the sources disclose enough information so that dates may be given for the beginning *and* end of his reign, even though some uncertainty remains regarding exactly when his brief tenure came to a close.

---

237. A translation can be found in *ANET* 567. The text may locate Antiochus's assumption of the crown in the same month, although the eighth month (also mentioned there) is more likely (see O. Mørkholm, *Antiochus IV of Syria,* Classica et mediaevalia, dissertationes 8 [Copenhagen: Gyldendalske, 1966], 41–44).

238. Habicht, *2. Makkabäerbuch,* 215.

239. Josephus, as noted above, has little to report about Onias III. A reason for this is, as most scholars recognize, that he did not use 2 Maccabees as a source. It is possible that Onias III is the Onias mentioned in a list of high priests in 4QpsDan^c ar 1 i 9.

The unsettled conditions resulting from the conflict between Onias III and Simon, whatever role Heliodorus's visit played, are the backdrop for Jason's successful coup. While Onias was away, presenting his case in the capital, his brother Jason "obtained the high-priesthood by corruption" (2 Macc 4:7). It is perhaps not surprising that, in light of Heliodorus's unsuccessful attempt to commandeer funds in Jerusalem, Jason received the royal nod as high priest because he offered a substantial payment for the appointment. As Tcherikover notes, Jason may automatically have begun serving as surrogate high priest when his brother Onias departed for Antioch, just as some years later Lysimachus played a similar role when his brother Menelaus was away from Jerusalem (2 Macc 4:29).[240]

Although he may have been acting high priest in his brother's absence, Jason took a bold step in trying to wrest the position from Onias while the latter was visiting the king. Second Maccabees relates that he obtained the high priesthood from the new king Antiochus,

> promising the king at an interview[241] three hundred and sixty talents of silver, and from another source of revenue eighty talents. In addition to this he promised to pay one hundred fifty more if permission were given to establish by his authority a gymnasium and a body of youth for it, and to enroll the people of Jerusalem as citizens of Antioch. When the king assented and Jason came to office, he at once shifted his compatriots to the Greek way of life. (4:8-10)

Jason's Hellenizing of Jerusalem has, of course, stimulated endless discussion regarding its character,[242] how much of an innovation it was, and the like; but at least he is credited with receiving royal permission to establish quintessential Hellenistic institutions in Jerusalem, institutions that apparently did not exist there before this time. The character of these institutions and the per-

---

240. *Hellenistic Civilization and the Jews*, 466 n. 17.

241. This may not be the best translation of δι᾽ ἐντεύξεως, which could mean "through a petition" (Goldstein, *II Maccabees*, 216). It is unlikely that Jason would have left Jerusalem to secure the high priesthood when it was precisely Onias's absence that had provided him with the opportunity to usurp the office. It is not impossible, though, that he did travel to the capital.

242. See the helpful summary of the positions articulated by various scholars (for example, Bickerman, Tcherikover, Goldstein) in Grabbe, *Judaism from Cyrus to Hadrian*, 1.250–55. Compare also the general comments of Seth Schwartz, "The Hellenization of Jerusalem and Shechem," in M. Goodman, ed., *Jews in a Graeco-Roman World* (Oxford: Clarendon, 1998), 37–46; he emphasizes the public and rather nominal Hellenism found in cities that became Greek and that the native religion continued to be practiced.

sonal role requested by Jason with regard to them would have entailed a
change in the duties of the high priesthood. A gymnasium was the fundamental educational organ in a Greek city, and the ephebate was a body of
youth who were trained in a gymnasium to become citizens. Moreover, "education in the *ephebeion* was bound up with no small expense and therefore
became in the Hellenistic period more or less the monopoly of the sons of the
wealthy. The fact that, together with the opening of the *gymnasion*, Jason built
an *ephebeion*, shows with complete clarity which were the classes among the
people of the new polis for whose education he was providing."[243] It seems
important, too, that Jason wished to have these institutions under his control
(if "by his authority" refers to Jason's, not the king's, power); he would in this
way have become the leader of a Hellenistic political and educational community, and he would have had the authority to determine the membership
list in the new organization.[244]

The amounts of money that Jason offered to the king tempt one to tie
2 Macc 4:8-9 to the report at the end of the Tobiad Romance about an event
that also occurred when Antiochus IV assumed the throne: "As for Hyrcanus,
seeing how great was the power which Antiochus had, and fearing that he
might be captured by him and punished for what he had done to the Arabs, he
ended his life by his own hand. And all his property was seized by Antiochus."
(*Ant.* 12.4, 11 [§236]). It is reasonable to think that Hyrcanus's death may have
made his deposit in the Jerusalem temple accessible to the royal treasury (a 100
percent death tax) and that Jason was the instrument for carrying out the
transfer.

While 2 Maccabees presents a relatively clear scenario for Jason's unnat-
ural assumption of the high priesthood, Josephus leaves a different picture.
Dealing with the beginning of Antiochus's reign, he writes: "About this same
time the high priest Onias also died, and Antiochus gave the high priesthood
to his brother; for the son whom Onias had left was still an infant" (*Ant.* 12.5,
1 [§237]). Unlike 2 Maccabees, Josephus's source reported a peaceful, legitimate transfer of the office: just as when Simon I died and his son Onias II was
too young to serve, Simon's brother took the office, so now when Onias III
died and his son (Onias IV) was too young, his brother Jason became the high
priest. Which picture is correct—usurpation (2 Maccabees) or legitimate

---

243. Tcherikover, *Hellenistic Civilization and the Jews*, 162. On the gymnasium and the
ephebate related to it, see Hadas, *Hellenistic Culture: Fusion and Diffusion*, 65–67.
244. Rooke thinks Jason's appointment as high priest and as Seleucid agent represents a
change in the high priesthood from what had prevailed before this time (*Zadok's Heirs*, 273–74).
It does seem that his position differed in some ways from that of his predecessors, but, as we have
seen a number of times, most of them appear also to have exercised political power.

transfer (Josephus)? The disagreements do not stop here. Josephus goes on to relate that it was Menelaus and the Tobiads who, several years later when Menelaus was high priest, went to Antiochus and requested the right to adopt a Greek way of life, including having a gymnasium in Jerusalem (*Ant.* 12.5, 1 [§§240–41]).

There are reasons for thinking that 2 Maccabees has the more reliable report on this point and that Josephus's source or Josephus himself, for whatever reason, offers a confusing, less trustworthy account. Josephus's presentation of the high-priestly family at this juncture in *Antiquities* is strange. The historian says not only that Antiochus gave the high priesthood to Jason upon Onias's death, but also that the king, when he later became angry with Jason, gave the post to his younger brother named *Onias*. Realizing that he needed to explain the odd situation of a family with two sons named Onias, he wrote: "for Simon [= Simon II] had three sons, and the high-priesthood came to all three of them, as we have shown. Now Jesus changed his name to Jason, while Onias was called Menelaus" (*Ant.* 12.5, 1 [§§238–39]).[245] Here, nothing is said about the youthfulness of Onias III's son as a reason for conferring the office on Menelaus. In 2 Maccabees, Menelaus is, of course, presented as the brother of Onias III's opponent Simon, not as Onias's brother.

Assuming that 2 Maccabees has the more reliable account (and more on this later), we may assess Jason's appointment and his program. For one, the influence of Greek ways, as many have shown, was hardly a novelty at this time.[246] Second, the impetus for the so-called Hellenistic reform came from a high-ranking Jewish priest, not from the Seleucid government. Possibly Jason effected a change that powerful and wealthy Judeans had hoped for but could not realize while Onias III, "a zealot for the laws" (2 Macc 4:2), reigned as high priest. First Maccabees 1:11 indicates, apparently about this event, that "certain renegades came out from Israel and misled many, saying, 'Let us go and make a covenant with the Gentiles around us, for since we separated from them many disasters have come upon us.'" The change in kings may also have been seen as an opportune time for proposing the new plan, especially as Onias III may have harbored pro-Ptolemaic views. Antiochus was not the rightful heir of Seleucus IV (both were sons of Antiochus III) and apparently encountered some opposition when he first claimed the throne.[247] Establishing a Hellenistic city in Jerusalem posed an advantage for him:

---

245. Josephus calls him by the same name elsewhere, for example, in *Ant.* 20.10, 3 (§235).

246. Hengel has made the point overwhelmingly in *Judaism and Hellenism*.

247. See Mørkholm, *Antiochus*, 38–50; Gera, *Judaea and Mediterranean Politics*, 109–17; Hengel, *Judaism and Hellenism*, 1.277 and 2.183.

The king readily acceded to the wishes of the Jerusalem aristocracy and their new head for preparations to found the new *polis* 'Antioch in Jerusalem', since this served to establish the multi-national Seleucid state. One cannot speak of a deliberate policy of Hellenization on the part of the Seleucids or Antiochus IV, but it was useful when orientals adopted Greek customs and became Hellenes. Furthermore, he attached importance to stable conditions on his southern border in the face of the revanchist Egyptians. Not least, this royal mark of favour was honoured with an additional one hundred and fifty talents. Thus it is easy to understand that during his reign the king granted similar rights to a further eighteen cities, including Babylon.[248]

The move to make Jerusalem a polis was a political one with religious overtones. For the author of 2 Maccabees, however, it defied the divine laws (4:11, 17) and later events he saw as God's retribution for the ways of Jason and his supporters. In 1 Maccabees, which never mentions Jason, we learn the apostates "abandoned the holy covenant" and "sold themselves to do evil" (1:15). Specific charges that 2 Maccabees lodges against them are that noble young men wore the Greek hat and that the priests were more interested in the wrestling arena than the temple altar (2 Macc 4:12-16); 1 Maccabees adds that some removed the marks of circumcision (1:15). Second Maccabees also charges Jason with sending three hundred drachmas of silver for a sacrifice to Hercules at the Tyrian quadrennial games, events attended by the king himself. Only a decision by those who actually transported the money prevented it from being used for the purpose intended by the rather ecumenical Jason (4:18-19).

While there were these sides to the reform, or rather these results, it seems that Jason did not attempt to rid Jerusalem of its traditional cult, although 1 and 2 Maccabees may present him as doing so. Instead, by making Jerusalem into a polis, he seems to have added the new but kept the old.[249] At least, there is no reference to terminating the traditional temple worship or objections to the reform (apart from the judgments of the later authors of 1 and 2 Maccabees); in fact, one could conclude the opposite. Some three years after Jason took office and received permission to institute the reform,[250] Antiochus him-

---

248. Hengel, *Judaism and Hellenism*, 1.277.

249. See, for example, Tcherikover, *Hellenistic Civilization and the Jews*, 165–67; and Klaus Bringmann, *Hellenistische Reform und Religionsverfolgung in Judäa: Eine Untersuchung zur jüdisch-hellenistischen Geschichte (175–163 v. Chr.)*, Abhandlungen der Akademie der Wissenschaften in Göttingen, Philologisch-historische Klasse, Dritte Folge 132 (Göttingen: Vandenhoeck & Ruprecht, 1983), 67–68.

250. The event is dated by the reference in 2 Macc 4:21 to the coronation (τὰ πρωτοκλίσια) of Ptolemy VI Philometor; no such ceremony is known for this king who began to reign in

self visited the city. Rather than arousing opposition, "[h]e was welcomed magnificently by Jason and the city, and ushered in with a blaze of torches and with shouts" (2 Macc 4:22). Tcherikover has interpreted the king's visit to the transformed city as the appearance of its founder: "Antiochus' visit to Jerusalem formed a suitable pretext for proclaiming officially and with great pomp the foundation of the Greek city 'Antioch-at-Jerusalem.'"[251]

We learn no more about Jason's activities as high priest, and, in the year 172 BCE (perhaps), he was removed from office by the king and replaced by Menelaus, the brother of the Simon who had earlier opposed Onias III. The royal move changed the already anomalous situation into an even stranger one: Onias III was the first living ex-high priest of whom we know, and now his brother Jason joined him in that exclusive club. Jason receives heavy criticism from the author of 2 Maccabees, who supplemented his claim that he obtained the office "by corruption" (4:7) with several other evaluations. "He set aside the existing royal concessions to the Jews, secured through John the father of Eupolemus, who went on the mission to establish friendship and alliance with the Romans; and he destroyed the lawful ways of living and introduced new customs contrary to the law" (4:11). The "existing royal concessions to the Jews" may be a reference to the decree by Antiochus III, Antiochus IV's father, permitting Jews to live according to their ancestral customs.[252] The author continues by mentioning "the surpassing wickedness of Jason, who was ungodly and no true high priest" (4:13); he is "the vile Jason" who sent the money for the sacrifice to Hercules (4:19; compare v. 20). As noted above, the writer of 1 Maccabees never mentions Jason, and Josephus refers to him only briefly.

We will hear more about Jason later. He lost his recently acquired position as high priest when, "after a period of three years,"[253] he made the mistake of sending Menelaus, brother of Simon, as an envoy to convey money to the king and to transact business (2 Macc 4:23). While there, Menelaus succeeded in

---

181–180 BCE, well before Antiochus became king. See Mørkholm, *Antiochus*, 68 n. 18: "*Proto-clisia* undoubtedly refers to a banquet presided over by the young Egyptian king, but we have no possibility of dating this incident." Compare Goldstein, *II Maccabees*, 234–35. Second Maccabees 4:23 does mention a period of three years just after Antiochus's visit to Jerusalem; hence the visit took place no later than 172 BCE.

251. *Hellenistic Civilization and the Jews*, 165.

252. Note that the text does not say that John was the one who established friendship and alliance with the Romans; rather he is here identified as the father of the man who, according to 1 Macc 8:17, was one of the two emissaries later sent by Judas Maccabeus to negotiate such an agreement with the Romans.

253. Jochen Gabriel Bunge ("Zur Geschichte und Chronologie des Untergangs der Oniaden und des Aufstiegs der Hasmonäer," *JSJ* 6 [1975]: 4) thinks the time unit *three years* means only that he held the office for parts of three consecutive years.

purchasing the high-priestly office for himself. "So Jason, who after supplant-
ing his own brother was supplanted by another man, was driven as a fugitive
into the land of Ammon" (4:26). It will be recalled that, according to Josephus,
he lost the position when Antiochus became angry with him (*Ant.* 12.5, 1
[§238]). It is possible that Jason had difficulty raising the money he had
promised to pay for his new post and Jerusalem's changed status, although this
is not said in the sources. He had, however, by purchasing the high priesthood,
set a dangerous precedent that was to cost him dearly in more than one way.
That his place of refuge was Ammon is perhaps not accidental: it was the location of the Tobiad Hyrcanus's former residence, and Jason, now out of favor
with the Seleucid king, may have fled there in the hope of gaining support.

15. Menelaus (172–162 BCE)

Menelaus, beginning: Menelaus became the high priest when he promised
a substantial amount of money for the royal coffers. Jason had sent him to
deliver money to the royal treasury. "But he, when presented to the king,
extolled him[254] with an air of authority, and secured the high-priesthood for
himself, outbidding Jason by three hundred talents of silver. After receiving the
king's orders he returned, possessing no qualification for the high-priesthood,
but having the hot temper of a cruel tyrant and the rage of a savage wild beast"
(2 Macc 4:24-25). Here and elsewhere, the author of 2 Maccabees exudes nothing but the deepest contempt for the man who served as high priest for the
decade[255] that was to see some of the most turbulent events in Jewish history.
The comment that he had "no qualification for the high-priesthood [τῆς μὲν
ἀρχιερωσύνης οὐδὲν ἄξιον φέρων]" should be read in light of the discussion
concerning his brother Simon's family connections. If Simon was indeed from
the priestly clan of Bilgah, as suggested above, then Menelaus, too, was a priest
(4:25 denies his worthiness to be high priest, not that he was a priest). But, as
the author declares, he was not from the Oniad family that, to this point, held
an exclusive right to the high priesthood. In fact, Menelaus is the first recorded
high priest in the Second-Temple period to belong to a different family than the
one directly descended from Joshua, the first high priest. As we have seen, Josephus confuses the matter by mistakenly regarding Menelaus (whom he also
calls *Onias*) as another brother of Onias III and Jason, something quite

---

254. It is not absolutely clear whom Menelaus is extolling, himself or the king. See Abel, *Les
livres des Maccabées*, 338, and Goldstein, *II Maccabees*, 236, both of whom favor the interpretation that he was making himself appear important.

255. See 2 Macc 4:7 with 4:23 and 13:1 but especially Josephus *Ant.* 12.9, 7 (§385): "he had
served as high priest for ten years."

contrary to the information in 2 Maccabees.[256] This could be seen as an attempt on the part of his source to lend legitimacy to Menelaus, but it is more likely that other causes have led to the confusion (see below).

It may be too much to expect that 2 Maccabees would offer an objective picture of Menelaus, but the next event recorded has to do with financial problems that arose when he failed to "pay regularly any of the money he promised to the king" (2 Macc 4:27). The captain of the citadel in Jerusalem, Sostratus, was commissioned to press him for payment, and, when his efforts did not produce the desired result, Menelaus and Sostratus were summoned to the capital (4:28-29). Lysimachus, another brother of Menelaus, was appointed "as deputy in the high-priesthood [τῆς ἀρχιερωσύνης διάδοχον]" (4:29). This is the first time we meet the notion of a deputy high priest, although as mentioned above, Jason may have been left as deputy when his brother Onias III went to Antioch to explain the situation in Jerusalem. It should be noticed that 2 Macc 4:28 gives us an early reference to a Seleucid military presence in Jerusalem, one manned by at least some Cypriots (4:29). It was the duty of the officer in charge of the citadel to collect the revenue due the government; he, too, had to appoint a deputy while away from his post (4:29). As Goldstein notes, "[t]o prevent a Jewish subordinate from repeating his own exploit, Menelaus may have seen to it that henceforth the garrison commander should receive the tax money and send it on to the king."[257]

Against this backdrop, we once again meet Onias III, who had apparently remained in the area of Antioch after he was ousted as high priest in 175 BCE and who seems to have kept himself informed about events in Jerusalem. When Antiochus IV had to leave Antioch to put down a revolt in the cities of Tarsus and Mallus,[258] in his absence he appointed Andronicus, "a man of high rank, to act as his deputy [τὸν διαδεχόμενον]" (2 Macc 4:31). In this unusual situation with three leaders away from their normal posts and three deputies representing them, Menelaus determined to do away with Onias III, who was perhaps still, in some people's minds, the legitimate high priest. As 2 Maccabees relates it, Menelaus, while the king was away, "thinking he had obtained

---

256. It has been suggested that *Onias* was Menelaus's Hebrew name and that he was somehow related to the family of Onias III—perhaps he married a sister of Onias III and Jason and thus was a brother-in-law, not a brother as Josephus thought. Being related to the high-priestly family could have been a factor in his appointment (see, for example, Schunck, "Hoherpriester und Politiker?" 507–8). Of course, this is speculative.

257. *II Maccabees*, 237, but he does qualify this by saying the reference could be to the money for which Menelaus was in arrears (Bickerman understands διαφόρων here in this way, "Héliodore au temple de Jérusalem," 164).

258. The event is not mentioned in other sources.

a suitable opportunity, stole some of the gold vessels of the temple and gave them to Andronicus; other vessels, as it happened, he had sold to Tyre and the neighboring cities" (4:32). Presumably, he had sold valuables to raise money; now he used other precious objects to influence the king's deputy.

Menelaus's high-handed ways with temple property spurred Onias III to action.

> When Onias became fully aware of these acts, he publicly exposed them, having first withdrawn to a place of sanctuary at Daphne near Antioch. Therefore, Menelaus, taking Andronicus aside, urged him to kill Onias. Andronicus came to Onias, and resorting to treachery, offered him sworn pledges and gave him his right hand; he persuaded him, though still suspicious, to come out from the place of sanctuary; then, with no regard for justice, he immediately put him out of the way. (2 Macc 4:33-34)

In this way, the last member of the Oniad house to have received the high priesthood as a hereditary right met his end after seeking asylum in what appears to have been a pagan sanctuary.

This remarkable passage has raised a number of questions, especially in light of the sequel in which Antiochus IV returns to Antioch, hears strong complaints from both Jewish people and others about Andronicus's act, publicly humiliates his deputy, and then executes him in the place where he had killed Onias (2 Macc 4:35-38). It is understandable that Menelaus would have felt threatened by Onias, who could claim to be the rightful high priest and presumably had support in the Jewish community of Antioch and perhaps elsewhere. With Onias openly critical of his efforts, Menelaus decided to act decisively. It has surprised some commentators that the ex-high priest Onias, a man of such pious reputation (even Antiochus, who had deprived Onias of his office, is said to have wept "because of the moderation and good conduct of the deceased" [4:37]), retired to a pagan sanctuary (apparently the temple of Apollo in Daphne), but he may have seen no other way to save his life.[259]

---

259. So Menahem Stern, "The Death of Onias III," *Zion* 25 (1959–60): 2 (Hebrew). As Stern explains, some have argued that the writer of 2 Maccabees invented this episode to discredit the temple of Onias in Egypt, which was founded by Onias III's son, Onias IV. It is difficult to imagine, however, why the author would attribute such an act to a legitimate high priest. Stern thinks the author reported it because it was a familiar and necessary part of the story. Tcherikover, apparently finding it incredible that Onias fled to a pagan sanctuary, maintained that, as there was a synagogue at Daphne, Onias more likely fled there (*Hellenistic Civilization and the Jews*, 469 n. 39). As Goldstein comments, "[i]f the place of asylum had been a synagogue . . . , our writers probably would have mentioned the fact" (*II Maccabees*, 239).

The major problem posed by the passage is that, while non-Jewish sources document Antiochus's execution of Andronicus, they offer a different reason for it. According to Diodorus (*Library of History* 30.7, 2), "Andronicus, who assassinated the son of Seleucus [= Seleucus IV's son] and who was in turn put to death, willingly lent himself to an impious and terrible crime, only to share the same fate as his victim."[260] It seems from a later report by John of Antioch that Antiochus was suspicious of his nephew, who could be regarded as the rightful heir of his father's throne, and had him murdered but covered his part in the execution by attributing it to others whom he then dispatched.[261] Stern argues that the explanation in 2 Maccabees for Andronicus's death is not to be rejected; it may be that he was already suspected of having killed the young prince and that his execution of Onias gave the king a pretext for dispensing with him.[262] If so, Onias's death and that of Prince Antiochus may have occurred at about the same time. The Seleucid king list dates the death of the prince to some time between July 31 and August 28, 170 BCE; that year is probably the one in which the former high priest was executed.[263]

However his death is to be explained, Onias III died,[264] and the event left its imprint on other sources. So, for instance, Dan 9:26 is often thought to refer to it. In the angel Gabriel's explanation of the predicted seventy weeks of years, he says: "After the sixty-two weeks, an anointed one shall be cut off and shall have nothing, and the troops of the prince who is to come shall destroy the city and the sanctuary." The "anointed one" is regularly taken to be Onias,[265] and

---

260. Francis R. Walton, *Diodorus of Sicily* 11, LCL (Cambridge: Harvard Univ. Press, 1957), 289.

261. See Stern, "The Death of Onias III," 3; Bevan, *The House of Seleucus*, 2.128.

262. "The Death of Onias," 3–5; compare Tcherikover, *Hellenistic Civilization and the Jews*, 469 n. 40.

263. For views on the date, see Bunge, "Zur Geschichte und Chronologie," 3–5; he places the event in the Babylonian Seleucid year 140 (171–170 BCE); Mørkholm, *Antiochus*, 71; Gera, *Judaea and Mediterranean Politics*, 129–30. Gera, however, considers the connection of Onias III with these events to be fictitious and thinks the story in 2 Maccabees is a doublet of the one about the prince's death. This seems implausible and hardly dispenses with Stern's arguments. V. Keil, among others, has also argued against the historical reliability of the story about the death of Onias III in 2 Maccabees; see his essay "Onias III.—Märtyrer oder Tempelgründer?" *ZAW* 97 (1985): 221–33.

264. For more on the Josephan passages, which say he simply died, see below.

265. Among many modern commentators, see James A. Montgomery, *A Critical and Exegetical Commentary on the Book of Daniel,* ICC (Edinburgh: T. & T. Clark, 1927), 381, 393–94; John J. Collins, *Daniel,* Hermeneia (Minneapolis: Fortress Press, 1993), 356–57. As both note, the interpretation of the following phrase (וְאֵין לוֹ) is disputed; Collins favors the translation "with no one to help him," which is parallel to Dan 11:45. The dating of the cutting off of an anointed one (after sixty-two weeks of years) would not fit the chronology for the Second-Temple period

the implication is that his death[266] was a decisive event in postexilic history, one of the few turning points identified in the angelic interpretation. The context in Daniel 9 places the death of Onias in relation to the decrees of Antiochus (the "prince" of 9:26), as if the two defined the critical time in this history. It may be that Dan 11:22 also intends Onias III, calling him "the prince of the covenant": "Armies shall be utterly swept away and broken before him, and the prince of the covenant as well."[267] Here, too, the context is the reign of Antiochus IV. Finally, it is also possible that *1 Enoch* 90:8, part of the Animal Apocalypse, alludes to Onias's death: "And I saw in the vision how the ravens flew upon those lambs, and took one of those lambs, and dashed the sheep in pieces and devoured them."[268] The lambs are a pious group of Jews, while the ravens are a symbol for the Seleucids in this vision. Reference to the high priest's death in sources as diverse as 2 Maccabees and

---

as reconstructed by modern experts. If Onias's death occurred not far from 170 BCE, sixty-two weeks of years before this would be 604 BCE, far too early a starting point for the chronology (the order to rebuild Jerusalem) on any interpretation of Dan 9:24-27. Fausto Parente has argued that Josephus's tradition making Onias III the founder of the Leontopolis temple is correct and that 2 Maccabees, which speaks of his absence in Antioch and eventual execution there, is tendentious. He ("Onias III' [sic] Death and the Founding of the Temple of Leontopolis," in *Josephus and the History of the Greco-Roman Period: Essays in Memory of Morton Smith*, ed. F. Parente and J. Sievers, StPB 41 [Leiden: Brill, 1994], 69–98) comments: "The news of Onias' flight into Egypt seems to have been removed from 2 Maccabees at some stage after the text had been completed, since the gap [between 4:6 and 4:7] is still visible. Therefore it follows that the report of his murder was added afterwards" (98). It seems more likely that 2 Maccabees is accurate and that Josephus, for identifiable reasons, has confused some characters in the story. See below.

266. It is difficult to take the strong verb כרת in a lesser sense as meaning only that he lost his office (as Josephus claims). See Bunge, "Zur Geschichte und Chronologie," 4 n. 6. Wellhausen, however, understood Dan 9:26 as saying that not a high priest but the high priesthood was exterminated. It serves as an end to the period begun by "until the time of an anointed" when Jerusalem was ruled by the legitimate high priests, although in troubled times. (*Israelitische und jüdische Geschichte*, 236–37 n. 2). Keil ("Onias III.," 226–28) also understands כרת in a weaker sense.

267. Montgomery, *Daniel*, 451; Collins, *Daniel*, 382.

268. The translation is from Michael A. Knibb, *The Ethiopic Book of Enoch*, 2 vols. (Oxford: Clarendon, 1978), 2.213. For the identification, see, for example, Matthew Black, *The Book of Enoch or I Enoch*, SVTP 7 (Leiden: Brill, 1985), 276. Goldstein, who accepts the Daniel passages as references to Onias's death, thinks that 1 Enoch 90:8 could hardly refer to Onias, as it is speaking about events at the end of the third century and, moreover, the author of the apocalypse who had a negative view of the Second-Temple cult would not have entertained a favorable view of a high priest who presided over it (*II Maccabees*, 239–40). An older objection is that if Onias III were meant in this passage, he would have been represented as a sheep, not a lamb, to be consistent with the imagery of this apocalypse. See, however, Patrick A. Tiller, *A Commentary on the Animal Apocalypse of* I Enoch, SBLEJL 4 (Atlanta: Scholars, 1993), 353–54, who finds the lamb imagery to be appropriate because by this time Onias III had been removed from office.

the apocalyptic works of Daniel and 1 Enoch implies that the murder made a deep impression on a range of observers; all of them combine to offer early testimony against Josephus's report that Onias simply died and was succeeded by Jason.[269]

Second Maccabees says nothing about whether Antiochus IV suspected Menelaus's role in the murder of Onias. It does proceed, though, to relate a succeeding event—one that must not have been much later and perhaps was almost simultaneous with Onias's death; in this case the king did become suspicious. While Lysimachus was apparently still in charge in Jerusalem but, says the author, with the connivance of Menelaus, "many acts of sacrilege had been committed in the city" (4:39), and these led to an uprising against Lysimachus. The latter met the disturbance with force; yet, though his opponents were poorly armed, the deputy high priest's troops were defeated, and he was killed (4:40-42). It is interesting that 2 Maccabees calls Lysimachus "the temple robber"; surely, we are to remember Heliodorus here, and that the earlier would-be temple thief also received his just reward—both at the place of their crime, the temple treasury. Following the battle in Jerusalem, "[c]harges were brought against Menelaus about this incident. When the king came to Tyre, three men sent by the Jewish senate [τῆς γερουσίας] presented the case before him" (4:43). This is one of the few references in the sources to a senate, and it is here pictured as acting in opposition to the high priest and on behalf of a popular uprising.

Menelaus is portrayed in a consistent way in 2 Maccabees. As he had done on the earlier occasion with Andronicus, now he again resorted to bribery. He offered money to a key aide of the king, Ptolemy son of Dorymenes,[270] who succeeded in changing the king's mind about Menelaus. Rather than executing the real culprit, we learn, Antiochus had the representatives of the senate killed. The rage of the author is transparent:

> Menelaus, the cause of all the trouble,[271] he acquitted of the charges against him, while he sentenced to death those unfortunate men, who

---

269. It may be that Onias III is the Onias who is mentioned in 4Q245 i 9 in a list of high priests. For the text, see John J. Collins and Peter W. Flint, "245. 4Qpseudo-Daniel^c ar," in *Qumran Cave 4 XVII Parabiblical Texts, Part 3,* consulting ed. J. VanderKam, DJD 22 (Oxford: Clarendon, 1996), 159–61.

270. See 2 Macc 8:8, where he is the governor of Coele-Syria and Phoenicia, and 1 Macc 3:38.

271. Josephus reports that at the end of his life, the Seleucid authorities also became convinced that Menelaus was "the cause of the mischief," this time meaning the Maccabean uprising and its aftermath (*Ant.* 12.9, 7 [§384]), in that he was the one responsible for persuading Antiochus IV to ban the practice of Judaism.

would have been freed uncondemned if they had pleaded even before Scythians. And so those who had spoken for the city and the villages and the holy vessels quickly suffered the unjust penalty. Therefore even the Tyrians, showing their hatred of the crime, provided magnificently for their funeral. But Menelaus, because of the greed of those in power, remained in office, growing in wickedness, having become the chief plotter against his compatriots. (4:47-50)

To this point, the writer has charged Menelaus with purchasing the office of high priest, theft of temple valuables, and two cases of bribery that led to murder. Such expensive ways hardly helped the financial status of a person who had agreed to pay a steep price for the high-priestly office.[272]

As we have seen, Josephus credits the introduction of Hellenistic institutions to Menelaus and his Tobiad supporters, not to Jason (as in 2 Maccabees); as we have also noted, there is reason to be uneasy about his narrative at this point, because he presents Menelaus as a brother of Onias III even though he gives the two the same name. The two sources agree that the change was made by a brother of Onias III but disagree about the identity of that brother. Since Josephus places these events at the time of Antiochus's first invasion of Egypt, it will be useful first to examine what 2 Maccabees reports about it and then to adduce Josephus's version(s).

Second Maccabees 5:1 speaks of Antiochus's second invasion (ἔφοδον = approach, onset, attack) of Egypt—a time when apparitions of cavalry were seen in the air over Jerusalem (v. 2). The word ἔφοδον is not the normal one for *invasion*, and it is possible that, by referring to the event as the second of these, the author is reminding the reader of the incident in 4:21-22 when, in 171 BCE, Antiochus made preparations for war with Egypt and came to Jerusalem and Phoenicia.[273] First Maccabees 1:16-24 dates the military maneuver to the Seleucid year 143 (v. 20), which would be 169 BCE. The occasion is mentioned to provide the background for the reappearance in the story of Jason, the deposed high priest. Although he had lost his position in 172 BCE, he now perceived an opportunity to regain it:

272. Menelaus's promise of large sums of money in exchange for the high priesthood should probably not be viewed against the backdrop of ongoing Seleucid payments of the war indemnity to Rome, since Antiochus IV had paid off the entire amount outstanding in 173 BCE. See Gera, *Judaea and Mediterranean Politics*, 117–19.

273. Goldstein, *II Maccabees*, 246–47, although it is difficult to accept his added idea that terming this the second departure, while 1 Macc 1:20-24 identifies it as his first invasion, was meant to protect the veracity of Dan 11:25-28, 29-30.

When a false rumor arose that Antiochus was dead, Jason took no
fewer than a thousand men and suddenly made an assault on the city.
When the troops on the wall had been forced back and at last the city
was being taken, Menelaus took refuge in the citadel. But Jason kept
relentlessly slaughtering his compatriots, not realizing that success at
the cost of one's kindred is the greatest misfortune, but imagining
that he was setting up trophies of victory over enemies and not over
compatriots. He did not, however, gain control of the government; in
the end he got only disgrace from his conspiracy, and fled again into
the country of the Ammonites. (5:5-7)

Jason's attempt must be seen against the backdrop of Antiochus's invasion of
Egypt. The Seleucid king took Egypt and laid siege to Alexandria itself before
he decided to withdraw. We do not know how or why Jason heard the rumor
about the king's death, but Antiochus was the one who had appointed
Menelaus as high priest, and, if the monarch were dead, Menelaus would no
longer have had his powerful support. The low number given for Jason's
troops implies that he expected more help from within Jerusalem. Menelaus is
reported to have retired to the citadel, the place from which the Seleucid
authorities exercised their control over Jerusalem. Second Maccabees 1:7-8,
part of the first letter prefixed to the book, refers to "the critical distress that
came upon us in those years after Jason and his company revolted from the
holy land and the kingdom and burned the gate and shed innocent blood." (In
its account of this campaign to Egypt, 1 Maccabees does not mention Jason's
revolt.) Jason, after returning to Ammon, was forced to flee from there to
Egypt and, interestingly, from there to *Lacedaimonia* "in hope of finding protection because of their kinship" (2 Macc 5:9; compare the Spartan correspondence from the time of Onias I). He died in exile (v. 10).[274] Second
Maccabees is almost silent about any control Jason may have exercised over
Jerusalem,[275] for how long this lasted (note "in the end"), and any contact
Menelaus may have had with Seleucid authorities at this time.

Antiochus IV took poorly to the news from Jerusalem—his appointee
there was under siege from someone whom the king had deposed several years
earlier. He believed that Judea was in revolt against him and acted accordingly.
Second Maccabees 5:11-14 recounts his capture of Jerusalem and large-scale

---

274. The burial cave that is known as Jason's Tomb appears unrelated to the high priest
Jason. Coins found in it indicate that it began to be used in the early first century BCE (L. Y. Rahmani, "Jason's Tomb," *IEJ* 17 [1967]: 61–100).

275. But see 2 Macc 1:8, quoted above, where he is said to have burnt the gate, although it
does not further identify the gate.

slaughter of its inhabitants (eighty thousand killed or sold into slavery). Then, in a passage redolent of the author's convictions, he tells of the violence Antiochus committed at the temple, assisted shockingly enough by the high priest Menelaus:

> Not content with this, Antiochus dared to enter the most holy temple in all the world, guided by Menelaus, who had become a traitor both to the laws and to his country. He took the holy vessels with his polluted hands, and swept away with profane hands the votive offerings that other kings had made to enhance the glory and honor of the place. Antiochus was elated in spirit, and did not perceive that the Lord was angered for a little while because of the sins of those who lived in the city, and that this was the reason he was disregarding the holy place. But if it had not happened that they were involved in many sins, this man would have been flogged and turned back from his rash act as soon as he came forward, just as Heliodorus had been, whom King Seleucus sent to inspect the treasury. (2 Macc 5:15-18)

The writer implies and hardly needed to say how strongly Menelaus's conduct contrasted with that of Onias III just a few years earlier. The king is said to have confiscated eighteen-hundred talents from the temple and to have become blasphemously proud of his accomplishments (5:21). First Maccabees 1:20-24 offers less detail about the human casualties and more about the loss of property: it says that Antiochus took the golden altar, the lampstand and related utensils, the table of the bread of the presence, cups for libations, bowls, gold censers, the curtain, crowns, even the gold decoration adorning the front of the temple. It adds that he also seized "the hidden treasures that he found" (v. 23; see also Dan 11:28).

The fact that so many valuables and so much money were removed from the temple makes one wonder whether there were still some unresolved issues having to do with the sums that Menelaus had promised to pay. After all, this was the second time that he was implicated in robbery of temple goods, and it is not clear how plundering the temple could be regarded as support offered by Antiochus on behalf of his appointee Menelaus.

Antiochus's violent actions in Jerusalem in 169 BCE were not to be the end of the matter. "He left governors to oppress the people: at Jerusalem, Philip, by birth a Phrygian and in character more barbarous than the man who appointed him; and at Gerizim, Andronicus; and besides these Menelaus, who lorded it over his compatriots worse than the others did" (2 Macc 5:22-23). The presence of this Philip indicates that Menelaus, after this point at least, did not exercise the supreme political office in Jerusalem, apparently unlike his predecessors.[276] But for reasons that are not enumerated, the king is credited with additional measures against the Jewish people.

> In his malice toward the Jewish citizens, Antiochus sent Apollonius, the captain of the Mysians, with an army of twenty-two thousand, and commanded him to kill all the grown men and to sell the women and boys as slaves. When this man arrived in Jerusalem, he pretended to be peaceably disposed and waited until the holy sabbath day; then, finding the Jews not at work, he ordered his troops to parade under arms. He put to the sword all those who came out to see them, then rushed into the city with his armed warriors and killed great numbers of the people. (5:23-26)

First Maccabees describes the same event in 1:29-40, dating it to the equivalent of 167 BCE, two years after Antiochus's attack on the city.[277] There, the leader is called "a chief collector of tribute,"[278] and he and his troops "plundered the city, burned it with fire, and tore down its houses and its surrounding walls" (v. 31). In a fateful move, they also "fortified the city of David with a great strong wall and strong towers, and it became their citadel. They stationed there a sinful people, men who were renegades. These strengthened their position; they stored up arms and food, and collecting the spoils of Jerusalem they stored them there, and became a great menace" (1:33-35). The citadel was to be a problem until the time of Simon, the third Hasmonean leader and second high priest (1 Macc 14:36-37). All of this precedes Antiochus's decrees banning the practice of Judaism; these follow immediately in 1 Maccabees (1:41-61) and after a short notice about Judas Maccabeus (5:27) in 2 Maccabees (6:1-11). Whether the punitive expedition and the decrees were connected is not said, but they are juxtaposed in the sources.

The decrees of Antiochus IV against Judaism are not presented in exactly the same way in 1 and 2 Maccabees. The latter says the king sent an envoy "to compel the Jews to forsake the laws of their ancestors and no longer to live by the laws of God" (6:1). For 1 Maccabees, the king's policy was empire-wide,

---

276. Schunck, "Hoherpriester und Politiker?" 509.

277. The precise chronology of events at this time has been a point of dispute. Bringmann (*Hellenistische Reform und Religionsverfolgung in Judäa*, 15–28) argues that all Seleucid dates in 1 Maccabees are calculated from an autumn 312 BCE inception of the Seleucid era. In his system, Antiochus's second Egyptian campaign was in 168 BCE and the religious edicts followed in the same year. He also thinks the temple was rededicated in 165, not 164, BCE.

278. The two readings, chief of the Mysians, and chief collector of tribute, have arisen from the same consonants vocalized differently (שר מסים).

with certain Jews being the only ones to oppose it. He is supposed to have written to all peoples in his realm, "that all should be one people, and that all should give up their particular customs" (1:41-42). The two works do agree that traditional sacrifices were banned, the sanctuary defiled, Sabbaths and festivals profaned or banned, and circumcision ruled illegal (1 Macc 1:45-50; 2 Macc 6:2-6, 10-11). Where Menelaus was in all of this we are not told, but there is no mistaking the fundamental change in the way in which worship took place in the temple where he was high priest.[279]

What motivated this repressive step some two years after Antiochus himself had pillaged Jerusalem and slaughtered and enslaved many inhabitants? There have been varied proposals, but (or rather, because) the source material is not especially full or helpful. Any solution must reckon with the fact that a sizable number of Jews accepted the changes, while a significant number opposed them.

1. Bickerman and Hengel:[280] According to these scholars, the protagonists of the religious reform were extreme Hellenists such as Menelaus and the Tobiads; they wished to rid Judaism of the practices that made them different from their neighbors, practices that qualified them as barbarians. First Maccabees 1:11 attributes such a sentiment to certain "renegades" who "came out from Israel and misled many, saying, 'Let us go and make a covenant with the Gentiles around us, for since we separated from them many disasters have come upon us.'" Bickerman also identified the residents of the citadel as Syrians who would have been opposed to distinctive Jewish customs. A problem here is that, while the sources do identify some Jewish people as instigators of the *Hellenistic* reform, they do not credit the *religious* persecution to their urging. Only the Seleucid government is held responsible for that.

2. Tcherikover thought there was a Hasidic revolt in Jerusalem, with the traditionalists opposing both Menelaus and Jason. Antiochus, seeing that the Jewish religion was the root cause of the repeated problems in the area, decided to ban it. In this, he was seconded by the inhabitants of the citadel who were probably Syrians. They would have had a say in the religious policy of the city of which they were now residents and would have had no interest in retaining distinctive Jewish practices.[281]

---

279. As Rooke observes, Menelaus is not said to be an agent in the persecution at this point, but "the fact that he apparently managed to remain in office throughout the persecution implies that he did not actively oppose the measures taken by Antiochus, whether or not he actually cooperated with them or even instigated or suggested them" (*Zadok's Heirs*, 278).

280. Bickerman, *Der Gott der Makkabäer: Untersuchungen über Sinn und Ursprung der makkabäischen Erhebung* (Berlin: Schocken, 1937; ET 1979); Hengel, *Judaism and Hellenism*, vol. 1.

281. *Hellenistic Civilization and the Jews*, 175–203.

While the issue is too complicated to grapple with here, Tcherikover's reading does point in a helpful direction, even though he did not exploit the range of evidence that may be brought to bear on the problem. Here, it will be useful to take a somewhat different approach to the issue by discussing the evidence about Onias IV, apparently the oldest surviving son of Onias III and thus, under normal circumstances, the rightful heir to the high priesthood. There are confusing, conflicting claims about him in the sources, but it is possible that they contain a clue to the severity of Antiochus IV's reactions in 167 BCE. It is not certain that Onias IV ever served as high priest in Jerusalem, but he may have done so before fleeing to Egypt and establishing the Jewish temple in Leontopolis.

[Onias IV?][282] Josephus is our primary source of information about Onias IV and the origins of the Jewish temple at Leontopolis in the nome of Heliopolis, but, since the historian recorded several conflicting accounts about these events, the history of the man and of the temple he founded (if indeed he was the one who established it) continues to be a matter of dispute among scholars. We should examine the relevant sections and attempt, if possible, to recover the course of events.[283]

1. Passages in *The Jewish War*: Josephus begins his historical survey in *War* with a brief statement about the events in question.

At the time when Antiochus, surnamed Epiphanes, was disputing with Ptolemy VI. the suzerainty of Syria, dissension arose among the Jewish nobles. There were rival claims to supreme power, as no individual of rank could tolerate subjection to his peers. Onias, one of the chief priests [τῶν ἀρχιερέων], gaining the upper hand, expelled the

---

282. Although the debated point about the identity of this Onias has been whether he was Onias III or Onias IV, Émil Puech has defended a new approach in "Le grand prêtre Simon (III) fils d'Onias III, le Maître de Justice?" in *Antikes Judentum und Frühes Christentum: Festschrift für Hartmeut Stegemann zum 65. Geburtstag,* ed. B. Kollmann, W. Reinbold, and A. Steudel, BZNW 97 (Berlin: de Gruyter, 1999), 137–58. He argues that the Onias who founded the temple in Egypt was the son of Simon (Menelaus's brother). He was frustrated when Menelaus selected his brother Lysimachus as the second-ranking priest and therefore went to Egypt and founded his own temple. There is no textual support for this theory; it is based on the hypothesis that Josephus confused names for this period.

283. For a study of the relevant passages, see, for example, Smith, "A Study of the Zadokite High Priesthood," 74–101; M. Delcor, "Le temple d'Onias en Égypte: Réexamen d'un vieux problème," *RB* 75 (1968): 188–203; Robert Hayward, "The Jewish Temple at Leontopolis: A Reconsideration," *JJS* 33 (1982): 429–43; and J. Taylor, "A Second Temple in Egypt: The Evidence for the Zadokite Temple of Onias," *JSJ* 29 (1998): 297–310. Her reading of the evidence seems implausible (she, unlike Smith, Delcor, Hayward, and many others, thinks Onias III founded the temple).

sons of Tobias from the city. The latter took refuge with Antiochus and besought him to use their services as guides for an invasion of Judaea. The king, having long cherished this design, consented, and setting out at the head of a huge army took the city by assault, slew a large number of Ptolemy's followers, gave his soldiers unrestricted licence to pillage, and himself plundered the temple and interrupted, for a period of three years and six months, the regular course of the daily sacrifices. The high priest [ὁ δ᾽ ἀρχιερεύς] Onias made his escape to Ptolemy and, obtaining from him a site in the nome of Heliopolis, built a small town on the model of Jerusalem and a temple resembling ours. We shall revert to these matters in due course. (1.1, 1 [§§31–33])

The time to which Josephus assigns these events can be narrowed down to some extent. Disputed sovereignty over Coele-Syria was a cause of the Sixth Syrian War in 169–68 BCE.[284] Presumably, this is what is meant by the opening sentence. The circumstances of the Seleucid-Ptolemaic conflict are crucial to the passage: the ousted Tobiads sided with King Antiochus and assisted him as he invaded, while Onias, when he was forced from Jerusalem, fled to King Ptolemy. Tcherikover thought that Josephus confused Jason with Onias.[285] He could, of course, show that Jason had done a number of the actions attributed here to Onias: he had driven the Tobiads from Jerusalem, at which time they went to Antiochus (*Ant.* 12.5, 1 [§§237–41]). Tcherikover thought that Josephus had not only confused the names but also the events of 171 BCE when, according to Josephus, Onias expelled the Tobiads, and the events of 168 when Jason attacked Jerusalem and locked Menelaus in the fortress. "It may then be concluded that the passage is based on the events of 171, but Josephus, desiring to shorten the story and to pass on quickly to the account of the persecutions of Antiochus, embodied them in the second war of Jason and transferred the whole affair to the time of Antiochus's Egyptian campaign."[286]

If one compares the events of this paragraph of *War* with the chronology in 1 Maccabees, Josephus telescopes events, so that what happened over a two-

---

284. It is often suggested that περὶ ὅλης Συρίας in Josephus's text is a mistake for περὶ κοίλης Συρίας (see Tcherikover, *Hellenistic Civilization and the Jews*, 536 n. 28).

285. *Hellenisitic Civilization and the Jews*, 468 n. 36. See the summary of his argument on this point on 392–95, an analysis originally published in "War 1.1, 1 as a Historical Source," *Madaʿe-Hay-yahadut* 1 (1926): 179–86 (Hebrew). Tcherikover argues there that most problems with the notice in *War*, in comparison with the other sources, disappear if one changes *Onias* to *Jason*; but he also maintains that Josephus here was writing from memory and not only confused these two characters but also forgot that Antiochus fought twice against Egypt.

286. *Hellenistic Civilization and the Jews*, 393–94.

year period (169–167 BCE) is presented as though it were one series of events transpiring in rapid succession. In comparison with 2 Maccabees, the paragraph covers events from about 175 to 167 BCE, if it does fail to distinguish Onias III from Onias IV. Whatever the problems may be with the section, the source connects Onias's flight to Egypt with the events that included the religious decrees of 167 BCE. The departure is, however, noted only after the chronological detail that the daily sacrifices ceased for three and one-half years (167–164 BCE), so that it may be implied that his departure was no earlier than 164 BCE. Interestingly, Onias is called the high priest (ὁ ἀρχιερεύς) when he leaves Jerusalem. This could hardly be Onias III, who was no longer living at the time.

As he said he would at the end of the passage, Josephus returns to the origins of the Oniad temple in Egypt at a later point in *War*: 7.10, 2–4 (§§420–36). Here, he calls Onias the "son of Simon" (this would be Onias III, according to the high-priestly genealogy in *Antiquities*) and repeats that he was "one of the chief priests at Jerusalem" (§423). In this passage, too, he flees from Antiochus, who was at war with the Jews, and to Ptolemy, who hated Antiochus. In Egypt, Onias speaks of making the Jewish nation Ptolemy's ally and mentions the Seleucid king's sacking the Jerusalem temple (§425). After describing the temple in Heliopolis, Josephus writes: "In all this, however, Onias was not actuated by honest motives; his aim was rather to rival the Jews at Jerusalem, against whom he harboured resentment for his exile [φυγῆς], and he hoped by erecting this temple to attract the multitude away from them to it" (§431). Onias, who can only be Onias IV despite Josephus's identification of him as a son of Simon, is thus the subject of a partially negative report.

In this statement, Josephus adds detail but pictures Onias in virtually the same way as he did in *War* 1. Although he names Simon as his father, it is a mistake he will later correct in *Antiquities* in line with his own high-priestly genealogy in which Onias III, not Onias IV, is the son of a Simon. In *War* 7, the historian does not refer to the Tobiads as the opponents of this Onias (IV).

2. Passages in *Antiquities*: If the two sections in *War* were our only sources, the resulting problems would be minimal, but the matter becomes more complex when Josephus's reports in *Antiquities* are added to the mix. There, in Book 12.9, 7 (§§387–88), he assigns Onias's flight to Egypt to the time when Menelaus was executed and Alcimus appointed to the high priesthood (162 BCE).

> Then Onias, the son of the high priest, who, as we said before, had been left a mere child when his father died [see 12.5, 1 (§237)], seeing that the king had slain his uncle Menelaus and had given the high priesthood to Alcimus, although he was not of the family of high

priests, because he had been persuaded by Lysias to transfer the office from this house to another, fled to Ptolemy, the king of Egypt. (§387)

The historian adds that Onias received land in the nome of Heliopolis where he built a temple (§388). In this passage, Josephus changes his earlier claim that Onias was the son of Simon by identifying his father as Onias whose death he had noted in 12.5, 1 (§237). As he had there, he considers Menelaus the uncle of Onias IV, while 2 Maccabees relates him to a different family.

The picture becomes more complex with the addition of *Ant.* 13.3, 1–3 (§§62–73), where the Flavian historian devotes a longer section to Onias and supplies new information. The section is lodged directly after the notice about the death of King Demetrius (Demetrius I) in 150 BCE, although Josephus's summary statement concluding this and the following section—also concerning Jews in Egypt—suggests that he is simply recording events that occurred during Ptolemy Philometor's long reign (181–180 to 164, 163–145 BCE), whatever their precise dates may have been. Josephus again (§62) calls Onias (IV) the son of Onias (III) and says that he was living in Alexandria. Apparently while he was there, he heard what the Seleucids were doing in Judea and asked permission to build a temple like the one in Jerusalem. Of considerable interest is the first sentence in the letter Onias wrote to Ptolemy and Cleopatra: "Many and great are the services which I have rendered to you in the course of the war, with the help of God, when I was in Coele-Syria and Phoenicia" (§65). Marcus thought that the reference was to the conflict between Ptolemy VI Philometor and Ptolemy VIII Euergetes II,[287] but mention of Coele-Syria and Phoenicia makes that highly unlikely. In this passage, the time of temple construction in Egypt may be put later than is implied in Josephus's other reports.

Finally, in *Ant.* 20.10, 3 (§§235–36), when dealing with the execution of Menelaus (whom Josephus continues to call *Onias* and identifies as a brother of Onias III), he writes that the transfer of the high priesthood in 162 BCE was the first time a high priest's son was excluded from succeeding his father: "In consequence of this, Onias, who was the nephew of the deceased Onias [= Menelaus] and who bore the same name as his father, made his way to Egypt, where he won the friendship of Ptolemy Philometor and Cleopatra his queen, and persuaded them to build a temple to God in the nome of Heliopolis" (§236).[288]

---

287. *Josephus* 7, 258 n. a.

288. This statement, too, seems strange in light of what Josephus writes in *Ant.* 15.3, 1 (§§40–41) regarding King Herod's removal of a high priest: "But in this he [= Herod] acted unlawfully, for never had anyone been deprived of this office [= the high priesthood] when once

Although we may not be able to piece together an accurate account of what happened from these partially conflicting sections, there are several points that follow from them.

1. The events took place in the 160s BCE, in the context of renewed Seleucid-Ptolemaic hostilities and of conflicts in Judea between supporters of one or the other of the Hellenistic kingdoms. It is difficult to determine from the *War* passages when Onias's flight from Jerusalem to Egypt took place, but it seems that it was after the years of the religious persecution, and in this they appear to be consistent with *Antiquities*.
2. The Onias who fled Jerusalem and eventually founded the temple in Heliopolis was Onias IV, not Onias III. Josephus conveyed incorrect genealogical information in *War*; this he later corrected in *Antiquities*. In this respect, he became consistent in *Antiquities* with the claim in 2 Maccabees that Onias III was dead by this time.
3. Josephus gave Onias IV the title *high priest*, thus providing some evidence that he at least claimed that title at some point.
4. Once he was in Egypt, Onias reminded the king and queen of the military services he had rendered for them while he was still in Coele-Syria (he would serve in a similar capacity at a later time in Egypt). If he left Coele-Syria in 162 BCE, then his war efforts preceded that date and would have occurred between 168 and 162 BCE. This may seem to raise a problem with *Ant.* 12.5, 1 (§237) where, at the death of his father (placed at the time of the transfer of the high priesthood to Jason, that is, 175 BCE), Onias (IV) was "still an infant." The translation may not be accurate, however. Josephus called Onias a νήπιος, a term that can mean "infant" but may also refer generally to someone who is a "minor, not yet of age."[289] He also calls him a παῖς "boy, youth"[290] (*Ant.* 12.5, 1 [§237] and 12.9, 7 [§387]). If the more general meaning is intended in these passages, then Onias IV, though he would have been a minor in 175 BCE, could have been old enough to command troops in the period 168–162 BCE. As we have seen, the information in *Ant.* 12.5, 1 is quite confused in comparison with the data of 2 Maccabees. This raises the possibility that Josephus has garbled matters in this passage.

It will be recalled that in *Ant.* 12.2, 5 (§§43–44) Josephus had recorded the case of the high priest Simon I who left a son Onias (Onias II) who was "an

___
he had assumed it, except that Antiochus Epiphanes had violated this law first when he removed Jesus and appointed his brother Onias . . . ."

289. BAG, 539.
290. BAG, 609.

infant" (νήπιον υἱόν); as a result, the high priesthood passed temporarily to Simon's brother. It may be that Josephus was misled by the earlier passage to confuse matters here: it could have induced him to call Onias's father Simon, and the fact that the high priesthood had passed from Onias III to his brother Jason caused him to assume that, as before in the comparable situation, the reason for this unusual procedure was the presence of an underage son. Consequently, the assertion that Onias IV was too young to assume office in 175 BCE may not be a documented historical statement but a mistaken inference by Josephus who would not have known from his primary source, 1 Maccabees, what had transpired in the last pre-Maccabean years.

On the basis of the Josephan passages and the points argued above, the following is a plausible historical reconstruction. When Onias III lost the high priesthood in 175 BCE and his brother Jason took office, Onias's son Onias IV, the true heir to his father's position, remained in Jerusalem. With his supporters, he harbored anti-Seleucid (and anti-Jason) feelings, and these grew stronger after the murder of Onias III in Antioch in 170. At that time, Onias IV's unhappiness with the Seleucid overlords increased when the high priesthood, although it was taken from Jason, was not given to him by rightful succession but to the unrelated Menelaus. Menelaus, as Josephus tells us, had the support of the Tobiads (presumably not Hyrcanus's side of the family). At this time, Onias IV took measures into his own hands. Now that he was of age, he claimed the high priesthood for himself (hence Josephus calls him the high priest), and, using troops loyal to the high-priestly family, he drove the rival high priest Menelaus and his Tobiad faction from power. How this may have correlated, if it did, with Jason's revolt, we do not know;[291] but Onias IV may have been a military presence in Judea in those times—a factor that could have had something to do with Antiochus IV's decision in 167 BCE to issue the religious decrees banning the practice of Judaism. The late dating of the king's decision is not well motivated in 1 and 2 Maccabees, neither of which mentions Onias IV. There may be tendentious reasons why the authors chose not to mention him: the writer of 2 Maccabees wanted to focus attention on the illegal high priests and Judas's cleansing of the one and only temple in Jerusalem; the compiler of 1 Maccabees wished to place all honor on Judas and his brothers and to justify the Maccabean high priesthood. But, judging from Josephus, more was happening in Judea than 1 and 2 Maccabees report: the

---

291. Bunge thinks that Onias IV joined forces with Jason and concludes that the only conceivable time when Onias IV could have obtained his ancestral dignity would have been the short Oniad interregnum in the fall of 169 BCE ("Zur Geschichte und Chronologie," 10).

legitimate high priest was attempting to gain his rightful position and was successfully using military force to do so.

All of the above might be acceptable, but Josephus throws one more obstacle in the way of our historical reconstruction. In *Antiquities*, just after the passage in which he claims that all three of Simon II's sons became high priests and reports that Antiochus gave the high priesthood to Jesus/Jason before depriving him of it in favor of his brother Menelaus, Josephus writes:

> And when the former high priest Jesus rose against Menelaus, who was appointed after him, the populace was divided between the two, the Tobiads being on the side of Menelaus, while the majority of the people [τὸ δὲ πλέον τοῦ λαοῦ] supported Jason; and being hard pressed by him, Menelaus and the Tobiads withdrew, and going to Antiochus informed him that they wished to abandon their country's laws and the way of life prescribed by these, and to follow the king's laws and adopt the Greek way of life. Accordingly, they petitioned him to permit them to build a gymnasium in Jerusalem. And when he had granted this, they also concealed the circumcision of their private parts in order to be Greeks even when unclothed, and giving up whatever other national customs they had, they imitated the practices of foreign nations. (12.5, 1 [§§239–41])

Here Josephus credits to Menelaus and the Tobiads what 2 Maccabees attributes to Jason. Moreover, and in this he is consistent in his accounts, he ties events closely with the Tobiads and with pro-Ptolemaic and pro-Seleucid factions—something that is not said but at times can be inferred from 2 Maccabees.

If, however, we place this section from Josephus side-by-side with 1 Macc 1:11-15, Josephus's source, we gain a better impression of what the Flavian historian has done.

And when the former high priest Jesus rose against Menelaus, who was appointed after him, the populace was divided between the two, the Tobiads being on the side of Menelaus, while the majority of the people [τὸ δὲ πλέον τοῦ λαοῦ] supported Jason; and being hard pressed by him, Menelaus and the Tobiads withdrew, and going to Antiochus

In those days certain renegades came out from Israel and misled many, saying, "Let us go and make a covenant with the Gentiles around us, for since we separated from them many disasters have come upon us." This proposal pleased them, and some of the people eagerly went to the king, who authorized them to observe the ordinances of the

informed him that they wished to abandon their country's laws and the way of life prescribed by these, and to follow the king's laws and adopt the Greek way of life. Accordingly, they petitioned him to permit them to build a gymnasium in Jerusalem. And when he had granted this, they also concealed the circumcision of their private parts in order to be Greeks even when unclothed, and giving up whatever other national customs they had, they imitated the practices of foreign nations. (*Ant.* 12.5, 1 [§§239–41])

Gentiles. So they built a gymnasium in Jerusalem, according to Gentile custom, and removed the marks of circumcision, and abandoned the holy covenant. They joined with the Gentiles, and sold themselves to do evil. (1 Macc 1:11-15)

It is evident that Josephus is here offering an interpretation of his source and, wherever he saw fit, supplying names of individuals and groups, which are lacking in the vague account of 1 Maccabees. That is, he does not appear to have had an independent source from which he was drawing information; he simply added his own details to 1 Maccabees. This was noted already by Büchler, who wrote in connection with these two passages, after observing the agreement of the two in the main points, that 1 Macc 1:13 lacks mention of the author of this insertion in which just "some of the people" appears. Josephus, however, without much thought, inserted the Tobiads, about whom he had just spoken, for the general designation. In this way the contradiction with the report in 2 Maccabees arose.[292]

It just may be that Josephus preserves evidence of an attempt by Onias IV, the son of Onias III and a pro-Ptolemaic leader, to gain the high priesthood for himself, an attempt that may have been successful for a short time but soon was halted through the measures adopted by Antiochus IV with the assistance of Menelaus and his Tobiad supporters. This would be a coup beyond the one carried out briefly by Jason and one not recorded in 2 Maccabees; it has the potential for providing a satisfactory explanation for why Antiochus reacted as he did in 167 BCE, two years after he had taken the city: A man with a hereditary claim to the high priesthood (Onias IV) had ousted Menelaus. In view of the troubles he had encountered before in Jerusalem, Antiochus determined to attack the problem at the root and drive out both Onias IV and the traditional Jewish practices with which he was associated.

---

292. *Die Tobiaden und die Oniaden*, 111.

It seems wisest to accept the general picture of 2 Maccabees but to admit the possibility that Josephus may have preserved additional historical information. This may be the case especially for the events around the year 169 BCE and the cause(s) that led Antiochus to respond so forcefully in Jerusalem.

Whatever may have been the course of events, the family of Mattathias, a priest from the clan of Joiarib and a descendant of a man named *Asamonaios* (*Ant.* 12.6, 1 [§265]; hence the name *Hasmonean* for the family), and his sons (especially Judas nicknamed *Maccabeus*) led the famous uprising known as the Maccabean revolt. By the year 164 BCE (or 165), after several battles with Seleucid forces, these rebels managed to recapture the temple precinct and rededicate the sanctuary to the traditional form of worship. Their efforts made it very difficult indeed to enforce the religious bans of King Antiochus. Menelaus was officially the high priest during these years, but for at least some of the time he could not have carried out sacerdotal functions at the temple because it was in enemy hands.

Menelaus, continued: In fact, we hear little about Menelaus in the remaining years of his life. During the time when the Seleucid decrees were in force (167–164 BCE, possibly 168–165), worship at the temple would have been deeply compromised, but Menelaus and his work in connection with the temple are not part of the record.[293] In fact, the next mention of the high priesthood in 2 Maccabees contains no reference to Menelaus, although it is an interesting passage for understanding what the high priesthood may have meant to the Seleucid government. After the Maccabean recapture and cleansing of the temple and subsequent victories, the Seleucid official Lysias invaded with a large force.[294] "He intended to make the city a home for Greeks, and to levy tribute on the temple as he did on the sacred places of the other nations, and to put up the high priesthood for sale every year" (2 Macc 11:2b-3). Lysias suffered a crushing defeat (11:6-12), so his plan was not put into action, but it may be that annual sale of the high priesthood was an accepted practice elsewhere in the Hellenistic world—a practice that may have been a model for

---

293. Bringmann (*Hellenistische Reform und Religionsverfolgung in Judäa*, 66–140) thinks the Hellenistic reform ended when Menelaus, the enemy of Jason who had instituted it, took over as high priest. He argues that Menelaus, to retain his position after alienating the city, was the one who proposed the religious decrees and thus deprived his priestly opponents of their power base (the traditional cult had continued under Jason). At this time, Menelaus presided over a new, probably Phoenician cult (like that of the military contingent stationed in Jerusalem). Antiochus agreed to his proposals for political and financial reasons. On this interpretation, the Hellenistic reform and the religious decrees had no connection with each other.

294. The relative date of Lysias's invasion is a problem because 1 Macc 3:38—4:35 places it before the rededication of the temple, while in 2 Maccabees it figures after the first Hanukkah.

Antiochus IV in his earlier dealings with Jason and Menelaus, however contrary it was to the Jewish tradition.[295]

Menelaus also appears in the third of the four letters situated in 2 Maccabees 11. As commentators have long noted, the letters do not appear in their correct chronological order, but the third of them includes the name of Menelaus and divulges something about the part he played in the years when Judaism was banned. Second Maccabees puts the document in the reign of Antiochus V (164–162 BCE), the period in which it locates all four letters, but from the date and contents it seems much more likely that the letter belongs to the reign of Antiochus IV.[296] It may also be the case, as Habicht has argued, that the third letter precedes the first and fourth letters in date.[297] Wherever it fits, it describes a role for Menelaus that does not come to expression elsewhere in 2 Maccabees, which is consistently negative about him.

> King Antiochus, to the senate of the Jews and to the other Jews, greetings. If you are well, it is as we desire. We also are in good health. Menelaus has informed us that you wish to return home and look after your own affairs. Therefore those who go home by the thirtieth of Xanthicus will have our pledge of friendship and full permission for the Jews to enjoy their own food[298] and laws, just as formerly, and none of them shall be molested in any way for what may have been done in ignorance. And I have also sent Menelaus to encourage you. Farewell. The one hundred forty-eighth year. Xanthicus fifteenth. (2 Macc 11:27-33)

Here, Menelaus is clearly the mediator between the Jews and the Seleucid government. He had communicated to the central authority the Jewish desire to

---

295. E. J. Bickerman, *Institutions des Seleucides,* Service des Antiquités Bibliothèque archéologique et historique 26 (Paris: Librairie orientaliste Paul Geuthner, 1938), 114–15. Bickerman mentions the passage in dealing with the regular taxes and explains that sale of priestly honors was the practice at the time and is attested in several cities in Asia Minor. The Ptolemies required that one buy the authorization to carry out the various functions of the Egyptian cult (115).

296. The four letters have been the subjects of several studies. For a recent overview, see Gera, *Judaea and Mediterranean Politics,* 239–53. Gera puts three of the four letters in the reign of Antiochus IV (or at least at a time when he was still believed to be alive); Letter 2 is the obvious exception in that it refers to Antiochus's death.

297. Christian Habicht, "Royal Documents in Maccabees II," *HSCP* 80 (1976): 14–15.

298. The meaning of δαπανήμασι is not entirely clear. NRSV follows the suggestion that it refers to a means of living, thus to food; but it may mean "expenditures" (Mørkholm, *Antiochus,* 156 n. 63). Goldstein emends to διαιτήματα (customs, way of life) (*II Maccabees,* 421).

resume the previous way of life. In order to encourage and secure this, the king defined a period when, without penalty, Jews could return to their homes (a total of fifteen days).[299] Among the favors granted by Antiochus was permission for Jews to follow their own laws concerning food (?) and other matters. This sounds very much like a retraction of the earlier decrees, or at least some of them, and indicates that the letter was meant to include people who opposed those decrees.

The letter is addressed to the Jewish senate (γηρουσία) and thus not to rebels such as the Maccabees. Hence, we have documentary evidence here that the senate was in existence, thus favoring the assumption that it had continued to exist through the years of the decrees[300] and that the king was now working through standard, official channels.[301] Although he was not the addressee of the letter, Menelaus played an important role in bringing about the royal concessions. It is not said how and where he reported the matter to the king, but Antiochus IV was far off in the east at this time, so that if Menelaus traveled to see him in person, his was a long journey indeed. The king believed that there was some point in sending Menelaus to "encourage you" (παρακαλέσοντα ὑμᾶς). Perhaps the meaning is that he was to reassure the recipients about the measures contained in the letter.[302] It may be that, as Gera argues, Menelaus feared his influence was fading with the victories of Judas Maccabeus and that the solution he encouraged was to revoke the religious decrees so that support for the rebels would weaken. In the end, the strategy proved unsuccessful, but it was tried for a short time.[303] If the king's letter dates to a time before the rededication of the temple, the response of the Maccabean forces was hardly conciliatory; if it was written after the rededication, the policy was still a failure.

We next meet Menelaus in a dated context. Second Maccabees 13:1-2 mentions the year of the Seleucid Era 149 (164–163 BCE) as the time when Judas Maccabeus heard about a great invasion of Judea by Antiochus V Eupator (164–162) and Lysias; 1 Macc 6:20 dates what seems to be the same event to the Seleucid year 150 (163–162):

> Menelaus also joined them and with utter hypocrisy urged Antiochus on, not for the sake of the country's welfare, but because he thought

---

299. See Gera, *Judaea and Mediterranean Politics*, 244, for parallels for such a period of time.
300. See M. Stern, *The Documents of the Maccabean Revolt*, 71.
301. See Mørkholm, *Antiochus*, 156; Gera, *Judaea and Mediterranean Politics*, 248.
302. Abel takes the term in the sense "tranquilliser" (*Les livres des Maccabées*, 430, 431).
303. Gera, *Judaea and Mediterranean Politics*, 247–48. Compare also Schunck, "Hoherpriester und Politiker?" 509–10.

that he would be established in office. But the King of kings aroused the anger of Antiochus against the scoundrel; and when Lysias informed him that this man was to blame for all the trouble, he ordered them to take him to Beroea and to put him to death by the method that is customary in that place. For there is a tower there, fifty cubits high, full of ashes, and it has a rim running around it that on all sides inclines precipitously into the ashes. There they all push to destruction anyone guilty of sacrilege or notorious for other crimes. By such a fate it came about that Menelaus the lawbreaker died, without even burial in the earth.[304] And this was eminently just; because he had committed many sins against the altar whose fire and ashes were holy, he met his death in ashes. (2 Macc 13:3-8)

It appears from this passage that Menelaus at the time lived in Antioch.[305] This would be understandable because, according to the preceding contexts in both 1 and 2 Maccabees, the temple had been captured by the Maccabean forces (leading to the rededication, 1 Macc 4:36-61; 2 Macc 10:1-8), and there is no indication that they had relinquished control of it. First Maccabees 4:60-61a says that they had "fortified Mount Zion with high walls and strong towers all around, to keep the Gentiles from coming and trampling them down as they had done before. Judas stationed a garrison there to guard it" (see also 1 Macc 6:7, 26). According to 1 Macc 5:54, Judas and his men returned safely to Mount Zion after a long campaign (compare 2 Macc 12:31-32, where they celebrate Pentecost [the festival of Weeks] in Jerusalem). The immediate cause of the Seleucid invasion of Antiochus V and Lysias was Judas's resolve to destroy the forces in the citadel who "kept hemming Israel in around the sanctuary" (1 Macc 6:18); and the king and his army, after the battle at Beth Zur, encamped against Judas "in Judea and at Mount Zion" (6:48), specifically before the sanctuary (6:51). So, they held the sanctuary area at that time. The king is said to have torn down the wall around Mount Zion before returning to Antioch (6:62). The letter of Antiochus V to Lysias, which restores the temple to the Jews (2 Macc 11:25), seems simply to be a concession to the status quo on this point (see 2 Macc 13:23).

The armed attempt by the Seleucids to retake Jerusalem and Judea was cut short by troubles in Antioch, but at some point during or after the campaign,

---

304. See Habicht, *2. Makkabäerbuch*, 267, where he gives references to the sources attesting the method by which Menelaus was executed; and Abel, *Les livres des Maccabées*, 451. It was a Persian way of killing people for religious offenses.

305. See Abel, *Les livres des Maccabées*, 450.

Menelaus met his end in the ashes of Beroea (= Aleppo). Although, 2 Maccabees reports, he hoped to "be established in office" (13:3), his fate was to be quite different. It is noteworthy that Lysias, the great Seleucid officer, is said to be the one who by then had perceived that Menelaus "was to blame for all the trouble" (13:4). In this paragraph we get our only hint that he had ever conducted high-priestly duties at the temple, and it is worded so as to express the author's belief in retribution: "because he had committed many sins against the altar whose fire and ashes were holy, he met his death in ashes" (13:8). Josephus, who follows 1 Maccabees (which does not mention Menelaus), adds to his source a reference to the end of the high priest. He places it at a point after the troops of Antiochus V had torn down the wall around the sanctuary area but in other respects his description resembles the one in 2 Maccabees: [306]

> After doing this, he returned to Antioch, taking with him the high priest Onias, who was also called Menelaus. For Lysias had advised the king to slay Menelaus, if he wished the Jews to remain quiet and not give him any trouble; it was this man, he said, who had been the cause of the mischief by persuading the king's father to compel the Jews to abandon their fathers' religion. Accordingly, the king sent Menelaus to Beroea in Syria, and there had him put to death; he had served as high priest for ten years, and had been a wicked and impious man, who in order to have sole authority for himself had compelled his nation to violate their own laws. The high priest chosen after the death of Menelaus was Alcimus, also called Jakeimos. (*Ant.* 12.9, 7 [§§383–85])

So Josephus reproduces a source that blames Menelaus for the change from the ancestral religion; the reference should be to the decrees of 167 BCE.

Depending on which date for the Seleucid invasion is correct, Menelaus died in 163 or 162 BCE. Thus ended the ten-year reign of the high priest who ruled during the decrees of Antiochus IV and the Maccabean response.

16. Alcimus (162 to 160 or 159 BCE)

A priest with the Greek name Alcimus and the Hebrew name Yaqim (= Yakeimos)[307] succeeded Menelaus in office and presided for some three

---

306. The author of 2 Maccabees stresses divine intervention, while in Josephus, the removal of Menelaus is seen more as a calculated political act. See Abel, *Les livres des Maccabées*, 450.

307. The Hebrew name יָקִים or יוֹיָקִים has a variant form, אֶלְיָקִים which may lie behind the choice of the Greek name Ἄλκιμος. See Goldstein, *I Maccabees*, 333.

years. He, unlike Menelaus, is mentioned in both 1 and 2 Maccabees, and Josephus refers to him a number of times. Despite the variety of sources for him and his career, some questions remain about his background and his high-priestly tenure.

As 1 Maccabees presents the matter, at the time when Demetrius I (162–150 BCE), son of Seleucus IV and nephew of Antiochus IV, seized the Seleucid throne from Antiochus V and Lysias, "there came to him all the renegades and godless men of Israel; they were led by Alcimus, who wanted to be high priest [βουλόμενος ἱερατεύειν[308]]. They brought to the king this accusation against the people: 'Judas and his brothers have destroyed all your Friends, and have driven us out of our land. Now then send a man whom you trust; let him go and see all the ruin that Judas has brought on us and on the land of the king, and let him punish them and all who help them'" (1 Macc 7:5-7). Alcimus's first appearance in the book is, then, as head of an anti-Maccabean delegation, all of whom had been exiled from the land by Judas and his forces and looked to the new Seleucid king as their protector. The author also identifies for us Alcimus's motive—he wanted to be high (?) priest. We learn in the immediate sequel that the king did as requested: he sent Bacchides, governor of Beyond the River (which included Judea), to settle matters, and he named[309] "the ungodly Alcimus" (7:9) as high priest. Since Demetrius became king in the Seleucid year 151 (162–161 BCE),[310] Alcimus's appointment or, perhaps more likely, only his confirmation as high priest seems to have taken place in that year as well.

Josephus, however, complicates matters somewhat. He does follow 1 Maccabees in saying that Alcimus succeeded Menelaus in office after Antiochus V condemned the latter to death (*Ant.* 12.9, 7 [§385]: "the high priest chosen after the death of Menelaus was Alcimus, also called Jakeimos"), but just two paragraphs later he puts Alcimus's appointment, not in the reign of Demetrius, but in that of his predecessor, Antiochus V. The event is synchronized with the flight of Onias IV to Egypt. Onias (Menelaus's nephew, according to Josephus) took his leave from Judah upon seeing that the king

---

308. It seems overly specific to translate the infinitive as "to be *high* priest." BAG defines the word as "hold the office or perform the service of a priest" (372); LSJ gives "to be a priest or priestess." Perhaps the NRSV translates from context.

309. It is possible that the verb ἔστησεν in 1 Macc 7:9 means only "confirmed" and does not imply that he was first appointed at this time. See Abel, *Les livres des Maccabées*, 131, and also the analysis of the passage below. Goldstein translates with "confirmed" (*I Maccabees*, 326). The importance of this point will become evident later.

310. For the dates, see Schürer, *The History of the Jewish People*, 129–30; Antiochus V is still named as king on a cuneiform document of October 17, 162 BCE (see Goldstein, *I Maccabees*, 329).

(Antiochus V) "had given the high priesthood to Alcimus, although he was not of the family of high priests, because he had been persuaded by Lysias to transfer the office from this house to another" (*Ant.* 12.9, 7 [§387]).[311] It is reasonable to conclude that Alcimus did indeed become high priest in 162 BCE during the reign of Antiochus V and that when Demetrius came to the throne he needed to be reconfirmed in office.[312] The present forms of 1 and 2 Maccabees do not mention the earlier appointment; only Josephus does.

In 1 Maccabees 7, a dramatic scene follows once Bacchides, Alcimus, and the royal troops arrived in Judah.

> Then a large group of scribes appeared in a body before Alcimus and Bacchides to ask for just terms. The Hasideans were first among the Israelites to seek peace from them, for they said, "A priest of the line of Aaron has come with the army, and he will not harm us." Alcimus[313] spoke peaceable words to them and swore this oath to them, "We will not seek to injure you or your Friends." So they trusted him; but he seized sixty of them and killed them in one day. (1 Macc 7:12-16)

In verse 17, the event is interpreted in connection with Ps 79:2-3 regarding the deaths of "your faithful ones [חסידיך]," thus supplying the Hebrew word lying behind the Greek Ασιδαῖοι of verse 13.[314] The passage cited from the psalm speaks of corpses with no one to bury them, a fate that is implied for the sixty slain Hasideans. Of both Alcimus and Bacchides, it is said that there "is no truth in them" (v. 18).

Bacchides soon withdrew but left a contingent of troops to help Alcimus gain control of the country. Although Alcimus became the ruler of the land (v. 20: καὶ κατέστησεν τὴν χώραν τῷ Ἀλκίμῳ), he had difficulties after Bacchides's departure.

---

311. As we will see, 1 Macc 7:14 says that the Hasideans considered Alcimus a priest from Aaron's line; this need not entail, though, that he was from the branch of that line that produced high priests. Or, as Josephus's list of high priests in *Antiquities* 20 puts it: "Jacimus, who was of Aaron's line but not of the same family as Onias" (20.10, 3 [§237]).

312. See Abel, *Les livres des Maccabées*, 457; Goldstein, *II Maccabees*, 482–83; Habicht, *2. Makkabäerbuch*, 270–71 n. 3 a.

313. The text has only a pronoun, which the translator of the NRSV has taken to mean Alcimus; Josephus, however, understood it as referring to Bacchides, who was thus guilty of the executions, not Alcimus (*Ant.* 12.10, 2 [§396]).

314. Although the NRSV here translates the introduction to the citation from the psalm as "in accordance with the word that was written," the Greek text reads: κατὰ τὸν λόγον, ὃν ἔγραψεν αὐτόν. Goldstein (*1 Maccabees*, 332-33) thinks the text claims that Alcimus wrote Ps 79, but to make his case he must assume a different Hebrew original for the curious Greek clause.

Alcimus struggled to maintain his high priesthood, and all who were troubling their people joined him. They gained control of the land of Judah and did great damage in Israel.[315] And Judas saw all the wrongs that Alcimus and those with him had done among the Israelites; it was more than the Gentiles had done. So Judas went into all the surrounding parts of Judea, taking vengeance on those who had deserted and preventing those in the city from going out into the country. When Alcimus saw that Judas and those with him had grown strong, and realized that he could not withstand them, he returned to the king and brought malicious charges against them. (1 Macc 7:21-25)

The language of the report is vague in places, but it leaves a clear picture of a fundamental division in Judah between the royally appointed leader Alcimus and the forces of Judas. Alcimus not only received his position from the king, but he also needed muscular royal support to maintain it. In fact, even with that backing, he could not hold it. Nicanor, the next Seleucid official sent to rectify the situation in Judea, met a crushing defeat at the hands of Judas (7:26-49).

After concluding an alliance with the Romans and thus against Demetrius I (1 Maccabees 8), Rome's enemy,[316] Judas faced another challenge when the king sent Bacchides and Alcimus on a second mission into Judea. They reached Jerusalem in the first month of the Seleucid year 152, that is, in the fall of 161 BCE (9:1-3). The ensuing battle cost Judas Maccabeus, the "savior of Israel," his life (9:21). The summary at the end of the account has an odd ring to it: "Now the rest of the acts of Judas, and his wars and the brave deeds that he did, and his greatness, have not been recorded, but they were very many" (9:22).

Bacchides appears, then, to have succeeded in conquering the land and erecting fortresses in key areas. The Maccabean forces, now under the

---

315. At this point, Josephus has more detail than 1 Maccabees: "But Alcimus, wishing to strengthen his authority, and perceiving that by making the people feel friendly toward him he would govern with greater security, led them on with kind words, and speaking to everyone in a pleasant and gracious manner, very soon indeed acquired a large body of men and a force behind him, who were for the most part from the irreligious and renegades, and these he used as his attendants and soldiers in going through the country; and all those whom he found in it siding with Judas he slew" (*Ant.* 12.10, 3 [§§398–99]). Judas's actions described next are therefore only a balanced response to Alcimus's attempt to destroy his opponents.

316. Regarding the credibility of the agreement in this historical context and the general authenticity of the wording of the Roman document, see Gera, *Judaea and Mediterranean Politics*, 303–12. For an unconvincing economic interpretation of the agreement, see Wolf Wirgin, "Judah Maccabee's Embassy to Rome and the Jewish-Roman Treaty," *PEQ* 101 (1969): 15–20. He believes there is a precedent for establishing a trading relationship in the Areus-Onias letter.

leadership of Judas's brother Jonathan, retired to the wilderness across the Jordan (1 Macc 9:23-53). In these circumstances, we meet Alcimus once more.

> In the one hundred and fifty-third year, in the second month, Alcimus gave orders to tear down the wall of the inner court of the sanctuary. He tore down the work of the prophets! But he only began to tear it down, for at that time Alcimus was stricken and his work was hindered; his mouth was stopped and he was paralyzed,[317] so that he could no longer say a word or give commands concerning his house. And Alcimus died at that time in great agony. When Bacchides saw that Alcimus was dead, he returned to the king, and the land of Judah had rest for two years. (9:54-57)

The event is dated to the second month of the Seleucid year 153, which was in the late fall of 160 BCE (May 159, if the Babylonian Seleucid reckoning is used). Some commentators understand the temple remodeling that Alcimus proposed to be removal of "the wall separating the inner court, to which only Jews had access, from the outer court, to which Gentiles were admitted. Its demolition was thus a gesture of internationalism such as Antiochus Epiphanes would have approved; but it was an abomination to the orthodox, the more so since the wall had been set up by the prophets Haggai and Zechariah."[318] Josephus adds that he had served as high priest for four years (*Ant.* 12.10, 6 [§413]), although his high-priestly list in *Ant.* 20.10, 3 (§237) allows him only

---

317. Josephus says that "a sudden stroke from God seized him" (*Ant.* 12.10, 6 [§413]).

318. John Christopher Dancy, *A Commentary on I Maccabees,* 137 (the two prophets did not build the wall, of course, but they did encourage the rebuilding of the temple). Bickerman argued that the desecration of the temple in 167 BCE (see 1 Macc 4:38, 48) had involved removing the barrier between courts and had thus made the Jerusalem temple like Greek ones, which had only one or no enclosures (*Der Gott der Makkabäer,* 110–11). T. A. Busink adopted Bickerman's position and applied it to 1 Macc 9:54 as well (*Der Tempel von Jerusalem von Salomo bis Herodes,* 2 vols., SFSMD 3 [Leiden: Brill, 1980], 2.877–78, 883–84). See also Abel, *Les livres des Maccabées,* 174. Goldstein, however, has countered that the word *court* is used here only of the area adjacent to the house and that therefore "the barrier which Alcimus sought to remove must have belonged to the inner court" (*I Maccabees,* 391). He adds: "Even if Alcimus had not been pious, there could be no issue of introducing gentiles or Greek practices to the inner court" (392). How he knows either that the word *court* refers only to the area immediately around the house or that there could be no question of introducing Gentiles is not at all clear. Paolo Sacchi believes the wall was one dividing priests from the laity; its removal could thus mean either laicizing or a complete sacralizing of the people (*The History of the Second Temple Period,* JSOTSup 285 [Sheffield: Sheffield Academic, 2000], 245). Compare Smith, "A Study of the Zadokite High Priesthood," 70–72 (he considers it the wall separating Jew and Gentile).

three years. It is not impossible that both numbers are correct, with the higher number calculating part of a year as a full one.[319]

The story of Alcimus is also told in 2 Maccabees, where it follows lines similar to those in 1 Maccabees yet in places differs significantly from it. Both books report something about an official action regarding his high priesthood at the beginning of Demetrius I's reign (2 Macc 14:1-4; compare 1 Macc 7:1-11).

> Now a certain Alcimus, who had formerly been high priest [τις προ-γεγονὼς ἀρχιερεύς] but had willfully defiled himself in the times of separation, realized that there was no way for him to be safe or to have access again to the holy altar, and went to King Demetrius in about the one hundred fifty-first year, presenting to him a crown of gold and a palm, and besides these some of the customary olive branches from the temple. (2 Macc 14:3-4)

As noted above, 1 Maccabees implies the same year for Alcimus's first contact with Demetrius and his confirmation as high priest.

A problem posed by 2 Macc 14:3 is the designation of Alcimus as a *former* high priest, since he does not appear in any high-priestly list or story before this time, and 1 Maccabees also does not refer to an earlier stint in office for him (though Josephus does). It may be that 2 Maccabees is implying merely that, when Menelaus died, Alcimus became high priest but that, because of conditions caused by the Maccabean forces, he had not been able to exercise the duties of the office. This may also explain the claim in 1 Maccabees that Alcimus wanted to be high (?) priest when he first visited Demetrius (7:5, that is, he wanted to serve as high priest). It should be said, though, that neither 1 nor 2 Maccabees reports the appointment of Alcimus immediately after the death of Menelaus; this is obvious for 1 Maccabees, which never mentions Menelaus, and 2 Maccabees puts the death of Menelaus in the Seleucid year 149 (13:1) but the first reference to Alcimus in the Seleucid year 151, or, as 2 Macc 14:1 words it, "[t]hree years later." Presumably, he became high priest shortly after Menelaus perished but had not succeeded in claiming the prize or perhaps had subsequently been driven from his office. The action of Demetrius, then, would have had the effect only of confirming him in the post that was already his, not of making the initial appointment,[320] although royal

---

319. So Marcus, *Josephus* 7, 215 n. j.

320. Another possibility is presented by the absence of the definite article before ἀρχιερεύς. The anarthrous form may imply that he had become a leading/chief priest, not the high priest. But see below on Alcimus's statement in 2 Macc 14:7.

confirmation came at no small price. Here we should recall that Josephus does, in fact, place his installation in an earlier time, during the reign of Antiochus V (on this, see below).[321]

Another issue raised by 2 Macc 14:3 has to do with the meaning of the words "had willfully defiled himself in the times of separation." The times in question have occasioned lengthy debate among the commentators. The preferred reading appears to be ἀμιξία ("not mixing" with others), while some witnesses have ἐπιμιξία ("mixing" with others).[322] Abel took the passage to mean that Alcimus had defiled himself during the time of Antiochus IV by engaging in Hellenism,[323] yet others have countered that this is unlikely because the Hasideans found no problem with Alcimus's appointment as high priest (although this point is made in 1 Maccabees, not 2 Maccabees).[324] Habicht may well be correct in arguing that the time of separation or disunity ("in der Zeiten der Uneinigkeit" in his rendering) was the period when the Hasideans and Judas and his party had separated regarding the appointment of Alcimus. Alcimus's defilement was his breaking the pact and executing sixty of the Hasideans (which led to the reunification of the Hasideans and Judas; see 2 Macc 14:6).[325]

A major difference between 1 and 2 Maccabees is that the latter has no equivalent of 1 Macc 7:8-24, the section having to do with Bacchides's campaign, the murderous encounter with the Hasideans, and the efforts to place Alcimus securely in charge.[326] Rather, it moves directly to an account of Alcimus's trip to the capital that resulted in Nicanor's campaign. The issue has been studied in detail by Mölleken,[327] who has departed from many commentators by not rejecting the version in 2 Maccabees in favor of the one in 1 Maccabees. That is, he does not think it is correct to say that 2 Maccabees omitted the section; he thinks that 1 Maccabees has moved part of it from its correct, original position at the end of chapter 6 and another part from chapter 9 to their present location in chapter 7 for tendentious reasons.

---

321. See Smith, "A Study of the Zadokite High Priesthood," 65–66 (in 68–70, he refutes the suggestion of Büchler that Alcimus was simply a civil ruler, not the high priest in the Jewish sense of that term).

322. Abel, Les livres des Maccabées, 457–58.

323. Ibid.

324. Habicht, 2. Makkabäerbuch, 271; Goldstein, II Maccabees, 484.

325. Habicht, 2. Makkabäerbuch, 271.

326. See Goldstein for a discussion of possible reasons why this material does not appear in 2 Maccabees (II Maccabees, 479–81).

327. W. Mölleken, "Geschichtsklitterung im I. Makkabäerbuch (Wann wurde Alkimus Hoherpriester?)," ZAW 65 (1953): 205–28.

According to Mölleken, 1 Macc 7:8-24 is not a unity but consists of segments that the author has drawn together from two contexts. The first part of it, verses 12-18 (Bacchides, Alcimus, and the Hasideans), and verses 20-24 (efforts to establish Alcimus and Judas's response) should be moved to the passage regarding the peace agreement between Antiochus V/Lysias and the Jews in 6:55-61. In this way, he realigns the text to illustrate how he understands its original form to have been worded, but the reconstruction runs into some difficulties, such as the failure of the resulting text to mention Alcimus before referring to him with a pronoun.[328] Also, Mölleken has to remove the reference to Bacchides in 7:12 and understand the role of the scribes here as offering advice on Alcimus's fitness for the office of high priest. The parallel context in 2 Maccabees (13:23—14:1) lacks a notice about Alcimus and the execution of sixty pious ones; this, however, Mölleken did not see as evidence against his reading of the end of 1 Maccabees 6. Instead, he attributed the omission of these elements to the *Tendenz* of the author of 2 Maccabees.[329] In his overall reconstruction, he places the appointment of Alcimus in the context of the peace negotiations with Antiochus V and Lysias and in this way thinks he has combined all of the evidence from 1 and 2 Maccabees, once 1 Macc 6:55—7:24 is restored to its original form.[330]

He then moves 1 Macc 7:8-11, 19 (where Bacchides is mentioned) to 1 Maccabees 9, where a campaign of this eminent Seleucid official is narrated;[331] but here again, Mölleken is forced to change the text to make the material from chapter 7 fit the context in chapter 9 (for example, removal of the words "Bacchides and Alcimus" from 9:1). Yet, he does find that this rearrangement (or recovery of the original order) solves problems in the text. In particular, he mentions several geographical difficulties and the fact that 1 Macc 7:9 speaks of Demetrius's "confirmation (ἔστησεν)" of Alcimus, not his "appointment" (for which a form of καθιστάναι would have been used).[332] He concludes that the author did violence to the historical fact in his source in order to lower the date when Alcimus, who was inconvenient for the Hasmoneans, assumed office; by doing so the writer was also able to give the false impression that Alcimus had exploited the change of kings in Antioch to usurp the high priesthood.[333]

---

328. Ibid., 214–15. He deals with the issue on 214 n. 4 (see also 216–18) but has to assume an earlier reference to Alcimus that has dropped from the text.
329. Ibid., 218.
330. See his outline in ibid., 221–23.
331. Ibid., 223–24.
332. Ibid., 227.
333. Ibid., 227–28.

Mölleken's hypothesis, while impressively argued, encounters too many obstacles to make it acceptable. Apart from the arbitrary textual emendations (whether moving sections around or deleting words and phrases), the purpose that supposedly motivated such large-scale changes is not convincing. Why would Alcimus's achieving appointment as high priest at the time of a change on the Seleucid throne place him in a more negative light? Furthermore, both 1 and 2 Maccabees leave some hints about a claim by Alcimus to the office, before he first appealed to Demetrius.

In 2 Maccabees, as in 1 Maccabees, Alcimus acts as a spokesman for the Jews. He was invited by the king "to a meeting of the council and was asked about the attitude and intention of the Jews" (2 Macc 14:5). Responding to this invitation, Alcimus delivered an impassioned speech:

> Those of the Jews who are called Hasideans, whose leader is Judas Maccabeus, are keeping up war and stirring up sedition, and will not let the kingdom attain tranquillity. Therefore I have laid aside my ancestral glory—I mean the high-priesthood[334]—and have now come here, first because I am genuinely concerned for the interests of the king, and second because I have regard also for my compatriots. For through the folly of those whom I have mentioned our whole nation is now in no small misfortune. Since you are acquainted, O king, with the details of this matter, may it please you to take thought for our country and our hard-pressed nation with the gracious kindness that you show to all. For as long as Judas lives, it is impossible for the government to find peace. (14:6-10)

The king sent Nicanor to remove Judas, scattering his troops, and to make Alcimus "high priest of the great temple" (v. 13).

There follows a time when Nicanor and Judas appear to be friends, in fact as signatories to a covenant (2 Macc 14:18-25). As this went against Alcimus's wishes, he brought to the king an accusation that Nicanor was not serving his sovereign. The wording here is suggestive. Alcimus, arguing from the covenant between Nicanor and Judas, "told him that Nicanor was disloyal to the government, since he had appointed that conspirator against the kingdom, Judas, to be his successor" (14:26). Is Alcimus (called "that depraved man" by the narrator) here accusing Nicanor of having named Judas high priest? This point will be addressed below. At any rate, the king disapproved of the agreement

---

334. A statement such as this, whatever its historical veracity, suggests that the author of 2 Maccabees was not using the word ἀρχιερεύς in 14:3 in the sense of "a chief priest."

between Nicanor and Judas and ordered Nicanor to dispatch Judas to Antioch as a prisoner (v. 27). The reader is informed that Nicanor was displeased with the king's command, yet had no choice but to obey it. When Judas noticed a cooling of their relations, he and some troops went into hiding. This scene is the last one in 2 Maccabees in which Alcimus appears.

This is the place to mention Bunge's analysis of some chronological problems in the narratives about Alcimus in our three sources about him. Bunge, like Mölleken with whom he partially agrees, uncovers difficulties with the presentation of Alcimus's career in 1 Maccabees.[335] He accepts three years (*Ant.* 20.10, 3 [§237]) as the correct length for his reign, considering the four years of *Ant.* 12.10, 6 (§413) to be the result of Josephus's revising his source. So, Alcimus's tenure as high priest extended from 149–152 of the Seleucid Era (= S.E.). Against this, 1 Maccabees, as Bunge reads the text, has him assume office in 151 and die in 153 S.E.[336]

In order to explain the discrepancy, he examines 1 Maccabees 7–9 which is, he thinks, a section of the book problematic both for its sources and calendar. The author had three kinds of dates: purely Greek ones expressing only year numbers and derived from the Seleucid chronicle; Jewish months that the writer combined with the year numbers from the Seleucid chronicle; and dates that the author inferred from valid year numbers and with which he filled gaps in his presentation.[337]

Armed with these assumptions, Bunge examines the year numbers in 1 Maccabees. In 9:54, one reads the date "the one hundred and fifty-third year, in the second month" as the time for Alcimus death. The date is the year after the one in which, Bunge thinks, Alcimus died. Since it is a year number, it should come from the Seleucid chronicle, but the date lacks any context taken from that chronicle and refers only to an internal Jewish event. He concludes that both the date in 9:3 (the first month in 152 S.E.) and the one in 9:54 belong to no genuine literary tradition and thus came from the author of 1 Maccabees (the third category of dates).[338]

To determine how the author arrived at these dates, he examines 1 Maccabees 7, which, on his view, provides the information necessary for understanding 9:3. Nicanor's campaign is dated to 151 S.E. (7:1), with Nicanor Day falling on Adar 13 (Adar is the twelfth month of the year). First Maccabees 7:50 reports that, after this, the land had rest for a few days, and then 9:3 follows by dating Bacchides's campaign to the first month of 152 S.E. Alcimus's

---

335. Ibid., 10–27 (the section on Alcimus).
336. Ibid., 15–16.
337. Ibid., 17.
338. Ibid., 18.

death, which should (if he died in 152 S.E.) fall in the next month, is curiously moved to the next year (153 S.E.).[339]

He agrees with Mölleken that there are difficulties regarding the section about the appointment of Alcimus in 1 Maccabees 7, but he thinks there are also difficulties with the report about Alcimus's death in 1 Macc 9:54-57, a section that breaks up the context. He finds it strange, for instance, that the story about the death of Alcimus, who was most closely related to Judas, not Jonathan, and who was mentioned only briefly at the beginning of the chapter, occurs immediately after a list of the cities Bacchides fortified. Also, it is odd that 9:57 concludes the death story with the notice that Bacchides, on seeing that Alcimus was dead, returned to the king. To add to the puzzle, Bacchides a short time later returns on his own initiative. In historical fact, argues Bunge, Bacchides made only one campaign; he did not return to Antioch but remained in Judah, attacking the last centers of opposition loyal to Jonathan. The narrative about the one campaign is now broken up by 9:54-57.[340]

The lack of order in 1 Maccabees 7 is worse. Bunge does not agree with Mölleken that 7:7, (12), 13-18, 20-24 contain the missing report about the appointment of Alcimus and that this was the subject of the negotiations between Bacchides and the Hasideans. Rather, a closer look at the passage shows that the scribes simply asked Bacchides for peace and assumed the presence of Alcimus with the army would protect them. Second Maccabees 14:6, which identifies the Hasideans as Judas's allies, clarifies the point: the passage in 1 Maccabees 7 deals with the desertion of some of Judas's adherents to Bacchides. The installation of Alcimus (7:20-25) is entirely independent of this episode. So, he sees the Hasidean story as belonging to the time of Bacchides's campaign but 7:20-25 should be detached from it. He argues that 7:20a, 21-25 (the appointment of Alcimus) should be connected with the context of 6:62-63 where Antiochus V weakens the fortifications around Mount Zion and then returns home. This order provides a reasonable setting for 7:5-7 (the renegades and Alcimus, who wanted to be high priest, go to King Demetrius) and, unlike our form of 1 Maccabees, explains why Demetrius *confirmed* (rather than appointed) Alcimus as high priest (7:9). So, the Hasidean episode had nothing to do with Alcimus's becoming high priest.[341]

Bunge thinks that the campaign of Bacchides and the campaign of Nicanor (1 Macc 7:26-49) were two phases in a single military action. Why did the author transpose the Hasidean tale, which is associated with this cam-

---

339. Ibid.
340. Ibid., 19.
341. Ibid., 21–22.

paign, to an earlier point in the narrative (7:12-18)? Second Maccabees 14–15, which parallels 1 Maccabees 7, points the way to the answer. It is not simply a matter of manipulating sources or some problem in them; the reason for the change was the writer's desire to present Alcimus as negatively as possible. First Maccabees's failure to mention the pre-Hasmonean high priests (other than Alcimus) was intentional. Although the author probably knew that Alcimus had been appointed by Antiochus V, he purposely moved the Hasidean story to the time of Demetrius's accession to imply that the forcible appointment of Alcimus was purchased with the blood of the sixty Hasideans—a crime for which Alcimus indirectly shared the guilt. When one realizes that the author of 1 Maccabees was otherwise well disposed toward the Hasideans (see 2:42), one cannot avoid concluding that he predated the event from where it belongs in chapter 9 (Bacchides's campaign) to chapter 7 to free the Hasideans from the charge of betraying Judas.[342]

First Maccabees 7 thus becomes for Bunge the negative counterpart of chapter 10, where a Seleucid king appoints Jonathan high priest. If one reads 1 Maccabees 7 and 9:54-57, he would have to conclude that Alcimus (and with him probably the other pre-Hasmonean high priests) was unworthy of the office and that Jonathan was fully in the right in taking it. Bunge thinks we may not be able to discern where 1 Macc 9:54-57 originally belonged, but we can say that the author placed it where he did because he had an eight-year gap for which he had little to report and this he tried to fill by attributing Alcimus's death to the year 153 s.e.[343]

Bunge's case is no more convincing than Mölleken's and shares some of its weaknesses, such as the unsupported relocations in the text. His thesis also rests on questionable assumptions about the sources at the disposal of the person who wrote 1 Maccabees (would his Jewish source have no year dates?). It is also not obvious why Alcimus would be pictured more negatively in the present form of 1 Maccabees than he would have been in the supposed original form: in either case, he would share blame for the death of the Hasideans. Finally, there is no need to assume an arbitrary invention of a year date (153 s.e.) on the part of the author, simply because he wished to fill a gap in his sources. 2 Maccabees does not mention Alcimus's death and thus does not date it; the date in 1 Maccabees is acceptable and does not necessarily contradict Josephus's evidence that he ruled three or four years, both of which could be correct, depending on how one counted partial years. The years of the high priest Alcimus were, then, 149–153 s.e., or 162–159 bce.

---

342. Ibid., 23–25.
343. Ibid., 26–27.

Before leaving Alcimus and his brief reign as high priest, we should note that he has been suggested as the character underlying a story told in several rabbinic texts. For example, in *Gen. Rab.* 65.26, which deals with Isaac's mistaking Jacob for Esau in Gen. 27:23-27 (especially the phrase "the smell of my son is like the smell of a field that the LORD has blessed" [v. 27]), the example of two men, Joseph Meshitha and Yaqim of Serurot, is adduced. This Yaqim was a nephew of Yose b. Yoezer of Seridah. About him we read:

> As to Yose, when the time came that the enemies wanted to enter the mountain of the house [of the sanctuary], they said, "Let one of them go in first." They said to Yose, "Go in. Whatever you take out will belong to you." He went in and took out the golden candelabrum. They said to him, "It is not proper for an ordinary person [הדיוט] to make use of such a thing, so go in a second time, and what you take out will belong to you." But he did not agree to do so. Said R. Phineas, "They offered him the taxes for three years, but he did not agree to go in." He said, "It is not enough for you that I have made my God angry once, should I now outrage him yet a second time?" What did they do to him? They put him on a carpenter's vice and they sawed him in two, and he cried out, "Woe, woe that I angered my creator!"
>
> Yaqim of Serurot was the son of the sister of R. Yose b. Yoezer of Seridah. He was riding on his horse. He passed before the beam on which [Yose] was to be hanged. He said to him, "Look at the horse on which my master has set me riding and look at the horse on which your master has set you riding!" He said to him, "If that is what he does for those who spite him, how much more will he do for those who do his will!" He said to him, "And has anyone done his will more than you have?" He said to him, "And if that is what happens to those who do his will [that they are tortured to death], all the more so will he do for those who spite him."
>
> That statement penetrated into his heart like the venom of a snake, and he went and applied to himself the four modes of the death penalty applied by a court, namely, stoning, burning, decapitation, and strangulation. How did he accomplish it? He brought a beam and stuck it into the ground, and put up a wall of stones around it, then tied a cord to it. He made a fire in front of the beam and put a sword in the middle of the post. He first hung himself on the post. The cord burned through, and he was strangled. Then the sword caught his body, and the wall of stones fell on him, and he burned up.

Yose b. Yoezer of Seridah dozed off and he saw the bier of the other flying through the air. He said, "By a brief interval he reached the Garden of Eden before me."[344]

Goldstein, who follows others in identifying this Yaqim as Alcimus, thinks that the story may reflect a disagreement between the two relatives regarding collaboration with the Seleucids, as Alcimus had done.[345] Yet, the facts that such a story is told in none of the early sources and that there is no evidence the high priest Alcimus is intended, make one doubt the connection, even though the tale is put in the context of foreign violation of the temple.

---

344. Jacob Neusner, *Genesis Rabbah: The Judaic Commentary to the Book of Genesis: A New American Translation,* vol. 2, BJS 105 (Atlanta: Scholars, 1985), 400–401.

345. Goldstein, *I Maccabees,* 336. We should also recall that Alcimus has been suggested as the model for the high priest Jehoiakim in Bar 1:7.

4

The Hasmonean High Priests
(152–37 BCE)

Preliminary Issues

The reigns of Jason, Menelaus, and Alcimus marked a period (175–159 BCE) when the royal administration took a direct hand in the high-priestly succession and provoked a strong reaction from some elements in Judea. The Seleucid sovereigns would continue their involvement in the office in subsequent years, but a new era was soon to dawn when the descendants of the priest Mattathias, the pioneering leader of the revolt according to 1 Maccabees, succeeded in taking the office. First Maccabees reports that the first member of the family to be appointed high priest was Jonathan, who donned the sacred vestments in 152 BCE; it says nothing about Judas, his brother and predecessor as leader of the Maccabean forces, serving as high priest. The point may seem self-evident, as Judas died in 161 BCE when Alcimus was still in office (he continued to occupy it until 159 BCE). Yet, the two had been bitter enemies, and it is possible that Judas operated as a rival high priest to Alcimus for some time. This is only a possibility, not a demonstrable conclusion, but there are a few hints in the literature pointing toward it. This matter should be explored before we turn to the period of the official Hasmonean[1] high priesthood. A second preliminary problem that will be treated is the so-called *intersacerdotium*, that is, the years 159 (death of Alcimus) to 152 (accession of the Hasmonean Jonathan) when, to judge by the high-priestly lists, no one occupied the office.

---

1. As noted before, Josephus lists a certain Asamonaios (= Hebrew חשמון) as an ancestor of Mattathias (*Ant.* 12.6, 1 [§265]); for this reason the family is known as the Hasmoneans.

Judas Maccabeus[2] *as High Priest?*

The primary reason for suspecting that Judas may have served as high priest is that Josephus several times says he did. In his list of Second-Temple high priests in *Antiquities* 20, he does not include Judas; rather, he passes immediately from Alcimus to a period of vacancy for the office: "Now Jacimus [= Alcimus] died after holding the high priesthood for three years. No one succeeded him [διεδέξατο δ᾽ αὐτὸν οὐδείς]; and the city continued for seven years without a high priest" (*Ant.* 20.10, 3 [§237]). The next high priest he mentions is Jonathan (§238).[3] However, Josephus contradicts his own list in his narrative for the period in question. He follows his source, 1 Macc 9:11-22, in relating Judas's death in a battle against the Seleucid commander Bacchides (*Ant.* 12.11, 2 [§§426–34]) but supplements it with a number of laudatory words about Maccabeus, including these: "And such was the prowess of this man that he left behind him the greatest and most glorious of memorials—to have freed his nation and rescued them from slavery to the Macedonians. And he had held the high priesthood for three years when he died [τὴν δ᾽ ἀρχιε-ρωσύνην ἔτος τρίτον κατεσχὼν ἀπέθανεν]" (*Ant.* 12.11, 2 [§434]). This surprising statement is not the only time the historian connects Judas with the office. Earlier, in *Ant.* 12.10, 6 (§§413–14), where he wrote about the sudden death of Alcimus (following 1 Macc 9:54-57), he added to his source: "he died, having been high priest for four years. And when he died, the people [ὁ λαός] gave the high priesthood to Judas" (§414). Josephus next describes the treaty between Rome and the Jewish nation, the subject of 1 Maccabees 8. After quoting the decree of the Roman senate, he writes without backing from 1 Maccabees: "The decree was signed by Eupolemus, the son of Joannes, and by Jason, the son of Eleazar, Judas being high priest of the nation [ἐπὶ ἀρχιερέως μὲν τοῦ ἔθνους Ἰούδα], and his brother Simon commander" (§419).

Josephus, therefore, had evidence from a source other than 1 Maccabees (whatever that source may have been), or he inferred from his source(s) that Judas had served as high priest, but the official list of high priests did not include his name. Neither 1 nor 2 Maccabees ever stakes such a claim for Judas, despite the great admiration that their authors had for him. Josephus himself may have deduced from some hints in 1 Maccabees that Judas, who

---

2. The writer of 1 Maccabees gives Judas the epithet Maccabeus in 1 Macc 2:4 (compare 8:20). A widely accepted view is that it means "hammerer."

3. In *Life* 1.4, Josephus also says that Jonathan was the first member of the Hasmonean family to become high priest.

was certainly acting as leader of some entity in concluding an agreement with the Romans, must have been high priest. Judas sent messengers to propose an alliance to the senate, and those envoys, in a formal situation, are said to have introduced their business thus: "Judas, who is also called Maccabeus, and his brothers and the people of the Jews have sent us to you to establish alliance and peace with you, so that we may be enrolled as your allies and friends" (1 Macc 8:20). In their official response, the senators did not refer to Judas at all, only to the Jewish people (1 Macc 8:23-32).

Second Maccabees adds some tantalizing details. It will be recalled that when King Demetrius, after consulting with Alcimus, sent Nicanor to restore order in Judea, he gave him "orders to kill Judas and scatter his troops, and to install Alcimus as high priest of the great temple" (2 Macc 14:13). That is, the way to put Alcimus in office was to remove Judas who had apparently driven him out (14:6-7, 10). Rather than killing Judas, Nicanor made a covenant with him (14:18-20), an agreement that aroused Alcimus's ire. He took the agreement to the king and "told him that Nicanor was disloyal to the government, since he had appointed that conspirator against the kingdom, Judas, to be his successor [διάδοχον]" (14:26). It does sound from Alcimus's words as if he thought the covenant between Nicanor and Judas involved the appointment of Judas as high priest in his place.[4] The ensuing narrative seems to confirm what Alcimus claimed. When the king ordered Nicanor to jettison the covenant and imprison Judas, Nicanor unwillingly attempted to capture him. Judas hid, but Nicanor went to find him and assumed he was at the temple: "he [Nicanor] went to the great and holy temple while the priests were offer-

4. While the meaning of διάδοχος is clear enough (successor, deputy [for this latter sense of the term, see 2 Macc 4:29]), there is some textual and exegetical uncertainty regarding the pronoun αὐτοῦ, which appears near it. F.-M. Abel (Les livres des Maccabées, EBib [Paris: Gabalda, 1949], 464) followed the manuscript evidence that places the word after βασιλείας and translated: "car l'adversaire même de son royaume, Judas, il l'avait promu diadoque." There is other manuscript evidence that places αὐτοῦ after Ιουδαν: his successor Judas. If this is the correct reading, it would still leave an ambiguity: was Alcimus charging that Nicanor had appointed Judas his own successor or the successor of Alcimus? The context favors the latter option (so Sidney Tedesche and Solomon Zeitlin, The Second Book of Maccabees, Jewish Apocryphal Literature (New York: Harper, 1954], 233). Jonathan A. Goldstein understands the text to be saying that Nicanor had appointed Judas as his own deputy (II Maccabees, AB 41A [Garden City, N.Y.: Doubleday, 1983], 472). Christian Habicht correctly observes that the statement by Alcimus presupposes that, as the king had directed in 2 Macc 14:13, Alcimus has indeed been installed in the post (so Judas was not the official high priest; 2. Makkabäerbuch, JSHRZ 1.3 [Gütersloh: Gütersloher, 1979], 274 nn. a)-b) to v. 26). As for the referent of αὐτοῦ, he notes that the naming of Judas as either Nicanor's or Alcimus's successor did not lie within Nicanor's area of authority; such appointments would have required royal action.

ing the customary sacrifices, and commanded them to hand the man over" (14:31). Nicanor threatened to level the sanctuary if they refused (v. 33). If Alcimus had been in charge of the temple, it is difficult to believe Nicanor would have thought Judas was hiding there.

It may be that Judas, after taking control of the temple from Seleucid authorities (1 Macc 4:36-61 [165 or 164 BCE]), never lost it except perhaps for a brief time when Antiochus V demolished the wall that surrounded it (1 Macc 6:51-54). This seems to have been the reason why Alcimus was unable to assume the high priesthood, despite royal appointment of him. We should also pay attention to the seemingly bland word that Josephus uses for the group that gave the high priesthood to Judas—the people (ὁ λαός). As we will see in the section on Simon below, this may be a designation, not for the entire populace, but for the Maccabean troops who were instrumental in the appointments of Jonathan and Simon.

> Perhaps it is acceptable to say that Judas functioned as a rival high priest to Alcimus and that he enjoyed control of the temple. Josephus says that the people appointed him high priest—certainly an unofficial though effective act—and this would again mean that his army had appointed him to the position. One must be cautious, however, because . . . Josephus does not consistently use λαός where his source does. Nevertheless, it is an intriguing possibility—and not at all an unlikely one—that Judas's army did select him as high priest after the death of Menelaus. His name would not have appeared on official lists of high priests (such as the one in *Antiquities* 20 or in those of 1–2 Maccabees) because Judas lacked royal confirmation—something that clearly would not have stopped him from acting in the capacity of high priest. In placing his elevation after Alcimus's death, Josephus may have assumed that the two could hardly have been high priests at one time and that therefore Judas must have assumed office after the former high priest died. He then tried in places to introduce this conclusion into his chronology for the high priests but did it rather poorly and inconsistently.[5]

---

5. James VanderKam, "People and High Priesthood in Early Maccabean Times," in *The Hebrew Bible and Its Interpreters,* ed. W. H. Propp, B. Halpern, and D. N. Freedman, BJS 1 (Winona Lake, Ind.: Eisenbrauns, 1990), 221; reprinted in VanderKam, *From Revelation to Canon: Studies in the Hebrew Bible and Second Temple Literature,* JSJSup 62 (Leiden: Brill, 2000), 219.

With Judas's death, Alcimus became high priest without a rival, but he still had to contend with opposition from adherents of the Maccabean movement.[6]

The Intersacerdotium

The seven-year span between when Alcimus died in 159 BCE and when Jonathan assumed office in 152 is known as the *intersacerdotium*, the time when no high priest, at least not one named in the records, served at the Jerusalem temple. As nearly as we can tell, this was the first time in the long history of the Second Temple when such a vacancy had occurred. The sources that should contain information about these years are 1 Maccabees and Josephus (largely dependent on 1 Maccabees), but they are not very helpful. We learn from the former that, after his death, Judas's friends chose Jonathan to deal with their external and internal enemies, "to take his place as our ruler and leader, to fight our battle" (1 Macc 9:30). He accepted the offer and assumed the roles of "ruler and leader," but nothing is said about the high priesthood. Later in the same chapter, we read about Alcimus's death (9:54-57) in the year 159 BCE. Jonathan and his brother Simon subsequently led their forces to a decisive victory over Bacchides and his Jewish allies and concluded a peace treaty with the Seleucid commander (9:58-72). The result is phrased in a traditional manner by the author: "Thus the sword ceased from Israel. Jonathan settled in Michmash and began to judge the people; and he destroyed the godless out of Israel" (9:73). The very next verse is set in the year 152 BCE (10:1). So, following Alcimus's death, 1 Maccabees is silent about the high priesthood until Jonathan's royal appointment in 152.

Josephus is more explicit about an *intersacerdotium*. When Jonathan received a letter from Alexander (Balas; on him see below) appointing him high priest in 152 BCE, the historian writes: "this being four years after the

6. Emil Schürer doubts that "Judas ever exercised the functions of High Priest" (*The History of the Jewish People in the Age of Jesus Christ (175 B.C.—A.D. 135)*, 3 vols., rev. and ed. G. Vermes and F. Millar with M. Black [Edinburgh: T. & T. Clark, 1973–87], 170–71); rather he was "the effective leader of the Jewish community." He adds in a footnote (n. 31 on p. 170): "It is not in itself inconceivable that Judas also usurped the functions of the High Priest. But I Maccabees says nothing about it; in addition, a legitimate claimant was present in the person of Onias IV . . . , who would probably be respected as such by Judas." We actually have no information on this last point. We should add that according to the Groningen Hypothesis, which posits a series of Wicked Priests in the Qumran texts, Judas was included among them, entailing that he was considered a high priest by the writer of Pesher Habakkuk (see, for example, A. S. van der Woude, "Wicked Priest or Wicked Priests? Reflections on the Identification of the Wicked Priest in the Habakkuk Commentary," *JJS* 33 [1982]: 349–59, esp. 353–54).

death of his brother Judas—for there had been no high priest during this time [καὶ γὰρ οὐδὲ κατὰ τοῦτον τὸν χρόνον ἀρχιερεύς τις ἐγεγόνει]" (*Ant.* 13.2, 3 [§46]). So at this point, Josephus allows for a four-year *intersacerdotium*, since he continues to include Judas's three-year high priesthood after Alcimus's term in his chronology. However, in *Antiquities* 20 where he is reproducing a high-priestly list, he says: "Now Jacimus [= Alcimus] died after holding the high priesthood for three years. No one succeeded him; and the city continued for seven years without a high priest [διεδέξατο δ' αὐτὸν οὐδείς, ἀλλὰ διετέλεσεν ἡ πόλις ἐνιαυτοὺς ἑπτὰ χωρὶς ἀρχιερέως οὖσα]" (20.10, 3 [§237]). From this, it seems to follow that there was a gap in the official occupation of the high-priestly office for a number of years, probably seven—although Josephus alone is explicit about it.

Such a gap has struck a number of scholars as implausible. One reason is that the high priest had certain essential duties, prominent among which were leading and participating in the ceremonies on the Day of Atonement when he entered the Holy of Holies itself.[7] In fact, Stegemann terms such a situation "impossible" and writes:

> In 164 B.C. the Maccabees had reintroduced, along with the tradi-
> tional worship, the annual observance of the Jewish feasts in the Tem-
> ple. The highest Holy Day is Yom Kippur, the Day of Atonement,
> which simply cannot be observed in conformity with the Torah with-
> out a high priest, as long as the Temple exists (Leviticus 16). Further-
> more, in 157 B.C. the insurgent Maccabees had concluded a peace
> with the Seleucids, so that the country was calm now, and there could
> be no grounds for doing without the annual celebration of the Day of
> Atonement or the high priest, who was absolutely necessary for that
> celebration.[8]

It seems likely that the *functions* of the high priest would have continued even if no one held the position officially, that is, by royal appointment.[9] Goldstein

---

7. See, for example, Hartmut Stegemann, *Die Entstehung der Qumrangemeinde* (Bonn: privately printed, 1971), 213–20.

8. *The Library of Qumran: On the Essenes, Qumran, John the Baptist, and Jesus* (Grand Rapids: Eerdmans, 1998), 147. He discusses the Teacher of Righteousness, known from the Qumran texts, as high priest on 147–48. He grants that we do not know whether the Teacher was the immediate successor of Alcimus in 159 BCE; he does think, however, that we now have evidence that he was Jonathan's immediate predecessor.

9. A suggestion has been that the סגן הכהנים or some other replacement carried out the essential duties of the high priest (for example, Joseph Derenbourg, *Essai sur l'histoire et la géographie de la Palestine d'après les Thalmuds et les auteurs rabbiniques* [Paris: Imprimerie impériale, 1867], 66; reprinted, Hildesheim: Gerstenberg, 1975).

hypothesizes that the "Seleucid government could find no satisfactory person to fill the high priesthood and sought to avoid trouble by leaving the position vacant."[10] There was, of course, a legitimate candidate—Onias IV—but by this time he was ensconced in Egypt in addition to having family connections that probably would not have recommended him to the government.

Because we know nothing certain about it, it may seem wiser to drop the topic of the *intersacerdotium*, and this would be possible had it not become a subject of debate in connection with discussions about the origins of the Dead Sea Scrolls community. In fact, several scholars have suggested that the Teacher of Righteousness, apparently the founder of the group that eventually settled at Qumran, was high priest or at least acting high priest during the seven-year period and that his name has been expunged from the official list as an act of *damnatio memoriae*. The point, as all must admit, is highly speculative, but we should pause briefly to examine the evidence adduced for it.

Two types of information have been tapped in support of the thesis. Hartmut Stegemann has argued from data in several Qumran texts, while Jochen Gabriel Bunge and Jerome Murphy-O'Connor have drawn attention to evidence in the letter of the Seleucid king Demetrius I in 1 Macc 10:25-45.

Stegemann finds backing for his thesis that the Teacher was a high priest in what he regards as the *titular* use of the word הכוהן with respect to him. He maintains that the term alone, with no adjective or accompanying noun, is employed to designate preexilic chief priests at various shrines (for example, Eli) in both pre- and postexilic sources, while in postexilic texts, the absolute הכוהן designates the Aaronic high priest then in office.[11] The Teacher is called simply הכוהן in 1QpHab 2.8; 4QpPsᵃ 2.19; 3.15 and was therefore a high priest.[12] If the Teacher was a high priest, the *intersacerdotium* is the logical time when he would have served. A look at the data shows, nevertheless, that the point does not follow. Among other difficulties, if simple use of הכוהן entailed that someone so designated was the high priest, some individuals who are not more explicitly called high priests would have to be added to the

---

10. Jonathan A. Goldstein, *I Maccabees* AB 41 (Garden City, N.Y.: Doubleday, 1976), 394.

11. A good example is Sir 50:1, which refers to the high priest Simon as הכהן; the Greek translation renders as ἱερεὺς ὁ μέγας. For the texts, see Francesco Vattioni, *Ecclesiastico: Testo ebraico con apparato critico e versioni greca, latina et siriaca* (Pubblicazioni del Seminario de Semitistica; Naples: Instituto Orientale di Napoli, 1968).

12. *Die Entstehung der Qumrangemeinde*, 102. He includes the evidence for his claim in two lengthy footnotes, nn. 328–29 (pp. A 79–83) and says that in post-exilic Judaism the titular, absolute use of הכוהן could designate only the reigning high priest. Exceptions are those places where the form occurs in contexts where a current or previouisly mentioned priest is so designated (102). The Qumran passages where the term occurs do not fall into the last kinds of contexts he mentions and thus, for him, they indicate that the writers regarded him as a high priest.

list: Ezra (Ezra 7:11; 10:10, 16; Neh 8:2, 9; 12:26), Meremoth (Ezra 8:33), and Shelemiah (Neh 13:13). In other words, the definite form of the noun alone does not serve as a consistent, foolproof means for identifying someone as a high priest.[13] Michael Wise has surveyed the instances adduced by Stegemann and many more from sources such as coins and inscriptions and concluded: "The great mass of evidence—from the usage for known early postexilic high priests to the Hasmonean coins and the ossuary inscriptions—points to the conclusion that the way to say 'high priest' was HKHN HGDL. The conclusion has to be that the references to the T[eacher] of R[ighteousness] as HKHN do not intend to suggest that he was ever a functioning—or nonfunctioning— high priest."[14]

Bunge, nevertheless, accepted Stegemann's arguments for identifying the Teacher of Righteousness as a high priest and built upon this foundation.[15] His major contribution was to introduce the letter of Demetrius I (1 Macc 10:25-45) into the discussion. We will examine that letter below in connection with the appointment of Jonathan to the high priesthood, but here we should note that Bunge dates it to the year 152 BCE (with 1 Maccabees), which, for him, was two years before Jonathan became high priest.[16] Since the letter, which mentions a high priest twice (vv. 32, 38), was written two years before Jonathan became high priest, Jonathan's predecessor must be intended. If Stegemann is right that Jonathan's immediate predecessor was the Teacher, then the high priest in Demetrius's letter must be the Teacher whose existence would thus be attested independent of the Qumran texts.[17]

As Bunge understands the course of events, Jonathan set himself up at Michmash while the Teacher was serving as high priest in Jerusalem. When the dispute between the Seleucid king Demetrius I (162–150 BCE) and the claimant to his throne, Alexander Balas, broke out, Jonathan took advantage of the king's permission to recruit and arm troops. With those troops he entered Jerusalem. Since Jonathan, under these conditions, could hardly have served as a second to the high priest, the Teacher soon fled. When the victorious Alexander summoned Jonathan to meet him in Ptolemais (1 Macc 10:59-

---

13. See the assessment of John J. Collins, "The Origin of the Qumran Community: A Review of the Evidence," in *To Touch the Text: Biblical and Related Studies in Honor of Joseph A. Fitzmyer, S.J.*, ed. M. Horgan and P. Kobelski (New York: Crossroad, 1989), 165-66.

14. "The Teacher of Righteousness and the High Priest of the Intersacerdotium: Two Approaches," *RevQ* 14 (1990): 602.

15. "Zur Geschichte und Chronologie des Untergangs der Oniaden und des Aufstiegs der Hasmonäer," *JSJ* 6 (1975): 27.

16. First Maccabees 10 dates the letter and the appointment of Jonathan to the same year, with the appointment preceding the letter. Bunge reverses the two.

17. "Zur Geschichte und Chronologie," 34.

66), Jonathan was able to gain his favor with gifts and also received the high priesthood from him. A delegation opposed Jonathan. These people would have been partisans of the Teacher; they charged Jonathan with driving out the rightful claimant to the high priesthood. Alexander ignored their charges and thus Jonathan became high priest at the expense of the Teacher.[18] The author of 1 Maccabees, who wished to justify Jonathan's takeover, reordered material in chapter 10 to make it seem that Jonathan began serving as high priest two years before he actually did.[19]

Soon after the appearance of Bunge's essay, Murphy-O'Connor subjected his conclusions to critical analysis.[20] He agreed with Bunge that there is just one letter of Demetrius in 1 Maccabees 10 and that it antedated Jonathan's appointment as high priest. He found those inferences to be very important but wanted to verify whether the letter in 10:25-45 was authentic. If it was not, of course there would be no historically reliable evidence for a predecessor of Jonathan serving as high priest in 152 BCE. After comparing Demetrius's letter with the letter that Antiochus III (223–187 BCE) had sent to Zeuxis (preserved in *Ant.* 12.3, 4 [§§148–53]),[21] he concluded that the parts of Demetrius's letter that are phrased impersonally (for example, v. 31 "Jerusalem and its environs . . . shall be holy and free from tax") constitute the original document, while those couched in the first person are interpolations serving later Hasmonean interests.[22] In most details, then, the letter is authentic, but as for the two references to the high priest, the one in verse 32 (releasing control of the citadel to him) is redactional and the one in verse 38 (three Samarian districts under the control of the high priest) is authentic. As a result, the letter does indeed attest in one passage that a high priest was in place in 152 BCE, before Jonathan took office.[23] "It thus refers to the personage who occupied the office after the death of Alcimus and who, when forced out by Jonathan, became the Teacher of Righteousness of the Essenes."[24]

Wise, though he refuted Stegemann's argument from a titular use of הכוהן, has, nevertheless, accepted the principal arguments of Bunge and

---

18. Ibid., 35–39.

19. Ibid., 42–43.

20. "Demetrius I and the Teacher of Righteousness (*I Macc.*, x, 25-45)," *RB* 83 (1976): 400–420.

21. The letter, addressed to the governor Zeuxis, deals with transport of two thousand Jewish families from Mesopotamia and Babylonia to Lydia and Phrygia and with the provisions to be made for them there.

22. "Demetrius I," 402–6, 416–17.

23. Ibid., 417–19.

24. Ibid., 420.

Murphy-O'Connor. He moved beyond their positions by formulating a more specific case for identifying the Teacher of Righteousness as the high priest of 1 Macc 10:32, 38 and hence of the *intersacerdotium*.[25] On his reading of the evidence, the Teacher was the author of the Temple Scroll, and the Temple Scroll and the wording of Demetrius's letter in 1 Macc 10:34-35 exhibit some agreements. King Demetrius authorized: "All the festivals and sabbaths and new moons and appointed days, and the three days before a festival and the three days after a festival—let them be days of immunity and release for all the Jews who are in my kingdom. No one shall have authority to exact anything from them or annoy any of them about any matter" (10:34-35). The references to festivals with three-day periods surrounding them are probably to pilgrimage festivals so that the king would be exempting his subjects from paying the potentially very high taxes on products they brought for the holidays. This would also, Wise thinks, entail more income for the temple, as pilgrims would feel freer to come with livestock and tithes. But why should the time period specified have been *three* days?

The Temple Scroll mentions three-day periods in more than one passage. In 43.12–15, in a context where sabbaths and festivals are being discussed, the writer stipulates: "Those who live within a distance of three days' walk from the sanctuary shall bring whatever they can bring. If they cannot carry it, they shall sell it for money and buy with it corn, wine, oil, cattle, and sheep, and shall eat them on the days of the festivals."[26] Then in TS 52.13–14 we read: "You shall not slaughter clean cattle or sheep or goat in any of your towns, within a distance of three days' journey from my sanctuary. It is rather in my sanctuary that you shall slaughter it." As these three-day journey prescriptions are not attested in other sources, "[o]ne could build a case that the explanation for these striking commonalities is simply that the letter of *1 Macc* was written to please the same man who wrote the *TS*. In other words, this link between *1 Macc* and the *TS* may establish a link between the T[eacher] of R[ighteousness] and the high priest of the Intersacerdotium."[27] Wise does

---

25. "The Teacher of Righteousness," 602–13. See also his *A Critical Study of the Temple Scroll from Qumran Cave 11,* SAOC 49 (Chicago: University of Chicago, 1990), 189–94 for the same arguments.

26. Translation of Geza Vermes, *The Complete Dead Sea Scrolls in English* (New York: Penguin, 1997), 204 (the following translation is also from Vermes, 209). Wise refers only to the material in lines 12–13, not to the conditional sentence ("If they cannot . . ."), which weakens his case by providing for monetary conversion of offerings.

27. "The Teacher of Righteousness," 611–12.

recognize that the conclusion is problematic and that the three-day phenomenon is subject to other explanations.[28]

As Wise notes, the detail regarding a three-day journey derives from Exod
3:18 (see 8:23) and is not therefore unique to the Temple Scroll.[29] Whatever its
derivation, though, it remains interesting that a period of three days around
festivals is found in both Demetrius's letter and in the Temple Scroll. But, they
do seem to be talking about different subjects, with the letter centering on
three-day periods on both sides of the festival, and the Temple Scroll with the
distance of a three-day trip. If the purpose of Demetrius's concession was to
ease the passage of pilgrims carrying sacrificial items with them, what would
have been the purpose of the three-day period after a festival? When these
problems are coupled with all the other uncertainties in his case—that the
Teacher authored the Temple Scroll, that the Teacher was a high priest and
serving in the *intersacerdotium*, that the letters are reversed in 1 Maccabees 10,
the argument turns out not to be convincing.

Below, we present evidence that suggests the order of letters in 1 Maccabees 10 is correct as it stands. If so, the letter of Demetrius I would not document the presence of a high priest in 152 bce before Jonathan began serving
in that capacity—a view that also misses the point of why the king did not
mention Jonathan as an addressee. In addition, if, as noted above, Stegemann's
arguments for identifying the Teacher of Righteousness as a high priest are
unconvincing, we have no textual evidence that anyone, much less the Teacher,
was Jonathan's immediate predecessor. This does not entail that the office was
vacant or that the Teacher could not have served at least acting as high priest
before Jonathan; it means only that we have no secure evidence in favor of
either thesis.[30]

---

28. Ibid., 612–13.

29. Yigael Yadin had drawn attention to this in his edition of the scroll, *The Temple Scroll*,
3 vols. with Supplement (Jerusalem: IES, the Institute of Archaeology of the Hebrew University
of Jerusalem, and the Shrine of the Book, 1983), 2.183. See Wise, "The Teacher of Righteousness,"
611 n. 77. Menahem Stern pointed to *Ant.* 16.2, 3 (§27), where Jews in Ionia complain about
being compelled to appear in court on holy days (see also 16.2, 4 [§45]) and to 16.6, 2 (§163),
where Augustus confirms their right "that they need not give bond (to appear in court) on the
Sabbath or on the day of preparation for it (Sabbath Eve) after the ninth hour" (*The Documents
on the History of the Hasmonaean Revolt with a Commentary and Introduction* [Tel Aviv: Hakkibbutz Hameuchad, 1965], 103–4 [Hebrew]). This enlargement of the time around the Sabbath is
roughly parallel to Demetrius's statement. He also notes that the word ἀτελείας (NRSV "immunity," 1 Macc 10:34) does not mean a freedom from taxes (LSJ: exemption from public burdens).

30. Émile Puech has proposed a variation on the theme that the Teacher of Righteousness
was the high priest of the seven-year period in question. As we saw in the preceding chapter, he
maintains that Josephus has confused some characters with similar names and that the Onias

The Hasmonean High Priests (152–37, 35 BCE)

Following the seven-year period for which no reliable source names a high priest, the office experienced a significant change when the first high priest from the Hasmonean line officially took the position. Jonathan's appointment as high priest inaugurated a period of more than a century during which members of his family held the post.

17. Jonathan (152–142 BCE)[31]

The first Hasmonean included in the high-priestly list and consistently so recognized in the narrative sources is Jonathan, the fifth and apparently youngest son of Mattathias (1 Macc 2:5, where he is "Jonathan called Apphus").[32] He, for unstated reasons, became the leader of the Maccabean forces after Judas died, even though older siblings were alive and active (for example, Simon). Judas's death led to a desperate time for his followers, when their enemies, supported by Bacchides, were firmly in control of Judea (1 Macc 9:19-27, 32-53). Under the circumstances, "all the friends of Judas assembled and said to Jonathan, 'Since the death of your brother Judas there has been no one like him to go against our enemies and Bacchides, and to deal with those of our nation who hate us. Now therefore we have chosen you today to take his place as our ruler [ἄρχοντα] and leader [ἡγούμενον], to fight our battle.'[33] So

who founded the temple in Egypt was not a son of Onias III (he was a son of Simon, the captain of the temple in 2 Macc 3:4). Rather, the *unnamed* son of Onias III, who was very young when his father was murdered, was probably called Simon (a case of papponomy with Simon II); he was the one who legitimately took over the functions of high priest after Alcimus's death, by which time this Simon was of age. So, the high priest of the period 159–152 BCE was Simon III who, after being driven from office by Jonathan in 152, became the Teacher of Righteousness of the Qumran community. Jonathan expunged his name from the records ("Le grand prêtre Simon [III] fils d'Onias III, le Maître de Justice?" in *Antikes Judentum und Frühes Christentum: Festschrift für Hartmut Stegemann zum 65. Geburtstag,* ed. B. Kollmann, W. Reinbold, and A. Steudel, BZNW 97 [Berlin: de Gruyter, 1999], 137–58). His case finally requires rejecting statements in the texts in favor of hypothetical identifications. It is simpler to interpret Josephus's admittedly difficult assertions about the two Oniases as above.

31. The number given to each high priest in the heading corresponds to the List of High Priests, pp. 491–92.

32. Abel derives the nickname from חפּיץ, which he understood as "loved, favorite" (*Les livres des Maccabées,* 32; see his survey of other views on 31–32); compare Goldstein, who thinks the derivation may be correct (*II Maccabees,* 231).

33. Josephus says he was appointed "commander [στρατηγός] of the Jews" (*Ant.* 13.1, 1 [§6]).

Jonathan accepted the leadership at that time in place of his brother Judas" (9:28-31). At this juncture (no date is attached), he assumed control of Judas's army; the text says nothing about succeeding to the high priesthood in his brother's stead—just as we would expect because Alcimus was the reigning high priest (see 9:54-57) and now enjoyed greater security than before. The Maccabean forces had been driven from Judea across the Jordan, and Bacchides reinforced his control of the land by fortifying several places in it (9:43-53). First Maccabees 9:57 says there was a period of tranquility for two years after the death of Alcimus, that is, until 157 BCE (see *Ant.* 13.1, 5 [§22]).

The situation soon changed when Jonathan and his brother Simon were able to defeat Bacchides and conclude a peace treaty with him (1 Macc 9:58-72). A quaint reminiscence of the days of the judges[34] follows: "Thus the sword ceased from Israel. Jonathan settled in Michmash[35] and began to judge the people; and he destroyed the godless out of Israel" (9:73). According to Josephus, he "administered the affairs of the people and punished the wicked and godless, and so purged the nation of them" (*Ant.* 13.1, 6 [§34]). At least, we may infer that Maccabean supremacy did not meet with everyone's satisfaction and that Jonathan's authority was not yet that of the official ruler of the country. He was influential, but his only appointment at this stage had come from his own faction.[36]

Jonathan's prominent place in Judea serves as the background for the further change in his fortunes depicted in 1 Maccabees 10. The first verse of the chapter dates the events to 160 S.E. (153–152 BCE). The immediate occasion for Jonathan's rise to the high priesthood was a contest for the Seleucid throne pitting the reigning monarch Demetrius I (162–150 BCE) against "Alexander Epiphanes, son of Antiochus" (1 Macc 10:1).[37] As the two sides assembled

34. Goldstein, *I Maccabees*, 377, 395. There are other such references in the context. Goldstein points to the positions given to Jonathan—ruler and leader—in 1 Macc 9:30 and comments: "Jonathan is to be a latter-day Judge" (377). The friends' last words in 9:30 "to fight our battle" echo the people's plan for a king in 1 Sam 8:20.

35. The place is located some eight miles north of Jerusalem, so Jonathan was close to but not in the capital city.

36. Schürer suggests that Jonathan set up a rival government in Michmash, while the Sanhedrin in Jerusalem was still controlled by the Hellenizing party (*History*, 1.177).

37. For the ancient information about his identity, see Edwyn R. Bevan, *The House of Seleucus,* 2 vols. (London: Arnold, 1902; reprinted: New York: Barnes & Noble, 1966), 2.207–10, and Appendix M (300–301); Schürer, *History of the Jewish People,* 1.177–78 n. 11; Goldstein, *I Maccabees,* 397–98. It was widely believed he was not actually the son of Antiochus IV. The fact that 1 Maccabees seems to accept the claim that Alexander was Antiochus IV's son makes the situation all the more ironic: the alleged son of the archenemy of the Maccabean family now appoints a Maccabean to the high priesthood. If the author did know the doubts about Alexander's family connections, it was not in his interest, as a defender of the Hasmonean family, to mention the point.

armies to settle the dispute, the backing of Jonathan, an experienced commander of battle-tested veterans, became a prize coveted by both. Demetrius and Alexander dispatched letters to him to solicit his support. In the case of Demetrius (the text of whose first letter is not preserved), the situation was more delicate because he naturally assumed that Jonathan was a confirmed enemy. To encourage Jonathan, the king "gave him authority to recruit troops, to equip them with arms, and to become his ally; and he commanded that the hostages in the citadel should be released to him" (1 Macc 10:6; see *Ant.* 13.2, 1 [§§37–38]).[38]

Although the two were hardly on friendly terms, Jonathan exploited the royal concessions. He entered Jerusalem and read the king's letter in public, whereupon the alarmed residents of the citadel delivered the hostages to him. We learn that the news also caused the foreigners in the strongholds that Bacchides had set up to abandon them and return to their homes. In this way, Jonathan was suddenly in control of the land, with the exception of Beth Zur (Josephus adds Jerusalem [*Ant.* 13.2, 1 (§42)]). He also took care to improve the defenses of Jerusalem and Mount Zion in particular (1 Macc 10:10-11), some ten years after Antiochus V had torn down the wall around it (1 Macc 6:62).[39]

Jonathan improved his situation further by dealing with the other side in the struggle for the Seleucid throne. After accepting and acting on Demetrius's concessions, he received a letter from the man to whom 1 Maccabees already in this context (10:15) gives the royal title: "King Alexander to his brother Jonathan, greetings. We have heard about you, that you are a mighty warrior and worthy to be our friend. And so we have appointed you today to be the high priest of your nation [ἀρχιερέα τοῦ ἔθνους σου]; you are to be called the king's Friend[40] and you are to take our side and keep friendship with us"

---

38. First Maccabees 9:53 reports that Bacchides had taken hostages from the leading families and placed them under guard in the citadel.

39. Erecting such defenses shows that Jonathan was acting as head of the nation in the capital city (see Goldstein, *I Maccabees*, 399).

40. "Friend of the king" was an important honor and indicated a close relationship with and ready access to the monarch. The title was given to someone who was a part of the court and personally attached to a particular king; to such people, the ruler granted the right of wearing a purple robe. Bacchides was a Friend of the king (1 Macc 7:8). On the title, see E. J. Bikerman, *Institutions des Séleucides*, Service des Antiquités Bibliothèque archéologique et historique 26 (Paris: Geuthner, 1938), 40–50. As Bikerman notes (p. 44), Jonathan was unusual in that he moved to different levels in the ranks of the Friends, as successive kings honored him. See below for the subsequent appointments of Jonathan as royal Friend. Menahem Stern ("The Days of Jonathan and Demetrius II," in *Hasmonaean Judaea in the Hellenistic World: Chapters in Political History*, ed. D. Schwartz [Jerusalem: Zalman Shazar Center for Jewish History, 1995 (Hebrew)],

(1 Macc 10:18-20; see *Ant.* 13.2, 2 [§45]). To these extraordinary benefits, he added a purple robe and golden crown. Once he had quoted Alexander's letter, the writer of 1 Maccabees makes a laconic but eloquent comment: "So Jonathan put on the sacred vestments[41] in the seventh month of the one hundred sixtieth year, at the festival of Booths, and he recruited troops and equipped them with arms in abundance" (10:21). The combination of sacerdotal and military roles was to characterize much of the history of the Hasmonean high priesthood. The festival of Booths would have been a particularly grand occasion for Jonathan to wear the spectacular clothing of the high priest and appear before a large number of pilgrims at the temple.[42]

In this context, 1 Maccabees says nothing about whether Onias IV was a viable candidate to become high priest (he is never mentioned in the book) or whether another person held the office after Alcimus. Josephus (*Ant.* 13.2, 3 [§46]), however, adds that Jonathan "put on the high-priestly robe, this being four years after the death of his brother Judas—for there had been no high priest during this time." As we have seen, his statement presupposes his understanding that Judas had served as high priest for three years after Alcimus (12.11, 2 [§434]).

Alexander's appointment of Jonathan as high priest[43] inspired Demetrius to offer sweeping concessions to "the nation of the Jews" (1 Macc 10:25), although Jonathan is not listed among the recipients of his largess. It seems that he realized Jonathan was lost to the enemy camp; therefore, he campaigned for the support of others and perhaps hinted, by not naming Jonathan as an addressee of the letter,[44] at placing someone else in the high-

---

49–50 n. 3) has shown, however, that titles such as Friend of the King, Brother, and so forth did not all belong to one system, so that we cannot always determine whether one title was loftier than another. There is evidence, too, that a person could hold more than one of these titles at the same time.

41. It seems doubtful that "vestments" is the correct translation of στολή alone.

42. See Abel, *Les livres des Maccabées,* 184; Jeffrey L. Rubenstein, *The History of Sukkot in the Second Temple and Rabbinic Periods,* BJS 302 (Atlanta: Scholars, 1995), 63–64. Joseph Sievers suggests that Jonathan may have been the one to instigate the offer from Alexander (*The Hasmoneans and Their Supporters: From Mattathias to the Death of John Hyrcanus I,* SFSHJ 6 [Atlanta: Scholars, 1990], 83–86). He also thinks it is strange that Jonathan began serving as high priest just after the Day of Atonement when the high priest would have had his most visible role and that the brevity of the notice about his appointment provides a hint that it was controversial at the time.

43. It is curious that in *Ant.* 20.10, 3 (§238) Josephus reports that "the descendants of the sons of Asamonaios" appointed Jonathan high priest. This contradicts *Ant.* 13.2, 2–3 (§§45–46), where he relates Alexander's nomination of Jonathan as in 1 Macc 10:20-21.

44. Abel (*Les livres des Maccabées,* 185) thought that Demetrius omitted Jonathan's name because the Maccabean brother did not have the support of the entire nation. As the king did not

priestly office.[45] In his letter, addressed "to the nation of the Jews," note these provisions that pertain to the priests and even to the high priest:[46]

1. "Jerusalem and its environs, its tithes and its revenues, shall be holy and free from tax" (1 Macc 10:31).
2. "I release also my control of the citadel in Jerusalem and give it to the high priest, so that he may station in it men of his own choice to guard it" (1 Macc 10:32). Josephus appears to have missed the point of the wording of Demetrius's letter by having him write: "And the citadel I place in the hands of your high priest Jonathan" (*Ant.* 13.2, 3 [§51]).[47]
3. "All the festivals and sabbaths and new moons and appointed days, and the three days before a festival and the three days after a festival—let them be days of immunity and release for all the Jews who are in my kingdom" (1 Macc 10:34).
4. "As for the three districts that have been added to Judea from the country of Samaria, let them be annexed to Judea so that they may be considered to be under one ruler and obey no other authority than the high priest" (1 Macc 10:38).[48]

The king also specified a number of other grants that were to the financial advantage of the temple (1 Macc 10:39-44).[49]

Whatever group received the royal epistle, "Jonathan and the people," that is, Jonathan and his troops (on this, see below), rejected the proposals,

---

wish to antagonize the sizable opposition to him, he did not name Jonathan the high priest. See Goldstein, *I Maccabees*, 405.

45. This seems to be a better way of understanding the letter than Bunge's theory that it is the text of the letter mentioned but not quoted in 1 Macc 10:6. See above.

46. There is no need to decide whether the concessions are believable, since they were never implemented, and one can no longer tell whether Demetrius was able or intended to follow through on them. For the debate about whether the letter is an addition to 1 Maccabees from Roman times, see Schürer, *History of the Jewish People*, 1.178–79 n. 14. For arguments in support of the letter's authenticity and reasons for its similarity with Demetrius II's letter (1 Macc 11:30-37), see M. Stern, *Documents*, 85–86. Murphy-O'Connor, as explained earlier, separates an authentic letter phrased impersonally from added elements worded in the first person ("Demetrius I," 402–19).

47. Abel, *Les livres des Maccabées*, 187–88.

48. Josephus reads quite differently: "it shall be the concern of the high priest that not a single Jew shall have any temple for worship other than that at Jerusalem" (*Ant.* 13.2, 3 [§54]).

49. In 1 Macc 10:39, Demetrius gives to the Jewish nation the city of Ptolemais and its environs so that the revenue from them could cover the costs of the temple. Since Ptolemais was under Alexander's control and served as his headquarters even after he became king, the gift appears to have been meaningless or perhaps hints that the addressees should try to take the city. See Abel, *Les livres des Maccabées*, 189; M. Stern, *Documents*, 85.

choosing to remain on Alexander's side (1 Macc 10:46-47). We should add that Demetrius's letter names no governor or other official alongside the high priest. As it transpired, Jonathan had read the signs of the times correctly: Alexander defeated Demetrius in battle, and the king lost his life in the course of the fighting (1 Macc 10:48-50).[50]

First Maccabees, then, dates Jonathan's assumption of the high-priestly dignity to the year 160 s.e., that is, 152 BCE, and places it in the seventh month, the month with the largest number of festival days.[51] There may seem to be no problem with this, but Bunge has argued that Jonathan did not actually receive his royal appointment until two years later (150 BCE), when Alexander officially became king (150–145 BCE).[52] Although 1 Macc 10:1 dates Alexander's arrival at and occupation of Ptolemais to 152 BCE, the following material in the chapter deals, Bunge believes, with events that happened in the decisive year 150 BCE, when the armies of Alexander and Demetrius fought and the latter died (see 1 Macc 10:57, which gives the equivalent of this date [162 s.e.] for the wedding of Alexander, which occurred shortly after he became king).

Bunge thinks that the erroneous date for Jonathan's appointment as high priest in 1 Maccabees is the result of an intentional move on the part of the author, who combined the year-date for Alexander's arrival in the region (160 s.e.) with the month-date for Jonathan's investiture, which derived from a Jewish tradition known to him. Bunge cites conflicts between the two royal letters and their contexts to reinforce his case. For example, the fact that Jonathan received the first offer from Demetrius (1 Macc 10:3-7) contradicts 10:47 where Jonathan and his men "favored Alexander, because he had been the first to speak peaceable words to them." Bunge also believes that the letter men-

---

50. At this point, Josephus inserts a story about a dispute between Jews and Samaritans of Alexandria, with the two sides presenting their cases before Ptolemy Philometor and his council. The issue was which temple, the one in Jerusalem or that on Mount Gerizim, had been built according to Moses' Law (*Ant.* 13.3, 4 [§§74–79]). The Jewish disputant Andronicus, on his way to victory in the debate, "began with proofs from the Law and the succession of the high priests, showing how each had become head of the temple by receiving that office from his father, and that all the kings of Asia had honoured the temple with dedicatory offerings and most splendid gifts" (*Ant.* 13.3, 4 [§78]).

51. Klaus-Dietrich Schunck observes that Jonathan thus received the high priesthood in the same way that Jason, Menelaus, and Alcimus did—appointment by a foreign king (although he strangely thinks he was not an Aaronide) and that he now put political goals before the religious ones of the Maccabean uprising as a result ("Hoherpriester und Politiker? Die Stellung der Hohenpriester von Jaddua bis Jonatan zur jüdischen Gemeinde und zum hellenistischen Staat," *VT* 44 [1994]: 511–12).

52. The following paragraphs summarize the arguments that he offers in "Zur Geschichte und Chronologie," 29–43.

tioned in 10:6 is the one whose text is given in 10:25-45. So, on his view, the letter of 10:25-45 belongs in the context of 10:1-6 (see above for the implications of his understanding of the original text for the question whether there was a high priest during the years 159–152 BCE).

For Bunge, then, Alexander's letter, in which he makes Jonathan high priest, fits, not in the circumstances of the year 152 BCE, but in the context of 150 BCE, the year in which he became king in Demetrius's place. Neither the letter nor the context suggests that Jonathan switched loyalties; only the present order of the text implies that he did, first accepting concessions from the desperate Demetrius and then from his rival Alexander. Hence, Alexander appointed Jonathan high priest in the year 150 BCE at a time when he actually had the royal authority to do so.

Bunge's reconstruction of events entails that Jonathan was placed in a delicate position in 150 BCE when Alexander defeated Demetrius and succeeded him on the Seleucid throne. At that time Jonathan would have been Demetrius's ally, a commander pledged to raising troops in this capacity; yet he did not come to the king's assistance in the battle with Alexander's troops. So, as Bunge reads the evidence, Alexander did not just invite Jonathan to his wedding later in the year; he summoned him, and Jonathan was able to survive only by giving Alexander costly gifts. So successful was Jonathan on this occasion that Alexander named him high priest, though another person still held the office (see above, on the *intersacerdotium*).

Bunge finds further verification for Jonathan's appointment in 150 BCE in *Ant.* 20.10, 3 (§238), where Josephus credits Jonathan with a high-priestly reign of seven years. The historian did not take this number from 1 Maccabees, which implies a ten-year reign for Jonathan. Nevertheless, Josephus's number is correct: from his appointment in the seventh month of the Seleucid (Babylonian) year 162 to his death at the end of the Seleucid (Babylonian) year 169 is seven full years. That is, 1 Maccabees suggests that Jonathan died between January and March of 142 BCE, which would be the end of the Seleucid (Babylonian) year 169.

Why did the writer of 1 Maccabees rearrange historical events? He had at his disposal, Bunge thinks, a Jewish work about Jonathan's high priesthood, the Seleucid chronicle, and the two royal letters. As a partisan of the Hasmoneans, he wished to justify Jonathan's becoming high priest and to do so he combined the month-number from his Jewish source and the year-numbers from the Seleucid chronicle in such a way that he antedated his high priesthood by two years. The Seleucid chronicle was favorable to Alexander and regarded him as king already in 152 BCE when he reached Ptolemais (see 1 Macc 10:1 "there he began to reign"). So, it was not difficult for the author of 1 Maccabees to move the beginning of Jonathan's tenure to 152 BCE, whereas he had in fact received the office only in 150 BCE. The writer did this to whitewash the reputation of Jonathan.

Did this editorial intervention occur so that we should date the inception of Jonathan's reign to the year 150 BCE against the clear statement of 1 Macc 10:21? Here, as with Bunge's argument regarding the dates for Alcimus's reign, his learned case fails to convince. By the nature of his claim, there would be no manuscript evidence for a form of 1 Maccabees that would have had the original order, but basic questions may be asked about what he proposes. First, is there really a contradiction between Demetrius's initial concessions to Jonathan and 1 Macc 10:47, which says Alexander was the first to offer peaceable words? There may be a problem in this respect, but there are other ways of viewing the text. Abel thought that the lost Hebrew original of 1 Macc 10:47 read the consonants שלום, which the Greek translator understood as peace (εἰρηνικῶν) but which the author meant as compensation, payment (šillûm). In other words, Alexander would be credited with being one who offered, not words of peace, but talk of remuneration—probably meaning the high priesthood.[53] While this is possible, it may be preferable to examine the difficult word ἀρχηγός (= "the first" in the NRSV). Goldstein translates "They favored Alexander, because he was the original cause of their opportunity for peaceful discussions" and explains that his rendering makes everything logical.[54] By introducing the notion of "opportunity for," however, he seems to be doing more than translating.

If one looks at what is said about Demetrius's original offer to Jonathan, a simpler solution suggests itself. There is nothing about "peaceful words" in 1 Macc 10:6; there, the talk is only about military preparation and assistance, together with an offer of hostage release. The wording of Alexander's letter could much more properly be understood as expressing peaceful words (appointment as a royal Friend, reference to friendship), and perhaps this is all that is meant by 10:47.

Second, do Jonathan's actions in 1 Macc 10:7-11 presuppose the contents of the letter in 10:25-45? It seems that they do not. In 1 Macc 10:6, Demetrius gives Jonathan the right to:

---

53. Abel, Les livres des Maccabées, 192. He finds the same confusion in Mic 7:3 and relates this verse to the situation of 1 Maccabees 9–10. Dancy, who considers the idea that the text means to say Alexander was first in merit, not in time, accepts Abel's proposal (A Commentary on 1 Maccabees, 148), which is repeated in F.-M. Abel and Jean Starcky, Les livres des Maccabées, rev. 3rd ed., La Sainte Bible (Paris: Cerf, 1961), 166.

54. 1 Maccabees, 403, 414.

- recruit and arm troops
- be his ally
- receive hostages

The letter in 1 Macc 10:25-45 grants the nation, among many other concessions, these rough parallels:

- enrollment of up to thirty thousand troops in the royal army
- control of the citadel (hostages are not mentioned)

That is, even the related provisions in the letter are different from the ones implied for Demetrius's initial communication by Jonathan's actions in verses 7-11. In verses 7-11, he has the right to recruit troops and he receives hostages, as the king in 10:6 authorized. His rebuilding of the city and his command to construct walls and fortify Mount Zion could be seen as a response to the provisions in 10:44-45 (although the latter verses envision broader building projects in Judea and do not mention fortifications specifically on Mount Zion), but they could also be interpreted as reasonable steps taken by a military leader at a time of impending war.

Third, does Bunge's hypothetical order of events make sense? It seems that it creates more problems than does the narrative in 1 Maccabees 10. On his view, Jonathan would have raised an army as an ally of Demetrius, yet somehow, when Demetrius needed his assistance, he was allowed to stand on the sidelines—this when there is some evidence that the battles between Demetrius and Alexander continued for some time.[55] Then, according to Bunge, Jonathan, who had actually done Alexander a favor by failing to help Demetrius, was nevertheless summarily called to account by Alexander who ordered him to meet him at Ptolemais where he had to bribe his way to success. Alexander, one would think, might rather have greeted Jonathan with rich gifts for having made his victory easier (as 1 Maccabees suggests was the case).

Fourth, it is difficult to understand how moving Jonathan's appointment two years earlier would have polished his reputation more than taking office in 150 BCE would have entailed.

When the evidence is considered, Bunge's case falls. There appears to be no compelling reason for rejecting 152 BCE, the date given in 1 Maccabees, as the year when Jonathan became high priest.

For some time after becoming high priest in 1 Macc 10:21, Jonathan remains the protagonist in the narrative of 1 Maccabees, just as he had been

---

55. See Bevan, *House of Seleucus*, 2.210–11.

since Judas's death, but we learn little about what he did as the leader of the national cult. The author focuses more on his diplomatic and military roles than on his strictly priestly ones. The subsequent accounts picture Jonathan as the ruler of the nation and in this way indicate that the diverse powers he had received from both Demetrius and Alexander remained his. Alexander invited Jonathan[56] to meet himself and Ptolemy (VI Philometor) at Ptolemais where Alexander's marriage to Ptolemy's daughter, Cleopatra, was being celebrated in the year 150 (10:57). Jonathan was able to impress the two kings with expensive presents (10:59-60). Even though he had attained the highest priestly office in the land and held the political and military power, Jonathan was not yet free of internal enemies. When "malcontents from Israel, rene-gades,[57] gathered together to accuse him" (10:61), King Alexander refused to believe them; instead, he clothed Jonathan in purple and gave orders that no one was to bring charges against him (10:62-64). "Thus the king honored him and enrolled him among his chief Friends, and made him general [στρατη-γόν] and governor of the province [μεριδάρχης]" (10:65). These titles added a royal imprimatur to the powers that Jonathan had already been exercising for some time.[58]

Strengthened by his high offices, Jonathan played a prominent role in dis-putes about the Seleucid throne for a number of years. The next incident in which he figures came three years later (147 BCE [10:67; Ant. 13.4, 3 (§86)]) when Demetrius I's son, soon to be known as Demetrius II, tried to take the Seleucid throne from Alexander. Apollonius, the governor of Coele-Syria for this latter Demetrius,[59] wrote to the high priest Jonathan (1 Macc 10:69), accusing him of remaining loyal to Alexander and challenging him to fight his forces in the plain (10:70-73). A series of victories by Jonathan and Simon gave them control of parts of the coastal region and further endeared Jonathan to

---

56. *Ant.* 13.4, 2 (§83) adds the title "the high priest," which is lacking in 1 Macc 10:59.

57. The Greek text reads ἄνδρες παράνομοι. Although the adjective can be a general term for evildoers (a term whose meaning depends on the user's point of view), it seems an odd one to employ if, as Bunge thinks, these men were partisans of the Teacher of Righteousness. He and his followers were noted for their devotion to the Law, not violation of it. In 1 Macc 1:11, the same term designates those who wished to do away with Israel's distinctive laws, and in 11:21 it is employed for the men who complained to the king about Jonathan's attack on the citadel in Jerusalem. These other usages have led commentators to identify the opponents in 10:61 as a Hellenizing group who now found themselves in a difficult situation (for example, Abel, *Les livres des Maccabées*, 195).

58. See Schürer, *History of the Jewish People*, 1.180. Note that a "chief Friend" may be a pro-motion for Jonathan who had earlier been named a Friend of the king.

59. Josephus, *Ant.* 13.4, 3 (§88), says Apollonius was Alexander's governor, but that would make little sense in the account. See Marcus, *Josephus* 7, 269 n. d; and *Ant.* 13.4, 4 (§102).

Alexander (10:74-89). As he was before he became high priest, so after he took the office Jonathan remained a military commander. Before he became high priest, nothing was said about any problem with his being a priest and also engaging in battles where there was the likelihood of corpse contamination; the same is the case after he became high priest and continued his role as general. Ptolemy VI soon took some of the coastal cities from Jonathan, but the high priest managed to remain on peaceful terms with him (11:1-8).

Upon the deaths of Alexander[60] and Ptolemy VI in 145 BCE (1 Macc 11:13-19), Demetrius II (145 to 140–139) took the throne. This turn of events could have put Jonathan, the friend and ally of Alexander and Ptolemy, in an awkward position, but remarkably he exploited the moment to besiege the ever-troublesome citadel in Jerusalem.[61] In this context, we again meet "certain renegades who hated their nation"; they told the king about Jonathan's action (11:21). The angry monarch ordered an end to the siege and summoned Jonathan to meet him at Ptolemais, where Jonathan secured his favor with gifts and even requested three Samarian provinces from him (he received them). As a result, the king treated him well. "He confirmed [ἔστησεν] him in the high-priesthood and in as many other honors as he had formerly had, and caused him to be reckoned among his chief Friends" (11:27; see *Ant.* 13.4, 9 [§124]). First Maccabees 11:30-37 is a copy of Demetrius II's letter confirming his grants to the Jews.[62] The address reads "King Demetrius to his brother Jonathan and to the nation of the Jews, greetings" (v. 30). This letter is the first official document addressed to a Hasmonean ruler and the Jewish nation (in that order), a practice that will become standard.[63] Yet, though his place as head of the nation is evident from the order in which the entities are listed in the address, the king does not mention Jonathan's official titles. We should observe, though, that at the end of the letter the monarch instructs: "Now therefore take care to make a copy of this, and let it be given to Jonathan and put up in a conspicuous place on the holy mountain" (v. 37).

By this time we have, then, two instances in which a Seleucid monarch dealt with Jonathan in connection with the high-priestly office: Alexander

---

60. Josephus says he was "surnamed Balas" (*Ant.* 13.4, 8 [§119]); see Marcus, *Josephus* 7, 284 n. a, for other references to this name.

61. Here again, Josephus adds the title *high priest* (*Ant.* 13.4, 9 [§121]) to Jonathan's name. Schürer sees in Jonathan's siege of the citadel an attempt by him to break away from the Seleucid Empire (*History*, 1.181).

62. The letter to Jonathan and the Jewish nation is a copy of the one the king sent to Lasthenes, a high official in his administration (see Abel, *Les livres des Maccabées*, 209).

63. Goldstein, *I Maccabees*, 431 (see also his discussion of high-priestly powers, 431–32); M. Stern, *Documents*, 107. The remission of taxes granted by the king made the Jews a privileged *ethnos* (Goldstein, *I Maccabees*, 432).

named him to the post, and Demetrius II confirmed him in it. There is no doubt that the Jewish high priest owed his office to the Seleucid monarch, but it is also clear that Jonathan's military powers permitted him wide latitude in dealing with weak kings, monarchs desperate to retain the throne.

Jonathan managed to survive the succession of intrigues around the throne in Antioch for several more years, although the forces that would bring about his end were already in place. Demetrius II became vastly unpopular when he dismissed his troops (Josephus adds that he "reduced their pay" [*Ant.* 13.4, 9 (§129)]), and Trypho,[64] a supporter of the late Alexander, began making arrangements for Alexander's son Antiochus to take over the throne. Jonathan[65] is credited with sending three thousand soldiers to protect Demetrius II against his own subjects in Antioch, but the king later reneged on the rewards he had promised (for example, removal of troops from the Jerusalem citadel and the strongholds) and became estranged from Jonathan (1 Macc 11:38-53). In these circumstances, the troops of Trypho managed to put his protégé Antiochus VI (145–142 BCE) on the throne after defeating Demetrius II (11:54-59). Perhaps because his relations with Demetrius had cooled, Jonathan retained his office, despite the change of regimes: "Then the young Antiochus wrote to Jonathan, saying, 'I confirm [ἵστημι] you in the high priesthood and set you over the four districts and make you one of the king's Friends.' He also sent him gold plates and a table service, and granted him the right to drink from gold cups and dress in purple and wear a gold buckle. He appointed Jonathan's brother Simon governor from the Ladder of Tyre to the border of Egypt" (1 Macc 11:57-59; compare *Ant.* 13.5, 4 [§§145–46]).

In the wake of another string of military triumphs (including a victory over officers of Demetrius [1 Macc 11:60-74]), Jonathan sent an embassy to renew the friendship his brother Judas had first made with the Romans (see 1 Maccabees 8; *Ant.* 13.5, 8 [§§163–70]).[66] His emissaries entered the senate with the message: "'The high priest Jonathan and the Jewish nation have sent us to renew the former friendship and alliance with them'" (12:3). He also

---

64. Josephus calls him "Diodotus, surnamed Tryphon" (*Ant.* 13.5, 1 [§131]).

65. As he does elsewhere, Josephus applies the title *high priest* to Jonathan in *Ant.* 13.5, 2 (§133), where 1 Macc 11:41 lacks it.

66. See M. Stern, *Documents*, 90–91, regarding why this was the first opportune time for Jonathan to renew ties with Rome. For the somewhat confusing terminology for the kind of relationship the Hasmonean state established with the Romans and the reality lying behind it, see Sara Mandell, "Did the Maccabees Believe That They Had a Valid Treaty with Rome?" *CBQ* 53 (1991): 202–20. She concludes: "The diplomatic agreement concluded was not and had never been a treaty of friendship, although the Maccabees and the ἔθνος of the Jews interpreted it as such" (219).

dispatched a letter to the Spartans; it began: "'The high priest Jonathan, the senate of the nation, the priests, and the rest of the Jewish people to their brothers the Spartans, greetings'" (12:6). That letter recalled the earlier letter from the Spartan king Areus to the high priest Onias (considered above in chapter 3 under Onias I), advocated reviving "family ties" with them, reported on events since the earlier correspondence, and told them about the renewal of relations with Rome. The original letter from King Areus was appended to this letter (12:5-23).[67] It is perhaps no accident that shortly before this, in 146 BCE, the Romans had defeated the Achaean League, a victory that improved the position and prestige of Sparta.[68]

While both the statement of the messengers to the Roman senate and the letter to the Spartans place the name of Jonathan and his title *high priest* first among those sending the message, the letter to the Spartans is especially interesting in that it, unlike the communication with Rome, includes "the senate of the nation [ἡ γερουσία τοῦ ἔθνους]" alongside the high priest and the larger groups in Judean society. The high priest is the first name in diplomacy, but he was not to the only entity involved in international relations.

Jonathan and Simon continued to be successful on the battlefield against supporters of the former king Demetrius II (1 Macc 12:24-34). These struggles, though they resulted in victories, highlighted for the brothers the need for improved defenses in their own country and put them in a position to build them. Included in their efforts were raising and repairing the wall of Jerusalem and erecting a high barrier to separate the citadel from the city (12:35-38).[69]

Trypho, who by now wished to take the crown for himself, was wary of Jonathan, who had been confirmed as high priest by Antiochus VI and could therefore be a supporter of the young king. As they approached each other with armies, Trypho, most inexplicably, was able to make Jonathan dismiss almost all of his forty thousand troops; then, when the warrior-high priest entered Ptolemais to meet Trypho, he and the one thousand soldiers left with him were ambushed (1 Macc 12:39-48). Jonathan survived the attack but was

---

67. After the section on communications with Rome and Sparta, Josephus inserts a brief section on the three "schools of thought among the Jews"—Pharisees, Sadducees, and Essenes—and contrasts their views on "fate" (*Ant.* 13.5, 9 [§§171–73]).

68. M. Stern, *Documents*, 91.

69. According to *Ant.* 13.5, 11 (§§181–83), Jonathan assembled the people in the temple and encouraged them to "repair the walls of Jerusalem, and to set up again the part of the wall round the temple which had been thrown down, and to fortify the temple precincts by high towers, and, in addition, to build still another wall in the midst of the city to keep the garrison in the citadel from reaching the city, and in this way cut off their large supply of provisions" (§§181–82). The temple wall had been destroyed by Antiochus V (1 Macc 6:62).

a prisoner of Trypho for his remaining days.[70] Although his brother Simon sent one hundred talents of silver and Jonathan's two sons as hostages, a ransom Trypho had demanded, he did not release Jonathan; rather, he soon thereafter executed him at Baskama northeast of the Sea of Gennesaret (13:12-23).[71] Simon then arranged the burial of his brother in their hometown of Modein. "All Israel bewailed him with great lamentation, and mourned for him many days" (13:26).

No date is attached to the end of Jonathan's life and high priesthood, but 1 Macc 13:41-42 synchronizes the first year of Simon, his successor as high priest, with 170 S.E.; hence, Jonathan died in 143–142 BCE.[72] At the end of his account Josephus says: "Now when Jonathan died as high priest, he had been ruler of the nation for four years" (*Ant.* 13.6, 6 [§212]). The number is puzzling, as is the one in *Ant.* 20.10, 3 (§238), where he wrote about the time after the seven-year gap in the high priesthood: "Then the descendants of the sons of Asamonaios, entrusted with the leadership of the nation, after war had been waged against them and they had taken the offensive against the Macedonians, resumed the tradition, appointing as high priest Jonathan, who held office for seven years." If the chronological conclusions defended above are correct, both of Josephus's numbers are wrong and correspond to no time when an official act of appointment was made by a king; they also do not harmonize with a time when the Maccabean forces might have appointed Jonathan. From the dates in 1 Maccabees, we may infer that his high priesthood lasted about ten years.[73]

Before leaving Jonathan, the first Hasmonean high priest, we should consider briefly the information about him in the Qumran texts.[74] The data fall under two headings: references or possible references to Jonathan, and Jonathan as the leading candidate for the position of Wicked Priest.

---

70. Josephus says that Trypho(n) himself took Jonathan (*Ant.* 13.6, 2 [§192]).

71. Josephus (*Ant.* 13.6, 6 [§§209–10]) wrote that Trypho(n) "invaded Galaaditis, where he killed Jonathan and ordered that he be buried, and then returned to Antioch. But Simon sent to the city of Basca and brought back the bones of his brother, which he buried in Modeei [*sic*], his birthplace, while all the people made great lamentation over him."

72. Jonathan's capture and death were part of Trypho's moves to obtain the throne. First Maccabees 13:31-32, which follows immediately on the notice about the burial of Jonathan, mentions that Trypho killed Antiochus and took the throne for himself. This happened in 142 or 141 BCE. See Schürer, *History of the Jewish People*, 1.130–31; Peter Green, *Alexander to Actium: The Historical Evolution of the Hellenistic Age*, HCS 1 (Berkeley: Univ. of California Press, 1990), 714.

73. See Marcus, *Josephus* 7, 332–33 n. b, for a discussion of how the number *four* may have entered the text; considering it a corrupt misreading of δ᾽ (meant as an abbreviation for δέκα) does not explain the number *seven* in *Antiquities* 20.

74. See Sievers, *Hasmoneans*, 88–92 for a brief overview of the anti-Hasmonean standpoint expressed in some of the scrolls.

First, there are references or possible references to Jonathan in the scrolls: His name may appear in 4Qpseudo-Daniel^c ar (4Q245). The editors, who date the handwriting on the fragments remaining from this manuscript to the early first century CE, disagree with the first interpreters who thought the text was part of the one represented on 4Q243-44.[75] The relevant piece of text is fragment 1 column 1, of which only the ends of lines have survived. At the top of the fragment just a few words are legible; among them are the name *Daniel* in line 3 and, in line 4, reference to a writing that was (is) given. Then, in lines 5–10, there are names familiar from priestly lists, while in lines 11–13, the names of a few kings survive. Too little of the text is available for us to discern how the parts were connected, if they were. As the editors read the priestly section, we have the following names:

5.	Lev]i Qahat
6.	]Bukki Uzzi
7.	Zado]k Abiathar
8	]Hi[l]kiah
9.	] [ ] and Onias
10.	Jona]than Simon

It would be helpful to know how wide the full column was, but there are no sure means for calculating it. If one attempts to reconstruct the list of priests, using the one in 1 Chr 6:1-15 (MT 5:27-41), lines 6 and 7 would have about thirty-nine and thirty-five letter spaces respectively, but the presence of Abiathar in line 7 shows that the Chronicles list is not the basis for this one. Also, there are problems in 1 Chronicles 6 (MT 5) after the name *Zadok*. At any rate, one would not be able to fit all of the names of the list (or of other, related lists) into the available spaces for lines 8–10, if our fragment contained the full high-priestly list.

As a result, we do not know how many names separated Onias and Jonathan; we also cannot be sure which Onias is meant. The reading *Jonathan* is not certain, since only part of the penultimate letter and all of the final letter are legible, but it is a reasonable one, especially with the name *Simon* following it.[76] Nothing in the surviving text indicates why these particular names were cited or what the author thought of any member of the list. The editors attempt to relate the priestly and kingly lists of names to the issue of

---

75. John J. Collins and Peter W. Flint, "245. 4Qpseudo-Daniel^c ar," *Qumran Cave 4 XVII Parabiblical Texts, Part 3*, consulting ed. J. VanderKam, DJD 22 (Oxford: Clarendon, 1996), 154–55.

76. See the comments of Collins and Flint, "245. 4Qpseudo-Daniel^c ar," 160.

maintaining the separation between the high priesthood and kingship; this is speculative but possible for a community that separated the two offices in its expectation of a messiah from Aaron and one from Israel/David.[77]

Émil Puech has argued that 4Q523 (4QJonathan) fragments 1–2 also contain a reference to Jonathan the Maccabee. He dates the semicursive scribal hand to the years 150–125 BCE and thinks it was written early in this time period.[78] In the fragmentary text, he finds Jonathan pictured as the Wicked Priest, a conclusion arising from the negative associations in the lines of the column where his name appears. Here, too, the reading *Jonathan* is not entirely certain, but it is likely.

The name *Jonathan* occurs in line 2 after what appears to be a verb: [. The verb is not at all clear in meaning, but Puech relates it to יגה II (it parallels הגה II) which, in the causative stem, means "remove." So, he considers either "they removed Jonathan" or "I would remove Jonathan" as possible renderings.[79] Line 3 refers to armies that have stolen, line 4 to forks, line 5 to Gog and Magog, line 9 may refer to treasures, and line 12 possibly mentions a deposit; the rest are even more unclear. Peuch explains that the Jonathan of 4Q523 is best understood as Jonathan the Maccabee after the time of his nomination as high priest by Alexander Balas. Contemporary writers like Josephus usually situate Gog and Magog in the northeast. The text would be referring to theft of temple vessels by an impious hand, perhaps Jonathan's. So, after being faithful at the beginning of his career, Jonathan became the Wicked Priest as Pesher Habakkuk labels him. [80]

Although Puech has drawn large consequences from the few surviving words of 4Q523, caution is in order. Since the verb that precedes the name *Jonathan* is uncertain and the connection of Jonathan with the words of the following lines is unknown, we should not infer much from it. Then, too, we do not know that the Jonathan of line 2 is Jonathan the Hasmonean, although he may be. No source connects Jonathan with robbery of temple vessels, nor can we be sure that Gog and Magog refer to the Seleucids who appointed Jonathan as high priest.[81]

---

77. Collins and Flint, "245. 4Qpseudo-Danielc ar," 157–58. See also the treatment of this text by Peter W. Flint, "4Qpseudo-Daniel arc (4Q245) and the Restoration of the Priesthood," *RevQ* 17 (1996): 137–50, especially 140–43. There, too, it is seen as addressing the separation of kingship and high priesthood.

78. "523. 4QJonathan," *Qumrân Grotte 4 XVIII Textes Hébreux (4Q521–4Q528, 4Q576–4Q579)*, DJD 25 (Oxford: Clarendon, 1998), 75.

79. Ibid., 78.

80. Ibid., 76.

81. Puech has elaborated his thoughts on the text at greater length in "Jonathan le Prêtre Impie et les débuts de la Communauté de Qumrân. 4QJonathan (4Q523) et 4QPsAp (4Q448),"

Second, we should note that, in the opinion of many scholars, Jonathan was the Wicked Priest of the Qumran texts—an inference that seems to be correct.[82] This unnamed person (or persons, as some think) is relevant to the history of the high priesthood because his title הכוהן הרשע appears to be a play on one of the attested titles for the high priest—הכוהן הראש (Ezra 7:5; 2 Chr 31:10).[83] The Wicked Priest came into direct and violent contact with the also unnamed Teacher of Righteousness and thus is associated with the early days of the group.

Despite the fact that much has been written about the Wicked Priest, the full title appears only seven times in the scrolls, and in only six of them is there any context to help identify who he was.[84] It is likely that he is also meant by the word הכוהן, which figures in some of the contexts where the full title is found. The following are the relevant passages.[85]

1. 1QpHab 8.8–13: Commenting on Hab 2:5-6 (an arrogant man who seizes wealth but at whom the nations will jeer): "Interpreted, this concerns the Wicked Priest who was called by the name of truth when he first arose. But when he ruled over Israel his heart became proud, and he forsook God and betrayed the precepts for the sake of riches. He robbed and amassed the riches of the men of violence who rebelled against God, and he took the wealth of the peoples, heaping sinful iniquity upon himself. And he lived in the ways of abominations amidst every unclean defilement." It may be that his being called by the name of truth at first refers to the time before Jonathan became high priest. This would make good sense of the following line: "But when he ruled over Israel . . ." The wealth acquired by the Wicked Priest could be the loot taken by Jonathan in his many battles ("he took the wealth of the peoples"), but there is also mention of what appears to be confiscation of money from others ("the men of violence"). In addition, the commentator charges him with living contrary to purity laws. This may include Jonathan's work at the temple, but

---

RevQ 17 (1996): 241–70, although he has no more concrete evidence for his position. In that article, he also argues that 4Q448 mentions Jonathan the Maccabee. It seems more likely that the text is dealing with Alexander Jannaeus, and it will be treated in the section on his reign as high priest.

82. Early proponents of this view were Geza Vermes, *Les manuscrits du désert de Juda* (Paris-Tournai: Desclée, 1953), 90–102; J. T. Milik, *Ten Years of Discovery in the Wilderness of Judaea*, SBT 26 (London: SCM, 1959), 65–69.

83. The first to offer this explanation in print appears to have been Karl Elliger, *Studien zum Habakuk-Kommentar vom Toten Meer*, BHT 15 (Tübingen: Mohr/Siebeck, 1953), 198.

84. In 4QpIsa^c (4Q163) the title appears on fragment 30 line 3, but only a few words survive and nothing besides the title on the third line.

85. Translation of Vermes, *The Complete Dead Sea Scrolls in English*, 482–85, 489–90.

it could encompass more—for example, a high priest who in battle would be in danger of corpse defilement.

2. 1QpHab 8.16—9.2: The very next comment (on Hab 2:7-8, which mentions oppression by the nations) does not use the full title but almost certainly intends the Wicked Priest: "[Interpreted, this concerns] the Priest who rebelled [and violated] the precepts [of God . . . to command] his chastisement by means of the judgements of wickedness. And they inflicted horrors of evil diseases and took vengeance upon his body of flesh." It may be that Jonathan's death at the hands of Trypho(n) is intended here, although 1 Maccabees does not refer to torture that he may have suffered while he was held prisoner.

3. 1QpHab 9.9–12 (comment on Hab 2:8b, which speaks of violence done to the inhabitants of the land): "Interpreted, this concerns the Wicked Priest whom God delivered into the hands of his enemies because of the iniquity committed against the Teacher of Righteousness and the men of his Council, that he might be humbled by means of a destroying scourge, in bitterness of soul, because he had done wickedly to His elect." Again, the language may point to the unpleasant end of Jonathan's life when he was at the mercy of his enemies.

4. 1QpHab 11.4–8 (on Hab 2:15, understood as referring to someone who makes others drink and gazes at their festivals): "Interpreted, this concerns the Wicked Priest who pursued the Teacher of Righteousness to the house of his exile that he might confuse him with his venomous fury. And at the time appointed for rest, for the Day of Atonement, he appeared before them to confuse them,[86] and to cause them to stumble on the Day of Fasting, their Sabbath of repose." In this familiar passage, it is evident that the Wicked Priest and Teacher observed the Day of Atonement at different times; that is, they had different calendars by which to date their holidays. At a time when the Teacher and his group could not defend themselves and would not have suspected trouble, the Wicked Priest attacked.

5. 1QpHab 11.12–15 (on Hab 2:16, where the cup of the Lord's wrath will be poured out on the wicked person): "Interpreted, this concerns the Priest whose ignominy was greater than his glory. For he did not circumcise the foreskin of his heart, and he walked in the ways of drunkenness that he might quench his thirst. But the cup of the wrath of God shall confuse him, multiplying his . . . and the pain of . . ." The reference to drunk-

---

86. The verb is לבלעם, which seems more graphic in meaning than "to confuse them." Its sense is "to swallow/devour them."

enness by the priest who seems to be the Wicked Priest has led some to understand the passage as pointing to Simon (1 Macc 16:11-17), Jonathan's successor, on the grounds that Simon was murdered while drunk at a dinner party, whereas there is no textual evidence of Jonathan's having a drinking problem. Little should be made of this, however, because the text may not be speaking literally; moreover, even if it is, we know nothing about the drinking habits of Jonathan, though there is no reason to think he was a teetotaler.

6. 1QpHab 12.2–10 (commenting on Hab 2:17, which alludes to violence done to Lebanon, the land, the city, and its inhabitants): "Interpreted, this concerns the Wicked Priest, inasmuch as he shall be paid the reward which he himself tendered to the Poor. For *Lebanon* is the Council of the Community; and the *beasts* are the simple of Judah who keep the Law. As he himself plotted the destruction of the Poor, so will God condemn him to destruction. And as for that which He said, *Because of the blood of the city and the violence done to the land*: interpreted, *the city* is Jerusalem where the Wicked Priest committed abominable deeds and defiled the Temple of God. *The violence done to the land*: these are the cities of Judah where he robbed the Poor of their possessions." The Wicked Priest is pictured as a violent opponent of the community, as one who took their property; he is again charged with defiling the temple.

7. 4QpPsᵃ (4Q171) 4.7–12 (a comment on Ps 37:32-33, where the wicked watches for a chance to kill the righteous, but the Lord will not abandon the latter): "Interpreted, this concerns the Wicked [Priest][87] who [watched the Teacher of Righteousness] that he might put him to death [because of the ordinance] and the law which he had sent to him. But God will not *aban[don him and will not let him be condemned when he is] tried*. And [God] will pay him his reward by delivering him into the hand of the violent of the nations, that they may execute upon him [judgement]." It is a pity that the text is so broken but the Wicked Priest is a secure reading. It is intriguing that a law was sent by someone (the Teacher, apparently) to the Wicked Priest. This, it has been suggested, may have been 4QMMT. At any rate, the Wicked Priest is again to be handed over to the "violent of the nations" as Jonathan was.

Jonathan was, then, not only the first high priest from the Hasmonean family but also the first about whose political power there can be no

---

87. The brackets are incorrectly placed in Vermes's translation, since the last two consonants of הכוהן are preserved (the ה is only partially visible).

question.[88] He already had his own army when Alexander Balas appointed him high priest, and he exercised governmental control for some ten years under titles such as general and governor of the province (see 1 Macc 10:65). Although he was high priest during those ten years, we read of no specifically priestly act that he performed.[89] If he was the Wicked Priest of the Qumran pesharim, then we know about an attempt he made to quell internal dissent and that his high priesthood did not meet with everyone's approval. Jonathan did not become the first in a hereditary line of high priests; rather, when he was killed, his office was transferred to his brother Simon.[90]

18. Simon III (142–134 BCE)

When Jonathan met his end at the hands of Trypho(n), the reins of power fell to his older and last surviving brother, Simon (see 1 Macc 13:4). We do not

---

88. After studying the terms used in the LXX for the leading priests (the word ἀρχιερεύς is rare) and contrasting this evidence with 1 Maccabees, which quite consistently uses ἀρχιερεύς for the Hasmonean high priest, Rooke suggests that this supports the inference that the word "came into use to meet the new situation under the Hasmoneans whereby the high priesthood was given to the person who already had the authority of leadership among the people as a way of defining that leadership" (Zadok's Heirs, 293). This is unlikely to be the case because ἀρχιερεύς was employed by sources such as Hecateus, the Letter of Aristeas, and the Tobiad Romance—all of which may be pre-Hasmonean in date or at least pre-First Maccabees. There was a change with the rise of the Hasmoneans, but the change does not seem to have been from a high priest with purely cultic functions to one with both cultic and governmental duties.

89. Rooke writes: "Just as the 'deliverer' and therefore the monarchic paradigm is stressed more than the 'Phinehas' paradigm for the Hasmonean rise to power, in the exercise of their office both Jonathan and his successors are portrayed more as sacral kings than as ruling priests" (Zadok's Heirs, 289). This is true insofar as 1 Maccabees dwells much more on the military, administrative sides of their positions than on the priestly aspect. But, this is a product of the nature of 1 Maccabees (and thus of Josephus's narrative that is based on it), whatever role Jonathan's (and later Simon's) high-priestly office actually played in his career and whatever contribution it made to his prestige.

90. The priestly line to which the Hasmoneans belonged is traced to Joiarib in 1 Macc 2:1, and Joiarib is the first of the twenty-four priestly groups in 1 Chr 24:7-19. The groups in 1 Chronicles 24 are divided into two, with sixteen from the line of Eleazar and eight from Ithamar (v. 5); Zadok is listed as being from Eleazar (v. 3). The chapter offers no further evidence for which of the twenty-four belonged to which line, but it is likely (two chances out of three) that Joiarib and hence the Hasmoneans were Zadokites. Also, the appeal to the zeal of Phinehas in 1 Macc 2:26, 54 could point in the same direction, as Phinehas was Eleazar's son. For these arguments, see Rooke, Zadok's Heirs, 281–82. The possibility, even the likelihood, that the Hasmoneans were Zadokites should be emphasized in opposition to the frequently repeated idea that they were non-Zadokites (see, for example, Smith, "A Study of the Zadokite High Priesthood," 107–108). They were perhaps not Oniads, but they may indeed have been Zadokites.

know why he had failed to assume leadership of the Maccabean forces at an earlier time, since he was the elder brother of both Judas and Jonathan. Moreover, in his testament, his father Mattathias had said to his sons: "'Here is your brother Simeon who, I know, is wise in counsel; always listen to him; he shall be your father'" (1 Macc 2:65). Whatever the case may have been, he became the leader in 142 BCE, while Jonathan was still alive but a captive. We know that Jonathan had sons because Simon was able to send two of them to Trypho as hostages as part of the unsuccessful negotiations to procure the release of Jonathan (1 Macc 13:15-19); but neither 1 Maccabees nor Josephus says anything about the traditional hereditary nature of the high priesthood at this point, and the fate of his sons is unknown. Rather than passing from father to son, the office passed from brother to brother, and we hear no hint that anyone in the Hasmonean camp thought it should be otherwise.

Already during the reign of Jonathan, Simon had attained high office. Jonathan had been named ruler and leader (1 Macc 9:30), but he and Simon together commanded the Maccabean forces (9:33-49, 62-65; 10:74-85; 11:64-66; 12:33-34, 38). Antiochus VI, after confirming Jonathan in the high-priestly office, appointed Simon "governor [στρατηγόν] from the Ladder of Tyre to the borders of Egypt" (11:59).[91]

While his brother languished in captivity, Simon took vigorous steps to thwart the intent of the surrounding nations to exploit Jonathan's absence. They are quoted as saying, "'They have no leader or helper. Now therefore let us make war on them and blot out the memory of them from humankind'" (1 Macc 12:53). Simon received word about an imminent invasion led by Trypho and "saw that the people were trembling with fear. So he went up to Jerusalem, and gathering the people together he encouraged them" (1 Macc 13:2-3a) with a speech about the noble exploits of his family for the nation and with a pledge to defend them in the same way his deceased brothers had. The address had the desired effect: "The spirit of the people was rekindled when they heard these words, and they answered in a loud voice, 'You are our leader [ἡγούμενος] in place of Judas and your brother Jonathan. Fight our battles, and all that you say to us we will do'" (13:7-9). At this point, nothing is said about Simon assuming the high priesthood or acting as deputy high priest for Jonathan, who was still alive.[92]

---

91. Simon had also served as a military commander in the time of Judas when he led a successful campaign into Galilee (1 Macc 5:21-23).

92. Menahem Stern, "Simon: An Independent Judaea," in his *Hasmonaean Judaea in the Hellenistic World: Chapters in Political History,* ed. D. Schwartz (Jerusalem: Zalman Shazar Center for Jewish History, 1995 [Heb.]), 74.

Simon made preparations for the inevitable military conflict (1 Macc 13:10-11) and soon had to cope with the danger posed by Trypho's invasion. Apparently, no actual battle took place as the two armies maneuvered parallel to each other, but when the Seleucid force moved northward after an unexpected snowfall, Trypho had Jonathan executed. Not long after this, Trypho also murdered Antiochus VI and made himself king (13:31-32).[93] Simon continued fortifying Judea and also appealed to Demetrius II, still a rival king, for help against Trypho (13:33-34). Demetrius responded favorably to Simon's overtures and sent yet another royal letter, one that has a surprising beginning to the address:

> King Demetrius to Simon, the high priest [ἀρχιερεῖ] and friend of kings, and to the elders and nation of the Jews, greetings. We have received the gold crown and the palm branch that you sent, and we are ready to make a general peace with you and to write to our officials to grant you release from tribute. All the grants that we have made to you remain valid, and let the strongholds that you have built be your possession. We pardon any errors and offenses committed to this day, and cancel the crown tax that you owe; and whatever other tax has been collected in Jerusalem shall be collected no longer. And if any of you are qualified to be enrolled in our bodyguard, let them be enrolled, and let there be peace between us. (13:36-40)

So the king simply addresses Simon as high priest; he does not claim to be appointing him to the post.[94] While he may not have exercised any effective control in the area, Demetrius's letter in effect freed Judea from Seleucid taxes and thus Seleucid control.[95]

Whatever may have transpired between Demetrius II and Simon, we next meet in 1 Maccabees reference to a crucial turning point in Judean history: "In the one hundred seventieth year [143–142 BCE] the yoke of the Gentiles was removed from Israel, and the people began to write in their documents and contracts, 'In the first year of Simon the great high priest and commander and

---

93. The date is October of 142 BCE (ibid., 75).

94. Compare Goldstein, *I Maccabees*, 477. He thinks the writer is covering the fact that Simon had already been installed as high priest by a large number of Jews and wants to lend legitimacy to Simon by having him royally appointed. Yet, the text does not say Demetrius II here appoints Simon. See below for further discussion of the matter.

95. Schürer writes: "With this, the political independence of Judaea was acknowledged" (*History*, 1.190). See also M. Stern, *Documents*, 124–26.

leader of the Jews'" (13:41-42).[96] Evidently, with the peace treaty negotiated with Demetrius, a new era dawned (literally), one that entailed counting years by a system other than the Seleucid era (although in 1 Maccabees, the Seleucid reckoning continues to be used).[97]

Simon followed the agreement with the conquest of Gazara (1 Macc 13:43-48), whose population he replaced with "those who observed the law" (13:48).[98] But a more significant event may have been expelling the residents from the citadel in Jerusalem and cleansing the site that had been set up at the time of Antiochus IV's decrees (1 Macc 1:33-40): "On the twenty-third day of the second month, in the one hundred seventy-first year [late 141 BCE], the Jews entered it with praise and palm branches, and with harps and cymbals and stringed instruments, and with hymns and songs, because a great enemy had been crushed and removed from Israel. Simon decreed that every year they should celebrate this day with rejoicing. He strengthened the fortifications of the temple hill alongside the citadel, and he and his men lived there" (13:51-52). So, Simon accomplished something none of his brothers had been able to do and thus removed the symbol and center of Seleucid control in Jerusalem.

A note about preparations for war between Kings Trypho and Demetrius II in the 172 S.E. (= 141–140 BCE) and the imprisonment of the latter in Parthia precedes a poem about the peace that Simon introduced (1 Macc 14:4-15). It celebrates his virtuous rule, his conquests, and the idyllic conditions that resulted—describing them in traditional language (for example, "the people sat under their own vines and fig trees, and there was none to make them afraid" [v. 12]). Simon is also praised for seeking out the Law,[99] getting rid of "all the renegades and outlaws" (v. 14), and making the sanctuary

---

96. Josephus says: "And so great was the respect of the people for Simon that in their contracts with one another, as well as in public documents, they dated them 'from the first year of Simon, the benefactor [τοῦ εὐεργέτου] and ethnarch of the Jews'" (*Ant.* 13.6, 7 [§214]).

97. See M. Stern, "Simon," 77–79.

98. John, Simon's son and the future high priest, lived in Gazara where he served as commander of his father's forces (1 Macc 13:53). It is generally agreed that 1 Maccabees is speaking about Gazara, although the manuscripts of the book read *Gaza*; Josephus gives the correct reading in *Ant.* 13.6, 7 (§215; see also 1 Macc 13:53). M. Stern deals with the significance of this conquest and also with the inscription found there that seems to be a curse on Simon ("Simon," 79–80).

99. The phrase τὸν νόμον ἐξεζήτησεν is interesting in light of the Qumran title דורש התורה; in fact, Goldstein (*I Maccabees*, 491) thinks the "author here may be attacking the sect for its opposition to the Hasmonaeans," with Simon being the real interpreter of the Law. At least, it points to a role of the high priest as one who exposits the Torah.

glorious. None of the actions for which he is lauded is specifically tied to his rank as high priest, although the Law and the sanctuary are natural associations with it.[100] Adding still more to the splendor of his name, the Romans and Spartans heard of Jonathan's death and Simon's appointments (including becoming high priest) and renewed their friendship and alliance. The author of 1 Maccabees quotes the letter the Spartans sent in response to a Jewish delegation dispatched to renew their friendship. It begins in the now customary way: "The rulers and the city of the Spartans to the high priest [ἱερεῖ μεγάλῳ][101] Simon and to the elders and the priests and the rest of the Jewish people, our brothers, greetings" (14:20). The letter ends by mentioning that a copy had been sent to the high priest [τῷ ἀρχιερεῖ] Simon (14:23). Simon also dispatched an envoy to Rome to confirm their alliance and to present a "large gold shield weighing one thousand minas," though no document is quoted in connection with the occasion (14:24; see 15:15-24).

All of this focus on Simon's accomplishments at home and abroad sets the stage for the remarkable circumstances described in 1 Macc 14:25-49.[102] In this section, the writer of 1 Maccabees tells us, among other topics, that Simon did not receive the high priesthood by genealogical succession, installation by Jewish officials, or in the first place by royal appointment; rather, he received it from *the people* (ὁ λαός [1 Macc 14:35]). A natural question to ask is whether it is possible to determine from the surviving evidence who these people were and what legal or *de facto* authority they possessed (or someone thought they possessed) to take so momentous a step. In the following pages, an effort will be made to identify the people who engaged in this remarkable act through a study of those passages in 1 Maccabees that describe Simon's rise and through an analysis of how the author uses the term ὁ λαός in these and other pericopes.

The logical starting point for the inquiry is the document in 1 Macc 14:27b-45, in which one encounters the claim that initially Simon owed his appointment as high priest to the people. Verses 25-26 provide an editorial

---

100. Rooke thinks the passage "expresses ideas which are very reminiscent of Psalm 72, another royal psalm," although the examples she lists are only generally similar (*Zadok's Heirs*, 298–300). This is all part of her argument that the Hasmonean high priests, who were a new phenomenon, are presented chiefly on the model of sacral kingship. Such ruling priests were unknown in Judea before this. We have seen some evidence that renders such a conclusion unlikely. The Hasmonean brothers were probably not the first ruling high priests, but their rule, reinforced by an army, took a more muscular form.

101. The same form is used in the Spartan letter quoted in Jonathan's missive to them in 1 Macc 12:20. See Rooke, *Zadok's Heirs*, 292.

102. This section regarding 1 Macc 14:25-49 is a slightly revised version of VanderKam, "People and High Priesthood." On this assembly, see also Sievers, *Hasmoneans*, 119–27.

introduction to what follows: "When the people [ὁ δῆμος] heard these things, they said, 'How shall we thank Simon and his sons? For he and his brothers and the house of his father have stood firm; they have fought and repulsed Israel's enemies and established its freedom.' So they made a record on bronze tablets and put it on pillars on Mount Zion." The document itself, obviously meant for public consumption, is then quoted in verses 27b-49. It records both the occasion (vv. 27b-28) and the content of a decree that was made relative to Simon. The occasion was a "great assembly" in Simon's third year as high priest (140 BCE);[103] it was attended by priests, people, rulers of the nation, and elders of the country. At that meeting, someone announced (ἐγνώρισεν) to those present ("us") the material found in verses 29-45—a document that had been composed by an unnamed group or individual. The process of ratification is described in verses 46-49: all the people agreed to it, Simon himself accepted the almost unlimited powers accorded him, and orders were given that the decree itself be placed on bronze tablets in the temple area and that copies be placed in the treasury for Simon and his sons. The decree itself takes a rather standard form:[104] a whereas-section, which explains the grounds for the honors to be granted, precedes a description of the honors given the hero. In this case, the whereas-section begins in verse 29 with the word ἐπεί and extends through verse 40; in verse 41 one finds, it seems, the beginning of the honors, although the true function of the verse has been obscured by the presence of ὅτι in nearly all witnesses to the text. That is, as the text now reads, verses 41-43 are also parts of the whereas-section. It seems likely, however, that they form the beginning of the second part of the decree.[105]

The decree first summarizes some major Maccabean accomplishments (1 Macc 14:29-34). Verse 29 quickly notes the military bravery of Simon and his brothers (Judas is never mentioned by name) on behalf of the sanctuary, law, and nation. Jonathan's career is lightly touched upon in verse 30, where three actions are noted: he gathered the nation, became high priest, and died. Then one reaches the reign of Simon, which is transparently the center of interest (verses 31-40) in the whereas-section. The decree mentions that he took command when Israel's enemies determined to invade (after Jonathan's removal) and notes that he fortified the cities of Judea, Beth Zur, Joppa, and Gazara, spending large amounts of his own money to pay his soldiers. These events can be located in the previous chapters (1 Macc 12:53—13:48),

103. The exact date in 1 Macc 14:27 is Elul 18 in S.E. 172 (Elul is the sixth month of the year). This is synchronized with Simon's third year as high priest, thus indicating that he had become high priest already in the year 142 BCE.

104. Abel, *Les livres des Maccabées*, 155.

105. See Stern, *Documents*, 132–39; and Goldstein, *I Maccabees*, 500–509.

although Simon captured Beth Zur in 11:65-66 when Jonathan was still the leader (this passage does not mention his fortifying it; compare 14:7). After these notices in verses 31-34, the decree states (v. 35): "The people [ὁ λαός] saw Simon's faithfulness and the glory that he had resolved to win for his nation, and they made him their leader and high priest, because he had done all these things and because of the justice and loyalty that he had maintained toward his nation. He sought in every way to exalt his people [τὸν λαὸν αὐτοῦ]."

The text then turns to Simon's momentous act of driving the residents of the citadel from this bastion and his refortification of the citadel and of Jerusalem itself (1 Macc 14:36-37; see 1 Macc 13:49-52). Simon's accomplishments led to his confirmation as high priest by Demetrius II and his enlistment as one of the king's Friends (vv. 38-40; compare 1 Macc 13:36-40). Here, the whereas-section concludes. The honors that follow include Simon's being leader (ἡγούμενον), high priest forever, governor (στρατηγόν), and the one in charge of the sanctuary (vv. 41-45). His position as high priest, which he had already occupied for at least two years,[106] was confirmed, according to this document, by three parties: Demetrius II (v. 38), the Jews and the priests (v. 41), and the people who ratified this decree (v. 46).

One conclusion of some importance that emerges from a study of the decree is that the accomplishments of Simon are not listed in order, or, at least, they do not appear in the same order as in the preceding narrative. A case in point arises in 1 Macc 14:35-40, where the removal of the Gentiles from the citadel is related before Demetrius's confirmation of Simon's high priesthood. In 1 Maccabees 13, the two events are reversed. Also, Gazara is listed among the cities that Simon had fortified and in which he settled Law-keeping Jews (v. 34)—an event that is presented as one of the motives why the people appointed him high priest (v. 35). However, in the narrative of 1 Maccabees, this event figures in 13:43-48—after Demetrius had confirmed Simon's investiture (13:36-40). All of this suggests that the military exploits of Simon may be arranged topically rather than in strict chronological order.[107] Other reasons for doubting the order of events in the decree will be presented below.

The essential point for the present purposes is that according to the wording of the document in 1 Macc 14:27-45, the people (ὁ λαός) were the first to install Simon in the high-priestly office. Chapter 14 provides more information about the sort of group that these people were. From it, it is apparent that the term ὁ λαός can be used in a specific sense that includes neither the entire body of people present at the assembly nor the nation as a whole. It is note-

106. That is, the assembly occurred in his third year as high priest (1 Macc 14:27).
107. See M. Stern, *Documents*, 136–37.

worthy that the writer employs the word δῆμος in verse 25 for those who wished to honor Simon on this occasion; it is also found elsewhere for the citizenry of a nation in official documents (for example, in the correspondence with the Romans and Spartans in 1 Maccabees).[108] The participants in the great assembly that conferred honors upon Simon are identified as priests, people (λαός), rulers of the nation, and elders of the country (v. 28). The facts that *the people* are distinguished from the other groups and occupy second position in the list are perhaps significant. In order to define more exactly who these people were and what authority they had or claimed, it would be helpful if the account about the occasion when they made Simon high priest could be located.

Although the solemn decree in 1 Macc 14:27b-45 unambiguously names the people as the party that was originally responsible for Simon's investiture as high priest, the preceding narratives that deal with Simon contain no passage in which the author explicitly describes the time when the people made their appointment. When one bears in mind the importance of the office—far and away the highest in the land—and the status of Simon in 1 Maccabees (2:65; 5:17, 20-23; 11:59, 64-65; 12:33; and so forth), it seems unlikely that the writer would have left the event unrecorded. It is plausible, though, to suppose that he did narrate the occasion but that, for whatever reason(s), he declined to mention the high priesthood at that particular stage in Simon's rise.[109] After all, as noted earlier, the manner in which he acquired the office deviated in some respects from the normal procedure. According to the decree of 1 Macc 14:27-45, the people's appointment of Simon preceded royal *confirmation* (ἔστησεν), and 1 Macc 13:36-40 indicates that their action must also have antedated Demetrius's letter to Simon, since in it the king, without comment, calls Simon "high priest" (v. 36). First Maccabees 13:41-42 then adds that in 170 s.e. (= 142 BCE) "the people [ὁ λαός] began to write as the dating formula in bills and contracts, 'In the first year, under Simon, high priest, commander, and chief of the Jews'" (v. 42). All of this entails that Simon became high priest at the very beginning of his period of leadership, probably not after every one of the accomplishments listed at the beginning of the decree. That the assembly met in his third year as high priest confirms the point.

The sequence within the decree itself (if it is chronological in this case) and the order in the preceding narratives strongly favor the thesis that the people appointed Simon as high priest at the meeting described in 1 Macc 13:1-9. It is worthwhile to study the larger context of this pericope because it is crucial for identifying who the people of 1 Macc 13:1-9 were. The preceding chapter

108. Goldstein, *I Maccabees*, 500.
109. Compare ibid., 476–77.

relates the events that led to Trypho's deceptive capture of Jonathan. When
Jonathan came to meet this Seleucid general with some forty-thousand troops
(1 Macc 12:41, 46; compare *Ant.* 13.6, 1 [§190]), Tryphon asked, "Why did you
put all these people [πάντα τὸν λαὸν τοῦτον] to so much trouble when we are
not at war?" (1 Macc 12:44). Jonathan dismissed all but one thousand of his
men. He was then promptly seized and the one thousand remaining soldiers
were executed (vv. 46-48). Next, Tryphon dispatched units of his troops whose
assignment was to take the two thousand soldiers of Jonathan's army who had
been left in Galilee, but the Jewish soldiers managed to elude them and return
to Judea where they mourned for Jonathan and the one thousand who had
perished in Ptolemais (vv. 49-52). One then reads the enthusiastic words that
the author places on the lips of the hostile neighboring forces: "They have no
leader or helper. Now, therefore, let us make war on them and blot out the
memory of them from humankind" (1 Macc 12:53b). This is the situation,
incidentally, that is mentioned at the beginning of the decree in 1 Maccabees
14. The anti-Seleucid elements in Judea were thrown into a worse quandary
when they heard that Trypho was assembling a large force intending "to
invade the land of Judah and destroy it" (1 Macc 13:1b; compare v. 12). The
story about the meeting in question at which Simon addressed the people then
follows immediately.

The context indicates, therefore, that the people whom Simon rallied at
the Jerusalem gathering described in 1 Macc 13:1-9 were those members of the
Maccabean forces who had escaped to Judah. As noted above, Jonathan's army
had been called *the people* (1 Macc 12:44), and the crowd of 13:1-9 is also
called *the people*: "he saw that the people [τὸν λαόν] were trembling with fear.
So he [Simon] went up to Jerusalem, and gathering the people [τὸν λαόν]
together he encouraged them" (13:2-3a). He managed to revive their fainting
spirits by recalling the singular contributions that his family had made to their
welfare. As the last of them, he, too, was willing to sacrifice himself for the
cause of the nation and sanctuary. The people [τοῦ λαοῦ, v. 7] then took heart
from his words and exclaimed, "You are our leader [ἡγούμενος] in place of
Judas and your brother Jonathan. Fight our battles, and all that you say to us
we will do" (1 Macc 13:8b-9). It should be added that the title ἡγούμενος specified here is the very one that is given in 1 Macc 14:35 with ἀρχιερέα as an
office or honor that the people had originally bestowed upon Simon. This provides extra support for the thesis that 1 Macc 13:1-9 depicts the occasion when
Simon became high priest, though the author fails to mention the title.

It seems likely, then, that the people appointed Simon their leader and
high priest at the assembly described in 1 Macc 13:1-9 and that the people
there were the remnants of the Maccabean army that had been under

Jonathan's command. The language of these people in 1 Macc 13:8b-9 lends added force to the argument that Hasmonean troops were the ones who first gave Simon his offices. Their exclamation echoes the words of Judas's military companions who had, some years before, appointed Jonathan to succeed his fallen brother (Judas's death is related in 1 Macc 9:18):

1 Macc 9:30: Now therefore we have chosen you today to take his place as our ruler [ἄρχοντα] and leader [ἡγούμενον], to fight our battle.

1 Macc 13:8b-9a: You are our leader [ἡγούμενος] in place of Judas and your brother Jonathan. Fight our battles . . .

The context of 1 Macc 9:30 shows that the group that passed along the Maccabean mantle did not consist of all anti-Seleucid Judeans but only of Judas's friends who were in need of a new general (1 Macc 9:28-29). Similarly, it is most likely that the people of 1 Macc 13:1-9 who designated Simon as Jonathan's successor were the Maccabean party and more specifically the Hasmonean army. The people were neither all the residents of Jerusalem nor even all its anti-Seleucid inhabitants. They were Hasmonean soldiers.

These are not the only passages in 1 Maccabees in which the potentially very general term ὁ λαός has the specific meaning *soldiers*. Before turning to some of them, it should be noted that λαός at times clearly has its familiar inclusive sense (for example, 1 Macc 14:46); but, there is a series of cases (besides those mentioned above) in which it must have a more restricted referent. For example, 1 Macc 3:55 says that Judas appointed commanders of thousands, hundreds, fifties, and tens over the people (τοῦ λαοῦ); 5:43 relates that Judas and all the people (πᾶς ὁ λαός), during a military campaign, swam across a river—hardly an exercise for an entire populace of men, women, and children but one that would be feasible for an army. Other instances include: 1 Macc 5:61, which designates the defeated troops of the subordinate officers Joseph and Azariah *the people* (ἐν τῷ λαῷ); 6:19-20, which reports that all the people (πάντα τὸν λαόν) laid siege to the citadel; and 7:6, in which the high priest Alcimus, in the course of bringing charges against Judas and his band, denounced the people (τοῦ λαοῦ) to the king (compare also 7:26, 48; 10:7, 46).

The practice of calling an army *the people* has a long history both in Greek and Hebrew sources. Homer uses the term frequently in the Iliad "specifically for the army, the soldiers, especially in distinction from their leaders"—a usage that later disappears from Greek texts.[110] In the Hebrew Bible, military

---

110. Herrmann Strathmann, with R. Meyer, "λαός," in *TDNT* 4.30.

units are often labeled הָעָם,[111] and presumably this word appeared in the Hebrew original of 1 Maccabees wherever ὁ λαός in its various forms now stands. Good examples can be found in many biblical war stories. In Josh 6:3-5, Joshua receives battle instructions from the Lord:

> You shall march around the city, all the warriors circling the city once. Thus shall you do for six days, with seven priests bearing seven trumpets of rams' horns before the ark. On the seventh day you shall march around the city seven times, the priests blowing the trumpets. And when they make a long blast with the ram's horn, as soon as you hear the sound of the trumpet, then all the people [הָעָם = ὁ λαός in the LXX] shall shout with a great shout; and the wall of the city will fall down flat, and all the people [הָעָם = ὁ λαός] shall charge straight ahead (see also vv. 7, 8, 10, 20; 8:1, 5, 10-11, 14, 16, 20; 10:21, 33; 1 Sam 30:21).

Second Samuel 1:4 should also be quoted: "'The army [הָעָם] fled from the battle, but also many of the army [הָעָם] fell and died." This list of passages is merely illustrative, not exhaustive.

If one may, therefore, conclude that the people of 1 Macc 13:1-9 were the remnants of Jonathan's army and that they named Simon high priest in his brother's stead, then some new light is shed on the great assembly in chapter 14. The people, that is, the Maccabean army, conferred the high priesthood on Simon as part of the general transfer of Jonathan's authority—a procedure that they had effected earlier when Jonathan had succeeded Judas. The situation was more complicated in the present case, though, because Jonathan had acquired the high-priestly office after taking over the leadership of the Maccabean forces. It may be that the appointment of Simon by the people was provisional—perhaps a temporary measure, depending on Jonathan's fate (his death is reported later, in 13:23). There were precedents in the Second-Temple period, as we have seen, for a brother or another relative of a high priest to assume the office temporarily under special circumstances. For instance, 2 Macc 4:29 reports that Menelaus, when he had to be away from Jerusalem, left his brother Lysimachus as his substitute (see below).

If this was the nature of Simon's appointment in 142 BCE, it would have required confirmation later from other power groups in order to make it appear fully legitimate. But, his soldiers were the first body to recognize him as cultic chief, and they were the ones who began, after Jonathan's death was

---

111. Liver, "עם," אנציקלופדיה מקראית (vol. 6; Jerusalem: Bialik, 1971), 237–38.

confirmed (1 Macc 13:25), to write on contracts: "In the first year of Simon the great high priest and commander and leader of the Jews" (1 Macc 13:42b). By this time, Simon had been recognized as high priest by the Seleucid monarch Demetrius II, as the greeting in his letter to Simon shows (1 Macc 13:36). Confirmation and elaboration of Simon's positions were subsequently given by Jewish authorities as well and approved by the δῆμος in the events of chapter 14 (v. 25). At that meeting, the high-priestly office was made Simon's in perpetuity—that is, the succession reverted to the traditional hereditary form (Simon was the last surviving son of Mattathias). The Hasmonean family had thus replaced the Oniad line as the high-priestly clan.

If Simon did, in fact, first gain recognition as high priest at the meeting with Jonathan's terrified soldiers (1 Macc 13:1-9), why did the author of 1 Maccabees fail to mention the office in his account? Simon was his hero, and one would think that he would have been delighted to write that, immediately after Jonathan's removal, the people made him the heir of all his brother's positions. The writer does not, of course, explain his omission, but some suggestions can be made. He would have wished to avoid giving the impression that there was anything illegal about Simon's assumption of the high priesthood. Since the high priest in Jerusalem was a notable official in the Seleucid realm, it was necessary that the king make the appointment even if his act meant no more than that he set his seal of approval on the result of a legal Jewish process of nomination. It would not have been proper—or at least not traditional—for an army to usurp the king's right to appoint a high priest. This may have been one reason why the author does not name the high priesthood in 1 Macc 13:1-9. Rather, he allows Demetrius II to be the first person in his narrative to address Simon as high priest (1 Macc 13:36). In this way, Simon's investiture receives royal legitimation.[112]

While this and perhaps other factors may have motivated the author not to mention the high priesthood in 1 Macc 13:1-9, he did not remove from his book all traces of Simon's earlier elevation. He used as a source the document now found in 1 Macc 14:29-45 and did not alter it significantly, perhaps because of its official character. It did include a reference to Simon's appointment as high priest by the people, but perhaps it was thought that the note could safely be left at this later point in the book, whereas it would have raised uncomfortable questions if it had appeared at the beginning of chapter 13. One possibly unintended result of using the word λαός for the group that first

---

112. See Goldstein, who argues that the author of 1 Maccabees omitted Simon's earlier appointment by the people "to conceal Simon's and the Jews' desertion of Antiochus VI's cause" (*I Maccabees*, 476–77).

made Simon high priest was that, to later readers, he appeared to have been chosen high priest by popular acclaim. Josephus understood the passage in this sense. He does not reproduce the decree of chapter 14, but in his paraphrase of 1 Macc 13:1-9 he writes: "Thereupon Simon, seeing that the people of Jerusalem [τοὺς Ἱεροσολυμίτας] were dismayed at these happenings . . . , called the people [τὸν δῆμον] together in the temple" (Ant. 13.6, 3 [§197]). Later, when summarizing the end of 1 Maccabees 13, he observes: "And Simon, after being chosen high priest by the populace [τοῦ πλήθους] . . ." (Ant. 13.6, 7 [§213]).

According to 1 Maccabees 14, then, Simon held the following positions:

- high priest forever (v. 41)
- leader (ἡγούμενος, vv. 35, 41)
- governor (στρατηγός, v. 42)
- ethnarch (14:47; see vv. 41-44)
- protector (τοῦ προστατῆσαι, v. 47) in charge of the country and sanctuary, including appointing officials over both (v. 42).

It adds that all were to obey him, that all contracts should be written in his name, and that he should wear purple and gold (vv. 41-44). The stated need for all to obey him raises the suspicion that there was some opposition to Simon's elevation. First Maccabees 14:44-45 confirms the suspicions: "None of the people or priests shall be permitted to nullify any of these decisions or to oppose what he says, or to convene an assembly in the country without his permission, or to be clothed in purple or put on a gold buckle. Whoever acts contrary to these decisions or rejects any of them shall be liable to punishment."[113] The Maccabean triumph seems to be complete with Simon's success, but there is reason to think not everyone shared the author's enthusiasm for the new situation.[114]

---

113. Some scholars consider Simon the Wicked Priest of the Qumran pesharim (for example, Frank Moore Cross, *The Ancient Library of Qumran*, 3rd rev. ed. [Sheffield: Sheffield Academic, 1995], 101–20). Cross had defended this view already in the first edition of the book which appeared in 1958. Walter Franklin Smith ("A Study of the Zadokite High Priesthood within the Graeco-Roman Age: From Simeon the Just to the High Priests Appointed by Herod the Great" [Ph.D. diss., Cambridge: Harvard University, 1961], 109–62) provides a lengthy defense for the idea that Simon's permanent removal of the Zadokite high priesthood as depicted in 1 Maccabees 14 is the event that precipitated the exile of the Qumran Essenes and their opposition to the Hasmonean high priests. He also maintains that Simon was the Wicked Priest. While that identification seems less likely, with Jonathan being the more probable candidate, we should recall that Simon is mentioned directly after Jonathan in 4Q245 i 10 in a list of high priests.

114. See Sievers, *Hasmoneans*, 124–27, 133–34.

Almost all of 1 Maccabees 15–16 is devoted to the few years of Simon's rule as supreme leader. His position continued to be influenced by events in the Seleucid Empire, where dynastic struggles further weakened its already fading power. Another Antiochus, this one the younger brother of Demetrius II, wrote to Simon seeking his support as part of his preparations to invade and take over the Seleucid crown (15:2-9).[115] Antiochus's letter begins: "King Antiochus to Simon the priest[116] and ethnarch and to the nation of the Jews, greeting" (15:2). The future Antiochus VII Sidetes (138–129 BCE), like his predecessors, made sweeping grants to the Jewish people and confirmed previous ones. Besides remission of taxes (again), he permitted freedom to Jerusalem and the temple and recognized Simon's right to control the fortresses he had built. A new provision is: "I permit you to mint your own coinage as money for your country" (15:6). There is no evidence that Simon ever acted upon this important grant; it appears that his son John Hyrcanus was the first Hasmonean to mint coins.[117]

At some point in 138 BCE or later (see 1 Macc 15:10), the envoys whom Simon had sent to Rome returned with letters to the kings and countries in the area. The Roman letter acknowledged that the messengers had been sent by the high priest Simon, accepted the gift they had presented, and ordered that no one in the area harm the Jewish people. It added: "Therefore if any scoundrels have fled to you from their country, hand them over to the high priest Simon, so that he may punish them according to their law" (1 Macc 15:21). Again we have mention of opposition to Simon. Simon himself received a copy of the Roman letter.

First Maccabees relates that, during the struggle between Antiochus VII and Trypho, Simon sent Antiochus two thousand troops, money, and equipment, but the aspirant to the throne, for unclear reasons, refused them "and broke all the agreements he formerly had made with Simon, and became estranged from him" (15:27).[118] The cooling of relations led to a threat issued

---

115. For the background, see M. Stern, "Simon: An Independent Judaea," 81–82. Antiochus, who was not yet in Seleucid territory, may already have gained Roman support.

116. The form of the title (ἱερεῖ alone) is surprising in 1 Maccabees.

117. See Ya'akov Meshorer, *A Treasury of Jewish Coins from the Persian Period to Bar-Kochba* (Jerusalem: Yitzhak ben-Zvi, 1997), 29–31 (Hebrew).

118. Josephus reports the event differently, claiming that because of the money and provisions Simon provided to Antiochus's men, "for a short while he was considered one of his closest friends" (*Ant.* 13.7, 2 [§224]). But at this point, 1 Maccabees is no longer Josephus's source. M. Stern ties the king's change of policy to his greater sense of security now that Trypho had been deprived of most of the kingdom. At that point, an independent Judah became undesirable ("Simon," 83–84).

by the royal Friend Athenobius to Simon: he was either to hand over to the king the cities of Joppa and Gazara and the Jerusalem citadel along with their tribute (the king considered them his cities) or else to pay one thousand talents of silver to cover the costs of damage and lost revenue (15:28-31). When Athenobius delivered the ultimatum to Simon in Jerusalem, he was stunned at Simon's magnificence. Simon defended the justice of his taking possession of the disputed cities but did offer as a compromise to pay one hundred talents for Joppa and Gazara. Neither Athenobius nor Antiochus was amused and a Seleucid invasion of Judea led by Cendebeus ensued (15:32-41).

When his son John reported the invasion to his father, Simon summoned his two oldest sons (Judas and John) and gave them an assignment: "'My brothers and I and my father's house have fought the wars of Israel from our youth until this day, and things have prospered in our hands so that we have delivered Israel many times. But now I have grown old, and you by Heaven's mercy are mature in years. Take my place and my brother's, and go out and fight for our nation, and may the help that comes from Heaven be with you'" (1 Macc 16:2b-3). From Simon's words, we learn not only that he considered himself too advanced in years to lead the army[119] but also that Judas may have been his oldest son, though John was the military commander (see 13:53). Judas was, however, soon to die and thus did not have a chance to succeed his father. We are told that John led the troops and his cavalry (the first mention of cavalry in a Maccabean force) to victory over Cendebeus, his infantry, and his cavalry in a battle near Modein, the city of the Hasmoneans; in the fighting his brother Judas was wounded (16:4-10).

Simon's death is the subject of 1 Macc 16:11-17. The villain was a certain Ptolemy son of Abubus who had married a daughter of Simon and was governor in the district of Jericho. The writer describes him in an interesting way: "he had a large store of silver and gold, for he was son-in-law of the high priest" (16:11b-12). A motive is also attributed to him: "His heart was lifted up; he determined to get control of the country, and made treacherous plans

---

119. Josephus says something quite different: "But Simon, when he heard of Antiochus's lawless conduct, and though he was now an old man, nevertheless was aroused by the unjust treatment he had received from Antiochus, and being filled with a spirit stronger than his years, took command in the war like a young man" (*Ant.* 13.7, 3 [§226]). In the next line, he has Simon leading a different contingent of troops than the ones commanded by his sons. He says much the same in his summary section about Simon in *J.W.* 1.2, 2 (§§50–53). There, he adds that Simon, "after a brilliant victory was appointed high-priest and liberated the Jews from the Macedonian supremacy which had lasted for 170 years" (§53). It is strange that he should say Simon received the high priesthood after the victory over Cendebeus. His narrative shows by referring to the liberation that he is not being chronological in his report about Simon's days, but he does seem to tie the high priesthood to the campaign mentioned in 1 Macc 16:1-10.

against Simon and his sons, to do away with them" (16:13). As Simon was touring the area (this time with his sons Mattathias and Judas) and attending to the needs of the towns, he included Jericho in his circuit. There, Ptolemy entertained him in his stronghold named Dok where he planned to carry out his plot at a banquet. "When Simon and his sons were drunk, Ptolemy and his men rose up, took their weapons, rushed in against Simon in the banquet hall and killed him and his two sons, as well as some of his servants" (16:16).[120] The arrival of Simon and his sons in Jericho is dated to the eleventh month of the year 177 s.e., that is, in 134 bce (16:14).

Ptolemy hoped to secure both military help and control of the land from Antiochus VII, who may have supported his efforts;[121] he also sent forces to take Simon's son John and to capture Jerusalem and the temple precinct. However, someone managed to warn John of the planned assassination, and he was able to execute the people whom Ptolemy had sent to kill him in Gazara (1 Macc 16:18-22). The final two verses of 1 Maccabees provide a summary statement about the reign of this John as high priest (16:23-24).

With Simon's death in the month Shebat in the year 134 bce (after a reign of eight years, *Ant.* 13.7, 4 [§228]),[122] the last of Mattathias's remarkable sons passed from the scene. The hereditary principle, which had lain dormant since Onias III succeeded Simon II, now reasserted itself when his son John became the next high priest. Although he had been high priest of the nation for eight years, no text records a single priestly act that Simon performed while holding the office—true to the nature of 1 Maccabees, our primary source.

At the death of Simon III in 134 bce, the high priesthood once again became a hereditary office and continued to be a family possession (with a two-year gap from 37–35 bce) until 35 bce when King Herod had the last Hasmonean high priest, Aristobulus III, executed.

19. John Hyrcanus (134–104 bce)

Simon's son John became high priest after the murder of his father, and he enjoyed one of the longest high-priestly tenures of any member of the family. We have three narrative sources for events in his reign: 1 Maccabees, which

---

120. Josephus says that Simon was killed but that Ptolemy then imprisoned Simon's wife and two sons (*Ant.* 13.7, 4 [§228]).

121. M. Stern, "Simon," 86–87. Ptolemy wrote a report to the king directly after the murders (1 Macc 16:18).

122. In *Ant.* 20.10, 3 (§240) Josephus writes: "he held the high priesthood one year longer than his brother." Josephus had assigned Jonathan a reign of only seven years.

mentions him several times during his father's high priesthood,[123] deals briefly with his career after Simon's death (16:18-24); and *J.W.* 1.2, 3 (§54) to 1.2, 8 (§69) and *Ant.* 13.7, 4 (§228) to 13.10, 7 (§300) contain extended sections about him.[124] To these literary sources we may add numismatic evidence, since he now appears to have been the first Hasmonean ruler to mint coins bearing his name, and the Qumran scrolls, which probably contain a few references to him. He also figures in the Mishnah and Talmuds, and we will deal with those references as well.[125]

The three narrative sources, which relate the end of Simon's life at the hands of his son-in-law Ptolemy, all agree that John, who is called *Hyrcanus* only by Josephus, was not present at the stronghold of Dok where the assassination took place. John was with his troops at Gazara (= Gezer), and to that city Ptolemy sent men to kill him (1 Macc 16:19; *J.W.* 1.2, 3 [§54]; *Ant.* 13.7, 4 [§228]). In both of his books, Josephus calls John the third son of Simon. His intent may have been merely to distinguish him in this way from the other two (Mattathias and Judas) who met their end at Ptolemy's hands (either at the same time as Simon [1 Macc 16:16] or later [*J.W.* 1.2, 4 (§60); *Ant.* 13.8, 1 (§235)]) and not to indicate that he was the youngest. In fact, 1 Macc 16:2 refers to Judas and John as Simon's "two eldest sons."

Ptolemy's plan included not only eliminating Simon's family but also taking Jerusalem and the temple precinct.[126] John escaped the attempt on his life

---

123. See 1 Macc 13:53 where his father made him "commander of all the forces; and he lived at Gazara [= Gezer]"; 16:1-10 where he leads the troops to victory over Antiochus VII's general Cendebeus.

124. Steve Mason estimates that in *Antiquities* Josephus, who uses *War* as a source, "stretches it into a narrative that is about six times as long. . . . Where *Ant.* parallels *War*, the reproduction is more or less exact with respect to content but the formulation is new" (*Flavius Josephus on the Pharisees: A Composition-Critical Study,* StPB 39 [Leiden: Brill, 1991], 214). For a list of sources used and possibly used, see Clemens Thoma, "John Hyrcanus I as Seen by Josephus and Other Early Jewish Sources," in *Josephus and the History of the Greco-Roman Period: Essays in Memory of Morton Smith,* ed. F. Parente and J. Sievers, StPB 41 (Leiden: Brill, 1994), 131.

125. Although it does not mention John Hyrcanus, the letter preserved in 2 Macc 1:1-9 is dated to 188 S.E., that is, 124 BCE, a date in Hyrcanus's reign. It is a letter from the "Jews in Jerusalem and those in the land of Judea, To their Jewish kindred in Egypt" (1:1), and it urges them to keep "the festival of booths in the month of Chislev" (1:9), that is, Hanukkah. If authentic, the letter would be a witness to relations between Judea and the Egyptian Diaspora during the reign of Hyrcanus. It is possible that it contains a veiled warning to the Egyptian Jews about the Oniad temple there, as E. J. Bickermann argued, although he did not regard this as certain ("Ein jüdischer Festbrief vom Jahre 124 v. Chr. [II Macc 1 1-9]," *ZNW* 32 [1933]: 233–54, especially 249–52). On it, see also Goldstein, *II Maccabees,* 137–53.

126. There is no evidence that Ptolemy was himself a priest and that he aspired to the high priesthood. First Maccabees 16:11-13 says only that he was "governor over the plain of Jericho,"

because he was warned about it, and he is reported to have killed his would-be assassins (1 Macc 16:22), although Josephus says only that he escaped. At this point, for reasons that are not clear, 1 Maccabees ends with a summary statement whose wording may imply that the book itself was completed during Hyrcanus's pontificate: "The rest of the acts of John and his wars and the brave deeds that he did, and the building of the walls that he completed, and his achievements, are written in the annals of his high-priesthood [βιβλίῳ ἡμερῶν ἀρχιερωσύνης αὐτοῦ], from the time that he became high priest after his father" (1 Macc 16:23-24). From these formulaic, biblically shaped lines, we learn that there was an official written record of Hyrcanus's reign as high priest.[127]

Josephus becomes the only narrative source for the reign of Hyrcanus once 1 Maccabees ends. Although at this stage he still refers to John as a "youth [νεανίσκος]" (*J.W.* 1.2, 3 [§55]; *Ant.* 13.7, 4 [§229]), he seems to have been a resourceful young man. Josephus's story about John's first days as high priest, unlike the accounts of his predecessors' careers, contains a reference to a priestly act that he performed.

> This youth, forewarned of their approach, hastened to reach the city [Jerusalem], fully confident of the people's [τῷ λαῷ] support, both from their recollection of his father's achievements and their hatred of Ptolemy's enormities [παρανομίας].[128] Ptolemy also rushed to gain entrance by another gate, but was repelled by the populace [τοῦ δήμου], who had with alacrity already admitted Hyrcanus. Ptolemy forthwith withdrew to one of the fortresses above Jericho, called Dagon; while Hyrcanus, having gained the high priestly office held by his father before him, offered sacrifice[129] to God and then started in haste after Ptolemy to bring aid to his mother and brethren. (*J.W.* 1.2, 3 [§§55–56]; *Ant.* 13.7, 4 [§229] to 13.8, 1 [§230] is very similar)

John attempted to rescue his imprisoned family members but was forced to withdraw when Ptolemy tortured them as he looked on helplessly. Moreover,

---

was rich since he was the high priest's son-in-law, and that he wanted to take control of the country.

127. See Abel, *Les livres des Maccabées*, xxvi–xxvii, 283.

128. Crossmann Werner notes that John's popularity had also been secured by his military achievements during his father's reign (*Johann Hyrkan: Ein Beitrag zur Geschichte Judäas im zweiten vorchristlichen Jahrhundert* [Wernigerode: Angersteins, 1877], 10).

129. *Ant.* 13.8, 1 (§230) says he "propitiated God with sacrifices." Werner thinks he presented the sacrifice required by Leviticus 8–9 for a new high priest (*Johann Hyrkan*, 23–24).

a sabbatical year arrived at that time, as Josephus reports.[130] Hyrcanus apparently lifted the siege under these circumstances, despite his mother's brave protests, but Ptolemy executed his mother and brothers anyway (*J.W.* 1.2, 4 [§§57–60]; *Ant.* 13.8, 1 [§§230–35]). Josephus stresses the strong feeling of empathy experienced by Hyrcanus as he saw his mother terribly misused.

John's failure to rescue his mother and brothers preceded more difficulties for the young high priest. The next event recorded by Josephus is the devastating invasion by Antiochus VII Sidetes.[131] The military campaign is not directly pertinent to his high priesthood apart from the fact that in *Antiquities* the historian gives a precise date for the invasion and synchronizes it with the first year of Hyrcanus's reign. The event obviously transpired early in John's tenure in office because Antiochus was still responding to Simon's actions against him. The invasion occurred "in the fourth year of his [Antiochus's] reign and the first of Hyrcanus' rule, in the hundred and sixty-second Olympiad" (*Ant.* 13.8, 2 [§236]). Antiochus became king in 138 BCE and Hyrcanus began to rule in 134 BCE, but Olympiad 162 corresponded with the years 132–129 BCE.[132] It does not seem possible to reconcile the regnal years with the Olympiad reference; the Olympiad number, in view of the year in the reigns of the two leaders and other factors in Antiochus's career, is probably incorrect.[133]

---

130. The reference to a sabbatical year has stimulated debate for two reasons. One is chronological, the other concerns legislation for the seventh year. On the chronological front, there are references to two sabbatical years in the sources for this period: 1 Macc 6:49, 53 (during the short reign of Antiochus V [164–162 BCE]); and the present one. The exact year of the former one is not certain. It would make good sense of the chronology if the sabbatical year early in Hyrcanus's reign began in the latter part of 134 BCE; if so, the one in 1 Macc 6:49, 53 fell in 162 BCE. On the evidence for the sabbatical cycles, see Ben Zion Wacholder, "The Calendar of Sabbatical Cycles during the Second Temple and the Early Rabbinic Period," *HUCA* 44 (1973): 153–96; reprinted in his *Essays on Jewish Chronology and Chronography* [New York: Ktav, 1976], 1–44). As for the legislation, Sievers notes that Josephus "supposed that in a sabbatical year *all* work was prohibited 'as on the sabbath days.' Hence he concluded that the advent of the sabbatical year prevented Hyrcanus from continuing the siege. But no such prohibition is known to biblical or rabbinic law. Furthermore, there is no evidence that fighting was ever suspended during the sabbatical year" (*Hasmoneans*, 135–36 n. 3). See also Werner, *Johann Hyrkan*, 25; he notes the problems and suggests that, besides concern for the welfare of his captive family members, John withdrew in anticipation of a retaliatory attack by Antiochus VII.

131. Ptolemy, the assassin of Simon, was allied with Antiochus VII or at least sought his assistance (1 Macc 16:18); see Werner, *Johann Hyrkan*, 10–11. Whether this request for help bore any relation to the invasion is not known, but he does seem to offer the king what he had demanded from Simon in 1 Macc 15:30-31. On the textual problems in 16:18, see Goldstein, *I Maccabees*, 525–26.

132. See Marcus, *Josephus* 7, 346–47 n. c; Schürer, *History of the Jewish People*, 1.608; and E. J. Bickerman, *Chronology of the Ancient World*, 2nd ed., AGRL (Ithaca, N.Y.: Cornell Univ. Press, 1968), 119.

133. Schürer offers an extended discussion and adduces and analyzes the relevant sources

In *War,* Josephus gives only a swift summary of Antiochus's victory over John. He writes that John robbed the valuables from King David's tomb and with them bribed Antiochus to end the siege of Jerusalem (1.2, 5 [§61]). He also records in the same passage that John, with the surplus from David's tomb, paid "a mercenary force, being the first Jew to start this practice" (see also *Ant.* 13.8, 4 [§249] and compare 7.15, 3 [§393]).

The war with Antiochus occupies far more space in the *Antiquities,* which describes in detail the straits to which Antiochus reduced his Judean foes. There, Josephus says that the Seleucid king not only ravaged the country but also besieged Jerusalem and constructed one hundred manned towers on its north side. To enforce the siege his men dug a ditch to keep Jerusalem's residents from fleeing. Under these circumstances, Hyrcanus, when he saw that the large number of people in the city exhausted the scant supplies too quickly, "separated from the rest those who were useless, and drove them out, and retained only those who were in the prime of life and able to fight" (*Ant.* 13.8, 2 [§240]). The ones expelled endured terrible sufferings, ended only by some extraordinary events related to a holiday: "the festival of Tabernacles came round," at which point the people in the city took back the wretches caught between the lines. "And Hyrcanus sent to Antiochus, requesting a truce of seven days on account of the festival, which Antiochus, deferring to his piety toward the Deity, granted and moreover sent a magnificent sacrifice, consisting of bulls with gilded horns and cups of gold and silver filled with all kinds of spices" (13.8, 2 [§242]). The historian contrasts this act of Antiochus VII with the behavior of Antiochus IV and says this was why all called him *Eusebes* (§§243–44). The incident will not be the only example of Antiochus VII's piety in Josephus's history.

The Seleucid monarch's reaction to the festival induced Hyrcanus to "request that he restore to the Jews their native form of government" (13.8, 3 [§245]). Antiochus offered a truce, with the conditions being that the Jews "hand over their arms, pay tribute to him for Joppa [compare 1 Macc 15:28, 35] and the other cities bordering on Judaea, and receive a garrison" (§246). That is, he demanded what he had earlier required from Simon (1 Macc 15:28-31). In contrast to the response from Simon, this time the Jews agreed to the demands but objected to another garrison in Jerusalem "since they did not come into contact with other peoples because of their separateness [ἀμιξίαν]" (§247). The two sides came to an agreement that the Jews would pay five hundred silver talents and deliver hostages (instead of accepting a garrison),

---

(*History,* 1.202–3 n. 5). See also Werner, who changes the ordinal so that Josephus would be referring to Olympiad 161, not 162 (*Johann Hyrkan,* 18). Werner also thinks John's reign began in 135 BCE.

including one of Hyrcanus's brothers. As a precaution, Antiochus ordered that the city walls be dismantled.[134]

The sequence of the events that followed is not entirely clear, but at some point Hyrcanus entertained Antiochus and his troops on a lavish scale in Jerusalem (*Ant.* 13.8, 4 [§§249–50]). This would be most unexpected, if the siege that had produced food shortages had just been lifted.[135] *Antiquities* gives the impression that this happened after Antiochus withdrew and mentions it just before noting that Hyrcanus accompanied the Seleucid king on his Parthian campaign, which began perhaps several years later (130 BCE). So, a different occasion may be in view. At any rate, in both *War* and *Antiquities,* we read about Hyrcanus's opening of David's tomb in this context: in *War* part of the treasure was used to bribe Antiochus to raise the siege, part to pay mercenaries (1.2, 5 [§61]); in *Antiquities* (in this passage) only the mercenaries are paid from it (13.8, 4 [§249], but see 7.15, 3 [§393]).

In whatever way all of this may have happened, Antiochus and Hyrcanus became allies, and the Jewish high priest took part in the great campaign that Antiochus led against the Parthians. Their collaboration provided the second occasion on which Antiochus demonstrated his respect for Jewish religious customs and another opportunity for us to see John Hyrcanus himself observing a festival. The sources have left an impressive picture of the vast host that

---

134. The meaning seems to be that the walls themselves, not just the tops of them, were destroyed, despite Josephus's use of the term τὴν στεφάνην. See Schürer, *History of the Jewish People,* 204 n. 6; Marcus, *Josephus* 7, 352 n. b. First Maccabees 16:23 lists rebuilding the walls as one of John's great achievements. Diodorus refers to Antiochus VII's siege of Jerusalem in his *Library of History* 34—35.1, 1–5: "the Jews held out for a time, but when all their supplies were exhausted they found themselves compelled to make overtures for a cessation of hostilities. Now the majority of his friends advised the king to take the city by storm and to wipe out completely the race of Jews, since they alone of all nations avoid dealings with any other people and look upon all men as their enemies." After his advisors refer to what they take to be the history of the Jews and also mention the time Antiochus IV entered the Holy of Holies, what he found there and what punitive measures he took as a result (including forcing the high priest to eat pork), the historian continues: "Rehearsing all these events, his friends strongly urged Antiochus to make an end of the race completely, or, failing that, to abolish their laws and force them to change their ways. But the king, being a magnanimous and mild-mannered person, took hostages but dismissed the charges against the Jews, once he had exacted the tribute that was due and dismantled the walls" (Francis R. Walton, *Diodorus* 12, LCL [Cambridge: Harvard Univ. Press, 1967]). As Menaham Stern suggests, the information in Josephus and Diodorus may ultimately rest on a common source, perhaps Posidonius (Stern, *Greek and Latin Authors on Jews and Judaism,* 3 vols. [Jerusalem: Israel Academy of Sciences and Humanities, 1974–84], 1.184).

135. Sievers, *Hasmoneans,* 140. Werner (*Johann Hyrkan,* 28–29) argues that Antiochus was pressured to withdraw from Jerusalem by the Parthian threat to his realm but that he also wanted Jewish support for his campaign and thus was generous in his treatment of them.

Antiochus led, whether of troops or others, and of the great wealth and luxury of the king's way of life, even on a military mission. Antiochus VII, the son of Demetrius I and brother of Demetrius II (who was still being held in a rather comfortable confinement by the Parthians), was the last great Seleucid king. At this time he felt sufficiently secure to move eastward in an attempt to regain that part of the Hellenistic empire. His army won a number of victories early in the campaign, but soon the tide changed and in the eventual defeat he and thousands in his train lost their lives (129 BCE).[136]

According to Josephus, at first "Hyrcanus set out with him. On this we have the testimony of Nicolas of Damascus, who writes as follows. 'After defeating Indates, the Parthian general, and setting up a trophy at the Lycus river, Antiochus remained there two days at the request of the Jew Hyrcanus because of a festival of his nation on which it was not customary for the Jews to march out.' Nor does he speak falsely in saying this; for the festival of Pentecost had come round, following the Sabbath, and we are not permitted to march either on the Sabbath or on a festival" (*Ant.* 13.8, 4 [§§249–52]).[137] The fact that this Pentecost fell on a Sunday (the day after the Sabbath) is interesting in connection with the ancient debates about when the holiday was to be celebrated. According to the Sadducean position, it always fell on a Sunday, whereas that was just one of several days on which it could fall in the rabbinic system. While some have attempted to relate the point to Hyrcanus's subsequent attachment to the Sadducees, it would be precarious to base the conclusion on this one occurrence, for which the day of the week could have been an accident and of which no further note is taken by Josephus or his source.[138]

Hyrcanus must have left Antiochus at some point during the campaign. When he heard of the king's death, John exploited the power vacuum in the Seleucid realm (despite the release and return of Demetrius II) by moving militarily against a number of targets (*J.W.* 1.2, 6 [§§62–63]; *Ant.* 13.9, 1 [§§254–56]). Both of Josephus's accounts credit him with surmising correctly that the Syrian cities would be short of able-bodied defenders in wake of Antiochus VII's disaster in Parthia; and both sources say that his forces went to Madaba, Samago/Samoga, Shechem, Mount Gerizim where the Cutheans lived, and the Idumean cities of Adora and Marisa (with others).[139] The

---

136. Bevan, *The House of Seleucus*, 2.242–46; Glanville Downey, *A History of Antioch in Syria from Seleucus to the Arab Conquest* (Princeton: Princeton Univ. Press, 1961), 125–26.

137. Leviticus 23:21 forbids work on the festival of Weeks (= Pentecost).

138. See Werner, *Johann Hyrkan*, n. 102 (13–14 of the Anmerkungen); Marcus, *Josephus* 7, 354 n. a.

139. Menahem Stern ("The Relations between Judea and Rome during the Reign of John Hyrcanus," *Zion* 26 [1961]: 8–9 [Hebrew]) raises questions about the claim that there would have been a shortage of manpower in Seleucid cities and that John's major conquests in the center and

narrative in *War* is brief, while in *Antiquities* Josephus expands the report by explaining about the temple on Gerizim: it was "built after the model of the sanctuary at Jerusalem, which Alexander permitted their governor Sanaballetes to build for the sake of his son-in-law Manasses, the brother of the high priest Jaddua, as we have related before. Now it was two hundred years later that this temple was laid waste" (13.9, 1 [§256]). If his numbers are precise, the temple was constructed in about 329 BCE and destroyed in about 129 (the date of Antiochus's death and Hyrcanus's military actions). No explanation for why Hyrcanus decided to destroy the temple is given,[140] but it is difficult to see how it could have improved relations with those who worshiped there. If he destroyed the "Cutheans" who worshiped on Mount Gerizim, the purpose could hardly have been to convince them to change their allegiance to the Jerusalem temple, and, as for the others who may have used the sanctuary, there is no indication that they started traveling to Jerusalem for festivals and

---

south of the land and in Transjordan would have occurred in 129–128 BCE. Demetrius II at this very time was active militarily and even marched against Egypt. He thinks that Josephus simply provides a continuous list of John's conquests to a certain point and only then does he turn to external events. Hence, his conquests probably took a longer time than the brief period immediately after Antiochus VII's death in 129.

140. Despite the lack of an explanation in the sources, scholars have speculated about John's motives in destroying the temple. One suggestion is that the Samaritan temple attracted Jews living nearer to it than to the one in Jerusalem; hence Hyrcanus decided to level the competing shrine (Menahem Mor, "Samaritan History: The Persian, Hellenistic and Hasmonaean Period," in *The Samaritans*, ed. A. D. Crown [Tübingen: Mohr/Siebeck, 1989], 16). It is not impossible (though undocumented) that the Samaritans had supported Antiochus VII when he invaded Judea and John was taking his revenge (James D. Purvis, *The Samaritan Pentateuch and the Origin of the Samaritan Sect*, HSM 2 [Cambridge: Harvard Univ. Press, 1968], 113–15). Purvis sees the event as the point when a complete break between Jews and Samaritans occurred; he also argues that the Samaritan Pentateuch was edited in the late Hasmonean period. Some scholars have concluded that John razed the Samaritan temple later than the time implied by Josephus's narrative in *Antiquities*—at the time when he destroyed Samaria near the end of his reign (for some references, see B. Hall, "Samaritan History: From John Hyrcanus to Baba Rabbah," in *The Samaritans*, ed. A. D. Crown [Tübingen: Mohr/Siebeck, 1989], 33–34). The historian does clearly separate the events but the specifics of the chronology remain unclear. I. Magen's excavations at the site have produced new data even if they have not solved the problem of when the destruction occurred. The archaeologist found thousands of coins from the Seleucid period, including 153 from Antiochus VII, 139 from Alexander Zebinas, and 82 from Antiochus VIII. There are, on Magen's calculations, some 412 coins now identified as dating from after Antiochus VII's death, with the last from 111–110 BCE (later he writes 112–111 BCE). There were also 546 coins from the Hasmonean rulers. From this, he concludes that the final destruction of the site occurred in 112–111 BCE. He does not think the evidence allows one to support the thesis of two destructions there in Hyrcanus's time, although he thinks the siege was protracted and that Hasmonean troops were stationed there to prevent the worshipers from returning ("Mt. Gerizim—Temple City," *Qad* 33 [2000]: 114–15, 118 [Hebrew]).

sacrifices. Reconciliation between the two religious communities was most improbable after Hyrcanus's action.[141]

Another side of his religious policy may be seen from a different addition in *Antiquities* beyond the terse lines of *War*. Hyrcanus, "after subduing all the Idumaeans, permitted them to remain in their country so long as they had themselves circumcised and were willing to observe the laws [νόμοις; variant: νομίμοις = customs] of the Jews. And so, out of attachment to the land of their fathers, they submitted to circumcision and to making their manner of life conform in all other respects to that of the Jews. And from that time on they have continued to be Jews" (§§257–58). Presumably, such measures were not necessary for the community around Mount Gerizim, and, in the case of Idumea, there would have been no temple to rival the one in Jerusalem. In both cases, Hyrcanus can be seen extending Jewish practices over territories that he controlled and in this way incorporating into the nation sizable populations who lacked a Jewish past and whose status was to be controversial, at least to some.[142]

One of the disputed points in the study of Hyrcanus's career concerns his relations with the Romans and which documents preserved in *Antiquities* relate to his reign. In *Ant.* 13.9, 2 (§§259–66), John follows the practice of his Hasmonean forebears (Judas, Jonathan, Simon) by renewing ties of friendship with Rome. He dispatched an embassy, which the senate received and to whom it responded in written form. The Jewish ambassadors, according to the Roman document, had requested that the cities disputed with Antiochus VII be granted to them. They asked "that Joppa and its harbours and Gazara and Pegae and whatever other cities and territories Antiochus took from them in the war, contrary to the decree of the Senate, be restored to them, and that the soldiers of the king be not permitted to march through their country or those of their subjects, and that the laws made by Antiochus during this same war contrary to the decree of the Senate be annulled, and that the Romans send envoys to bring about the restitution of the places taken from the Jews by Antiochus and to estimate the value of the territory ruined during the war" (13.9, 2 [§§261–63]). The senate did indeed renew the alliance (§264) but declined to respond at the time to the other issues raised (§265). Instead, the

---

141. Compare Sievers, *Hasmoneans*, 142–43. It is likely that Megillat Taʿanit for Kislev 21 relates to this event ("the day of Mount Gerizim").

142. See Part I of Seth Schwartz, *Imperialism and Jewish Society, 200 B.C.E. to 640 C.E.,* JCMAMW (Princeton: Princeton Univ. Press, 2001). For a discussion of whether the Idumeans were forced to become circumcised (as is so regularly asserted in the scholarly literature) or many already were, see the section on Aristobulus I below and his treatment of the Itureans.

Roman authorities gave the Jewish representatives money for the return journey and pledges of safety during their travels.

M. Stern has formulated a detailed, impressive case that this embassy, far
from being the only one in Hyrcanus's time as a reader might infer from Josephus and one that followed his conquests in Samaria and Idumea, was actually the middle one of three delegations he dispatched to Rome. The
documents relating to the other two are indeed recorded by our historian, but
he mistakenly placed them in the reign of Hyrcanus II (an understandable
confusion of two men with the same name). According to Stern, the most
plausible order of the documents is as follows:

1. Upon assuming office in 134 BCE, John, as one did at such times, sent
   ambassadors to Rome to renew existing ties with the great world power.
   The relevant document regarding the mission is the *senatus consultum*
   now found in *Ant.* 14.8, 5 (§§145–48) where it has nothing to do with its
   context and does not fit the time of Julius Caesar and Hyrcanus II to
   which Josephus assigns it. The Roman document addressed no specific
   issue because the occasion called for no decision other than "renewing the
   relation of goodwill and friendship" between the Romans and the Jews
   (§146).[143]

2. Around the years 128–127 BCE, at the time of intense rivalry between
   Demetrius II and Alexander Zebinas (see below), rivals for control of the
   Seleucid kingdom, John sent the embassy depicted in *Ant.* 13.9, 2
   (§§260–66; see above). As Rome was not yet ready to decide definitively
   regarding the situation around the Seleucid throne, the senate did not
   accede to John's requests.[144]

3. In 113–112 BCE, when Antiochus IX Cyzicenus (see below) was still a
   threat, John sent a third embassy to Rome, requesting his ally's help. The
   senatus consultum for that occasion appears in *Ant.* 14.10, 22 (§§247–55),
   where it is embedded in a decree by the people of Pergamum honoring the
   high priest Hyrcanus and the Jews. At that time, the senate gave "King
   Antiochus, son of Antiochus" various orders, including returning to the
   Jews whatever territory he had taken from them.[145]

---

143. M. Stern, "Relations," 3–6. Werner reviews earlier discussions and with others places
this document in the time of Simon (*Johann Hyrkan*, 34–35).

144. Stern, "Relations," 7–12. Werner also thinks the document belongs at the earlier point
in his reign after John had returned from the Parthian campaign and desired Roman support for
throwing off the Seleucid yoke and for expanding his borders—that is, it belongs before these
conquests (*Johann Hyrkan*, 31–34).

145. Stern, "Relations," 12–19. Werner considers the document spurious (*Johann Hyrkan*,
35–36).

The reconstruction indicates that John was eager to confirm and, if possible, exploit the Jews' pact with the Romans in his relations with the Seleucids.

As this sketch also implies, during Hyrcanus's reign, the Seleucid government went through tumultuous times, with various upheavals and the by now all too familiar rivalry for the throne. Josephus records the military activities and death of Demetrius II, the rise and fall of Alexander Zabinas (or Zebinas; 128–123 BCE) who, he says, became "friends with the high priest Hyrcanus" (*Ant.* 13.9, 3 [§269]), whereas Demetrius had been interested in attacking him (§267). Zabinas, however, soon lost his life fighting Demetrius's son Antiochus VIII Grypus (he ruled jointly with his mother Cleopatra from 125–121 BCE and then ruled a part of the kingdom alone until 96 BCE). The latter, continuing the policy of his father, wished to invade Judea but refrained from doing so because his step-brother and cousin Antiochus IX Cyzicenus (114–95 BCE) contended with him for the kingship of the Seleucid realm.

All of the conflict surrounding the throne in Antioch had important repercussions for John Hyrcanus. Josephus says that, throughout the years that Antiochus VIII and IX fought each other,

> Hyrcanus lived in peace; for after the death of Antiochus (Sidetes [129 BCE]) he too revolted from the Macedonians, and no longer furnished them any aid either as a subject or as a friend; instead, his government progressed and flourished greatly during the reign of Alexander Zebinas and especially under these brothers. For the war between them gave Hyrcanus leisure to exploit Judaea undisturbed, with the result that he amassed a limitless sum of money. Moreover, when Cyzicenus ravaged his land, he openly showed his intention, and seeing that Antiochus had been deserted by his Egyptian allies and that both he and his brother were faring badly in their struggle with each other, he showed contempt for both of them" (13.10, 1 [§§272–74]). Although the Seleucid dynastic situation was complicated,[146] for Hyrcanus the circumstances were simple. Despite some times of danger,[147] he could afford to snub the once mighty Seleucids, aggrandize himself at home, and expand Judea's boundaries into the surrounding regions.

---

146. M. Stern offers a detailed account of the struggles for the throne in Antioch in part II, chaps. 5 and 6 of his *Hasmonaean Judaea*.

147. Although Josephus's words may seem inconsistent with parts of Stern's reconstruction given above, Stern was able to marshal evidence from other sources (for example, coins indicating the cities he controlled and when) that show the problem that Antiochus IX posed for Hyrcanus early in the Seleucid monarch's reign ("Relations," 15–17).

His campaign into Samaria and the area around it forms the subject of
J.W. 1.2, 7 (§§64–66) and *Ant.* 13.10, 2–3 (§§275–83). According to the latter,
"he attacked and besieged it vigorously; for he hated the Samaritans as
scoundrels because of the injuries which, in obedience to the kings of Syria,
they had done to the people of Marisa,[148] who were colonists and allies of the
Jews" (13.10, 2 [§275]). Both sources relate that John had a wall constructed
around the besieged city and left his sons Antigonus and Aristobulus (the
future high priest) in charge of the siege (*J.W.* 1.2, 7 [§64]; *Ant.* 13.10, 2
[§276]). In their dire distress, the Samaritans summoned the Seleucid king,[149]
whom the Hasmonean forces defeated and chased to Scythopolis. The story is
one more illustration of the depths to which Seleucid power had sunk at this
stage in history. In *Antiquities,* Josephus mentions a second time the Samaritans asked Antiochus for help; the king in turn requested assistance from
Ptolemy IX Soter II who dispatched six thousand men. Despite their destructive raids in Judea, they could not force an end to the siege of Samaria. The two
commanders left by Ptolemy when he withdrew fared no better (§§278–80).
Hyrcanus took the city of Samaria after a one-year siege, reduced the survivors
to slavery, and effaced any sign of the city from the earth (§281). The story of
the siege says nothing about Hyrcanus's high priesthood but says much about
relations with people in the area of Samaria.

Without parallel in *War*, at this point in *Antiquities* Josephus relates a tale
about a revelation granted to Hyrcanus the high priest (13.10, 3 [§§282–83]),
not the only story he preserves about the special status of John.

> Now about the high priest Hyrcanus an extraordinary story is told
> how the Deity communicated with him, for they say that on the very
> day on which his sons fought with Cyzicenus, Hyrcanus, who was
> alone in the temple, burning incense as high priest,[150] heard a voice

---

148. On the problem with the location of this city, see Marcus, *Josephus* 7, 366 n. a.

149. In *J.W.* 1.2, 7 (§65), he is Antiochus VIII Grypus (called Aspendius, after the place
from which he came); in *Ant.* 13.10, 2 (§276), he is Antiochus IX Cyzicenus. See Schürer, *History
of the Jewish People*, 1.209–10.

150. The offering seems to be the one depicted in Exod 30:1-10; the altar of incense is
placed "in front of the curtain that is above the ark of the covenant" (30:6). On it, Aaron was to
offer incense in the morning and evening. Note that the talmudic parallel cited below says that
John heard the voice coming from the Holy of Holies, which would have been very easy to do if
he was making the offering of Exod 30:7-9. Hebrews 9:4 says that the altar of incense was actually in the Holy of Holies. C. Houtman attributes this claim to the "less than lucid wording of the
text (30:36; 40:5; cf. also Lev. 16:12)" (*Exodus*, vol. 3, HCOT [Leuven: Peeters, 2000], 555). For
the placement of this altar in various sources and possible ambiguities about it, see Harold W.
Attridge, *The Epistle to the Hebrews,* Hermeneia (Philadephia: Fortress Press, 1989), 234–35.
Although Joseph Blenkinsopp ("Prophecy and Priesthood in Josephus," *JJS* 25 [1974]: 251–52)

saying that his sons had just defeated Antiochus. And on coming out of the temple he revealed this to the entire multitude, and so it actually happened. This, then, was how the affairs of Hyrcanus were going.

Josephus's version makes an attempt to prove the veracity of the story by saying John revealed the message immediately to the crowd at the temple, before the report had arrived from the battlefield. It is one of the few tales about supernatural encounters for high priests in the Second-Temple period (Jaddua and Onias III are also said to have had them) and the first hint in the sources that John was thought to have prophetic gifts.

Parallels to the story have survived in rabbinic literature (*t. Soṭah* 13:5; *y. Soṭah* 24b; *b. Soṭah* 33a). In fact, John is the first Hasmonean high priest to whom there are specific references in the writings of the sages.[151] In *b. Soṭah* 33a, the story is repeated in connection with a discussion whether one can pray in any language, with Aramaic in particular being in dispute. "Behold it has been taught: Joḥanan, the High Priest, heard a *Bath Ḳol* issue from within the Holy of Holies announcing, 'The young men who went to wage war against Antioch[us] have been victorious.'"[152] The point is that since the announcement was made in Aramaic, the ministering angels must have understood it.[153]

After *Antiquities* relates how Queen Cleopatra of Ptolemaic Egypt put the two sons of Onias (IV) in charge of her army (13.10, 4 [§§284–87]), the two books of Josephus report that the successes of John and his sons sparked opposition among their envious fellow countrymen. In *War*, Josephus refers to meetings, agitation, and even fighting (1.2, 8 [§67]); in *Antiquities*, he adduces the Pharisees as a strong example of the opposition Hyrcanus encountered.[154] Before relating the story about the break between the high

---

holds that the event would have occurred on Yom Kippur (so also Werner, *Johann Hyrkan*, 44), that does not seem the most likely interpretation of the passage in Josephus.

151. See Y. Gafni, "The Hasmoneans in Rabbinic Literature," in *The Hasmonean Period*, ed. D. Amit and H. Eshel, Sederet 'Idan 19 (Jerusalem: Yitzhak ben-Zvi, 1995), 269 (Hebrew). The rabbis refer to the earlier Maccabean revolt and purification of the temple but do not relate the material to a specific individual—only to the Hasmonean house or to the sons of Hashmon.

152. Gafni thinks that the sages derived the story from the source from which Josephus drew it ("The Hasmoneans in Rabbinic Literature," 270). Werner presents a similar case; he thinks the story with the one in *b. Qidd.* 66a (see below) came from the (Hebrew) source on Hyrcanus's reign to which 1 Macc 16:23-24 refers (*Johann Hyrkan*, 23–24).

153. See n. 8 to the rendering in the Soncino Talmud from which the translation of the passage is taken; A. Cohen, *Soṭah*, The Babylonian Talmud, ed. I. Epstein, 3/6 (London: Soncino, 1936).

154. For the way in which Josephus in *Antiquities* inserts the account of the break between John and the Pharisees into the parallel framework in *War*, see Mason, *Flavius Josephus on the Pharisees*, 215–16. It is, however, difficult to accept his conclusion that the Pharisees are

priest and the Pharisees, the historian writes about the latter: "so great is their influence with the masses that even when they speak against a king or high priest, they immediately gain credence" (*Ant.* 13.10, 5 [§288]). The passage not only introduces the Pharisees as being at the heart of the opposition to John but also distinguishes the two offices—ruler and high priest—that were to be at the center of the dispute in the story to follow, although "king" was not a title claimed by John. Hyrcanus, we learn here for the first time, was prior to the split "a disciple of theirs, and was greatly loved by them" (§289).

At a feast whose guest list included Pharisees, Hyrcanus made the mistake of asking them to tell him whether he was doing anything wrong so that he could correct the error (§290). All of the Pharisees managed to answer in harmony with the spirit of the occasion: "they testified to his being altogether virtuous, and he was delighted with their praise" (§290). But one guest (possibly a Pharisee), badly misjudging the situation, spoke his mind:

> Eleazar, who had an evil nature and took pleasure in dissension, said: "Since you have asked to be told the truth, if you wish to be righteous, give up the high-priesthood and be content with governing the people." And when Hyrcanus asked him for what reason he should give up the high-priesthood, he replied, "Because we have heard from our elders that your mother was a captive in the reign of Antiochus Epiphanes. But the story was false, and Hyrcanus was furious with the man, while all the Pharisees were very indignant. (§§290–92)

It is understandable that Eleazar's blunt words would cause trouble between him and Hyrcanus, but the Pharisees soon also became implicated in his imprudent attack on the most powerful man in the state. Note that at the end of this citation we are not told who or what the object of the Pharisees' indignation was.

As Josephus relates the story, matters soon went from bad to worse when "a certain Jonathan, one of Hyrcanus' close friends, belonging to the school of Sadducees, who hold opinions opposed to those of the Pharisees, said that it had been with the general approval of all the Pharisees that Eleazar had made his slanderous statement; and this, he added, would be clear to Hyrcanus if he inquired of them what punishment Eleazar deserved for what he had said" (*Ant.* 13.10, 6 [§293]).

---

presented negatively in the introductory §288 (218–19, 222–30, 245). Daniel R. Schwartz also interprets the paragraph as expressing a negative attitude toward the Pharisees and attributes it to Nicolaus of Damascus ("Josephus and Nicolaus on the Pharisees," *JSJ* 14 [1983]: 158–62).

The high priest followed his friend's advice, and when the Pharisees proposed what was taken to be a mild penalty ("stripes and chains" [§294]), he thought he had proof of their collaboration—a conclusion encouraged by Jonathan. "And Jonathan in particular inflamed his anger, and so worked upon him that he brought him to join the Sadducaean party and desert the Pharisees, and to abrogate the regulations which they had established for the people, and punish those who observed them. Out of this, of course, grew the hatred of the masses for him and his sons" (§§295–96). Josephus appends to this story an explanation of the Pharisees' "regulations" and Sadducean opposition to them (§§297–98).

What appears to be the same story is told, not about John but about his son Alexander Jannaeus (Yannai) in *b. Qidd.* 66a. The context there is a discussion about the testimony of one or two witnesses in cases such as alleged adultery. In this instance, the matter in question is the charge that the high priest's mother had fallen captive to the nations in Modein.

It once happened that King Jannai went to Ḳohalith in the wilderness and conquered sixty towns there. On his return he rejoiced exceedingly and invited all the Sages of Israel. Said he to them, "Our forefathers ate mallows when they were engaged on the building of the [second] temple; let us too eat mallows in memory of our forefathers." So mallows were served on golden tables, and they ate. Now, there was a man there, frivolous, evil-hearted and worthless, named Eleazar son of Po'irah, who said to King Jannai, "O King Jannai, the hearts of the Pharisees are against thee." "Then what shall I do?" "Test them by the plate between thine eyes." So he tested them by the plate between his eyes. Now, an elder, named Judah son of Gedidah, was present there. Said he to King Jannai, "O King Jannai! Let the royal crown suffice thee, and leave the priestly crown to the seed of Aaron." (For it was rumoured that his mother had been taken captive in Modi'im.) Accordingly, the charge was investigated, but not sustained, and the Sages of Israel departed in anger. Then said Eleazar b. Po'irah to King Jannai: "O King Jannai! That is the law even for the most humble man in Israel, and thou, a King and a High Priest, shall that be thy law [too]!" "Then what shall I do?" "If thou wilt take my advice, trample them down." "But what shall happen with the Torah?" "Behold, it is rolled up and lying in the corner: whoever wishes to study, let him go and study!" Said R. Naḥman b. Isaac: Immediately a spirit of heresy was instilled into him, for he should have replied,

"That is well for the Written Law; but what of the Oral Law?"
Straightway, the evil burst forth through Eleazar son of Po'irah, all the
Sages of Israel were massacred, and the world was desolate until
Simeon b. Sheṭaḥ came and restored the Torah to its pristine
[glory].[155]

The section concludes with a discussion of the witnesses to the charge that
Jannaeus's mother had been a captive.

The story about the breach between a Hasmonean high priest/ruler and
the Pharisees has undergone intense scrutiny, especially at the hands of those
who are concerned with the history of the Pharisees and with the attitude(s)
toward them in the writings of Josephus. Our concern here is not so much
with these issues as with the story's bearing on the high priesthood.

It is likely that John Hyrcanus was the original Hasmonean ruler of the
story, not Alexander Jannaeus.[156] One reason is that Josephus, who connects it
with Hyrcanus, provides the earliest evidence for it[157]—evidence that appears
in a historical narrative, not a later talmudic discussion about the fate of the
sages and rules about witnesses. Also, if we accept Josephus's account of the
relations between the Hasmoneans and the Pharisees, it would make no sense
to place the break between them in the reign of Jannaeus who was their enemy
from the beginning. Finally, it is likely that *b. Ber.* 29a preserves a memory of
the actual relations. In a discussion of whether to remove a reader who makes
a mistake in the "blessing" of Minim, the case of Samuel the Lesser, who composed it, is raised along with the possibility that he might have recanted. So,
the question is whether a good man can become bad:

For lo, Johanan the High Priest officiated as High Priest for eighty
years and in the end he became a Min[.] Abaye said: Johanan is the
same as Jannai. Raba said: Johanan and Jannai are different; Jannai

---

155. H. Freedman, trans., *The Babylonian Talmud,* ed. I. Epstein, 3/8 (London: Soncino,
1966).

156. See, for example, Schürer, *History of the Jewish People,* 1.214; Jacob Neusner, *The Rab-
binic Traditions about the Pharisees before 70,* 3 vols. (Leiden: Brill, 1971; reprinted: Atlanta:
Scholars, 1999), 1.173–76; Joshua Efron, "Simeon Ben Shataḥ and Alexander Jannaeus," in his
Studies on the Hasmonean Period, SJLA 39 (Leiden: Brill, 1987), 161–89.

157. R. Travers Herford (*The Pharisees* [Boston: Beacon, 1962], 39–40) is correct in saying
that this reason alone is not sufficient evidence for accepting Josephus's version and rejecting the
talmudic one, as the language of the story in the *baraita* has some archaic features. Yet, *Antiquities* is a different kind of source than *b. Qidd.* 66a. It should be added that Herford thought the
talmudic story had confused Hyrcanus with Jannaeus and that the break in relations had actually occurred in the time of Hyrcanus (pp. 41–45).

was originally wicked and Johanan was originally righteous. On Abaye's view there is no difficulty, but on Raba's view there is a difficulty?—Raba can reply: For one who was originally righteous it is also possible to become a renegade.[158]

Here Raba is aware of John's favorable rating by the Pharisees early in his reign and of his break with them later, while Abaye advances the implausible suggestion that the two names are used for the same person.[159]

If we accept Josephus's assignment of the event to Hyrcanus's time, we may conclude that before the banquet he aligned himself with the Pharisaic viewpoint. That is, they were prominent enough already during his reign to exercise influence on the top-ranking man in Judea; indeed, he could even be called their disciple (μαθητής). Also, the high priest's standing with the populace is supposed to have been tied to his support of Pharisaic beliefs and practices. His shift to the Sadducees, one learns, led to hostile relations between the Hasmoneans and the masses—something that would become painfully evident when John's son Alexander Jannaeus became high priest and king. It is apparently to the rebellion caused by the rupture with the Pharisees that Josephus refers in *J.W.* 1.2, 8 (§67),[160] although in the earlier book he does not supply the story about the disastrous banquet.

---

158. M. Simon, trans., *The Babylonian Talmud*, ed. I. Epstein, 1/1 (London: Soncino, 1948).

159. This seems the more likely interpretation of Abaye's statement הוא ינאי הוא יוחנן. See, for example, A. Baumgarten, "Rabbinic Literature as a Source for the History of Jewish Sectarianism in the Second Temple Period," *DSD* 2 (1995), 30. M. Geller's suggestion that Abaye means only that "this account of Hyrcanus is the same account as that regarding Jannaeus in bQidd. 66a" does not seem to follow from the wording (Geller, "Alexander Jannaeus and the Pharisee Rift," *JJS* 30 [1979]: 206), although Abaye is the one credited with the story in *b. Qidd.* 66a. He thinks Raba's point was, not that Hyrcanus and Jannaeus were different individuals, but "that the two accounts of banquets are separate, with each being true" (207). Geller also thinks the reference to the mother's captivity in Modein in the talmudic version could refer to Aristobulus I's imprisonment of his (and Jannaeus's) mother there, but there is no evidence for this claim (209–10). Another advocate of the talmudic account as preferable to Josephus's story was Gedalia Alon, *Jews, Judaism and the Classical World: Studies in Jewish History in the Times of the Second Temple and Talmud* (Jerusalem: Magness, 1977), 23–28. For a helpful summary of reasons for regarding the talmudic account as "a secondary, garbled version of the story found in Josephus," see John P. Meier, *A Marginal Jew: Rethinking the Historical Jesus*, vol. 3: *Companions and Competitors*, ABRL (New York: Doubleday, 2001), 351 n. 24. Compare also Efron, "Simeon Ben Shatah and Alexander Jannaeus," 176–86.

160. In *J.W.* 1.2, 8 (§67), he calls the outbreak of opposition to Hyrcanus στάσις, while in *Ant.* 13.10, 7 (§299) he says, after the banquet story, that Hyrcanus put down the στάσις. As D. Schwartz points out ("Josephus and Nicolaus on the Pharisees," 158–59), one needs the passage in *War* to understand Josephus's reference to στάσις in *Antiquities*.

A second point worthy of note is Josephus's formulation of Eleazar's argument why Hyrcanus should give up the high priesthood. He does not claim there was something wrong with one person holding both the leading civil and religious positions; rather, his reason is the alleged captivity of Hyrcanus's mother during the reign of Antiochus IV.[161] The charge was that Simon's wife was captured and possibly defiled during the war—something that, though it goes unmentioned in the historical sources, would, so it seems from this passage, have disqualified her children from the priesthood. Marcus claims that the captivity of Hyrcanus's mother "would have been a violation of the laws, based on Lev. xxi.14, concerning the genealogical qualifications of the high priest."[162] In *Against Apion,* Josephus himself provides the earliest evidence of how the rule was understood (see also *Ant.* 3.12, 1 [§276], where he includes "a prisoner of war" in his version of Lev 21:7, and §277 on the high-priestly rules]). In a context in which he is explaining the great care taken for the purity of the priesthood, he writes: "In the not infrequent event of war, for instance when our country was invaded by Antiochus Epiphanes, by Pompey the Great, by Quintilius Varus, and above all in our own times, the surviving priests compile fresh records from the archives; they also pass scrutiny upon the remaining women, and disallow marriage with any who have been taken captive, suspecting them of having had frequent intercourse with foreigners" (*Ag. Ap.* 1.34–35). *M. Ketub.* 2:9 mandates: "If a woman was imprisoned by gentiles for an offence concerning property she is still permitted to her husband; but if it was for a capital offence she is forbidden to her husband. If a city was overcome by a besieging troop all women therein of priestly stock become ineligible [for marriage with a priest]." Rashi understood Lev 21:14-15 in this sense, noting that the words ולא יחלל זרעו in verse 15 imply that if the high priest married a woman who fell into one of the forbidden categories in verse 14, his children with her would be profaned with the result that they would not be qualified for the priesthood.[163] So, the point of Eleazar's charge has to do with Hyrcanus's mother, not with any general theory that no one person should be both high priest and head of state. The talmudic account misses the point of Eleazar's claim by having Judah son of Gedidah urge the ruler-high priest to "leave the priestly crown to the seed of Aaron." Hyrcanus (and Jannaeus) was, of course, from the seed of Aaron.

---

161. If Josephus's specification of the time as the reign of Antiochus IV is correct, the Hasmonean ruler of the story could hardly have been Jannaeus because of the obvious chronological problem.

162. *Josephus* 7, 374 n. a.

163. Abraham ben Isaiah and Benjamin Sharfman, *The Pentateuch and Rashi's Commentary,* vol. 3: *Leviticus* (Brooklyn: S. S. & R., 1950), 213.

Josephus gives no support to those who hold that some theoretical or philosophical difference led to the break between the Hasmoneans and the Pharisees.[164] While there is no compelling reason to think that Josephus has reproduced all the relevant information about the relations between them,[165] he explains the rift from a personal insult delivered to Hyrcanus by Eleazar, who may or may not be a Pharisee in the story. It is possible that behind Hyrcanus's eventual move against the Pharisees lies a political motif. Lee Levine, for example, has formulated a detailed case that John wished to enlist the support of the Sadducees, who included priests with high military positions, while the Pharisees, who generally lacked such qualifications, proved less useful to him. In other words, the initiative would have come from the side of Hyrcanus, and the banquet scene was hardly the whole story, whatever its historical value. That would make good sense, but the evidence for it is definitely indirect and, at least in this context, it is not supported by Josephus.[166] Levine

---

164. Louis H. Finkelstein thought that Pharisaic pacifism led them to oppose the Hasmoneans and their conquests (*The Pharisees: The Sociological Background of Their Faith* [Philadelphia: JPS, 1938], 248–53). He, like others, believed that on this occasion Hyrcanus drove the Pharisees from the Sanhedrin (606–9), though Josephus says nothing about this. Hyrcanus's coins (see below) say he was the head of the Judean חבר, but what this group was and who its members were remain unknown. Schürer, who thought the חבר was the γερουσία, found the wider reason for Hyrcanus's break with the Pharisees in the nature of the two groups: "The more his political interests came to the fore, the more those concerned with religion receded into the background. But he was correspondingly obliged to move away from the Pharisees and closer to the Sadducees. For in view of the distinctly worldly character of his policies, no sincere association with the Pharisees was in the long run possible" (*History*, 1.213). Victor Tcherikover (*Hellenistic Civilization and the Jews*, trans. S. Applebaum [New York: Atheneum, 1970], 254–57) thought that "here was no chance quarrel which had broken out at the royal court owing to the discourtesy of a guest at a banquet, but the perpetuation of the ancient feud between the priests and the scribes" (256). All of these views assume we know more about the Pharisees and Sadducees in this period than the sources disclose. Thoma even claims: "The essential point of Josephus is that in the case of John Hyrcanus the questionable double-office of high priest and ruler of the people was not directed against God's will. On the contrary, God has confirmed the double-office by bestowing the gift of prophecy on Hyrcanus" ("John Hyrcanus I," 129). He misses the point that a practical, not a theoretical, objection was directed at his holding both offices. The Qumran community, however, may have opposed the concentration of the two offices in one person as suggested by their notion of a messiah of Aaron and a messiah of Israel.

165. Compare Werner, *Johann Hyrkan*, 53.

166. Lee I. Levine, "The Political Struggle between Pharisees and Sadducees in the Hasmonean Period," *Jerusalem in the Second Temple Period: Abraham Schalit Memorial Volume*, ed. A. Oppenheimer, U. Rappaport, and M. Stern (Jerusalem: Yitzhak ben-Zvi, Ministry of Defence, 1980), 61–83 (Hebrew). He builds on M. Stern's study ("The Relations"), in which he showed that the delegates sent by the Hasmoneans on missions especially to Rome came from the same families over several generations and that Greek names were the norm among them. That is true, but it hardly follows that they were Sadducees. Also, his argument that the names of these people

and others have highlighted a number of problems with the story as presented in *Antiquities* and with how it fits (or does not fit) in its context.[167] Perhaps the most we can say about its historical value is that it documents a change in John's political alignment and supplies evidence that some opposed his serving as high priest because of questions about the purity of his line.[168]

In both *War* and *Antiquities*, Josephus quickly ends the account of Hyrcanus's reign by noting that he lived out his days in prosperity, after crushing the revolt, and that he died after ruling well for thirty-one years[169] and fathering five sons. Both works add a note about John's unique status. He was

> truly a blessed individual and one who left no ground for complaint against fortune as regards himself. He was the only man to unite in his person three of the highest privileges: the supreme command of the nation [τήν τε ἀρχὴν τοῦ ἔθνους], the high priesthood [τὴν ἀρχιερωσύνην], and the gift of prophecy [προφητείαν]. For so closely was he in touch with the Deity, that he was never ignorant of the future; thus he foresaw and predicted that his two elder sons would not remain at the head of affairs. (*J.W.* 1.2, 8 [§§68–69]; // *Ant.* 13.10, 7 [§§299–300])

So Josephus knew of two stories relating to predictions by John about two of his sons (see above on the *bat qol* he received). Although he merely alludes to the second one here, he explains it more fully in *Ant.* 13.12, 1 (§§320–23). There, writing about the end of Hyrcanus's son Aristobulus's brief reign, he records that Aristobulus's wife, Salina (apparently Salome Alexandra), appointed his brother Jannaeus king in his stead. The historian tells the reader that Jannaeus had been

---

were common among priests at the time also does not show that they were priests. The names could have been common among other groups as well.

167. "Political Struggle," 71–72.

168. Werner (*Johann Hyrkan*, 45-60) has a lengthy discussion about John and the Pharisees. He concludes that John eventually repented of leaving the Pharisees and returned to them. He found evidence for this conclusion in the largely favorable statements about him in talmudic literature and the claim in *Talmud Yerushalmi* that he reestablished the Pairs. Josephus, of course, says nothing about such a change of heart by Hyrcanus, and the violent relations between John's son Alexander Jannaeus and the Pharisees also argue against a return to them by his father.

169. Some manuscripts of *War* (1.2, 8 [§68]) have thirty-three years, but *Ant.* 20.10, 3 (§240), from an official list of high priests, also assigns him thirty-one. Josephus mentions "the tomb of John the high priest" on a number of occasions in *War*. For example, in 5.6, 2 (§259), Titus decided to assault Jerusalem opposite this tomb, which appears to be that of Hyrcanus (so for example, Thackeray, *Josephus* 3, 281 n. b). See also *J.W.* 5.7, 3 (§304); 5.9, 2 (§356); 5.11, 4 (§468); and 6.2, 10 (§169). In *J.W.* 5.11, 4 (§468), he puts it on the north side of the city.

hated by his father [John Hyrcanus] from the time he was born, and never came into his sight so long as he lived. Now the reason for this hatred is said to have been as follows. Of all his sons Hyrcanus loved best the two elder ones, Antigonus and Aristobulus; and once when God appeared to him in his sleep, he asked Him which of his sons was destined to be his successor. And when God showed him the features of Alexander, he was grieved that this one should be the heir of all his possessions, and so he let him be brought up in Galilee from his birth. (§§321–22)[170]

John's offices of ruler and high priest[171] are familiar from the preceding parts of Josephus's account of his reign, but his prophetic gifts (Josephus does not actually call him a prophet) have understandably attracted scholarly comment.[172] The attribution is interesting in light of Josephus's claim elsewhere that the exact succession of prophets had ceased after the time of King Artaxerxes (*Ag. Ap.* 1.41), although this is not quite the same as saying that prophecy had ended during the Persian period.[173] Josephus was familiar with a tradition according to which John, by virtue of private and apparently frequent communications with God, knew the future.[174] In this connection, scholars have drawn attention to Josephus's assertion in *Ant.* 3.8, 9 (§218).[175]

---

170. As Werner comments, John, possessor of so many virtues, lacked the good fortune of knowing he was bequeathing his position to a reliable successor (*Johann Hyrkan*, 60–61). The fact that he wanted his wife to succeed him perhaps suggests a lack of confidence in any of his five sons.

171. The fact that these two offices are distinguished (as they also are in the story of John's dispute with the Pharisees) entails for Rooke that the two were different and distinguishable (*Zadok's Heirs*, 310–11). They are indeed distinguishable, with separate titles used for them, but this need have no implications for the situation in the pre-Hasmonean period. Rooke's thesis that John's rule should be assessed as primarily that of a king, not as a high priest (p. 313), is difficult to reconcile with the evidence of the coins which mention his high-priestly title first; and, of course, John did not, so far as we know, claim to be a king.

172. Thoma ("John Hyrcanus I," 127) observes that Josephus grants no such fullness of honors to any other person.

173. For example, Louis H. Feldman, "Prophets and Prophecy in Josephus," *JTS* 41 (1990): 400–401.

174. Josephus claimed similar revelations for himself in *J.W.* 3.8, 3 (§§352–54); 3.8, 9 (§§400–401); and *Life* 42.209. For a detailed but not entirely convincing evaluation of how Josephus's own experiences may have influenced his account of the first Hasmonean high priests, see Joan Annandale-Potgieter, "The High Priests in I Maccabees and in the Writing of Josephus," in *VII Congress of the International Organization for Septuagint and Cognate Studies, Leuven 1989*, ed. C. E. Cox, SBLSCS 31 (Atlanta: Scholars, 1991), 393–429.

175. See Blenkinsopp, "Prophecy and Priesthood in Josephus," 240, 252–55; Rebecca Gray, *Prophetic Figures in Late Second Temple Jewish Palestine: The Evidence from Josephus* (Oxford: Oxford Univ. Press, 1993), 16–23.

There in §§214–18, he inserts some details about the high priest's special vestments, details he had earlier omitted. He says that when God was present at a sacred ceremony the sardonyx worn on the high priest's right shoulder would begin to shine, while the twelve stones in his breastplate would burst forth in brilliant light when God came to the aid of the army. "Howbeit, *essên* [= breastplate] and sardonyx alike ceased to shine two hundred years before I composed this work, because of God's displeasure at the transgression of the laws" (§218).[176] Rebecca Gray concludes that this was Josephus's own view, one differing from other ancient theories about the end of priestly divination; his chronology puts the cessation around the time of Hyrcanus's reign. It seems that "Josephus used two hundred as a round number, and that he believed that priestly divination of the sort he describes in *Antiquities* 3.214–18 had ceased at the conclusion of John's reign."[177] She also shows that this would be in harmony with Josephus's understanding of John as the last great priestly ruler, one who retained this superior form of government and who did not claim the royal crown as his successors did.[178] If so, we would have another indication that Josephus believed John, more than those who followed him, had a special relation with God. Priestly divination may not be a classical form of prophecy, but Josephus and others considered its verdicts more irrevocable than a prophetic message.[179]

Josephus's claim that John alone combined the three "privileges" in his person is reflected, according to some scholars, in other literature composed around his time. R. H. Charles, for example, concluded that the *Testaments of the Twelve Patriarchs* was written during John's reign. He pointed to passages in the work that refer to Levi as both priest and king (*T. Reu.* 6:10-11 with *T. Sim.* 5:5); and *T. Levi* 8:15, he believed, added the office of prophet. As no other ruler held all these offices, the text was composed in the time of Hyrcanus.[180] Obviously, other conclusions could be drawn from the evidence he cited, but *T. Levi* 8:14 speaks of a new king from *Judah's* line; he is the one who establishes a new priesthood whose leader will apparently in some sense resemble

---

176. Translation of H. St. J. Thackeray, *Josephus* 4, LCL (Cambridge: Harvard Univ. Press, 1967). Thackeray (as have others) points out that Josephus's figure of two hundred years would lead back to the reign of Hyrcanus, as he wrote *Antiquities* in 93–94 BCE (see pp. 420–21 n. b). Compare also Blenkinsopp, "Prophecy and Priesthood in Josephus," 240; and Feldman, "Prophets and Prophecy in Josephus," 402–3.

177. Gray, *Prophetic Figures*, 20.

178. Ibid., 21–22.

179. Ibid., 23.

180. See conveniently his treatment of the issue in the edition of the *Testaments* in his *APOT* 2.289. Thoma ("John Hyrcanus I," 135–40) also sees Hyrcanus behind references in the *Testament of Levi*.

a prophet. This would hardly fit the situation of Hyrcanus, who was neither king nor from the tribe of Judah.[181]

This John, a man of so many distinctions, accomplishments, and gifts, appears in more sources than Josephus's two histories. The coins minted in his name constitute the first category of references outside of Josephus. Until recently, the most widely accepted view had been that John had not minted coins and that the ones with the name יהוחנן were from his grandson Hyrcanus II; this was a revision of still earlier claims assigning those coins to Hyrcanus I. Discoveries in the last several years have now changed that picture and make it quite likely that the יהוחנן coins are to be attributed to John Hyrcanus.

Meshorer lists four Hebrew names that are found on the Hasmonean coins: Jehohanan the high priest; Judah the high priest; Jehonathan the king + Alexander, or Jehonathan (Jonathan) the high priest; and Mattityah the high priest. The ones in the first category he had earlier assigned to Hyrcanus II, but two archeological finds have rendered that conclusion invalid. First, in Galilee a trove of about seven hundred bronze coins has come to light. Among them were many Hasmonean *perutot*, a few independent coins from Akko, and a number of Seleucid coins. All of the Hasmonean coins have the name יהוחנן on them, while none of the other coins is later in date than 110 BCE. This entails that the יהוחנן coins are from the same period and thus should be attributed to John Hyrcanus. Second, as we have seen above, the Samaritan city on the summit of Mount Gerizim, where the temple was destroyed by Hyrcanus's forces in about 113–111 BCE, has yielded coins from second-century Seleucid kings. They date from before 113 BCE. There, a considerable number of יהוחנן coins were uncovered, and these must be from John Hyrcanus.[182]

Meshorer thinks, on the basis of the historical evidence, that John Hyrcanus began minting coins in the year 128 BCE.[183] On the ten categories of coins that he assigns to him, Meshorer finds two different inscriptions, surrounded in each case by a wreath:

- יהוחנן הכהן הגדול וחבר היהודים,
  Jehohanan the high priest and the assembly of the Jews

- יהוחנן הכהן הגדול ראש חבר היהודים,
  Jehohanan the high priest, the head of the assembly of the Jews[184]

---

181. Although *T. Levi* 8:11 says that Levi's descendants would be divided into three offices, 8:17 mentions high priests, judges, and scribes.

182. Meshorer, *A Treasury of Jewish Coins,* 30–31.

183. Ibid., 35.

184. Ibid., 35–36.

There has been debate about the meaning of the noun חבר in these inscriptions. Does it refer to the entire Jewish community or is it the name of a ruling institution presided over by the high priest? According to Schürer, its meaning is "now generally accepted to be 'congregation', i.e. the γερουσία of the Jewish nation known from later documents as the Sanhedrin."[185] That would be an important point if true, although certainty eludes us; nevertheless, it is perhaps not an accident that the first office listed on the coins is that of high priest.[186] And, whatever this "congregation" was, the high priest was the leader (ראש) of it.

On John's coins, the most prominent symbols are a pair of cornucopias, connected at the base and with pomegranates between them; this may be a unique Jewish creation. There are also types showing lilies or palm branches and ones with a war helmet.[187]

A second source of information outside the writings of Josephus comes from archeological excavations. One prominent building project that may have begun during the reign of Hyrcanus is the Hasmonean winter palace complex in the area of Jericho. In the vicinity of Tulul Abu el-'alayiq near the mouth of the Wadi Qelt, excavators headed by Ehud Netzer of the Hebrew University of Jerusalem found an area extending some six acres in which there were many remains of palaces, aqueducts, and swimming pools. Although the complex reached its fullest development in the Herodian period, it appears that the first stage of construction took place during the reign of John Hyrcanus.[188] The palace complex provides evidence of Hasmonean wealth and luxury and gives concrete witness to the claims in the literature that these high priests became very rich indeed.

Although Josephus's accounts of John Hyrcanus's reign are positive, he does indicate that opposition arose. Among the opposition groups we may be able to number the authors of some texts found in the Qumran caves. He could be named in 4Q331 1 i 7 (line 6 mentions "the priest"): .] יוחנן לבי אל As the editor, Joseph Fitzmyer, writes: "Though this Yoḥanan might be someone else, it is probably the youngest son of Simon Maccabee, John Hyrcanus

---

185. *History*, 1.211. See n. 25 where older views are noted.

186. Uriel Rappaport, "The History of the Hasmonean State—From Jonathan to Mattathias Antigonus," in *The Hasmonean Period*, ed. D. Amit and H. Eshel, Sideret 'Idan 19 (Jerusalem: Yitzhak ben-Zvi, 1995), 65–66 (Hebrew).

187. Meshorer, *A Treasury of Jewish Coins*, 37–39.

188. Ehud Netzer, "The Winter Palaces of the Judean Kings at Jericho at the End of the Second Temple Period," *BASOR* 228 (1977): 1–13; idem, "Jericho: Tulul Abu el-'alayiq," in *NEAEHL* 2.682–91; and idem, *Hasmonean and Herodian Palaces at Jericho*, vol. 1 (Jerusalem: IES, 2001).

I."[189] Also, Hyrcanus is the most likely candidate for the title "man of Belial" in 4QTest where biblical passages about the future prophet, ruler, and priest are cited and perhaps directed against the claim that John held these offices.[190]

Hyrcanus's name appears a number of times in rabbinic literature (in addition to the story related above about the voice from the sanctuary). Especially prominent in those references are a series of abrogations credited to him. For example, in *m. Maʿas. Š.* 5:15 we read: "Johanan the High Priest did away with the Avowal[191] concerning the Tithe. He too made an end also of the 'Awakeners' and the 'Stunners'. Until his days the hammer used to smite in Jerusalem. And in his days none needed to inquire concerning *demai*-produce."[192] As Danby explains the references (following *b. Soṭah* 48a), the avowal regarding the tithe means "So that a man need not say, 'I have given it to the levite', for Ezra had enacted that, as a punishment to the levites who did not go up with him to Jerusalem, the First Tithe should be given to the priests." The awakeners is a term for "the daily singing by the levites of the verse (Ps. 44[23]) 'Awake, why sleepest thou, O Lord?' because of its unseemliness." The stunners were the individuals responsible for stunning sacrificial animals before they were killed. "This was abolished as likely to cause a forbidden blemish in the beast." The smiting hammer is supposed to mean that even for the middle days of the seven-day festivals, John forbade necessary work, while the *demai*-produce is produce about which there is doubt whether a tithe had been taken from it. John "issued the ruling that (Sot. 48a) only Heave-offering of Tithe and Second Tithe need be taken account of in *demai*-produce."[193]

Lieberman devoted a short study to two of the edicts attributed to John. He noted that the reason stated for laws is not necessarily the real explanation for them and that these rulings from the high priest are examples. The

---

189. "331. 4QpapHistorical Text C," in *Qumran Cave 4 XXVI Miscellanea, Part 1*, DJD 36 (Oxford: Clarendon, 2000), 277. The Hasmonean name *Shelamzion* is mentioned in 1 ii 7.

190. Hanan Eshel, "The History of the Qumran Community and the Historical Details in the Dead Sea Scrolls," *Qad* 30 (1997): 91.

191. Saul Lieberman adduced evidence showing that the term הודייה, which Danby and others render as "avowal," actually means "declaration" (*Hellenism in Jewish Palestine: Studies in the Literary Transmission, Beliefs and Manners of Palestine in the I Century b.c.e.–IV Century c.e.*, Texts and Studies of the Jewish Theological Seminary of America 18 [New York: Jewish Theological Seminary of America, 1962], 140 n. 11).

192. Herbert Danby, *The Mishnah* (Oxford: Oxford Univ. Press, 1933), 82. The same text occurs in *m. Soṭah* 9:10.

193. Danby, *Mishnah*, 82 nn. 4–8. Schürer took these rulings to express John's opposition to the Pharisees, but that seems unlikely especially for the *demai* ruling (*History*, 1.214). See Geller, "Alexander Jannaeus and the Pharisees Rift," 204–5. For the rulings, compare also Werner, *Johann Hyrkan*, 49–60; Derenbourg, *Essai*, 71–72; Thoma, "John Hyrcanus I," 133–34.

"Stunners" were in fact abolished, he maintained, because this was a heathen custom (*t. Soṭah* 13:10 is explicit about this). The same was the case for the "Awakeners," though again another explanation is stated. He concluded that the evidence he marshaled "makes it very probable that the object of some of the abrogations of Johanan was to purify the Temple service and to keep out of it all traces of pagan worship. For reasons of tact he did not divulge his purpose to the public. But the desired effect was achieved, and the Rabbis gave him the deserved praise for it."[194]

The mishnaic ruling about stunning sacrificial animals before slaughtering them has become the object of renewed discussion in connection with 11QT[a] 34.6, particularly in light of the interpretation of the passage in *y. Soṭah* 9:11, 24a: "As for the 'Stunners', those who would strike [upon] the calf between its horns. Johanan the High Priest cried to them: How long will you feed the altar with blemished animals and thereupon he made rings for them. Rabbi Ba said in the name of R. Judah (R. Johanan): He made rings for them, wide at the bottom and narrow at the top" (compare *t. Soṭah* 13:10). In 11QT[a] 34.6, part of a column dealing with the slaughtering house at the temple, such rings for holding animals are mentioned: ואוסרים את קרני[195] הפרים אל הטבעות. Yadin held that, rather than describing a contemporary practice, the writer was making a case for introducing the rings: "it was the commands of the scroll—or the concept behind them favoured by the author and his sect—that influenced John Hyrcanus to make changes in the Temple in their spirit."[196]

---

194. "Three Abrogations of Johanan the High Priest," in *Hellenism in Jewish Palestine*, 143 (the chapter is on pp. 139–43). He added some notes about the *demai* issue, holding that it too could be an example of the practice he had isolated. "The generally accepted opinion is that during the priesthood of Johanan, the tithes were given to (or forcibly taken by) the priests instead of the Levites. The statement of Deut. 26:13 (*And I gave it to the Levite etc.*) in the Declaration would therefore be untrue. Accordingly, the High Priest, who most probably supported the priesthood, was opposed to the Declaration because it would remind the worshipper that he broke the law by letting the tithes go to the priests, and therefore abolished it altogether. However, it is very unlikely that Johanan revealed his motive publicly. He probably found some other excuse. Perhaps his pretext is preserved in a different tradition (see *Tosefta, TP* and *TB* ibid.): he claimed that the people in general did not strictly observe the laws of the tithes (i. e. gave them neither to the Levites nor to the priests), and he therefore canceled the Declaration in order not to cause some people to utter a lie in the Temple" (143 n. 28). According to Yadin (*The Temple Scroll*, 1.388–89 n. 3), 11QT[a] 43, which combines Deut 14:22-23 and 26:12-13, "deletes the text of the avowal concerning the tithe."

195. Yadin reads ראשי (*Temple Scroll*, 2.145), but Elisha Qimron's reading given above is perhaps slightly better (see his *The Temple Scroll: A Critical Edition with Extensive Reconstructions*, JDS [Beer Sheva: Ben-Gurion Univ. of the Negev Press, 1996], 49), although it is difficult to read the letters on the photograph.

196. Yadin, *Temple Scroll*, 1.388. Yadin found various strands of evidence from which he

We have, then, several sources that attribute cultic innovations to Hyrcanus, some of which would probably have been acceptable to the Pharisees and some perhaps not (for example, the rings).

Apart from the abrogations, *m. Parah* 3:5 offers another reference to John: "If they did not find the ashes from the seven [earlier] Sin-offerings, they could use them from six, or from five, or from four, or from three, or from two, or from one. Who had prepared them? Moses prepared the first, Ezra prepared the second, and five were prepared after Ezra. So R. Meir. But the Sages say: Seven since Ezra. And who prepared them? Simeon the Just and Johanan the High Priest prepared two each, and Eliehoenai the son of Hakkof and Hanamel the Egyptian and Ishmael the son of Phiabi prepared one each." The interesting point about this Mishnah is that John is paired with the highly honored Simeon the Just as the only two high priests who prepared two red heifers (see Num 19:1-10), although his eventual opposition to the Pharisaic teachings might have led one to expect otherwise.

Finally, in *m. Yad.* 4:6, part of a section listing disputes between Sadducees and Pharisees, we encounter his name as a striking example: "The Sadducees say, We cry out against you, O ye Pharisees, for ye say, 'The Holy Scriptures render the hands unclean', [and] 'The writings of Hamiram do not render the hands unclean'. Rabban Johanan b. Zakkai said, Have we naught against the Pharisees save this!—for lo, they say, 'The bones of an ass are clean, and the bones of Johanan the High Priest are unclean'. They said to him, As is our love for them so is their uncleanness—that no man may make spoons of the bones of his father or mother. He said to them, Even so the Holy Scriptures: as is our love for them so is their uncleanness; [whereas] the writings of Hamiram which are held in no account do not render the hands unclean."[197] John's bones are here cited as a parallel to the scriptures as two positive entities, which have the interesting result of rendering something impure.

So, John Hyrcanus was a unique figure in the list of Jewish high priests and his legacy cast a long shadow over several bodies of literature. He was

---

concluded that the Temple Scroll was composed "in the days of John Hyrcanus or shortly earlier [*sic*]" (*The Temple Scroll*, 1.390). One such argument came from the section on the law of the king (56.12—59.21), which legislates not only about offensive and defensive wars (John fought both types) but also rules that the royal guard be Jewish, whereas John was the first to hire mercenaries.

197. Danby, *Mishnah*, 784. *Tg. Ps.-J.* Deut 33:11, a verse from the blessing on Levi, reads: "Bless, O Lord, the sacrifices of the House of Levi, those who give the tenth from the tithe, and receive with pleasure the oblation from the hand of Elijah the priest which he offered on Mt. Carmel. Break the loins of Ahab, his enemy, and the neck of the false prophets who rose against him. As for the enemies of John the High Priest, may they have no foot to stand on" (quoted from Schürer, *History of the Jewish People*, 1.215 n. 33).

surely one of the greatest of the Hasmoneans and yet a man who, like his father Simon, did not claim the office of king for himself. In fact, Josephus tells us that John left his wife in charge of the land (*J.W.* 1.3, 1 [§71]), not one of his sons. Derenbourg thought this might provide a hint that the Pharisaic argument about separating the offices had had some influence on John;[198] yet, as we will see, family problems may rather be the explanation.

20. Aristobulus I (104–103 BCE)

After the long and distinguished career of John Hyrcanus ended, he was succeeded by his son Aristobulus I, who reigned for a shorter time than any of the other Hasmoneans. For Aristobulus, whose Hebrew name was Judas (*Ant.* 20.10, 3 [§240]), our sources are *J.W.* 1.3, 1 (§70) to 1.3, 6 (§84) and *Ant.* 13.11, 1 (§301) to 13.11, 3 (§319), with the brief notice in *Ant.* 20.10, 3 (§§240–41). Josephus claims Aristobulus was the eldest son of Hyrcanus, and, as John had reigned for thirty-one years, Aristobulus may not have been very young when he inherited his father's offices.

Aristobulus was mentioned as a military leader already in the days of his father. Hyrcanus appointed Antigonus and Aristobulus to oversee the siege of Samaria (*Ant.* 13.10, 2 [§276]). He is credited with defeating Antiochus (either VIII or IX), who came to relieve the city from the Hasmonean siege against it (*Ant.* 13.10, 2 [§277]), with his brother joining the pursuit of the defeated king—the incident that was behind the story of the *bat qol* heard by Hyrcanus (*Ant.* 13.10, 3 [§§282–83]).

The succession to Hyrcanus surfaced strong tensions in the family. Josephus reports regarding his family members that Aristobulus honored his next-oldest brother Antigonus, while "the rest he imprisoned in chains. His mother also, who had disputed his claim to authority, John having left her mistress [κυρίαν] of the realm, he confined in bonds and carried his cruelty so far as to starve her to death" (*J.W.* 1.3, 1 [§71]; see *Ant.* 13.11, 1 [§302]).[199] Even his relations with Antigonus would soon dissolve into jealousy, suspicion, and finally execution. It does appear from Josephus's statement that Hyrcanus designated his wife as his successor, something that will recur at the end of Jannaeus's reign. Naturally, Hyrcanus's spouse could succeed him only as the

---

198. *Essai*, 85.

199. Julius Wellhausen thought the mother and brothers in question were his stepmother and stepbrothers and adds since if his wife was much older than Jannaeus, he probably was as well. This explains his affection for Antigonus, his actual brother of a similar age (*Israelitische und jüdische Geschichte*, 2nd ed. [Berlin: Reimer, 1895], 264 n. 1).

secular ruler, not as high priest; Aristobulus, then, would have inherited the high priesthood and military leadership but not the political supervision of the realm. By starving his mother to death, Aristobulus dispensed with the division of power ordered by his father and took the temporal sovereignty for himself as well.[200]

Despite the short reign of Aristobulus, Josephus says that he "transformed the government into a monarchy, and was the first to assume the diadem, four hundred and seventy-one years[201] and three months after the return of the people to their country, when released from servitude in Babylon" (*J. W.* 1.3, 1 [§70]; compare *Ant.* 13.11, 1 [§301]; *Ant.* 20.10, 3 [§241]). Two issues arise here: the change in government, and the date for the change.

The change in the Hasmonean ruler's title from a lesser one to that of king may have marked an important stage in the evolution of the Hasmonean state. It appears that the roles of Aristobulus's predecessors differed from those of kings in little more than name, but they apparently refrained from adopting the title. In view of the declining power of the Seleucid kingdom, Hyrcanus, at least, could have taken that step, but no source says that he did. Also, even at the great assembly that accorded high honors to Simon (1 Macc 14:25-49), nothing is said about kingship. If we examine the titles used for the earlier Hasmonean rulers, they are:

Jonathan: general, governor of the province (στρατηγός, μεριδάρχης; 1 Macc 10:65; compare also 9:30 where he is ἄρχων)
Simon: governor of Ladder of Tyre to the border of Egypt (στρατηγός; 1 Macc 11:59)
    Leader (ἡγούμενος; 1 Macc 13:8, 42; 14:35, 41)
    Governor (στρατηγός; 14:42)
    Ethnarch (ἐθνάρχης; 14:47; 15:1-2)
John: rule of the nation (ἄρχη, τὸ ἄρχειν; *Ant.* 13.10, 5, 7 [§§291, 299])

So, Aristobulus, according to Josephus, was the first to take the next step and adopt the title of king. The historian mentions participation by no national or other governing body in making this decision.

If we had only Josephus's narratives, we would not be aware of a problem with this claim. However, Strabo in his *Geography* 16.2, 40 says: "At any rate [he had just mentioned a number of characters who had received instructions from the gods and included Moses among them], when now Judaea was under the rule of tyrants, Alexander was first to declare himself king instead of priest

---

200. See Schürer, *History of the Jewish People*, 1.216.
201. *Ant.* 13.11, 1 (§301) gives 481 years.

[πρῶτος ἀνθ᾿ ἱερέως ἀνέδειξεν ἑαυτὸν βασιλέα ᾿Αλέξανδρος]; and both Hyrcanus and Aristobulus were sons of his; and when they were at variance about the empire, Pompey went over and overthrew them."[202] Strabo's reference to Alexander's two sons and their encounter with Pompey demonstrates that the Alexander in question was Jannaeus. Although some historians prefer Strabo's testimony over that of Josephus,[203] his seemingly straightforward statement is not without difficulties: the Hasmonean sovereign clearly did not relinquish the high priesthood when adopting the title of king, as he indicates. Also, because of the lack of source material, it is not evident how much Strabo knew about the Hasmoneans who governed before Jannaeus, none of whom he names. It seems likely that Josephus is the more reliable historian here because he had the data to write a much fuller account of the Hasmonean rule, whereas Strabo mentions just a few individuals and episodes in it, including the inaccuracy just noted. Also, Josephus's assertion is a sort of narrative *lectio difficilior,* in that it would be more difficult to explain his attribution of kingship to the short-lived and relatively obscure high priest Aristobulus than to the more famous, not to say notorious, Alexander Jannaeus, who reigned a much longer time.[204]

The surviving numismatic evidence offers no help regarding the question whether Aristobulus assumed the title of king. As one might expect, for an individual who reigned for about one year, the number of coins minted, preserved, and identified from his term in office is not large. In his case, there is the added difficulty that another Aristobulus served as both king and high priest (Aristobulus II [67–63 BCE]) and may have minted coins. As we have seen, Josephus says that Aristobulus's Hebrew name was Judah, and a small number of Hasmonean coins with the name Judah are available. Meshorer divides them into two categories that differ somewhat epigraphically but, apart from spelling, bear the same legend:

Category K (20 coins)   יהודה כהן גדול וחבר היהודים
Jehudah high priest and the assembly of the Jews
Category L (7 coins)   יהודה הכהן הגדל וחבר היהדים
Jehudah the high priest and the assembly of the Jews

---

202. Cited from Menahem Stern, *Greek and Latin Authors on Jews and Judaism,* 3 vols. (Jerusalem: Israel Academy of Sciences and Humanities, 1974–78), 1.301–302. The Greek text for these lines is on p. 296.

203. See, for example, Eduard Meyer, *Ursprung und Anfänge des Christentums,* 3 vols. (Stuttgart: Cotta, 1921), 2.275, especially n. 6; Rappaport, "The History of the Hasmonean State," 69.

204. See the discussion of Menahem Stern, *Greek and Latin Authors,* 1.307.

He is not certain whether they should be attributed to Aristobulus I or II and finds the coins numismatically of little significance. They are all of the same small value (one *perutah*), with the inscription inside a wreath on one side of the coins and cornucopiae with pomegrantes between them on the other. At any rate, none of the coins has an inscription with the title *king*. The first time that title appears on Hasmonean coins is during the reign of Alexander Jannaeus (103–76 BCE).[205]

Regarding the chronology that Josephus gives (471 or 481 years after the return from Babylonian captivity), his numbers in both sources are too large to fit the modern understanding of postexilic chronology. If, indeed, Josephus is referring to the return in the first year of Cyrus (539 BCE), then 471 years later would bring us to 68 BCE, while the variant in *Antiquities* would put Aristobulus's assumption of the crown in 58 BCE. Although the number is probably inaccurate or inaccurately transmitted, it does at least show that not all ancient Jewish writers believed the time from the exile to the Hasmonean rule was a short one. In fact, Josephus consistently has too many years to fit the period.

Josephus's number has been related to an early interpretation of Daniel's seventy weeks of years or 490 years (Dan 9:24-27).[206] If one accepts the number 481 (plus three months) as the correct reading in Josephus and adds the one year of Aristobulus's reign, one could conclude that Alexander Jannaeus began his rule in the last heptad of the seventy year-weeks of Daniel's prophecy. Naturally, this would reflect very poorly on Jannaeus, and, it has been claimed, the chronology stems from his enemies the Pharisees early in his reign. The length of Jannaeus's reign soon gave the lie to this prediction. While all of this is possible, there are too many uncertainties connected with it (for example, the variant reading 471 in Josephus) to assign much weight to it.

Much space in Josephus's brief narratives about Aristobulus is devoted to the tragic deterioration in his relations with his favored brother Antigonus, a story in which a high-priestly duty plays a part. In fact, the story occupies almost all of the Aristobulus section in *War* (1.3, 2 [§72] to 1.3, 6 [§84]). Josephus sees retribution at work for the king's cruelty to the other members of his family. To be sure, he blames the break between Aristobulus and Antigonus on "knavish courtiers" (§72), but the eventual murder of his beloved brother is said to have hastened Aristobulus's death. At first, Aristobulus recognized the

---

205. Meshorer, *Treasury*, 39–40; see also 183–84 for a catalog of all the examples.

206. See the helpful summary of the arguments in William Adler, "The Apocalyptic Survey of History Adapted by Christians: Daniel's Prophecy of Seventy Weeks," in *The Jewish Apocalyptic Heritage in Early Christianity*, ed. J. VanderKam and W. Adler, CRINT 3.4 (Minneapolis: Fortress Press, 1996), 211–12.

character of the negative reports he received about his brother—they arose from envy. Then, matters reached a turning point at the festival of Tabernacles.

> [O]ne day when Antigonus had come in pomp from a campaign to attend the festival at which, according to national custom, tabernacles are erected in God's honour, Aristobulus happened to be ill; and, at the close of the ceremony, Antigonus, surrounded by his bodyguard and arrayed with the utmost splendour, went up (to the Temple) and offered special worship on his brother's behalf. Thereupon these villains went off to the king and told him of the military escort and of Antigonus's air of assurance, grander than became a subject, and that he was coming with an immense body of troops to put him to death, disdaining the mere honours of royalty when he might occupy the throne itself. (*War* 1.3, 2 [§§73–74])

It is likely that in this passage we have one of the few witnesses to the practice that a high priest, when unfit to officiate at a temple ceremony, would be replaced by his brother. That is, the special worship that Antigonus offered was not "on his brother's behalf," as Thackeray renders it, but "in place of his brother [ὑπὲρ τἀδελφοῦ]." Aristobulus's sickness (a repeated theme in the narrative) prevented him from carrying out his high-priestly duties; hence his brother replaced him temporarily.[207] The story also serves as a reminder that, at least while the high priests were also the civil rulers, such occasions could give birth to serious suspicions and worries on the part of the high priest who was replaced if only for a short time.

This time Aristobulus believed the charges brought to his attention and set up a test. The king placed his own bodyguards in a subterranean passage and invited Antigonus to visit him. The guards were ordered to allow him to enter the castle Baris, where Aristobulus was bedridden, if he came unarmed; if he came armed, the guards were to execute him. Aristobulus himself, we learn, instructed Antigonus to come without his arms (1.3, 3 [§75]). Aristobulus's wife, however (called the queen [βασίλισσα]), conspired with Antigonus's enemies. They induced the king's messengers to omit his instruc-

---

207. The parallel in *Ant.* 13.11, 1 (§304) is worded differently: "Antigonus, arrayed in great splendour and with his heavy-armed soldiers about him, went up to the temple to celebrate the festival and to pray earnestly for his brother's recovery." *B. Yoma* 47a records an occasion when the high priest Simon son of Kamithos was defiled by an Arab's spittle on the evening before Yom Kippur began; his brother served as his replacement for the day. See Joachim Jeremias, *Jerusalem in the Time of Jesus: An Investigation into Economic and Social Conditions during the New Testament Period,* trans. F. H. Cave and C. H. Cave (Philadelphia: Fortress Press, 1969), 153 esp. n. 24, for the references.

tions about arms. Instead, they told Antigonus "that his brother had heard that he had procured for himself some very fine armour and military decorations in Galilee; that illness prevented him from paying a visit of inspection; 'but now that you are on the point of departure, I shall be very glad to see you in your armour'" (§76). Antigonus suspected nothing and promptly marched to his death at the hands of Aristobulus's bodyguards in a "dark passage, called Strato's Tower" (§77). The mention of Strato's Tower allows Josephus the opportunity to tell the story about the Essene Judas who had predicted the place and day of the event (1.3, 5 [§§78–80]).

When Aristobulus heard what had happened, his health declined further until he died "after a reign of no more than a year" (1.3, 6 [§84]). In *Antiquities,* Josephus tells the same story but adds a section about the accomplishments and character of Aristobulus. He mentions that he had the "title of Philhellene, he conferred many benefits on his country, for he made war on the Ituraeans and acquired a good part of their territory for Judaea and compelled the inhabitants, if they wished to remain in their country, to be circumcised and to live in accordance with the laws of the Jews" (*Ant.* 13.11, 3 [§318]). He also cites the testimony of Strabo (via Timagenes) that Aristobulus was "a kindly person" (§319; Strabo is also the authority for the report about circumcising some of the Itureans). So, Josephus claims that, for the Itureans, Aristobulus pursued the same policy that his father had for the Idumeans (*Ant.* 13.9, 1 [§§257–58]). About this, there is serious question whether Josephus understood the matter correctly. His citation from Strabo says: "This man was a kindly person and very serviceable to the Jews, for he acquired territory for them, and brought over [ὠκειώσατο; it can mean "to make someone a friend"] to them a portion of the Ituraean nation, whom he joined to them by the bond of circumcision." Josephus infers that Aristobulus forced circumcision upon the Itureans, but it is not clear that Strabo said the same. It may be that Strabo says no more than that some Itureans, a people who may have practiced circumcision, were also brought into political association with the Jews.[208] The same may have been the case for the Idumeans in John Hyrcanus's time. If this is the case, then it is possible that Josephus's inference is drawn from the presumably anti-Hasmonean Nicolaus of Damascus, although that is hardly the only conclusion one could reach.[209]

---

208. See the detailed discussion of this much-debated issue, including the evidence of an otherwise unknown Ptolemy, in Shaye J. D. Cohen, *The Beginnings of Jewishness: Boundaries, Varieties, Uncertainties,* HCS 31 (Berkeley: Univ. of California Press, 1999), 110–29.

209. M. Stern, *Greek and Latin Authors,* 1.267. As Stern notes about this passage from Strabo, it "may show how one can use Strabo's tradition to correct the picture that emerges from Nicolaus" (1.271). For the relation between Strabo and Nicolaus, see Schürer, *History of the Jewish People,* 1.26.

Mention of the Itureans indicates that Aristobulus's troops took territory to the north of Galilee, perhaps in the region of the Beqa Valley. However far his conquests or annexations went, the Hasmonean state was clearly expanding northward.

21. Alexander Jannaeus (103–76 BCE)

The ancient sources for the reign of Alexander Jannaeus are primarily Josephus's two books (*J.W.* 1.4, 1–8 [§§85–106]; *Ant.* 13.12, 1 to 15, 5 [§§320–405]), with *Antiquities* having the much longer account. There are some references to him in rabbinic literature, and a multitude of coins bearing his name and titles have survived. It is highly likely that he is called "the angry young lion," particularly in 4QPesher Nahum (4Q169). Josephus provides some information regarding his role as high priest, although most of the narratives catalogue his seemingly endless battles against neighboring cities and states.

As he reaches the time of Aristobulus's premature death, Josephus mentions no son who might have served as his heir. Perhaps he had no sons or, if he did, he (or they) might have been too young to be considered for the succession. Whatever Aristobulus's family situation may have been, his spouse took an active role in the direction of the kingdom, as Hyrcanus's widow had attempted to do at his death. *Jewish War* 1.4, 1 (§85) does not supply her name, but according to *Ant.* 13.12, 1 (§320) she was called Salina (variant: Salome).[210] She "released his [Aristobulus's] imprisoned brothers and placed on the throne Alexander who had the double advantage over the others of seniority and apparent moderation of character.[211] However, on coming to

---

210. There is no proof for it, but she does appear to be the woman who became Jannaeus's wife and, twenty-seven years later, succeeded him on the throne of Judea. If she was both the widow of Aristobulus and the wife of his brother Jannaeus, the two roles raise the issue whether Jannaeus married her in obedience to the levirate law (which would imply that she and Aristobulus had no sons). *Ant.* 13.15, 5 (§404) says that Jannaeus was forty-nine years of age when he died, implying that he would have been twenty-two or twenty-three years old when he began to reign; *Ant.* 13.16, 6 (§430) records that Alexandra was seventy-three when she died, after reigning nine years following Alexander's death. That is, if she is the same woman, she would have been thirty-seven years of age when Jannaeus began his reign and at which time they were presumably married. Wellhausen commented: "Er zählte 24 [*sic*], sie 37 Jahre, woraus man die Art der Ehe erkennt" (*Israelitische und jüdische Geschichte*, 264). Joseph Sievers ("The Role of Women in the Hasmonean Dynasty," in *Josephus, the Bible, and History*, ed. L. H. Feldman and G. Hata [Leiden: Brill, 1989], 135–36) points out that Lev 21:14 prohibits a high priest from marrying a widow and mentions possible solutions to the problem.

211. The Greek word behind "moderation of character" is μετριότης, which, as Marcus notes, can also mean "knowing his place" (*Josephus* 7, 389 n. d). Yet, there is no indication in the text of Josephus's two books that she attempted to seize political power for herself, leaving Jannaeus with the high priesthood alone. See Sievers, "Role of Women," 135.

power, he put to death one brother, who had aspirations to the throne; the survivor, who was content with a quiet life, he held in honour" (*J.W.* 1.4, 1 [§85]; compare *Ant.* 13.12, 1 [§§320, 323]).

Into this brief opening statement about Jannaeus drawn from *War*, Josephus (as we saw above) inserts a short addition about him in *Antiquities*: "but it had been his fate to be hated by his father from the time he was born, and never to come into his sight so long as he lived. Now the reason for this hatred is said to have been as follows. Of all his sons Hyrcanus loved best the two elder ones, Antigonus and Aristobulus; and once when God appeared to him in his sleep, he asked Him which of his sons was destined to be his successor. And when God showed him the features of Alexander, he was grieved that this one should be the heir of all his possessions, and so he let him be brought up in Galilee from his birth. God, however, did not deceive Hyrcanus" (13.12, 1 [§§321–22]).

The many wars of Jannaeus will not concern us here other than to note that his victories (there were also a number of defeats) resulted in an expansion of the territory of Judea to the west, north, and east, yielding a kingdom whose size rivaled that claimed for the united monarchy of biblical Israel. Despite or rather because of his many foreign conquests, Jannaeus aroused much dissatisfaction at home. The massive drain on human and economic resources eventually sparked violent protests, and, in the narratives about them, his role as high priest plays a part. Yet, the issue of corpse impurity for a high priest in battle never surfaces in the ancient accounts about him.

After relating the battles between Jannaeus and Ptolemy IX (Soter II) Lathyrus (he ruled Egypt in 116–107 and 88–81 BCE and Cyprus alone in 107–88) and how Jannaeus became allied against him with Cleopatra III, Ptolemy's mother, Josephus relates a story that is supposed to express the high esteem in which Alexander was held by Jews in both Judea and the Diaspora. When Jannaeus presented gifts to Cleopatra, some of her advisors urged her to accept them but also to invade his country and take control of it. However, Ananias, one of Onias IV's sons who was a commander of her forces, countered their proposal. He said "that she would commit an injustice if she deprived an ally of his own possessions, especially one who is our kinsman. For I would have you know that an injustice done to this man will make all us Jews your enemies" (*Ant.* 13.13, 2 [§354]). The queen followed his advice and made an alliance with Jannaeus (§355). From this statement (if it is reliable), it appears that any antagonism felt by the Oniads for the Hasmoneans had disappeared.

When Josephus's long expansion in *Antiquities* ends and he rejoins the narrative of *War*, the occasion is the revolt of the Judeans against Jannaeus (beginning at *J.W.* 1.4, 3 [§88]; *Ant.* 13.13, 5 [§372]). It will be helpful to have the parallel accounts before us.

J.W. 1.4, 3 (§§88–89)	*Ant.* 13.13, 5 (§§372–74)
After his reduction of these places to servitude, the Jewish populace rose in revolt against him at one of the festivals; for it is on these festive occasions that sedition is most apt to break out.	As for Alexander, his own people revolted against him—for the nation was aroused against him—at the celebration of the festival, and as he stood beside the altar and was about to sacrifice, they pelted him with citrons, it being a custom among the Jews that at the festival of Tabernacles everyone holds wands made of palm branches and citrons—these we have described elsewhere; and they added insult to injury by saying that he was descended from captives and was unfit to hold office and to sacrifice; and being enraged at this, he killed some six thousand of them, and also placed a wooden barrier about the altar and the temple as far as the coping (of the court) which the priests alone were permitted to enter, and by this means blocked the
It was thought that he would never have quelled this conspiracy, had not his mercenaries come to his aid. These were natives of Pisidia and Cilicia; Syrians he did not admit to the force on account of their innate hatred of his nation. After slaying upwards of six thousand of the insurgents . . .	people's way to him. He also maintained foreign troops of Pisidians and Cilicians, for he could not use Syrians, being at war with them.

The festival of Tabernacles, since it is one of the three pilgrimage festivals, would have attracted a large crowd to the temple in Jerusalem. And, as Josephus notes, such occasions were rich in potential for mischief. In this case, the pilgrims took advantage of the fact that they were carrying citrons or lemons—surely an usettling circumstance for any leader;[212] they threw them at the high priest as he was about to offer sacrifice (*War* does not provide this detail). Neither of Josephus's accounts explains specifically why they did this on this particular celebration of the festival, rather than, say, at the one the

---

212. See Rubenstein, *The History of Sukkot*, 82, who observes that this is the "earliest attestation of the citron as the 'fruit of goodly trees' of Lev. 23:40."

year before.[213] But in *Antiquities,* Josephus adds their charge that he was unfit to serve as high priest because he was born from captives. This reminds one of the charge directed against his father Hyrcanus by Eleazar (*Ant.* 13.10, 5 [§292]), although it is phrased more generally in the present case ("descended from captives"). One could argue that Josephus did not know which Hasmonean high priest was the object of the charge and hence leveled it against two of them, but if John Hyrcanus would have been ineligible to serve as high priest because his mother had been a captive of war, that experience would have rendered his sons ineligible as well. We should also recall that the talmudic parallel to the story of Hyrcanus's break with the Pharisees attaches it to Jannaeus, where he is the one falsely accused of being descended from a captive.

Josephus may not be our only source for the story about showering Jannaeus with lemons. A somewhat similar story figures in *b. Yoma* 26b and *b. Sukkah* 48b and may be under consideration in *m. Sukkah* 4:9. The mishnaic paragraph deals with the water libation performed on each of the days of the festival of Tabernacles.

> 'The Water-libation, seven days'—what was the manner of this? They used to fill a golden flagon holding three *logs* with water from Siloam. When they reached the Water Gate they blew [on the *shofar*] a sustained, a quavering and another sustained blast. [The priest whose turn of duty it was] went up the [Altar-]Ramp and turned to the right where were two silver bowls. R. Judah says: They were of plaster, but their appearance was darkened because of the wine. They had each a hole like to a narrow snout, one wide and the other narrow, so that both bowls emptied themselves together. The bowl to the west was for water and that to the east was for wine. But if the flagon of water was emptied into the bowl for wine, or the flagon of wine into the bowl for water, that sufficed. R. Judah says: With one *log* they could perform the libations throughout eight days. To the priest who performed the libation they used to say, 'Lift up thine hand!' for once a certain one poured the libation over his feet, and all the people threw their citrons at him.[214]

---

213. Derenbourg thought, on the basis of the passages in Josephus and the talmudic ones (see below), that Jannaeus's intent was to show his contempt for the custom of pouring a libation on the altar—a custom that was important to the Pharisees (*Essai,* 98).

214. The translation is from Danby, *Mishnah,* 179. The text of the last part of the quotation reads: ולמנסך אומרים לו הגבה ידך שפעם אחת ניסך אחד על גבי רגליו ורגמוהו כל העם באתרוגיהן (cited from Philip Blackman, *Mishnayot,* vol. 2 *Order Moed,* 2nd ed. [Gateshead: Judaica, 1983], 339).

B. Sukkah 48b (see also *y. Sukkah* 4:8, 54d), commenting on this passage, uses the same wording as the end of the Mishnah but identifies the "certain one" who poured the libation over his feet as a Sadducee, and *t. Sukkah* 3:16 calls him a Boethusian. In no case, however, does a rabbinic text identify this priest as a high priest and certainly not as Jannaeus. In fact, the only striking parallel between the rabbinic references and the story in Josephus is the pelting with lemons,[215] since Josephus says nothing about Jannaeus's pouring a libation on his feet. In the context in Josephus, it appears that the people are more concerned with his war-like ways than with his ritual performance.[216]

In *Antiquities* and *War,* Josephus says that Jannaeus's mercenary forces slaughtered some six thousand people on this occasion. The story furnishes the first indication of open rebellion among the king's Jewish subjects whom Josephus does not define more precisely. They are simply "the Jewish populace" or "the nation." It also exhibits the brutal character of the king and his troops, something that will be witnessed repeatedly in the following stories.

Jannaeus, besides responding with force, altered the architecture of the temple to protect himself from future attacks. Josephus says that he "placed a wooden barrier [δρύφακτον δὲ ξύλινον] about the altar and the temple as far as the coping (of the court) which the priests alone were permitted to enter, and by this means blocked the people's way to him." The translator in the Loeb edition, Robert Marcus, was puzzled by the notice, "since such a barrier (called γείσιον or θριγκός) had been built by Solomon, according to Josephus, *Ant.* viii. 95, and was presumably found in the second, as in Herod's temple, *cf. B.J.* v. 226."[217] Perhaps Josephus means a fence of some sort different than the barrier mentioned elsewhere. T. A. Busink thinks Jannaeus's new barrier was higher than the others: This part reserved for the priests was separated in Herod's temple and probably also in the Second Temple by a low railing from

---

215. Throwing lemons at someone as an insult is more widely attested. See Rubenstein, *The History of Sukkot,* 121–22 n. 68, for references and bibliography.

216. Jeffrey L. Rubenstein ("The Sadducees and the Water Libation," *JQR* 84 [1994]: 417–44) provides a survey of views about the issue in the rabbinic texts and the solutions proposed by scholars. Whatever the issue with pouring a water libation at or on one's feet may have been and whoever the priest in question was, it is not at all clear that any of this is relevant for Josephus's story about Jannaeus. Rubenstein recognizes this point and wonders "whether the Rabbis adapted a popular Josephan tale for their own purposes. This does not deny that the Rabbis recalled a dispute over some aspect of how the libation was to be performed. But it raises the possibility that a minor, rather technical, disagreement, no different from any other of the myriad mishnaic disputes, was read into the Josephan story (or a popularized version of that account) and became exaggerated through the addition of the legendary trope of citron pelting" (423–24).

217. *Josephus* 7, 413 n. g.

the part accessible to the laity. In its place Alexander Jannaeus erected a high wooden partition.[218]

The next evidence for the dreadful relations between Alexander and his subjects follows a brief account of his battles with various Arab opponents east of the Jordan and Sea of Galilee. He nearly met his end in a rough encounter with "a multitude of camels"; *War* says that he lost his entire army in the episode (*J.W.* 1.4, 4 [§90]; *Ant.* 13.13, 5 [§375]).

> He himself escaped to Jerusalem, but the magnitude of his disaster provoked the nation, which had long hated him, to insurrection. Yet once again he proved a match for them, and in a succession of engagements in six years killed no fewer than fifty thousand Jews. His victories, however, by which he wasted his realm, brought him little satisfaction; desisting, therefore, from hostilities, he endeavoured to conciliate his subjects by persuasion. But his change of policy and inconsistency of character only aggravated their hatred; and when he inquired what he could do to pacify them, they replied "Die; even death would hardly reconcile us to one guilty of your enormities."
> (*J.W.* 1.4, 4 [§§90–92]; see *Ant.* 13.13, 5 [§§375–76])

Here, as in the episode regarding the citrons, Josephus does not identify Jannaeus's opponents other than to call them "the nation," "Jews," or "his subjects."[219] Judging by the numbers of those said to have been executed by the king, the opposition to him was widespread indeed.

The prolonged period of murdering his subjects serves as the backdrop in both of Josephus's works for an appeal by the Jewish opponents of Jannaeus to the Seleucid king Demetrius III Eucerus.[220] Demetrius was a son of Antiochus VIII Grypus, and Ptolemy Lathyrus had made him king in Damascus in 96 BCE, although a rival monarch, Philip, Demetrius's brother, reigned in

---

218. T. A. Busink, *Der Tempel von Jerusalem von Salomo bis Herodes*, 2 vols., SFSMD 3 (Leiden: Brill, 1980), 2.889. He also concludes from the passage that at this time, as in the fourth century, the inner court of the temple was not yet divided.

219. Despite Josephus's failure to name the Jewish enemies of the king, it is common to read in the literature that the Pharisees were Alexander's opponents (for example, Schürer, *History of the Jewish People*, 1.223). As we will see, there is evidence from elsewhere in Josephus and in other sources to believe Pharisees were active opponents of Jannaeus, but, if Josephus's numbers for those killed by him are at all accurate, the opposition was more extensive and not confined to one relatively small group.

220. His epithet was εὔκαιρος, "timely, fortunate," but Josephus uses ἄκαιρος, "untimely," which perhaps more accurately reflects what little is known about him.

Antioch (see *Ant.* 13.13, 4 [§§369–70]) and two others ruled elsewhere.[221] It is usually thought that the appeal to Demetrius took place around 88 BCE. The reasoning is that the episode occurred at least six years (the years mentioned in *J.W.* 1.4, 4 [§91]; *Ant.* 13.13, 5 [§376]) after the battle of Gaza (*Ant.* 13.13, 3 [§§358–64]), which in turn took place in approximately 96 BCE, near the time when Antiochus VIII Grypus died (see *Ant.* 13.13, 4 [§365]).[222] It was no later than 88 BCE, because Demetrius was exiled to Parthia at some point in that year.

Demetrius may have commanded no great military force, but it is a dramatic sign of changing times that Jewish people would turn to a Seleucid king for help against a Hasmonean ruler. Demetrius accepted their invitation, invaded Jannaeus's territory with his army and the Jews who had turned to him, and defeated Jannaeus's forces (composed of mercenaries and Jews) near Shechem (*J.W.* 1.4, 5 [§§92–95]; *Ant.* 13.14, 1 [§§377–78]). Although Demetrius's side was victorious, his Jewish allies soon abandoned him and six thousand Jews who felt sympathy for the defeated Jannaeus joined their king who had fled to the hills. As a result, Demetrius withdrew from the land. Jewish opposition to Alexander continued, however, and led to one of the most notorious events in Hasmonean history. Josephus retells it in both books, though he provides more explanation in *Antiquities*.

J.W. 1.4, 6 (§§96–98)	*Antiquities* 13.14, 2 (§§379–83)
The remainder of the people, however, did not, on the withdrawal of their allies, drop their quarrel, but waged continuous war with Alexander, until, after killing a very large number of them, he drove the rest into Bemeselis; having subdued this town, he brought them up to Jerusalem as prisoners. So furious was he that his savagery went to the length of impiety. He had eight hundred of his captives crucified in the midst of the city, and their wives and children butchered before their eyes, while	But later on the Jews fought against Alexander and were defeated, many of them dying in battle. The most powerful of them, however, he shut up and besieged in the city of Bethoma, and after taking the city and getting them into his power, he brought them back to Jerusalem; and there he did a thing that was as cruel as could be: while he feasted with his concubines in a conspicuous place, he ordered some eight hundred of the Jews to be crucified, and slaughtered their children and wives he

---

221. See Green, *Alexander to Actium*, 551–52. Green comments about the complicated struggles for the Seleucid crown: "Fragmentation of command could scarcely go farther" (552). M. Stern provides a detailed survey of the period in "The Seleucid Kings, 104–83 BCE," which is chap. 6 in his *Hasmonaean Judaea*, 108–17.

222. See, for example, Schürer, *History of the Jewish People*, 1.221, 223–24.

looked on, drinking, with his concubines reclining beside him.

Such was the consternation of the people that, on the following night, eight thousand of the hostile faction fled beyond the pale of Judaea; their exile was terminated only by Alexander's death.

before the eyes of the still living wretches. This was the revenge he took for the injuries he had suffered; but the penalty he exacted was inhuman for all that, even though he had, as was natural, gone through very great hardships in the wars he had fought against them, and had finally found himself in danger of losing both his life and his throne, for they were not satisfied to carry on the struggle by themselves but brought foreigners as well, and at last reduced him to the necessity of surrendering to the king of the Arabs the territory which he had conquered in Moab and Galaaditis and the strongholds therein, in order that he might not aid the Jews in the war against him; and they committed countless other insulting and abusive acts against him. But he still seems to have done this thing unnecessarily, and as a result of his excessive cruelty he was nicknamed Thrakidas (the "Cossack") by the Jews.

Then his opponents, numbering in all about eight thousand, fled by night and remained in exile so long as Alexander lived.

As he relates the gruesome tale, Josephus continues his practice of referring to Jannaeus's Jewish opponents with general terms (the remainder of the people, his captives, the people, the hostile faction in *War*; the Jews, the most powerful of them, his opponents in *Antiquities*). Although many students of Josephus had concluded that his opponents were Pharisees, basing themselves on later sections regarding Jannaeus and his wife Alexandra, the case for identifying at least some of Alexander's most vigorous opponents as Pharisees has received what many regard as confirmation from 4Q Pesher Nahum. The first column of the pesher begins in this way (3–4 i 1–9):

> I [*Where is the lions' den and the cave of the young lions?*] (ii, 11).
> [Interpreted, this concerns]. . .a dwelling place for the ungodly of the nations.

Whither the lion goes, there is the lion's cub, [with none to disturb it] (ii, 11b).

[Interpreted, this concerns Deme]trius king of Greece who sought, on the counsel of those who seek smooth things, to enter Jerusalem. [But God did not permit the city to be delivered] into the hands of the kings of Greece, from the time of Antiochus until the coming of the rulers of the Kittim. But then she shall be trampled under their feet . . .

The lion tears enough for its cubs and it chokes prey for its lionesses (ii, 12a).

[Interpreted, this] concerns the furious young lion who strikes by means of[223] his great men, and by means of the men of his council.

[*And chokes prey for its lionesses; and it fills] its caves [with prey] and its dens with victims* (ii, 12a–b).

Interpreted, this concerns the furious young lion [who executes revenge] on those who seek smooth things and hangs men alive, . . . formerly in Israel. Because of a man hanged alive on [the] tree, He proclaims, '*Behold I am against [you, says the Lord of Hosts'*].[224]

The similarities of the pesher to Josephus's account are obvious.

1. Both name Demetrius, who is a Greek king, although the first part of his name must be restored in the Hebrew text.
2. Both texts attribute an invasion to this Demetrius.[225]
3. Both place the event in roughly the same period. Josephus situates the story precisely, while the pesher dates it to a time between when Antiochus took Jerusalem and when the Kittim (= Romans) took it (63 BCE). If the Antiochus in question is Antiochus IV, then the event occurred between the early 160s and 63, while if Antiochus VII is intended, it happened between the late 130s and 63.
4. Both refer to hanging people alive. Josephus says that Jannaeus crucified the eight hundred men while dallying with his concubines; the pesher

---

223. Vermes's translation is dubious here. "His great men" is preceded by the preposition *bet* which, with the verb "strikes," indicates the ones struck, not the means through which the blow is delivered. For an extended review and discussion of the evidence, see Gregory L. Doudna, *4Q Pesher Nahum: A Critical Edition,* JSPSup 35 (Sheffield: Sheffield Academic, 2001), 363–70.

224. Cited from Vermes, *The Complete Dead Sea Scrolls in English,* 474.

225. See Doudna, *4Q Pesher Nahum,* 347–48. He translates "Demetrius . . . sought to come to Jerusalem" and argues that it means he intended to come there without actually reaching it, and that it does not imply he was ever near Jerusalem or actually attacked it.

relates the incident as it interprets the reference to lionesses in the text of Nahum.

It is likely that the "furious young lion" (or Lion of Wrath [כפיר החרון])
is Alexander Jannaeus.[226] The argument is based on the resemblance of the
scene pictured in the pesher to the one in Josephus's accounts. The case can be
strengthen by appeal to another text, 4Q167 (4QpHos[b]) 2.2, although the context is far too broken to derive a connected sense from it. The Lion of Wrath is
mentioned in an interpretation of Hos 5:13-14a. The citation of Hos 5:13 ends
on fragment 2.1 and the first letter of the term introducing the interpretation
also survives on that line. Then on line 2, כפיר החרון can be read just before
the citation of Hos 5:14a begins (it extends to line 3). In this verse, the image
of the כפיר (one of two words for lion in the verse) is used to symbolize the
way in which the Lord will act toward the house of Judah. The first words of
the interpretation have not survived, but, when the fragmentary text resumes,
something in Hos 5:14a is being interpreted as "the last priest" (כוהן האחרון)
who will extend his hand to strike/defeat Ephraim. A solid argument can be
constructed that *Ephraim* in the pesharim is another code name for the Pharisees. The intriguing element here is the content of the biblical lemma where
the figure of the Lion of Wrath and the last priest appear: "When Ephraim saw
his sickness and Judah his wound, then Ephraim went to Assyria, and sent to
the great king [Hebrew: a king who will contend]. But he is not able to cure
you or heal your wound. For I will be like a lion to Ephraim, and like a young
lion to the house of Judah" (Hos 5:13-14a). The picture here is like the one in
Pesher Nahum, where the ones who seek smooth things invite Demetrius, a
foreign king, to assist them; in Hosea, Ephraim (= the Pharisees in Qumran
exegetical literature) goes to a foreign king who contends but cannot deliver
them. In such a context, the Lion of Wrath puts in an appearance. It is possible that the phrase "the last priest [כוהן האחרון]" is a play on the title "the Lion
of Wrath [כפיר החרון]."

Although it is widely accepted in scholarship on Pesher Nahum that the
Lion of Wrath (כפיר החרון) of the text is Alexander Jannaeus, Doudna has
formulated a lengthy case that the angry lion is not an Israelite leader but a
future, foreign conqueror.[227] He has correctly noted that the verbs of which
כפיר החרון is the subject (4QpNah 3–4 i 5, 7) are in the imperfect tense, not
the past as they are at times translated.

---

226. For a recent survey of the evidence, see Håkan Bengtsson, *What's in a Name? A Study
of the Sobriquets in the Pesharim* (Uppsala: Uppsala Univ., 2000), 271–80.

227. *4Q Pesher Nahum*, 363–433, especially 363–88.

There are, nevertheless, no compelling reasons to understand כפיר החרון as a foreign ruler and none to understand him as a future conqueror. The text is broken so that some of our questions cannot be answered, but the surviving words do not determine the ethnicity of the character. Doudna claims: "There is nothing in the text which has Demetrius contemporary with the Lion of Wrath; rather, it is implied that Demetrius is one of the kings of Yavan of the past, and the Lion of Wrath is to be associated with the Kittim who come after the kings of Yavan. The Lion of Wrath does not make war against *Demetrius* but against the *rulers of Jerusalem. That* is the issue, *that* is the motif of the text."[228] Apparently, on his view, we are to assume that if the Lion of Wrath is fighting against the great ones (*Jerusalem* has to be supplied for Doudna's theory), then he must be a foreign conqueror. The surviving parts of the text say nothing about an association between the Kittim (the Romans) and the Lion of Wrath. Furthermore, the lacunae in the text do not allow us to identify the "great ones" whom the Lion of Wrath is striking; that is, the text does not say to which group or party the great ones belong. In the only other passage in Pesher Nahum where "great ones" occurs in context, they are associated with Manasseh (probably the Sadducees), while "the men of his council" makes one think of the seekers of smooth things (= Ephraim = Pharisees [see for the term עצה with suffixes in such contexts 4QpNah 3–4 i 2; 3–4 ii 6, 9; 3–4 iii 7; it is never used with Manasseh]). The imperfect tense of the verbs need not point to the future, only to ongoing acts; moreover, they may simply reflect the tense of the participles in Nah 2:13a, as the perfect tense verb in Nah 2:12b is echoed in the reference to Demetrius as a figure who acted in the past.

Among the exegetical issues relating to the pesher, one that has received an especially large amount of attention is the identity of the people termed "seekers of smooth things [דורשי החלקות]." The phrase appears in Pesher Nahum and in four other texts found in the Qumran caves (CD 1.14—2.1; 1QH^a 10.31–38; 12.9–11; 4Q177 [Catena^a] 2.12–13; 4Q163 [4QpIsa^c] 23 ii 10–12). These other four texts leave the reader with a fairly general picture of the seekers as ones who interpret the law in a way contrary to the one advocated by the people of the scrolls, who reject the strong claims made by the Teacher of Righteousness, and who teach the people incorrect lessons, but they do not provide enough information to identify these opponents more precisely. The references to the seekers of smooth things in Pesher Nahum have been crucial to the argument because of the close parallels with the story about Jannaeus's crucifying the eight hundred who, claim many scholars, were Pharisees. As we have seen, though it would be likely to find Pharisees among Alexander's opponents after his father John Hyrcanus's treatment of and

---

228. Ibid., 380.

experience with them, Josephus, to this point in his narratives, has never said they were in fact Pharisees. Yet, from both the pesher and Josephus's narrative, a fairly strong case can be constructed for the thesis that the people whom Jannaeus crucified were Pharisees.[229]

It is highly likely that the epithet "seekers of smooth things" is an insulting name given to the Pharisees by the writers of the Qumran texts. In addition to the evidence supplied by Pesher Nahum, other texts associate the group indirectly with legal decisions and practices that are probably to be tied to the Pharisees. Furthermore, the derisive name given to them—דורשי החלקות—seems to be a pun on the term given to the Pharisees's legal rulings—הלכות.[230]

We should now examine those subsequent sections in Josephus's two histories, bearing in mind the question whether the eight hundred crucified men were Pharisees.[231] Both *War* and *Antiquities* devote the next sections to other events in Jannaeus's reign—mostly international history and more battles by Alexander—that are not relevant to our subject; we reach the salient parts at the point where the narrative deals with Alexander's last days and the problem of the succession. The account in *War* is again briefer. Here, Josephus chides Alexandra, Jannaeus's wife and successor, for her excessive reliance on the Pharisees who rose to great power during her reign (*J. W.* 1.5, 2 [§§110–12]). As an example of the Pharisees' authority while she ruled, he mentions the case of Diogenes, whom they executed. He was "a distinguished man who had been a friend of Alexander"; this man they accused "of having advised the king to crucify his eight hundred victims. They further urged Alexandra to make away with the others who had instigated Alexander to punish those men; and as she from superstitious motives always gave way, they proceeded to kill whomsoever they would. The most eminent of the citizens thus imperiled sought refuge with Aristobulus" (1.5, 3 [§§113–14]).[232] So, in this section we

---

229. Levine argues that Josephus, with an eye toward his Roman readers, purposely did not identify Jannaeus's opponents as Pharisees so as not to mention them specifically in connection with rebels and people who undermine the national order ("The Political Struggle between Pharisees and Sadducees in the Hasmonean Period," 69).

230. The position identifying the seekers as Pharisees has been adopted by many. For a recent summary of the evidence and arguments, see VanderKam, "Those Who Look for Smooth Things, Pharisees, and Oral Law," in *Emanuel: Studies in Hebrew Bible, Septuagint, and Dead Sea Scrolls in Honor of Emanuel Tov*, ed. R. Kraft, S. Paul, L. Schiffman, and W. Fields, VTSup 94 (Leiden: Brill, 2003), 465–77.

231. The following paragraphs are drawn from VanderKam, "Pesher Nahum and Josephus," in *When Judaism and Christianity Began: Essays in Memory of Anthony J. Saldarini*, ed. A. Avery-Peck, D. Harrington, and J. Neusner (Leiden: Brill, 2004), 1.299–311.

232. Aristobulus was one of Alexander and Alexandra's two sons. The other was named Hyrcanus.

have explicit testimony that Pharisees were the ones concerned to punish those who had advised Jannaeus to kill the eight hundred. This is not the same as saying the eight hundred were Pharisees, but, at least the Pharisees felt some responsibility for affording them belated revenge.[233]

Antiquities again supplements the brief account in *War*. In his later work, Josephus adds a deathbed discussion between Alexander and Alexandra, during which the king urged her to allow the Pharisees greater power in her administration.[234] The issue was how she could retain the throne for herself and their children, when the nation was so hostile to him (as she pointed out). He said that she should not only capture fortresses but also "she should yield a certain amount of power to the Pharisees, for if they praised her in return for this sign of regard, they would dispose the nation favourably toward her. These men, he assured her, had so much influence with their fellow-Jews that they could injure those whom they hated and help those to whom they were friendly; for they had the complete confidence of the masses when they spoke harshly of any person, even when they did so out of envy; and he himself, he added, had come into conflict with the nation because these men had been badly treated by him" (*Ant.* 13.15, 5 [§§401–2]). Here, Jannaeus confesses late in life that he had mistreated the Pharisees and that his miscalculation had led to the troubles he had experienced with his own people. The Pharisees, as he understood the situation, were the cause of the revolts and unrest.

To this advice, King Alexander added another interesting suggestion, one concerning the treatment of his body. "'And so,' he said, 'when you come to Jerusalem, send for their [= the Pharisees'] partisans [text: soldiers],[235] and showing them my dead body, permit them, with every sign of sincerity, to treat me as they please, whether they wish to dishonour my corpse by leaving it unburied because of the many injuries they have suffered at my hands, or in their anger wish to offer my dead body any other form of indignity'" (13.15, 5

---

233. See Albert I. Baumgarten, "Seekers After Smooth Things," in *EDSS*, 858. E. P. Sanders has shown from various details in the stories from the time of John Hyrcanus to that of Alexandra that the opponents of Jannaeus "included the Pharisees, probably as their leaders" (*Judaism: Practice and Belief 63 BCE–66 CE* [Philadelphia: Trinity Press International, 1992], 382). In the same place, he adds that the seekers of smooth things in Pesher Nahum are Pharisees.

234. On the deathbed plan, see Mason, *Flavius Josephus on the Pharisees*, 248–54. He thinks the language of Jannaeus's speech is anti-Pharisaic and pro-Hasmonean and hence probably comes from Josephus, not Nicolaus of Damascus (250). Or, as he puts it: "Josephus must have formulated (or freely invented) Alexander's deathbed speech." This is hardly the only way of reading the scene. Jacob Neusner writes: "The version in *Antiquities* of the Pharisees-in-power story is strikingly revised in favor of the Pharisees" (*From Politics to Piety: The Emergence of Pharisaic Judaism* [Englewood Cliffs, N.J.: Prentice-Hall, 1973], 60; see also his comments on 63).

235. On the textual problem, see Marcus, *Josephus* 7, 431 n. a.

[§403]). The plan worked: Alexandra turned his body over to the Pharisees (we do not learn what they did with it), and they supported her, even praising her departed husband (13.16, 1 [§§405–6]).

This bizarre story about Alexander's corpse is what tips the scales in favor of identifying the eight hundred men whom Alexander Jannaeus had crucified as Pharisees. The argument goes this way: Alexander had mistreated the bodies of the crucified men; this is the most specific statement about abusing the bodies of his enemies because regarding all of the others we learn only of their deaths, not how they died. Now, he was allowing fellow Pharisees to avenge his brutality against their colleagues by turning over his corpse to them, to be treated however they chose. The gesture seems to be a case of quid pro quo: surviving Pharisees were invited to mistreat Jannaeus's body as he had abused the bodies of the eight hundred Pharisees whom he hanged alive.

Anthony Saldarini and others have been correct to urge caution here because, as they have pointed out, Josephus never does explicitly call the eight hundred who were crucified *Pharisees*; that point has perhaps not been appreciated sufficiently in the literature.[236] Saldarini's reminder that we should not limit our reconstructions of Jewish divisions to the three groups mentioned by Josephus is also a useful one, just as we should remember that we do not know what membership in one of the groups may have involved at this time or how loosely or precisely such terms were used.

In a case like this one, we must ask the question of historicity. Did the deathbed conversation between Jannaeus and Alexandra take place and did it contain the advice about the Pharisees, including the suggestion that she surrender his body to them? After all, Josephus says nothing about this in *War*; it appears only in *Antiquities* in which the treatment of the Pharisees may be more highly tendentious.[237] Also, speeches, as we know, provided the ancient historian with rich opportunities for invention and even mischief.

---

236. *Pharisees, Scribes, and Sadducees in Palestinian Society: A Sociological Approach* (Wilmington, Del.: Glazier, 1988), 278–80; the book has been reissued in the Biblical Resource Series (Grand Rapids: Eerdmans, 2001) under the same title and with the same pagination. See also Chaim Rabin, "Alexander Jannaeus and the Pharisees," *JJS* 7 (1956): 3–11.

237. This is a much controverted point. For scholars who think that Josephus adopted a consistent attitude towards the Pharisees in both works, see, for example, Saldarini, *Pharisees, Scribes, and Sadducees*, 83, 85–133; Ellis Rivkin, *A Hidden Revolution: The Pharisees' Search for the Kingdom of God Within* (Nashville: Abingdon, 1978). For an extended argument that Josephus is consistently negative about them, see Mason, *Flavius Josephus on the Pharisees*. As representatives of the thesis that he presents the Pharisees more positively in *Antiquities* than in *War* in order to commend them to the Romans as the sort of people best suited to lead Jewish society after the disaster of 70 CE, see Morton Smith, "Palestinian Judaism in the First Century," in *Israel: Its Role in Civilization*, ed. M. Davis (New York: Jewish Theological Seminary of America,

We cannot, of course, prove that Jannaeus gave Alexandra the advice Josephus credits to him. But, it is reasonable to think that something of the sort occurred because of the sequel. The Pharisees, according to both *War* and *Antiquities*, became dominant in Alexandra's regime and took energetic steps to punish those involved in crucifying the eight hundred victims. We have no proof that the king's corpse was given to the Pharisees, but their drastic switch of allegiance—from all-out opposition to Alexander to ardent support of Alexandra—must have had some cause. If the ones who tried to avenge the eight hundred were indeed Pharisees (as the sources assert), we have some reason for thinking the eight hundred were fellow Pharisees. If the story about Alexander's body is authentic (as *Antiquities*, our only source for details about the transfer of power to Alexandra, attests), then the case becomes that much stronger.

The Pharisaic opposition to Alexander Jannaeus has left its imprint in later literature. The rabbinic sages, who saw the Pharisees as their predecessors, recorded the disfavor in which they held him in several passages. We have already reviewed some of these in connection with his father John Hyrcanus (the break in relations with the Pharisees [*b. Qidd.* 66a], the claim that Johanan was Yannai [*b. Ber.* 29a]).[238] One character who looms large in such references is Simeon ben Shetah, who was thought to be the brother of Queen Salome Alexandra, Jannaeus's wife. So, in *b. Soṭah* 47a one reads: "When King Jannaeus put the Rabbis to death, Simeon b. Shetah was hid by his sister." Building on this information, the following story is told in *b. Ber.* 48a:

1956), 67–81; and Jacob Neusner in several publications. Examples are *From Politics to Piety*, 60–63 (specifically on our story); and idem, "Josephus' Pharisees: A Complete Repertoire," in *Josephus, Judaism, and Christianity*, ed. L. H. Feldman and G. Hata (Detroit: Wayne State Univ. Press, 1987), 274–92. For a somewhat different understanding, see Seth Schwartz, *Josephus and Judaean Politics*, CSCT 18 (Leiden: Brill, 1990). He finds that *Antiquities* "does not consistently propagandize for the Pharisees. Yet, despite the work's sloppiness and episodic character, it clearly *is* propagandistic, and its tendencies can be demonstrated with certainty because much of the work can be compared with its sources" (215). For him, the new leadership group supported by Josephus has much in common with the Pharisees though they are not called Pharisees; they appear to be the early rabbis (216). Another angle on the issue of the Pharisees in *War* and *Antiquities* has been expressed by Daniel R. Schwartz, who thinks that "*BJ* reflects Josephus' attempt to portray the Pharisees, incorrectly but safely, as uninvolved in politics and certainly as uninvolved in rebellion." In *Antiquities* and *Life*, which have the same viewpoint and were written after the revolt against Rome had receded farther into the past, Schwartz observes that "Josephus was less cautious and therefore much source material, which indicated Pharisaic involvement in politics and even in rebellion, found its way into these books" ("Josephus and Nicolaus on the Pharisees," 169).

238. There it is also said that "Jannai was originally wicked."

King Jannai and his queen were taking a meal together. Now after he
had put the Rabbis to death, there was no-one to say grace for them.
He said to his spouse: I wish we had someone to say grace for us. She
said to him: Swear to me that if I bring you one you will not harm him.
He swore to her, and she brought Simeon b. Shetah, her brother. She
placed him between her husband and herself, saying. See what honour
I pay you. He replied: It is not you who honour me but it is the Torah
which honours me, as it is written, Exalt her and she shall promote
thee, [she shall bring thee to honour when thou dost embrace her]. He
[Jannai] said to her: You see that he does not acknowledge any authority! They gave him a cup of wine to say grace over. He said: How shall
I say the grace? [Shall I say] Blessed is He of whose sustenance Jannai
and his companions have eaten? So he drank that cup, and they gave
him another and he said grace over it.[239]

There may also be a distorted reflection of the death-bed conversation
between Jannaeus and Alexandra in *b. Soṭah* 22b: "King Jannai said to his wife,
'Fear not the Pharisees and the non-Pharisees but the hypocrites who ape the
Pharisees; because their deeds are the deeds of Zimri but they expect a reward
like Phineas.'" At any rate, there are also references suggesting that the king
subjected himself to the rulings of authorities such as Simeon ben Shetah. In
b. Sanh. 19a, a passage that pointedly distinguishes the kings of Israel from the
kings of David's line and associates Alexander with the former, Jannaeus is
forced to accompany to the law court a servant who had killed a man. The
leader of the court in the story is Simeon.

As noted above, more coins on which Jannaeus's name is stamped have
survived than for any other Hasmonean ruler, and they, too, cast some light on
his career as high priest. In his study of the Alexander coins, Meshorer divides
them into ten categories, *mem* through *tav*.[240] While Jannaeus continued his
father's practice of minting *perutot* with an inscription and cornucopias, he
also innovated. In the coins in Meshorer's group *ayin*, there is a lily on one side
and an anchor on the other—a combination found previously only in a series
of coins that Hyrcanus may have issued in 130–129 BCE in the name of Antiochus VII Sidetes. The inscription on Jannaeus's coins in this category reads:
יהונתן המלך, and its Greek equivalent ΑΛΕΞΑΝΔΡΟΥ ΒΑΣΙΛΕΩΣ. Meshorer
thinks the anchors, besides their Hellenistic meaning of arriving at a safe

---

239. In another meal story (*b. Ker.* 28b), Jannaeus and Alexandra disagreed on whether the
flesh of a goat or a lamb was better and submitted their dispute to one Issachar of Kefar Barkai
who is said to be the high priest!

240. *Treasury*, 40–43; the full catalog of the coins with their inscriptions is on 184–91.

haven, symbolized Jannaeus's conquests on the Mediterranean coast.[241] However that may be, it is important here to observe that these coins and many
others of Jannaeus make no mention of his high priesthood, only of his status
as king (see groups *mem* [less m 17], *nun, samekh, ayin, pe*). Yet, on another set
of coins, the inscription has no reference to his kingship, only to his office of
high priest (*ṣade* [יהונתן הכהן הגדל וחבר היהדים]; see also *qof–tav*). One exceptional coin type (all instances are from the same stamp) is his m 17, which
bears the words כהן המלך (the words could be read in reverse order), with an
unclear symbol (it is not *he*) before כהן. Meshorer regards the coin type as a
curiosity.

Another novel feature on some of Jannaeus's coins is the use of Aramaic
for the inscription (group *nun*, see also group *samekh*). They are unique
among Jewish coins not only in using the Aramaic language and script (the so-
called paleo-Hebrew script is used in the Hebrew ones), but also in giving the
date in the monarch's reign—his twenty-fifth year (79–78 BCE): מלכא
אלכסנדרוס שנת כה. Meshorer interprets the data in light of Josephus's descriptions of Jannaeus's last years. He thinks the use of Aramaic at this late point in
his reign reflects an attempt to appease the Pharisees, in that the king used on
these coins a language and script more widely known, not the ancient script
that had been used on Hasmonean coins, which could be read only by a few.[242]
This is possible, although Josephus puts such gestures by Jannaeus at the very
end of his life, not more broadly in the last years of his reign.

One other complication regarding the Alexander coins is worth noting.
Meshorer, echoing others, has raised the possibility that some of the coins
attributed to Jannaeus were actually minted by his son, Hyrcanus II whose
Hebrew name is unknown but could have been Jonathan, like Alexander's. We
will consider this possibility below in the chapter on Hyrcanus II. Here we
should note that not all of the many coins thought to be from Jannaeus may
actually have been minted by him. Some, especially those with the name
spelled in the shorter form ינתן may have been issued by his successor as high
priest.[243]

---

241. Some of the coins in the *mem* group have an anchor on one side, with a star surrounded by a diadem on the other. Jannaeus's name and royal title are written between the points
of the star. In this way, he was able to express his kingly position (for the star as royal symbol, see
Num 24:17), while at the same time honoring the prohibition of placing an image of himself on
the coins (Meshorer, *Treasury*, 41).

242. Ibid., 42–43. Meshorer thinks the numbers of them suggest that this type of coin,
though it mentions his twenty-fifth year, continued to be minted by Jannaeus for the remaining
years of his rule.

243. Ibid., 31–32.

In concluding our study of Jannaeus, we should consider 4Q448 (4QApocryphal Psalm and Prayer), a text that probably refers to Jannaeus by name, although he is not called the high priest in it. The small piece of parchment contains three compositions: a previously unknown Hallelujah psalm, Psalm 154, and a prayer that mentions Jonathan. The editors have translated the last-named item in this way:

1. Guard (or: Rise up), O Holy One
2. over King Jonathan [יונתן המלכ] (or: for King Jonathan)
3. and all the congregation of Your people
4. Israel
5. who are in the four
6. winds of heaven.
7. Let them all be (at) peace
8. and upon Your kingdom
9. may Your name be blessed.[244]

They have also read the name and title ליונתן המל]ך in column 3.8, although the reading there is more difficult (the context speaks of blessing for the kingdom, perhaps at a time of war).[245]

As we have seen, Jannaeus's Hebrew name Jonathan was stamped on his coins as יהונתן most often, but there are coins that bear the spelling ינתן. There are also two bullae with the inscription ינתן כהן גדל ירשלם מ.[246] To the extent of our knowledge at present, there was no Hasmonean whose Hebrew name was Jonathan and who officially held the title *king*, other than Alexander Jannaeus. Hence the person mentioned in 4Q448 and the bullae is with the highest probability to be interpreted as Jannaeus.[247]

If, as we should, we accept the identification, we encounter the problem why a text that may be read as wishing a blessing on Jonathan should be found at Qumran, where the normal stance appears to have been strongly anti-Hasmonean. The editors have adopted the explanation that the text was brought

244. Esther Eshel, Hanan Eshel, and Ada Yardeni in *Qumran Cave 4 VI Poetical and Liturgical Texts, Part 1*, consulting ed. J. VanderKam and M. Brady, DJD 11 (Oxford: Clarendon, 1998), 421.

245. *Qumran Cave 4 VI*, 423.

246. Nachman Avigad, "A Bulla of Jonathan the High Priest," *IEJ* 25 (1975): 8–12; idem, "A Bulla of King Jonathan," *IEJ* 25 (1975): 245–46.

247. Vermes has suggested that Jonathan the king is Jonathan the first Hasmonean high priest (*The Complete Dead Sea Scrolls in English*, 331) and that the text refers to the beginning of his reign when, according to 1QpHab 8.8–9, he was known by the name of truth. This seems unlikely, as Jonathan is never, in our sources, called "king."

to Qumran from elsewhere and hence does not express the views of the people residing around Khirbet Qumran.[248] That, however, is not entirely satisfactory as it would, no matter its place of origin, still be a part of the Qumran library. We do not know why such a text was preserved at Qumran, but one possibility is that the people of Qumran approved of Jannaeus's stern measures against their opponents, the Pharisees. The editors of 4Q448 think the pesharim picture the Lion of Wrath (= Jannaeus) negatively because of his violent treatment of opponents, but there is nothing in those texts that requires such a reading.[249]

It is surely possible that the attitude of the covenanters at Qumran toward the Hasmonean rulers changed as circumstances did; nevertheless, the other evidence on this matter shows only negative views about the reigning house. In this respect, the approach to 4Q448 defended by E. Main seems to point in a more helpful direction. According to Main, a study of the biblical usage of the phrasing found in line 1 (עור על) demonstrates that the prayer asks God to fight against King Jonathan but to bless his people.[250]

When Alexander died of an illness in 76 BCE, he had reigned for twenty-seven or twenty-eight years. Yet, true to the more political nature of our sources, little is said about his acts as high priest. As a warrior-king, Jannaeus extended the borders of his land well beyond what his predecessors had accomplished, but his excesses aroused tremendous internal hostility. His seemingly interminable battles raise in the most acute form among the Hasmonean rulers the problem of a high priest in the presence of corpses. As with his ancestors, nothing is reported about how Jannaeus handled the danger of this type of impurity while continuing to officiate at the altar in Jerusalem.[251]

---

248. "4QApocryphal Psalm and Prayer," 414–15. Their claim—that Jannaeus may have ceased using the title *king* in deference to the Pharisees and that this is reflected in the fact that some of his coins bearing the title king are restamped but with the high-priestly title (see group *tav*)—seems farfetched. We have no literary evidence for such a move, and Salome Alexandra continued to have a royal title after his death.

249. See Yigael Yadin, "Pesher Nahum (4Q pNahum) Reconsidered," *IEJ* 21 (1971): 1–12.

250. "For King Jonathan or Against? The Use of the Bible in 4Q448," in *Biblical Perspectives: Early Use and Interpretation of the Bible in Light of the Dead Sea Scrolls*, ed. M. E. Stone and E. G. Chazon, STDJ 28 (Leiden: Brill, 1998), 113–35. The same interpretation is advocated by André Lemaire, "Le roi Jonathan à Qoumrân (4Q448 B–C)," in *Qoumrân et les manuscrits de la mer Morte*, ed. E.-M. Laperrousaz (Paris: Cerf, 1997), 57–70.

251. For an interesting discussion of the question, based mostly on rabbinic texts, see Victor Aptowitzer, *Parteipolitik der Hasmonäerzeit im rabbinischen und pseudoepigraphischen Schrifttum*, Veröffentlichungen der Alexander Kohut Memorial Foundation 5 (Vienna: Kohut Foundation, 1927), 1–65. Although Aptowitzer thought it was a reason why some opposed centering the civil and religious leadership in a single person, Josephus at least does not name it as

22. Hyrcanus II (76–67, 63–40 BCE)

For the second time in her career, Salome Alexandra seized control of the succession when her royal husband died.[252] The agreement between herself and Alexander, according to *Antiquities* (our only record), entailed that she would become the civil ruler but would give the Pharisees a measure of power. This seems a strange procedure in a dynasty because Alexandra and Alexander had two sons, the older of whom would be the one to succeed his father. Yet, in his lengthy deathbed instructions, Jannaeus said nothing about a role for his sons (although see *Ant.* 13.15, 5 [§400] where their children are mentioned). Alexandra is the only family member who receives consideration, or, as *J.W.* 1.5, 1 (§107) puts the matter: "Alexander bequeathed the kingdom to his wife Alexandra, being convinced that the Jews would bow to her authority as they would to no other, because by her utter lack of his brutality and by her opposition to his crimes she had won the affections of the populace." It may be that Alexander did not think either of his sons would be an effective or appropriate ruler.

The parallel in *Antiquities* is more explicit about the sons and provides a sketch of their differing characters. "Now although Alexander had left two sons, Hyrcanus and Aristobulus, he had bequeathed the royal power to Alexandra. Of these sons the one, Hyrcanus, was incompetent to govern and in addition much preferred a quiet life, while the younger, Aristobulus, was a man of action and high spirit. As for the queen herself, she was loved by the masses because she was thought to disapprove of the crimes committed by her husband" (13.16, 1 [§407]). Alexandra could succeed her husband upon the throne, but as a woman she was automatically disqualified from serving as high priest, a post reserved for the sons of Aaron.

The queen apportioned roles to her sons in accordance with their natures. "Of the two sons whom she had by Alexander, she appointed the elder,

---

a cause for asking either Hyrcanus or Jannaeus to give up the high priesthood. It may be the case that the Hasmoneans appealed to the zeal of their ancestor Phineas as the model for their warlike priesthood (compare 1 Macc 2:24-26).

252. J. Geiger compares the succession and the part of Salome after the deaths of John Hyrcanus and of Aristobulus with the roles of women in similar situations in various Hellenistic dynasties; "The Hasmonaeans and Hellenistic Succession," *JJS* 53 (2002): 1–17. He considers the possibility that Aristobulus I had two wives and one son (Hyrcanus II). The childless wife would have become Alexander Jannaeus's spouse (compare also Wellhausen, *Israelitische und jüdische Geschichte*, 264 n. 1). This theory has the advantage of accounting for the strong opposition between brothers and Josephus's claim that Hyrcanus II was some eighty years of age when he died in 30 BCE. Geiger's appeal to amphimetrism is interesting but, as he admits, is contrary to or goes beyond what Josephus reports.

Hyrcanus, high priest out of consideration alike for his age and disposition, which was too lethargic to be troubled about public affairs;[253] the younger, Aristobulus, as a hot-head, she confined to a private life" (*J.W.* 1.5, 1 [§109]; compare *Ant.* 13.16, 2 [§408] on the appointment of Hyrcanus: "because of his greater age but more especially because of his lack of energy"). That is, Hyrcanus seemed a safer appointment as high priest to Alexandra, who was concerned about her own position. In this context, both of Josephus's works refer to the power enjoyed by the Pharisees under the rule of Alexandra.

This unimpressive introduction brings Hyrcanus II onto the stage of history. Despite his reputed personality and the major upheavals that occurred during his long tenure, he proves to be one of the most interesting high priests of the Second-Temple period. We read about him during his mother's reign and, of course, in more detail after her death in 67 BCE. By the time Alexandra died, Hyrcanus had been reigning as high priest for nine years, but the sources provide no account of any priestly act that he performed during that span. Presumably, the Pharisees were a powerful force in the kingdom, and perhaps they exercised influence on Hyrcanus, but the sources say nothing about this—in sharp contrast to modern scholars who see Hyrcanus as a high priest of whom the Pharisees approved.[254] Josephus does not mention the Pharisees during his long reign.

The supposedly lethargic Hyrcanus, we learn to our surprise, received the royal crown from his mother while she was still alive (*J.W.* 1.6, 1 [§120]). *Antiquities* does not furnish the same detail but resorts to a detailed chronological statement about the beginning of his reign as king: "Now when Hyrcanus assumed royal power, in the third year of the hundred and seventy-seventh Olympiad, the Roman consuls being Quintus Hortensius and Quintus Metallus, the same who was surnamed Creticus, Aristobulus promptly declared war on him" (14.1, 2 [§4]). The 177th Olympiad included the years 72–69 BCE, meaning that the year in question was 70 or early 69

---

253. Daniel R. Schwartz questions Thackeray's translation here, noting that ἐνοχλεῖν is active; "Josephus on Hyrcanus II," in *Josephus and the History of the Greco-Roman Period: Essays in Memory of Morton Smith,* ed. F. Parente and J. Sievers, StPB 41 (Leiden: Brill, 1994), 222. He translates: "he was too lethargic to give trouble about the whole." As we shall see, these summaries of Hyrcanus II's character are the first in a series of similar statements, mostly in *Antiquities* but with some in *War.* Whether they fit the nature of the man evident in the narratives is another matter—one that Schwartz treats in detail in "Josephus on Hyrcanus II." We will return to this issue below.

254. See, for example, Peter Richardson, *Herod: King of the Jews and Friend of the Romans,* SPNT (Columbia: University of South Carolina, 1996), 79.

BCE.[255] The date is consistent with *War*'s statement that Hyrcanus succeeded his mother on the throne before her death. It produces a conflict, nevertheless, with other information in *Antiquities* and may be an additional case (like that for Hyrcanus I) in which Josephus was inaccurate in his synchronizations.[256] While we do not know, then, exactly how long Hyrcanus II wielded royal power, it is clear that, at least for a short time near Alexandra's death (perhaps only three months), he, like his male predecessors, was both high priest and king.

As was to happen so regularly in his career, Hyrcanus was soon put at a disadvantage by a more vigorous leader, in this instance his brother, Aristobulus II. Aristobulus quickly took control of most of the nation's fortresses while his mother remained alive, but the battle between the forces of the brothers probably took place after her death. Most of Hyrcanus's troops deserted, but he and his supporters took Aristobulus's wife and children as hostages and found refuge in the Antonia[257] in Jerusalem (*J.W.* 1.6, 1 [§§120–21]). *Antiquities* says that Alexandra had already taken her daughter-in-law and grandchildren hostage at this fortress that overlooked the temple (13.16, 5 [§426]; compare 14.1, 2 [§5]). Under the circumstances, a truce was arranged:

> before any irreparable harm was done, the brothers came to terms, to the effect that Aristobulus should be king and Hyrcanus, while abdicating the throne, should enjoy all his other honours as the king's brother. The reconciliation on these terms took place in the temple. In the presence of the surrounding crowd they cordially embraced each other, and then exchanged residences, Aristobulus repairing to the palace, Hyrcanus to the house of Aristobulus. (*J.W.* 1.6, 1 [§§121–22])

Antiquities attributes the initiative for the agreement to Hyrcanus and adds that they sealed the agreements with "oaths and pledges" (14.1, 2 [§§6–7]). On this surprising note, Hyrcanus's first stint as high priest ended.

---

255. See, for example, Bickerman, *Chronology of the Ancient World*, 119.

256. See the detailed discussion in Schürer, *History of the Jewish People*, 1.200–201 n. 1; Marcus, *Josephus* 7, 450–51 n. c. The lengths of reigns that Josephus attributes to the brothers (Hyrcanus three months [*Ant.* 15.6, 4 (§180)], Aristobulus three years and six months [*Ant.* 14.6, 1 (§97)]) before Pompey settled their dispute would not fill the years from 70–69 to 63 BCE.

257. This was a name later given by King Herod to the place earlier called the Baris.

23. Aristobulus II (67–63 BCE)

In neither history at this juncture does Josephus say anything about transfer of the *high priesthood* from Hyrcanus II to Aristobulus II, but elsewhere our historian makes precisely that claim. As we will see, Josephus later records two instances in which Aristobulus was captured by the Romans and sent to Rome, adding about the second case: "there he was kept in chains, after being king and high priest [βασιλεύσας μὲν καὶ ἀρχιερατεύσας] three years and six months" (*Ant.* 14.6, 1 [§97]). Later yet, in describing Herod's reign, Josephus notes the first time the king removed a high priest from office and says this had never occurred apart from that particular time and two earlier ones: when Antiochus Epiphanes removed Jason[258] and "the next was Aristobulus, who removed his brother Hyrcanus" (15.3, 1 [§41]). Finally, in his list of high priests in *Antiquities* 20, he encapsulates Hyrcanus II's reign thus: "She [Alexandra] gave the high priesthood to Hyrcanus and herself occupied the throne for nine years, after which she died; her son Hyrcanus held the high priesthood for an equal period. For after her death, Hyrcanus' brother Aristobulus made war upon him, defeated him, deprived him of his office and himself became both king and high priest of the nation [ἐβασίλευέ τε καὶ ἀρχιεράτευεν τοῦ ἔθνους]. When he had reigned two years and three months,[259] Pompey came and took the city of Jerusalem by storm and sent him and his children to Rome in bonds. Pompey also restored [ἀποδούς] the high priesthood to Hyrcanus and permitted him to have the leadership of the nation, but forbade him to wear a diadem. Hyrcanus ruled for twenty-four years, in addition to the nine years of his previous rule" (*Ant.* 20.10, 4 [§§242–44]).[260] Hence, the period from approximately 67–63 BCE resembled the one in 175–172 when a brother (Jason) replaced a brother (Onias III) as high priest, with the deposed high priest (Onias III) offering opposition to the new claimant of the office (Jason). A difference is that Hyrcanus regained the post, whereas Onias did not.

The truce between the brothers proved to be a brief lull in their lengthy struggle, with the throne being the prize sought. The years from Alexandra's death in 67 until 63 BCE, when Pompey captured Jerusalem, were marked by armed conflict between the siblings. Josephus credits the reinvigorization of Hyrcanus's cause to Antipater,

---

258. Why he does not mention the removal of Onias III in 175 BCE is not clear.

259. The text says literally "in the third year of the rule and the same months." As we have just seen, *Ant.* 14.6, 1 (§97) assigns him three years and six months.

260. See Schürer, *History of the Jewish People,* 1.233–34.

an old and bitterly hated foe [of Aristobulus, apparently]. An Idumaean by race, his ancestry, wealth, and other advantages put him in the front rank of his nation. It was he who now persuaded Hyrcanus to seek refuge with Aretas, king of Arabia, with a view to recovering his kingdom, and at the same time urged Aretas to receive him and to reinstate him on the throne." (*J.W.* 1.6, 2 [§§123–24])[261]

Aretas, under heavy pressure from Antipater, raised an army of fifty thousand men to force the return of Hyrcanus to the kingship in Jerusalem (1.6, 2 [§§124–26]).[262] *Antiquities* adds that Hyrcanus, who had first sent Antipater to Aretas to receive assurances about his own safety, also promised Aretas "that if he were restored and received his throne, he would return to him the territory and the twelve cities which his father Alexander had taken from the Arabs" (14.1, 4 [§18]). For a force of fifty thousand troops and cavalrymen, Aristobulus's army was no match. As Josephus relates,

Defeated in the first encounter he [Aristobulus] was driven into Jerusalem, and would there have been speedily captured through the storming of the city, had not Scaurus the Roman general, intervening at this critical moment, raised the siege. The latter had been sent into Syria from Armenia by Pompey the Great, then at war with Tigranes." (*J.W.* 1.6, 2 [§§126–27])

---

261. While the question of Josephus's sources is an important one throughout his works, it becomes especially acute when one reaches this point in his history because now the family of King Herod begins to play a significant role. The historian of Herod, Nicolaus of Damascus, was used as a source by Josephus before this in his narrative, but beginning with Antipater, Herod's father, Nicolaus was writing about a subject on which he could not afford to be objective. Josephus himself was aware of this. In introducing Antipater in *Antiquities* he writes, after calling Antipater "a man of action and a trouble-maker" (14.1, 3 [§8]): "Nicolas of Damascus, to be sure, says that his family belonged to the leading Jews who came to Judaea from Babylon. But he says this in order to please Antipater's son Herod" (14.1, 3 [§9]). Josephus adds that Jannaeus and his wife had appointed Antipater governor of Idumea (14.1, 3 [§10]). In this context, *Antiquities* supplies another characterization of Hyrcanus when it says he did not believe Antipater's claim that Aristobulus wanted to kill Hyrcanus to make his own rule more secure: "But Hyrcanus gave no credence to these words, for he was naturally a decent man and because of his kindliness did not readily listen to slander. But his ineffectualness and weakness of will made him seem ignoble and unmanly to those who observed him. Aristobulus, however, was of the opposite nature, being a man of action and alert spirit" (14.1, 3 [§13]).

262. We may be somewhat suspicious of what motivated Antipater to back Hyrcanus, but Smallwood goes beyond what our sources say in her assertion: "Antipater was a friend of Hyrcanus, but a friend from interested motives. Well aware of Hyrcanus' poor potential as a ruler, he made it his ambition to rule himself through Hyrcanus as puppet-king" (E. Mary Smallwood,

With this short narrative Josephus brings events to the dawn of the Roman era in Judea.[263]

Aristobulus bribed Scaurus into supporting his cause,[264] and the general responded by ordering an end to the siege of Jerusalem. Aretas complied in great fear, withdrew, and thus deprived Hyrcanus of his main support. Once the Romans had left the area and returned to Damascus, Aristobulus attacked his enemies and defeated them (*J.W.* 1.6, 3 [§§128–30]).[265]

This is the setting for the scene in which both Hyrcanus and Aristobulus presented their cases before Pompey in Damascus.[266] Antipater and Hyrcanus "implored him to show his detestation of the violence of Aristobulus, and to restore to the throne the man whose character [!] and seniority entitled him to it" (1.6, 4 [§131]). *Antiquities* presents a fuller picture of the circumstances when Pompey arrived in Damascus:

The Jews under Roman Rule: From Pompey to Diocletian—A Study in Political Relations, SJLA 20 [reissued, Boston: Brill, 2001]), 20. Several incidents in the later stories demonstrate that Hyrcanus was more than a puppet-king.

263. *Antiquities* inserts an entire episode around this point. Josephus there says that Aretas, Hyrcanus, and their forces besieged Aristobulus and his supporters in the temple. The citizens joined Hyrcanus, while only the priests were loyal to Aristobulus (scholars have also imported party loyalties into this scene: the priests were supposedly Sadducees as was Aristobulus, though Josephus does not so identify them [see Richardson, *Herod*, 79]). In this context, Josephus also relates the story of a certain Onias who had once by prayer induced the deity to end a drought and who now was pressured to put a curse on Aristobulus and his side; he refused and was stoned to death. This was also the time of Passover, but the besieged priestly faction had no lambs for sacrifice. The Jews on Hyrcanus's side are said to have extorted huge sums from them for each lamb they provided and, upon receiving the money, failed to deliver the lambs. A terrible storm that destroyed the crops was their punishment (*Ant.* 14.2, 1–2 [§§21–28]). The Passover sacrifice is the first time a priestly act is even suggested in connection with either of the two brothers.

264. This is another case in which Hyrcanus appears in a different light in *Antiquities* than in *War*. In *Antiquities*, Josephus adds that though "Hyrcanus promised him [Scaurus] no less a sum, he accepted the offer of Aristobulus, for he was both wealthy and generous and asked for more moderate terms, whereas Hyrcanus was poor and niggardly and held out untrustworthy promises for greater concessions" (14.2, 3 [§§30–31]).

265. See Smallwood, *The Jews under Roman Rule*, 21.

266. Only *Antiquities* mentions Aristobulus's spectacular gift to Pompey, valued at five hundred talents, although, in quoting Strabo about the present, Josephus includes his statement that "Alexander, the king of the Jews" had sent it (14.3, 1 [§§34–36]). Why the statement mentions Alexander rather than Aristobulus is puzzling. For the discussion regarding a Roman coin, dated to the equivalent of 55 BCE, with the caption Bacchius Iudaeus and whether it is related to Aristobulus II's gift, see Meshorer, *A Treasury of Jewish Coins*, 33–34. If this Iudaeus is Aristobulus II, then his Hebrew name may well have been Judah and some or all of the Jewish coins with that name could be his. As we have seen, however, these coins may have been minted by Aristobulus I whose Hebrew name we know was Judah.

he heard the case of the Jews and their leaders Hyrcanus and Aristobulus, who were quarrelling with one another, while the nation was against them both and asked not to be ruled by a king, saying that it was the custom of their country to obey the priests of the God who was venerated by them, but that these two, who were descended from the priests, were seeking to change their form of government in order that they might become a nation of slaves. (*Ant.* 14.3, 2 [§41])[267]

Antiquities has Hyrcanus complain, not only about the loss of his rights as the older brother, but also about the fact "that he had but a small part of the country under his rule" (14.3, 2 [§42]).[268] Antipater had also supplied him with "more than a thousand of the most reputable Jews" (14.3, 2 [§43]) to fortify his point of view.[269] Aristobulus seems not to have wanted to appear too servile to the Romans and left the place before Pompey had reached a decision about the brothers' dispute. This angered the conqueror, who pursued Aristobulus, with the latter entering the fortress Alexandreion. From there, he negotiated with Pompey while Hyrcanus was with the Roman forces (the brothers argued about the crown). Nothing is said in these sections about whether Aristobulus, who feared Pompey might restore the throne to Hyrcanus, was also concerned that he might give back the high priesthood to him.[270] Eventually,

---

267. Diodorus, *Library of History* 40.2, supports this general picture: "During Pompey's stay in Damascus of Syria, Aristobulus, the king of the Jews, and Hyrcanus his brother came to him with their dispute over the kingship. Likewise the leading men, more than two hundred in number, gathered to address the general and explain that their forefathers, having revolted from Demetrius [the text has "the temple"], had sent an embassy to the senate, and received from them the leadership of the Jews, who were, moreover, to be free and autonomous, their ruler being called High Priest, not King. Now, however, these men were lording it over them, having overthrown the ancient laws and enslaved the citizens in defiance of all justice; for it was by means of a horde of mercenaries, and by outrages and countless impious murders that they had established themselves as kings" (from M. Stern, *Greek and Latin Authors*, 1.185–86). He continues with Pompey's criticism of Hyrcanus's party for lawless acts and attacks on Romans. Compare also Strabo, *Geography* 16.2, 40.

268. We do not know what that small part might have been. Some have surmised that it was the area of Idumea; Abraham Schalit, *King Herod: Portrait of a Ruler* (Jerusalem: Bialik, 1962 [Hebrew]), 9 n. 31 = *König Herodes: Der Mann und sein Werk,* 2nd ed. (Berlin: de Gruyter, 2001), 9–10; Smallwood, *The Jews under Roman Rule,* 22 n. 4; Richardson, *Herod,* 98.

269. If Hyrcanus's charge that Aristobulus had committed "acts of piracy at sea" is factual, this would be the only case of a Jewish high priest who was so occupied (14.3, 2 [§43])! Pirates on the Mediterranean Sea were one of the problems that Pompey had come to address in the East.

270. Dio says about the brothers: "Their rulers were two brothers, Hyrcanus and Aristobulus, who were quarrelling themselves, as it chanced, and were creating factions in the cities on account of the priesthood (for so they called their kingdom) of their god, whoever he is" (*Roman*

he managed to reach Jerusalem to await the inevitable response of Pompey, made the more frightening by the refusal of Aristobulus's side to pay a promised sum of money (*J.W.* 1.6, 4–5 [§§132–37]; *Ant.* 14.3, 3–4, 1 [§§46–57]).

The Romans soon laid Jerusalem under siege. The city was a formidable place to storm, and it took a great deal of planning and work to ready the attack. Josephus says that while the Romans were preparing, "sedition broke out within the walls; the partisans of Aristobulus insisting on a battle and the rescue of the king, while those of Hyrcanus were for opening the gates to Pompey" (1.7, 2 [§142]; compare *Ant.* 14.4, 2 [§58]). It seems Aristobulus's side fared more poorly in the dispute, with the result that they fled to the temple compound and cut the bridge that connected it with the city. With them out of the way, Hyrcanus's suppporters let the Romans into the city (see also Dio, *Roman History* 37.16, 1). Now, the Romans had only the temple mount to capture, not the entire city. They arranged themselves to take it, with a certain Piso in command. "In this work the friends of Hyrcanus keenly assisted him with their advice and services" (1.7, 2 [§144]; *Ant.* 14.4, 2 [§60]).

The Romans took advantage of Jewish laws against Sabbath labor and attack to set up their siege-works.[271] Their position allowed them to observe the service at the altar that continued to function in the temple. Pompey not only admired the bravery of the Jewish defenders, but was also impressed by

> the way in which they carried on their religious services uncurtailed, though enveloped in a hail of missiles. Just as if the city had been wrapt in profound peace, the daily sacrifices, the expiations and all the ceremonies of worship were scrupulously performed to the honour of God. At the very hour when the temple was taken, when they were being massacred about the altar, they never desisted from the religious rites of the day. (1.7, 4 [§148]; *Ant.* 14.4, 3 [§§65–67])

Whether their dedication is in any way to be attributed to Aristobulus's leadership or to priestly custom is not said.

In *Ant.* 14.4, 3 [§66], Josephus dates the Roman capture of the temple to "the third month, on the Fast Day, in the hundred and seventy-ninth

---

History 37.15, 2, cited from M. Stern, *Greek and Latin Authors*, 2.350). Dio also mentions that Pompey "immediately won over Hyrcanus without a battle, since the latter had no force worthy of note."

271. Defensive warfare was permitted, but it was apparently considered illegal to counter preparations for battle by the enemy (see M. Stern, *Hasmonaean Judaea in the Hellenistic World*, 209).

Olympiad, in the consulship of Gaius Antonius and Marcus Tullius Cicero." The third month and the Fast Day, if by this term is meant the Day of Atonement (observed on tenth day of seventh month, Lev 16:29-30), would not harmonize, but here "the third month," to judge from *J.W.* 1.7, 4 (§149), refers to the third month of the siege. The Olympiad in question began in July 64 BCE, with the first year of it therefore including the first half of the year 63. If that information is accurate, the day when the temple was taken could not be the Day of Atonement, which would occur in September or October. L. Herzfeld suggested and others have agreed that Josephus took the reference to "the Fast Day" from a source,[272] the author of which thought that Jews fasted on the Sabbath.[273] Whatever the time may have been, it is interesting that Josephus mentions the Holy of Holies, which Pompey and others entered—something that, the historian repeats, "was permitted to none but the high priest" (*J.W.* 1.7, 6 [§152]; compare *Ant.* 14.4, 4 [§72]). Of course, even the high priest was permitted to go into the room only on the Day of Atonement.

So, after a brief reign as high priest and king, Aristobulus II lost both offices when Pompey defeated and removed him. He will continue to play a part in the story for another twelve years, as he seems never to have lost the hope of regaining his high position.[274]

Hyrcanus II (Second Term, 63–40 BCE)

Having taken the temple and entered its most sacred place, Pompey still won praise for his piety by ordering the "custodians to cleanse it and to resume the

---

272. "Wann war die Eroberung Jerusalems durch Pompejus, und wann die durch Herodes?" *MGWJ* 4 (1855): 109–15.

273. See Marcus, *Josephus* 7, 480–81 n. c. As Cassius Dio reports that Jerusalem fell to Pompey on a Sabbath (*Roman History* 37.16, 4), this seems a reasonable solution. See M. Stern, *Hasmonaean Judaea in the Hellenistic World*, 210; *Greek and Latin Authors*, 1.276–77. For Dio's text, see *Greek and Latin Authors*, 2.349 and Stern's comments on pp. 352–53, where he raises the possibility that Dio made an incorrect inference from the references to the Roman military labors on the Jewish Sabbath.

274. We do not know whether Aristobulus II minted coins in his own name. His uncle Aristobulus I was named Judah, and two series of coins identifying the high priest as Judah have been found (see the section on Aristobulus I above). We do not know the Hebrew name of Aristobulus II and thus have no reason to assign these coins to his reign. See Meshorer, *A Treasury of Jewish Coins*, 39–40, 183–84; but see also his argument about a Roman coin (noted above) that may suggest that Aristobulus II's Hebrew name was Judah (pp. 33–34). If it was, then we may have coins from his reign as high priest. On these coins, only the title high priest occurs, not that of king.

customary sacrifices. He reinstated [αὖθις δ' ἀποδείξας][275] Hyrcanus as high priest, in return for his enthusiastic support offered during the siege, particularly in detaching from Aristobulus large numbers of the rural population who were anxious to join his standard" (*J.W.* 1.7, 6 [§153]). The restoration presumably meant that he returned to Hyrcanus the high priesthood and effective control of the temple itself, which for some time—since his flight to Aretas in Petra—had been in the hands of Aristobulus and his faction. Josephus says nothing here about restoration of the crown to Hyrcanus (but see *Ant.* 15.6, 4 [§180]),[276] although Dio says: "The kingdom was given to Hyrcanus and Aristobulus was carried away."[277] As we will see, in subsequent narratives about events in the time of Caesar, Hyrcanus is called king several times.

Pompey's redistribution of territories, including freeing a number of cities the Hasmoneans had captured over the decades and confining the Judean nation "within its own borders" (*Ant.* 14.4, 4 [§74]; *J.W.* 1.7, 7 [§155]), and his imposition of tribute on Judea are the backdrop for Josephus's assessment (only in *Antiquities*) of the cause for the calamity:

> For this misfortune which befell Jerusalem Hyrcanus and Aristobulus were responsible, because of their dissension. For we lost our freedom and became subject to the Romans, and the territory which we had gained by our arms and taken from the Syrians we were compelled to give back to them, and in addition the Romans exacted of us in a short space of time more than ten thousand talents; and the royal power which had formerly been bestowed on those who were high priests by birth became the privilege of commoners. (14.4, 5

---

275. The parallel passage in *Ant.* 14.4, 4 (§73) reads ἀπέδωκεν. Strabo, *Geography* 16.2, 46, preserves a record of Pompey's appointment of Hyrcanus, though through a corruption the text reads "Herod" instead of "Hyrcanus": "Now Pompey clipped off some of the territory that had been forcibly appropriated by the Judaeans, and appointed Herod to the priesthood." For an analysis of the passage, see M. Stern, *Greek and Latin Authors*, 1.310 (the translation is on p. 304).

276. In *Ant.* 20.10, 4 (§244), Josephus writes that "Pompey also restored the high priesthood to Hyrcanus and permitted him to have the leadership of the nation, but forbade him to wear a diadem." As Richardson comments (*Herod*, 100), Hyrcanus, if he did not receive back the crown, failed to get the office that was the heart of the dispute between the brothers.

277. *Roman History* 37.16, 4 (M. Stern, *Greek and Latin Authors*, 2.350). See Stern's comment on this passage, which he takes to be inaccurate (p. 353). The historian Florus (*Epitome* 1.40, 30) wrote: "Being appointed arbitrator between the two brothers, who were disputing the throne, he decided in favour of Hyrcanus and threw Aristobulus into prison, because he was seeking to restore his power" (Stern, *Greek and Latin Authors*, 2.133). Ammianus Marcellinus, *Res Gestae* 14.8, 12, says Pompey left the rule to a governor (Stern, *Greek and Latin Authors*, 2.604).

[§§77–78]; compare *J. W.* 5.9, 4 [§396] where he refers to the madness of the two brothers)[278]

Pompey appointed Scaurus governor of Syria, a large region that included Judea, and deported Aristobulus in chains, with his children in tow (*J. W.* 1.7, 7 [§157]; *Ant.* 14.4, 5 [§79]).[279] These firm measures should have solved many problems, but one of Aristobulus's two sons, Alexander, who seems to have been a true heir of his father, managed to escape and to resume Aristobulus's military ways (*J. W.* 1.7, 7 [§158]; *Ant.* 14.4, 5 [§79]).

Hyrcanus and Antipater continued to collaborate, now in cooperation with the Roman authorities. Josephus says they assisted Scaurus with a supply of grain when his forces, who were ravaging Arabia around Petra, were in danger of starving (*J. W.* 1.8, 1 [§159]; *Ant.* 14.5, 1 [§80]).[280] But Hyrcanus was not able to maintain control of Jerusalem, because Alexander, his nephew, had succeeded in raising an army and overran Judea. Aristobulus and his sons, who represented for many an anti-Roman stance and who never seem to have had difficulty assembling an army in Judea, proved to be persistent enemies of the new Roman order.[281] Alexander "caused Hyrcanus serious annoyance by his raids upon Judaea. Having already advanced to Jerusalem and had the audacity to begin rebuilding the wall which Pompey had destroyed, he would in all probability have soon deposed his rival, but for the arrival of Gabinius,

---

278. D. Schwartz ("Josephus on Hyrcanus II," 217–25) thinks that Josephus's assessment of Hyrcanus II in *Antiquities* relates to his actions regarding his brother and later regarding Herod. "*Antiquities* consistently teaches that politics is a nasty game, and one should either play it as it is to be played or leave it; Hyrcanus did neither. He was by nature unsuited to political life but did not leave it; the result was that during most of his career he engaged in στάσις against his brother, a στάσις which provided for the loss of the Hasmonean state and the Herodian takeover" (p. 225).

279. Aristobulus was one of the captives who were included in Pompey's triumph in Rome. Plutarch, who describes the event, twice calls Aristobulus a king (*Life of Pompey* 39.3; 45.5), and Appian assigns him the same title (*Syriaca* 50.252). In his *Mithridaticus* 117:578, however, Appian claims that Pompey executed Aristobulus directly after his triumph (see M. Stern, *Greek and Latin Authors*, 2.183–84)—an assertion that does not harmonize with Josephus's subsequent narratives.

280. At least in the version in *Antiquities*, Hyrcanus *orders* Antipater to deliver the grain; in *War*, he merely *sends* him to do so.

281. Uwe Baumann, *Rom und die Juden: Die römisch-jüdischen Beziehungen von Pompeius bis zum Tode des Herodes (63 v. Chr.–4 v. Chr.)*, Studia Philosophica et Historica 4 (Frankfurt am Main: Lang, 1983), 51, 58; Richardson, *Herod*, 100. Joseph Klausner (*The History of the Second Temple*, 5 vols., 6th ed. [Jerusalem: Achiasaf, 1963], 3.235–39) stresses this point, regarding the Jews who supported Aristobulus and his sons as freedom fighters against the Romans with their collaborators Antipater and Hyrcanus.

who had been sent to Syria as successor to Scaurus" (*J.W.* 1.8, 2 [§160]; *Ant.* 14.5, 2 [§82] says that "Hyrcanus was no longer able to hold out against the strength of Alexander"). Whether Alexander, when in Jerusalem, actually executed high-priestly functions is not said.[282] Gabinius eventually defeated Alexander's forces and besieged him in the fortress Alexandreion. At the request of Alexander's mother, who apparently was not in Rome but was deeply concerned about the welfare of her husband and children imprisoned there, Gabinius demolished this and two other fortresses so that they would not serve as bases for future military operations (*J.W.* 1.8, 5 [§168]; *Ant.* 14.5, 4 [§90]).

Pacifying Alexander provided Gabinius with an opportunity to alter the governmental structure of the area. "After this Gabinius reinstated Hyrcanus in Jerusalem and committed to him the custody of the Temple. The civil administration he reconstituted under the form of an aristocracy. He divided the whole nation into five unions [συνόδους];[283] one of these he attached to Jerusalem, another to Gadara, the third had Amathus as its centre of government, the fourth was allotted to Jericho, the fifth to Sepphoris, a city of Galilee. The Jews welcomed their release from the rule of an individual and were from that time forward governed by an aristocracy" (*J.W.* 1.8, 5 [§§169–70]; *Ant.* 14.5, 4 [§§90–91]).[284] Schürer understands this to mean that Gabinius thereby deprived the ineffective Hyrcanus of his civil duties and left only the temple and its supervision to the high priest,[285] but some later evidence suggests, as we will see, that Hyrcanus did still exercise some wider political power. Yet, the Romans seem not to have had much confidence in Hyrcanus's ability to control the region. The reforms of Gabinius can be seen as effecting the proposals made by the Jewish emissaries to Pompey six years earlier when they asked for an end of kingship and a return to a rule by priests,[286] although we know nothing about the duties of the local sanhedrins (possibly they collected taxes) and how long they continued to exist.

A revolt headed by Aristobulus, who with his son Antigonus had escaped from Rome (56 BCE), and another led by the once-defeated Alexander (55 BCE), Aristobulus's other son, led to further changes. Hyrcanus and Antipater appear at this time as strong supporters of the Roman cause (see *J.W.* 1.8, 7

---

282. Richardson (*Herod*, 102) thinks Alexander served as high priest for a short time, although he recognizes that Josephus does not report this.

283. They are called συνέδρια in *Antiquities*.

284. Marcus writes that by "aristocracy" Josephus "means priestly rule, as he explains in *Ant.* xi.111" (*Josephus* 7, 495 n. g).

285. *History*, 1.268–69; Baumann, *Rom und die Juden*, 55–56.

286. Baumann, *Rom und die Juden*, 55.

[§175]; *Ant.* 14.6, 2 [§99]) with consequences for the way in which many Judeans viewed them.[287] Following his victories over the leaders of the two uprisings,[288] "Gabinius then proceeded to Jerusalem, where he reorganized the government in accordance with Antipater's wishes" (*J.W.* 1.8, 7 [§178]; see all of 1.8, 6–7 [§§171–78]; *Ant.* 14.6, 1–4 [§§92–103]). This may be the time when Antipater received the title ἐπιμελητής.[289]

We continue to receive no information about Hyrcanus's duties as high priest. When Crassus replaced Gabinius as governor of the large province of Syria in 54 BCE, he looted the Jerusalem temple to provide funds for his campaign against the Parthians. *War* has a brief report, saying only that he "stripped the temple at Jerusalem of all its gold, his plunder including the two thousand talents left untouched by Pompey" (1.8, 8 [§179]). *Antiquities* provides a fuller statement by relating the story of a priest Eleazar, called "the guardian of the money" (ὁ τῶν χρημάτων [variant: θησαυρῶν] φύλαξ ἱερεύς). This Eleazar is credited with buying Crassus off so that he would not steal more of the sanctuary's valuables (14.7, 1 [§§105–9]).[290]

In an inauspicious way, Josephus introduces for the first time into his accounts a name that will dominate them both—Herod. After Crassus's defeat and death and Cassius's accession to the governorship of the Syrian province (53–51 BCE), the latter put down a continuation of Aristobulus's revolt led by a certain Peitholaus, whose execution Antipater recommended.[291]

> Antipater had married a lady named Cypros, of an illustrious Arabian family, by whom he had four sons—Phasael, Herod, afterwards king, Joseph, and Pheroras—and a daughter, Salome. He had, by kind offices and hospitality, attached to himself persons of influence in

---

287. For the textual problem here, see Marcus, *Josephus* 7, 499 n. f.

288. Gabinius sent both Aristobulus and Antigonus back to Rome. As he had agreed with their mother, Gabinius later arranged for her children to return from Rome. They and their mother stayed in Ashkelon. It has been thought on the basis of a vague allusion in Cassius Dio, *Roman History*, 39.56, 6, that Julius Caesar might have supported the uprisings led by Aristobulus and his sons, but the evidence is too sparse to be sure (see Baumann, *Rom und die Juden*, 62 n. 51).

289. See Baumann, *Rom und die Juden*, 62–64.

290. Crassus had also looted a temple in Hierapolis (Plutarch, *Crassus* 17).

291. Baumann suspects that Aristobulus's son Alexander was behind the revolt but wisely chose not to demonstrate this openly until he saw how matters developed (*Rom und die Juden*, 67 n. 73). Cassius is supposed to have sold some thirty thousand inhabitants of Galilee into slavery. The leader Peitholaus, whom Josephus had mentioned before, appears to be the פיתלאיס in 4Q468e 3 (John Strugnell, "The Historical Background to 4Q468g [= 4QHistorical B]," *RevQ* 73 [1999]: 137–38; the siglum g was earlier assigned to the text). Line 2 of the fragment refers to someone killing a multitude of people.

every quarter; above all, through this matrimonial alliance, he had won the friendship of the king of Arabia, and it was to him that he had entrusted his children when embarking on war with Aristobulus. (*J.W.* 1.8, 9 [§181]; compare *Ant.* 14.7, 3 [§§121–22])

The narratives soon turn to the time of Julius Caesar (he crossed the Rubicon in 50 BCE, the year when the civil wars began) who released Aristobulus and even supplied him with two legions to oppose and weaken Pompey's partisans in Syria (compare Dio, *Roman History* 41.18, 1). A short time later in the same year, Aristobulus met his death by poison and was, after some delay, buried in the royal sepulchres in Jerusalem on Mark Antony's orders (*J.W.* 1.9, 1 [§§183–84]; *Ant.* 14.7, 4 [§§123–24]). Aristobulus's son Alexander, too, was executed at Pompey's behest by Q. Metellus Scipio, proconsul of Syria and Pompey's father-in-law; after being condemned in a trial, he was beheaded (*J.W.* 1.9, 2 [§185]; *Ant.* 14.7, 4 [§125]). Caesar's victory over Pompey at Pharsalus and the latter's subsequent death in Egypt (48 BCE) put leaders such as Hyrcanus and Antipater in a difficult position, because they had energetically supported the Roman officials appointed in the wake of Pompey's victory in 63 BCE.[292] Now that Caesar was in the ascendancy and had tried (unsuccessfully) to exploit Aristobulus's influence against the Pompeians, the two opponents of Aristobulus had to make a decision. They proved skillful enough to chart their course successfully through the troubled waters, because we soon find them offering much-needed assistance to Caesar himself when he was in tight circumstances in Egypt (beginning in October of 48 BCE).

We learn little about the specifics involved in their transfer of loyalties, but *War* mentions that "Antipater, on the death of Pompey, went over to his opponent and paid court to Caesar" (1.9, 3 [§187]). No reference is made here to Hyrcanus, though a summary statement about the subject in *Antiquities* typically casts matters in a somewhat different light: "When Caesar, after his victory over Pompey and the latter's death, was fighting in Egypt, Antipater, the gover-

---

292. As is well known, the *Psalms of Solomon* offers strong poetic expressions of the author's hatred for Pompey and for those who had supported him. He does not name names, but the Hasmoneans receive heavy criticism. For the capture of Jerusalem and the death of Pompey, see 2:22-29; 8:1-22 (vv. 16-17 say he was well received by the local leaders). In 17:6-9, the Hasmoneans are pictured thus: "With pomp they set up a monarchy because of their arrogance; they despoiled the throne of David with arrogant shouting. But you, O God, overthrew them, and uprooted their descendants from the earth, for there rose up against them a man alien to our race. You rewarded them, O God, according to their sins; it happened to them according to their actions. According to their actions, God showed no mercy to them; he hunted down their descendants, and did not let even one of them go" (R. B. Wright, "Psalms of Solomon," *OTP* 2.666).

nor of the Jews, under orders from Hyrcanus proved himself useful in many ways" (14.8, 1 [§127]).[293] If this is accurate, then Hyrcanus was in a position of authority over Antipater, despite the latter's role as ἐπιμελητής of the Jews.[294]

Antipater, as befitted his office, was the one to lead troops in support of Caesar's cause, and he displayed extraordinary valor in doing so, but *Antiquities* again adds a note that suggests a greater influence possessed by Hyrcanus, or at least that Antipater sensed Jewish people would place a higher premium on the high priest's authority. Mithradates, a king of Pergamum, led a force to aid the beleaguered Caesar in Egypt, but as he reached the border his way was blocked by the Jews from the district of Onias.

J.W. 1.9, 4 (§190)	*Ant.* 14.8, 1 (§§131–32)
Antipater, however, prevailed on them not only to refrain from opposition, but even to furnish supplies for the troops;	Antipater, however, persuaded them too to side with his party on the ground of their common nationality, especially when he showed them a letter[295] from the high priest Hyrcanus, in which he urged them to be friendly to Caesar and receive his army hospitably and furnish it with all things necessary. And so, when they saw that Antipater and the high priest had the same wish, they complied. And when those in the
with the result that no further resistance was encountered even at Memphis, whose inhabitants voluntarily joined Mithradates.	neighbourhood of Memphis heard that these Jews had joined Caesar's side, they too invited Mithradates to come to them.

293. Smallwood (*The Jews under Roman Rule*, 37) argues that the assistance Hyrcanus offered to Caesar was a response to Caesar's confirming him as high priest already in 48 BCE. That is, she, with others, dates the document recorded in *Ant.* 14.10, 4 (§199) to the year 48 (on this text, see below). The titles given to Caesar in it are compatible with that date, though they would also fit several later years. Smallwood believes that conferring the title of high priest alone (the only title given to Hyrcanus in the document) logically precedes his appointment in 47 BCE as ethnarch as well. Her thesis is possible but contrary to the narrative order and to the order of the decrees. Naturally, neither of these objections is decisive.

294. This statement in *Antiquities* raises some doubt about Schürer's claim that "Antipater cannot have been a political officer in the service of Hyrcanus because the latter no longer had any political standing after the time of Gabinius's enactment. So if he acts ἐξ ἐντολῆς Ὑρκανοῦ, *Ant.* 14.8, 1 (127), this is perhaps to be explained by the spiritual authority which Hyrcanus had as High Priest" (*History of the Jewish People*, 1.270–71 n. 13). The authority attributed to him in the present case does not look very spiritual.

295. Although Marcus translates "a letter," the Greek text has τὰς . . . ἐπιστολάς.

In *Antiquities,* the Oniad Jews agree only when they learn that Hyrcanus and Antipater concurred in wanting them to support Mithradates. We have no way of knowing whether Hyrcanus actually sent such letters, as *Antiquities* is our only source for them, but at least the claim reveals the lofty estimation in which the high priest was held or thought to have been held, even beyond the borders of Judea.

Both of Josephus's histories praise Antipater's bravery and, like Mithradates himself, credit him with not only averting a disaster but winning a great victory. Mithradates lauded Antipater to Caesar, with the result that he was rewarded for his extraordinary efforts. *War* reports:

> Later, when Caesar had settled affairs in Egypt and returned to Syria [47 BCE], he conferred on Antipater the privilege of Roman citizenship with exemption from taxes, and by other honours and marks of friendship made him an enviable man.[296] It was to please him that Caesar confirmed [ἐπεκύρωσεν] the appointment of Hyrcanus to the office of high priest. (1.9, 5 [§194])

The section of *Antiquities* that parallels this one supplies similar information, including Caesar's confirmation of Hyrcanus as high priest, although it somewhat abbreviates the lines about Antipater's honors. But, to it *Antiquities* attaches some new information that, according to Josephus, enjoyed the support of Strabo.

> It is said by many writers that Hyrcanus took part in this campaign [the one of Mithradates] and came to Egypt. And this statement of mine is attested by Strabo of Cappadocia, who writes as follows, on the authority of Asinius. 'After Mithradates, Hyrcanus, the high priest of the Jews, also invaded Egypt.' And again this same Strabo in another passage writes as follows, on the authority of Hypsicrates. 'Mithradates went out alone, but Antipater, the procurator of Judaea, was called to Ascalon by him and provided him with an additional three thousand soldiers, and won over the other princes; and the high

---

296. It may be that there were official documents confirming the grants Caesar gave to Antipater and that Josephus, for whatever reason, did not include them in the series of texts he cites in *Ant.* 14.10, 1–26 (§§185–267). A possible reason why he did not reproduce them is that they did not deal with the Jewish nation, the criterion for inclusion there (see §186). Josephus does mention the order that the honors given to Antipater be recorded in the Capitol (*J.W.* 1.10, 3 [§200]).

priest Hyrcanus also took part in the campaign.' These are Strabo's own words. (14.8, 3 [§§138–39])[297]

Strabo, then, transmitted information to the effect that the Jewish high priest was a military figure who cooperated actively in the campaign for which *War* names only Antipater as a participant. Moreover, Caesar himself confirmed the point in an official document that refers to the campaign (*Ant.* 14.10, 2 [§§190–95]; see below). Whatever Hyrcanus's part in it may have been and whatever the reasons why he did so,[298] we do have confirmation that the new Roman power, Caesar, saw fit to keep Hyrcanus in his position as high priest of the Jews.

It appears, then, that Hyrcanus and Antipater had succeeded in switching sides in the great Roman conflict with no loss of position or prestige. In the next sections of both *War* and *Antiquities*, however, we read again about Antigonus, the surviving son of Aristobulus II. He attempted to exploit the potentially volatile political circumstances to his advantage—not an unreasonable plan in view of his father's favorable relations with Caesar. He thought that by recalling the previous loyalty of Hyrcanus and Antipater to Pompey, Caesar's enemy, he would succeed in being appointed his father's heir as high priest and ruler in their place. Naturally, he complained to Caesar about the fate of his late father and brother but he said more:

> he came forward and accused Hyrcanus and Antipater. They had, he said, in utter defiance of justice, banished him and his brothers and sisters[299] from their native land altogether; they had, in their

297. On the passages from Strabo, see M. Stern, *Greek and Latin Authors*, 1.282–83. If, as Stern and others do, one assumes that Nicolaus of Damascus was Josephus's main source for the account in *War*, then we have a discrepancy between Strabo's sources and Nicolaus. Asinius was a friend of Herod. Strabo's information from Asinius comes from his history of the civil wars in Rome (see Stern, *Greek and Latin Authors*, 1.212). For Hypsicrates, a first-century BCE historian and grammarian, see 1.220.

298. Baumann (*Rom und die Juden*, 93, esp. n. 83) lists several reasons for doubting that Hyrcanus was present and physically involved in the campaign. The strongest of them seems to be that if he had been present, there would have been no need for Antipater to present letters from him. One could, however, imagine circumstances in which written messages might have been in order, but the matter remains uncertain, as Baumann agrees. Richardson (*Herod*, 106–108) thinks Hyrcanus must have been present during the campaign. This is, of course, hardly be the first time a high priest is credited with military action.

299. Josephus was more precise than Thackeray's translation. Antigonus appears to have had one brother. Josephus wrote τῶν ἀδελφῶν, which means "siblings" here.

insolence, repeatedly done outrage to the nation; they had sent supports into Egypt, not from any goodwill to Caesar, but from fear of the consequences of old quarrels and to obliterate the memory of their friendship for Pompey. (*J.W.* 1.10, 1 [§§195–96])

Antiquities abbreviates his charges, most importantly by omitting mention of their "friendship for Pompey" (14.8, 4 [§140]). Antigonus may well have been correct in his accusations, but Antipater was able to convince Caesar that Antigonus, like his father, was a revolutionary at heart and that he (Antipater) had served Caesar well.

> After hearing both speakers, Caesar pronounced Hyrcanus to be the more deserving claimant to the high-priesthood,[300] and left Antipater free choice of office. The latter, replying that it rested with him who conferred the honour to fix the measure of the honour, was then appointed viceroy (ἐπίτροπος) of all Judaea.[301] He was further authorized to rebuild the ruined walls of the metropolis. Orders were sent by Caesar to Rome for these honours to be graven in the Capitol, as a memorial of his own justice and of Antipater's valour. (*J.W.* 1.10, 3 [§§199–200])

Antiquities says that Caesar granted the right to rebuild the walls of Jerusalem to Hyrcanus who had requested the favor (14.8, 5 [§144], but, in 14.9, 1 [§156], Antipater does the rebuilding).[302] It appears that at this time Caesar conferred the office of ethnarch of the Jews on Hyrcanus.[303] In his later work,

---

300. *Ant.* 14.8, 5 (§143) says only that he "appointed Hyrcanus high priest," something that would seem redundant at this point, as he already was the high priest. Some of the Roman documents cited by Josephus at a later point add that Hyrcanus was to have all the traditional privileges that custom afforded the high priest (see 14.10, 2 [§195]; 4 [§199]; 6 [§203]).

301. For the title, see Baumann, *Rom und die Juden*, 95, who considers the rank an undetermined one that allowed Antipater to become involved in all important political situations; and Smallwood, *The Jews under Roman Rule*, 39, who notes that the term, in imperial times, translated the Latin *procurator*, an office that was concerned with the collection of taxes. Compare also Richardson, *Herod*, 106.

302. In the fragmentary document preserved in *Ant.* 14.10, 5 (§§200–201), Caesar allows certain men (presumably Jews) to rebuild the walls and Hyrcanus to live in the city in whichever way he chose. The document may, however, date to the year 44 BCE (see below).

303. Although he does not mention it in the narratives, Josephus does include at a later point in *Antiquities* the official document in which Caesar, in 47 BCE after the adventures in Egypt, verifies the appointment (*Ant.* 14.10, 2 [§§190–95]). See Schürer, *History of the Jewish People*, 1.271; Klausner, *The History of the Second Temple*, 3.241; Smallwood, *The Jews under Roman Rule*, 38–39; Baumann, *Rom und die Juden*, 94.

Josephus also adds what he took to be the text of the Senate's decree (14.8, 5 [§§145–48]), but, as we saw in surveying the reign of Hyrcanus I, he imported a document that belongs in the time of Hyrcanus I, not in the 40s BCE. It has nothing to do with the situation depicted in the present context.

Josephus also includes in this setting a decree from the Athenian people in honor of Hyrcanus (*Ant.* 14.8, 5 [§§149–55]). Like the one before it, its placement in the time of Hyrcanus II is in doubt. So, for instance, Marcus points out that Agathocles's archonship (§150), the time for the decree, occurred in 106–105 BCE, that is, in the time of Hyrcanus I.[304] Josephus says that the honors came to Hyrcanus "for he had been of service to them" (§149)—something we know of elsewhere for neither Hyrcanus I nor Hyrcanus II. The decree itself contains a specific identification of the honoree: "Hyrcanus, son of Alexander, the high priest and ethnarch of the Jews" (§151); this could refer only to Hyrcanus II. His virtues to which the Athenian decree responded were that he

> has continued to show goodwill to our people as a whole and to every
> individual citizen, and to manifest the greatest zeal on their behalf,
> and when any of the Athenians come to him either on an embassy or
> on a private matter, he receives them in a friendly manner and sends
> them on their way with precautions for their safe return. (§151)

His rewards were a golden crown, a bronze statue of himself erected in the precincts of a temple, and public announcement of the honors at various festivals and games (§153). An embassy was to convey the good news to him. The text, then, says little about Hyrcanus other than his two titles, which are attested elsewhere, and his international contacts.[305]

We may infer from the introduction to the official documents recorded at a later point in *Antiquities* that Hyrcanus dispatched a delegation to Rome in the year 47 BCE, after Caesar's settlement of Judean matters and his return to Rome. At that time he requested that Caesar "should confirm the treaty of

---

304. *Josephus* 7, 527 n. c; compare 526 n. a. For the list, see, for example, W. Dinsmoor, *The Archons of Athens in the Hellenistic Age* (Amsterdam: Hakkert, 1966 [reprint of the 1931 edition]), 252–94. There is no archon named Agathocles attested for any time during the reign of Hyrcanus II.

305. Klausner (*The History of the Second Temple*, 3.242) thinks the Athenian honors came to Hyrcanus II in the wake of the return of ports to Judea by Caesar and thus the return of traders from places such as Athens. Hyrcanus is supposed to have welcomed them and thus received the benefits noted in the text. A number of features in the document resemble ones found in the Decree of the People of Pergamum (*Ant.* 14.10, 22 [§§247–55]), which definitely belongs to the reign of Hyrcanus I.

friendship and alliance with him" (*Ant.* 14.10, 1 [§185]). *Antiquities* 14.10, 3 (§§196–98) may contain the text of Caesar's response.

While some details in the preceding sections made it appear that Hyrcanus was Antipater's superior, the next ones describe situations in which Antipater appears as the power behind Hyrcanus. He rebuilt the wall of Jerusalem, as Caesar had permitted, and then proceeded through the country suppressing uprisings (about which we know nothing),[306]

> and everywhere combining menaces with advice. Their support of Hyrcanus, he told them, would ensure them a prosperous and tranquil existence, in the enjoyment of their own possessions and of the peace of the realm. If, on the contrary, they put faith in the vain expectations raised by persons who for personal profit desired revolution, they would find in himself a master instead of a protector, in Hyrcanus a tyrant instead of a king, in the Romans and Caesar enemies instead of rulers and friends; for they would never suffer their own nominee to be ousted from his office. (*J.W.* 1.10, 4 [§§201–2]; see *Ant.* 14.9, 1 [§§156–57])

Antipater worked diligently to enforce the *pax romana* in Judea and thus to strengthen himself and Hyrcanus in their offices. A striking fact here is that Antipater is quoted as calling Hyrcanus a *king*. It is unlikely that Caesar restored the royal title to him, as it is never used in the official documents relating to these times (see *Ant.* 14.10, 2–7 [§§190–212]), yet we will meet it several more times at later points in the narrative.[307]

In the immediate sequel, though he had taken pains to bolster the standing of Hyrcanus, Antipater reorganized the government upon seeing that Hyrcanus was "indolent and without the energy necessary to a king [βασιλείας ἀτονώτερον]" (*J.W.* 1.10, 4 [§203]; *Ant.* 14.9, 2 [§158] lacks any mention of kingship). Antipater, to address the shortage of energy, appointed two of his sons as governors[308]—his oldest, Phasael, he made governor of Jerusalem and its territory, and his second son, Herod, he appointed governor of Galilee,

---

306. The uprisings may have been connected with Antigonus's maneuvers.

307. Thackeray (*Josephus II*, 95 n. a) simply calls *king* an incorrect term (referring to *J.W.* 1.10, 4 [§203]), while Marcus (*Josephus 7*, 532 n. a) suggests the more likely interpretation that "[b]y the Jews he was called 'king,' by the Romans, 'ethnarch.'" So also Smallwood, *The Jews under Roman Rule*, 39 (his subjects called him by the unofficial title of king).

308. It is tempting to suspect a long-term, dynastic plan on Antipater's part, but Josephus does not encourage such thinking and Antipater may have had other motives (for example, security in the face of opposition to his now official position [so Baumann, *Rom und die Juden*, 107–108]). Galilee and Jerusalem would have been the most likely places for opposition to arise.

"though a mere lad" (*J.W.* 1.10, 4 [§203]).[309] Here begins the age when Herod, who would soon end the Hasmonean dynasty, held high office and exercised his powers with brilliance and brutality.[310]

The young governor of Galilee first distinguished himself in clearing "bandits" from the border region between Galilee and Syria. He captured Ezekias, their leader, and executed him along with many of his followers—a development that pleased the Syrians (note, not the Galileans).[311] His vigorous measures came to the attention of Sextus Caesar, then governor of Syria and a relative of Julius Caesar. Herod's brother Phasael is credited with governing Jerusalem well (*J.W.* 1.10, 5 [§§204–6]; *Ant.* 14.9, 2 [§§159–61]). "Antipater, in consequence, was courted by the nation as if he were king and universally honoured as lord of the realm. Notwithstanding this, his affection for Hyrcanus and his loyalty to him underwent no change" (*J.W.* 1.10, 5 [§207]; *Ant.* 14.9, 2 [§162]). That is, the picture we receive is of Antipater as a diplomatic leader, loyal to his Roman overlords and faithful to his Jewish coruler, and without aspirations to evict Hyrcanus from his position.[312]

---

309. *Antiquities* 14.9, 2 [§158] says he was about fifteen years of age. But, as scholars have noted, Josephus elsewhere records that when Herod died (4 BCE), he was about seventy years (*Ant.* 17.6, 1 [§148]); hence, in 47 BCE he would have been around twenty-five years old (see, for example, Walter Friedrich Otto, *Herodes: Beiträge zur Geschichte des letzten jüdischen Königshauses* [Stuttgart: Metzlersche Buchhandlung, 1913], 18; Marcus, *Josephus* 7, 533 n. d).

310. Antipater and Phasael say later that Hyrcanus was the one who made Herod's appointment possible (*Ant.* 14.9, 5 [§181]).

311. There has been much speculation about the identity and family connections of this Ezekias, especially because of the relations between him and the later leaders of the fourth philosophy. Klausner (*The History of the Second Temple*, 3.251–53) thought he and his band were freedom fighters who had formerly supported the Hasmoneans. For a summary of various hypotheses, see Martin Hengel, *The Zealots: Investigations into the Jewish Freedom Movement in the Period from Herod I until 70 A.D.* (Edinburgh: T. & T. Clark, 1989), 313–15. From the passage in *Antiquities* regarding the pleas for help directed to Hyrcanus in Jerusalem by the mothers of the slain "bandits," he concludes that a considerable number of Ezekias's group were from respectable Jerusalem families; the same is suggested by the Sanhedrin's dealing with the case. Baumann (*Rom und die Juden*, 108) and others think the phenomenon of robbers in Galilee was a local reaction against Herod as a foreign rival to the Hasmoneans. Sean Freyne (*Galilee from Alexander the Great to Hadrian 323 BCE to 135 CE: A Study of Second Temple Judaism* [Edinburgh: T. & T. Clark, 1998 (paperback version of the 1980 volume)], 63) supposes that Ezekias was "in all probability, one of the Hasmonaean nobles of Galilee who opposed both Roman and Herodian domination" and that his execution by Herod probably "caused the Hasmonaean aristocracy that was prepared to go along with Roman rule to join Antigonus rather than Hyrcanus." But our sources say nothing about this. Why would the "bandits" have operated on the Syrian-Galilean border, if they were opposing Herod? For a more likely view, see Richardson, *Herod*, 110–11.

312. See Schalit, *King Herod*, 35–36 = *König Herodes*, 51–52.

The rise of the Antipatrids to enormous influence in the areas of Jewish settlement led nevertheless to tensions with the partisans of Hyrcanus. *War* (influenced by Nicolaus of Damascus, Herod's court historian) credits those tensions to Hyrcanus's envy at Herod's many honors and to "a number of malicious persons at court, who had taken offence at the prudent behaviour either of Antipater or of his sons" (1.10, 6 [§208]). This is a case in which *War* is more positive to Antipater, Phasael, and Herod than *Antiquities* is. In the latter, the ones who incite Hyrcanus to action are "the leading Jews"[313] who were concerned not only with the popularity enjoyed by the Idumean family but also with the revenues Hyrcanus was losing. The issue was control (under Rome's watchful eye, following Caesar's arrangements for governing the area) of the territories included in Hyrcanus's realm: was he the king in fact or in name only, with Antipater and his sons the actual rulers? Herod's bold handling of the "bandits" exacerbated their worries about the Idumeans.

> No longer masquerading as viceroys, they had now openly declared themselves masters of the state, thrusting him aside; seeing that, without either oral or written instructions from Hyrcanus, Herod, in violation of Jewish law, had put all this large number of people to death. If he is not king but still a commoner, he ought to appear in court and answer for his conduct to his king and to his country's laws, which do not permit anyone to be put to death without trial. (*J.W.* 1.10, 6 [§209])[314]

Antiquities refers specifically to the requirement of a trial before the *Sanhedrin* (14.9, 3 [§167]).[315]

---

313. From his study of the term οἱ ἐν τέλει, W. Buehler ("The Pre-Herodian Civil War and Social Debate: Jewish Society in the Period 76–40 B.C. and the Social Factors Contributing to the Rise of the Pharisees and the Sadducees" [Ph. D. diss., Basel, 1974], 51–56) concludes that those bringing the charges in *Antiquities* may have been members of the Sanhedrin or lower councils. Individuals similarly designated later brought charges against Herod before Antony in both Bithynia and Daphne in Syria (*Ant.* 14.12, 2 [§302]; *J.W.* 1.12, 5 [§243]). They were Jewish aristocrats who had much to lose from the rise of Antipater and his sons, and they consistently opposed them and supported Hyrcanus.

314. *Antiquities* has the leading Jews mention an occasion when Antipater, who had become a friend of the Roman generals, urged Hyrcanus to give them money but then presented the money to them as if it were from him. "Hyrcanus heard of this but gave the matter no thought; on the contrary, he was actually pleased" (14.9, 3 [§165]). This is example in which Hyrcanus in *Antiquities* is portrayed in a more negative light than in *War*.

315. James S. McLaren finds a contradiction within *Antiquities*: it says on the one hand that Herod killed someone without the Sanhedrin's verdict and on the other that he had acted apart from Hyrcanus's permission; *Power and Politics in Palestine: The Jews and the Governing of their*

The debates in Hyrcanus's court[316] set the scene for the much-studied trial of Herod by the Sanhedrin—a scene in which we may well see Hyrcanus function in one of the high-priestly roles, the leader of the Sanhedrin. Josephus's two accounts share a basic framework for the story (*J.W.* 1.10, 7–9 [§§210–15]; *Ant.* 14.9, 4–5 [§§168–84]), though they differ on a number of particulars.

1. Hyrcanus summoned Herod to trial.
2. Herod, on the advice of Antipater, came to Jerusalem with troops but only a limited number of them so that it would not appear he intended to depose Hyrcanus.
3. Sextus Caesar, governor of Syria,[317] intervened, ordering Hyrcanus to acquit Herod.
4. Hyrcanus, who loved Herod[318] and desired his acquittal, complied with the order.
5. Herod left Jerusalem, yet there was a possibility that he would be summoned to appear before the Sanhedrin a second time.[319]
6. Herod returned with an army,[320] but his father and brother convinced him not to attack his benefactor and friend Hyrcanus.
7. Herod withdrew with his army.

Items 4 and 5 in this summary are not as clear as one might wish. If Herod was acquitted (as both texts say), why would he be summoned a second time to face the same charges? *Antiquities* says that Hyrcanus had ordered a delay in the proceedings.

Antiquities alone provides a report of what happened when Herod appeared in person before the Sanhedrin. "But when Herod stood in the

---

Land 100 BC–AD 70, JSNTSup 63 (Sheffield: JSOT Press, 1991), 71. But, as we do not know the relation between Hyrcanus's authority and that of the Sanhedrin, this need not follow.

316. Josephus inserts a scene in which the mothers of the men whom Herod had executed called upon "the king and the people" to bring Herod to trial in the Sanhedrin. Such pleas moved Hyrcanus to summon Herod (*Ant.* 14.9, 4 [§168]).

317. As Sextus Caesar was murdered in 46 BCE, this incident could be not later than that year (see *Ant.* 14.11, 1 [§268]).

318. *Antiquities* 14.9, 4 (§170) adds that he loved him as a son.

319. In *War*, Herod believed that Hyrcanus had not wished his escape. Also, it was "knaves at court" who continued anti-Herodian propaganda at this time (1.10 [§212]). It may be that in *Antiquities* he returns because members of the Sanhedrin called him back, although this is not really clear (14.9, 5 [§§178–80]).

320. In both accounts, Herod increased his power while away because Sextus appointed him governor of Coele-Syria (*Ant.* 14.9, 5 [§180]; *J.W.* 1.10, 8 [§213] adds Samaria to his realm). Only *Antiquities* says that Herod paid him for the additional territories.

Synhedrion with his troops, he overawed them all, and no one of those who had denounced him before his arrival dared to accuse him thereafter; instead there was silence and doubt about what was to be done" (*Ant.* 14.9, 4 [§171]). While everyone was cowed into silence, "someone named Samaias,[321] an upright man and for that reason superior to fear" (*Ant.* 14.9, 4 [§172]), spoke to the group. This man, who plays no role in *War*, noted that Herod's appearance differed completely from the humble demeanor of those whose cases were tried by the council.

> But this fine fellow Herod, who is accused of murder and has been summoned on no less grave a charge than this, stands here clothed in purple, with the hair of his head carefully arranged and with his soldiers round him, in order to kill us if we condemn him as the law prescribes, and to save himself by outraging justice. But it is not Herod whom I should blame for this or for putting his own interests above the law, but for you and the king for giving him such license. Be assured, however, that God is great, and this man, whom you now wish to release for Hyrcanus' sake, will one day punish you and the king as well. (*Ant.* 14.9, 4 [§§173–74])[322]

---

321. For suggestions (they can be no more) about the identity of this man (is he perhaps the Shemaiah who was paired with Avtalion or the Shammai of Hillel-Shammai fame?), see Schalit, *King Herod*, 358 n.151 = *König Herodes*, 45 n. 151. Klausner argued at length that he was Shammai (*The History of the Second Temple*, 3.253–55; so, too, Derenbourg, *Essai*, 149–50). In *Ant.* 15.1, 1 (§§3–4), Samaias is called a disciple of Pollion, with Pollion, said to be a Pharisee, being credited with giving the speech in the Sanhedrin (Klausner thought Pollion was a corruption of the name Hillel). The two also figure in *Ant.* 15.10, 4 (§370) where again Pollion is called a Pharisee and Samaias is his disciple.

322. McLaren thinks that the differences between *War* and *Antiquities* are a product of Josephus's inserting the Samaias scene, which necessitated other changes (*Power and Politics in Palestine*, 76–77): "The reference to a law court in *Antiquities of the Jews* was essential to provide an audience for the speech of Samaias. Josephus's decision to describe this institution as the *synedrion* should be understood as nothing more than an imposition in the narrative to meet a particular requirement." Compare Richardson, *Herod*, 111. However, if we do not know the relation between Hyrcanus's acquittal of Herod and actions by the court, his thesis is weakened. He is correct in observing that Hyrcanus makes the important decisions, but that hardly implies that the court/Sanhedrin was not involved. The historicity of Samaias's speech is another question, one for which we have no other evidence. In this connection, it is exceptionally difficult to accept the claim, first advanced by Derenbourg (*Essai*, 146–48), that the largely different story in *b. Sanh.* 19a (the trial of Jannaeus's servant for killing someone; Jannaeus himself was summoned to appear) is a parallel to the present tale about Hyrcanus II, Herod, and the Sanhedrin (for references, see Schürer, *History of the Jewish People*, 1.276 n. 31; Schalit, *King Herod*, 358 nn. 152–53 = *König Herodes*, 45–46 nn. 152–53; both Schürer and Schalit accepted the suggestion). It is even more difficult to agree with Mantel that the talmudic account preserves a more reliable version

The longer account in *Antiquities* relates that Hyrcanus, when he saw that the Sanhedrin wished to execute Herod, "postponed the trial to another day, and secretly sent to Herod, advising him to flee from the city, for in that way, he said, he might escape danger" (14.9, 5 [§177]). So, perhaps we are to believe that Hyrcanus had rendered his verdict while the council itself had not yet done so. This would be consistent with Herod's concern that he would be recalled to face the Sanhedrin, something he refused to do. The members of that august body did indeed want Herod to reappear, but Hyrcanus, who is said to suffer from "cowardice and folly" (*Ant.* 14.9, 5 [§179]), feared that Herod would come to depose him. Hyrcanus proved correct, and only strong intervention by Antipater and Phasael kept Herod from resorting to violence.

This story gives us our first opportunity to learn details about a court or sanhedrin in Jerusalem. Josephus always calls it "the" Sanhedrin in the present context (once "this" Sanhedrin), never "a" sanhedrin. Hyrcanus had the right to summon an accused individual, even a governor of the region of Galilee, to face the Sanhedrin,[323] although it is not said explicitly that the high priest was a member of it or chaired its sessions. The story implies that the Sanhedrin could go against his wishes, and it is not evident what relation Hyrcanus's acquittal of Herod might have had with any decision taken by the Sanhedrin. The only detail about anyone in the court is the name Samaias, who is not identified as being a member of a particular group (for example, the Pharisees).[324]

If this picture mirrors reality, it shows Hyrcanus, whatever character defects Josephus attributes to him, as the central man in the government. He was the one to whom various factions turned, the one who exercised a certain control over Herod, the one who was able to summon a prominent suspect to the Sanhedrin but who was also able to circumvent its wishes, and the one through whom the leading Roman official Sextus Caesar acted.[325] Yet, while

---

of the episode than the ones in Josephus's works (Hugo Mantel, *Studies in the History of the Sanhedrin*, HSS 17 [Cambridge: Harvard Univ. Press, 1965], 72–73).

323. This shows that Herod was in some sense under Hyrcanus's jurisdiction, a fact recognized by Antipater in his advice to his son (so McLaren, *Power and Politics in Palestine*, 69).

324. The subject of a/the Sanhedrin has been endlessly debated by scholars, with the scant and varied evidence giving rise to a multitude of theories. One difficult problem has been how, if at all, to use *m. Sanhedrin* in studies of the Greco-Roman period. Although a number of scholars have proposed that there was a division of labor between two sanhedrins—one political and one religious—the stories in Josephus's writings and in the New Testament do not favor such a theory. For convenient surveys, see A. Saldarini, "Sanhedrin," *ABD* 5.975–80; Schürer, *History of the Jewish People*, 2.199–226. Mantel is a defender of the thesis that there were two sanhedrins (*Studies in the History of the Sanhedrin*, 54–101).

325. For several of these points, see McLaren, *Power and Politics in Palestine*, 77–79. Buehler says that from this time on, the "Jerusalem aristocracy, although backing Hyrcanus,

the incidents show his central role, they also paved the way for his eventual ouster by Herod, whose power was much more than theoretical.[326]

Events of enormous consequence for the Roman Empire, including the murder of Julius Caesar on March 15, 44 BCE, at the hands of Cassius and Brutus, form the backdrop for the next developments in Judea. Just before Caesar's assassination, a Jewish embassy sent by Hyrcanus had reached Rome (see *Ant.* 14.10, 5–6 [§§200–210]) to present requests to the dictator. As Caesar's executioners moved to the east, Cassius took control of Syria and began exacting impossible sums of money from his subjects to fund the anticipated war with partisans of Caesar. These were to be raised by the individual rulers in the area, but the quotas were so large that only unscrupulous leaders like Herod were able to comply swiftly.[327] Once again, Antipater and others were faced with the practical need to change sides in order to survive. So, we find Antipater making hasty arrangements to raise the money demanded by Cassius, a murderer of Caesar, Antipater's benefactor. For the purpose, he appointed not only his sons but also other acquaintants, among whom was a man named Malichus. He seems to be the individual mentioned earlier in *Ant.* 14.5, 2 (§84) // *J.W.* 1.8, 3 (§162), when he had a detachment of Jewish troops under his control during the battle against Alexander, Aristobulus II's son, in the mid-50s. By the time Cassius took control of Syria, Malichus had clearly become an important leader, as we can see from his being named one of those responsible for raising the enormous sums demanded. Although Antipater designated him to carry out the task, the two were opposed to one another (see *Ant.* 14.11, 2 [§273]). Malichus was tardy in securing the money demanded and was in danger of having Cassius execute him when Antipater (*J.W.* 1.11, 2 [§222]), or rather Hyrcanus through Antipater (*Ant.* 14.11, 2 [§276]), paid one hundred talents to spare him. He must have been important to merit such treatment. Despite Antipater's help, Malichus, according to Josephus, "plotted against Antipater, thinking that his death would make for the security of Hyrcanus' rule" (*Ant.* 14.11, 3 [§277]).[328] Schalit understands him to have been an old

---

always appear in opposition to Antipater and his family" ("The Pre-Herodian Civil War," 54, compare 56).

326. At a place after the trial and before the death of Caesar, Josephus inserts a section containing official documents relating to Hyrcanus and the Jews (*Ant.* 14.10, 2–25 [§§190–264]). These have been mentioned several times above, but the entire section is treated in more detail at the end of this chapter.

327. It may be, as Baumann (*Rom und die Juden*, 118) maintains, that Herod believed the heavy taxation was a lesser evil than the alternative faced later by a number of cities that failed to comply (*Ant.* 14.11, 2 [§§274–75]).

328. *War* reads quite differently: "Malichus, far from remembering this service of Antipater, concocted a plot against the man who had often saved his life, impatient to remove one who

and trusted friend of Hyrcanus, who aspired to take Antipater's place in the regime.[329] Oddly enough, he had enough power to force Antipater across the Jordan to raise an army, although his son Phasael ruled in Jerusalem and Herod controlled the armory there (*J.W.* 1.11, 3 [§224]; *Ant.* 14.11, 3 [§278]).[330] Neither text of Josephus is explicit about Hyrcanus's relations with Malichus, but at some point the latter is credited with fomenting revolution in Judea and again courting death from Murcus, then the proconsul of Syria. Inexplicably, Antipater interceded for him once more.

When Malichus heard that Cassius and his colleague Murcus had appointed Herod prefect (ἐπιμελητής) of Coele-Syria (so *Ant.* 14.11, 4 [§280]; the area was Syria according to *J.W.* 1.11, 4 [§225]) and had given him an army with a promise to make him king of Judea[331] after they had defeated Octavian and Mark Antony, he put his plot into effect. He "bribed one of the royal butlers[332] to serve poison to Antipater" at a banquet at Hyrcanus's palace (*J.W.* 1.11, 4 [§226]); Antipater soon died from the effects (43 BCE).[333] No attempt seems to have been made to assassinate his sons at this time. In both histories, Josephus praises Antipater, perhaps even more strongly in *Antiquities*: he was "a man distinguished for piety, justice, and devotion to his country" (14.11, 4 [§283]). In *War,* he was "a man of great energy in the conduct of affairs, whose crowning merit was that he recovered and preserved the kingdom [τὴν ἀρχήν] for Hyrcanus" (1.11, 4 [§226]).

In the sequel, we find Hyrcanus attempting to exercise both his civil authority and his power as high priest. Malichus understandably feared Herod's reaction to his father's murder. Phasael, as usual, counseled moderation when Herod planned an armed response. Herod eventually returned to "Jerusalem, then keeping festival, at the head of his troops. Instigated by

---

was an obstacle to his malpractices" (1.11, 3 [§223]). This is an example that is cited in the debate about the pictures of Antipater and Hyrcanus in Josephus's two histories. In this instance, *War,* which is supposed to be based on Nicolaus of Damascus, is more concerned with Antipater, while in *Antiquities,* Josephus speaks more favorably about Hyrcanus.

329. *King Herod,* 34–35 = *König Herodes,* 49; Baumann, *Rom und die Juden,* 120.

330. Richardson (*Herod,* 115–16) cites the incident as challenging "views that exaggerate Antipater's power and minimize Hyrcanus's" (116).

331. Doubt has been expressed about their promising him the kingship. The argument goes that one could read this as propaganda fashioned to put Herod's monarchy in the worst possible light: it was promised to him by Cassius, the Roman who, after Pompey, was the most hated by the Jews (see, for example, Baumann, *Rom und die Juden,* 121–22). But, if the throne in fact was given to Herod at a later time by the Roman Senate, as Josephus says, it is difficult to see how this point stands. The promise of Cassius remained just that, a promise, nothing more.

332. *Ant.* 14.11, 4 (§281) identifies him as Hyrcanus's butler.

333. For the date, see Schürer, *History of the Jewish People,* 1.277 n. 39; Otto, *Herodes,* 22.

Malichus, who was alarmed at his approach, Hyrcanus sent orders forbidding him to intrude aliens upon the country-folk during their period of purification. Herod, scorning the subterfuge and the man from whom the order came, entered by night" (*J.W.* 1.11, 6 [§229]). *Antiquities* lacks the slighting reference to Hyrcanus and points out that Hyrcanus allowed himself to be persuaded by Malichus (14.11, 4 [§285]). So, Hyrcanus as high priest issued an order based on purity concerns, even if he was doing so for ulterior motives. The story again raises the question of the relation between Hyrcanus and Malichus,[334] as they here acted in league against Herod. Herod's contempt for the authority of the high priest-ruler appears unchanged from the time when he intimidated the Sanhedrin.

Herod eventually dispatched Malichus who, at this late stage in his life, when desperation "stimulated him to conceive yet grander schemes . . . had dreams of raising a national revolt against the Romans, while Cassius was preoccupied with the war against Antony, of deposing Hyrcanus without difficulty, and of mounting the throne himself" (*J.W.* 1.11, 7 [§232]; compare *Ant.* 14.11, 6 [§290]). This seems to mark a new development in his aspirations. Herod, operating with Cassius's permission and military assistance, had Malichus executed after a dinner with Hyrcanus. Hyrcanus's reaction to the event is described in an interesting way. *War* 1.11, 8 (§§234–35) says: "Hyrcanus from sheer fright instantly swooned and fell; when brought, not without difficulty, to himself, he asked Herod by whom Malichus was killed. One of the tribunes replied 'By Cassius's orders.' 'Then,' said Hyrcanus, 'Cassius has saved both me and my country, by destroying one who conspired against both.' Whether he expressed his real opinion or from fear acquiesced in the deed, was uncertain" (see *Ant.* 14.11, 6 [§§292–93], where there is no fainting, only temporary speechlessness).

The Malichus affair did not end here. A friend of Malichus attacked Phasael while Herod was in Damascus. Phasael was able to defeat him, but again Hyrcanus was in the background of the events. Phasael "reproached Hyrcanus for ingratitude both in abetting the rebel and in allowing the brother of Malichus to take possession of the fortresses. Quite a large number of these had been taken, including Masada, the largest of all" (*J.W.* 1.12, 1 [§237]). *Antiquities* says that the citizens took up arms for Helix, Malichus's brother, whom Phasael confined in a tower but then released. Herod later recovered the fortresses (*Ant.* 14.11, 7 [§296]; *J.W.* 1.12, 2 [§238]). It does appear that Hyrcanus was working clandestinely to rid himself of the Antipatrids.

---

334. Hyrcanus did not try to avenge Antipater's murder nor did he hand Malichus over to the Sanhedrin, as one might think he should (see Baumann, *Rom und die Juden*, 123 n. 30). Compare Otto, *Herodes*, 22.

At around this time (42 BCE),[335] amid the unrest and eruptions of violence against the Idumean brothers, a familiar figure returned to the scene—Antigonus, son of Aristobulus II, who had earlier appeared before Julius Caesar in an attempt to snatch control from Hyrcanus and Antipater. Marion, whom Cassius had appointed prince of Tyre, was an enemy of Herod. He had briefly taken three fortresses in Galilee, which Herod at some point recovered; the latter also tried to discredit Marion by treating the captured Tyrians leniently. This Marion was involved in bringing Antigonus back to his own land, as was Fabius, governor of Syria whom Antigonus had bribed. A third ruler who collaborated in the restoration was Ptolemy the son of Mennaeus, ruler of Chalcis in Lebanon, who was married to Antigonus's sister Alexandra. All of this help notwithstanding, Herod was able to defeat the forces of Antigonus in an opening battle somewhere in Judea and to drive him from the region. Herod returned to Jerusalem to great applause, as "Hyrcanus and the people wreathed his head with crowns" (*Ant.* 14.12, 1 [§299]). Hyrcanus had much to fear from Antigonus and would therefore have been grateful for the rescue, even if it came from Herod. Herod further endeared himself to Hyrcanus's side by betrothing Mariamme, who was the granddaughter of both Hyrcanus II and his brother Aristobulus II through the marriage of their children (Alexandra, Hyrcanus's daughter, to Alexander, Aristobulus's son).[336] Josephus reports that this made him a "kinsman of the king" (*J.W.* 1.12, 3 [§241])—another reminder that, at least in some circles, Hyrcanus held the royal title. Although Mariamme and Herod did not marry for five years, the union gave Herod some legitimacy as ruler and, at the time of Antigonus's attack, it may also have served to align him more closely with Hyrcanus, whose relations with Herod may have been strained following the death of Antipater and its aftermath.

Events continued to move at a swift pace in the empire. The armies of Mark Antony and Octavian defeated the opposing forces led by Brutus and Cassius at Philippi (both committed suicide there) in October of 42 BCE. The new circumstances required yet another switch of loyalties by Herod, his

---

335. The situation was made the more chaotic by Cassius's departure from Syria (Schürer, *History of the Jewish People*, 1.277).

336. We could speculate that the marriage between Alexander and Alexandra had been arranged in view of Hyrcanus's failure to father a son, although Josephus writes nothing about the matter. It seems implausible to imagine the wedding effected a union between the house of Aristobulus and that of Hyrcanus, but Smallwood thinks it "will have helped to heal the family feud, and satisfied Aristobulus' faction by giving Alexander good prospects of succeeding Hyrcanus, who had no son, as High Priest" (*The Jews under Roman Rule*, 36 n. 51). The information in Josephus's writings permits no time when such a reconciliation would have occurred and depicts Alexander as fighting to remove Hyrcanus twice.

brother Phasael, and Hyrcanus. While Octavian returned to Italy, Antony advanced to the east, and in Bithynia embassies from the subject states called on him. Among them was a delegation of "Jewish leaders, who accused Phasael and Herod of usurping the government and leaving to Hyrcanus merely titular honours" (*J.W.* 1.12, 4 [§242]). They saw in the new circumstances an opportunity to rid themselves of Herod and Phasael; they apparently supported Hyrcanus, whom they did not accuse before Antony. Herod was able to deflect any injury from himself and his brother by bribing Antony handsomely. Later, when Antony was in Ephesus, "the high priest Hyrcanus and our nation sent an embassy to him" (*Ant.* 14.12, 2 [§304]), requesting that he undo the harm they had suffered from Cassius: to free Jews who had been sold, to retain the privileges granted by Antony and Dolabella (see *Ant.* 14.10, 9 [§§217–18]), and receive back from the Tyrians the Jewish property they had taken. Antony agreed to do so. This is the second context in *Antiquities* in which Josephus augments the shorter narrative of *War* by inserting official documents (*Ant.* 14.12, 3–5 [§§306–22]). The first of these documents is addressed only to Hyrcanus (though there is a textual problem), whose high-priestly title appears before that of ethnarch; the Idumean brothers are not mentioned.[337] For a treatment of those documents in which Antony grants the Jewish petitions, see the end of the chapter.

War continues the narrative with another embassy of Jewish leaders to Antony, this time when he was at Daphne near Antioch in Syria. One hundred officials brought complaint against Herod and Phasael, while a certain Messala (who would later defend Herod in Rome) and Hyrcanus (listed in that order) defended Herod. The high priest's motivation in supporting Herod was the marriage alliance with him. Antony heard both sides but asked Hyrcanus

> who was the best qualified ruler. Hyrcanus pronouncing in favour of Herod and his brother, Antony was delighted, because he had formerly been their father's guest and had been hospitably entertained by Antipater when he accompanied Gabinius on his Judaean campaign. He, accordingly, created the brothers tetrarchs, entrusting to them the administration of the whole of Judaea. (*J.W.* 1.12, 5 [§244]; compare *Ant.* 14.13, 1 [§§324–26])[338]

What their offices entailed for Hyrcanus's powers is not said, but he did remain the ethnarch of the Jews as Antony's official response to him indicates

---

337. See Richardson, *Herod*, 123.

338. In *Antiquities*, Messala defends Herod in Hyrcanus's presence, though here, too, Hyrcanus opts for Herod.

(*Ant.* 14.12, 3 [§306]).[339] The delegation was soon followed by a larger one (one thousand members), but Antony persisted in his decision and treated the messengers with violence, just as he had punished the previous embassy when its members complained about his decision. Josephus says that Hyrcanus, who with Herod had urged the men not to oppose Antony, was the one who arranged burial for the dead and medical attention for the wounded (*J.W.* 1.12, 6–7 [§§245–47]; *Ant.* 14.13, 2 [§§327–29] where Herod's bribe to Antony is mentioned).[340] The stories provide graphic evidence of the amount of opposition there was to Herod and Phasael in Judean society and the bravery of their enemies who risked (and in some cases lost) their lives in making their case. The iron hand of Rome provided Herod's and Phasael's support, not the populace or the aristocracy.

International events once more weighed heavily on Judea. 40 BCE was the year in which Rome's great eastern rival, Parthia, invaded the Levant, conquering Syria and much of Asia Minor. In Antony's absence, Pacorus, the crown prince, and the satrap Barzapharnes led the Parthian forces and provided an ideal occasion for yet another attempt by Antigonus, Aristobulus II's son, to wrest control of Judea from Hyrcanus, Herod, and Phasael. Lysanias, the successor of Ptolemy in Chalcis, forged an agreement with Barzapharnes to seat Antigonus on the throne. Either Lysanias (according to *War*) or Antigonus (so *Antiquities*) promised the satrap one thousand talents and five hundred women if he would remove Hyrcanus (and Herod and his supporters in *Ant.* 14.13, 3 [§331]), thus making Antigonus king. Josephus says the payment was not made but the Parthians nevertheless proceeded to help Antigonus gain control.[341] As had happened several times before, the appearance of a member of Aristobulus's family inspired a large number of Jewish people to flock to his support.[342] A pitched battle against Hyrcanus and

---

339. Richardson (*Herod*, 124 n. 119) suggests they held posts beneath Hyrcanus.

340. *War* mentions a bribe from Herod at the time of the first delegation, as does *Antiquities*.

341. Klausner (*The History of the Second Temple*, 3.260) attributes the story about the women to Nicolaus of Damascus, who aimed to discredit Antigonus and in so doing to present Herod more favorably. Josephus then naïvely copied from his source the story charging Antigonus with making the offer. Klausner thought the contradiction about who—Lysanias or Antigonus—extended the promise and the fact that it was not carried out proved his interpretation. Klausner generally thought that Antigonus was a character far superior to his portrait in Josephus's writings. At least we may say that he attracted a large number of Jewish supporters to his side.

342. They may have been disaffected already because of Antony's policy of fleecing the East for his personal aggrandizement and the support of his huge army. Herod and Phasael would

Phasael took place in Jerusalem, and Herodian troops came to their assistance, confining the forces of Antigonus to the temple area (*J.W.* 1.13, 2 [§§250–52]; *Ant.* 14.13, 3 [§§335–36]). The whole situation was complicated by the arrival of many pilgrims for the festival of Weeks (= Pentecost). Judging from the places where the factions were entrenched, Hyrcanus would not have been functioning as high priest at the temple during the holiday.

After many skirmishes and the customary slaughter in Jerusalem, "Antigonus petitioned for the admission of Pacorus [this Pacorus was the Parthian king's cupbearer and a general] as mediator. Phasael consented, and received into the city and offered hospitality to the Parthian, who, with five hundred horsemen, had come ostensibly to put an end to strife, in reality to support Antigonus" (*J.W.* 1.13, 3 [§254]; *Ant.* 14.13, 4 [§340]). Disastrously, Phasael agreed to accompany Pacorus to Barzapharnes in order to continue the negotiations, and Hyrcanus joined him, despite Herod's arguments to the contrary (he suspected a trap and thought Phasael should kill Pacorus—or so we are told). Of course, Herod was right, as the other two were soon to learn.[343]

Eventually, Phasael and Hyrcanus discovered the truth about the situation and heard of the payment Lysanias and/or Antigonus had promised (the women of Herod's, Phasael's, and Hyrcanus's households were included in the five hundred [*J.W.* 1.13, 4 (§257); *Ant.* 14.13, 10 (§365)]). Phasael was urged to flee, but, says Josephus, he "could not bring himself to desert Hyrcanus" (*J.W.* 1.13, 5 [§259]; see *Ant.* 14.13, 5 [§346]). Following the family custom, Phasael promised Barzapharnes a larger bribe than Antigonus could offer. "Immediately after, certain Parthians who had been left behind, with orders to do so, arrested Phasael and Hyrcanus, the prisoners cursing them bitterly for their perjury and breach of faith" (*J.W.* 1.13, 5 [§260]; *Ant.* 14.13, 6 [§348]). Herod, always more attuned to harsh reality, when informed of what had happened to Phasael, refused to walk into the trap set for him, and in this he was assisted by Alexandra, Hyrcanus's daughter and the mother of Mariamme, Herod's betrothed (*War* says it was Mariamme who provided the advice).

---

have been the local leaders responsible for collecting the vast sums of money. See Baumann, *Rom und die Juden*, 137–39.

343. It would be simple to dismiss Josephus's reports as a reflection of Nicolaus of Damascus's flattery of Herod, as Klausner does (*The History of the Second Temple*, 3.261), but Herod does appear to have been more adept at dealing with reality than Phasael and Hyrcanus were. M. Stern's suggestion (*Hasmonaean Judaea in the Hellenistic World*, 257) that Phasael and Hyrcanus II may have expected they could secure their positions during the change in rule from the Romans to the Parthians, just as Antipater and Hyrcanus II had switched their loyalties several times before, seems unlikely, since the Parthians were backing Antigonus, who could hardly coexist with Hyrcanus.

Herod then set out on the long flight that was, with many adventures, to lead him to Masada (where he left his family), Nabatea, Egypt, and finally to Rome where, apparently to his surprise,[344] the Senate, at the behest of Antony and Octavian, named him king of Judea.

Meanwhile, with no protector, Phasael and Hyrcanus were left to their fates. The Parthians ravaged the land and pillaged what they could, although Josephus claims they spared Hyrcanus's treasure that was a modest three hundred talents (*J.W.* 1.13, 9 [§268]; *Ant.* 14.13, 9 [§363]). But, more was to follow. The Parthians,

> not content with raising Antigonus to the throne,[345] delivered up to him Phasael and Hyrcanus, in chains, for torture. Hyrcanus threw himself at the feet of Antigonus, who with his own teeth, lacerated his suppliant's ears, in order to disqualify him for ever, under any change of circumstances, from resuming the high priesthood; since freedom from physical defect is essential to the holder of that office. (*J.W.* 1.13, 9 [§§269–70])

Antiquities presents the matter somewhat differently. There, Josephus writes that Antigonus, disappointed by the escape of the women whom he meant to give to the Parthians and fearful that the people would restore Hyrcanus to the throne, "went up to him where he was being guarded by the Parthians, and cut off his ears, thus taking care that the high priesthood should never come to him another time, because he was now mutilated, and the law requires that this office should belong only to those who are sound of body" (14.13, 10 [§366]).[346]

---

344. According to *Ant.* 14.14, 5 (§§386–87), Herod had come to Rome to claim the kingship for Aristobulus III, his wife Mariamme's brother.

345. Dio, *Roman History* 48.26, 2, writes: "He [Pacorus] then invaded Palestine and deposed Hyrcanus, who was at the moment in charge of affairs there, having been appointed by the Romans, and in his stead set up his brother Aristobulus as a ruler because of the enmity existing between them" (from M. Stern, *Greek and Latin Authors*, 2.357). Dio confused Aristobulus and his son Antigonus, though he correctly refers to Antigonus in 48.41, 4–5.

346. The law about the physical requirements for a priest is in Lev 21:16-23. A priest was to have no physical blemish; the passage lists twelve types of them, no one of which is laceration or amputation of ears. A descendant of Aaron with a physical defect was prevented from making offerings. It may be that Lev 21:23 is specifically directed to the high priest (see Jacob Milgrom, *Leviticus 17–22* [AB 3A; New York: Doubleday, 2000], 1821–32). Milgrom refers to 4Q266 (4QD^a) 5 ii where this passage from Leviticus is under discussion. There, line 5 refers to a priest who is in captivity to Gentiles; apparently this disqualifies him from serving at the altar (see J. Baumgarten, *Qumran Cave 4 XIII: The Damascus Document [4Q266–273]*, DJD 18 [Oxford: Clarendon, 1996], 50–51). See also *m. Bek.* 7:1–7 (in 7:4, problems with ears are noted but it does not mention cutting them off).

However Hyrcanus suffered the injury,[347] his high priesthood ended in 40 BCE with his nephew's cruel disfigurement of him.

This was not to be the end of his eventful life. Phasael seems to have committed suicide, an act of valor that, according to *War* (that is, Nicolaus of Damascus), was a credit to him (a true brother of Herod) and cast Hyrcanus as "the most ignoble of men" (1.13, 10 [§271]). The Parthians brought Hyrcanus as a prisoner to their land (1.13, 11 [§273]).

Antiquities relates a few details about the remaining decade of his life. When the Parthians transported him to their country, King Phraates "treated him very leniently because he had learned of his distinguished and noble lineage" (15.2, 2 [§14]). He allowed Hyrcanus to live in a large Jewish community in Babylon. "These men honoured Hyrcanus as their high priest and king, as did all the Jewish nation occupying the region as far as the Euphrates" (15.2, 2 [§15]).

Hyrcanus remained content with his new circumstances until he heard that Herod had become king of Judea (that is, in 37 BCE or later).[348] It may seem inexplicable, but Herod's assumption of power filled him with hope, for, as Josephus relates, he thought Herod was in his debt for saving him from the Sanhedrin's death sentence some ten years earlier. At least the presence of Herod as king in Judea was more encouraging than Antigonus as king and high priest. Babylonian Jews attempted to dissuade Hyrcanus from returning to Judea,

> mentioning the services and honours given him, and saying that among them he would lack nothing in the way of high-priestly or kingly honours and, what was more important, that over there he could not have these things because of the mutilation of his body, suffered at the hands of Antigonus, and that favours received by commoners [such as Herod] are not returned by them in like manner when they become kings. (*Ant.* 15.2, 2 [§17])

Hyrcanus insisted on returning and Herod, by correspondence, encouraged him in his plan. Herod even wrote about his "virtually sharing the kingship" with him (*Ant.* 15.2, 3 [§18]) in repayment for Hyrcanus's past kindnesses to him. Josephus alerts the reader, though, to what the king was

---

347. Baumann (*Rom und die Juden*, 142) thinks it more likely that the Parthians cut off Hyrcanus's ears, as such amputations were a Parthian form of punishment (referring to Tacitus, *Annales* 12.14, 3).

348. *J.W.* 1.22, 1 (§434) says that the marriage of Mariamme and Herod (in 37 BCE, during the siege of Jerusalem) made Hyrcanus optimistic.

thinking: "His zeal did not, however, spring from these motives but from the fact that he himself had no just claim to rule and he feared that a change might be made with good reason; and so he was eager to get Hyrcanus into his power or even to put him out of the way altogether" (15.2, 3 [§20]). It is reasonable to think that Herod worried about Hyrcanus, not only because the royal and priestly Hasmonean was out of his reach, but also because he could become a focal point of a Parthian attack, backed by the large Jewish population in Babylon, against himself and his kingdom. The conflict between Rome and Parthia had not ended; in the year 36 BCE, Parthia dealt Antony a defeat. Hyrcanus, with all the associations his name and line aroused and the honor in which he was held among Mesopotamian Jews, may have played a small part in the international calculations of the time.[349]

Hyrcanus did make the journey to his homeland, with the approval of King Phraates and the financial assistance of Babylonian Jews. When he arrived, Herod played his part to the full: he "received him with all honour, assigned him the first place in meetings, gave him the most honoured seat at the banquet-table and called him Father; thus he quite deceived him and in a variety of ways managed to keep his treacherous designs from being suspected" (*Ant.* 15.2, 4 [§21]).

This is the last we hear of Hyrcanus for a number of years. During the latter half of the 30s BCE, Herod continued to struggle with the Hasmoneans with whom he was related by marriage. His quarrels with Alexandra and Mariamme were ongoing, with their hatred brought to a boiling point by Herod's drowning of Mariamme's brother Aristobulus III, the last Hasmonean high priest, in the year 35 BCE (on him, see below). The end came for Hyrcanus II in the aftermath of the battle of Actium, where the armies of Octavian defeated the forces of Antony, Herod's benefactor (September, 31 BCE). With the death of his principal support whom Herod had even tried to help militarily at Actium, all seemed lost for the Idumean monarch. His enemies sensed a great opportunity, and he himself despaired of his future. Under these dark clouds, Herod's thoughts turned to the former high priest and king.

> And Herod himself, seeing that Hyrcanus was the only one left of royal rank, thought it would be to his advantage not to let him stand as an obstacle any longer. He believed that, if, on the one hand, he were to survive and escape danger, it would be safest not to have a man who was worthier than himself of obtaining the kingship wait to seize his opportunity at such a time of difficulty for himself; if, on the

---

349. Klausner, *The History of the Second Temple*, 4.11.

other hand, he were to suffer death at Caesar's [= Octavian] hand, he wished because of envy to remove the only man who might succeed him as king. (15.6, 1 [§164])[350]

Perhaps Herod reasoned that Caesar and Hyrcanus had enjoyed close relations and that his adoptive son Octavian might turn to his great-uncle's ally to replace Herod, the friend of Antony.

Josephus says that Hyrcanus's daughter Alexandra, far more aggressive than her father, urged him to take advantage of the situation by writing to Malchus, the ruler of the Arabs and, of course, Herod's enemy of longstanding, and asking him for protection. "For, she said, if they got away and things turned out badly for Herod, as was likely in view of Caesar's enmity to him, they would be the only candidates for the royal power both because of their lineage and because of the goodwill of the masses toward them" (*Ant.* 15.6, 2 [§167]). Hyrcanus refused at first but eventually relented. He gave a letter to a certain Dositheus, his friend; in the letter, he asked Malchus to send some horsemen to escort them to the Dead Sea. Dositheus, though he had many reasons to hate Herod, proved a traitor to Hyrcanus by divulging the letter to Herod. Herod ordered him to deliver it to Malchus as if the plan was proceeding in order to check the Arab's response. Malchus wrote that

> he would receive both Hyrcanus himself and all his party and as many of the Jews as sympathized with his cause, and that he would send a force to bring them in safety, and Hyrcanus would lack nothing for which he asked. When Herod received this letter, he immediately sent for Hyrcanus and questioned him about the agreements which he had made with Malchus. When the other denied having made any, Herod showed the letters to the Council [τῷ συνεδρίῳ] and had the man put to death. (15.6, 2 [§§172–73])

At this point in his narrative, Josephus does something unusual: he says that he took the preceding account from Herod's Memoirs but that other sources do not agree with it, "for they hold that it was not for such reasons that Herod killed Hyrcanus but rather that he did so after bringing charges against him which were invented with characteristic trickery" (*Ant.* 15.6, 3 [§174]). He then reports what the other sources say.

Once, while they were at a banquet, Herod, without giving Hyrcanus any ground for suspicion, put the question to him whether he had

---

350. See Otto, *Herodes*, 52.

received any letters from Malchus, and when Hyrcanus admitted having received greeting-cards from him, he asked also whether he had taken any gift from him, and the other replied that he had received nothing more than four beasts for riding, which Malchus had sent him. This act Herod construed as evidence of bribe-taking and treason, and ordered the man to be strangled. (15.6, 3 [§§175–76])[351]

Josephus also adds the reasons why his other informants disagreed with Herod's self-serving account and found their story more credible. They appealed to the mild, nonreckless character evident throughout Hyrcanus's long life, whether as a young man and even while a king when he had ceded most of the power to Antipater. Moreover, says Josephus, he was eighty-one years of age at the time of his death, a time when Herod was secure in his reign. Neither of these statements is true: Hyrcanus, if eighty-one in the year 30 BCE, would have been born in 111, some eight years before his parents were married (seventy-one is a more plausible age). Also, Herod was anything but secure in his reign after Antony's defeat and before Herod's trip to meet Caesar. The sources also pointed out that when Hyrcanus left Babylonia, he left a crowd of supporters and put himself entirely in Herod's power, entailing that he hardly could have had revolutionary thoughts. "It is therefore most unlikely and out of keeping with his nature, they say, that he should have attempted anything like revolutions, and these charges were a pretext invented by Herod" (*Ant.* 15.6, 3 [§178]; in 15.6, 5 [§183] he says that Herod got Hyrcanus out of the way). Presumably Herod, like Octavian/Augustus, reshaped the past to his greater honor and glory, distorting events that might mar the visage he wished to present. This is one of several cases in which Josephus proves that he did not approach sources uncritically.

Once he has dealt with the conflicting stories about the end of Hyrcanus's life, Josephus adds a summary of his career. He notes his appointment as high priest by his mother, an office that he held for nine years before he became

---

351. *War* is much briefer about the fate of Hyrcanus. In the course of documenting Herod's troubles at home despite his public success, the text traces his domestic problems to his Hasmonean wife Mariamme (1.22, 1 [§§431–32]). One example of such difficulties was Hyrcanus's death. "Next he put to death, on suspicion of conspiracy, Hyrcanus, Mariamme's grandfather, who had come back from Parthia to Herod's court. Hyrcanus had been taken prisoner by Barzapharnes when the latter overran Syria, but had been liberated through the intercession of his compassionate countrymen living beyond the Euphrates. And had he but followed their advice not to cross the river to join Herod, he would have escaped his tragic fate; but the marriage of his grand-daughter lured him to his death. He came relying upon that and impelled by an ardent longing for his native land, and roused Herod's resentment not by making any claim to the throne, but because it actually belonged to him by right" (§§433–34).

king around the time of his mother's death. After ruling as monarch for three months, he lost the kingship to his brother Aristobulus. The historian includes a generalizing comment that is inconsistent with his earlier narratives: "When it [= the throne] was restored to him later by Pompey, he received all his honours back and continued to enjoy them for forty years more" (*Ant.* 15.6, 4 [§180]). According to the narratives, Pompey restored Hyrcanus to the high priesthood but he did not give him the crown. Moreover, the time from Pompey's restoration of his honors to the time when he lost them to Antigonus was twenty-three or twenty-four years, not forty (63–40 BCE).[352] After surveying the final decade of his life, Josephus says:

> But what was most painful of all, as we have said before, was that in his old age he came to an unworthy end. For he seems to have been mild and moderate in all things and to have ruled by leaving most things for his administrators to do, since he was not interested in general affairs nor clever enough to govern a kingdom. That Antipater and Herod advanced so far was due to his mildness, and what he experienced at their hands in the end was neither just nor an act of piety. (*Ant.* 15.6, 4 [§§181–82])[353]

That seems true enough!

For a man who ruled as high priest for as many years as Hyrcanus did (thirty-three), many of them also as king (whether officially or de facto), we would expect that he minted coins. No ancient source records what his Hebrew name was (if he had one), and this has complicated matters. As we have seen, Meshorer now assigns the coins with the name Yohanan to Hyrcanus I; they had earlier been assigned to Hyrcanus II on the assumption that his Hebrew name also was Yohanan, like his grandfather. At this time, we have no firm evidence that either Alexandra, his mother, or Hyrcanus II minted coins in their own names. Meshorer thinks it possible that two categories of coins bearing the name Yonatan (rather than the longer form Yehonatan, the Hebrew name of Alexander Jannaeus) came from Hyrcanus II. The shorter form of the name would have been intended to distinguish him from his

---

352. In *Ant.* 20.10, 4 (§245), he correctly assigns him a rule of twenty-four years for the post-63 BCE period.

353. For his characterization by Josephus, see Schwartz, "Josephus on Hyrcanus II," 227–32, especially p. 232: "Josephus turned the notion of Hyrcanus' incapacity, which Nicolaus had applied—invented?—in order to explain and justify the rise of the Antipatrids, not into a weapon to condemn the Antipatrids . . . but into one to condemn Hyrcanus, and blame him for the fall of the Jewish national state."

father. The categories in question he labels *shin* and *tav*. All of them (with some corruptions) bear the legend: ינתן הכהן הגדול וחבר היהודים. He thinks a clue pointing in this direction lies in the fact that the coins in one of these categories are stamped upon older coins from Jannaeus (type *ayin*). In the end, he is unable to decide.[354]

Documents relating to Hyrcanus II

An important subject in the study of Hyrcanus II's high priesthood and one deserving special notice is the series of official Roman documents quoted by Josephus in *Antiquities* without parallels in *War*. They appear in two contexts, the first concerning Hyrcanus's contact with Julius Caesar and the second documenting his relations with Mark Antony.

Documents from Julius Caesar and others relating to them: These documents are inserted at the point in the narrative after Herod was dissuaded by his father and brother from attacking Hyrcanus in Jerusalem in the aftermath of the Sanhedrin fiasco. This set of documents occupies *Ant.* 14.10, 2 (§190) to 14.10, 25 (§264). Josephus lodges the long section at the place in the history where Caesar is about to travel to Africa in his campaign against the Pompeians Scipio and Cato (47 BCE). At this time, writes Josephus, "Hyrcanus sent to him with the request that he should confirm the treaty of friendship and alliance with him. And here it seems to me necessary to make public all the honours given our nation and the alliances made with them by the Romans and their emperors, in order that the other nations may not fail to recognize that both the kings of Asia and of Europe have held us in esteem and have admired our bravery and loyalty" (*Ant.* 14.10, 1 [§§185–86]). The historian, who is explicit about his apologetic aim, stresses that Roman documents were both authoritative and verifiable: "for they are kept in the public places of the cities and are still to be found engraved on bronze tablets in the Capitol" (14.10, 1 [§188]). He first cites the Caesar's texts regarding "Hyrcanus and our nation" (§189) and then adds a number of related documents—or at least ones he thought were related.

Josephus takes pains to underscore the authenticity of these documents. At the beginning of the section, he reminds the reader how they were publicly

---

354. *A Treasury of Jewish Coins*, 31–32, with the catalogue on 189–91. In the text of his discussion, Meshorer says that the coins of category *shin* are the ones stamped on the older Jannaeus coins, while in the catalogue he identifies those of category *tav* in this way. For his discussion of whether Alexandra minted coins, see pp. 43–44.

available, and at the end of it he reasserts the point, referring to "those decrees engraved on bronze pillars and tablets which remain to this day and will continue to remain in the Capitol" (§266). He says that there are others like them but that, rather than tax the reader inordinately, he has cited only some: "for I cannot suppose that anyone is so stupid that he will actually refuse to believe the statements about the friendliness of the Romans towards us, when they have demonstrated this in a good many decrees relating to us, or will not admit that we are making truthful statements on the basis of the examples we have given" (*Ant.* 14.10, 26 [§267]; compare 14.12, 6 [§323]). His language suggests there were such detractors, and the debate about the genuineness of the documents has continued to the present.

The documents take different forms, and, of course, each must be examined on its own merits. In his study of *senatus consulta*, R. Sherk refers to ones cited by Josephus and says about them: he "has given us what he claims are true copies of those *senatus consulta* which concerned Jewish history. They may be regarded in general as genuine, but whether he changed anything or was guilty of mistakes in transcription is a matter of conjecture. Even the texts he gives may be mere copies of copies."[355] The documents that he has in mind are *Ant.* 13.9, 2 (§§260–64; Hyrcanus I); 14.8, 5 (§§145–48; Hyrcanus I); 14.10, 10 (§§219–22; decree of the Senate). Smallwood, speaking more generally of all the documents in §§190–264 (and those in *Antiquities* 16), says their authenticity "is hardly in doubt."[356] Indeed, it is fair to say that contemporary opinion inclines toward accepting the cited documents as genuine, official Roman texts.[357]

---

355. *Roman Documents from the Greek East: Senatus Consulta and Epistulae to the Age of Augustus* (Baltimore: Johns Hopkins, 1969), 6. He agrees with a number of scholars who think Josephus found these documents in books 123–24 of Nicolaus of Damascus's *Historiae* (*Roman Documents*, p. 6 n. 7).

356. *The Jews under Roman Rule*, 558 (part of her Appendix B, "The Documents Quoted by Josephus in *Antiquitates Judaicae*," pp. 558–60). Scholars have usually suggested that Josephus could have examined a number of the documents in Rome where he lived for several decades after 70 CE and wrote *Antiquities*, or he could have found them in his source, Nicolaus of Damascus. See the short summary in Smallwood, 558–59. M. Pucci Ben Zeev defends a third possibility, namely, he used local archives of Diaspora communities where copies were kept, though he may not himself have consulted the originals but got copies from friends and acquaintances, thus accounting for the fragmentary nature of some texts and the mistakes found in them ("Greek and Roman Documents from Republican Times in the Antiquities: What Was Josephus' Source?" *Scripta Classica Israelica* 13 [1994]: 46–59). It is widely recognized that there are *textual* problems in some of the documents as they have reached us; most of these involve names and titles. See, for example, K. Noethlichs, *Das Judentum und der römische Staat: Minderheitenpolitik im antiken Rom* (Darmstadt: Wissenschaftliche Buchgesellschaft, 1996), 82.

357. See M. Pucci Ben Zeev, "Caesar and Jewish Law," *RB* 102 (1995): 29–30, and the literature she cites. There she has in mind the material in §§190–212.

We may divide the documents here into three categories: (1) §§190–212, decrees of the Senate or Roman rulers relating to Hyrcanus and the Jewish nation; (2) §§213–46, rescripts from provincial officials in answer to questions relating to Jewish rights; and (3) §§247–64, resolutions from cities regarding Jewish rights.[358] Hyrcanus's name plays a prominent role in many of them, whether as the one to whom the document is addressed and who receives honors or as the one who protects the interests of Jews living in different cities outside Judea.

1. Decrees of the Senate or Roman rulers:
   a. Caesar to the Sidonians (*Ant.* 14.10, 2 [§§190–95]): The text relates directly to Hyrcanus's part in the campaign to aid Caesar in Egypt. It is addressed to the "magistrates, council and people of Sidon" (§190) because an official record was to be kept there (see 14.10, 3 [§197]; 14.10, 6 [§203] says tribute was to be paid in Sidon). As Caesar wrote: "I am sending you a copy of the decree, inscribed on a tablet, concerning Hyrcanus, son of Alexander, the high priest and ethnarch of the Jews, in order that it may be deposited among your public records. It is my wish that this be set up on a tablet of bronze in both Greek and Latin" (§191). The text of the decree, agreed to by Caesar and the council, then follows. "Whereas the Jew Hyrcanus, son of Alexander, both now and in the past, in time of peace as well as in war, has shown loyalty and zeal toward our state, as many commanders have testified on his behalf, and in the recent Alexandrian war came to our aid with fifteen hundred soldiers, and being sent by me to Mithradates, surpassed in bravery all those in the ranks, for these reasons it is my wish that Hyrcanus, son of Alexander, and his children shall be ethnarchs of the Jews and shall hold the office of high priest of the Jews for all time in accordance with their national customs, and that he and his sons shall be our allies [συμμάχους] and also be numbered among our particular friends; and whatever high-priestly rights or other privileges exist in accordance with their laws, these he and his children shall possess by my command. And if, during this period, any question shall arise concerning the Jews' manner of life, it is my pleasure that the decision shall rest with them. Nor do I approve of troops being given winter-quarters among them or of money being demanded of them" (14.10, 2 [§§192–95]).[359]

---

358. *Rom und die Juden*, 74.

359. Augustus confirmed such Jewish rights at a later time, when, in response to a complaint from the Jews of Asia and Cyrenaica, he wrote: "Since the Jewish nation has been found

The titles claimed by Caesar in the text (before the part cited above) point clearly to 47 BCE as the date.[360] The document consists of two parts: Caesar's letter accompanying the decree (§§190–91) and Caesar's decree regarding Hyrcanus and the Jews (§§192–95).[361] The authenticity of the document has been debated, with Baumann assigning it a "+" indicating a positive assessment of its historical worth.[362] It already presupposes that Hyrcanus possesses the title *ethnarch*, as that is the way in which Caesar refers to him (§191). The specific privileges given to Hyrcanus are: (1) he and his children are to be ethnarchs of the Jews, that is, the office is to be hereditary; (2) they are forever to hold the office of high priest of the Jews in line with national custom;[363] (3) he and his sons are to be allies and particular friends of the Romans; (4) any high-priestly rights and privileges dictated by their customs were to belong to Hyrcanus and his children. The reference to sons of Hyrcanus is surprising, since, to the best of our knowledge, he had no sons, only a daughter (Alexandra).[364] Perhaps the phrase is traditional in such documents; whatever the case may be, it is repeated frequently in the ones Josephus cites.

Pucci Ben Zeev has shown that there are parallels to Caesar's granting such benefits in return for military assistance and has concluded from the evidence that the grants had legal validity, giving Jews the

---

well disposed to the Roman people not only at the present time but also in time past, and especially in the time of my father the emperor Caesar, as has their high priest Hyrcanus, it has been decided by me and my council under oath, with the consent of the Roman people, that the Jews may follow their own customs in accordance with the law of their fathers, just as they followed them in the time of Hyrcanus, high priest of the Most High God" (*Ant.* 16.6, 2 [§§162–63]).

360. See, for example, Schürer, *History of the Jewish People*, 1.272; Baumann, *Rom und die Juden*, 95; M. Pucci Ben Zeev, "Caesar's Decrees in the Antiquities: Josephus' Forgeries or Authentic Roman *Senatus Consulta*?" *Athenaeum* 84 (1996): 73–74 (specifying September of 47 BCE as the date of Caesar's letter in §§190–91).

361. Pucci Ben Zeev, "Caesar's Decrees," 73–76, where she also demonstrates that both parts have the formal elements expected in such documents. The decree itself has, as she shows, strong similarities with three nearly contemporary ones (between 42 and 30 BCE) written by Octavian about a certain Seleucus of Rhosos. See her essay "Seleukos of Rhosos and Hyrcanus II," *JSJ* 26 (1995): 113–21.

362. *Rom und die Juden*, 87.

363. As Baumann observes, he here rejects the claims of Antigonus on the high priesthood (*Rom und die Juden*, 95–96).

364. We have no ancient information about the matter, but one wonders whether the fact that Hyrcanus had no sons played into calculations in Aristobulus's family about the succession to the office.

right to live according to their ancestral laws as the Romans permitted to a number of other groups.[365]

b. Grants, concessions and awards made by Caesar (*Ant.* 14.10, 3 [§§196–98]): The short section opens with a general introduction, perhaps by Josephus and not part of the document: "The following are the grants, concessions and awards made by Gaius Caesar, Imperator and Consul." The remaining sections contain part of an authentic *senatus consultum*[366] confirming the grants given by Caesar (in §§192–95) in response to the delegation sent to Rome by Hyrcanus (see 14.10, 1 [§185]). The circumstances are not entirely clear, but Hyrcanus may have requested an official relation of συμμαχία for his people, not just for himself, and Caesar would then have referred the matter to the Senate for confirmation.[367] The document would then date from any of the years when Caesar was consul (46–44 BCE would be the relevant ones); it largely repeats what Caesar had granted in 47 BCE. Or, the *senatus consultum* may simply confirm Caesar's earlier decree—a procedure that is attested a number of times.[368] "That his children shall rule over the Jewish nation and enjoy the fruits of the places given them, and that the high priest, being also ethnarch, shall be the protector of those Jews who are unjustly treated. And that envoys be sent to Hyrcanus, son of Alexander, the high priest of the Jews, to discuss terms of friendship and alliance" (14.10, 3 [§§196–97]). Baumann thinks that §§208 and 212 may refer to the same *senatus consultum*.[369]

c. Caesar on the high priesthood (*Ant.* 14.10, 4 [§199]): This document also refers to Caesar as consul and thus, if the detail is correct, would date from 48, 46, 45, or 44 BCE.[370] It reads: Caesar, "in recognition of the honour, virtue and benevolence of Hyrcanus, son of Alexander, and in

---

365. "Caesar and Jewish Law," 30–37.

366. See Pucci Ben Zeev, "Caesar's Decrees," 77. The correct Greek term for a *senatus consultum* (δόγμα) is used in §198.

367. Baumann, *Rom und die Juden*, 96–98. This would explain the short time between 47 BCE when Caesar regulated Jewish affairs and the embassy to Rome.

368. Pucci Ben Zeev, "Caesar's Decrees," 77–79. She apparently thinks that the letter of Caesar in §§190–91 is later than both his decree and the *senatus consultum*, making §§192–98 earlier than September of 47 BCE.

369. *Rom und die Juden*, 98. He suggests that originally the Senate had denied the Jews the alliance they requested (98–99).

370. For suggestions why the ordinal numbers specifying which time it was he held the office (for example, consul for the third time) are omitted, see Pucci Ben Zeev, "Caesar's Decrees," 79–80.

the interest of the Senate and people of Rome, has granted that both he and his sons shall be high priests and priests of Jerusalem and of their nation with the same rights and under the same regulations as those under which their forefathers uninterruptedly held the office of priest." The document, then, confirms the hereditary right of Hyrcanus's family to the high priesthood with its traditional perquisites. It may, with the previous paragraphs, be another fragment of the *senatus consultum* confirming Caesar's decrees of 47 BCE.[371]

d. Caesar on Jerusalem and taxes (*Ant.* 14.10, 5 [§§200–201]): He gives permission to fortify Jerusalem and for Hyrcanus to live in it; the tax concession mentioned here may have been meant to finance the building project. The text may date, though an emendation would be needed, to 47 BCE (see *J.W.* 1.10, 3–4 [§§199–201]; *Ant.* 14.8, 5 [§144], 14.9, 1 [§156] for permission to build the walls at that time) or, following the reference to Caesar's fifth consulship, to 44 BCE.[372] If that is the correct year as the text indicates, then the tax reduction could have been connected with the beginning of a sabbatical year.

e. Caesar on other Jewish privileges (*Ant.* 14.10, 6 [§§202–10]): Items d. and e. (and f.?) may belong to the same document, which would have been written shortly before Caesar's death in 44 BCE (when he was consul for the fifth time [so §200], though §202 presents problems).[373] If one follows a common emendation of "Imperator for the second time" (a meaningless ordinal with the permanent office Imperator) to "Imperator, dictator for the second time" (with the Latin text of *Antiquities*), the date would be 47 BCE.[374] Besides legislating that some tax relief was to be offered during sabbatical years and other related matters, Caesar granted permission to rebuild Jerusalem's walls and ruled "that Hyrcanus, son of Alexander, the high priest and ethnarch of the Jews, shall occupy it [= Jerusalem] as he himself may choose" (§200). Also, he ordered that Jews should "pay tithes to Hyrcanus and his sons, just as they paid to their forefathers" (§203). The city of Joppa was

---

371. Pucci Ben Zeev, "Caesar's Decrees," 80–81. She does not rule out the possibility that this text dates to 48 BCE and is thus the earliest of the documents in the context.

372. See Marcus, *Josephus* 7, 554 n. b; Pucci Ben Zeev, "Caesar's Decrees," 81–82. She adds that the text may be another fragment of a *senatus consultum* dated to February 9, 44 BCE (see §222).

373. See Marcus, *Josephus* 7, 555 n. f.; Schürer, *History of the Jewish People*, 1.273–74; Baumann includes §211 in it and considers it a *senatus consultum* relating to the embassy sent to Caesar shortly before his death (*Rom und die Juden*, 99).

374. For the evidence and a discussion, see Pucci Ben Zeev, "Caesar's Decrees," 82–83.

returned to Jewish control with the added proviso that "for this city Hyrcanus, son of Alexander, and his sons shall pay tribute, collected from those who inhabit the territory, as a tax on the land, the harbour and exports, payable at Sidon in the amount of twenty thousand six hundred and seventy-five *modii* every year except in the seventh year, which they call the sabbatical year" (§206). Although there are textual uncertainties in the passage,[375] the high priest is brought into some sort of financial relation with Joppa. Hyrcanus and the Jews were also given villages in the plain (of Esdraelon, apparently). Caesar stipulated that "the ancient rights which the Jews and their high priests and priests had in relation to each other should continue" (§208), and he returned to them territories that had been given, probably by Pompey, to kings in Syria and Phoenicia. The section closes with another interesting grant: "to Hyrcanus and his children and to the envoys sent by him shall be given the right to sit with the members of the senatorial order as spectators of the contests of gladiators and wild beasts; and that when they request permission of the Dictator or Master of the horse to enter the Senate chamber, they shall admit them and shall give them an answer within ten days at the latest from the time when a decree is passed" (§210).[376]

f. Caesar on the loyalty of the Jews (*Ant.* 14.10, 7 [§§211–12]): This section, too, comes from early 44 BCE (Caesar is consul for the fifth time)[377] and contains a speech in which Caesar deals with the rights of Hyrcanus the high priest and ethnarch of the Jews. Caesar says: "Inasmuch as the high commanders in the provinces before me have testified on behalf of Hyrcanus, the high priest of the Jews, and of the Jews themselves before the Senate and people of Rome, and the people and Senate have expressed thanks to them, it is fitting that we too should be mindful of this and provide that there be given by the Senate and people of Rome to Hyrcanus and the Jewish nation and the sons of Hyrcanus a token of

---

375. See nn. g and h in Marcus, *Josephus 7*, 557.

376. Pucci Ben Zeev thinks that §199, §§202–10, and §§196–98 all belong to the same *senatus consultum* that confirmed Caesar's decree made in 47 BCE (its text is in §§192–95). "As for paragraphs 190–191, they represent the final stage, namely, the letter written by Caesar which accompanied both his own decree and its confirmation in the decree of the senate" ("Caesar's Decrees," 85).

377. See Schürer, *History of the Jewish People*, 1.272–73; Baumann, *Rom und die Juden*, 105. He was made dictator for life (a title mentioned in the text) between January 26 and February 15, 44 BCE (Pucci Ben Zeev, "Caesar's Decrees," 85). Pucci Ben Zeev therefore associates it with the *senatus consultum* of February 9, 44 BCE (and thus with §§196–98) and sees this text as giving Caesar's proposal of a *senatus consultum* (pp. 85–86).

gratitude worthy of their loyalty to us and of the benefits which they have conferred upon us" (§212). The document is short on specifics about what the token of gratitude might have been, unless we follow the view that this paragraph belongs to the same document as §§196–98.

2. Rescripts from provincial officials regarding Jewish rights:

g. Julius Gaius to the people of Parium (*Ant.* 14.10, 8 [§§213–16]): This document, whoever the sender was,[378] differs from the preceding ones in that it is addressed to a specific place from which complaints have been raised by Jews who were not being permitted to observe their customs and rites. The authorities are ordered to revoke any such decisions. It resembles the series of such documents in §§217–46.

h. Decree of the Senate recommended by Antony and Dolabella after Caesar's death (*Ant.* 14.10, 10 [§§219–22]):[379] Just before Caesar was murdered, Hyrcanus sent another delegation to Rome to make requests, apparently including a petition for a treaty of friendship. The Senate, after his death, complied with their requests (§§217–18) and the decree follows. It simply confirms Caesar's enactments that had not yet been recorded in the treasury.[380] The section closes with a list of the four Jewish delegates, some of whom we will meet again.

i. Letter of Dolabella to Ephesus (43 BCE), responding to Hyrcanus's requests (*Ant.* 14.10, 12 [§§225–27]): One of Hyrcanus's delegates to Rome also asked Dolabella, who had become governor of Syria (Josephus calls him "governor of Asia"), to exempt Jews from military service and to allow them to live according to their native customs. We learn that Dolabella immediately agreed to the request and wrote to cities in Asia; Josephus includes his missive to Ephesus. The letter credits Hyrcanus's messenger with explaining matters convincingly to Dolabella: Jews could not serve in the military "because they may not bear arms or march on the days of the Sabbath; nor can they obtain the native foods to which they are accustomed" (§226). Here we see Hyrcanus carrying out the function granted by Caesar that he was to be "the protector of those Jews who are unjustly treated" (§197).

j. Lentulus the consul in 49 BCE gives a ruling about Jews in Ephesus, followed by a similar statement from the legate Titus (*Ant.* 14.10, 13 [§§228–30]); see also 14.10, 16 (§234): This text appears to be related to

---

378. For the difficulties with names and titles, see Marcus, *Josephus* 7, 561 nn. d and e.

379. Sherk (*Roman Documents from the Greek East*, 6) considers it a *senatus consultum*. It dates from April 11, 44 BCE, handing over to the quaestors Caesar's *senatus consultum* of February 9. See also Baumann, *Rom und die Juden*, 105; Schürer, *History of the Jewish People*, 1.273.

380. See Sherk, *Roman Documents from the Greek East*, 8.

the subject of the previous one. Most if not all of the documents in §§228–40 deal with this issue.

k. Decree of the people of Delos (*Ant.* 14.10, 14 [§§231–32]): They accept Lentulus's ruling regarding people here called "Jews who were Roman citizens" (§232).

l. Gaius Fannius to the magistrates of Cos (*Ant.* 14.10, 15 [§233])

m. Lucius Antonius to Sardis (*Ant.* 14.10, 17 [§235])

n. Marcus Publius on Alexandrian Jewish exemption from military service (*Ant.* 14.10, 18 [§§236–37])

o. Lentulus on Ephesian Jewish exemption from military service (*Ant.* 14.10, 19 [§§238–40])

p. Magistrates of Laodicea to the proconsul Gaius Rabirius regarding a letter from Hyrcanus requesting permission for Jews to live according to their native laws (*Ant.* 14.10, 20 [§§241–43]): Another envoy of Hyrcanus (not one of the four delegates to Rome mentioned earlier) named Sopatrus delivered a letter to the magistrates from the consul Gaius Rabirius "in which you have informed us that certain persons have come from Hyrcanus, the high priest of the Jews, bringing documents concerning their nation, to the effect that it shall be lawful for them to observe their Sabbaths and perform their other rites in accordance with their native laws, and that no one shall give orders to them, because they are our friends and allies, and that no one should do them injury in our province" (§§241–42). The letter was deposited in the archives. The following ones to the end of the section (§264) are similar in character.

q. Publius Servilius Galba to the people of Miletus allowing Jews to live according to their customs (*Ant.* 14.10, 21 [§§244–46]): Hyrcanus is not mentioned in this section, but it may be related to the previous one because Tralles appears in both.

3. Resolutions from cities regarding Jewish rights:

r. Decree of the people of Pergamum (*Ant.* 14.10, 22 [§§247–55]), which belongs to the time of Hyrcanus I

s. Decree of the people of Halicarnassus (*Ant.* 14.10, 23 [§§256–58]): Hyrcanus does not figure by name but, in imitation of the Romans, they allow Jews to live by their customs.

t. Decree of the people of Sardis (*Ant.* 14.10, 24 [§§259–61]): Here, we have a similar situation as in the preceding text.

u. Decree of the people of Ephesus (*Ant.* 14.10, 25 [§§262–64]): This, too, resembles the preceding one. It appears that the Roman decree of rights to the Jews led to the decisions by these various cities.

Documents from Mark Antony: These texts figure in the narrative after the victory by Antony and Octavian over Cassius at Philippi in 42 BCE. Antony then traveled into Asia Minor where he received delegations from many peoples. When he was at Ephesus,

> the high priest Hyrcanus and our nation sent an embassy to him, bringing a golden crown and requesting that he would write to the provincial governors to set free those Jews who had been taken captive by Cassius in violation of the laws of war, and restore to them the territory of which they had been deprived in the time of Cassius. These demands Antony decided the Jews were justified in making, and so he immediately wrote to Hyrcanus and the Jews. He also sent to the Tyrians a decree to the same effect. (*Ant.* 14.12, 2 [§§304–305])

a. The first document is his missive to Hyrcanus and the Jews (*Ant.* 14.12, 3 [§§306–13]): The decree is addressed "to Hyrcanus, high priest and ethnarch, and to the Jewish nation"[381] and refers to envoys who met Antony in Ephesus. Two of these delegates were among those whom Hyrcanus had earlier sent to Rome (see §219), a fact noted by Antony himself. Antony identified with the Jewish concerns about the sufferings imposed on them by Cassius and, now that the world was recovering from the depredations caused by them, he wished to help the Jews. "Having, therefore, in mind to promote the welfare both of you and your nation, I shall take care of your interests. And I have also sent notices throughout the cities that if any persons, whether freemen or slaves, were sold at auction by Gaius Cassius or by those subordinate to him, they shall be released; and it is my wish that you shall enjoy the privileges granted by me and Dolabella. And I forbid the Tyrians to use violence against you, and command that they restore whatever they possess belonging to the Jews. As for the crown which you have sent, I have accepted it" (§§312–13). Here again, Hyrcanus is presented as protecting Jewish interests, wherever the need arose.

b. The second document is his letter to the Tyrians (*Ant.* 14.12, 4 [§§314–18]): The decree seems to be the one mentioned by Antony in his message to Hyrcanus in the previous section. Antony says that he was apprised of the situation by "the envoys of Hyrcanus, the high priest and ethnarch" (§314), and he ordered the Tyrians to return what they had

---

381. As Marcus indicates, most manuscripts read "to Hyrcanus, high priest and ethnarch of the Jews," so that the decree would have been sent to Hyrcanus alone (*Josephus* 7, 611 n. g). Just above in §305, however, Josephus says it was for Hyrcanus and the Jews.

recently taken from the Jews—anything belonging to Hyrcanus the ethnarch of the Jews. He also promised to adjudicate any disputes when he came to the area.

c. The third document is Antony's second letter to the Tyrians (*Ant.* 14.12, 5 [§§319–22]): He commands that the text of his edict—ordering the release of enslaved people and of property to the Jews—be displayed publicly in Latin and Greek forms.

Josephus records that he wrote in the same way to the people of Sidon, Antioch, and Aradus (14.12, 6 [§323]).

The sum total of these texts leaves us with the impression that Hyrcanus, high priest and ethnarch of the Jews, was a valued friend whom the Romans, in the time of Julius Caesar and immediately after, were pleased to have serve in the highest posts (which he was to pass to his children) and a vigorous promoter of the rights of Jews living in the Diaspora. If the documents are genuine, he hardly seems to have been the passive, inept character that Josephus, in a series of formulaic passages,[382] sets before our eyes.

Hyrcanus II served as high priest longer than any of the Hasmoneans, exceeding the term of his grandfather John Hyrcanus by two years. He held the office through turbulent times when radical changes in Judea occurred. He was the first high priest to regain the office after losing it and the first to lose it a second time. As he left no son to succeed him, the high-priestly office passed into a new phase in its long history.

24. Antigonus (40–37 BCE)

In the year 40 BCE, Antigonus, the second and only surviving son of Aristobulus II, became both king and high priest as his father had been for a short time (67–63 BCE). As we have seen, he was able to wrest the high priesthood and civil leadership of Jewish territory from Hyrcanus II, Herod, and Phasael through the military might of the Parthians. We had encountered him prior to that date in connection with the high priesthood. He had appeared before Julius Caesar in 47 BCE in an attempt to win back the family's ancestral offices then held by Hyrcanus and Antipater (*J.W.* 1.10, 1–2 [§§195–98]; *Ant.* 14.8, 4 [§§140–42]; compare also *Ant.* 14.6, 1 [§96]). He hoped that, because of

---

382. Those passages are: *Ant.* 13.16, 1 (§407); 13.16, 2 (§408; and *J.W.* 1.5, 1 [§109]); 14.1, 3 (§13); 14.2, 3 (§31); *J.W.* 1.10, 4 (§203); and *Ant.* 14.9, 2 (§158); 14.9, 5 (§179); 15.6, 4 (§181–82).

Caesar's support of his father and brother Alexander, he would be appointed high priest and ruler by Caesar, who could be expected to oppose Hyrcanus and Antipater, men who owed their positions to Pompey and his faction. But Antigonus's timing proved dreadful: Hyrcanus and Antipater had just distinguished themselves in Caesar's service during the campaign in Egypt. As a result, Antigonus's arguments fell on deaf ears, and he was forced to bide his time until a more favorable opportunity arose.

Five years later (42 BCE), he thought the time had come (see above). The oppressive Cassius had left Syria to meet his doom at Philippi, and in his absence chaos reigned in the region. In those circumstances, some local dynasts, backed by the governor of Syria, conspired to restore Antigonus to his homeland. Marion of Tyre and Ptolemy of Chalcis were the individuals at the center of the plan, and Antigonus had assured there would be no opposition from the governor of Syria by bribing him (*Ant.* 14.12, 1 [§§297–98]). Despite the extensive scheming, the attempt failed when Herod's forces were able to defeat the troops fighting for Antigonus.

Success for him was not to come until the year 40 BCE, when the Parthians, Rome's mighty neighbor to the east, invaded lands along the Mediterranean coast. Antigonus won their support for installing him on the throne in Jerusalem and thus removing the pro-Roman Hyrcanus and Herod (*Ant.* 14.13, 3 [§331]). We have already noted the bribe that he may have offered to procure their backing: one thousand talents and five hundred women. Fighting between the two sides in Jerusalem led to no decisive battle, but the situation changed in Antigonus's favor when Phasael and Hyrcanus were lured into a Parthian trap (14.13, 4 [§§340–41]) and Herod fled from the city (14.13, 7 [§§352–53]). As we have seen, at that time Antigonus disfigured Hyrcanus so that he could no longer serve as high priest (14.13, 10 [§366]), and himself became king and presumably high priest as well. The narrative here does not mention Antigonus's offices, but elsewhere we read that the Parthians made him king (for example, *Ant.* 14.14, 3 [§379, in Herod's report to Antony in Rome]; *J.W.* 1.13, 11 [§273] says they "installed Antigonus as master"; compare *J.W.* 1.14, 4 [§284]). As for the high-priestly office, Josephus never actually says he took it, but we may infer that he did from the fact that the historian names him among the high priests in his list in *Ant.* 20.10, 4 (§245), where he is also called king. Since in his narratives Josephus never calls him high priest, we should not be surprised that he describes no high-priestly act performed by him. On his coins, however, Antigonus does designate himself high priest (see below).

The entire sections of *War* and *Antiquities* devoted to the time of Antigonus as ruler center around the war between him and Herod for the throne. Herod had traveled to Rome where Antony, with Caesar's consent, decided he was the man to exercise Roman dominion in Jerusalem and saw to his appointment as king of the Jews.[383] "Besides admiration for Herod, he had as strong an incentive in his aversion for Antigonus, whom he regarded as a promoter of sedition and an enemy of Rome" (*J.W.* 1.14, 4 [§282]). Caesar "convened the Senate, to which Mesalla, seconded by Atratinus, presented Herod and dwelt on the services rendered by his father and his own goodwill towards the Roman people; demonstrating at the same time that Antigonus was their enemy, not only from the earlier quarrel which they had had with him, but because he had also just been guilty of contempt of Rome in accepting his crown from Parthian hands. These words stirred the Senate, and when Antony came forward and said that with a view to the war with Parthia it was expedient that Herod should be king, the proposal was carried unanimously" (*J.W.* 1.14, 4 [§284]; see *Ant.* 14.14, 4 [§§381–85]). The account makes it abundantly clear that the Romans countered their archenemy's move of making Antigonus king by crowning Herod as monarch.[384] *Antiquities*, which notes the bribe Herod promised to Antony, also adds that Antony was "anxious to co-operate in the things which Herod wished" (14.14, 4 [§383]).

These comments, if historically reliable, suggest that Herod sought kingship from the Romans, although a later statement casts a different light on the situation. In the very next paragraph, Josephus writes: "But this was the greatest sign of Antony's devotion to Herod, that not only did he obtain the kingship for him, which he had not hoped for—he had come to the capital not to claim the kingship for himself, for he did not believe the Romans would offer it to him, since it was their custom to give it to one of the reigning family, but to claim it for his wife's brother who was a grandson of Aristobulus on his father's side and of Hyrcanus on his mother's[385]—but he also made it possible for Herod in only seven days altogether to obtain these unexpected grants and leave Italy" (14.14, 5 [§§386–87]). However this should be assessed,[386] we are

---

383. *Ant.* 14.14, 4 (§382) says that Herod made the decision easier for Antony by promising him money for the crown.

384. For the evidence regarding the date of his appointment (late 40 BCE), see Schürer, *History of the Jewish People*, 1.281–82 n. 3. For reacting to the Parthian installation of Antigonus, see Richard D. Sullivan, *Near Eastern Royalty and Rome, 100–30 B.C.,* Phoenix Supplementary Volume 24 (Toronto: Univ. of Toronto Press, 1990), 223.

385. Although he does not name him here, his wife Mariamme's brother was Aristobulus III, who was to become high priest for a short time in 35 BCE (see below).

386. It is difficult to believe that Herod would expend so much energy to obtain the crown for someone else, much less a person from the line that had caused him serious problems and represented the chief rival to himself. Yet, see M. Stern, *Hasmonaean Judaea in the Hellenistic World*, 259–61.

reminded here of the concern Herod felt about the legitimacy of the Has-moneans as opposed to his lack of it—a concern that would long dictate his policy toward the old royal family.

The conflict between the two great world powers, Rome and Parthia, forms the backdrop for the brief reign of Antigonus. Herod moved quickly to secure the crown the Senate had given him and to rescue his family besieged by Antigonus at Masada. He had Roman assistance in doing so, although that aid was limited because of both the larger need to cope with the Parthian threat and the venality of the Roman officers sent to help Herod.[387]

The Roman officer Ventidius, whose mandate was to repel the Parthians (something he did in 39 BCE),[388] made a detour into Judea

> ostensibly to give aid to Joseph [Herod's brother in charge of Masada], but in reality the whole business was a device to obtain money from Antigonus; at any rate he encamped very near Jerusalem and extorted from Antigonus as much money as he wanted.[389] Then he himself withdrew with the greater part of his force; but in order that his extortion might not be detected, he left Silo behind with a certain number of soldiers; to him also Antigonus paid court in order that he might not cause any trouble, hoping at the same time that the Parthians would once more give him some help. (*Ant.* 14.14, 6 [§§392–93]; compare *J.W.* 1.15, 2 [§§288–89])

We need not pursue the gory details of the three-year war between kings Antigonus and Herod. With bribes liberally spread around on all sides, the conflict continued longer than one might have anticipated. Herod seemed to have the upper hand in that he had not only his own troops and supporters but also the might of Rome behind him; yet the sources indicate widespread opposition to him from considerable parts of the Jewish populace who fought for Antigonus. Antigonus's bribes assured that Roman support for Herod

---

387. This charge could be leveled against all the leading characters in the story; bribery was a way of life in the politics of the time.

388. Sullivan, *Near Eastern Royalty*, 312.

389. Dio says that Ventidius, who did defeat the Parthians, "occupied Palestine without trouble, after he had frightened the king, Antigonus, out of the country. Besides accomplishing all this he exacted large sums of money from the rest individually, and large sums also from Antigonus and Antiochus and Malchus the Nabataean, because they had given help to Pacorus" (*Roman History* 48.41, 4–5 [M. Stern, *Greek and Latin Authors*, 2.358–59]). Stern quotes the Loeb translation (by E. Cary), but it does not appear that Dio says Ventidius drove Antigonus from the country (which would be contrary to Josephus's accounts) but only that he frightened him (ἐκφοβήσας).

would be unreliable (for example, *J.W.* 1.15, 3 [§291]; 1.15, 6 [§§297, 302]; *Ant.* 14.15, 1 [§395]; 14.15, 3 [§§406, 412]). At one point, as Herod's forces were besieging Jerusalem, he ordered that a proclamation be made to those trapped inside that he had come for their benefit and would punish no one who had opposed him. *War* notes only that Antigonus made a counterproclamation (1.15, 5 [§§295–96]), ordering the people not to listen to Herod's message or to desert to him. *Antiquities* adds specifics of what Antigonus is supposed to have said:

> But Antigonus in answer to Herod's proclamation told Silo and the Roman army that it would be contrary to their own notion of right if they gave the kingship to Herod who was a commoner and an Idumaean, that is, a half-Jew, when they ought to offer it to those who were of the (royal) family, as was their custom. And, he argued, if they were now ill-disposed toward him and were determined to deprive him of the kingship on the ground that he had received it from the Parthians, there were at least many of his family who might lawfully receive the kingship, for they had committed no offence against the Romans, and they were priests; and thus they would be unworthily treated if they were deprived of this rank. (*Ant.* 14.15, 2 [§§403–4])[390]

Antigonus's line of argument recalls the earlier claim in *Antiquities* that the Romans normally appointed rulers from the existing royal family, and it points to the center of the Romans' objection to him—he was a Parthian appointee. Antigonus appears ready to abdicate if rule could remain in his family. In a noteworthy way, he appeals to the fact that the men in his line were priests as a factor qualifying them to rule. His theory, hardly a new one (compare *Ant.* 14.3, 2 [§41]), will recur in subsequent intrigues around the high priesthood.

The situation changed when Ventidius succeeded in expelling the Parthians from the area; the immediate result was that the Romans could afford to lend more military assistance to Herod in his struggle for the throne (*J.W.* 1.16, 6 [§317]; *Ant.* 14.15, 7 [§434]). Antony dispatched Machaerus to help Herod, but the officer apparently accepted yet another of Antigonus's bribes and in the process incurred the suspicion of both Herod and Antigonus (*J.W.* 1.16, 6–7 [§§317–20]; *Ant.* 14.15, 7 [§§435–38]). Herod soon left the region to complain about Machaerus to Antony, who was then present at the Roman

---

390. Otto thinks it plausible that Antigonus and Silo held negotiations about his abdicating in favor of another Hasmonean (*Herodes*, 30).

siege of Samosata, and there he further ingratiated himself with the ruler of
the east and freed up more Roman help. But in Herod's absence, his brother
Joseph made a disastrous attempt to capture the grain supply in Jericho, losing his men, the Roman troops with him, and his own life. We learn that
Antigonus violated Joseph's dead body by decapitating it (J.W. 1.17, 1–2
[§§323–25]; Ant. 14.15, 10 [§§448–49]). To judge from Josephus's narratives,
the desecration of his brother's corpse became perhaps the driving force
behind Herod's renewed determination to oust Antigonus.

After Samosata, Antony appointed Sossius governor of Syria with orders
to assist Herod. Sossius sent two legions to Herod and began to march toward
the battle zone with additional forces (J.W. 1.17, 2 [§327]; Ant. 14.15, 9
[§447]). Herod's armies won a number of victories and many came to his side
(War says that one motivation was their hatred for Antigonus [1.17, 6
(§335)]). The Herodian and Roman movements toward Jerusalem led
Antigonus to think of abandoning the city (J.W. 1.17, 6 [§339]; Ant. 14.15, 12
[§461]). When Herod finally subjected the capital to siege, it was three years
after his appointment as king (J.W. 1.17, 8 [§343]; compare Ant. 14.15, 14
[§465]), making the time the spring of the year 37 BCE. So confident was he of
victory that Herod, after making arrangements for the siege, went to Samaria
where he married the Hasmonean princess Mariamme (Antigonus's niece) to
whom he had been betrothed five years earlier (J.W. 1.17, 8 [§344]; Ant. 14.15,
14 [§467]).[391] Although he may not have fully appreciated it at the time, the
wedding created an opportunity for intense opposition to himself from within
his own family. The overwhelming power at the disposal of Sossius and Herod
made the fall of Jerusalem a foregone conclusion, though the defenders fought
courageously until they were confined to the temple area and the upper city.
Antiquities mentions that after the first and second walls had been scaled by
attackers, "some of the porticoes round the temple were burnt, which Herod
accused Antigonus of setting on fire, making an effort to draw upon him the
hatred of the Jews by this charge" (14.16, 2 [§476]). Carnage ensued, with the
victors killing and plundering all around. Herod is supposed to have tried to
stop the Romans, who were enraged by the length of the siege, from ravaging
the city and from slaughtering its surviving residents.[392]

---

391. Compare Sullivan, Near Eastern Royalty, 225, for the significance the marriage had for
Herod. As Otto, Herodes, 23, pointed out, the betrothal five years early had benefited Herod by
elevating him above his older brother, and now, in 37 BCE, his connection with the old royal family had advantages for him. At least he could not be as easily opposed on the grounds that he was
a usurper of the kingship.

392. Richardson, Herod, 158–60.

Although the defenders struggled valiantly and, according to *Antiquities*, "they were resisting strongly for the sake of Antigonus' kingship" (14.16, 2 [§478]),[393] the city fell.[394] Antigonus, who had not left Jerusalem, then emerged.

> In this scene [of general carnage] Antigonus, regardless alike of his former fortune and that which now was his, came down from the castle and threw himself at the feet of Sossius. The latter, far from pitying his changed condition, burst into uncontrollable laughter and called him Antigone. He did not, however, treat him as a woman and leave him at liberty; no, he was put in irons and kept under strict guard. (*J.W.* 1.18, 2 [§353]; *Ant.* 14.16, 2 [§481])

Under the circumstances, Antigonus should have had no hope of release or milder treatment. Both of Josephus's works assert that Sossius made an offering of a gold crown to God and left with Antigonus in chains to bring him to Antony (then in Antioch) for resolution of his case. *War* says tersely that he, "clinging with forlorn hope to life, fell beneath the axe, a fitting end to his ignominious career" (1.18, 3 [§357]).[395] *Antiquities* expands on the occasion of his death.

---

393. This note appears at the point where Herod had agreed to allow sacrificial victims to be brought to the Jews ensconced in the temple so that the daily offering could continue (§477). As noted by Otto (*Herodes*, 33), the nobility of Jerusalem also realized that a victory by Herod would mean the end of them, as they had opposed him in the past.

394. The exact date of its fall to Herod and Sossius is much debated because the ancient evidence is not unified. For a summary, see Schürer, *History of the Jewish People*, 1.284–86 n. 11; Otto, *Herodes*, 33–37 n.; Schalit, *King Herod*, Appendix 4, 509–11 = *König Herodes*, Anhang IX, 764–68.

395. Dio has an account that resembles the one in Josephus in some details (*Roman History* 49.22, 3–5). He refers to So[s]sius who "conquered in battle Antigonus, who had put to death the Roman guards that were with him, and reduced him by siege when he took refuge in Jerusalem. The Jews, indeed, had done much injury to the Romans, for the race is very bitter when aroused to anger, but they suffered far more themselves. The first of them to be captured were those who were fighting for the precinct of their god, and then the rest on the day even then called the day of Saturn. And so excessive were they in their devotion to religion that the first set of prisoners, those who had been captured along with the temple, obtained leave from Sosius, when the day of Saturn came round again, and went up into the temple, and there performed all the customary rites, together with the rest of the people. These people Antony entrusted to a certain Herod to govern; but Antigonus he bound to a cross and flogged—a punishment no other king had suffered at the hands of the Romans—and afterwards he slew him" (from M. Stern, *Greek and Latin Authors*, 2.360; the last verb [ἀπέσφαξεν] could mean to slit the throat). See also Strabo as Josephus quotes him in *Ant.* 15.1, 2 (§§9–10); Strabo stresses the high regard in which the Jews held Antigonus and their refusal, even under torture, to accept Herod as king. The execution was an attempt to make the Jews change their minds. Plutarch also mentions the beheading of Antigonus (*Life of Antony* 36.4 [Stern, *Greek and Latin Authors*, 1.568–69]).

But Herod feared that if Antigonus were kept under guard by Antony and brought to Rome by him, he might plead the justice of his cause before the Senate and show that he was descended from kings while Herod was a commoner, and that his sons ought to reign by virtue of their lineage, even though he himself had committed offences against the Romans; and because of this fear Herod gave Antony a large bribe and persuaded him to put Antigonus out of the way. (14.16, 4 [§§489–90])[396]

Here, *War* is more closely representative of the strongly pro-Herodian stance of the king's court historian, Nicolaus of Damascus, while *Antiquities* gives voice to a more pro-Hasmonean view expressed by a descendant of that house, Josephus himself. Yet, while both statements articulate biases, the one in *Antiquities* has a ring of verisimilitude in that Herod for years after remained neurotic about the possible restoration of the Hasmoneans. Josephus says elsewhere that Antigonus reigned for three years and three months (*Ant.* 20.10, 4 [§246]).

Josephus ends his account of the capture of Jerusalem by Herod and the death of Antigonus with a reflection on the Hasmonean age. He considered this its termination, declaring that

the rule of the Asamonaean line came to an end after a hundred and twenty-six years.[397] Theirs was a splendid and renowned house because of both their lineage and their priestly office, as well as the things which its founders achieved on behalf of the nation. But they lost their royal power through internal strife and it passed to Herod, the son of Antipater, who came from a house of common people and from a private family that was subject to the kings. Such, then, is the account we have received of the end of the Asamonaean line. (*Ant.* 14.16, 4 [§§490–91])

Although he reigned just a few years, Antigonus did mint coins; in fact, some of the most beautiful and certainly the most unusual Hasmonean coins

---

396. In *Ant.* 15.1, 2 (§§8–9), he says that Antony had decided to parade him in his forthcoming triumph in Rome but upon hearing that the Jews had remained faithful to Antigonus because they hated Herod, he beheaded him in Antioch. Otto (*Herodes*, 37) doubts that Herod's money drove Antony, who had not planned on doing so, to execute this enemy of Rome.

397. If accurate, the figure would lead one back to the year 163 BCE. See Marcus, *Josephus* 7, 703 n. b, who connects that date with the time when Onias IV fled to Egypt. Note that Josephus does not say the Hasmonean high priesthood lasted 126 years, only that Hasmonean rule did.

bear his name. It is the coins that verify Josephus's claim that he served as high priest. He was the only Hasmonean high priest-king to bear the name Antigonus (Aristobulus I's brother Antigonus was at most only a substitute high priest) with the result that the coins with that name must be assigned to him. They use both his Hebrew name (Mattityah) and his Greek one (Antigonos) and bear inscriptions in Hebrew and in Greek. The Hebrew is (with variations): מתתיה הכהן הגדול וחבר היהודים, Mattityah the high priest and the assembly of the Jews (some lack the reference to חבר היהודים), while the Greek reads: ΒΑΣΙΛΕΩΣ ΑΝΤΙΓΟΝΟΥ, of King Antigonus. His coins are distinguished by the varieties in their values. Meshorer explains Antigonus's most impressive coins as reflecting the time of struggle with Herod. He points out that, while the throne was in dispute, it was important for both sides to exploit the propaganda value of coins to assert in the most graphic way who was the true ruler. Herod's coins, too, were large and beautiful only during these years (40–37 BCE). There was also probably an exceptional need for a large quantity of coins at that time to pay the huge numbers of troops involved in the fighting. Interestingly, some of Antigonus's coins have a picture of the table of showbread on the obverse and a seven-branched menorah from the temple on the reverse.[398]

---

398. Meshorer, *A Treasury of Jewish Coins*, 30, 34, 50–56.

5

The High Priests in the Herodian Age (37 BCE to 70 CE)

25. Ananel (37–35, 35 to about 30? BCE)[1]

The death of Antigonus need not have meant the end of the Hasmonean high priesthood, because there were males of the family who could have assumed the office. Hyrcanus, of course, was ineligible due to his physical defect, although he did return to Jerusalem in 37 BCE after Antigonus's removal. We have seen that Herod was suspicious of the influence Hyrcanus might still wield, but he managed to keep his designs from the former high priest as he continued the lengthy process of securing his own control of the land. Another Hasmonean of whom we know was Aristobulus III, a son of Alexander and Alexandra and thus a brother of Mariamme, Herod's wife. As he was just fourteen or fifteen years of age at the time, however, he may not have been considered a viable candidate for the position.[2] But, even if he had been of age, Herod

---

1. The number given to each high priest in the heading corresponds to the List of High Priests, pp. 491–92.

2. Compare Abraham Schalit, *King Herod: Portrait of a Ruler* (Jerusalem: Bialik, 1962 [Hebrew]), 62 with n. 18 (376) = *König Herodes: Der Mann und sein Werk*, 2nd ed. (Berlin: de Gruyter, 2001), 101–2 with n. 18. Herod later says his youth was the reason why he did not appoint Aristobulus at the beginning of his reign (*Ant.* 15.2, 7 [§34]). We know of no age limits on high priests, but there is some reason to think priests could not serve until they were twenty years of age. See Emil Schürer, *The History of the Jewish People in the Age of Jesus Christ (175 B.C.— A.D. 135)*, 3 vols., rev. and ed. G. Vermes, F. Millar, and M. Black (Edinburgh: T. & T. Clark, 1973–87), 2.243–44. Herod was soon to violate this principle, but under special circumstances.

would have had second and third thoughts about appointing him then. The new monarch's primary concern was securing his own position.

Josephus tells us that Herod's deceptive treatment of Hyrcanus was not his only hostile act toward the Hasmonean survivors. "He also practiced other wiles to the advantage of his rule, but the result was only dissension in his own household. For example, because he wanted to avoid appointing a distinguished person as high priest of God, he sent for a rather undistinguished priest from Babylon, named Ananel [Ἀνάνηλον], and gave him the high priesthood" (*Ant.* 15.2, 4 [§22]). With this brief notice, Josephus announces Herod's new policy: the high priesthood was removed from the Hasmonean family, and, because the occupant of the office could be influential, he wished to have someone without the appealing associations of the former (and legitimate) ruling family, qualities that were liable to put Herod at a disadvantage. By assuming the kingship, he had removed the possibility of there being another high priest-king as had happened frequently in the Hasmonean period. Now, he wished to downgrade the office of high priest to insure that the incumbent would not be a rival to him.[3] Or, as Josephus says, he "assigned the office to some insignificant persons who were merely of priestly descent" (*Ant.* 20.10, 5 [§247]).

There has been uncertainty among scholars about who his appointee Ananel was, due in part to the fact that Josephus gives what appears to be conflicting information about him in two passages. After calling him "a rather undistinguished priest [ἱερέα τῶν ἀσημοτέρων] from Babylon" (*Ant.* 15.2, 4 [§22]), he adds at a later point: "And so Herod immediately took the high priesthood away from Ananel, who was, as we have said before, not a native (of Judaea) but (was descended) from the Jews who had been transported beyond the Euphrates, for not a few tens of thousands of this people had been transported to Babylonia; and Ananel, who came from there, was of a high-priestly family [ἀρχιερατικοῦ γένους] and had long been treated by Herod as a valued friend. Just as he once had honoured him, when he took over the kingship, so he now dismissed him in order to end his domestic troubles" (*Ant.* 15.3, 1 [§§39–40]). The problem is simple: how could a member of a "high-priestly" family be an "undistinguished priest"?

---

3. See Schalit, *King Herod*, 62 = *König Herodes*, 101–2. Schalit (*König Herodes*, Zusatz XVI, 696) rightly disagrees with Otto's judgment that Herod's action did not express an opposition in principle to the Hasmonean house (Walter Friedrich Otto, *Herodes: Beiträge zur Geschichte des letzten jüdischen Königshauses* [Stuttgart: Metzlersche, 1913], 38–39). Martin Goodman, *The Ruling Class of Judaea: The Origins of the Jewish Revolt against Rome A.D. 66–70* (Cambridge: Cambridge Univ. Press, 1987), notes it was customary in the Hellenistic period for rulers to change individuals in such offices as their political needs dictated.

One could explain the two passages in more than one way. One possibility is to consider them contradictory and to accept one and dismiss the other; a number of scholars opt for this approach and regard the slighting reference to the status of Ananel's family as Josephus's way of casting aspersions on the quality of Herod's appointment.[4] Accepting the latter of Josephus's two descriptions seems the more popular option, though some have doubted it as well.[5] As we will see, there have been several attempts to trace a noble priestly lineage for Ananel. Another option is to examine Josephus's terms in context. The adjective ἄσημος (used in both *Ant.* 15.2, 4 [§22] and 20.10, 5 [§247]) means "unknown, obscure, insignificant" in connection with individuals.[6] By referring to Ananel with the term, Josephus could simply be saying he was not known in Israel or had no connections there. He says as much in *Ant.* 15.3, 1 (§39), where he comments that he was not a native of the land. His second adjective, ἀρχιερατικός designates something or someone with high-priestly connections, that is, "membership of the legitimate priestly nobility."[7] It may have been the case that Ananel was a ranking priest in the Babylonian Jewish community—perhaps even a Zadokite, while at the same time he was unknown in Jerusalem. If we read the passages in context, the terms are used at places where we learn about contact between Babylonian Jews and Herod in connection with Hyrcanus's return to Judea. It makes some sense to suppose that Herod made the appointment of Ananel in consultation with Hyrcanus, who had spent three years in that Diaspora community.[8] It is not clear which period Josephus means when he says Herod had treated him as a friend. The word πάλαι need not point to the more distant past; perhaps he means that, in his two years as high priest, Herod had acted in a friendly way toward him.

---

4. For example, Peter Richardson, *Herod: King of the Jews and Friend of the Romans,* SPNT (Columbia: Univ. of South Carolina Press, 1996), 242 n. 8. Gustav Hölscher (*Die Hohenpriesterliste bei Josephus und die evangelische Chronologie,* SHAW, 1939–40, 3. Abhandlung [Heidelberg: Winter, 1940], 9) thought the negative reference came from the so-called anonymous source of Josephus.

5. Otto, *Herodes,* 38.

6. BAG 114. Joachim Jeremias prefers to go a step farther (with Klausner, see below) by saying the term must point to the Zadokite family (*Jerusalem in the Time of Jesus,* trans. F. H. Cave and C. H. Cave [Philadephia: Fortress Press, 1969], 193). He rightly notes that Josephus does not say in §22 that Ananel was from low priestly stock. Walter Franklin Smith ("A Study of the Zadokite High Priesthood within the Graeco-Roman Age: From Simeon the Just to the High Priests Appointed by Herod the Great" [Ph.D. diss., Harvard Univ., 1961], 172) thinks he must have been a Hasmonean or Zadokite and, as he was not a Hasmonean, he was from the Zadokite line. This assumes, of course, that the Hasmoneans were not Zadokites—an uncertain proposition.

7. Gottlob Schrenk, "ἱερός, etc.," in *TDNT* 3.272.

8. Richardson, *Herod,* 162, 242.

A second problem arises because, while Josephus clearly says Ananel was from Babylon, *m. Parah* 3:5, in a list of individuals who are supposed to have been high priests and who had prepared a red heifer, names "Hanamel the Egyptian [וחנמאל המצרי]." Some regard Ananel and Hanamel as the same person despite the difference in spelling of the names and in the places from which they are said to have come. So, for example, Joseph Klausner identifies the two and bases some speculative suggestions on the sparse data. He thinks it possible that Ananel was related to the leading priests from before the exile (referring to *Ant.* 15.3, 1 [§40]) and that, by appointing him, Herod was trying to accomplish something major: restoring the high priesthood to its rightful owners, the sons of Zadok who took precedence over the Hasmoneans in antiquity and rank. A priest with such an ancestral right Herod summoned from Babylon or Egypt; he had no roots in Israel or relatives in Jerusalem (see the discussion of the Greek adjectives above) and thus would not endanger Herod. To this, Klausner adds that Herod himself was related to the Babylonian Jews from the time of the first destruction, perhaps even to their priests.[9] To reconcile the conflicting information about the places from which Ananel/Hanamel came, Klausner suggests he was a Babylonian Jew who lived in Egypt.[10]

Schalit is no less speculative. While he does think Josephus's claim about the lofty status of Ananel's line is open to doubt, he believes Ananel's family had an ancient and noble pedigree. He even considers it possible that this man was a descendant of the Hanamel who sold family property to Jeremiah (Jeremiah 32). Jeremiah's relative was probably a priest and could have been exiled to Babylon, or he may have gone to Egypt where Jeremiah would have been held in honor after his prophecies proved true. These possibilities may account for the double tradition about Ananel's place of origin.[11]

Both Klausner and Schalit, with others who identify the man named by Josephus and the individual of *m. Parah* 3:5, place too much reliance on a detail in the Mishnah. The paragraph in question lists persons who had prepared red heifers (see Num 19:1-10). The first ones are Moses and Ezra, and after Ezra we find Simon the Just, Johanan the high priest, Eliehoenai the son of Hakkof, Hanamel the Egyptian, and Ishmael the son of Phiabi. All of the

---

9. He probably had in mind *Ant.* 14.1, 3 (§9) where Josephus quotes Nicolaus of Damascus as saying Antipater's family "belonged to the leading Jews who came to Judaea from Babylon"— a statement suspected already by Josephus himself as being fabricated to please Herod, Nicolaus's employer.

10. Joseph Klausner, *The History of the Second Temple*, 5 vols., 6th ed. (Jerusalem: Achiasaf, 1963), 4.12 (Hebrew).

11. Schalit, *King Herod*, 62 and n. 17 (376) = *König Herodes*, 101 with Zusatz XV, 693–95.

post-Ezra individuals were high priests: we have already met the first two, and Eliehoenai and Ishmael will appear in the list below. This makes it nearly certain that Hanamel is understood to be a high priest, though the order of names would not be chronological. But, it is advisable methodologically to accept the earlier testimony of Josephus, which makes sense in context. Some later high priests came from Egypt, but it is more likely that Ananel was from Babylon. Moreover, in *m. Parah* 3:5, the adjective *Egyptian* may have moved from its rightful place after Phiabi, who possibly was from Egypt (see below).[12] So, the first Herodian high priest was named Ananel (Hebrew חננאל; the word is attested as the name of a tower in Jerusalem [for example, Neh 3:1; 12:39]), and he came from the large Diaspora community in Babylon.[13]

Herod appointed him high priest in 37 BCE but removed him from office a short time later, perhaps in 35 BCE. Soon thereafter, he restored him to office following the murder of Aristobulus III. Ananel may have reigned during his second term until approximately 30 BCE, although we hear no more about him. He provides us with the first example of Herod's way of handling the high priesthood: it was no longer a hereditary office, only an appointive one. How this was reconciled with the requirement in the Torah that the position was to pass from father to son (for example, Exod 29:29-30) is not stated.

26. Aristobulus III (35 BCE)

A last gasp for the Hasmonean dynasty came in the year 36, or more likely 35 BCE, when Herod, against his better judgment, appointed a member of the family, Aristobulus III, as high priest and removed Ananel from the post. Aristobulus was a grandson of both Hyrcanus II and Aristobulus II and was also Herod's brother-in-law, now that the king had married Mariamme. He had been, as we have seen, the leading Hasmonean candidate to succeed Antigonus when the latter was executed in 37 BCE, but at the time considerations of both policy and age may have militated against Herod's naming him to the position.

The high priesthood of Aristobulus was doomed from the start. Herod appointed him at the insistence of his mother Alexandra (Hyrcanus II's daughter) and his sister Mariamme, Herod's wife. In *War*, Josephus merely

---

12. Smith, "A Study of the Zadokite High Priesthood," 175–76; Richardson, *Herod*, 244 n. 18.

13. As Schürer says about the mishnaic Hanamel the Egyptian, both the form of the name and the country of origin are incorrect (*History*, 2.229 n. 5). See also Jeremias, *Jerusalem*, 66. Joseph Derenbourg's suggestion that the name חנמאל of the Mishnah is actually Anan = Annas, the high priest who was the father of five other high priests (see below) is implausible (*Essai sur l'histoire et la géographie de la Palestine d'après les Thalmuds et les autres sources rabbiniques* [Paris: Imprimerie impériale, 1867], 155 n. 1).

alludes to the episode without providing many details (1.22, 2 [§437]), although there we learn that the young man's Hebrew name was Jonathan. According to this short passage, Mariamme, who hated Herod as passionately as he loved her, castigated him some years later for how he had treated her grandfather Hyrcanus and her brother. Since Hyrcanus II was executed in 30 BCE, the conversation would have taken place in that year or later. Besides Herod himself, she also attacked his mother Cyprus and sister Salome who responded in kind.

> [T]he women, seething with indignation, brought against her the charge which was bound in their opinion to touch Herod most nearly, that of adultery. Among much else which they invented to convince him, they accused Mariamme of having sent her portrait to Antony in Egypt and of carrying wantonness so far as to exhibit herself, though at a distance, to a man with a madness for her sex and powerful enough to resort to violence. (*J.W.* 1.22, 3 [§§438–39])

So, in *War* Josephus says that a story about Mariamme's portrait being sent to Antony in Egypt was invented by her hated in-laws.

The longer account in *Antiquities* traces the events to Alexandra, Mariamme's and Aristobulus's mother, who considered the appointment of Ananel as high priest "an unendurable insult" (15.2, 5 [§23]). Josephus then spells out the family connections of Alexandra and speaks about her children: she and Alexander (a son of Aristobulus II) had two children, "an extraordinarily handsome son, named Aristobulus, and Mariamme, the wife of Herod, who was famed for her beauty. She was disturbed and aggrieved by the indignity offered her son that while he was still alive someone should be called from abroad and be given the office of high priest. And using the help of a certain singer to get the letter delivered, she wrote to Cleopatra, asking her to request Antony to obtain the high priesthood for her son" (15.2, 5 [§§23–24]). Cleopatra was a veteran enemy of Herod and, of course, the best person for getting Antony's attention. In this context in *Antiquities*, it is Alexandra who contacts Cleopatra.

The plan misfired (Antony paid little attention to the request), but a new opportunity soon presented itself. In a story that a number of scholars find incredible, Josephus relates that Dellius, whom Dio identifies as Antony's lover,[14] "came to Judaea on some business, and when he saw Aristobulus, he was amazed[15] at his charm and was filled with admiration of his height and

---

14. See Marcus and Wikgren, *Josephus 8*, 14 n. a.

15. As Marcus and Wikgren indicate, a variant reading is "fell in love with" (*Josephus 8*, 14–15 nn. 2 and b).

beauty, and no less with (the beauty) of Mariamme, the king's wife" (15.2, 6 [§25]). He suggested to Alexandra that she could have her wishes fulfilled by Antony if she sent portraits of her children to him. For some reason, she was delighted by the thought that someone with the legendary, diverse sexual appetites of Antony would be attracted to her children, and had the portraits painted and sent. Antony is supposed to have felt embarrassed to send for Herod's wife and had no desire to get into trouble with Cleopatra for the act. "And so he instructed him [= Dellius] to send the lad in an outwardly respectable way, adding, 'if this be no burden.' When this was reported to Herod, he decided that it would not be safe for him to send Aristobulus, who was then most handsome—being just sixteen—and of a distinguished family, to Antony, who was more powerful than any Roman of his time, and was ready to use him for erotic purposes and was able to indulge in undisguised pleasures because of his power. He therefore wrote in reply that if the youth were merely to leave the country, the whole land would be filled with disorder and war, because the Jews had formed hopes of the overturn of the government and the rule of another king" (*Ant.* 15.2, 6 [§§28–30]). He then appointed Aristobulus high priest, removing Ananel from the office.[16]

So, *Antiquities* speaks of two episodes, both involving Alexandra (the letter to Cleopatra and the sequence around Dellius and the pictures for Antony). The latter bears some resemblance to the story in *War* but also differs from it significantly. The efforts of Alexandra form the background for the appointment of her son as high priest.

Schalit thinks the story in *War* is, as Josephus says, a product of the lies spread by Salome, Herod's sister, about Mariamme and that the version in *Antiquities* is a development of it. Neither, he contends, conveys historical fact. Rather, Herod's decision to place the young Hasmonean in the high priesthood was an act calculated, not to appease the old royal family, but to keep from it the true nature of his aim to exterminate the entire clan.[17] It is no simple task to disentangle from the conflicting accounts what might actually have happened, but it is also not difficult to believe that there was intense pressure on the king from the ranking Hasmonean women and that they might have tried to obtain support for their designs from the all-powerful Antony, to whom Herod owed his crown.

Whatever the course of events may have been, Herod did name Aristobulus III the high priest. *War* is characteristically brief, summarizing his term of

---

16. Klausner thinks the events were reversed, with Aristobulus's appointment as high priest preceding Herod's letter to Antony; but it is difficult to see why one should contradict our only source for the episode (*History*, 4.13).

17. *King Herod*, 62–65 = *König Herodes*, 102–8.

office in just a few sentences that clarify Mariamme's later reference to what Herod had done to her brother:

> For Herod had not spared even this poor lad; he had bestowed upon him in his seventeenth year the office of high priest, and then immediately after conferring this honour had put him to death, because, on the occasion of a festival, when the lad approached the altar, clad in the priestly vestments, the multitude with one accord burst into tears. He was, consequently, sent by night to Jericho, and there, in accordance with instructions, plunged into a swimming-bath by the Gauls and drowned. (1.22, 2 [§437])

Antiquities expatiates considerably on the events. Herod, as we have seen, decided to act on the appointment after dissuading Antony from summoning the young man. We also learn that the king did not want to leave either Aristobulus or Alexandra without honor, "especially because his wife Mariamme pressed him urgently to restore the high priesthood to her brother, and also because he thought it to his own advantage that Aristobulus, once placed in office, would not in fact be able to leave the country" (15.2, 7 [§31]). In other words, it sounds as if he wanted to treat Aristobulus as he was handling Hyrcanus: if they stayed within Herod's territory, he could control them. Elsewhere, they could cause dangerous problems for him, whether with the Parthians (Hyrcanus) or with Antony (Aristobulus). We know of no requirement that a high priest not leave the land (Onias III, John Hyrcanus, Alexander Jannaeus, Hyrcanus II, and Aristobulus II, for example, did), but his temple duties would tie him more closely with it and make departing more unlikely, especially if the high priest was no longer the civil ruler of the nation.[18] Both considerations of domestic harmony and royal policy, therefore, moved Herod to make the appointment.

Herod called a "council of his friends" before which he laid his plan. He took the opportunity to accuse Alexandra of not only plotting through Cleopatra and Antony to have her son become high priest but also of removing Herod so that the young man could govern as well. Having made his case, he tried to win public relations credits by putting on a show of magnanimity:

> But this purpose of hers, he said, was unjust, since her daughter [= Mariamme] at the same time would be deprived of the honour

---

18. Otto, *Herodes*, 40 n.; Schalit, *King Herod*, 378 n. 43 = *König Herodes*, 109 n. 43. He rightly notes the danger of contracting impurity outside the land.

which she now had, and she herself would be bringing disorder into a kingdom for which he had worked so hard and had acquired after undergoing no small danger. Nevertheless, he said, he would not keep in mind the improper things that she had done nor cease to treat them justly, but would even give the high priesthood to her son now, for he had earlier appointed Ananel only because Aristobulus was a mere lad. He spoke in these terms not thoughtlessly but with design and due deliberation, in order to deceive the women and the friends who had been called in for advice. (15.2, 7 [§§33–35])

We are, it seems from the sequel, supposed to imagine that Alexandra herself was present at this council, because she expressed her delight but also defended her actions. She admitted agitating for the high priesthood for the young man ("because of the dishonour") but denied having an eye on the throne. It was sufficient that the high priesthood was back in the family: "she now had enough honour because of the power which he held and the security which came to her whole family from the fact that he was better able to rule than any others" (*Ant.* 15.2, 7 [§36]). If she ever said such things, it was wishful thinking, as she was soon to learn. Family honor and security were her concerns and now, she thought, she had attained both. She pledged obedience and apologized for the frankness of her earlier criticisms.

Taking the office from Ananel, Herod gave it to Aristobulus. We hear of no contemporary who objected to the convenient removal of a high priest from the position that he was supposed to possess for life. But the priest Josephus, who here attributes the change in high priests to Herod's desire to end his domestic troubles, criticizes the king for his illegal action "for never had anyone been deprived of this office when once he had assumed it," with only three exceptions (this one and two earlier cases, *Ant.* 15.3, 1 [§§40–41]).[19]

Needless to say, domestic tranquility was short-lived. Herod was inherently suspicious of any threats to his power, and the Hasmoneans gave him good reason to worry. Herod, still concerned that Alexandra wanted to overthrow him, subjected her to an overly thorough house arrest (or rather, in this case, palace arrest), which she could not tolerate. She is supposed to have turned once more to her friend Cleopatra, who suggested that she with the young man escape to the seacoast where a ship could transport them to Egypt. They were to leave the city by hiding in coffins that were carried from Jerusalem at night; they were then to travel to the sea and board a waiting ship.

---

19. He notes the instances involving Jesus-Onias (= Jason-Menelaus, continuing his earlier confused identity of Menelaus as Jason's brother) and Aristobulus II-Hyrcanus II.

But, the scheme was uncovered because of the duplicity of an unreliable servant, and Herod caught them in the act. He did not punish Alexandra immediately out of fear of Cleopatra. "He was determined at all costs, however, to get the youth out of the way; but it seemed to him that he would be more likely to have his motives escape detection if he did not act at once or immediately after what had happened" (*Ant.* 15.3, 2 [§49]). It does seem strange that the mother and *the high priest* would take such bizarre measures to smuggle themselves out of Jerusalem. One wonders whether this story is a variant of Alexandra's earlier correspondence with Cleopatra when her son was not yet high priest. If this did happen during Aristobulus's high priesthood, it looks as if Alexandra and Aristobulus III did not consider the sacerdotal office enough for them. They wanted more. Mariamme is not mentioned in this account.

The end came soon for Aristobulus at what may have seemed a moment of triumph. At the celebration of the festival of Tabernacles (month seven, days fifteen to twenty-two), the high priest himself officiated at the altar[20] clothed in the glorious robes associated with the office. This may have been the first time he presided during a pilgrimage festival when crowds at the temple would be particularly large; also, at that time, Tabernacles may have been the most important festival of the sacred calendar. Several days of the lengthy holiday passed, during which Herod and the celebrants enjoyed the festivities.

> But it was the envy arising from this very occasion and clearly working within him that led him to carry out his purpose more quickly. For Aristobulus was a youth of seventeen when he went up to the altar to perform the sacrifices in accordance with the law, wearing the ornamental dress of the high priests and carrying out the rites of the cult, and he was extraordinarily handsome and taller that most youths of his age, and in his appearance, moreover, he displayed to the full the nobility of his descent. And so there arose among the people an impulsive feeling of affection toward him, and there came to them a vivid memory of the deeds performed by his grandfather Aristobulus.[21] Being overcome, they gradually revealed their feelings, showing joyful and painful emotion at the same time, and they called out to him good wishes mingled with prayers, so that the affection of the crowd became evident, and their acknowledgment of their emotions

---

20. Jonathan had become high priest at the festival of Tabernacles (1 Macc 10:21), and Alexander Jannaeus had offered sacrifice at the festival when he was attacked by worshipers who threw lemons at him (*Ant.* 13.13, 5 [§372]).

21. He was, Josephus may be implying, less like his other grandfather, Hyrcanus II.

seemed too impulsive in view of their having a king. As a result of all these things Herod decided to carry out his designs against the youth. (*Ant.* 15.3, 3 [§§50–53])[22]

It was not long after the festival concluded that Herod and Aristobulus were Alexandra's guests at the Hasmonean palace in Jericho. Herod tried to cover his treacherous intent by acting in a friendly way toward Aristobulus, whom he encouraged to drink. In the great heat of Jericho, they retired to the large swimming pools at the palace where Herod urged Aristobulus to join his servants who were playing in the water. He had instructed some friends to act as if they were having some good sporting fun by holding the young high priest underwater. They eventually succeeded in drowning him. "In this manner was Aristobulus done away with when he was at most eighteen years old and had held the high priesthood for a year. This office Ananel again obtained for himself" (*Ant.* 15.3, 3 [§56]).

Herod's best efforts to mask the drowning as if it were an accident misled no one, certainly not Alexandra.[23] His murderous act naturally increased the hatred she felt for Herod. His vendetta against the Hasmoneans was, of course, to continue some years later when he also executed Hyrcanus on what may have been manufactured charges of treason. The abhorrence felt by Alexandra and Mariamme for Herod eventually cost both of them their lives at the hands of the paranoid monarch (*Ant.* 15.7, 4 [§§222–31] for Mariamme; 15.7, 8 [§§247–52] for Alexandra; for other Hasmoneans see, for example, 15.7, 10 [§266]).[24] Neither had been hesitant about reminding him of the murders he had committed in their family and both continued agitating against Herod and for their family, delighting to remind the Herodians of their common origins. But after Aristobulus, no Hasmonean ever held the high priesthood.

Herod was summoned to Antony who was then in Laodicea to account for the death of Aristobulus. Although he feared the loss of his position and life, a

---

22. Jeffrey L. Rubenstein (*The History of Sukkot in the Second Temple and Rabbinic Periods,* BJS 302 [Atlanta: Scholars, 1995], 81) thinks the political danger attending the high priest's officiating at the great festival recalls the episode in which Antigonus, the brother and apparently substitute high priest for Aristobulus I, aroused suspicion that he might try to revolt against his brother. "Josephus reveals that Sukkot is the festival on which pomp, intrigue and political machinations take place. Because of the great numbers and impressive temple rituals, the high priest received such honor that his rivals felt threatened."

23. In *Ant.* 20.10, 5 (§248) Josephus wrote: "fearing that everyone would incline to Aristobulus, he put him to death at Jericho by contriving to have him strangled while swimming." Compare Otto, *Herodes,* 42.

24. Much later, Herod was also to execute Alexander and Aristobulus, the two sons whom Mariamme had borne to him (for the story of their deaths, see *Ant.* 16.11, 1–7 [§§356–94]).

bribe again helped win over the mighty Roman, and Herod returned to Jerusalem with his blessing, much to the chagrin of the Hasmonean ladies and Herod's other enemies (*Ant.* 15.3, 5–9 [§§62–87]).

Ananel (Reappointed, 35 to about 30? BCE)

Although he notes that Ananel regained the high priesthood after Aristobulus met his end (*Ant.* 15.3, 3 [§56]), Josephus records nothing about his second stint in office, not even about its termination—a rare phenomenon for the post-Hasmonean period.

27. Jesus Son of Phiabi (about 30? to between 24 and 22 BCE)

We cannot be absolutely sure of the point, but Ananel's immediate successor seems to have been a man whom Josephus calls Jesus, the son of Phabes. At any rate, he is the next high priest to be mentioned in the narrative. We have no information about his tenure in office and when he succeeded Ananel, if, in fact, he was the next high priest. The only mention of this Jesus in *Antiquities* comes as the final sentence in the story about Herod's appointment of the man who took over the office from him.

In that later passage, when Herod wished to make a certain Simon, the son of Boethus, the high priest (see below), nothing stopped him from doing so. "That is to say, he promptly removed Jesus, the son of Phabes, from the high priesthood and appointed Simon to this office, and contracted marriage with his daughter" (*Ant.* 15.9, 3 [§322]). The date for the end of Jesus's reign (between 24 and 22 BCE) can be estimated from the evidence for when Simon ruled (see below). The fact that Herod removed him from office shows that he continued to consider the high priesthood an appointive, not a lifelong, position.[25] There is no evidence that the office retained any significant political power under the Idumean king.

The name of Jesus's father occurs in various spellings in the manuscripts, but it is highly likely that the correct form is Phiabi.[26] We will meet this family name several times in connection with the high priesthood, as there were

---

25. Otto (*Herodes*, 115) and Schalit (*King Herod*, 160 = *König Herodes*, 312) speak of two rights denied to the high priests by Herod, who refused to allow any concentration of power apart from himself: the right of heredity, and the right of holding the office for one's lifetime.

26. See Schürer, *History of the Jewish People*, 2.229 n. 6; Marcus and Wikgren, *Josephus 8*, 154 n. a; Smith, "A Study of the Zadokite High Priesthood," 176.

two later high priests named Ishmael son of Phiabi (they ruled 15–16? and 59–61 CE); in fact, it was one of four families that supplied almost all of the last twenty-eight high priests in the Second-Temple period.[27] The paternal name figures both in *Antiquities* and in rabbinic texts (for example, *m. Soṭah* 9:15; *m. Parah* 3:5; *t. Menaḥ.* 13:21; *t. Parah* 3:6), and it has been found on a stone in a cemetery at Leontopolis in Egypt.[28] The last named fact has led some to conclude that the family of Phiabi was from Egypt[29] and that, by appointing a high priest from that family, Herod was trying to attract the support of Jews in Egypt, just as by his appointment of Ananel he had tried to gain the backing of Jews in Babylonia.[30]

28. Simon Son of Boethus (24–22 to 5 BCE)

As noted just above, Simon, son of Boethus, replaced Jesus, son of Phiabi, as high priest. The circumstances in which he attained the office are revealing about Herod's rather cavalier treatment of the high priesthood but also about the prestige the office retained.

Josephus says that Herod, moved by amorous desires, decided to marry again.

> There lived in Jerusalem a well-known priest named Simon, the son of one Boethus, an Alexandrian, who had a daughter considered to be the most beautiful woman of her time. And since there was much talk about her among the inhabitants of Jerusalem, Herod, as it happened, first became excited by what he heard, and then, on seeing her, was greatly smitten by the girl's loveliness, but he dismissed the thought of abusing his power in order to achieve his full desire, for he sus-

---

27. Jeremias, *Jerusalem*, 193–94.

28. For the epitaph in which the name figures, see William Horbury and David Noy, *Jewish Inscriptions of Graeco-Roman Egypt* (Cambridge: Cambridge Univ. Press, 1992), 69–70 (#33). The spelling in line 5 is φαβειτι. Horbury translates lines 3–6 of the words attributed to the entombed Arsinoe in this way: "For I was bereaved of my mother when I was a little girl; and when the flower of my youth dressed me as a bride, my father joined me in marriage with Phabeis, and Fate led me to the end of life in the travail-pain of my first-born child." As he notes (72), the name is Egyptian and so could refer to an Egyptian-Jewish husband or to an Egyptian one. The inscription dates from the mid-second to first century BCE.

29. Menahem Stern, "The Reign of Herod and the Herodian Dynasty," in *The Jewish People in the First Century,* ed. S. Safrai and M. Stern, CRINT I/1 (Philadelphia: Fortress Press, 1974), 274.

30. Richardson, *Herod*, 244–45.

pected with good reason that he would be accused of violence and tyranny, and so he thought it better to take the girl in marriage. And since Simon was, on the one hand, not illustrious enough to become related (to the king) but, on the other hand, too important to be treated with contempt, Herod fulfilled his desire in a rather reasonable way by increasing his and his daughter's prestige and making their position one of greater honour. That is to say, he promptly removed Jesus, the son of Phabes, from the high priesthood and appointed Simon to this office, and contracted marriage with his daughter. (*Ant.* 15.9, 3 [§§320–22])

The lovely lady in question was named Mariamme, usually called Mari-amme II[31] to distinguish her from Herod's earlier Hasmonean wife who was dead by this time.

The date when this Simon gained the high priesthood as a result of Herod's designs on his daughter can be ascertained to some extent from the order of events in *Antiquities*. In 15.9, 1 (§299), a drought is placed in Herod's thirteenth year, that is, 25–24 BCE. As conditions worsened, Herod was able to acquire grain from Petronius, then prefect of Egypt, an office the latter held from 24–21 BCE. The marriage to Mariamme II is noted a few paragraphs later with no intervening year dates. Then, after the marriage, Herod's construction of the city of Caesarea is described in 15.9, 6 (§§331–41). Paragraph 341 says that he finished it in twelve years (a figure preferable to the ten years mentioned in 16.5, 1 [§136]), with the completion coming in his twenty-eighth year (16.5, 1 [§136]), that is, 10–9 BCE. If the city reached completion in the year 10 BCE after construction for twelve years, he began building it in 22 BCE. As a result, Simon attained the high priesthood at some point between about 24 and 22 BCE.[32]

The man who received the high priesthood under such awkward circumstances was the first high priest from a family that was to provide many occupants of the office. In the passage quoted above, he is termed a resident of Jerusalem whose father Boethus was an Alexandrian; the Greek case endings show that Boethus, not Simon, was the Alexandrian.[33] Perhaps the connections

---

31. For the information regarding her, see Nikos Kokkinos, *The Herodian Dynasty: Origins, Role in Society, and Eclipse*, JSPSup 30 (Sheffield: Sheffield Academic, 1998), 217–23.

32. See Schürer, *History of the Jewish People*, 1.290–91; Hölscher, *Hohenpriesterliste*, 10; Marcus and Wikgren, *Josephus 8*, 165 n. d.

33. W. F. Smith ("A Study of the Zadokite High Priesthood," 178–79) claims that his prominence likely came from his being a Zadokite connected with the Oniad temple in Egypt. There is no record of this, however. We also have no secure information about whether this family of Boethus was connected with the Boethusians (see Smith, "A Study of the Zadokite High Priest-hood," 188–204; he also includes a lengthy discussion of the Bene Hezir inscription which men-

of the family with the great Alexandrian Jewish community were considered a bonus in his appointment. Unlike the earlier Ananel, he is said to have been well known, although his family at the time was not high-ranking. Once Herod elevated Simon to the high priesthood and married his daughter, the problem of the family's standing in society vanished.

Josephus's narratives divulge little about Simon during the course of his rather long incumbency. True to the actual reason for his appointment, he is mentioned several times only because Mariamme II was known as the high priest's daughter. For example, in *Ant.* 17.1, 2 (§14), Herod arranged the marriage of his son, also named Herod, and a granddaughter of Mariamme I. That younger Herod is identified as one "who had been born to him by the daughter of the high priest."[34]

While Simon served as high priest, Herod embarked on several construction projects, including rebuilding the temple itself (begun in 20 BCE). Remarkably, we do not read of any part Simon played in the entire episode; it was Herod's project, not the high priest's. We hear of the high priesthood only in connection with Herod's handling of the holy vestments. On the north side of the king's new temple was an especially strong citadel. "It was the kings and high priests of the Asamonaean family before Herod who had built it and called it *baris*. Here they had deposited the priestly robe which the high priest put on only when he had to offer sacrifice. This robe Herod kept safe in that place" (*Ant.* 15.11, 4 [§§403–4]). Josephus then adds details about the subsequent treatment of the high-priestly garments after Herod's death.[35] It is understandable that Herod would be wary of the robe, after his experience with the young, handsome Aristobulus III at the festival of Tabernacles. Whereas in Hasmonean times the vestments were kept safe by rulers who were also high priests (hence the garments were their own), Herod changed the practice by putting them under his control, much as the high priest was subordinate to him.[36]

---

tions the names of priests, several of which overlap with the high priests from the line of Boethus. Smith concludes, however, that the dissimilarities outweigh the similarities and that the names of the inscription are not those of the high-priestly Boethus family). According to *Avot of Rabbi Nathan* 5, the Boethusians are traced to Boethus, a disciple of Antigonos of Soko who followed Simon the Just. That is, the tradition in this text traces the origins of the group to a different person from a far earlier time.

34. See also *Ant.* 17.1, 3 (§19); *J.W.* 1.28, 4 (§562) where she is identified in the same way in a list of Herod's nine wives; 17.3, 2 (§53); *J.W.* 1.29, 2 (§573) where this Herod is named as the second successor to his father after Antipater (who, ironically, was married to the previous king Antigonus's daughter, *Ant.* 17.5, 2 [§92]; 18.5, 1 [§109]; 18.5, 4 [§136]; 19.6, 2 [§297]).

35. See below under the high priest Caiaphas for a treatment of this passage.

36. Otto, *Herodes*, 115.

The end of Simon's service as high priest came at a time determined by Herod and, appropriately enough, in connection with his daughter. After the death of Pheroras, Herod's brother, and in the course of uncovering an elaborate plot in which Antipater (Herod's heir), his mother, and Pheroras's wife were intimately involved, King Herod learned that the latter two were not the only women implicated. "And the high priest's daughter, who was the king's wife, was also accused of having been privy to all these plots and of having been eager to conceal them. For that reason Herod divorced her and struck her son out of his will, for he had been named to the throne. He also took the high priesthood away from his father-in-law Simon, the son of Boethus, and in his place appointed Matthias, the son of Theophilus, a native of Jerusalem" (*Ant.* 17.4, 2 [§78]). The parallel in *War* says that Herod had learned of Mariamme's complicity when he had subjected her brothers to torture (*J.W.* 1.30, 7 [§§599–600]). As a result, Simon received the office and lost it simply because of Herod's private, family concerns.

Removal of the high priest Simon from his post occurred at some time very late in Herod's reign, probably 5 BCE. Not long after relating the incident, Josephus describes the arrival of Antipater, Herod's son, in Jerusalem. Antipater, slated to be Herod's successor on the throne, had been sent to Rome as relations between himself and his father soured. When the king became convinced of Antipater's disloyalty, he lured him back to Jerusalem and promptly had him arrested. A trial established his guilt to Herod's satifaction; Antipater was to die in prison five days before his father's death. Josephus says that at "this time there happened to be in Jerusalem Quintilius Varus, who had been sent to succeed Saturninus as governor of Syria" (17.5, 2 [§89]; compare *J.W.* 1.31, 5 [§617]). Quintilius Varus was governor in Syria in approximately 6–4 BCE.[37] Varus was involved in the trial of Antipater, after whose imprisonment Herod clung to life for some time. At least one may say that Simon's removal followed the dedication of Caesarea in 10–9 BCE (*Ant.* 16.5, 1 [§136: Herod's twenty-eighth regnal year]) by a considerable span of time.

29. Matthias Son of Theophilus (5–4 BCE)

Matthias was a resident of Jerusalem and the fifth high-priestly appointment by Herod. Typically, we learn little about him, although Josephus does mention him in connection with two incidents.

The first (actually related second by Josephus) was an occasion when Matthias was rendered temporarily incapable of officiating as high priest after

37. Marcus and Wikgren, *Josephus 8*, 413 n. b; Jeremias, *Jerusalem*, 162 n. 48.

he had accidentally been rendered impure. "Now it happened during this
Matthias' term as high priest that another high priest was appointed for a single day—that which the Jews observe as a fast—for the following reason.
While serving as priest during the night preceding the day on which the fast
occurred, Matthias seemed in a dream to have intercourse with a woman, and
since he was unable to serve as priest because of that experience, a relative of
his, Joseph, the son of Ellemus, served as priest in his place. Herod then
deposed Matthias from the high priesthood" (*Ant.* 17.6, 4 [§§165–67]).

This case of nocturnal pollution disqualifying a priest before a day on
which he was to officiate reveals important information about the high priesthood and the rules that governed it. The story in *Antiquities* can be supplemented with parallel material in rabbinic texts. The occasion that Josephus
mentions was the night before a fast, and the fast was probably the Day of
Atonement.[38] The Mishnah preserves evidence of practices in connection
with the solemn fast on the tenth day of the seventh month, the day on which
the high priest had extensive temple duties that were mandated by the Torah
(Leviticus 16). For that reason, it was essential that he be in a state of purity to
carry out his roles. Naturally, the issue is discussed in the mishnaic tractate
Yoma. For example, it begins with the statement: "Seven days before the Day
of Atonement the High Priest was taken apart from his own house unto the
Counsellors' Chamber and another priest was made ready in his stead lest
aught should befall him to render him ineligible" (1:1).[39] Much of the remainder of the chapter is devoted to the preparations undertaken by the high priest
for the ceremonies of this solemn day.

In commenting on the appointment of a substitute priest so that he would
be ready to take the high priest's place if the latter became impure in some way,
the Tosefta cites R. Hananiah, the prefect of the priests, who said that the prefect was appointed for this purpose. The same passage notes that, after the

---

38. Marcus and Wikgren, *Josephus 8*, 447 n. b. think it was the fast of Esther on 11 Adar, but
there is no evidence in the context in *Antiquities* that any fast other than the best known one is
meant. Their dating arises from their assumption that the lunar eclipse mentioned in the context (*Ant.* 17.6, 4 [§167]) occurred just before Herod's death in March-April of 4 BCE. The fast of
Esther (whether one was observed at the time is doubtful) was the nearest one to this date. However, Schwartz correctly notes that the eclipse is connected, not with Herod's death, but with the
high priest Matthias's nocturnal defilement and is thus the one that took place in September
15–16 of 5 BCE. The Day of Atonement would have fallen on September 12–13 of that year and
is therefore the fast mentioned by Josephus (Daniel R. Schwartz, "Joseph ben Illem and the Date
of Herod's Death," in his *Studies in the Jewish Background of Christianity,* WUNT 60 [Tübingen:
Mohr/Siebeck, 1992], 157–66).

39. Herbert Danby, *The Mishnah* (London: Oxford Univ. Press, 1933), 162.

substitute serves, the high priest returns to his duties, and there is discussion about the status of the temporary replacement after his short stint as high priest. Rabbi Yose then refers to a story: "Joseph b. Elim of Sepphoris served in the place of the high priest for one hour" (*t. Yoma* 1:4).[40] Joseph son of Elim does seem to be the same name as Josephus's Joseph son of Ellemus, so that a single incident probably underlies the two texts. The incident also comes under consideration in the Talmuds. In *b. Yoma* 12b, commenting on the same Mishnah, the individual is also called Joseph son of Elam (here, the event is mistakenly put in Sepphoris rather than recognizing Sepphoris as Joseph's home) and there the same issue of the status of the substitute, once his temporary service ends, receives treatment (compare also *y. Yoma* 1:1, 38d).[41] It is understandable that an event so public as the temporary replacement of a high priest on the Day of Atonement would be remembered in the tradition.[42]

The second incident from Matthias's life concerns the reason Herod removed him from office. Late in the king's reign, when his illness and domestic woes were taking their heaviest toll (Josephus says he was about seventy years of age [*Ant.* 17.6, 1 (§148)]), his opponents were embolden to do what they had feared to try when he was less disabled. Two sages, Judas and Matthias (whom Josephus is careful to distinguish from the high priest; this one is the son of Margalothus [17.6, 2 (§149)]), encouraged their disciples to tear down Herod's constructions that violated the divine law. In particular, they ordered the young men to tear down the large, costly golden eagle that Herod had

---

40. The translation is from Jacob Neusner, *The Tosefta: Translated from the Hebrew with a New Introduction*, 2 vols. (Peabody, Mass.: Hendrickson, 2002), 1.542. Goodman claims that this Joseph is, among Herod's appointees as high priest, "the only incumbent who may have come from Palestine" rather than Egypt or Babylonia; whether he should be called an incumbent is debatable, but Josephus says explicitly that Matthias was a native of Jerusalem (*Ruling Class of Judaea*, 41–42). It is also strange that Goodman considers the brevity of Joseph's hold on the office as somehow indicative of Herod's cavalier policy about the high priesthood. He held office briefly because of the rules governing the replacement of a high priest who was temporarily incapable of exercising his functions. Herod had nothing to do with this.

41. See Jeremias, *Jerusalem*, 162–63.

42. One could make a case that this Joseph son of Ellemus should be included in the official list of high priests on the grounds that Josephus places him there (compare Hölscher, *Hohenpriesterliste*, 11–12; Jeremias, *Jerusalem*, 377, who lists him as the sixth high priest of the Herodian period). Josephus tells us that there were twenty-eight high priests who served from the time of Herod to the destruction of the temple (*Ant.* 20.10, 5 [§250]). To reach that number one must include this Joseph, even though he was only a temporary substitute as high priest. Placing him in the list, however, produces an inconsistency because in *Ant.* 20.10, 3 (§241), Josephus does not include Antigonus, the brother of Aristobulus I, although he seems on one occasion to have replaced his brother when the latter was ill. On the whole question and for other talmudic references to the incident, see Schürer, *History of the Jewish People*, 2.229 n. 7.

erected as a votive offering over the great gate of the temple—an offering that violated the second commandment. When they heard a rumor that the king was dead, they carried out their destructive act. But alas, Herod was not dead.

His officer took charge of the situation, arresting the two leaders and some forty of their followers. After the ringleaders made bold responses to the king's questions about the deed, Herod sent them in bonds to Jericho, where Jewish officials gathered at the amphitheater to hear the case. Herod brought the charges himself in a speech that, if authentic, discloses that he was still comparing himself in a defensive way with the Hasmoneans:

> lying on a couch because of his inability to stand, he recounted all his strenuous efforts on their behalf, and told them at what great expense to himself he had constructed the Temple, whereas the Hasmonaeans had been unable to do anything so great for the honour of God in the hundred and twenty-five years of their reign. He had also, he said, adorned (the Temple) with notable dedicatory offerings, and for these reasons he cherished the hope that even after his death he would leave behind a memorial of himself and an illustrious name. (17.6, 3 [§§161–63])

The king regarded their destruction of his offering as an act of sacrilege, while they considered it obedience to the Law of Moses.

For reasons not adequately explained, Herod then deposed the high priest Matthias "as being partly to blame for what had happened and in his stead appointed his wife's brother Joazar as high priest" (*Ant.* 17.6, 4 [§164]). It may be that Matthias was punished for no other reason than that the act of tearing down the eagle had occurred at the temple where he was in charge.[43] If he had been more directly implicated in the incident, he would not have escaped with so light a sentence, as the other Matthias, a leader of the young men who had pulled down the eagle, was burned alive along with some of his companions (17.6, 4 [§167]). The end of Matthias's brief term of office came early in the year 4 BCE. Josephus refers to an eclipse of the moon in the context—an eclipse that has often been dated to March 13, 4 BCE;[44] as we have seen, however, it was probably the one of the previous September. Herod died shortly after removing Matthias, and Josephus says that the king's life came to an end just before the time of Passover (17.9, 3 [§213]).

---

43. Schalit suggests Herod ousted him because he had been unable to prevent the incident (*King Herod*, 318 = *König Herodes*, 638).

44. Schürer, *History of the Jewish People*, 1.327; Marcus and Wikgren, *Josephus 8*, 449 n. b; Schalit, *King Herod*, 318 = *König Herodes*, 638.

30. Joazar Son of Boethus (4 BCE to 6 CE?)

Josephus, as we have just seen, follows his notice that Herod removed Matthias from office by writing: "and in his stead appointed his wife's brother Joazar as high priest" (*Ant.* 17.6, 4 [§164]). Because the referent of the possessive "his" in the phrase "his wife" is potentially ambiguous, there has been debate about just who this Joazar was. Does Josephus's formulation entail that he was the brother of *Herod's* wife (presumably Mariamme II) or that he was the brother of *Matthias's* wife? The former seems the far more likely conclusion in context, but the latter has found some defenders. So, for example, Mary Smallwood considers Joazar to be Matthias's brother-in-law, and Richard Horsley does as well.[45]

Schwartz has adduced several reasons in support of this interpretation and, as others have, deals with it in connection with an additional statement about the family of Boethus in *Ant.* 19.6, 2 (§§297–98).[46] Schwartz thinks the more likely reading of *Ant.* 17.6, 4 (§164) is that *Matthias's* wife was intended, because to refer to Herod's wife at this point would be singularly unhelpful (he had nine or ten of them). However, he fails to reckon with the fact that, in connection with the high priesthood, the wife of Herod who is meant consistently in the latter part of his reign is Mariamme II, as we have seen. True, Herod had divorced her by this time, but that need not mean he would avoid appointing another member of her family to the high priesthood, as Schwartz himself recognizes.[47] A further weakness of Schwartz's position is that he would be identifying someone in the narrative (Matthias's wife) whom Josephus had not noted before and about whom he adds nothing else. Since this Joazar is later called "Joazar, the son of Boethus" (*Ant.* 17.13, 1 [§339]) and Mariamme II's father Simon was also a son of Boethus, this seems the preferred identification in §164—a context in which Herod is clearly the subject of the actions.[48] We

---

45. E. Mary Smallwood, "High Priests and Politics in Roman Palestine," *JTS* 13 (1962): 17, 31, 33; Richard A. Horsley, "High Priests and the Politics of Roman Palestine: A Contextual Analysis of the Evidence in Josephus," *JSJ* 17 (1986): 32. See also W. F. Smith, "A Study of the Zadokite High Priesthood," 181.

46. Daniel R. Schwartz, *Agrippa I: The Last King of Judaea*, TSAJ 23 (Tübingen: Mohr/Siebeck, 1990), Appendix III "Simon Cantheras and the Boethus Family," especially 186–87. We will deal with the passage in *Antiquities* 19 at the appropriate juncture in the history below.

47. Kokkinos points to *J.W.* 1.30, 7 (§599), which says her brothers had denounced her under torture (*Herodian Dynasty*, 219). We do not know, however, whether any future high priest was among the brothers so abused.

48. See also Marcus and Wikgren, *Josephus 8*, 447 n. b (though the note is somewhat confused); Menahem Stern, "Aspects of Jewish Society: The Priesthood and Other Classes," in *The*

have no reason for thinking that Matthias's wife was from the family of Boethus.

So, the wife in question was probably Mariamme II, and Joazar was the second man from the family of Boethus to become high priest. He was the last person whom Herod installed in the office, since the monarch died almost immediately after the appointment, and he himself held the high priesthood only a very short time.

We next meet Joazar in connection with Archelaus's succession to his father in 4 BCE. Herod had finally designated this son as his successor after the death of the former heir apparent Antipater (*Ant.* 17.8, 1 [§188]). When he first took office, Archelaus won the goodwill of many people by a kindly speech, and on that occasion they asked him to lighten taxes and release prisoners. Some people who, Josephus says, had assembled "in their desire for revolutionary action" (17.9, 1 [§206]), were still mourning the deaths of those implicated in the eagle incident. They verbally abused the man whom the historian here calls "king," though he did not officially have the title.

> Then they came together as a body and demanded that they be avenged by Archelaus through the punishment of those men who had been honoured by Herod. And that first of all and most publicly he remove the high priest appointed by Herod and choose another man who would serve as high priest more in accordance with the law and ritual purity.[49] To these demands Archelaus assented in spite of his displeasure, for he was trying to restrain their impetuosity because of his intention of making a voyage to Rome as quickly as possible in order to observe what decision Caesar might make. (17.9, 1 [§§207–8]; *J.W.* 2.1, 2 [§§5–7])

Jewish People in the First Century, ed. S. Safrai and M. Stern, CRINT I/2 (Philadelphia: Fortress Press, 1974), 605; Schalit, *King Herod,* 318 = *König Herodes,* 638; Goodman, *Ruling Class of Judaea,* 139; Kokkinos, *Herodian Dynasty,* 219. It seems that the brothers of *Ant.* 19.6, 2 (§§297–98) are Joazar and Eleazar (see below).

49. In line with his theory about the political role of the high priests in this period, Horsley argues that these people were not demanding a high priest who confined himself to religious matters; rather, their charge was that he was "unjust politically, not unjustly political" ("High Priests," 32–33). As for the issue of purity, see Ernst Bammel, "Joasar," in his *Judaica: Kleine Schriften I,* WUNT 37 (Tübingen: Mohr/Siebeck, 1986), 30; he thinks there is an allusion here to "unüberbrückbare kultische Differenzen" [irreconcilable cultic differences] that would have separated Joazar from his opponents (in n. 12, he raises the possibility that differences of practice are meant and that the charge would therefore have been directed against all Boethusians, not just Joazar).

It seems that the crowd regarded Joazar as the deceased king's henchman, who was willing to permit a violation of the Law of Moses if it pleased Herod and to side with him as he punished those responsible for tearing down the golden eagle from atop the great gate of the temple.[50] In this regard, Joazar appears to contrast with Matthias, who may have been removed for not restraining those guilty of such dangerous vandalism. Joazar supported the ruling authority, no matter how dubious Herod's act was.

The tension escalated as Archelaus sent various messengers to persuade the crowd to be patient, and the arrival of Passover only made matters worse, because of the throng of celebrants who streamed into the city. After a contingent of his troops had been stoned by the crowd, he dispatched his entire army to quell the disturbance. They killed some three thousand people before order was restored. At that point, the ruler departed for Rome to await Augustus's verdict about the succession to Herod (17.9, 3 [§§213–23]). While he was away, widespread revolts broke out in the land; these the Roman officers sent to address the situation suppressed only with great difficulty (*Ant* 17.10, 1–10 [§§250–98]).

One of those officials, Varus, permitted a delegation of Jews to sail to Rome to petition Caesar for autonomy. This was at the very time when the emperor was trying to decide the succession to Herod, which Archelaus and others of the family were disputing, especially his brother Antipas. One of the charges brought by the Jewish delegation was Archelaus's responsibility for the deaths of the three thousand; they preferred for the land to become part of the province of Syria and thus to be governed from there (17.11, 2 [§§312–14]). The situation is strongly reminiscent of the one in 63 BCE, when Hyrcanus and Aristobulus contended for the throne before Pompey while a delegation of Jews asked to be delivered from both. In 4 BCE, Caesar finally decided to make Archelaus an ethnarch, not a king, and divided Herod's territory between him and two of Herod's other sons, Philip and Antipas (17.11, 4 [§§317–18]). He indicated that Archelaus could some day become king if he proved worthy of the crown.

When Archelaus arrived back in his reduced country, "he removed Joazar, the son of Boethus, from the high priesthood, blaming him for having supported the rebels [συστάντι τοῖς στασιώταις], and in his place appointed Joazar's brother Eleazar" (17.13, 1 [§339]). The charge against Joazar seems odd. The partisans of the Matthias who had pulled down the eagle wanted the high priest removed for religious reasons, and the disturbances that followed Archelaus's violent suppression of opposition to himself are pictured as a

---

50. See Smallwood, "High Priests," 17.

continuation of the eagle incident. Thus, it is not clear which rebels Joazar is accused of supporting. The temple had been damaged at one stage of the fighting; also, Sabinus, a procurator sent to the area while Caesar decided the issue of Herod's will, had provoked new rioting and had looted the temple (*Ant.* 17.10, 1–2 [§§250–64]; *J.W.* 2.3, 1–3 [§§39–50]). Whether these latter incidents led Joazar to side with these later Jewish rebels we do not know, but it may be that, in the difficult circumstances of the time, he threw in his lot with those who wished to introduce direct Roman control of Judea rather than rule by Herodians.[51] At any rate, though he did so for another reason, Archelaus gave those who demanded it what they had earlier requested by deposing Joazar (but see below for his reappointment).[52]

31. Eleazar Son of Boethus (4 BCE)

The third member of Boethus's family to become high priest was the first high priest appointed by Archelaus, a ruler who followed his father's policy of naming and removing occupants of the office as he saw fit or circumstances dictated. The simple fact that the ethnarch appointed Joazar's brother to be high priest demonstrates that the dismissal of Joazar was not directed against the family and whatever influence it exerted.[53] Eleazar was not given opportunity to serve for an extended time. In fact, the only other mention of him records the end of his reign: "Nor did Eleazar long remain in the (high) priesthood, for while he was still alive he was replaced by Jesus, the son of Seë" (*Ant.* 17.13, 1 [§341]). Just before this paragraph, Josephus had noted the marriage of Archelaus to Glaphyra, who had been his brother Alexander's wife and who had had children with Alexander. This latter fact made the marriage contrary to Deut 25:5-10. Whether Eleazar's removal was in any way related to the illegal marriage and whether he had brought it to Archelaus's attention *Antiquities* does not tell us.

With Eleazar, we meet our first example in the Herodian period of a high priest succeeding his brother (as Simon the Maccabee had succeeded Jonathan

---

51. See Bammel, "Joasar," 30–32. Smallwood ("High Priests," 20) thinks the charge was fabricated; compare Horsley ("High Priests," 33). Horsley adds that Joazar would not have been reappointed later if he had actually been involved in revolutionary activity (34). Given how little we know about the circumstances, the charge remains difficult to assess.

52. Hölscher rightly asks how replacement of a high priest, itself contrary to the law of Moses, could have pleased a group that wanted a high priest more observant of the law (*Hohenpriesterliste*, 12). He thinks that some problems like this arose from the imperfect fusion of sources by Josephus.

53. See, for example, Horsley, "High Priests," 34.

and Alexander Jannaeus had followed Aristobulus I). In the remaining years of the Second Temple, we will meet many other examples. Bammel[54] has shown that the same phenomenon is attested elsewhere in priesthoods of the Hellenistic-Roman world. In Judea, he thinks, this was a structural principle arising from family law. While he has correctly seen that the practice reflects a limited Roman interference with the high-priestly succession, it does not appear to have been a *principle* of succession. A number of brothers succeeded brothers as high priests, but other arrangements also prevailed. The overall picture is of a few families controlling the high priesthood, not of a principle of *Bruderfolge*.

32. Jesus Son of Seë [Σεέ] (4 BCE to ?)

Josephus records nothing more about this Jesus. All we are able to say about him, besides his appointment after Eleazar was deposed, is that he was replaced or died no later than 6 CE, by which time Joazar was again in office. We have no indication when the change of high priests took place, as Josephus uncharacteristically omits any such notice. Jeremias assumed that Jesus and the two first-century CE high priests who are not said to be related to any of the four dominant high-priestly families (Ananias son of Nedebaeus and Jesus son of Damnaeus) were related to them in some way.[55] It is tempting to propose a scribal error in the name of his father. Perhaps Σεέ [= ΣΕΕ] is a mistake for ΣΕΘ or ΣΕΘΙ who, as we will see, is listed as the father of Ananus. If so, he would indeed have been part of one of the great families.[56] Against this suggestion is the fact that Josephus says nothing about Ananus being the brother of this high priest or that Jesus was related to the family of Ananus that produced so many high priests, all of whom he lists in *Ant.* 20.9, 1 [§198]).

Joazar Son of Boethus (Reappointed in or before 6 CE)

One would think the removal of Joazar, the son of Boethus, in 4 BCE would have been the last we would hear of him as high priest, but it is not. In a puzzling reference, Josephus mentions him again as he writes about events that

---

54. Ernst Bammel, "Die Bruderfolge im Hochpriestertum der herodianisch-römischen Zeit," in his *Judaica: Kleine Schriften I*. WUNT 37 (Tübingen: Mohr/Siebeck, 1986), 21–27.

55. *Jerusalem*, 194.

56. See Hölscher, *Hohenpriesterliste*, 12, 21–22; M. Stern, "Aspects of Jewish Society," 606.

happened in 6 CE, just after Caesar deposed Archelaus and banished him to
Gaul. There can be no doubt that the immediate post-Archelean period is
under discussion here, because Quirinius was appointed as legate to Syria in 6
CE and ordered to make an assessment of people's property and to handle that
of Archelaus, while Coponius was sent to rule the Jews as their prefect.
"Quirinius also visited Judaea, which had been annexed to Syria, in order to
make an assessment of the property of the Jews and to liquidate the estate of
Archelaus" (*Ant.* 18.1, 1 [§2]). This is the setting for the next mention of Joazar
as high priest in the *Antiquities*. "Although the Jews were at first shocked to hear
of the registration of property, they gradually condescended, yielding to the
arguments of the high priest Joazar, the son of Boethus, to go no further in
opposition. So those who were convinced by him declared, without shilly-
shallying, the value of their property" (18.1, 1 [§3]). As Archelaus had deposed
Joazar in 4 BCE, he could, of course, still have been living ten years later in 6 CE,
although there is no indication in Josephus's narrative that he had recovered
the high priesthood. One might hypothesize that Josephus is here referring to
a former high priest as "the high priest" (as he does a number of times later in
his history; see the cases of Ananus and Jonathan below), but the next reference to him (his removal) seems to preclude that hypothesis.[57]

The same Quirinius is involved in the following appearance of Joazar as
high priest.

> Quirinius had now liquidated the estate of Archelaus; and by this
> time the registrations of property that took place in the thirty-
> seventh year after Caesar's defeat of Antony at Actium were complete.
> Since the high priest Joazar had now been overpowered by a popular
> faction [κατασταστιασθέντα ὑπὸ τῆς πληθύος], Quirinius stripped
> him of the dignity of his office and installed Ananus the son of Seth
> as high priest. (*Ant.* 18.2, 1 [§26])

The thirty-seventh year after Actium (31 BCE) should be 6 CE, the year when
Archelaus was banished and Rome took over more direct control of Judea.
Joazar therefore held the office at some time in 6 CE, but how long (if at all) he
held it before this we do not know. We should also like to know the identity of

---

57. Hölscher, *Hohenpriesterliste*, 13. Hölscher concluded that the appointment and reappointment of Joazar without mentioning his deposition resulted from a miscombining of
sources and that, with respect to the high-priestly list in this period, we can rely on the order of
names but not the chronology (13–14)—a solution based on very few data. In view of our ignorance about events in this period, it seems simpler to accept the idea of a reappointment and that
Josephus's source(s) failed to record the occasion for it.

the popular faction that had overpowered him and how and why they did so; on these matters too we are left frustrated.

The gap in our historical knowledge has left ample room for speculation regarding the reason(s) for Joazar's reappointment and second deposition from the office of high priest. As for his reappointment, Smallwood considers it more likely that Archelaus was the one responsible, not Quirinius or Coponius. She notes that Josephus had little information about the end of Archelaus's reign but much more for the first months of the new Roman province of *Judaea*. Hence, if Quirinius or Coponius had named Joazar high priest, Josephus would probably have recorded the fact.[58]

Why did Archelaus reappoint the man whom he had earlier deposed? Again, we do not know, but it may be that he wished to gain the support of a highly influential priest, possibly as a signal to the Romans that he was ruling in a more decisive way.[59] At any rate, one can imagine such a motivation.

It is more difficult to understand why Quirinius would have deposed the high priest who had just proved so helpful in making the census palatable to Judeans. Smallwood surmises that the legate of Syria may have preferred a less influential person in the office.[60] Or, perhaps to appease the radicals associated at that time with Judas the Galilean, Quirinius removed him and replaced him with someone more neutral, someone less closely identified with Rome.[61] Joazar would have been linked with imperial rule by his stand regarding the census, and this could well have earned him the hatred of some factions. At any rate, he had for a time served Roman interests and had thus acted as an aristocrat was expected to behave in the Roman imperial system.[62] He joins Hyrcanus II as the only high priests of the Second Temple who occupied the post, lost it, and regained it only to lose it a second time.

---

58. Smallwood, "High Priests," 20.

59. Horsley, "High Priests," 34; compare Smallwood, "High Priests," 21. She thinks that, at this point in his reign, Archelaus no longer cared about his reputation among his subjects.

60. Goodman, however, sees this as more evidence for his thesis that the high priests were not strong leaders, since Herod, who first named Joazar to the post, purposely appointed nonentities to the position (*Ruling Class of Judaea*, 43–44).

61. Horsley, "High Priests," 21.

62. See ibid., 35. Joazar's distinction of possibly having been appointed and deposed in both 4 BCE and 6 CE has led some scholars to suspect the presence of a doublet in *Antiquities*. Because the two dates involved are also the two at the center of the longstanding debate about the census of Quirinius (ca. 4 BCE according to the time presupposed in Luke 2; 6 CE according to Josephus), attempts have been made to offer a common solution to both. A detailed example is M.-J. Lagrange, "Où en est la question du recensement de Quirinius?" *RB* 8 (1911): 60–84; for a refutation of his arguments, see Smallwood, "High Priests," 18–20. See also Schürer, *History of the Jewish People*, 1.425–26.

33. Ananus Son of Seth/Sethi (6–15 CE)

Quirinius appointed Ananus ("Ανανος) to the office of high priest after completing the liquidation of Archelaus's estate and removing Joazar from the office (*Ant.* 18.2, 1 [§26]), that is, in 6 CE. This is the first recorded case of a governor of Syria making such an appointment. Ananus is a high priest about whom we have information from more than one source; he is mentioned not only by Josephus but also in the New Testament and probably in rabbinic literature.

Ananus took office in 6 CE, as the events associated with his appointment show. In the New Testament, we meet a high priest with a similar name—Annas[63]—who would have been ruling at the same time. So, for instance, in the sevenfold synchronism Luke offers to date the beginning of John the Baptist's public ministry, we read: "In the fifteenth year of the reign of Emperor Tiberius [28–29 CE][64] . . . during the high-priesthood of Annas ["Αννα] and Caiaphas" (3:1-2). Caiaphas was a son-in-law of Annas (see John 18:13); he became high priest (serving from 18 to 36–37 CE) during the procuratorship of Gratus, as we shall see. This Gratus was also the one who was to remove Ananus from office in the year 15 CE (*Ant.* 18.2, 2 [§§34–35]).

Why does Luke refer to "the high-priesthood of Annas and Caiaphas" as if two men shared the sacred office? We do not know the answer, but Fitzmyer states the options thus: "Since there was never more than one high priest at a time, the phrase raises a question again about either the accuracy of Luke's information or of his interpretation. On the other hand, it may have been customary to speak of an ex-high priest as such even when he was already out of office, and Luke may simply be referring to a period when Palestinian Jewry was dominated by two powerful figures."[65] His suggestions seem the most reasonable solution; there is no reason to think that Caiaphas had been removed from office in 28–29 CE (the year meant by Luke's chronological statement) and replaced by his father-in-law. In Luke, we probably have our first indication that a former high priest, perhaps especially one with close family connections to the incumbent, could be called a high priest.[66]

---

63. Below, this high priest is called *Ananus* when dealing with the information Josephus transmits and *Annas* when treating the New Testament reports.

64. A likely way of reading the statement is that Luke reckons from the death of Augustus (August 19, 14 CE) or the Senate vote acknowledging the succession of Tiberius (September 17, 14 CE), but there are other possibilities. See Joseph A. Fitzmyer, *The Gospel According to Luke I–IX,* AB 28 (Garden City, N.Y.: Doubleday, 1981), 455.

65. Ibid., 458.

66. As Raymond E. Brown observed, there are clear cases of this (*The Gospel According to*

Although Josephus reports little about him, other New Testament passages supply more indications that Annas continued to be associated with the
office while his son-in-law held the title of high priest. John 18 notes that he
was involved in the interrogation of Jesus directly after his arrest in the garden.
"So the soldiers, their officer, and the Jewish police arrested Jesus and bound
him. First they took him to Annas, who was the father-in-law of Caiaphas, the
high priest that year" (18:12-13). Annas appears to be the person designated
"the high priest" in the sequel. Simon Peter and the other disciple went into
the courtyard of the high priest because the other disciple was acquainted with
the official. It was there that Peter's denial occurred.

We might think that the interrogation took place before Caiaphas who
was the reigning high priest, but the text of John's Gospel contradicts such an
assumption. While John 18:19 says that the high priest conducted the questioning, verse 24, the last verse of the scene, reports: "Then Annas sent him
bound to Caiaphas the high priest." Hence, in the previous verses (18:19-23),
Annas is the person called the high priest;[67] in fact, Jesus, after he answered
Annas's questions, was struck on the face by a bystander who asked: "Is that
how you answer the high priest?" (v. 22).

The final reference to Annas in the New Testament continues the practice
of calling him the high priest, this time at a late point in the reign of Caiaphas.
As Jesus's disciples Peter and John were addressing a crowd at the temple after
Peter had healed a beggar who had been lame from birth (Acts 3), "the
priests,[68] the captain of the temple,[69] and the Sadducees" (4:1) came to them
and arrested them (4:1-3). "The next day their rulers, elders, and scribes
assembled in Jerusalem, with Annas the high priest, Caiaphas, John, and
Alexander, and all who were of the high-priestly family" (4:5-6). The groups
mentioned in this last passage constituted the Sanhedrin, a term that appears
in 4:15 in connection with this meeting. Hence, Annas and other members of

---

John XIII–XXI, AB 29A [Garden City, N.Y.: Doubleday, 1970], 820–21). We will encounter several of them in Josephus's subsequent narratives.

67. In order to counter this problem, some witnesses to the text of John read 18:24 directly
after 18:13, so that Caiaphas becomes the referent of the term "high priest" in the sequel; see
Brown, *John XIII–XXI*, 821.

68. Some manuscripts read "chief priests" instead of "priests," but this may have resulted
from harmonizing the passage with others in which the chief priests appear with the groups
mentioned here; see Joseph A. Fitzmyer, *The Acts of the Apostles*, AB 31 (Garden City, N.Y.: Doubleday, 1998), 297.

69. The captain of the temple was a very high-ranking officer, apparently the second highest, in the temple administration. The title ὁ στρατηγὸς τοῦ ἱεροῦ corresponds to סגן הכוהנים
in rabbinic literature.

his family were part of the Sanhedrin, as we might expect. Again, Annas seems
to receive the title "the high priest" in deference to his past occupancy of the
office and continued prominence, even at this late date.[70]

Ananus was the first[71] member of his family to hold the high priesthood,
and he was followed in the office by five of his sons (Eleazar, Jonathan,
Theophilus, Matthias, and Ananus) and by one son-in-law (Caiaphas). Josephus commented on the illustrious family when introducing the last of them,
the younger Ananus. "It is said that the elder Ananus was extremely fortunate.
For he had five sons, all of whom, after he himself had enjoyed the office for a
very long period,[72] became high priests of God—a thing that had never happened to any other of our high priests" (*Ant.* 20.9, 1 [§198]). These sons will
be treated in their historical sequence below.

Here, we should notice that the high-priestly house of Ananus may figure
in several rabbinic texts. In *t. Menaḥ.* 13:21, there is preserved a section, with
a parallel in *b. Pesaḥ.* 57a, containing a series of woes pronounced on priests
who took by force what did not belong to them (see 13.18–20):

> Concerning these and people like them and people similar to them
> and people who do deeds like their deeds did Abba Saul b. Biṭnit and
> Abba Yosé b. Yohanan of Jerusalem say, "Woe is me because of the
> house of Boethus. Woe is me because of their staves. Woe is me
> because of the house of Qadros. Woe is me because of their pen. Woe
> is me because of the house of Elhanan [Hanin in *b. Pesaḥ.* 57a]. Woe

---

70. Fitzmyer, *Acts*, 299; Bruce Chilton, "Annas," in *ABD* 1.257. Regarding Annas's role in
Jesus' condemnation in the Gospel of John, Rudolf Bultmann wrote: "Admittedly we know too
little of the events of the years 18–36 [the reign of Caiaphas as high priest] to be able to judge
whether Annas exercised high priestly functions, even though not recognised by the Romans as
High Priest. At all events it is conceivable that his prestige and his influence, even after his deposition, were so great that the community tradition could make him responsible for an event like
the condemnation of Jesus" (*The Gospel of John: A Commentary,* trans. G. R. Beasley-Murray
[Philadelphia: Westminster, 1971], 643 n. 3). Another approach to the problem has been to consider the words "and Caiaphas" in passages such as Luke 3:1-2 and Acts 4:6 as an addition and
the name Caiaphas as an interpolation in John 12 and 18; for a discussion and references to the
literature, see Hölscher, *Hohenpriesterliste,* 22–24. Naturally, this would entail a considerable
change in the generally accepted chronology for Annas and Caiaphas.

71. This is true unless Jesus son of Seë was actually Jesus son of Seth (see above), in which
case he would have been Ananus's brother.

72. It is a pity that Josephus is not more precise here about the length of Ananus's tenure as
high priest. The phrase ἐπὶ πλεῖστον hardly allows one to draw any conclusion regarding the
length of reign that Josephus assigns to him or the New Testament references to him as high
priest during the reign of Caiaphas.

is me because of their whispering. Woe is me because of the house of Ishmael ben Phiabi. For they are high priests, and their sons, treasurers, and their sons-in-law, supervisors, and their servants come and beat us with staves."[73]

The group designated "the house of Elhanan [Hanin]" may be the family of Ananus. If so, they are apparently charged with plotting and resorting to violent actions in taking portions not theirs. Later in Josephus's narratives, we will meet passages in which such incidents occur; presumably, the rabbinic tradition lodges the charge against later members of the family.

The end of Ananus's actual tenure as high priest came at the hands of the new Roman ruler in the area. A short time after becoming prefect of Judea, "Gratus deposed Ananus from his sacred office, and proclaimed Ishmaël, the son of Phabi, high priest" (*Ant.* 18.2, 2 [§34]; see also §33). The appointment of Gratus to his post had come from the emperor Tiberius, apparently not long after the death of Augustus (who died August 19, 14 CE). The process of naming him as prefect and his subsequent journey to Judea to assume office would have taken some time, so that it is unlikely he would have been in a position to remove the high priest until the year 15 CE. Gratus remained as prefect until 26 CE.[74] As Smallwood has suggested, there is no reason for thinking Gratus was dissatisfied with Annas's policy, since he was later to appoint others from his family.[75] It may be that Gratus thought removal of Annas would serve as a visible way of expressing his dominance over his new subjects. Later, we will meet several instances in which a new Roman ruler inaugurated his reign by making a change in the high priesthood.[76]

The tomb in which Annas was buried may have been located. Josephus wrote in *J.W.* 5.12, 2 (§506) about a wall that the Roman general and future

---

73. Neusner, *The Tosefta*, 2.1467–68.

74. In *Ant.* 18.2, 2 (§35), Josephus says that he served for eleven years. See Schürer, *History of the Jewish People*, 1.382.

75. E. Mary Smallwood, *The Jews under Roman Rule: From Pompey to Diocletian. A Study in Political Relations*, 2nd ed., SJLA 20 (Leiden: Brill, 1981), 159; compare her comments about Quirinius on 156.

76. Hölscher suggests that Josephus has an arrangement by content for the period from 6 CE to 37 CE, and, for that reason, appointments and removals of high priests are bunched together at what appear to be the beginnings and ends of the various Roman officials' terms of office (*Hohenpriesterliste*, 14–15). See also the extensive table of the pertinent information in Daniel R. Schwartz, "Pontius Pilate's Appointment to Office and the Chronology of Josephus' *Antiquities*, Books 18–20," in his *Studies in the Jewish Background of Christianity*, WUNT 60 (Tübingen: Mohr/Siebeck, 1992), 188–94 (his chronology for Gratus and Pilate is not accepted here). The data can, nevertheless, be assessed differently as there are exceptions to the pattern.

emperor Titus ordered constructed around Jerusalem during the siege in 70 CE. He says that it circled north of the city, then looped around the east side of Jerusalem before enclosing its southern end where "the line descended into the Valley of the Fountain, beyond which it ascended over against the tomb of Ananus the high priest." The wall then closed the circle by returning to the west side of the city. The area where Ananus's tomb was seems to be the site of the so-called Akeldama tombs, the most elaborate of which is situated in the middle of six others, has a triple entrance, and shows evidence of once having had a masonry façade that rose above the entrances. It has been identified as Ananus's family tomb.[77]

34. Ishmael Son of Phiabi (15–16 CE?)

Almost as soon as we learn that Gratus named Ishmael to be the high priest (the first time that a prefect of Judea appointed a high priest), we read that he removed him. "Not long afterwards he removed him also and appointed in his stead Eleazar, the son of the high priest Ananus" (*Ant.* 18.2, 2 [§34]). Ishmael was the second member of the sons of Phiabi to serve as high priest (see Jesus son of Phiabi above); later we will meet a second high priest by the name of Ishmael ben Phiabi.[78]

35. Eleazar Son of Ananus (16–17 CE?)

Apart from his family name, we learn little more about this Eleazar. He was the second member of the house of Ananus to hold the office of high priest and the first of Ananus's sons to do so. His appointment did not mark a revival of the old hereditary principle, as someone from outside the family served between the father-son pair. Josephus says that Eleazar retained the office for a year before Gratus removed him (*Ant.* 18.2, 2 [§34]).

---

77. See Leen Ritmeyer and Kathleen Ritmeyer, "Akeldama: Potter's Field or High Priest's Tomb?" *BAR* 20.6 (1994): 22–35, 76–78.

78. As we have seen above, *b. Pesaḥ.* 57a // *t. Menaḥ.* 13:21 preserves mention of the house of Ishmael son of Phiabi and accuses them of using their fists. Which of the two Ishmaels so identified is meant we do not know. Also *b. Ber.* 7a says that Rabbi Ishmael ben Elisha had a vision in the innermost place where he went to offer incense. The place in question appears to be the Holy of Holies, into which only the high priest could enter. However, no high priest named Ishmael was the son of Elisha. It may be that one of the Ishmaels ben Phiabi was intended. See Jeremias, *Jerusalem*, 149.

36. Simon Son of Camith (17–18 CE)

Eleazar's successor was no more a permanent presence on the high-priestly throne than he had been. "A year later he [Gratus] deposed him [Eleazar] also and entrusted the office of high priest to Simon, the son of Camith. The last-mentioned held this position for not more than a year and was succeeded by Joseph, who was called Caïaphas. After these acts Gratus retired to Rome, having stayed eleven years in Judaea. It was Pontius Pilate who came as his successor" (*Ant.* 18.2, 2 [§35]). The last two sentences vault over approximately eight years to the time when Pilate replaced Gratus as prefect of Judea (26 CE).

Simon the son of Camith seems to be the שמעון בן קמחית of various rabbinic texts. In *t. Yoma* 3:20 (commenting on *m. Yoma* 7:4), we learn: "Simeon b. Qimḥit went forth to speak with an Arab king, and spit spurt out of his [the king's] mouth and fell on his [Simon's] clothes. His brother went in and served in his stead as high priest. The mother of these [men] witnessed two [officiating] high priests [who were her sons] on the same day."[79] In *y. Yoma* 1:1, 38d and *y. Meg.* 1:12, 72a, which provide the same information, the name of the brother who served as substitute high priest is given as *Judah*.[80] There is some confusion in the texts about who the defiled high priest was because he is called R. Ishmael b. Kimhit in *b. Yoma* 47a, while in other clearly parallel passages, the high priest in question is not named (for example, *b. Nid.* 33b; *t. Nid.* 5:3, in both of which the one who spits on the high priest's clothing is a Sadducee). The unusual feature of this instance of defilement is that it took place on the Day of Atonement itself, not just before it, so that, if we follow *t. Yoma* and *y. Yoma*, two high priests served on the same day.[81]

Josephus's brevity entails that we are ignorant of the reasons that motivated the rapid replacement of high priests early in Gratus's term as prefect.[82] Although she realizes that it is speculative, Smallwood wonders whether a hint of Judean unrest supplied by Tacitus is related to the unsettled state of the lofty office. In *Annales* 2.42, 5, the historian says that when Germanicus[83] was in the

---

79. Neusner, *The Tosefta*, 1.561.

80. The mother is also called קמחית in this passage and she is said to have had seven sons, all of whom served as high priests. See also *y. Meg.* 1:12, 72a; *y. Hor.* 3:5, 47d. This is contrary to the information in the works of Josephus.

81. For other references, see Schürer, *History of the Jewish People*, 2.230 n. 11; Jeremias, *Jerusalem*, 153 n. 24.

82. As noted above, there is nothing to explain if we accept Hölscher's suggestion that the appointments are grouped together for thematic, not chronological, reasons (*Hohenpriesterliste*, 14–15).

83. Germanicus was Tiberius's nephew and adopted son; he had been appointed proconsul and sent to assume control of the eastern part of the empire. On him, see Fergus Millar, *The Roman Near East 31 BC–AD 337* (Cambridge: Harvard Univ. Press, 1993), 53–54.

east in the year 17 CE, "the overburdened provinces of Syria and Judaea" requested from him a reduction in their taxes. "Did the current High Priest encourage, or fail to discourage, the appeal, and so fall under Gratus' suspicion? It is mere conjecture."[84] Germanicus's response to the appeal is not recorded.

37. Joseph Caiaphas (18 to 36–37 CE)

As we have seen, John 18:13 identifies Caiaphas as the son-in-law of Annas (= Ananus).[85] He was therefore the third member of the illustrious family to serve as high priest and, judging by the length of his tenure, the first appointee with whom Gratus was satisfied. Josephus has little to say about him, but his name has become famous because of his part in the trial of Jesus. Also, the tomb of Caiaphas may have been found near Jerusalem.

Caiaphas (see above on Ananus/Annas) is mentioned together with Annas as high priest in Luke 3:2, where the year in question is probably 28–29 CE. John 11:45-53 (without a parallel in the Synoptic gospels) records an incident in which Caiaphas offered advice regarding Jesus during a meeting of Jewish leaders. A council convened when some Pharisees learned that Jesus had raised Lazarus.

> So the chief priests and the Pharisees called a meeting of the council, and said, "What are we to do? This man is performing many signs. If we let him go on like this, everyone will believe in him, and the Romans will come and destroy both our holy place and our nation." But one of them, Caiaphas, who was high priest that year, said to them, "You know nothing at all! You do not understand that it is better for you to have one man die for the people than to have the whole nation destroyed." He did not say this on his own, but being high priest that year he prophesied that Jesus was about to die for the nation, and not for the nation only, but to gather into one the dispersed children of God. So from that day on they planned to put him to death. (John 11:47-53)

Whether this was a formal meeting of *the* Sanhedrin is questionable because the term συνέδριον in verse 47 is not preceded by a definite article (contrary

---

84. Smallwood, *The Jews under Roman Rule*, 160.

85. That he was related to the family of Ananus/Annas is also suggested by Acts 4:6, where he appears to be included in the high-priestly family (compare David Flusser, "Caiaphas in the New Testament," *'Atiqot* 21 [1992]: 82).

to the translation of the NRSV),[86] although in other New Testament passages (for example, Acts 22:30—23:10), chief priests and Pharisees are components of *the* Sanhedrin. Caiaphas is introduced strangely: he is simply one of those present at the meeting and he is said to have been "high priest that year," that is, in the year in which Jesus was executed. But there is no evidence that the high priest's hold on the office had to be reconsidered or confirmed every year. This has led some commentators to conclude that John was simply mistaken about the nature of the high-priestly appointment;[87] others have more plausibly perhaps defended the Johannine statement as meaning something like "in that significant year."[88]

The claim that Caiaphas prophesied, if unwittingly, has also attracted attention.[89] We should recall that the high priest Jaddua saw a dream about the arrival of Alexander in Jerusalem, and Hyrcanus I had the gift of prophecy, according to Josephus—a gift that yielded several accurate predictions. The passage in John has reminded scholars of Philo's explanation of why, according to the Torah, difficult cases were referred to the priests (Deut 17:8-9): "Another possible reason for sending such cases to the priests is that the true priest is necessarily a prophet, advanced to the service of the truly Existent by virtue rather than by birth, and to a prophet nothing is unknown since he has within him a spiritual sun and unclouded rays to give him a full and clear apprehension of things unseen by sense but apprehended by the understanding" (*Spec. Laws* 4.36 [§192]).[90] John seems to be saying that the prophecy was connected with Caiaphas's role as high priest. One could also adduce those passages from the Hebrew Bible in which the *urim* and *tummim* enveloped in the high priest's vestments were thought to have predictive powers, but of course nothing of the sort is said in John 11. Here, Caiaphas was making a realistic political point, yet, for the evangelist, he was unconsciously giving voice to the true nature and significance of Jesus' death.[91]

---

86. See Raymond E. Brown, *The Gospel According to John I–XII*, AB 29 (Garden City, N.Y.: Doubleday, 1966), 440.

87. For example, Bultmann, *John*, 410 n. 10. Others have appealed to passages such as *b. Yoma* 9a, which refers to high priests whose tenure did not last for a full year, or *t. Yoma* 1:6–7, which says that kings appointed high priests every year; such passages, however, are not reliable historical sources and contradict the data in Josephus's history.

88. See Brown, *John I–XII*, 439–40. As he points out, this proposal is found already in Origen's commentary on John (28.12).

89. See Ernst Bammel, "ΑΡΧΙΕΡΕΥΣ ΠΡΟΦΗΤΕΥΩΝ," in his *Judaica et Paulina: Kleine Schriften II*, WUNT 91 (Tübingen: Mohr/Siebeck, 1997), 133–39 for references to related texts.

90. F. H. Colson, *Philo 8*, LCL (Cambridge: Harvard Univ. Press, 1939), 127. See also *T. Levi* 8:2, 15; *Ant.* 3.8, 1 (§192) refers to Aaron's prophetic gift.

91. See Brown, *John I–XII*, 442–43.

The Gospel of Matthew first mentions Caiaphas in 26:3 where "the chief priests and the elders of the people gathered in the palace of the high priest, who was called Caiaphas, and they conspired to arrest Jesus by stealth and kill him. But they said, 'Not during the festival, or there may be a riot among the people'" (26:3-5). This is not said to be an official gathering, say of the Sanhedrin, although it may have been. Later in the same chapter, Caiaphas is present at such a meeting.

Caiaphas makes his best known appearances during the trial of Jesus, although his name is used only in Matthew and John, not in Mark or Luke. In John 18, as we have seen earlier, Jesus was arrested in the garden (after Peter had cut off the right ear of the high priest's servant, 18:10 [also in Matt 26:51; Mark 14:47; Luke 22:50]) and then brought to Annas, identified as "the father-in-law of Caiaphas, the high priest that year" (18:13)—the second time John characterizes Caiaphas as "the high priest that year." In the same passage, Caiaphas is further described as "the one who had advised the Jews that it was better to have one person die for the people" (18:14, recalling 11:47-53). When Annas had completed his interrogation of Jesus regarding his disciples and teaching, he "sent him bound to Caiaphas the high priest" (v. 24). We learn nothing about any action Caiaphas took with Jesus; John says only that "they took Jesus from Caiaphas to Pilate's headquarters" (18:28). These passages articulate the judicial authority and responsibility of the high priest regarding the sorts of religious issues raised by Jesus and those around him.

The version of the story in Matthew 26 also has Jesus arrested in the garden, but, in the first Gospel, his captors bring him directly to the high priest Caiaphas (26:57). The other Synoptic gospels agree, without specifying the name of the high priest (Mark 14:53; Luke 22:54). The people who had assembled there are listed in different sequences in the Synoptics, but the same groups appear in each one: chief priests, scribes, elders, and the (whole) council. That is, at some point *the* Sanhedrin is gathered; all three Synoptics use the definite article, and Matthew and Mark refer to *the whole* Sanhedrin (Matt 26:59; Mark 14:55; Luke 22:52 has "their council").[92] In this meeting of the Sanhedrin, the high priest is the one who conducts the questioning. After witnesses charged Jesus with speaking of destroying the temple and rebuilding it in three days, the

---

92. For the idea that the Sanhedrin was the high priest's *consilium*, not a permanent body that met regularly, see Fergus Millar, "Reflections on the Trial of Jesus," in *A Tribute to Geza Vermes: Essays on Jewish and Christian Literature and History*, ed. P. R. Davies and R. T. White, JSOTSup 100 (Sheffield: JSOT Press, 1990), 378: "when the occasion arose the High Priest called together a group of citizens of his own choosing." See also Goodman, *Ruling Class of Judaea*, 115–16.

high priest stood up and said, "Have you no answer? What is it that they testify against you?" But Jesus was silent. Then the high priest said to him, "I put you under oath before the living God, tell us if you are the Messiah, the Son of God." Jesus said to him, "You have said so. But I tell you, From now on you will see the Son of Man seated at the right hand of Power and coming on the clouds of heaven." Then the high priest tore his clothes and said, "He has blasphemed! Why do we still need witnesses? You have now heard his blasphemy. What is your verdict?" They answered, "He deserves death." (Matt 26:62-66, parallels in Mark 14:60-64; Luke 22:66-71)

For our understanding of the high priesthood, the passage is important. The high priest is clearly the leader of the proceeding. He is not the only one who speaks, but the others are either the nameless witnesses or groups of people. Yet, while his questioning is decisive in moving the interrogation along, he asks the assembled body for its verdict; he does not himself pronounce it. The Sanhedrin declares Jesus worthy of death for blaspheming, as required by Lev 24:10-13 (where stoning is the prescribed method of execution), but they do not carry out the sentence. For that, the decision of Pilate, the prefect, was needed.

The final appearance of the name Caiaphas in the New Testament is in Acts 4, where he again works in connection with the Sanhedrin (the definite article is used, 4:15). As we noticed in the section about Ananus/Annas, Caiaphas is named in 4:6, but Annas is called the high priest. Here rulers, elders, and scribes assemble with members of the high-priestly family and form the Sanhedrin or council. They deliberate the case of Peter and John, who had healed a lame man in the temple and had proclaimed their message about Jesus of Nazareth. The two prisoners were permitted to speak while standing within the assembly, but they were sent outside the Sanhedrin when the leaders debated the case. After their deliberations, they recalled John and Peter and ordered them not to speak or teach in Jesus's name—only to have the two refuse to obey. Yet, we read, the Sanhedrin feared the reaction of the people who had witnessed the visible miracle (4:5-22). Here, no leading role is attributed to the high priest, regardless whether the writer considered Annas or Caiaphas to be the occupant of the office.

The next chapters in Acts contain a few references to the high priest but do not mention his name. The general chronology should entail that the high priest in question would be Caiaphas, but, as the author calls Annas the high priest in Acts 4:6, we cannot be sure of the point. In Acts 5:17-42, there is another confrontation between the apostles and the Sanhedrin in which the high priest plays a part. After the apostles had healed many and the numbers of those who believed in Jesus grew, "the high priest took action;[93] he and all who were with him (that is, the sect of the Sadducees), being filled with jealousy, arrested the apostles and put them in the public prison" (5:17-18).[94] The next day, when the apostles were found preaching in the temple area (Acts 5:19-20 says they had been released by an angel), the high priest and the others summoned them to a meeting of the Sanhedrin (5:21, 27), where the high priest questioned them about their disobeying the council's orders not to preach in the name of Jesus (vv. 27-28). This was the occasion when the Pharisee Gamaliel addressed his fellow members of the Sanhedrin after the apostles were sent outside (vv. 34-39). This time, too, the council recalled the prisoners, and, when they were again in the assembly, subjected them to flogging and repeated their orders to them (v. 40). Here once more, the high priest plays at least an important role as interrogator and as convener of the gathering; he is also associated with the Sadducees but not identified as one.

The high priest acts in a similar way with regard to Stephen. He, too, was brought before the council (see Acts 6:12, 15), where the high priest asked him whether the charges that he spoke against the temple and Mosaic Law were true (7:1). Following Stephen's lengthy response (7:2-53), "they" stoned him (7:58-59). That is, it is not said that this was the judgment issued by the council.[95]

Finally, Saul, later called Paul, is said to have sought from the high priest "letters to the synagogues at Damascus, so that if he found any who belonged to the Way, men or women, he might bring them bound to Jerusalem" (Acts 9:2). The later references to and retellings of the incident say that the chief priests were the ones who gave him the authority to carry out his plan (9:14, 21; 26:10, 12) or attribute the action to both the high priest and the council of elders (22:5-6). Acts 26:10-12 indicates that Saul received such authority, although commentators have often doubted that the high priest (and certainly chief priests) would have had legal control over Jews in the Diaspora.[96] The

---

93. Some Western manuscripts read, not Αναστας, but Αννας, yielding "Annas the high priest." However, the weight of the other manuscript evidence is against these witnesses (see Bultmann, *John*, 643 n. 3; Fitzmyer, *Acts*, 334).

94. Although some have claimed this passage proves that the high priest (here presumably Caiaphas) was a Sadducee (see, for example, Flusser, "Caiaphas," 82, 84), it indicates only that Sadducees on this particular occasion were with the high priest. We never learn whether he belonged to one of the so-called parties, and, if so, which one. Below we will see that the younger Ananus became the first high priest since John Hyrcanus to be explicitly identified as a Sadducee.

95. On the problems raised by the passage, see Fitzmyer, *Acts*, 390–91. Stoning was the prescribed punishment for blasphemy, but Acts does not identify the executioners beyond using "they" for them.

96. In reviewing the evidence, Fitzmyer draws attention to 1 Macc 15:16-21, which says that

time presupposed by the story may be at the end of Caiaphas's reign as high priest, during the short reign of his successor Jonathan, or in the high priesthood of Theophilus, son of Ananus.[97]

Returning to *Antiquities*, Josephus has little to say about Caiaphas. After his appointment, he next names him in connection with his account of Vitellius, who became legate of Syria in 35 CE, and his intervention in local affairs. Just this fact alone—that Caiaphas apparently did nothing that attracted the attention of Josephus's sources from the time of his appointment until the end of his relatively long reign, a time that included at least two crises—is intriguing.[98] He must have been acceptable to Gratus, and his successor as prefect, Pontius Pilate, did not remove him during his reign (26 to 36–37 CE). Josephus's silence about Caiaphas means that the historian fails to mention the high priest during two events in which we might have expected him to play an important part: the large-scale protests that arose when Pilate brought busts of the emperor into Jerusalem (*Ant.* 18.3, 1 [§§55–59]; *J.W.* 2.9, 2–3 [§§169–74]) and when he used funds intended for temple sacrifices to finance an aqueduct (*Ant.* 18.3, 2 [§§60–62]; *J.W.* 2.9, 4 [§§175–77]). In the latter case in particular, it seems the high priest should have had some role as the highest official at the temple.[99] Josephus does not tell us how Pilate managed to procure the funds and whether any Jewish official permitted the transfer; we learn only that he used them and that his action sparked a protest. What Caiaphas may have done during the crisis, we do not know.

The end of Pilate's tenure as prefect resulted from one of several protests against his heavy-handed ways. After he had sent his troops to Mount Gerizim, where an armed crowd had gathered to follow up the mountain a leader

the Romans gave the high priest Simon the right to extradite fugitives from foreign regions; he is not certain such a right would have extended to Jews of the Diaspora (*Acts*, 423).

97. Ibid., 422–23, 139. He suggests either Caiaphas or Jonathan.

98. See Goodman, *Ruling Class of Judaea*, 46; he takes the high priest's absence from these stories as evidencing the Jews' failure to have confidence in their leaders; instead of depending on them to mediate the crises, they tried to handle the situations themselves.

99. In *J.W.* 2.9, 4 (§175), Josephus calls it "the sacred treasure known as *Corbonas*," that is, קרבן. Smallwood (*The Jews under Roman Rule*, 163 n. 65) adduces *m. Sheqal.* 4:2 in this context. It says that from what remained in the sheqel chamber, various projects could be funded, including the wall of the city, its towers, and other communal needs. She concludes that the offense may have been Pilate's taking the funds without the approval of Jewish authorities or his taking more than the surplus mentioned in the Mishnah. She (p. 163) and others have considered it possible that Luke 13:1 refers to Pilate's response to the protest, but see Fitzmyer, *Luke X–XXIV*, 1006–7, who finds the suggestion unconvincing. On Pilate's handling of the crises during his reign and his depiction in Philo, Josephus, and the Gospels, see B. C. McGing, "Pontius Pilate and the Sources," *CBQ* 53 (1991): 416–38, esp. 428–38.

who claimed he would show them the sacred vessels Moses had deposited there, a battle ensued and a number of the crowd were killed. Later, Pilate imprisoned many of the participants and executed their leaders. In protest, members of the Samaritan council formally accused him before Vitellius.[100] Vitellius ordered Pilate to Rome to give the emperor an accounting of his actions and replaced him with someone named Marcellus. Pilate's reign in Judea, says Josephus, lasted ten years (26 to 36–37 CE). The time when Pilate was sent to Rome would have been in late 36 (possibly early 37) CE, because the emperor Tiberius (14–37 CE) died before Pilate reached the capital city (*Ant.* 18.4, 1–2 [§§85–89]).[101]

The end of Caiaphas's reign as high priest soon followed when Vitellius himself came to Jerusalem—at the time of Passover, says Josephus. The great man enjoyed a splendid reception and responded by remitting certain taxes on agricultural products. He also won Jewish favor by his dealing with the high-priestly vestments (see below). "After he had bestowed these benefits upon the nation, he removed from his sacred office the high priest Joseph surnamed Caiaphas, and he appointed in his stead Jonathan, son of Ananus the high priest. Then he set out on the journey back to Antioch" (*Ant.* 18.4, 3 [§95]).

The precise chronology of Pilate's departure from Judea and, by implication, Vitellius's appointment of a new high priest has been a disputed point because of some problems in Josephus's presentations. Smallwood, among others, has devoted a study to the issue and has formulated a plausible solution. Her argument runs this way.[102]

Vitellius made two visits to Jerusalem according to Josephus.

1. *Antiquities* 18.4, 3 (§90–95): At the Passover after he had dismissed Pilate, he allowed the high-priestly vestments to remain in Jewish custody, and he removed Caiaphas from his office.
2. *Antiquities* 18.5, 3 (§§120–24): At a traditional festival of the Jews, he stayed three days and then deposed the next high priest Jonathan (on him see below). On the fourth day, he received the news that the emperor Tiberius had died, an event that occurred on March 16, 37 CE.

---

100. These Samaritan leaders said the group had been trying to escape Pilate's persecution (*Ant.* 18.4, 2 [§88]).

101. The date of Tiberius's death was March 16, 37 CE. For the evidence indicating that Pilate left Judea in 36 CE, see Smallwood, *The Jews under Roman Rule*, 171–72, and also the discussion below.

102. E. Mary Smallwood, "The Date of the Dismissal of Pontius Pilate from Judaea," *JJS* 5 (1954): 12–21. See also her *The Jews under Roman Rule*, 171–72.

Some scholars have understood the two visits to have occurred on Passover of 36 CE and Passover of 37 CE, but this does not harmonize with two other pieces of information about Pilate: he *hurried* to Rome after Vitellius sent him there, and yet, by the time he reached Rome, Tiberius was dead (*Ant.* 18.4, 2 [§89]). If Pilate had left Judea around the time of Passover in 36 CE (in April), he would have dallied for about a year if he did not reach the capital until shortly after the emperor's death in March 37. But, Josephus says he hurried, so he clearly did not wait for a long time. Smallwood concludes (after adducing evidence for how long the trip to Rome took in the winter—at least three months), that Pilate departed Judea most probably in mid-December of 36 CE.

She adduces another item that further limits the options. Caiaphas's successor as high priest, Jonathan, after he was removed from office, was offered the position a second time some years later. He, however, declined the honor, saying, "I am content to have put on the holy vestments once" (ἅπαξ; *Ant.* 19.6, 4 [§314]). She understands "once" not to mean that he had served one term as high priest[103] but in the sense that he had worn the vestments just one time, that is, at just one festival (they were used at the three pilgrimage holidays and the Day of Atonement). If Caiaphas had been removed from the high priesthood shortly after Pilate left Judea (when Vitellius first came to Jerusalem) and Jonathan had officiated at only one festival when the robe would have been worn, that festival must have been the Passover of 37 when Vitellius came for his second visit.

Smallwood thinks Josephus made a mistake in linking Vitellius's first visit and hence Caiaphas's removal with a festival, but he did so for an understandable reason. The historian actually describes the first visit twice:

- *Antiquities* 15.11, 4 (§405, in the time of King Herod), where the history of the high-priestly vestments is told and Josephus allows himself to glance ahead to the time of Vitellius. Here, he says that when the Jews asked his permission to have custody of the vestments, Vitellius wrote to Tiberius about the matter, and Tiberius replied granting their request. No festival is mentioned.[104]

---

103. This seems a more natural understanding of the expression, but Smallwood's suggestion actually works well in the chronology of Jonathan's short high priesthood.

104. In *Ant.* 15.11, 4 (§§403–9), he dealt with the Baris, the strong citadel that Hyrcanus I had built north of the temple and where he normally lived. There, he says, the Hasmoneans kept their own high-priestly vestments, and Herod (who renamed the citadel Antonia after Antony) and the first Roman rulers of the area continued the policy. At that point in *Antiquities* 15, Josephus also described the procedure followed for the robe: it was kept under the high priest's and treasurers' seal; the treasurers would, with the Roman commander's permission, fetch it one day before a festival; and they would return it to its place under their seal directly after the holiday.

- *Antiquities* 18.4, 3 (§§90–95, the paragraphs mentioned above), in which Vitellius, at a Passover, simply granted the priests the right to have the vestments in their custody.[105]

Smallwood makes the sensible suggestion that Josephus confused two separate events: (1) Vitellius's first visit, which did not coincide with a festival: on this occasion the Jews requested the vestments and he wrote the emperor about the matter; and (2) Vitellius's second visit, at a Passover, when he was able to grant their request, having heard from the emperor in the meantime.

She infers therefore that this was the chronology:

- December of 36 CE: Pilate is dismissed by Vitellius
- 36–37 CE: Vitellius's first visit, dismissal of Caiaphas, and letter to the emperor about the vestments (no festival was involved)
- April of 37: Passover, Vitellius's second visit, dismissal of Jonathan, and granting of the request for the vestments.

The chronology offers a reasonable explanation of the data in Josephus. As a result, the reign of Caiaphas ended in the last days of 36, possibly in the first days of 37 CE.[106]

He adds that, after the change under Vitellius, Jewish control of the vestments continued until the time of King Agrippa I (king of Judea 41–44 CE).

105. Here, Josephus explains: "Seven days before each festival the vestments were delivered to the priests by the warden. After they had been purified, the high priest wore them; then after the first day of the festival he put them back again in the building where they were laid away before. This was the procedure at the three festivals each year and on the fast day. Vitellius was guided by our law in dealing with the vestments, and instructed the warden not to meddle with the question where they were to be stored or when they should be used" (*Ant.* 18.4, 3 [§§94–95]).

106. Compare Ernst Bammel, "Pilatus' und Kaiphas' Absetzung," in his *Judaica: Kleine Schriften I*, WUNT 37 (Tübingen: Mohr/Siebeck, 1986), 51–58. This economical solution, though it is not without problems, commends itself more than Otto's thesis that Josephus created a doublet when he combined two sources that spoke of one event—Vitellius's visit to Jerusalem at Passover of 37 CE (*Herodes*, 192–94, n.; Hölscher, without elaboration, accepted Otto's arguments, *Hohenpriesterliste*, 15–16). Otto, after reviewing the evidence and Josephus's procedure in this part of *Antiquities*, suggested that Josephus, following his principle of arrangement, mentions Vitellius's single visit twice: once while describing events in Judea, and the other time in connection with the Arabian campaign. He did recognize that his solution encountered a problem: Josephus mentions the removal of two high priests with different names in connection with Vitellius's visit(s) to Jerusalem—a circumstance suggesting two separate occasions. He was unable to counter the difficulty, proposing only that there were different traditions about the time when the two brothers-in-law were appointed. Daniel R. Schwartz has attempted to resurrect Otto's solution and to handle the problem it encountered; he has tried also to deal with the additional difficulty that two occasions are implied because at one point Vitellius wrote a letter

Josephus does not explain why Vitellius removed Caiaphas after he had held the office for an unusually long time. He also does not say explicitly that deposing the high priest was meant to be another benefit conferred on the nation by the great legate, though the order of the passage may imply that. At any rate, it was not disapproval of the high-priestly family that motivated the change, as Vitellius named a brother-in-law of Caiaphas as his replacement.

It may be that ossuaries of the family of Caiaphas have been found by archeologists. In the Peace Forest in the northern Talpiot area of Jerusalem, Zvi Greenhut excavated a burial cave in 1990.[107] In it were twelve ossuaries, six of which were untouched; in ossuary 8 was a coin dating from the sixth year of Agrippa (42–43 CE).[108] Among these six ossuaries were two bearing what may be the name of Caiaphas. One (number 6) of these has two inscriptions:

יהוסף בר קיפא (Jehoseph the son of qyp')

יהוסף בר קפא (= Jehoseph the son of qp')

Ossuary 3 reads just קפא. The skeletons of two infants, a toddler, a teenager, a young adult female, and a man in his sixties were found in the ossuary. Since Josephus says that Caiaphas's name was Joseph, the name on the ossuary may well be that of the high priest.[109]

---

to the emperor and only at a later time could he have received and acted on the reply from him ("Pontius Pilate's Suspension from Office: Chronology and Sources," in his *Studies in the Jewish Background of Christianity*, WUNT 60 [Tübingen: Mohr/Siebeck, 1992], 202–17). After an extended study of possible sources at this point in *Antiquities*, he concludes that Josephus himself was responsible for inserting the names of the two high priests after he had finished writing the narrative ("If Josephus returned to his narrative, sometime after composing it, he may well have forgotten that the two accounts refer to the same visit" [213]). So the historian simply added the names and thus confused his readers. Obviously, that is possible, but it is a weak solution to the difficulty with Otto's and Schwartz's thesis. As for the problem of the delay between Vitellius's writing Tiberius and receiving his answer, Schwartz simply asserts that *Ant.* 15.11, 4 (§405) was wrong about his writing a letter. *Antiquities* 18.4, 3 (§§90–95) does not mention the correspondence, but this is hardly strong reason for saying there was none and thus eliminating a problem.

107. Greenhut, "The 'Caiaphas' Tomb in North Talpiyot, Jerusalem," *'Atiqot* 21 (1992): 63–71; compare Ronny Reich, "Ossuary Inscriptions from the 'Caiaphas' Tomb," *'Atiqot* 21 (1992): 72–77; Joe Zias, "Human Skeletal Remains from the 'Caiaphas' Tomb," *'Atiqot* 21 (1992): 78–80; Greenhut, *The Akeldama Tombs: Three Burial Caves in the Kidron Valley, Jerusalem*, IAA Reports 1 (Jerusalem: Israel Antiquities Authority, 1996).

108. Greenhut, "The 'Caiaphas' Tomb," 70. Agrippa became king in 38 CE, although his territory then did not include Judea.

109. See Hillel Geva, "Jerusalem, Tombs," in *NEAEHL* 2.756; Craig A. Evans, "Caiaphas Ossuary," in *Dictionary of New Testament Background*, ed. C. A. Evans and S. E. Porter (Downers Grove, Ill.: InterVarsity, 2000), 179–80.

The case for the identification is not certain because, of course, the vocalization of קפא or קיפא is unknown and, if it is the name Caiaphas, the man in question could have been another Caiaphas. Also, the very reading of קיפא is in dispute, with some preferring to read a *vav* rather than a *yod* (that is, קופא). Since the form without a *vav* or *yod* is found twice, and the spelling with *vav* or *yod* just once, one could argue that all three instances attest the same pronunciation: Qepha or Qopha. However, the situation is complicated by the fact that New Testament witnesses are not unified in their spelling of the name *Caiaphas*: Codex Bezae, P[45], and a number of Latin copies read or reflect Καιφας.[110] Does this perhaps suggest a shorter and a longer pronunciation of the name or are other linguistic forces the cause of the difference? While the finds date from the first century CE, the absence of the term כהנא (priest) from the ossuaries and the poor character of the tomb have also been adduced as arguments against identifying it as the final resting place of the high priest.[111] However, the place where the ossuaries were found is an argument in favor of the identification with the high priest Caiaphas. Hence, while we cannot be sure, there is a decent chance that the ossuaries attest the name of the high priest Caiaphas (see further, below, on the name *Cantheras*).

38. Jonathan Son of Ananus (36 or 37 CE)

Vitellius removed Ananus's son-in-law Caiaphas from the high priesthood in 36–37 CE and named his brother-in-law Jonathan in his place (*Ant.* 18.4, 3 [§95]). After narrating the appointment, Josephus does not mention Jonathan's activities as high priest in his histories, other than to record the end of his official role a short time later. When Vitellius had received orders from Tiberius to attack Aretas, the king of Petra, he marched out with two legions supported by auxiliary troops and advanced toward Petra. His route would have taken him and the army through Jewish territory, a prospect that brought a deputation of high-ranking Jews to the enlightened legate. They objected that their tradition did not allow on their land the sorts of images on Roman military standards. Quite unlike Pontius Pilate,

---

110. BDF §37, p. 20. For a thorough discussion, see William Horbury, "The 'Caiaphas' Ossuaries and Joseph Caiaphas," *PEQ* 126 (1994): 36–38. He prefers the pronunciation Qopha for the name on the ossuaries and does not think the high priest Caiaphas is meant (40–41). Reich, after his review of the evidence, thinks the name is that of Caiaphas ("Ossuary Inscriptions from the 'Caiaphas' Tomb," 74–76).

111. Émil Puech, *La croyance des Esséniens en la vie future: Immortalité, résurrection, vie éternelle?* 2 vols., EBib 21-22 (Paris: LeCoffre, 1993), 1.193–95.

[y]ielding to their entreaty, he abandoned his original plan and ordered his army to march through the Great Plain, while he himself with Herod the tetrarch [= Antipas] and his friends, went up to Jerusalem to sacrifice to God during the traditional festival which the Jews were celebrating there. When he arrived there, he was greeted with special warmth by the Jewish multitude. He spent three days there, during which he deposed Jonathan from his office as high priest and conferred it on Jonathan's brother Theophilus. On the fourth day, when he received a letter notifying him of the death of Tiberius, he administered to the people an oath of loyalty to Gaius. (*Ant.* 18.5, 3 [§§122–24])

We might expect that the removal of a high priest would be precipitated by something of which the legate disapproved. So, for example, we might wonder whether Vitellius disliked some aspect of the way in which the standards issue was handled by the new high priest. As we will see, however, in the case of this Jonathan there is another possibility. Some years after he had left office and during the brief reign of Agrippa I as king over Judea (41–44 CE), we meet him again. Agrippa appointed several high priests, one of whom was "Simon son of Boethus, surnamed Cantheras" (*Ant.* 19.6, 2 [§297]; on him see below). When the king wished to remove him from office, he "proposed to restore it to Jonathan the son of Ananus, conceding that he was more worthy of the honour" (19.6, 4 [§313]). The former high priest's reaction to the offer was remarkable.

Jonathan, however, regarded the resumption of such an honour as unwelcome and declined it in the following words: "I rejoice, O king, to be honoured by you, and heartily appreciate this high prize offered me by your will, although God has adjudged me in no way worthy of the high priesthood. But I am content to have put on the holy vestments once,[112] for then I arrayed myself in them with more regard for sanctity than would be shown if I were to take them back.[113] But if

---

112. As we saw when dealing with Caiaphas and the date of his removal from office, Smallwood thinks this phrase means that Jonathan wore the vestments at just one pilgrimage festival ("The Date of the Dismissal of Pontius Pilate from Judaea," 16). It seems more likely that it means he had once been high priest, but, as a matter of fact, he does seem to have presided at a single holiday and thus to have had a very short term of office.

113. We do not know what is meant here, though it is possible the passage casts aspersions on the idea of resuming the office after being removed from it (as Joazar had regained it after he was deposed).

you desire that another, worthier than I, should receive the honour,
be instructed by me. I have a brother, pure of all sin against God and
against you, O king. Him I recommend as suitable for the honour."
(*Ant.* 19.6, 4 [§§313–15])

The passage has led Smallwood to think it possible Jonathan asked to be
replaced also when he held the office.[114]

He did not become high priest a second time, but Jonathan, understandably for an ex-high priest, did exercise considerable influence in subsequent
years. Some time later, when Cumanus was procurator (ca. 48–52 CE), a violent conflict erupted between Samaritans and Jews from Galilee, one that
began when some Jews were traveling through Samaritan territory to
Jerusalem for a festival and one of them was killed (*J.W.* 2.12, 3 [§§232–33]).
The deadly incident later was to involve Jonathan. In the aftermath of the first
conflict and following reprisals and Cumanus's ineffective handling of the crisis, leading Samaritan officials approached Ummidius Quadratus, who was
the governor of Syria. "The Jewish notables, including the high-priest
Jonathan, son of Ananus, also presented themselves, and maintained that it
was the Samaritans, by the murder in question, who had originated the disturbance, but that the responsibility for all that ensued lay with Cumanus for
refusing to take proceedings against the assassins" (*J.W.* 2.12, 5 [§240]). Later,
Quadratus "sent up to Caesar, along with two other persons of the highest
eminence, the high-priests Jonathan and Ananias [on him, see below],
Ananus, the son of the latter, and some other Jewish notables, together with
the most distinguished of the Samaritans" (*J.W.* 2.12, 6 [§243]).[115]

The same Jonathan from the family of Ananus was to prove influential in
an imperial appointment. According to *Ant.* 20.8, 5 (§§162–64), he met his
death because of his virtue and powerful position.

Felix [procurator from ca. 52–60 CE] also bore a grudge against
Jonathan the high priest because of his frequent admonition to
improve the administration of the affairs of Judaea. For Jonathan
feared that he himself might incur the censure of the multitude in

---

114. *The Jews under Roman Rule*, 173. The John who is mentioned directly after Caiaphas
in Acts 4:6 as a member of the high-priestly family may well have been our Jonathan (see
Fitzmyer, *Acts*, 299–300, who lists the manuscripts that read *Iōnathas* here).

115. The parallel in *Ant.* 20.6, 2 (§131) is quite different in that it says the Jewish leaders
around Ananias the high priest and the captain Ananus were sent to Rome in chains. Here, Josephus does not mention Jonathan. In §132, he refers to other Jewish and Samaritan leaders who
were sent to Rome but apparently not in chains; again Jonathan is not mentioned.

that he had requested Caesar [Claudius] to dispatch Felix as procurator of Judaea. Felix accordingly devised a pretext that would remove from his presence one who was a constant nuisance to him; for incessant rebukes are annoying to those who choose to do wrong. It was such reasons that moved Felix to bribe Jonathan's most trusted friend, a native of Jerusalem named Doras, with a promise to pay a great sum, to bring in brigands to attack Jonathan and kill him. Doras agreed and contrived to get him murdered by the brigands in the following way. Certain of these brigands went up to the city as if they intended to worship God. With daggers concealed under their clothes, they mingled with the people about Jonathan and assassinated him. (20.8, 5 [§§162–64]; see also *J.W.* 2.13, 3 [§256])[116]

So this Jonathan, like Ananus before him, remained a powerful figure well after his tenure as high priest, and, also like Ananus, continued to be called *the high priest,* though another held the office.

Schwartz has suggested what may have been King Agrippa's reasoning in wishing to replace Simon son of Cantheras with Jonathan. He has noted the good relations that the family of Ananus had with the Roman governors, with Jonathan being appointed by Vitellius, the legate of Syria. This Vitellius was a friend of the emperor Claudius. "It is reasonable, moreover, to suppose that Jonathan had some link with Pallas, Felix's brother, who was a very influential advisor of Claudius: such a connection could explain both Jonathan's access to Claudius and his recommendation of Felix, of all people, to the position. And it is just as reasonable for Agrippa, who knew what Rome was like, to prefer to have someone like that on his own side, as it were, by appointing him to the high priesthood."[117] The entire episode shows us a noble Jewish priest in close

---

116. Goodman (*The Ruling Class of Judaea*, 144–46) thinks that Ananias son of Nedebaeus (high priest from 48–59 CE) was behind the execution of Jonathan. When the two of them were sent to Rome (*J.W.* 2.12, 6 [§243]), "Jonathan may have achieved something of a political coup, for, by arranging that the next procurator should be the ex-slave Felix, he seems to have ensured that he (Jonathan) should be guaranteed a special place in his counsels (cf. *A.J.* 20.162 on his frequent advice to Felix). It would not be surprising if Ananias in retaliation and jealousy contrived to have Jonathan put out of the way by murder, particularly if he had also lost the high priesthood on Felix's arrival as governor." This is, as he realizes, quite conjectural and not directly supported by Josephus. We shall return to such issues in dealing with Ananias below. The fact that the account in *J.W.* 2 does not blame Felix for the assassination led Smallwood to think it implied Jonathan was killed because of his pro-Roman stance ("High Priests and Politics in Roman Palestine," 24–25). See Horsley, who also prefers the earlier account in *War* ("High Priests," 42–43).

117. *Agrippa I,* 71. He understands the king's reaction to Jonathan as showing that, while he often presented himself as Herod's successor and not as an official of Rome, he was not entirely

contact with the highest levels of the Roman administration and, in this case, coming to ruin because of it.

39. Theophilus Son of Ananus (37–41 CE)

When he removed Jonathan from office, Vitellius appointed his brother Theophilus to take his place (*Ant.* 18.5, 3 [§123]). Since the letter announcing the death of Tiberius arrived the next day, we have sound reason for thinking that Theophilus began to serve as high priest in 37 CE. In this way, the fifth member of the Ananean family took the office, so that their hold on the position ran, with two short exceptions, throughout the first decades of the Roman province *Judaea*: 6–15 CE (Ananus), 16–17 (Eleazar), 18 to 36–37 (Caiaphas), 36 or 37 (Jonathan), 37–41 (Theophilus).

Josephus gives us no additional information about this Theophilus other than the notice about his removal by King Agrippa I, a grandson of Herod the Great. When Agrippa, after a remarkable change in fortune, gained the throne of part of Herod's kingdom (but not Judea), he arrived in Palestine to take over his territories in 38 CE. Later, he was in Rome while the crisis caused by Caligula's wish to have his statue placed in the Jerusalem temple was being negotiated.[118] When Claudius became emperor in 41 CE, he enlarged Agrippa's territories in response to Agrippa's support of him. It was at this time that Agrippa received Judea and Samaria into his kingdom and thus control of Jerusalem with its temple. When he returned to his kingdom, he entered Jerusalem and went to the temple, where he offered sacrifices of gratitude. He also presented a gold chain to be hung over the treasure chamber in the temple—a chain given to him by Gaius Caligula equal in weight to the one that had bound him when the future king was a prisoner during Tiberius's reign (*Ant.* 19.6, 1 [§§292–96]). "Having thus fully discharged his service to God,

---

wedded to Herodian precedents. In appointing a member of Ananus's family as high priest, he was following Roman practice (see 69–71). On Jonathan and Pallas, see also Goodman, *The Ruling Class of Judaea*, 148.

118. Amazingly, the high priest is not mentioned in the stories about the Jewish response to Gaius's order that a statue of him as Zeus be installed in the temple in Jerusalem. As Smallwood comments, "this event should have been of deeper concern to the High Priests than any other in the century" ("High Priests and Politics in Roman Palestine," 23; compare Horsley, "High Priests," 38–39). Smallwood draws the reasonable conclusion that Jonathan, the former high priest, and Theophilus, the incumbent high priest, were among the leaders of the Jews to whom, according to Philo, Petronius the legate of Syria communicated the emperor's order (see *Embassy* 31.222 where he mentions that priests were among them).

Agrippa removed Theophilus son of Ananus from the high priesthood and bestowed his high office on Simon son of Boethus, surnamed Cantheras" (*Ant.* 19.6, 2 [§297]).

The statement sounds simple enough, but Schwartz has formulated a case for antedating Agrippa's removal of the high priest Theophilus from 41 CE, when Claudius added Judea to his holdings, to 38 CE when he was first appointed king over Herod Philip's and Lysanius's former territories.[119] He thinks that Josephus confused these two arrivals of King Agrippa, something that would have been easy for the historian to do, especially for events so similar and so close together in time.[120] In support of his thesis Schwartz gives four arguments.

First, the gold chain that Gaius Caligula had given to Agrippa and which commemorated his unjust imprisonment and rise to power would make more sense if the king had contributed it shortly after his release (that is, in 38 CE) rather than three years later (in 41). Moreover, a gift to the temple from Gaius would have been unthinkable after the statue crisis (that is, in 41), whereas there would have been no such concern in 38, before the incident.

Second, the man whom Agrippa appointed high priest, Simon Cantheras, seems to be the Simon the Just, who is said to have heard a voice from the Holy of Holies announcing the death of Caligula and the annulment of his decrees (see *b. Soṭ.* 33a; *t. Soṭ.* 13.6; *y. Soṭ.* 9.14, 24b; scholion to *Megillat Taʿanit* 22 Shebat [though Simon is not mentioned here]). If so, he was appointed high priest (note, the voice comes from the Holy of Holies where only the high priest could go) *during* Caligula's reign, not *after* it.

Third, Agrippa appointed Silas commander over his entire army. This Silas had shared Agrippa's troubles in the past, meaning apparently ones during Tiberius's time, that is, no later than 37 CE when Tiberius died. This appointment, too, would make more sense in 38 than in 41.

And fourth, since there was no governor in Judea between 37 and 41 CE (that is, after Pilate was removed and before Agrippa became king of the area), "it is not surprising that Agrippa would have been entrusted with some authority with regard to the Holy City and the Temple, although they were not within his kingdom."[121]

---

119. Schwartz, *Agrippa I*, 11–14.

120. Thus he finds Josephus committing an error the opposite of what he did for Vitellius's one (according to Schwartz) visit: here he makes two incidents into one, whereas there he turned one into two.

121. *Agrippa I*, 13. His argument that there was no prefect between 37 and 41 CE is on pp. 62–66.

Although Schwartz's case is plausible, it is improbable primarily because of the point he mentions in his fourth argument: Agrippa did not rule Judea and hence Jerusalem until the year 41 CE and for that reason he probably had no control over the high priesthood before that year. Schwartz thinks he would have been given such influence in 38 when there was no prefect in Judea, but Josephus never says that. It makes far more sense of Josephus's narrative to place Agrippa's removal of a high priest at a time when he was king over Jerusalem. If there was no prefect in the years 37–41 CE (and this is quite possible), the legate of Syria would more likely have been the one to appoint and remove high priests, as Vitellius had done. Schwartz's first argument is inconclusive: Agrippa may have waited to present his gift until he became king of Judea, and the gift was from him, not directly from Gaius.[122] Also, the appointment of Silas could well have been conditioned by the increase in Agrippa's domains; at any rate, his previous service to Agrippa would not make either 38 or 41 a more likely time for his appointment. In sum, Josephus's sequence of events is more likely than the one Schwartz defends.[123]

The act of replacing the reigning high priest, then, seems to have taken place as soon as Agrippa reached Jerusalem in 41 CE. He thus joins a list of several rulers (Quirinius, Gratus) who made such changes upon assuming office. A man named Matthias the son of Theophilus was to become high priest just before the revolt against Rome broke out (see below); whether he was a son of our Theophilus we do not know.

The name of this little-known Theophilus has been found in an inscription on the ossuary of his granddaughter Yehoḥanah. The text of the inscription has both Aramaic and Hebrew words.[124]

יהוחנה‎

יהוחנה ברת יהוחנן‎

בר ‎[125]תפלוס הכהן הגדל‎

---

122. Kokkinos suggests that "the golden chain of Caligula may adequately be explained as a kind of 'compensation' offered by Agrippa for the ex-emperor's attempted evil deed" (*Herodian Dynasty*, 283; see 282–84 for his refutation of Schwartz's arguments).

123. It is, of course, precarious to use a story in rabbinic texts as historical evidence in the absence of confirmation from Josephus or a similar source. There is no suggestion elsewhere that Simon Cantheras was considered Simon the Just, who seems to have been a high priest centuries earlier as we have seen.

124. Dan Barag and David Flusser, "The Ossuary of Yehoḥanah Granddaughter of the High Priest Theophilus," *IEJ* 36 (1986): 39–44.

125. Barag and Flusser indicate that the letter read as *tav* is uncertain; it looks much like a *ḥet* ("The Ossuary," 40 n. 6). But, if their drawing is accurate, it is clearly different from the other instances of *ḥet* in the inscription. Also, there is no high priest whose name would have the letters חפלוס‎.

"Yehoḥanah, Yehoḥanah, the daughter of Yehoḥanan the son of Theophilus the high priest." In this case, it is clear from Josephus's list of high priests that the title must apply to Theophilus, not to his son יהוחנן, as no high priest by that specific name served in the first century. As a result of the new evidence we may know the names of two of Theophilus's sons: Jehoḥanan the father of Yehoḥanah, and Matthias who became high priest (if the latter was indeed son of our Theophilus).[126]

40. Simon Cantheras Son of Boethus (41–42 CE)

This Simon, whom Josephus identifies as a son of Boethus, was Agrippa's choice as the new high priest when the king began to reign over Judea.[127] We had earlier encountered a Simon son of Boethus who reigned throughout a lengthy stretch of Herod's kingship (24–22 to 5 BCE) and was the monarch's father-in-law. Around the end of Herod's reign, Joazar son of Boethus held office (at least in 4 BCE) and resumed it later (at least in 6 CE); he was followed after his first term by his brother Eleazar son of Boethus (4 BCE). So, this second Simon son of Boethus was the fourth member of the family to become high priest, with the other three having served during Herod the Great's reign. The fact that the others were in office during the time of Herod has led Schwartz to conclude that Agrippa, in replacing a member of the Ananean family with one of Boethus's descendants, was "making a point: Agrippa was announcing, in so many words, that he was Herod's heir, not a Roman official."[128]

---

126. Derenbourg (*Essai*, 210–15) placed another high priest between Theophilus and the next high priest—Simon. *B. Pesaḥ.* 57a and 88b mention a certain Issachar of Kefar Barkai in a context of other high priests. Derenbourg thought Josephus omitted him from the list so as not to offend Agrippa II by writing how his father, Agrippa I, had punished a high priest by cutting off his hands for an act of disrespect to the monarch. There is no reason for accepting this reconstruction, which conflicts with Josephus's presentation.

127. That Josephus says Agrippa appointed Simon when he came to Jerusalem as king renders unlikely Schwartz's suggestion that Simon is the high priest of the story about Stephen in Acts 6–7. Schwartz, with others, has noted that no governor figures in those chapters and thus posits that the time in question was the period 39–41 CE when Agrippa was absent. Upon his return, he would have learned about Simon's unauthorized arrogation of power in executing Stephen and removed him (*Agrippa I*, 71–73). But Josephus, far from saying he removed him, writes that he appointed him. His removal came later. Schwartz's position is tied to his unconvincing arguments, surveyed above, that *Ant.* 19.6, 1–3 (§§292–99) relates to Agrippa's supposed arrival in Jerusalem in 38 CE, not his arrival in 41 with which Josephus connects the section. See *Agrippa I*, 11–14.

128. *Agrippa I*, 70. He thinks Agrippa's appointment of Silas as commander of his army probably points in the same direction.

Josephus did not leave the matter of Simon's important family connections to be inferred by the reader; rather, he detailed the members of the family and commented on the distinction they enjoyed. Directly after reporting Simon's appointment, he wrote: "Simon had two brothers and his father Boethus [whose][129] daughter was married to King Herod, as I explained earlier. Simon accordingly, as did his brothers and father, obtained the high priesthood, repeating the record of the three sons of Simon son of Onias under the Macedonian rule, as we reported in an earlier account" (*Ant.* 19.6, 2 [§§297–98]). It is interesting that the historian speaks in this way about the family of Simon; here, he repeats his earlier inaccurate understanding of the family connections of the high priests Onias III, Jason, and Menelaus.

Josephus's detailed statement about the family connections of the new high priest "Simon son of Boethus, surnamed Cantheras" has received a considerable amount of scholarly attention. The reasons are understandable because the statement is not without problems, impinges on interpretation of other statements in the *Antiquities*, and may relate to important priestly names, including that of Caiaphas.

As noted above, Josephus refers to our Simon (we will call him Simon *b*) as the son of Boethus, whose daughter was Herod's wife. We know from earlier passages (and Josephus refers us to them) that the father of Herod's wife was named *Simon son of* Boethus (for example, *Ant.* 15.9, 3 [§§320–22]), not *Boethus*. That Simon, who was clearly not our Simon (we will call this earlier high priest Simon *a*), was the father of Mariamme II and served as high priest from 24–22 to 5 BCE. Why then does Josephus say that Simon *b* was a son of Boethus, not a son of Simon *a*? If we make one simple assumption, we can explain Josephus's confusing statement in *Antiquities* 19: instead of "and his father Boethus whose daughter was married to King Herod," Josephus should have written (and perhaps he did): "and his father *Simon the son of* Boethus whose daughter was married to King Herod." The extant text may have resulted from a simple mistake of copying: in a context in which the names *Simon* and *Boethus* are used several times, an additional instance of *Simon* has fallen from the text.

If the suggested change is made, then the Boethean family members—a father and three sons, all four of whom were high priests—to which Josephus refers are:

---

129. Feldman's translation, which reads "Simon's" here, harmonizes this passage with Josephus's earlier references to Simon son of Boethus as father of Mariamme II. The text, however, places a relative pronoun after the name *Boethus*, suggesting that, here, Boethus is considered the father of Herod's wife.

- Simon *a* (he is identified as a member of the family of Boethus)
- Joazar (identified as a member of the family of Boethus)
- Eleazar (identified as Joazar's brother)
- Simon *b* (identified as a member of the family of Boethus)

This solution is doubly appealing, because it is economical and forms an exact parallel to the other case that Josephus cites in this passage: this Simon resembled the earlier Simon (Simon II) whose three sons followed him in office.

This simple emendation has not commended itself to all scholars. Schwartz[130] thinks that, while this one correction can solve the immediate issue, it does not explain other references in *Antiquities*. First, *Ant.* 17.6, 4 (§164), in narrating the change of high priests from Matthias the son of Theophilus (5–4 BCE) to Joazar, refers to the latter as "his wife's brother Joazar." We should recall that Schwartz understands this to mean that Joazar was the brother of Matthias's wife, not the brother of Herod's wife Mariamme II. We have also seen that his interpretation of the passage should be rejected and that the more likely reading is that Joazar was Mariamme's brother, both of whom are identified as belonging to the family of Boethus (something not said of Matthias's wife who is not mentioned elsewhere and whose family connections are unknown).

Second, there are some passages in which this Joazar is called "the son of Boethus," not "the son of Simon son of Boethus." One of these, *Ant.* 17.13, 1 (§339), immediately precedes the statement that his successor Eleazar was his brother. Schwartz thinks, on the basis of this paragraph, that both Joazar and Eleazar were, like Simon *a*, sons of Boethus and thus brothers. Here, we should object that calling Joazar a son of Boethus need mean no more than that he belonged to the house of Boethus.[131]

A third point noted by Schwartz is a chronological difficulty: if Simon *a* had a daughter (Mariamme II) of marriageable age in about 24–22 BCE, is it likely that a son of his would be appointed high priest more than sixty years later? Even Schwartz realizes this would be possible, since Josephus does not tell us when Simon *b* was born. For all we know, Simon *a* continued to have children after his daughter and Herod were married. This difficulty, though, has led others (for example, Smallwood) to posit that Simon *b* was more likely a son of one of the men whom they believe to be Simon *a*'s younger

---

130. *Agrippa I*, Appendix III: "Simon Cantheras and the Boethus Family," 185–89.

131. See, for example, Menahem Stern, "Social and Political Realignments in Herodian Judaea," *The Jerusalem Cathedra* 2 (1982): 52 with n. 83.

brothers—Joazar or Eleazar.[132] If one made such an assumption, however, it would not harmonize with Josephus's claim in *Ant.* 19.6, 2 (§§297–98) that he was talking about a father and his three sons. We learn nothing about any sons Joazar or Eleazar may have had and certainly nothing about sons of theirs who became high priests.

Schwartz moves from such evidence to treat the surname Cantheras (Κανθηρᾶς ἐπίκλησις) that Josephus gives to Simon *b*. Later, as we will see, the historian refers to another high priest whose name was Elionaeus the son of Cantheras (43–45 CE; τὸν τοῦ Κανθηρᾶ παῖδα [*Ant.* 19.8, 1 (§342)]). The form of the father's name given here is attested by the Latin version of *Antiquities*, while the Greek manuscripts favor Κιθαίρου;[133] however, in 20.1, 3 (§16), the same man is "surnamed Κανθήραν." So, we may be fairly sure that his surname or father's name was something resembling Cantheras.[134] To these references in Josephus, we should add *m. Parah* 3:5, which mentions among those high priests who prepared a red heifer Eliehoenai ben Hakkof, with a variant Hakayyaf (הקוף or הקיף). The relevance of this item is that the paternal name, if we accept the second reading which is actually that of the best manuscripts,[135] seems to be the name *Caiaphas*, with the ending expressed in this more familiar spelling being the Aramaic determined form paralleling the Hebrew definite article in HaQ-Qayyaph. If the names Cantheras and Caiaphas are thus associated, then Joseph, surnamed Caiaphas (the high priest from 18 to 36–37 CE), Simon *b*, and Elionaeus were all members of the house of Boethus, yet somehow connected with that of Ha-Qayyaph/Caiaphas.[136]

From all of these bits of data and inferences, Schwartz arrives at a solution. On his view, the unnamed wife of Matthias son of Theophilus had three brothers, all of whom became high priests: Simon *a*, Joazar, Eleazar (the father

---

132. Smallwood, "High Priests and Politics in Roman Palestine," 33–34. As noted before, she too drew the erroneous conclusion that Joazar was a brother of Matthias's wife.

133. This reading and the fact that *b. Pesaḥ.* 57a mentions the houses of Boethus and Catheras (= קתרוס) separately could entail that Cantheras (somehow related to the family of Boethus) and Cithras/Cathras were names of different families. See M. Stern, "Social and Political Realignments," 55.

134. For some of the evidence, see Feldman, *Josephus 9*, 376 with notes.

135. R. Brody, "Caiaphas and Cantheras," Appendix IV in Schwartz, *Agrippa I*, 190. Kokkinos (*The Herodian Dynasty*, 220–21) considers the possibility that Eliehoenai was a high priest from the pre-Herodian period because of the sequence of names in *m. Parah* 3:5, where his name is followed by that of Hanamel and Ishmael ben Phiabi. While that is possible, it would involve positing a high priest whom Josephus does not mention—not a recommended procedure.

136. For a more detailed treatment of the names mentioned in this paragraph, see below on Elionaeus.

The High Priests in the Herodian Age (37 BCE to 70 CE)   447

of all four was Boethus). Simon *b* was the son of Matthias and his wife, as was Elionaeus; the older brother of Simon *b* and Elionaeus was Joseph surnamed Caiaphas. If so, then Josephus's statement about a father and three sons occupying the high priesthood holds true:

Matthias
Joseph surnamed Caiaphas
Simon *b*
Elionaeus

Even a quick glance at Schwartz's theory shows it has virtually nothing on which to stand and contradicts several statements in Josephus.[137] First, as we have seen, he is probably wrong in thinking that Joazar was the brother of Matthias ben Theophilus's wife. Hence, there is no evidence she was from the family of Boethus. Just this simple conclusion destroys Schwartz's thesis, because Josephus explicitly connects each member of the family about which he wrote in *Ant.* 19.6, 2 (§§297–98) with the house of Boethus. Second, Josephus was talking about a *Simon* who had three sons, not about a *Matthias* who had three sons. The names Schwartz proposes do not fit. Third, Josephus never mentions that Matthias and his wife had sons who became high priests; if the family produced three such sons, it is likely he would have mentioned that important fact as he does in the case of the Boethus and Ananus families. Fourth, if Joseph surnamed Caiaphas of New Testament notoriety was the son of a high priest and was related to high priestly families on both his father and mother's side, would this item not have found its way into the text of Josephus, who in fact discloses nothing about his family connections?

In short, there seems no point in creating an elaborate scenario without support in Josephus and directly contradicting explicit statements in *Antiquities* when one simple change produces a clear statement in *Ant.* 19.6, 2 (§§297–98). The high priests Josephus deals with there are most likely Simon *a*, the father, and his three sons, Joazar, Eleazar, and Simon *b*. Below (under Elionaeus) we will approach the issue of the name *Cantheras*.

The specific deeds of Simon's high priesthood receive no mention in Josephus's books. As with several other high priests in this period, he records only Simon's appointment and his removal. We saw above that at some point King Agrippa saw fit to remove Simon from office and wished to replace him with the former high priest Jonathan the son of Ananus (*Ant.* 19.6, 4 [§313]).

---

137. For another firm rejection of Schwartz's conjectures, see Kokkinos, *Herodian Dynasty,* 219–21.

Jonathan, however, declined, and suggested that the king name his brother
Matthias (§§314–15). At any rate, that was the end of Simon's reign.

41. Matthias Son of Ananus (42–43 CE?)

With the installation of Matthias, a sixth member of Ananus's family assumed
the office of high priest. The fact that his brother Jonathan had nominated
him (*Ant.* 19.6, 4 [§§313–15], citing his purity before God and the king) is
another indication of Jonathan's ongoing influence in high places. Just after
noting Matthias's appointment, Josephus gives us a chronological peg for the
date of his assumption of office: he says that not long after this, Marsus
replaced Petronius (the man who had been instrumental in the crisis about
the emperor's statue) as legate in Syria. A probable date for Marsus's appointment is the year 42 CE.[138]

The next mention of Matthias is the notice about his removal, which
comes in the context of the stories about Agrippa's two conflicts with Rome.
The first resulted from the king's work in fortifying the walls of Jerusalem. His
efforts attracted the attention of Marsus, the legate of Syria, who notified the
emperor; Claudius in turn ordered Agrippa to desist from his project (*Ant.*
19.7, 2 [§§326–27]). The other incident was the assembly of client kings that
Agrippa organized in Tiberias in Galilee; again, Marsus was suspicious about
the intent of such a gathering and ordered the kings to return home (19.8, 1
[§§338–41]). Immediately after relating this story, Josephus writes: "Agrippa
felt very much hurt by this and henceforth was at odds with Marsus. He also
deprived Matthias of the high priesthood and appointed Elionaeus the son of
Cantheras to be high priest in his stead" (19.8, 1 [§342]). It may be that, in the
Antiquities, Josephus has reversed the order of the events, since in *War* he
claims that Agrippa's death stopped the wall project (2.11, 6 [§219];[139] but see
J.W. 5.4, 2 [§152] where he says that Agrippa stopped after laying the foundations, out of fear that Claudius would suspect what he intended). Whatever
the historical order may have been, does Josephus imply that Matthias's
removal was related to international events in which the legate of Syria
checked Agrippa's ambition?[140]

---

138. Louis H. Feldman, *Josephus* Vol. 9, *Jewish Antiquities Books 18–19,* LCL (Cambridge:
Harvard Univ. Press, 1965), 363 n. c; Schürer, *History of the Jewish People,* 1.263.

139. Schwartz, *Agrippa I,* 137, where he does not mention the passage in *War* 5, although he
does deal with it later (140–41).

140. Josephus mentions a Matthias, whom he calls τὸν ἀρχιερέα, in *J.W.* 4.9, 11 (§574).
However, this man was not our high priest, because later Josephus identifies this person (referring to the same incident of his asking Simon to enter Jerusalem during the revolt) as claiming

42. Elionaeus Son of Cantheras[141] (43?–45 CE)

The new high priest may have been a son or possibly a brother of the high priest Simon surnamed Cantheras; if so, he was yet another member of the family of Boethus who rose to the rank of high priest. In Josephus's history, however, he joins several other high priests in receiving no more notice than the report of his installation and of his dismissal.

The high priesthood of Elionaeus is the proper place in which to explore the meaning of the name *Cantheras* that Josephus specifies as his patronym. We should recall that he was not the first high priest to be associated with the name; Simon son of Boethus (= Simon *b*), the man who served as high priest before Elionaeus's immediate predecessor, had the name attached to him, although he is also said to have belonged to the house of Boethus. What does the name *Cantheras* signify when used together with the family name *Boethus* or without it, and what does it imply about family relations?

The name of the little-known Elionaeus also occurs in the Mishnah. It is so unusual (no other high priest had it) that when *m. Parah* 3:5 refers to a high priest with this name, it almost certainly intends the same man. There, we read that among those high priests who had prepared a red heifer was "Eliehoenai the son of Hakkof" (אֱלִיהוֹעֵינַי בֶּן הַקּוֹף). Although this is the reading of the editions, the superior reading in the manuscripts is אֱלִיהוֹעֵינִי בֶן הַקָּיָף.[142] The last word, which also appears with a single *yod*, is probably the Semitic form behind the name Καϊάφας in the New Testament and Josephus (note that it too has the definite article attached).[143] As a result, the one high priest Elionaeus is further defined by both the names Caiaphas and Cantheras, which are in turn also attested for Joseph surnamed Caiaphas and for Simon son of Boethus surnamed Cantheras (Simon *b*).

In addition, it is possible that *Cantheras* is reflected in a priestly name mentioned in *b. Pesaḥ.* 57a where, in a passage pronouncing woes on various

---

high-priestly ancestry. There, he calls him a son of Boethus (*J.W.* 5.13, 1 [§§527–31]), whereas our Matthias was from Ananus's house. The usage of τὸν ἀρχιερέα for one only of high-priestly lineage, not the high priest himself, is unusual. The Matthias of this passage is also not the second-to-last high priest Matthias, because Josephus clearly distinguishes the two of them in *J.W.* 6.2, 2 (§114).

141. The manuscripts read *Cithaerus*, while *Cantheras* comes from the Latin version; however, *Ant.* 20.1, 3 (§16) gives the name as *Cantheras* (see Feldman, *Josephus 9*, 376 n. a).

142. Brody, "Caiaphas and Cantheras," 190–91.

143. Horbury, "The 'Caiaphas' Ossuaries and Joseph Caiaphas," 37–40; Brody, "Caiaphas and Cantheras," 191–92. See also Derenbourg, *Essai*, 215; he thought Elionaeus was the high priest who presided over the proceedings that led to the death of James and the imprisonment of Peter in Acts 12:2-3.

high-priestly houses, one is called בֵּית קְתרוֹס (read בֵּית קְדרוֹס in the parallel in *t. Menaḥ.* 13:21). The talmudic spelling, if correct, would yield the form *Catheras*, which may underlie the other spelling of Elionaeus's patronymic, Cithaerus.[144] A form that appears to be the same name has also been found on a sherd discovered in the Burnt House in Jerusalem; the first-century CE inscription reads: דבר קתרס[(=]of the son of Qathros).[145]

Returning to Elionaeus, how can the same person be both son of Cantheras (so Josephus) and son of Caiaphas (so the Mishnah)? Brody has offered a detailed account of how this could have happened. He thinks that the two—Cantheras and Caiaphas—are actually the same name in different languages. After establishing that הקייף is the correct reading in *m. Parah* 3:5 and that the form should be vocalized *haq-qayyāph* (the vowel pattern indicates a person who belongs to a certain profession), he relates it to the noun קֻפָּה (*quppah*), meaning "basket." Thus a *qayyāph* is a basket person—either a maker of them or one who uses them to carry things. Brody does mention the problem that the term קֻפָּה is not related to the same triconsonantal root as הקייף (*qpp* vs. *qwp* or *qyp*), but he thinks that such a transfer between closely related roots is quite plausible in the spoken language. It is, however, a question mark that should be placed next to his proposal.

Cantheras he considers to be a Greco-Latin name and thinks it may represent either κανθήλια or κανθήλιος: the former means "pack-saddle"; the latter "pack-ass" (the definitions are from LSJ). Such an association assumes an l/r interchange (Canthel- and Canther-), which would not be impossible. But, he also adduces the Latin name Cant(h)erius = ass, mule. "κανθήλιος and cantherius do not basically refer to certain animals, but rather to the practice of using them as beasts of burden which carry baskets for this purpose."[146] If *Cantheras* is related to this word and if *Caiaphas* means porter, the two names have very similar meanings. With such a semantic overlap and with the same person (Elionaeus) being called both, a reasonable inference is that one of the names is a translaton of the other. He suggests that the Semitic form *qayyāph* is a rendering of Cantherius.[147]

---

144. Schwartz, *Agrippa I*, 187–88.

145. A photograph of the stone weight can be seen in Nahman Avigad, "Jerusalem: Burnt House (Area B)," *NEAEHL* 2.734. His transcription indicates that the *dalet* must be restored, but part of it is visible. A similar but not identical name has surfaced on a sherd from Masada: בת קתרא (Yigael Yadin and Joseph Naveh, *The Aramaic and Hebrew Ostraca and Jar Inscriptions*, Masada I: The Yigael Yadin Excavations 1963–1965, Final Reports [Jerusalem: IES, The Hebrew Univ. of Jerusalem, 1989], 22 n. 405 and pl. 22).

146. "Caiaphas and Cantheras," 194–95.

147. It seems unlikely that קוֹפאי or קפאי, a priest from the unknown Meqoshesh, in *t. Yebam.* 1:10 // *b. Yebam.* 15b, has the same name as הקייף. Horbury wishes to associate the two

Brody's argument is impressive and appealing, but whether it is convincing is another matter. For example, it is not at all certain that the name *Caiaphas* means *porter,* because of the problem with the triconsonantal root mentioned above but also because the word is not attested in Hebrew or Aramaic. In addition, we have to recall that the mishnaic passage is not free of problems: in the very same context as the one in which Eliehoenai the son of *Haq-qayyāph* appears, we meet Hanamel the Egyptian, which seems a mistake for Hananel the Babylonian (see under Ananel above).[148]

The uncertainties make it difficult to draw any firm conclusions. At least we may say there is good reason for saying that *Cantheras* is the name of a priestly house. It is possible that we should relate the names as Brody does and place Caiaphas, Simon *b,* and Elionaeus in a family tree. Possibly Simon and Elionaeus were sons of Joseph surnamed Caiaphas.[149] Or, if the names are not related, Elionaeus could have been a son or brother of Simon *b.* Why the name *Cantheras* (if it is not equivalent to *Caiaphas*) should have been applied to them is not known. At any rate, the evidence does not allow us to follow Schwartz's lead.[150] He thinks that Matthias son of Theophilus (high priest from 5–4 BCE) belonged to the family of Cantheras and that he had three sons who became high priest (see above on Simon *b*). While they received the name Cantheras from their father, their mother contributed the name Boethus. Hence, Simon *b* could be called both a son of Boethus and one surnamed Cantheras. We have, however, had opportunity to note that Josephus never relates this Matthias to a house of Cantheras and that Matthias's wife was probably not from the family of Boethus.

("The 'Caiaphas' Ossuaries and Joseph Caiaphas," 39), but see Brody, "Caiaphas and Cantheras," 191 n. 5. If the name is not the same, there is no basis for claiming, as M. Stern does, that Caiaphas's home town was Meqoshesh ("Aspects of Jewish Society: The Priesthood and Other Classes," in his *The Jewish People in the First Century,* 2.584; so also Flusser, "Caiaphas in the New Testament," 81).

148. See Horbury, "The 'Caiaphas' Ossuaries and Joseph Caiaphas," 40, 43.

149. M. Stern thinks that Elionaeus was his son ("Social and Political Realignments in Herodian Judaea," 55; so also Flusser, "Caiaphas in the New Testament," 81), and that the family of Cithaerus, the spelling in some manuscripts of *Antiquities,* was different from the family of Cantheras. For this latter point, he is able to cite *b. Pesaḥ.* 57a, which names both the house of Boethus and the house of Catheras (קתרוס). If Simon *b* was from the house of Boethus and surnamed Cantheras, this house was not the same as the house of Catheras/Cithaerus. The reading *Cantheras* in some places with respect to Elionaeus he regards as a corruption influenced by that very name. Yet if, as Schwartz thinks, the names Boethus and Cantheras are the correct ones, the talmudic passage need not be a problem because the two names, both used for Elionaeus, could point to the fusion of two high-priestly families.

150. *Agrippa I,* 186–89.

Elionaeus remained in office beyond the death of King Agrippa in 44 CE. Although he is not mentioned by name in connection with it, during his tenure as high priest there was another change in policy regarding the splendid vestments that only the chief pontiff could wear. Josephus relates that during the procuratorship of Cuspius Fadus (44–46? CE),[151] the first such official after Agrippa's death, the new ruler advised a change of policy for safeguarding the high-priestly garments. For some time, the Jews had maintained control over them—an agreement mediated by Vitellius, the legate of Syria, as we have seen. After Fadus had restored order by forcibly settling a dispute between the Pereans and the people of the city of Philadelphia, he "sent for the chief priests and the leaders of the people of Jerusalem and advised them to deposit the full-length tunic and the sacred robe, which it was the custom for the high priest alone to wear, in Antonia, which is a fortress. There they were to be entrusted to the authority of the Romans, as in fact they had been in times past" (*Ant.* 20.1,1 [§6]). Fadus's advice led Jewish leaders, who dared not oppose him, to request permission to send a delegation so that the matter could be adjudicated by the emperor. Fadus and Longinus, the ruler in Syria, agreed to their petition.[152]

The delegation went to Rome where King Agrippa's young son, later to be known as Agrippa II, helped them win Claudius's approval. The emperor communicated his decision in the form of a letter, which is recorded in *Ant.* 20.1, 2 (§§11–14). The information in that letter allows us to date it to the year 45 CE.[153] So, the custody of the vestments reverted to the Jews, in line with the precedent set by Vitellius (as Claudius noted).

Immediately after this, we read that Herod, the brother of Agrippa I and then the king of Chalcis (in the area of Lebanon), "asked Claudius Caesar to give him authority over the temple and the holy vessels and the selection of the high priests—all of which requests he obtained. This authority, derived from him, passed to his descendants alone until the end of the war [the revolt of 66–70 CE]. Herod accordingly removed the high priest surnamed Cantheras from his position and conferred the succession to this office upon Joseph the son of Camei" (*Ant.* 20.1, 3 [§§15–16]).

The fact that the deposed high priest is here said to be "surnamed Cantheras [τὸν ἐπικαλούμενον Κανθήραν]" rather than named "Elionaeus the son of Cantheras" as in *Ant.* 19.8, 1 (§342) has led to speculation that Josephus

151. For the dates, see Schürer, *History of the Jewish People,* 1.455.
152. The potential for trouble raised by Fadus's suggestion caused Longinus to come to Jerusalem with troops to prevent a violent Jewish reaction.
153. See Louis H. Feldman, *Josephus* Vol. 10, *Jewish Antiquities Book 20, General Index,* LCL (Cambridge: Harvard Univ. Press, 1965), 9 n. g, where he gives June 28 as the exact date.

may have omitted mention of the appointment of a high priest who had suc-
ceeded Elionaeus. Also, in *Ant.* 3.15, 3 (§§320–21) Josephus refers to a certain
Ishmael, who was high priest during the famine that occurred in the reign of
Claudius. Was there an Ishmael who was high priest after Elionaeus and who
was then the person said to be surnamed Cantheras and who was deposed by
Herod of Chalcis?

The famine in question occurred around the time of Agrippa I's death,[154]
and the removal of this high priest also happened at about that time. No less
an expert on the chronology of the period than Kirsopp Lake concluded that
Josephus had in fact neglected to mention the investiture of this Ishmael, surnamed Cantheras.[155] However, that seems a more complicated solution than
the slender evidence warrants. *Cantheras* could indeed have been a surname
of Elionaeus, since he belonged to this family; also, in *Ant.* 3.15, 3 (§320), it is
likely that Josephus wrote an incorrect name. There are two possibilities:
either he wrote *Claudius* when he should have written *Nero* (an Ishmael
became high priest during the time of Nero);[156] or, he wrote *Ishmael* when he
should have written *Elionaeus*. The latter is more likely because the point of
the story that Josephus tells in the passage in *Antiquities* 3 is that a famine was
in progress, and we know that there was a severe one in the time of Claudius,
not in Nero's reign.[157]

43. Joseph Son of Camei (45–48 CE)

The new high priest Joseph belongs to the growing list of high priests whose
names are noted only when they were appointed and deposed. The
patronymic is spelled in several ways in the manuscripts at *Ant.* 20.1, 3 (§16);
the ones that read Καμυδος, Καμοιδι, Κεμεδι, or Κεμεδη raise the possibility

---

154. For the date, see Schürer, *History of the Jewish People*, 1.457, especially n. 8. Jeremias,
however, argues for a later date for the famine—during the procuratorship of Tiberius Julius
Alexander (46–48 CE); see *Jerusalem*, 142. The debate centers upon the proper reading in *Ant.*
20.5, 2 (§101): ἐπὶ τούτοις as in all the manuscripts, or ἐπὶ τούτου, as in the Epitome. If, as is
reasonable to think, the manuscript reading is preferable, then Josephus, by writing the plural
demonstrative, would be placing the famine in the time of both Fadus and Tiberius Julius
Alexander, thus reporting that it began before the latter assumed office.

155. Lake, "The Chronology of Acts," in *The Beginnings of Christianity, Part I: The Acts of
the Apostles,* ed. F. Foakes-Jackson and K. Lake, 5 vols. (London: Macmillan, 1920–33), 5.455.

156. So H. St. J. Thackeray, *Josephus 4,* 474–75, n. a.

157. For more on this issue, see below. Jeremias (*Jerusalem*, 143), who puts the famine
between 46 and 48 CE, thinks that in *Antiquities* 3, Josephus incorrectly wrote *Ishmael* when he
should have used the name of one of his two predecessors, Joseph or Ananias.

that he belonged to the same family as Simon son of Camith (high priest in 17–18 CE).[158] This must remain uncertain, however, because of the variant forms in the Greek witnesses.

This Joseph remained high priest for only a few years. At some point while Tiberius Julius Alexander was procurator (46–48 CE), Herod of Chalcis removed his priestly appointee Joseph. The immediate context in which Josephus mentions the transfer of the office is suggestive but not specifically tied to the change. James and Simon, sons of Judas the Galilean who had led a revolt when Quirinius was taking his census in 6 CE, were crucified at the procurator's orders. Immediately after reporting this, Josephus writes: "Herod, king of Chalcis, now removed Joseph, the son of Camei, from the high priesthood and assigned the office to Ananias, the son of Nedebaeus, as successor" (*Ant.* 20.5, 2 [§103]). The events that the historian mentions in the following two sentences (20.5, 2 [§§103–4]) allow us to suggest a date for the end of Joseph's reign: Cumanus succeeded Tiberius Julius Alexander as procurator (in 48 CE), and Herod of Chalcis died in the eighth year of Claudius's reign (it included part of 48 CE).[159]

Hanan Eshel has suggested that Joseph son of Camei is mentioned in 4Q348 (4QDeed B heb?), a documentary text published by Ada Yardeni.[160] The extant parts of this badly damaged text, paleographically dated to later in the Herodian period (some point in the first century CE), contain mostly names, a number of which are well attested among priestly families. In line 13, Yardeni reads four midline circlets (they indicate the presence of illegible bits of ink) followed by וס כוהן גדול and three more midline circlets. She suggests that the three letters before *samekh* could be read as *waw* (as in the transcription), *yod*, and *dalet* or *resh*, that is, the word/name would be ר/דיוס, although she found no high-priestly name in the first century CE that would fit these letters. Eshel proposes that we read קומ]ודיוס, that is, Cam]ydus.[161] This is possi-

---

158. So Derenbourg, *Essai*, 230; Schürer, *History of the Jewish People*, 2.231 n. 16.

159. For the dates, see Schürer, *History of the Jewish People*, 1.458.

160. Hannah M. Cotton and Ada Yardeni, eds., *Aramaic, Hebrew, and Greek Documentary Texts from Naḥal Ḥever and Other Sites*, DJD 27 (Oxford: Clarendon, 1997), 300–303, with pl. LVIII.

161. Hanan Eshel, "4Q348, 4Q343, and 4Q345: Three Economic Documents from Qumran Cave 4?" *JJS* 52 (2001): 133. While Yardeni does not think the text comes from Qumran, Eshel thinks it does (p. 134). Yardeni was unable to determine whether the relevant part of 4Q348 belonged to the date formula, but Eshel interprets it this way and believes the text "proves that some people dated deeds according to the high priests' service. It can be assumed that these were Jews who were scrupulous in not using the years of the reign of Roman emperors when dating their documents" (133, where he cites *b. Giṭ.* 80a in support of this view). H. Cotton and E. Larson have now accepted Eshel's reading of the name ("4Q460/4Q350 and Tampering with Qum-

ble, although the various spellings of the name in the manuscripts of *Antiquities* require some hesitation about the identification. It is also not impossible that the next high priest's paternal name is reflected here.

44. Ananias Son of Nedebaeus (48–59 CE)

Ananias, the final high-priestly appointee of Herod of Chalcis, has left a larger legacy in the literature than did most other high priests of the age. We read about his activity already early in his relatively long reign, when he became involved in the violent dispute between Galilean Jews and Samaritans that resulted, Josephus says, from a Samaritan attack on Jewish pilgrims passing through their territory to celebrate a festival in Jerusalem. *Antiquities* says that many Galileans died, while some copies of *War* say that only one was killed (*Ant.* 20.6, 1 [§118]; *J.W.* 2.12, 3 [§232]). Cumanus, who was no stranger at this time to controversies with the Jewish people, handled the affair poorly in the eyes of many. He is supposed to have been bribed by the Samaritans (*Ant.* 20.6, 1 [§119]) and eventually attacked Jewish people with troops. Only persuasive intervention by unnamed leaders in Jerusalem quieted the incensed Jews and induced them and their brigand supporters to disperse (§§120–24; see *J.W.* 2.12, 4–5 [§§234–38]). Samaritan leaders then approached Ummidius Quadratus, governor of Syria, and asked him to punish the Jews who had caused such harm in their territory. A Jewish delegation also waited on him; among them was, as we saw earlier, the former high priest Jonathan the son of Ananus (*J.W.* 2.12, 5 [§240]; *Ant.* 20.6, 2 [§127] does not mention him by name). The Jewish delegates laid the blame at the feet of Cumanus.

Quadratus later appears to have determined that the Samaritans were at fault, but he executed the prisoners of both sides taken by Cumanus and others whose guilt he had ascertained. In *J.W.* 2.12, 6 (§243), Josephus says that Quadratus "sent up to Caesar, along with two other persons of the highest eminence, the high-priests Jonathan and Ananias, Ananus, the son of the latter, and some other Jewish notables, together with the most distinguished of the Samaritans." The account in *Antiquities* is parallel to this one but contains some important differences: "As for the high priest Ananias and the captain Ananus and their followers,[162] he put them in chains and sent them up to

---

ran Texts in Antiquity?" in *Emanuel: Studies in Hebrew Bible, Septuagint, and Dead Sea Scrolls in Honor of Emanuel Tov*, ed. S. Paul, R. Kraft, L. Schiffman, and W. Fields; VTSup 94 [Leiden: Brill, 2003], 118).

162. The translation may be misleading here. Josephus does not write that Ananias and Ananus were among those sent to Rome in chains but says: τοὺς δὲ περὶ Ἀνανίαν τὸν ἀρχιερέα

Rome to render an account of their actions to Claudius" (20.6, 2 [§131]).
Here, Josephus does not mention the ex-high priest Jonathan and adds that
the Jewish leaders were put in chains. Both accounts could be accurate, with
War simply omitting an embarrassing detail such as the chains. It is evident,
though, that Quadratus held Ananias and his son, who seems to have occupied
the second highest position in the temple hierarchy (that of סגן),[163] with other
eminent folk, responsible for the actions of those Jews who had taken up arms
to settle their dispute with the Samaritans.[164] They had failed to keep them in
check and now had to answer to the emperor for their misrule, as did
Cumanus himself, the tribune Celer, and the Samaritan officials.

Josephus records that Claudius, heavily influenced to do so by young
Agrippa, found the Samaritans to be at fault, executed their representatives,
banished Cumanus, and sentenced Celer, the tribune, to a gruesome death
(*J.W.* 2.12, 7 [§§245–46]; *Ant.* 20.6, 3 [§§134–36]). To replace Cumanus,
Claudius dispatched Felix to serve as procurator (52–60 CE) at the behest of
the former high priest Jonathan (see above), presumably when Jonathan was
in Rome with the delegation of Jewish leaders.

Despite all of this, Ananias managed to keep his high office, since we meet
him in the Book of Acts during the procuratorship of Felix. When the apostle
Paul returned to Jerusalem after what is known as his third journey, he was
arrested on the charge that he had defiled the temple by bringing Greeks into
it (Acts 21:28). After he was endangered by a Jewish crowd, the tribune
Claudius Lysias arrested him. Paul was allowed to address the crowd but was
later brought to the Sanhedrin, which the tribune, who had learned about
Paul's Roman citizenship, had convened in order to discover the nature of the
accusation against him (see Acts 22:30). Paul, who was standing, began to
address the council with a peculiar result:

> "Brothers, up to this day I have lived my life with a clear conscience
> before God." Then the high priest Ananias ordered those standing
> near him to strike him on the mouth. At this Paul said to him, "God
> will strike you, you whitewashed wall! Are you sitting there to judge
> me according to the law, and yet in violation of the law you order me
> to be struck?" Those standing nearby said to him, "Do you dare to

---

καὶ τὸν στρατηγὸν Ἄνανον δήσας. Thus, Quadratus dispatched those around or of the party of
these two leaders, not necessarily the leaders themselves (see Smallwood, "High Priests and Politics in Roman Palestine," 24 n. 2).

163. See Feldman, *Josephus 10*, 70–71 n. c.
164. See Horsley, "High Priests," 40–41.

insult God's high priest?" And Paul said, "I did not realize, brothers, that he was high priest; for it is written, 'You shall not speak evil of a leader of your people.'" (Acts 23:1-5)

Commentators have pointed out a number of improbabilities in the scene: would a tribune have been able to convene the Sanhedrin; how could Paul not have recognized the high priest? Such problems can be addressed satisfactorily.[165] We have no evidence that the tribune was unable to summon the Sanhedrin, and Paul's lengthy travels may well have kept him from knowing who was high priest at the time.[166] At least, he may not have known him by sight, and the high priest would not have been wearing his special garments for a meeting of the council. So, he would not have been identifiable in that way. The high priest's action of ordering Paul to be slapped is not explained (although see John 18:22), but it may be noteworthy that the text says nothing about Paul's having been given permission to speak. Perhaps he spoke out of turn, without leave from the council. However this may be, once more the high priest appears to be in charge of a session of the Sanhedrin.

The scene at the Sanhedrin, where Paul succeeded in dividing the assembly by appealing to belief in the resurrection of bodies, which he shared with the Pharisees and which the Sadducees rejected, was not to be his last encounter with the high priest Ananias. Soon after, we read about a plot against Paul's life in which the chief priests and the council were supposed to be involved (Acts 23:12-15); eventually Paul was spirited away by centurions and brought to Felix in Caesarea (23:23-35). "Five days later the high priest Ananias came down with some elders and an attorney, a certain Tertullus, and they reported their case against Paul to the governor" (Acts 24:1). A trial followed in which Tertullus spoke for the prosecution and Paul was allowed to defend himself (24:2-21).[167] Apart from more general complaints about the

---

165. On the scene, see Fitzmyer, *Acts*, 715, 716–18. Mantel's study of Acts 23 is thoroughly vitiated by an uncritical insertion of rabbinic material into the discussion (*Studies in the History of the Sanhedrin*, 290–98).

166. See F. F. Bruce, *The Acts of the Apostles*, 3rd ed. (Grand Rapids: Eerdmans, 1990), 464–65 for various suggestions about why Paul did not realize he was the high priest. The name of Ananias is attested in some copies of Acts 22:5, where Paul speaks of his intent in going to Damascus to capture followers of Jesus and bring them to the high priest. As Bruce notes, the reading can hardly be correct because Ananias was not high priest at the time of Paul's conversion (455).

167. There has been a dispute about what was happening in this scene because of uncertainty whether Acts 24:6b-8a was part of the earliest text. For the idea that Lysias had forcibly interrupted a Jewish legal proceeding in Jerusalem and that it is his case that was brought before Felix, see D. Béchard, "The Disputed Case against Paul: A Redaction-Critical Analysis of Acts 21:27—22:29," *CBQ* 65 (2003): 232–50.

trouble Paul had caused, Tertullus mentioned the defilement of the temple—perhaps the reason that the high priest was among those calling on Felix. Although Felix gave no decision in the case, he left Paul in a sort of custody for two years before being replaced as governor by Porcius Festus (24:27). Reference to the two-year period that was concluded by the change in governors permits one to date the trial before the Sanhedrin to about 58 CE,[168] since Felix's term as procurator probably ended in 60 CE when the emperor Nero recalled him.[169]

Ananias was, then, high priest yet in 58 CE, but he was not to hold the office much longer.[170] While Felix was still governor, yet very near the end of his tenure (after he had handled the dispute between the Syrians and Jews in Caesarea [*J.W.* 2.13, 7 (§§266–70); *Ant.* 20.8, 7 (§§173–78)]), Josephus reports that "King Agrippa conferred the high priesthood upon Ishmael, the son of Phiabi" (*Ant.* 20.8, 8 [§179]). This is an unusually short notice that does not even mention the name of the person whom the king thereby dislodged from office.

Although unnamed at this point, Ananias figures several times in later stories about the period after his high priesthood. Josephus notes that he exercised great influence during the reign of Albinus (62–64 CE) as procurator. He won the favor of the populace, so we learn, because of his wealth. "Now the high priest Ananias daily advanced greatly in reputation and was splendidly rewarded by the goodwill and esteem of the citizens; for he was able to supply them with money: at any rate he daily paid court with gifts to Albinus and the high priest.[171] But Ananias had servants who were utter rascals and who, combining operations with the most reckless men, would go to the threshing

---

168. This is the date Fitzmyer assigns to it (*Acts*, 140).

169. The exact date is debated, but Schürer considers 60 CE to be the most likely one; see the extended discussion of the issue in *History*, 1.465–66 n. 42. Also, see below under Ishmael son of Phiabi.

170. As in the cases of some of his predecessors, Ananias is not mentioned, though we might have expected him to appear, in connection with the handling of two crises that occurred during his reign, judging from the order of events in Josephus's histories: (1) the Passover at which a Roman soldier exposed himself to the Jewish crowd (*Ant.* 20.5, 3 [§108]; *J.W.* 2.12, 1 [§224] describes the incident differently: he raised "his robe, stooped in an indecent attitude, so as to turn his backside to the Jews, and made a noise in keeping with his posture"), and (2) the incident in which a Roman soldier tore up and burned a copy of the Torah (*Ant.* 20.5, 4 [§115]; *J.W.* 2.12, 1 [§229]). See Horsley, "High Priests," 40.

171. Mention of the high priest here implies that Ananias had an ongoing relationship with one of his successors that seems not to have been entirely negative. Like the earlier Jonathan, he continued to exercise influence upon powerful people, though he was no longer high priest. The high priest in question here is Jesus son of Damnaeus (see below) who ruled in 62–63 (?) CE.

floors and take by force the tithes of the priests; nor did they refrain from beating those who refused to give. The high priests were guilty of the same practices as his slaves, and no one could stop them. So it happened at that time that those of the priests who in olden days were maintained by the tithes now starved to death" (*Ant.* 20.9, 2 [§§205–7]).[172] Just after this, he mentions that "the secretary of the captain Eleazar—he was the son of Ananias[173] the high priest" (20.9, 3 [§208])—was kidnapped by *sicarii* (violent opponents of the Roman regime) and held for ransom. The wealthy Ananias was able to arrange with Albinus the release of ten associates of the kidnappers in exchange for his son's freedom. This, however, led to a predictable problem: the *sicarii* took to kidnapping members of Ananias's staff for similar exchanges (§§209–10). During the change of high priests in about 63 CE and the subsequent fighting between the new incumbent and his ousted predecessor (see below), Ananias is said to have had the greatest influence because of his wealth and therefore his ability to pay bribes (*Ant.* 20.9, 4 [§213]). Another son of Ananias, whose name was Simon, led a delegation to the procurator Florus near the beginning of the revolt (*J.W.* 2.17, 4 [§418]), though in this passage Ananias is not identified as the high priest. The purpose of that unsuccessful embassy was to urge Florus to send troops to crush the revolt before it became unstoppable. Another such delegation went to Agrippa who did send a force.

Ananias, who reigned for the longest time of any high priest after Caiaphas and who with his sons remained highly influential in later years, met his death when the revolutionaries turned on the wealthy and powerful in

---

172. Perhaps this is the origin of the words in *b. Pesah.* 57a: "The Temple Court also cried out: 'Lift up your heads, O ye gates, and let Johanan the son of Narbai, the disciple of Pinkai, enter and fill his stomach with the Divine sacrifices.' It was said of Johanan b. Narbai that he ate three hundred calves and drank three hundred barrels of wine and ate forty se'ah of young birds as a des[s]ert for his meal. It was said: As long as Johanan the son of Narbai lived, nothar was never found in the Temple." The editors suggest that this Johanan was Ananias son of Nedebaeus, although the names are not the same (see their n. 21). See also *b. Ker.* 28a–b; Derenbourg, *Essai*, 230–31.

173. There is also manuscript support for reading *Ananus* (see Feldman, *Josephus 10*, 110–11 nn. 3 and i). The variant conflicts with *J.W.* 2.17, 2 (§409), where he is identified as Ananias's son and is said to be the one who, while captain of the temple, persuaded those able to make such decisions to ban all sacrifices from foreigners—an act that led to stopping the daily sacrifice for the emperors. Josephus says the act was the "foundation" of the war against Rome. It is possible that the same Eleazar is the person called "Eleazar, son of the high priest Neus" in *J.W.* 2.20, 4 (§566). There is no high priest who was named Neus, and for that reason a number of scholars have proposed to read Ananias (Ἀνανιας) rather than Neus (Νεου). See Thackeray, *Josephus 2*, 540 n. a.

Jerusalem. Amid fighting between the revolutionaries and the troops sent by King Agrippa II, the rebels were able to drive the faction of Agrippa from the upper city of Jerusalem.

> The victors burst in and set fire to the house of Ananias the high priest and to the palaces of Agrippa and Bernice; they next carried their combustibles to the public archives, eager to destroy the money-lenders' bonds and to prevent the recovery of debts, in order to win over a host of grateful debtors and to cause a rising of the poor against the rich, sure of impunity. The keepers of the Record Office having fled, they set light to the building. After consuming the sinews of the city in the flames, they advanced against their foes; whereupon the notables and chief priests made their escape, some hiding in the underground passages, while others fled with the royal troops to the palace situated higher up, and instantly shut the gates; among the latter were Ananias the high-priest, his brother Ezechias and the members of the deputation which had been sent to Agrippa. (*J.W.* 2.17, 6 [§§426–29])

A few paragraphs later we learn the fate of Ananias. "On the following day [after 6 Gorpiaeus = a time in August/ September][174] the high-priest Ananias was caught near the canal in the palace grounds, where he was hiding, and, with his brother Ezechias, was killed by the brigands; while the rebels invested and kept strict watch on the towers, to prevent any soldier from escaping. But the reduction of the strongholds and the murder of the high-priest inflated and brutalized Menahem to such an extent that he believed himself without rival in the conduct of affairs and became an insufferable tyrant" (*J.W.* 2.17, 9 [§441]). In this way, Ananias died in 66 CE, fatally associated with the ruling class that the revolt decimated.

Or, so one would think from reading Josephus. Nevertheless, a very small inscription from Masada that may mention Ananias has led Michael Wise, building on sugestions from Smallwood, to conclude that Ananias was secretly allied with the *sicarii*, that he played a double game for some time, that he was at Masada or was expected to come there, but that he waited too long to reveal his true loyalties and thus fell victim to another rebel leader Menahem.[175]

---

174. So Thackeray, *Josephus 2*, 495 n. b.

175. "The Life and Times of Ananias Bar Nedebaeus and His Family," in his *Thunder in Gemini and Other Essays on the History, Language, and Literature of Second Temple Palestine*, JSPSup 15 (Sheffield: Sheffield Academic, 1994), 51–102.

Wise's argument is very hypothetical and finally unsupported, but we should examine the inscription and then deal with his case.

The inscription written on a piece of pottery reads: ‏ח]נני[ה כהנא רבא‏ ‏עקביא בריה‏.[176] The Aramaic form of the high-priestly title is fully preserved, although the name of the high priest must be partially restored. Among the relevant names from about this time, ‏חנניה‏ = Ananias seems the most likely candidate. So, on a jar at Masada, the names of a high priest and of his son are inscribed. Since Masada was a rebel stronghold, specifically of the *sicarii*, finding the high priest Ananias's name there is indeed surprising.

We should recall that Ananias's son Eleazar was the one responsible for ending the sacrifices of foreigners, including the emperor, and thus for inciting the revolt. Was Ananias himself somehow also involved with revolutionaries? If so, it would be understandable that another of his sons and perhaps Ananias himself were at Masada. This is what Wise argues. He understands the inscription on the jar to indicate possession of the item and that its owner naturally was at Masada where the jar was found.

But, why should one think that Ananias, whatever the sympathies of his otherwise unknown son Aqaviah, sided with the *sicarii*? Judging from Josephus's narrative, one would have to conclude the opposite: he opposed these revolutionaries who finally were involved in killing him. Wise correctly argues that there is evidence in Josephus for rivalry among the high-priestly families and that therefore it is possible Ananias aligned himself with the *sicarii* to gain leverage in his struggles with the other elite priests. He also maintains that the ideology of the *sicarii*, who included some well-to-do people in their numbers (like the Doras who arranged the murder of the former high priest Jonathan),[177] may have proved convenient for Ananias: they followed the creed "No ruler but God"; as a result, a theocratic regime, headed by a high priest, would have been desirable to them, and Ananias may have seen himself fulfilling that role some day.

One may grant the possibility of these points, but Josephus pictures Ananias as an opponent of the *sicarii* and indeed as an object of their attacks. As we saw above, they kidnapped the secretary of his son and members of Ananias's staff; paying their ransom demands was expensive for Ananias. And, of course, the *sicarii* brought about his death. All of this Wise explains as a double game by Ananias:[178] contrary to what Josephus plainly says, Ananias "had the

---

176. Naveh, *The Aramaic and Hebrew Ostraca and Jar Inscriptions*, 37 with pl. 30. Yadin had earlier read just ‏כהנא רבא עקביא‏, which seemed to produce a new high priest's name. Naveh later supplied the correct reading.

177. He is not, however, said to be a member of the *sicarii*; he merely used them.

178. This is Smallwood's idea, and she is frank about how it contradicts Josephus:

sicarii kidnap the secretary of his son, Eleazar. They then ransomed him by 'sending' to Ananias, saying that if he persuaded Albinus to release ten of their own now in prison, they would release the secretary. Ananias did what they had 'asked,' and the plan worked perfectly. By this device Ananias was simultaneously able to deflect certain suspicions that had apparently arisen that he was himself involved with the *sicarii*, and to prevent Albinus from prosecuting his program against the group. Indeed, the gambit worked so well that Ananias and his collaborators repeated it again and again, using, of course, members of Ananias' own household as the kidnap 'victims.'"[179] In other words, we must read the evidence backwards.

Wise goes on to say that, with powerful support among the elite and among the people, Ananias's forces (perhaps not the high priest himself) took Masada and then his son stopped sacrifices for the emperor at the temple. True, some members of Ananias's faction opposed the move; they were not yet aware of his double game. The delegation to Florus, which included Ananias's son Simon, was simply another of the former high priest's clever maneuvers. The duplicitous man *pretended* to oppose the cessation of sacrifices for the emperor. His son Eleazar called in *sicarii* to help in the struggle in Jerusalem. Menahem, however, ruined the whole plan when he took arms from Masada and returned to Jerusalem. He caught Ananias still carrying out his double identity by hiding with those who opposed the rebels. Ananias was killed before he could reveal his true sentiments. If he was playing a double game, he certainly lost.

This seems a remarkable conclusion to reach on the basis of a couple of words written on a jar at Masada. In this one interesting piece of evidence, whose exact meaning is not clear, Wise finds a key for unlocking the truth from Josephus's tendentious narrative. No one doubts that Josephus's narrative is tendentious and that he wished to defend Jewish leaders and make lower class rebels shoulder the blame for the revolt, but this does not justify reading

---

"Although Josephus says that Ananias acted under compulsion from the *sicarii*, collusion between the two sides seems obvious. Ananias appears, in fact, to have been playing a double game at this time: on the surface he, like most members of his class, remained on good terms with the Romans—and under a weak and venal procurator his money was useful for this purpose; but he secretly sympathized with the anti-Roman elements, and he used his influence over Albinus to further their cause" ("High Priests," 28). She wrote these words before the Masada discoveries were known. For her, the attitude of Ananias is indicative of the outwardly pro- but inwardly anti-Roman views of Jewish leaders just before the revolt. Horsley quite properly rejects Smallwood's suggestion, doubting that Ananias was in secret alliance with the *sicarii* ("High Priests," 46–47).

179. "The Life and Times of Ananias," 68.

his narrative in reverse—as though it were saying the opposite of what it says. Since Josephus's account is our only evidence about the actions of Ananias, Wise has to contradict it in order to make his point. That is problematic enough, but what is the significance of the jar inscription? Obviously, we do not know. Naveh conjectured that the inscription served to certify the contents as clean and thus suitable for holding sacred produce and that Aqaviah, to underscore his authority, included the name of his famous father.[180] One need not accept this explanation in order to reject Wise's thesis. We simply have no information about how such an object reached Masada: for all we know, *sicarii* stole the jar when destroying Ananias's palace and brought it to Masada. Whatever it means and however it reached the great wilderness fortress, the inscribed pottery piece hardly provides evidence that Ananias was on the side of the *sicarii*. Our sole historical source says the opposite.[181]

45. Ishmael Son of Phiabi (59–61 CE)

Ishmael, son of Phiabi, was the second high priest to bear exactly that name (they are not likely to have been the same person, as the first ruled in ca. 15–16 CE)[182] and the first person appointed to the position by Agrippa II. As we have seen, the short notice about his royal appointment (*Ant.* 20.8, 8 [§179]) lacks a reference to the one whom he replaced in office.

During the reign of Ishmael as high priest, a number of severe problems continued to afflict the Jews of Judea, both in their relations with each other and with the ruling authorities. With regard to internal issues, Josephus dates to this time a conflict between the elite and the ordinary priests.

> There was now enkindled mutual enmity and class warfare between the high priests, on the one hand, and the priests and leaders of the populace of Jerusalem, on the other.[183] Each of the factions formed

---

180. *The Aramaic and Hebrew Ostraca and Jar Inscriptions*, 38.

181. Wise makes a number of other claims that lack evidence to support them. For example, he writes: "Among the group taking control of Masada, Aqabiah bar Ananias undoubtedly figured prominently, perhaps indeed as commander" (71); or that Mur 19, which lists as a witness "Eleazar bar Hanana," is likely to have mentioned Eleazar bar Ananias. Although the name Hanana is, of course, related, it is not the same as Ananias.

182. He was the third high priest from the family of Phiabi, as Jesus son of Phiabi served as high priest during Herod's reign (perhaps between 30 and 24–22 BCE).

183. This does not appear to be what the text of Josephus says: the words ἐξάπτεται δὲ καὶ τοῖς ἀρχιερεῦσι ἔχθρα τις εἰς ἀλλήλους indicate that there was enmity and strife within the high-priestly class. The following words indicate that the same defects characterized their relations with the other groups. On this, see Wise, "The Life and Times of Ananias," 64–65.

and collected for itself a band of the most reckless revolutionaries and acted as their leader. And when they clashed, they used abusive language and pelted each other with stones. And there was not even one person to rebuke them. No, it was as if there was no one in charge of the city, so that they acted as they did with full licence. Such was the shamelessness and effrontery which possessed the high priests that they actually were so brazen as to send slaves to the threshing floors to receive the tithes that were due to the priests, with the result that the poorer priests starved to death. Thus did the violence of the contending factions suppress all justice. (*Ant.* 20.8, 8 [§§180–81])

There has been a long scholarly discussion about the meaning of the plural term *high priests* (ἀρχιερεῖς), which figures in this passage and elsewhere in the writings of Josephus and the New Testament.[184] Two general options are: (1) they were members of the Sanhedrin who belonged to the high-priestly families such as incumbent high priests, former high priests, and other members of their families;[185] or (2) they were priests who held the leading offices in the temple bureaucracy, such as the captain, treasurer, and so forth.[186] The two views are not mutually exclusive, as members of the families of high priests did hold top positions in the temple (see the example of Ananus, son of Ananias, who was the captain; *Ant.* 20.6, 2 [§131] with *J.W.* 2.12, 6 [§243]). Whatever may have been the range of meaning expressed by the plural *high priests*, they were undoubtedly the aristocrats among the clergy, people of rank and pedigree.

The issue of the tithes mentioned by Josephus is clear enough: wealthy priests sent their slaves to the place where tithes were collected by priests. Josephus does not say here that they used force to take tithes from other priests, but, however the slaves got the tithed food, the poorer priests, who lacked such help, lost their income and starved.

There are several biblical prescriptions about tithes, of which there were different kinds. The Levites received the first tithe of agricultural products, and from it they were to tithe to the priests (Num 18:20-32). This section of Numbers follows a related one in which the portion of the priests is described; it is not called a tithe there, but it was a stipulated allowance that had to be

---

184. For references, see BAG 112.
185. Schürer is usually listed as an advocate of this position. See, for example, *History*, 2.232–35. Goodman (*The Ruling Class of Judaea*, 119–20) and E. P. Sanders (*Judaism: Practice and Belief 63* BCE–66 CE [Philadelphia: Trinity Press International, 1992], 327–32) also find this explanation more convincing.
186. For this approach, see Jeremias, *Jerusalem*, 160–81.

given to the priest. The so-called second tithe is mandated in Deut 14:22-27 and was to be eaten at the sanctuary, with the tithe of the third year given to local Levites. There is some evidence in later texts that priests became the recipients of tithes (for example, Jdt 11:13; Tob 1:6-7), but it may be that the word *tithe* is being used in a broader sense in those passages to include any priestly dues such as those of Num 18:8-19.[187] Our passage may reflect that broader usage, entailing that it does not attest priestly appropriation of tithes that had once belonged to the Levites. The problem here may have to do with ready access, because the higher-ranking priests would have had more hands helping them obtain tithes from threshing floors than would the ordinary priests. Perhaps they even stationed their agents there. As we have seen in dealing with Ananias, a similar story can be found in *Ant.* 20.9, 2 (§§206–7), where physical violence is mentioned.[188] In our paragraph, Josephus does not say the servants used force, although that may be implied by the last sentence.

This story in Josephus's *Antiquities* (20.8, 8 [§§180–81], combined with the one in 20.9, 2 [§§206–7]) may be seen as the basis for the saying preserved in *b. Pesaḥ.* 57a: "Woe is me because of the house of Ishmael the son of Phabi, woe is me because of their fists! For they are High Priests and their sons are [Temple] treasurers and their sons-in-law are trustees and their servants beat the people with staves."[189]

Ishmael soon became involved in a dispute between the Jewish people and the rulers Agrippa II and Festus. The emperor Nero had replaced Felix with Porcius Festus, who served as procurator from 60 to 62 CE[190] (possibly a little earlier). While he was in office, Agrippa II "built a chamber of unusual size in his palace at Jerusalem adjoining the colonnade" (*Ant.* 20.8, 11 [§189]) from which he enjoyed watching what was happening in the temple area. Leading Jerusalemites took offense at the royal eavesdropping—something that Josephus says was contrary to tradition (§191)—and built a high wall to block his view. The wall did more than frustrate the king: it also blocked the view of the Romans who stationed guards in the western portico of the temple during festivals to "supervise the temple" (§192). Festus ordered those in charge to pull the wall down, but his command met with resistance: "they entreated him for permission to send an embassy on this matter to Nero; for, they said, they

---

187. For the evidence, see J. Baumgarten, "On the Non-literal Use of *maʿaser/dekate*," *JBL* 103 (1984): 245–51.

188. Smallwood, with others, wonders whether the two passages are duplicate accounts of the same event ("High Priests," 27).

189. A few lines later, the same text says: "The Temple Court also cried out: 'Lift up your heads, O ye gates, and let Ishmael the son of Phiabi, Phineas's disciple, enter and serve in the [office of the] High Priesthood.'"

190. See Schürer, *History of the Jewish People*, 1.467.

could not endure to live any longer if any portion of the temple was demolished. When Festus granted their request, they sent to Nero the ten foremost of their number with Ishmael the high priest and Helcias the keeper of the treasury" (§§193–94).

The embassy traveled to Rome where they enjoyed a favorable reception from Nero, who "not only condoned what they had done, but also consented to leave the building as it was. In this he showed favour to his wife Poppaea, who was a worshipper of God and who pleaded on behalf of the Jews. She then bade the ten depart but detained Helcias and Ishmael in her house as hostages. The king, on hearing this, gave the high priesthood to Joseph, who was surnamed Kabi, son of the high priest Simon" (*Ant.* 20.8, 11 [§§195–96]).[191]

It is reasonable to think that Ishmael was on the side of the people against Agrippa and Festus. If so, it is not surprising that Agrippa would remove him from office when Ishmael's enforced absence provided a convenient opportunity to take decisive action. It is a pity that Josephus does not tell us why Poppaea kept the two temple officials as hostages. Our Ishmael may be the person mentioned in *J.W.* 6.2, 2 (§114), where three of his sons are said to have escaped from Jerusalem, while Ishmael was beheaded at some unspecified time in Cyrene.[192]

We could drop the subject of Ishmael here, but he has become the subject of an essay by Daniel Schwartz, who has attempted a significant revision in the commonly accepted understanding of chronology in this period (as he has for earlier times; see above). One reference in Josephus and one in the Babylonian Talmud that conflict with the chronological picture presented above form the basis for his attempt.[193] Those two passages have been dis-

---

191. Smallwood recognizes that Ishmael opposed the rulers but did so only in this case in which Jewish traditions were protected. She also thinks that Nero detained Ishmael and the treasurer to give Agrippa a chance to appoint "a more amenable High Priest without having to risk antagonizing the Jews by deposing the man whose defence of the sanctity of the Temple will surely have been well received" ("High Priests," 25). Derenbourg thought the detention was to avoid embarrassing Agrippa II and that Josephus, in calling Ishmael a hostage, used the wrong word (*Essai,* 250–51).

192. *M. Soṭah* 9:15 says: "When R. Ishmael b. Phiabi died the splendour of the priesthood ceased." Recall, too, that an Ishmael son of Phiabi is said to have been one of those who prepared a red heifer (*m. Parah* 3:5). It would not be unlikely if the first passage referred to our Ishmael, though why he is called rabbi is not clear; the second could refer to either of the Ishmaels son of Phiabi. Another tradition about him suggests he was wealthy; *t. Yoma* 1:21: "Ishmael b. Phiabi's mother made for him a tunic worth a hundred maneh. And he would stand and make offerings on the altar wearing it" (see also *y. Yoma* 3:6; *b. Yoma* 35b).

193. "Ishmael ben Phiabi and the Chronology of the Province Judaea," *Tarbiz* 52 (1983): 177–200 (Hebrew). An English translation of the essay, "Ishmael ben Phiabi and the Chronology

cussed by many scholars and various solutions have been offered, but
Schwartz's article incorporates them with the other evidence into one system.
The argument is ultimately unsuccessful, because it dismisses what appear to
be straightforward historical statements in favor of ones that have a weaker
claim to such status.

The Josephan reference from which Schwartz begins is *Ant.* 3.15, 3
(§§320–21), in a context where he is summarizing the stories in the book of
Numbers. As he relates the story of the spies (Numbers 13–14) and the people's lack of faith in God's promise after hearing their report, he mentions the
divine judgment communicated through Moses that the Israelites were to
wander in the wilderness for forty years. They asked Moses to intercede for a
reduced sentence, but he refused and yet somehow calmed the crowd. This
leads to a digression on Moses's virtues and marvelous powers, which, says
Josephus, were still having their effects in his time. One example he cites is this:
"But yet again: shortly before [μικρὸν ἔμπροσθεν] the recent war, Claudius
being ruler of the Romans and Ishmael our high-priest, when our country was
in the grip of a famine so severe that an *assarôn* was sold for four drachms, and
when there had been brought in during the Feast of Unleavened bread [*sic*] no
less that seventy *cors* of flour—equivalent to thirty-one Sicilian or forty-one
Attic *medimni*—not one of the priests ventured to consume a crumb, albeit
such dearth prevailed throughout the country, from fear of the law and of the
wrath wherewith the Deity ever regards even crimes which elude detection."
Here, Josephus speaks of an Ishmael serving as high priest during Claudius's
reign (41–54 CE), whereas the only high priests named Ishmael in his narratives of the Roman period are Ishmael son of Phiabi (15–16 CE) and our Ishmael son of Phiabi (59–61 CE). The former held office during the reign of
Tiberius (14–37 CE), while the latter was high priest when Nero was emperor
(54–68 CE; Nero is mentioned in connection with his term as high priest).
Who then was this Ishmael from the time of Claudius? We have argued above
in the section devoted to Elionaeus that Josephus simply wrote the wrong
name for the high priest:[194] he should have written *Elionaeus*, a little-known
high priest who reigned only a short time, or *Joseph son of Camei*, a similarly
obscure high priest, but mistakenly wrote *Ishmael*, a more familiar name, and
thus bedeviled the work of future historians.

---

of Provincia Judaea," is included in his *Studies in the Jewish Background of Christianity*, 218–42.
References to both are included below.

194. Hölscher (*Die Hohenpriesterliste*, 16–18), after considering the evidence, concluded
that the dating of Ishmael in *Ant.* 3 is a mistake.

The second reference from which Schwartz starts is in *b. Yoma* 9a:

Rabbah b. Bar Hana[195] said: What is the meaning of the passage, The fear of the Lord prolongeth days, but the years of the wicked shall be shortened? [= Prov 10:27] 'The fear of the Lord prolongeth days' refers to the first Sanctuary, which remained standing for four hundred and ten years and in which there served only eighteen high priests. 'But the years of the wicked shall be shortened' refers to the second Sanctuary, which abided for four hundred and twenty years and at which more than three hundred [high] priests served. Take off therefrom the forty years which Simeon the Righteous served, eighty years which Johanan the high priest served, ten, which Ishmael b. Fabi served, or, as some say, the eleven years of R. Eleazar b. Harsum. Count [the number of high priests] from then on and you will find that none of them completed his year [in office].

These are the two texts in light of which Schwartz sets out to revise the accepted chronology for Ishmael son of Phiabi; they clearly conflict with the impression given in *Antiquities* 20 that Ishmael son of Phiabi served as high priest for a short time near the end of Felix's tenure and at the beginning of Festus's rule—all during the time of Nero. Yet, as should be obvious, the nature of these texts, especially the second, makes them a dubious basis for drawing historical conclusions. In other words, if it is history we are concerned about, we are off to a poor start.

Josephus's statement about a famine in the time of Claudius and Ishmael conflicts with data in his narratives that deal with the time in question. He records no high priest named Ishmael during the reign of Claudius and certainly not in the time of the famine. So, we are faced with a simple question: which is likelier to be accurate, a chronological statement that occurs out of context (as in *Antiquities* 3) or one that is based on a list of high priests and occurs in context (as in *Antiquities* 20)? The possibility that the isolated statement contains inaccuracies (perhaps because Josephus was relying on memory) should be kept in mind. Also, the chronological indicators in the passage may point in more than one direction: while Josephus associates Ishmael, the famine, and Claudius, he also says this happened "shortly before" the war, which began in 66 CE. This latter claim, while imprecise, is more compatible with a reign of Ishmael close to the onset of the revolt than with a time in the reign of Claudius, which ended twelve years earlier.

The talmudic passage, written down centuries after the lives of the individuals in question, should be recognized for what it is—a creative interpreta-

---

195. Although the Soncino translation reads this way, the text says Rabbah b. Bar Hana spoke in the name of R. Yohanan.

tion of Prov 10:27. The number of years assigned to Simeon the Righteous (forty) looks schematic, while those claimed for John Hyrcanus (eighty) are high by nearly fifty years. The ten years of Ishmael (or the eleven of R. Eleazar b. Harsum, who was not a high priest) are more plausible, but we should not overlook their function in the passage. The sage wishes to show that the high priests of the Second Temple (= the wicked of Prov 10:27) had short reigns. To do so, he somehow decides the number of high priests for the 420-year period (inaccurate by about 170 years) was 300+; from 420 he must subtract enough years to reduce it below 300, so he can claim that no high priest ruled even one full year, thus proving that the days of the wicked are shortened. Anyone wishing to derive historical data from this passage—for example, that Ishmael reigned ten years—should also hold that there were more than three hundred Second-Temple high priests, that John Hyrcanus ruled for eighty years, and that the Second Temple stood for 420 years. Of course, Schwartz does not do this, but he does not properly assess the context in which the ten-year reign of Ishmael appears. The numbers in the talmudic passage are multiples of ten. The forty years of Simeon the Righteous are mentioned several times in rabbinic texts, while the eighty years of John Hyrcanus (who was known to have reigned for a long time) allow the sage to reduce the 420 years to 300. Then, continuing to operate with units of ten, he needs only one such unit to drop the number under 300 so that he can claim the other three hundred high priests each ruled less than a year—a historically false conclusion but one delivering a homiletic point. In other words, it is prudent to recognize the passage for what it is and look elsewhere for chronological information.[196]

Despite the transparent problems with these two passages, Schwartz goes through a lengthy examination of Josephus's and Tacitus's narratives in an effort to show that Felix (given the dates 52–60 CE above) and Ishmael (given the dates 59–61 CE above) were appointed already in 49 CE, when the effects of the famine were still felt[197] and Claudius was emperor. If Ishmael was installed

---

196. In a footnote ("Ishmael ben Phiabi," 178 n. 8 = 219 n. 7) Schwartz tries to deal with this fundamental difficulty. He says that ten years (assigned to Ishmael in the passage) are not a round or typical number in rabbinic literature and that there is evidence for the accuracy of Rabbi Yohanan's claim about an annual change of high priests (he refers to an essay on the references in the gospel of John to "the high priest that year"). A look at the chronological information about high priests in Josephus's narratives provides abundant contrary information. Even a scholar like Klausner, who makes heavy use of rabbinic material in his work, rejects the ten years of this passage (and its calling R. Eleazar b. Harsum a high priest) as historically reliable information, since it conflicts with the information in Josephus (*History of the Second Temple*, 5.21).

197. Schwartz is not quite able to make Ishmael's appointment early enough to coincide with the famine, so he argues that, as the year 47–48 CE was a sabbatical year coming right after

in 49, then he could have served as high priest for ten years.[198] An obstacle to making such a case is that Felix's tenure as procurator is usually defined as 52–60 CE. Hence, his term began after the famine, although Claudius was still emperor. Schwartz adduces evidence showing to his satisfaction that Felix became procurator of Judea in 49 CE, not in 52.

It does seem that Josephus puts Ishmael's appointment near the end of Felix's reign. He notes Felix's commission by Claudius in *Ant.* 20.7, 1 (§137). In the very next sentence, he refers to the end of Claudius's twelfth year as emperor (53 CE), when he gave Agrippa II the tetrarchy formerly governed by Philip (§138). In other words, the context in *Antiquities* 20 suggests a time late in Claudius's reign as the point at which Felix received his assignment to govern Judea. After mentioning Felix's marriage to Drusilla[199] (*Ant.* 20.7, 2 [§§141–44]), Josephus records Claudius's death after a reign of over thirteen years (§148). This occurred on October 13, 54 CE.[200] There follow other events in Felix's time until, in 20.8, 8 (§179), Agrippa II confers the high priesthood on Ishmael. Only three paragraphs later (20.8, 9 [§182]), we learn that Festus succeeded Felix and that the Jewish leaders of Caesarea at this time went to Rome to accuse Felix. The latter was saved only through the intervention of his influential brother Pallas.

Schwartz argues that Josephus, despite where he locates the notice of Ishmael's appointment as high priest, does not imply that this occurred at the end of Felix's procuratorship. Josephus's practice was to place his information

---

the famine, the effects continued later ("Ishmael ben Phiabi," 196–97 = 236–37). Josephus's reference to the actual famine, however, puts it in the reign of Tiberius Alexander (46–48 CE) and possibly earlier, as we have seen (*Ant.* 20.5, 2 [§101]).

198. Compare Derenbourg, *Essai*, 235–36; he noted that some considered the ten years ascribed to Ishmael to be possible but added that the eleven years assigned to Eleazar b. Harsum could also fill the gap from 48 to 59 CE. As we will see, this is a misuse of the talmudic statements.

199. This Drusilla, the youngest daughter of Agrippa I, was born in 38–39 CE (since she was six years of age when her father died in 44 CE; *Ant.* 19.9, 1 [§354]). She was first married to Azizus king of Emesa and later to Felix. If Felix was procurator from 49 to 56, as Schwartz thinks, and if she was already married to Felix at least two years before Felix's term ended, as Acts 24 implies, then they were married no later than 54 CE when she was 16 or 17. This chronology would entail a very early age for her when she married Azizus (a union that followed the failure of the earlier plan to have her marry Epiphanes, son of Antiochus IV of Commagene), and it would have to allow enough time for her to weary of her marriage by the time Felix lured her away from her husband. All of this complicates although it does not disprove Schwartz's early chronology.

200. In *J.W.* 2.12, 8 (§§247–49), he mentions that Claudius sent Felix, enlarged Agrippa's territory, and died after reigning more than thirteen years. So here, too, the events are bunched together.

about high priests at the end of sections devoted to governors.²⁰¹ Moreover, the expression with which he introduces the appointment, κατὰ τοῦτον τὸν καιρόν, does not entail a strict chronological order. It refers merely to some time in Felix's reign, meaning the appointment of Ishmael could have happened long before the end of his rule.²⁰² That may be the case, but one can hardly avoid concluding that the appointment of Ishmael occurred in the reign of Nero, as Josephus is well into his account of events during that emperor's reign at this point (death of Claudius in 20.8, 1 [§148], Nero named emperor in 20.8, 2 [§§152–53], Ishmael appointed high priest in 20.8, 8 [§179]). It seems implausible that the Greek phrase would give one enough leeway to claim Josephus put Ishmael's appointment in the time of the wrong emperor—this for an event within Josephus's own lifetime.

Schwartz thinks that Ishmael was appointed high priest when Ananias, his immediate predecessor, was sent to Rome. As we have seen, Josephus, in the appointment notice, does not mention the name of Ishmael's predecessor. Agrippa would have wanted to appoint a new high priest as soon as possible in the physical absence of Ananias. All of this happened, he thinks, *at the beginning* of Felix's reign.

A problem with drawing such a conclusion (apart from the violence it does to the order of Josephus's narrative) is that it may be contradicted by another early source, the Book of Acts. There, Ananias is the high priest at the time of Paul's trial, a likely date for which was 58 CE (see above). If 58 CE is accurate and Ishmael was appointed after Ananias, then Ishmael did not become high priest before 58—far from the beginning of Felix's reign on any reckoning. Schwartz has to confront the fact that, in Acts 23:1-5, Paul appears before the Sanhedrin (the definite article is used, v. 1), before a man who is called "the high priest" with the definite article used twice (v. 2 ὁ δὲ ἀρχιερεύς; v. 4 τὸν ἀρχιερέα), and who is named Ananias (v. 2 Ἀνανίας; the same is the case in Acts 24:1). Although the textual evidence is overwhelming that Ananias is here considered the high priest, Schwartz notes only that, in Paul's reply in Acts 23:5, the words "high priest" are not preceded by the definite article. For him, this suggests Ananias was not yet functioning as the actual high priest, that is, the trial would have taken place before his official

---

201. We have seen, nevertheless, that this is not a universally followed principle in his history.
202. "Ishmael ben Phiabi," 180 = 221–22; see also his essay, "KATA TOYTON TON KAIPON: Josephus' Source on Agrippa II," *JQR* 72 (1982): 241–68. Even if the Greek expression has the function Schwartz assigns to it, how would we know that it referred to any time during *Felix's* reign, when the reign being discussed in this paragraph is that of Agrippa II? Kokkinos thinks that Agrippa II did not return to his newly acquired lands until 52 or 53 CE and thus could not have appointed Ishmael before this (*Herodian Dynasty*, 318–20).

appointment.[203] The passage says clearly he was *the* high priest and thus obviously opposes his conclusion.

Schwartz goes on to calculate when Felix became procurator. He was sent to the area by Claudius, and this occurred, to judge from Josephus, between the death of Herod of Chalcis (*Ant.* 20.5, 2 [§104]) in 48 CE and the enlargement of Agrippa II's territory in 53 (20.7, 1 [§138]). However, Schwartz thinks differently. He first turns to *Ant.* 20.5, 2 (§§103–4), where the appointments of Ananias and Cumanus and the death of Herod of Chalcis are mentioned in the same context, as if they happened around the same time. However, Schwartz thinks two sources are combined here—a circumstance that somehow is thought to weaken the link between the events.[204] At any rate, Cumanus assumed office early in 49 CE. He also thinks Cumanus ruled a very short time, less than one year (necessarily so if Felix, his successor, assumed office in the same year). His evidence comes from Josephus's reference to just one Passover while he was procurator.[205] Schwartz thinks it was the only Passover during his reign, whereas other scholars assume a time of peace before the disturbance at this Passover. In *Ant.* 20.5, 3 (§107), after saying that at a Passover (not identified as the first in his term) Cumanus, fearing trouble, stationed a company of soldiers at the temple, Josephus writes: "This had been in fact the usual practice of previous procurators of Judaea at the festivals." So, says Schwartz, as the text does not say Cumanus had done this before, this was his first festival. How this follows from Josephus's words is difficult to discern. Josephus's purpose here is to indicate that Cumanus did nothing out of the ordinary to provoke the pilgrims arriving for the festival. He did what others had done before him and for the same reason—fear of the crowd (see *J.W.* 2.12, 1 [§224] for this explanation). What sparked the violence was the soldier who exposed himself. In other words, we do not know whether this was the first, second, or third Passover while Cumanus ruled Judea.

From his reading of the data, Schwartz concludes that at the latest this was the Passover of 49 CE, while it could have been that of 48 or 47. His inference

---

203. "Ishmael ben Phiabi," 182 n. 27 = 223 n. 23.

204. One reason for suspecting two sources, one about the Herods, the other about the high priests, is that the second mention of Herod in these two paragraphs provides a fuller identification of him ("Ishmael ben Phiabi," 183 = 224). It remains a mystery, nevertheless, why the use of two sources should weaken the connection between two events reported in the same context.

205. As Schwartz realizes, Josephus actually mentions two of them in the time of Cumanus, with the second coming at the very end of his reign: the first, *Ant.* 20.5, 3 (§106) (= *J.W.* 2.12, 1 [§224]), and the second, *Ant.* 20.6, 2 (§133) (= *J.W.* 2.12, 6 [§244, where it is identified as Passover]). See Kokkinos, *Herodian Dynasty*, 319–20. Kokkinos, like others (for example, Schürer, *History of the Jewish People*, 2.458), puts Cumanus's reign in the years 48–52 CE.

follows only if we ignore Josephus's statement about the events of 48 and if we accept the possible but hardly necessary conclusion that this was the first time Cumanus had to cope with a Passover crowd. Schwartz believes that Cumanus and Ananias, therefore, would have arrived in Rome before Passover 49, while Agrippa II was in Rome and receiving appointment as his uncle's successor. Armed with his promotion, he would have wanted to exercise his right to appoint a high priest at once. By this means, Schwartz is able to infer that Felix was appointed procurator already in 49 CE and Ishmael received his office in the same year. One pointer in favor of this date, he thinks, is that Paul, when he appeared before Felix (the year 54 CE for Schwartz), said Felix had already judged the nation "many years" (Acts 24:10; on this see below).

The next problem for Schwartz is the chronology of Paul's ministry. He posits a minimal time lapse for events mentioned in the New Testament, in order to place Paul before Felix in 54 CE. Festus, the new procurator, then arrived two years later. But when did Festus become procurator? Schwartz thinks we have a difficult problem here because there are three items that are not easy to harmonize. First, Acts 24:27 says that Paul remained in prison after his hearings before Felix for two more years before Festus arrived. Second, Paul was tried in 54 CE (on Schwartz's view; for those who move the date later, the problem becomes worse). And third, Josephus says that after Festus replaced Felix, the Jews of Caesarea sent a delegation to Rome to complain about Felix before Nero but that Felix was saved by the influence of his brother Pallas: "He [Felix] would undoubtedly have paid the penalty for his misdeeds against the Jews had not Nero yielded to the urgent entreaty of Felix's brother Pallas, whom at that time he held in the highest honour" (*Ant.* 20.8, 9 [§182]). But Tacitus (*Annales* 13.14) reports that Pallas lost his high office at a time corresponding to the end of 54 or the beginning of 55 CE. Since the information about him shows that Pallas would hardly have been favored by Nero at the time Festus arrived in Judea (spring of 56) and Felix was arraigned, Schwartz suggests two corrections in this third item. First, it is doubtful Pallas was ever highly honored by Nero. If we alter Josephus's formulation and say he was still honored but not necessarily by Nero when his brother was arraigned, we do not have to limit ourselves to the time that ended with his removal (that is, before the end of 54 or the beginning of 55 CE). It may have been possible to speak of his enjoying prestige until the end of 55.[206] Second, in *J.W.* 2.13, 7

---

206. Mention of Pallas's decisive influence, a side note that could prove decisive in sorting out the chronology, is a problem for Schwartz, because he must assume that his influence continued despite his earlier demotion; it is an even larger problem for those who think Felix was charged later, in 58 or 60 CE. Perhaps M. Stern has said what needs to be said about this: "It should, however, be noted that his dismissal did not cancel his influence; and it may be assumed

(§270), there is reference to a delegation of Jews from Caesarea to Rome during (not at the end of) Felix's time; he sent representatives of the Syrian residents of the city and the Jews to the capital to have their quarrel adjudicated there. Schwartz thinks it makes better sense if just one delegation was sent, the one while Felix was in office; it was then that Pallas exercised his powerful influence on behalf of his brother.

Schwartz believes that his lower chronology makes better sense of Paul's words to Felix in Acts 24:10: "I cheerfully make my defence, knowing that for many years you have been a judge over this nation." His words "many years" would be inappropriate if we supposed Felix had not been appointed until 52 CE; but if he became procurator in 49, they make sense. In fact, Schwartz creates a little more difficulty for himself than defenders of the generally accepted dates encounter: for him "many years" means 49–54, while, for the other view, they refer to the period 52–58 CE.

Schwartz devotes much of the remainder of his article to the data on which scholars have based their conclusion that Felix became procurator of Judea in 52 CE. There are two sources of evidence. First, Josephus records his appointment (*Ant.* 20.7, 1 [§137]) between the exile of Cumanus (§136) and the enlargement of Agrippa II's territory (53 CE [§138]); hence scholars conclude Cumanus retained his office until some time close to 53. But, as Josephus dates only the enlargement of the kingdom, it is possible that some time elapsed between the arrival of Felix and the territorial enhancement. As we have seen, Schwartz thinks Cumanus did not serve more than one year.

The second source is Tacitus, from whom Schwartz thinks scholars have drawn the wrong conclusion. This is not the place to explore the problems presented by Tacitus's accounts of what happened in Judea in the 40s and 50s and the difficulties they have always presented (for example, his claim that Cumanus and Felix ruled at the same time, Felix over Samaria and Cumanus over Galilee, although earlier he had said that Felix ruled Judea: *Annales* 12.54,1–2). At least we may say that Tacitus mentions Felix when he talks about the events of 52 CE (*Annales* 12.54). After his lengthy study, Schwartz offers this chronology:[207]

that he retained a certain status so long as Burrus, the commander of the praetorian guard with whom he was on friendly terms, was alive, that is, until 62 C.E." ("Sources, Appendix: Chronology," in *The Jewish People in the First Century*, 76). Stern favors the year 60 as the end of Felix's tenure, although he does not rule out 58 or 59.

207. The items in bold print are the ones we have argued above are incorrect or, in the case of the last two, are incorrect by implication of the other dates we accept.

Before Passover 48	Cumanus appointed procurator of Judea
End of 48 or beginning of 49	death of Herod of Chalcis
Before Passover 49	**Cumanus and Ananias sent to Rome, Cumanus exiled, and Felix appointed in his place**
April–May 49	Claudius bequeathes the kingdom of Chalcis to Agrippa II, **Agrippa appoints Ishmael son of Phiabi high priest**
Early summer 54	**Paul tried before Felix**[208]
Fall 55	**delegation of Jewish nobles from Caesarea debates in Rome with representatives of the non-Jewish population and also accuses Felix; its arguments are rejected through the influence of Pallas**
End of 55	judgment of Pallas
Spring 56	**Festus appointed in Felix's place as procurator of Judea**[209]
58 or 59	**Ishmael son of Phiabi sent to Rome and held there by Poppea, Nero's wife**

His chronology is, as we have maintained, three years too early for Felix's appointment and ten years too early for that of Ishmael. It conflicts at key points with Josephus's placement of events and with the evidence from the book of Acts. When we recall that Schwartz began with the references to Ishmael in *Ant.* 3.15, 3 (§320–21) and *b. Yoma* 9a, we can see that he has failed to incorporate them into the other chronological evidence for the period, a result that is not surprising given the character of these two passages. When all is said and done, the traditional chronology makes far better sense of the data.

46. Joseph Son of Simon (61–62 CE)

Agrippa II saw fit to appoint Joseph high priest while Ishmael was detained in Rome (*Ant.* 20.8, 11 [§§195–96]). The high priest Simon who is said to be his father could be either of the two most recent Simons to hold the office, either Simon son of Camith (17–18 CE) or Simon Cantheras, son of Boethus (41–42

---

208. This proposed date shows why Schwartz denies Ananias was the high priest at Paul's trial, although the text clearly says he was. Ananias, on his view, lost the high priesthood in early 49 CE, so he could hardly be high priest in 54. But as Acts says he was, this is just one more indication of how poorly Schwartz's chronology fits the evidence.

209. For an analysis of the evidence, see Kokkinos, *The Herodian Dynasty*, Appendix 8: "Redating the Last Procurators and the Brother of Jesus," 385–86. He opts for a date of no later than summer of 58 CE for Festus's arrival, but the coins on which he bases his conclusion—ones from Nero's fifth year—do not specify the governor's name; hence, we do not know who minted them.

CE). His surname is spelled differently in the textual witnesses: Καβί, Καβεῖ, Κάμης, Καμί.[210] The last form suggests that the surname may be related to Camith (קמחית). So, his father may have been Simon son of Camith.[211]

Nothing more is said in *Antiquities* about this high priest apart from the notice about his removal from office. Josephus synchronizes the change with the appointment of Albinus as the procurator of Judea following the death of Festus (perhaps in 62 CE): "Upon hearing of the death of Festus, Caesar [= Nero] sent Albinus to Judaea as procurator. The king [Agrippa II] removed Joseph from the high priesthood, and bestowed the succession to this office upon the son of Ananus, who was likewise called Ananus" (*Ant.* 20.9, 1 [§197]). Here we have another case of replacing a high priest at the time the civil ruler was replaced, with the difference that it was not the new civil ruler who made the change but King Agrippa II, who had been ruling for a number of years before this.

Our Joseph may reappear in *J.W.* 2.20, 4 (§567), where there is mention of a Joseph son of Simon who at the beginning of the revolt was sent as commander to Jericho. It is also likely that Josephus mentions him in *J.W.* 6.2, 2 (§114), where he refers to "the chief priests[212] Joseph and Jesus" who escaped from the doomed city of Jerusalem after Josephus himself made his impassioned speech to the inhabitants.

47. Ananus Son of Ananus (62 CE)

The new high priest came from the family of Ananus, which (if we count Caiaphas among them) produced seven occupants of the office—a fact not missed by Josephus, who notes that the Ananeans were unique in the annals of the high priesthood (*Ant.* 20.9, 1 [§198]): "It is said that the elder Ananus was extremely fortunate. For he had five sons, all of whom, after he himself had previously enjoyed the office for a very long period, became high priests of God—a thing that had never happened to any other of our high priests." Although he was the last high priest from the house of Ananus, he hardly improved its reputation during his short tenure; later, however, he was to win Josephus's admiration for his role in the war against Rome.

The only act of his high priesthood mentioned by Josephus is a famous one that led to his dismissal.

> The younger Ananus, who, as we have said, had been appointed to the high priesthood, was rash in his temper and unusually daring. He fol-

210. Feldman, *Josephus* 9, 106 n. 1.
211. Hölscher, *Die Hohenpriesterliste*, 18.
212. It would also be possible to translate as "the high priests."

lowed the school of the Sadducees, who are indeed more heartless than any of the other Jews, as I have already explained, when they sit in judgement. Possessed of such a character, Ananus thought that he had a favourable opportunity because Festus was dead and Albinus was still on the way. And so he convened the judges of the Sanhedrin and brought before them a man named James, the brother of Jesus who was called the Christ, and certain others. He accused them of having transgressed the law and delivered them up to be stoned. Those of the inhabitants of the city who were considered the most fair-minded and who were strict in observance of the law were offended at this. They therefore secretly sent to King Agrippa urging him, for Ananus had not even been correct in his first step, to order him to desist from any further such actions. Certain of them even went to meet Albinus, who was on his way from Alexandria, and informed him that Ananus had no authority to convene the Sanhedrin without his consent. Convinced by these words, Albinus angrily wrote to Ananus threatening to take vengeance upon him. King Agrippa, because of Ananus' action, deposed him from the high priesthood which he had held for three months and replaced him with Jesus the son of Demnaeus. (*Ant.* 20.9, 1 [§§199–203])[213]

If the information in this passage is correct, we have evidence that, at least on the view of some, a high priest needed the procurator's permission to convene the Sanhedrin during this time; perhaps even Agrippa lacked authority to permit a high priest to summon the council. A second point of some significance is that, for the first time since the days of John Hyrcanus, Josephus mentions the party affiliation of a high priest. Ananus is said to have been a Sadducee, a group noted for its more severe penalties in legal cases.[214] Elsewhere, a high priest is mentioned *in connection with* Sadducees (for example, apparently Caiaphas in Acts 5:17), but none of them, after Hyrcanus, is specifically said to have been of the Sadducean persuasion. We should add that just because

---

213. Some have argued that the passage is a Christian interpolation (see, as an example, Tessa Rajak, *Josephus: The Historian and His Society* [Philadelphia: Fortress Press, 1984], 131 n. 73). Yet, it seems to fit in the context in which Josephus describes a number of high-priestly misdemeanors. See W. Poehlmann, "The Sadducees as Josephus Presents Them, or The Curious Case of Ananus," in *All Things New: Essays in Honor of Roy A. Harrisville,* ed. A. Hultgren, D. Juel, J. D. Kingsbury; WWSS 1 (St. Paul: Luther Northwestern Theological Seminary, 1992), 94–95.

214. See Poehlmann, "The Sadducees as Josephus Presents Them," 95–96 for the suggestion that the real reason for Ananus's removal was not his harshness, as the narrative may imply, but his failure to act properly as a Jewish leader under Roman rule.

Ananus son of Ananus was a Sadducee does not imply that his father or brothers belonged to that group.[215] Perhaps they did, but we have no evidence for such a conclusion.[216]

One conclusion that we may draw from the fact that Ananus had James executed is that it continues a pattern of opposition by members of the Ananean family toward Jesus and his followers. The elder Ananus and his son-in-law Caiaphas were, as we have noted, the authorities at the time of Jesus' trial(s), while Acts 4:6 mentions them and perhaps Ananus's son Jonathan as those who, with the council, tried John and Peter. It is possible, too, that Matthias son of Ananus was high priest when Agrippa I had James son of Zebedee killed (Acts 12:1-2).[217] Ananus son of Ananus added to these incidents by trying and executing James, the brother of Jesus and leader of the early church in Jerusalem.[218]

The younger Ananus, a few years after his removal from the high priesthood, figured prominently in the war against Rome (66–70 CE). Josephus says that following the disaster suffered by Cestius, the governor of Syria, at the beginning of the revolt (late in 66 CE), the Jews who had pursued him returned to Jerusalem and "partly by force, partly by persuasion, brought over to their side such pro-Romans as still remained; and, assembling in the Temple, appointed additional generals to conduct the war. Joseph, son of Gorion, and Ananus the high priest were elected to the supreme control of affairs in the city, with a special charge to raise the height of the walls" (*J. W.* 2.20, 3 [§§562–63]). Later, as part of war preparations during the winter of 66–67, we meet him again: "In Jerusalem Ananus the high priest and all the leading men who were not pro-Roman busied themselves with the repair of

---

215. One could cite many authors who claim that the high priests were Sadducees or usually Sadducees, despite the fact that the sources offer little to no support for the assertion. Schürer limits himself to saying that the chief priests were Sadducean (Acts 5:17 and this passage in *Antiquities* 20 are the only evidence he adduces [*History*, 2.414]), while Jeremias speaks of Sadducean high priests (for example, *Jerusalem*, 159). The issue of the supposed Sadducean beliefs of the high priests has played a part in the analysis of the "Caiaphas" ossuary.

216. Barag and Flusser ("The Ossuary of Yehoḥanah," 43–44) claim it is reasonable to assume the entire family was Sadducean because Ananus son of Ananus was. See also Flusser, "Caiaphas in the New Testament," 82–85. Kokkinos devotes a short appendix to "Sadducean High Priests and the Ananus Family" (*Herodian Dynasty*, 383–84), but he has no other support for his claim that "about twenty out of twenty-eight known high priests between c. 37 BCE and CE 66 would have been Sadducees" (383). He like others makes the mistake of believing that Acts 4:6 and 5:17 identify the high priests as Sadducees when they clearly fall short of doing that.

217. So Kokkinos, *Herodian Dynasty*, 383. Acts does not, however, name the high priest of the time or indicate that a high priest was in any way implicated in the execution.

218. Barag and Flusser, "The Ossuary of Yehoḥanah," 44.

the walls and the accumulation of engines of war" (2.22, 1 [§648]). Ananus was a member of the aristocracy who took part in the revolt, but, says Josephus, he "cherished the thought of gradually abandoning these warlike preparations and bending the malcontents and the infatuated so-called zealots to a more salutary policy; but he succumbed to their violence, and the sequel of our narrative will show the fate which befell him" (2.22, 1 [§651]).[219] In the very next section, Josephus mentions that Ananus and the magistrates sent an army against Simon son of Gioras to check his abusive treatment of people in the toparchy of Acrabatene. Simon then went to Masada, where he stayed until Ananus and others of his opponents had died (2.22, 2 [§§652–53]; see also 4.9, 3 [§§503–4]).

Ananus occupies a major amount of space in Book 4 of *War*. As the Romans advanced from the north having taken Galilee and a large number of escaping rebels poured south into Jerusalem, some leading citizens were murdered. This is the context in which Josephus speaks about the election of high priests by lot (see below). Ananus, here called the "senior of the chief priests, a man of profound sanity, who might possibly have saved the city, had he escaped the conspirators' hands" (4.3, 7 [§151]), tried to lead the populace against the brigands. Their reaction was to appoint Phanni high priest (see below). Several leaders tried to arouse the people against their opponents the Zealots who had occupied the temple; among those leaders was Ananus son of Ananus (4.3, 9 [§160]). The former high priest then made a long speech at the temple, trying to introduce some sanity into the situation by urging them to stop the Zealots, the villains within (4.3, 10 [§§162–92]). He could not tolerate the way in which the radicals were treating the temple. Here, it almost sounds as if he is still the high priest:

> Truly well had it been for me to have died ere I had seen the house of God laden with such abominations and its unapproachable and hallowed places crowded with the feet of murderers! And yet I who wear the high priest's vestments, who bear that most honoured of venerated names, am alive and clinging to life, instead of braving a death

---

219. In *Life* 38.193–94, Josephus says that Simon tried to get the high priests Ananus and Jesus, son of Gamalas, to remove him (Josephus) from his Galilean command. Ananus refused, citing testimonies to Josephus's skill and saying no charge could be brought against him. Only through bribery did Simon and his associates induce Ananus to order Josephus to be expelled from his post (39.195–96). See also 44.216. In 60.309–10, the historian says that popular feeling in Jerusalem had been aroused against Ananus for sending a delegation to Galilee to deprive Josephus of his command without the consent of the general assembly. The people even wanted to burn down his house.

which would shed lustre on my old age. If it must be then, alone will I go and, as in utter desolation, devote this single life of mine in the cause of God. (*J.W.* 4.3, 10 [§§163–64])

He contrasted the Roman enemy favorably with the vile misdeeds of fellow Jews and called on the people to fight for God and the sanctuary.[220]

His speech produced the desired effect. The people asked him to lead them against the Zealots (*J.W.* 4.3, 11 [§§193–95]). A battle of two desperate sides ensued, with Ananus and his supporters gaining the outer courts of the temple and the Zealots withdrawing to the inner parts (4.3, 12 [§§196–207]). "Ananus did not think fit to assail the sacred portals, especially under the enemy's hail of missiles from above, but considered it unlawful, even were he victorious, to introduce these crowds without previous purification; instead, he selected by lot from the whole number six thousand armed men, whom he posted to guard the porticoes" (4.3, 12 [§§205–6]). Even the horrible circumstances did not detract from the ex-high priest's concern for the sanctity and purity of the temple.

Ananus continued to lead his faction, but his work was soon undermined by Josephus's enemy John of Gischala, who, the historian tells us, faked allegiance with Ananus but secretly betrayed secrets to the Zealots (*J.W.* 4.3, 13 [§§208–15]). John embroidered charges that Ananus had convinced the people to summon Vespasian, the Roman general, to take the city; he also told the Zealots that Ananus would offer them peaceful terms but then would attack when they were not expecting it (4.3, 14 [§§216–23]). To all of this, he added an accusation of brutality against him (4.4, 1 [§224]). John's influence induced the Zealots to invite the Idumeans to Jerusalem to oppose Ananus and his group (4.4, 1 [§§224–32]). The former high priest and his forces closed the gates to the approaching Idumeans, whom Jesus, the priest next in rank to Ananus and also a deposed high priest as we shall see, addressed (4.4, 3 [§§238–69]). He denied the charge of complicity with the Romans, though he did not convince the Idumeans.

When a terrible storm struck at night, Ananus's side understood it as God directing affairs in their favor, while the Idumeans, locked outside the city, understood it as God's judgment on themselves (*J.W.* 4.4, 6 [§288]). Ananus's reputation for diligence in inspecting the sentries made the Zealots hesitant about sallying forth from the temple to open the city to their frustrated helpers

---

220. As scholars have noted, Ananus's speech and that of Jesus son of Gamaliel "resonate with Josephus' pro-Roman aims in his own speeches to the rebels in Jerusalem and with his general sentiments throughout *The Jewish War*" (Poehlmann, "The Sadducees as Josephus Presents Them," 96).

(4.4, 6 [§296]). But the horrendous weather seems to have kept him from his appointed rounds, the guards slept, and the Zealots escaped from their temple prison to let the Idumeans into Jerusalem. Josephus says this happened, "not through any remissness on his part, but by the over-ruling decree of destiny that he and all his guards should perish" (4.4, 6 [§297]).

The Idumeans found Ananus, whom they held in contempt for supporting the people, and Jesus, whose speech they resented, and executed them, even refusing them burial (*J.W.* 4.5, 2 [§§315–16]). Josephus ends his account of Ananus with a remarkable encomium on the man who had been high priest for only three months in 62 CE but who in the war proved a sensible and brave leader:

> I should not be wrong in saying that the capture of the city began with the death of Ananus; and that the overthrow of the walls and the downfall of the Jewish state dated from the day on which the Jews beheld their high priest, the captain of their salvation, butchered in the heart of Jerusalem. A man on every ground revered and of the highest integrity, Ananus, with all the distinction of his birth, his rank and the honours to which he had attained, yet delighted to treat the very humblest as his equals. Unique in his love of liberty and an enthusiast for democracy, he on all occasions put the public welfare above his private interests. To maintain peace was his supreme object. He knew that the Roman power was irresistible, but, when driven to provide for a state of war, he endeavoured to secure that, if the Jews would not come to terms, the struggle should at least be skilfully conducted. In a word, had Ananus lived, they would undoubtedly either have arranged terms—for he was an effective speaker, whose words carried weight with the people, and was already gaining control even over those who thwarted him—or else, had hostilities continued, they would have greatly retarded the victory of the Romans under such a general. With him was linked Jesus, who, though not comparable with Ananus, stood far above the rest. But it was, I suppose, because God had, for its pollutions, condemned the city to destruction and desired to purge the sanctuary by fire, that He thus cut off those who clung to them with such tender affection. So they who but lately had worn the sacred vestments, led those ceremonies of world-wide significance, and had been reverenced by visitors to the city from every quarter of the earth, were now seen cast out naked, to be devoured by dogs and beasts of prey. Virtue herself, I think, groaned for these men's fate, bewailing such utter defeat at the hands of vice. Such, however, was the end of Ananus and Jesus. (*J.W.* 4.5, 2 [§§318–25])

Scholars have debated the stance of Ananus with respect to the Romans. Smallwood thinks he was consistently anti-Roman and describes his summoning the Sanhedrin and executing James as an act of defiance against Rome, even a frontal attack. His attitude did not change when the war started, but he was a little older and wiser by that time and realized opposition was futile.[221] Exactly how his action with the Sanhedrin during an interim between procurators should be seen as an act of defiance against Rome is less than clear; he may just have been exploiting an opportunity that others determined was dangerous. Horsley thinks Ananus and other aristocratic priests remained pro-Roman and urged moderation as events moved in a frightening direction toward revolt.[222] All should admit, nevertheless, that we are at a point in Josephus's narrative where he is anxious to put himself and other aristocrats in a favorable light—though they supported the war at first, they did so to check the madness of the hotheads who were the real cause. Such tendentiousness makes it difficult for the historian to disentangle from Josephus's statements exactly how Ananus viewed the Romans and the frightening developments in a place for which he had major responsibilities.[223]

48. Jesus Son of Damnaeus (62–63 CE?)

This Jesus is another poorly documented high priest from the Roman period, one of the few whose family connections are unknown (Damnaeus is not otherwise attested). Agrippa II appointed him high priest when he removed Ananus son of Ananus from office (*Ant.* 20.9, 1 [§203]). His short reign left little impression on the historical records at our disposal. Josephus does refer to the high priest while Jesus was in office but does not mention him by name. While Albinus was procurator, the former high priest Ananias, son of Nedebaeus, exercised considerable influence among the Jews. "Now the high priest Ananias daily advanced greatly in reputation and was splendidly rewarded by

221. Smallwood, "High Priests," 28–31.

222. Horsley, "High Priests," 48–55.

223. See Shaye J. D. Cohen, *Josephus in Galilee and Rome: His Vita and Development as a Historian*, CSCT 8 (Leiden: Brill, 1979; reprinted 2002), 184–87. For a careful examination of the historical issue regarding both the stance of the moderate leaders during the early years of the revolt and Josephus's motives in writing his various accounts about them (including himself), see U. Rappaport, "The Jewish Leadership in Jerusalem in the First Part of the Great Revolt (66–68 CE)," in *The Ancient Period*, ed. I. Gafni, vol. 1 of *The Congregation of Israel: Jewish Independent Rule in Its Generations* (Jerusalem: Zalman Shazar Center for Jewish History, 2001 [Hebrew]), 75–83.

the goodwill and esteem of the citizens; for he was able to supply them with money: at any rate he daily paid court with gifts to Albinus and the high priest. But Ananias had servants who were utter rascals and who, combining operations with the most reckless men, would go to the threshing floors and take by force the tithes of the priests; nor did they refrain from beating those who refused to give. The high priests were guilty of the same practices as his slaves, and no one could stop them. So it happened at that time that those of the priests who in olden days were maintained by the tithes now starved to death" (20.9, 2 [§§205–7]). So the practice that Josephus had noted before continued during the reign of Jesus son of Damnaeus.

The only other information about his high priesthood in *Antiquities* has to do with his removal from office—although for the first time we learn that a deposed high priest did not go quietly. Josephus relates (*Ant.* 20.9, 4 [§§211–12]) some incidents through which Agrippa II, who spent vast sums on non-Jewish cities (Caesarea Philippi and Berytus), became unpopular among the Jewish people. In the next sentence, the historian writes: "And now the king deposed Jesus the son of Damnaeus from the high priesthood and appointed as his successor Jesus the son of Gamaliel. In consequence, a feud arose between the latter and his predecessor. They each collected a band of the most reckless sort and it frequently happened that after exchanging insults they went further and hurled stones. Ananias, however, kept the upper hand by using his wealth to attract those who were willing to receive bribes" (*Ant.* 20.9, 4 [§213]). Here, we have three high priests in one scene: two apparently fighting for the position, while the third—Ananias who had been deposed four years earlier—seems to have had the greatest influence. We do not read how the conflict was settled, but Jesus son of Gamaliel became the next high priest. Jesus son of Damnaeus appears to have been deposed while Albinus was still procurator, since his replacement by Florus is not mentioned until the next section in *Antiquities* (20.9, 5 [§215]), that is, in 63 or 64 CE.[224]

49. Jesus Son of Gamaliel (63–64 CE)

In *Antiquities*, we read about Jesus son of Gamaliel only when he was appointed and when he was removed from office. His dismissal came when the temple, begun by Herod in 20 BCE, finally reached completion. But, since some eighteen thousand workers would have been left unemployed if work

---

224. For the dates of Florus's fateful and hopelessly corrupt procuratorship (64–66 CE), see Schürer, *History of the Jewish People*, 1.470.

ceased entirely, the populace urged Agrippa to provide jobs for them by com-
missioning a project to raise the height of the eastern portico of the temple.
He declined to approve of what would have been a great engineering challenge
but did grant the right to pave the city with white stones. Directly after this
section about the temple, Josephus writes: "He also deprived Jesus the son of
Gamaliel of the high priesthood and gave it to Matthias the son of Theophilus,
under whom the war of the Jews with the Romans began" (*Ant.* 20.9, 7
[§223]). This was not long after Florus assumed office, perhaps in 64 CE.
Whether the removal of Jesus had something to do with the rejected building
project we are not told.

The deposed Jesus became, with Ananus the son of Ananus, a leader of
what Josephus presents as the moderate faction in Jerusalem early in the revolt
against Rome. So, when leading citizens urged the Jerusalemites to oppose the
Zealots, Jesus and Ananus exhorted the people to such an effort (*J.W.* 4.3, 9
[§160]). We have already noted Jesus' lengthy speech to the Idumeans, whom
the Zealots had summoned to their aid (4.4, 3 [§§238–69]). In it, he denied the
people had asked the Romans to take Jerusalem and outlined several more
useful options that were open to the Idumeans—such as helping the people
against the Zealots or laying down their arms. He was unsuccessful and met
his death with Ananus at the hands of the Idumeans, who deeply resented his
speech and refused burial for his corpse (4.5, 2 [§316]). As we have seen, in his
praise of Ananus, Josephus says this Jesus did not rank with Ananus but was
better than the rest (§323). He is also linked with Ananus in *Life,* where the two
are said to have succumbed to bribes to remove Josephus from office (38.193)
In *Life* 41.204, Josephus refers to Jesus in an interesting setting. When secret
arrangements were made in Jerusalem to remove Josephus, "[m]y information
reached me in a letter from my father, to whom the news was confided by
Jesus, son of Gamalas, an intimate friend of mine, who had been present at the
conference." Josephus, therefore, was at the time a close friend of a former high
priest.

Although Josephus has very little to say about Jesus son of Gamaliel as
high priest, rabbinic literature preserves information about him that provides an intriguing addition that may well be historically reliable.[225] *M.
Yebam.* 6 deals with some of the rules governing high-priestly marriages. In
6:2, for example, we learn that a widow may not become the wife of a high
priest, while 6:3 stipulates that a widow betrothed to a high priest may not eat
of the heave offering (see also 7:1). In this context, 6:4 contains a reference to
our Jesus: "A High Priest may not marry a widow [see Lev 21:14] whether she

---

225. For the references, see Derenbourg, *Essai,* 248–49 n. 2.

had become a widow after betrothal or after wedlock; and he may not marry one that is past her girlhood. But R. Eliezer and R. Simeon declare one that is past her girlhood eligible. He may not marry one that is not *virgo intacta*. If he had betrothed a widow and was afterward appointed High Priest, he may consummate the union. It once happened that Joshua b. Gamla betrothed Martha the daughter of Boethus, and he consummated the union after that the king appointed him High Priest. If a woman awaited levirate marriage with a common priest and he was appointed High Priest, although he had bespoken her he may not consummate the union. If the brother of the High Priest died, the High Priest must submit to *halitzah* and may not contract levirate marriage." If Martha who married Jesus son of Gamaliel was from the family of Boethus, then we have an instance of a marriage connection between high-priestly families.

Commenting on the mishnaic passage, *b. Yebam.* 61a discusses the scriptural basis for the decisions but adds about Jesus/Joshua that, though he was appointed high priest, he was not elected. "Said R. Joseph: I see here a conspiracy; for R. Assi, in fact, related that Martha the daughter of Boethus brought to King Jannai a tarkab of denarii before he gave an appointment to Joshua b. Gamala among the High Priests."[226] The passage does not inspire great confidence about its historical value when it refers to King Jannai (Jannaeus) rather than Agrippa; also, the verbs used for "appointed" and "elected" (piel and nitpael of מנה) may reflect the assumption, undocumented in our historical sources, that the former refers to political appointment, the latter to appointment by the religious authorities.[227] This case is not mentioned in the *Tosefta* to the passage, but it does reappear in *b. Yoma* 18a.

M. Yoma also mentions a high priest who seems to be our Jesus/Joshua. In the course of describing the procedure for the high priest on the Day of Atonement itself, the text (3:9) recounts a change he made: "He [= the high priest] came to the east, to the north of the Altar, with the Prefect on his right and the chief of the father's house on his left. And two he-goats were there and there also was a casket in which were two lots. They were of box-wood, but Ben Gamla made some of gold, and his memory was kept in honour."

Several passages mention the death of Martha, Jesus' extremely wealthy wife, amid the famine-like conditions in Jerusalem during the revolt (for example, *b. Giṭ.* 56a). *Lamentations Rabbah* 1.50 on Lam 1:16 calls her

226. See *b. Giṭ.* 56a which calls her one of the richest women in Jerusalem. Compare also *t. Yoma* 1:14.

227. So nn. 17–18 to the Soncino translation, *Yebamot*, I. W. Slotki, part 3, vol. 1 (London: Soncino, 1936). See n. 20 for the idea that the name Jannai is used for any Hasmonean or Herodian ruler.

"Miriam daughter of Boethus [בייתוס] whom Joshua ben Gamla married; when the king appointed him high priest, she once went in to see and said: I will go and see him when he reads on the day of atonement at the temple. They brought out rugs from the door of her house to the door of the temple so that her feet would not be exposed (get cold) but they were exposed. When Joshua her husband died the sages apportioned to her two seahs of wine per day" (author's translation; after further discussion, the text also refers to the dainty woman of Deut 28:56).

Jesus ben Gamla is also credited with an educational innovation.

[F]rom the time of the regulation of Joshua b. Gamala, of whom Rab Judah has told us in the name of Rab: Verily the name of that man is to be blessed, to wit Joshua ben Gamala, for but for him the Torah would have been forgotten from Israel. For at first if a child had a father, his father taught him, and if he had no father he did not learn at all. By what [verse of the Scripture] did they guide themselves?— By the verse, *And ye shall teach them to your children* [Deut 11:19], laying the emphasis on the word '*ye*'. They then made an ordinance that teachers of children should be appointed in Jerusalem. By what verse did they guide themselves?—By the verse, *For from Zion shall the Torah go forth* [Isa 2:3]. Even so, however, if a child had a father, the father would take him up to Jerusalem and have him taught there, and if not, he would not go up to learn there. They therefore ordained that teachers should be appointed in each prefecture, and that boys should enter school at the age of sixteen or seventeen. [They did so] and if the teacher punished them they used to rebel and leave the school. At length Joshua b. Gamala came and ordained that teachers of young children should be appointed in each district and each town, and that children should enter school at the age of six or seven. (*b. B. Bat.* 21a; Raba refers to the same ordinance later in 21a)

We have no way of confirming the story, although Klausner for one maintains that it is reliable. He thought it was impossible that the Talmud would have attributed so important a reform to the wrong person (especially a high priest for whom the office was purchased by his wife). Also, he argued that Josephus's failure to mention the reform is understandable in light of his focus on external events.[228]

---

228. *History of the Second Temple*, 5.22–24. Schürer, too, accepted the story and took it as evidence that before this time schools for boys existed (*History*, 2.418–19).

50. Matthias Son of Theophilus (64–66 CE?)

The notice about Matthias's appointment is the last we hear of him in *Antiquities*. The name of his father makes one wonder whether he was the high priest Theophilus son of Ananus who ruled from 37–41 CE. It is possible that he was and that Matthias was another member of the illustrious family;[229] yet it is curious that Josephus says nothing about the matter. He may be mentioned in *J.W.* 6.2, 2 (§114).

Presumably Matthias lost his position at some point early in the revolt, although Josephus does not report the event. He seems to have been the last high priest who received the position through what was then regarded as a normal appointment.[230]

51. Phannias Son of Samuel (68 CE?)

Josephus does not mention this man in his narrative in *Antiquities*, but, in the summary of the high priests that he provides in 20.10, 1–5 (§§224–51), he writes that Aaron was the first high priest and that the office was passed down in his family. "Wherefore it is also a tradition that none should hold God's high-priesthood save him who is of Aaron's blood and that no one of another lineage, even if he happened to be a king, should attain to the high priesthood. The total number of the high priests beginning with Aaron, who, as I have said, was the first, up to Phanasus, who during the war was appointed high priest by the revolutionary party, is eighty-three" (20.10, 1 [§§226–27]). This Phanasus, who is called Phanni in *War*, is the last high priest of whom we know.

Josephus presents the situation in these terms. The rebels at this time set up their headquarters in the temple (Josephus mentions the Holy of Holies). "To these horrors was added a spice of mockery more galling than their actions. For, to test the abject submission of the populace and make trial of their own strength, they essayed to appoint the high priests by lot, although, as we have stated, the succession was hereditary [or: by families]. As pretext for this scheme they adduced ancient custom, asserting that in the old days the high priesthood had been determined by lot; but in reality their action was the

---

229. A number of scholars assume he was a son of the earlier Theophilus. See, for example, Smallwood, "High Priests," 32; Barag and Flusser, "The Ossuary of Yehohanah," 42, 44; Kokkinos, *Herodian Dynasty*, 384.

230. Derenbourg, *Essai*, 249.

abrogation of established practice and a trick to make themselves supreme by getting these appointments into their own hands" (*J.W.* 4.3, 7 [§§153–54]). The rebels could claim a certain justification for their procedure from 1 Chronicles 24 where the priestly clans at least were organized and arranged by lot.[231]

In *War,* we learn more about the high priest whom the rebels selected. At the point in the narrative when the Romans had subdued Galilee and their opponents were entering Jerusalem in large numbers (therefore probably in 68 CE), Josephus spends some time describing the depraved conditions in the city. Within that account he says: "In the end, to such abject prostration and terror were the people reduced and to such heights of madness rose these brigands, that they actually took upon themselves the election to the high priesthood. Abrogating the claims of those families from which in turn the high priests had always been drawn, they appointed to that office ignoble and low born individuals [ἀσήμους καὶ ἀγενεῖς], in order to gain accomplices in their impious crimes; for persons who had undeservedly attained to the highest dignity were bound to obey those who conferred it" (*J.W.* 4.3, 6 [§§147–49]). The statement is interesting for several reasons. For one, it confirms what was apparent from the narratives, that a small number of families produced the high priests in the period from Herod to the revolt. For another, Josephus implies that more than one individual was appointed to the position by the rebels, although he never mentions another high priest whom they chose and calls Phanni the last. As a result, we might infer that there were others who served between Matthias son of Theophilus and Phanni; against this conclusion is, however, that Josephus says twenty-eight high priests held office during the 107 years from the beginning of Herod's reign until Titus burned the temple (see *Ant.* 20.10, 5 [§250]). If true, this would leave no space for any others between Matthias and Phanni.

Although he implied more than once that the lot fell on high priests, Josephus names only one and does so in the very next paragraph. "They accordingly summoned one of the high-priestly clans [ἀρχιερατικῶν φυλήν], called Eniachin, and cast lots for a high priest. By chance the lot fell to one who proved a signal illustration of their depravity; he was an individual named Phanni, son of Samuel, of the village of Aphthia, a man who not only was not descended from high priests, but was such a clown that he scarcely knew what the high priesthood meant. At any rate they dragged their reluctant victim out of the country and, dressing him up for his assumed part, as on the stage, put the sacred vestments upon him and instructed him how to

---

231. Klausner, *History of the Second Temple,* 5.208–9.

act in keeping with the occasion. To them this monstrous impiety was a subject for jesting and sport, but the other priests, beholding from a distance this mockery of their law, could not restrain their tears and bemoaned the degradation of the sacred honours" (*J. W.* 4.3, 8 [§§155–57]). The clan to which this Phanni belonged is otherwise unknown, though Josephus describes it as a high-priestly family (though curiously adding that he was not from high-priestly stock).[232]

While Josephus mentions Phanni (Pinhas) just in the one passage and treats him as if he were a buffoon, his name does surface in some rabbinic texts. *T. Yoma* 1:6–7, commenting on *m. Yoma* 1:2, specifically the words "for the High Priest has first place in offering a portion [of the animal-offerings] and has first place in taking a portion," says:

> It is the religious requirement of the high priest to be greater than his brethren in beauty, strength, wealth, wisdom, and good looks. [If] he is not, how do we know that his brethren should magnify him? Since it says, *And the priest who is higher by reason of his brethren* (Lev 21:10 [הכהן הגדול מאחיו])—that they should make him great. They said about Pinhas of Ḥabbata, on whom the lot fell to be high priest, that the revenuers and supervisors came along and found him cutting wood. So they filled up his woodshed with golden *denars*. R. Ḥanina b. Gamliel says, "Was he not a stonecutter? And was he not our father-in-law?[233] But they found him ploughing, as it says concerning Elisha, *So he departed from there, and found Elisha the son of Shaphat, who was plowing, with twelve yoke of oxen before him, and he was with the twelfth* (1 Kgs 19:19)." When [unacceptable] kings became many, they ordained the practice of regularly appointing high priests, and they appointed high priests every single year.[234]

The passage at least contains a reflection of Phanni's humble station and his election by lot.

---

232. One suggestion is that the form in *War* is a corruption of a name such as Yaqim, Elyaqim, or Yachin. See Thackeray, *Josephus 3*, 46–47 n. c; Klausner, *History of the Second Temple*, 5.208. The terms that Josephus uses in connection with Phannias (ignoble or undistinguished yet of a high-priestly family) remind one of those used to characterize Herod's appointments, particularly Ananel (*Ant.* 15.2, 4 [§22]; 15.3, 1 [§§39–40]; 20.10, 5 [§247]).

233. As R. Ḥanina b. Gamliel was from the patriarchal house and called Phineas his father-in-law, Klausner concluded he could hardly be a low-class character as Josephus presents him (*History of the Second Temple*, 5.209).

234. Neusner, *The Tosefta*, 1.542–43; see also *Sifra*, Emor 2 (113.1).

With this man, the history of the Second-Temple high priesthood whimpers to a sad end. Perhaps he served until the temple went up in flames in 70 CE, but Josephus has no more to say about him.

And so the Second-Temple high priesthood arrived at its conclusion, some 600 years after it began. The ancient office, so rich in sacerdotal and political associations, ended on a low note, never to be revived. Yet, though the historical form of the office ceased, the coming of an eschatological high priest had by this time, perhaps encouraged by failings among those who held the office, become an article of hope among some Jews and Christians. But that is another story, and here our study of the men who held the office of high priest may close.

The High Priests
of the Second Temple

The High Priests in Chronological Order

Chapter 1

1. Joshua (time of Cyrus [538–30] and the year 520 during the reign of Darius [522–486])

Chapter 2: Persian Period

2. Joiakim
3. Eliashib (mentioned in the year 444 in the time of Nehemiah)
4. Joiada
5. Johanan (mentioned in the year 410 in the Elephantine papyri)
6. Jaddua (contemporary of Alexander the Great [336–323]?)

Chapter 3: Early Hellenistic Period

7. Onias I (contemporary of Areus I [309–265]?)
8. Simon I
9. Eleazar (contemporary of Ptolemy II Philadelphus [283–246]?)
10. Manasseh
11. Onias II (contemporary of Ptolemy III Euergetes [246–221]?)
12. Simon II (contemporary of Ptolemy IV Philopator [221–204]?)
13. Onias III (?–175 BCE)
14. Jason (175–172 BCE)
15. Menelaus (172–162 BCE)
    Interlude: Onias IV?
16. Alcimus (162 to 160–159 BCE)

Chapter 4: Hasmonean High Priests

17. Jonathan (152–142 BCE)
18. Simon (142–134 BCE)
19. John Hyrcanus (134–104 BCE)
20. Aristobulus I (104–103 BCE)
21. Alexander Jannaeus (103–76 BCE)
22. Hyrcanus II (76–67, 63–40 BCE)
23. Aristobulus II (67–63 BCE)
24. Antigonus (40–37 BCE)

Chapter 5: Herodian Age

25. Ananel (37–35, 35–30? BCE)
26. Aristobulus III (35 BCE)
27. Jesus son of Phiabi (30–24/22 BCE)
28. Simon son of Boethus (24/22–5 BCE)
29. Matthias son of Theophilus (5–4 BCE)
30. Joazar son of Boethus (4 BCE?–6 CE)
31. Eleazar son of Boethus (4 BCE)
32. Jesus son of Seë (4 BCE to ?)
33. Ananus son of Seth/Sethi (6–15 CE)
34. Ishmael son of Phiabi (15–16 CE?)
35. Eleazar son of Ananus (16–17 CE?)
36. Simon son of Camith (17–18 CE)
37. Joseph Caiaphas (18–36/37 CE)
38. Jonathan son of Ananus (36 or 37 CE)
39. Theophilus son of Ananus (37–41 CE)
40. Simon Cantheras son of Boethus (41–42 CE)
41. Matthias son of Ananus (42–43 CE?)
42. Elionaeus son of Cantheras (43?–45 CE)
43. Joseph son of Camei (45–48 CE)
44. Ananias son of Nedebaeus (48–59 CE)
45. Ishmael son of Phiabi (59–61 CE)
46. Joseph son of Simon (61–62 CE)
47. Ananus son of Ananus (62 CE)
48. Jesus son of Damnaeus (62–63 CE?)
49. Jesus son of Gamaliel (63–64 CE)
50. Matthias son of Theophilus (64–66 CE?)
51. Phannias son of Samuel (68 CE?)

Families Supplying High Priests in the Herodian Age

Ananus (Annas)
1. Ananus son of Seth/Sethi (6–15 CE)
2. Eleazar son of Ananus (16–17 CE?)
3. Joseph Caiaphas (son-in-law of Ananus) (18–36/37 CE)
4. Jonathan son of Ananus (36 or 37 CE)
5. Theophilus son of Ananus (37–41 CE)
6. Matthias son of Ananus (42–43 CE?)
7. Ananus son of Ananus (62 CE)

Boethus

1. Simon son of Boethus (24/22–5 BCE)
2. Joazar son of Boethus (4 BCE?–6 CE)
3. Eleazar son of Boethus (4 BCE)
4. Simon Cantheras son of Boethus (41–42 CE)
5. Jesus son of Gamaliel (his wife was from the family of Boethus) (63–64 CE)

Phiabi

1. Jesus son of Phiabi (30–24/22 BCE)
2. Ishmael son of Phiabi (15–16 CE?)
3. Ishmael son of Phiabi (59–61 CE)

Bibliography

Abel, F.-M. "Alexandre le grand en Syrie et en Palestine (suite)." *RB* 44 (1935): 42–61.

———. *Les livres des Maccabées. EBib.* Paris: Gabalda, 1949.

Abel, F.-M., and Jean Starcky. *Les livres des Maccabées.* Revised 3rd ed. Paris: Cerf, 1961.

Ackroyd, Peter R. *Exile and Restoration: A Study of Hebrew Thought of the Sixth Century B.C.* OTL. Philadelphia: Westminster, 1968.

———. "The Jewish Community in Palestine in the Persian Period." In *Introduction: The Persian Period*, edited by W. D. Davies and L. Finkelstein, 160–61. *CHJ* 1. Cambridge: Cambridge Univ. Press, 1984.

———. "The Temple Vessels—A Continuity Theme." In *Studies in the Religion of Ancient Israel*, 166–81. VTSup 23. Leiden: Brill, 1972.

———. "Two Old Testament Historical Problems of the Early Persian Period." *JNES* 17 (1958): 13–27.

Adler, William. "The Apocalyptic Survey of History Adapted by Christians: Daniel's Prophecy of Seventy Weeks." In *The Jewish Apocalyptic Heritage in Early Christianity*, edited by J. VanderKam and W. Adler, 201–38. CRINT 3.4. Minneapolis: Fortress Press, 1996.

Albright, William F. "The Date and Personality of the Chronicler." *JBL* 40 (1921): 104–24.

Allan, N. "The Identity of the Jerusalem Priesthood during the Exile." *HeyJ* 23 (1982): 259–69.

Alon, Gedalia. *Jews, Judaism, and the Classical World. Studies in Jewish History in the Times of the Second Temple and Talmud.* Translated by I. Abrahams. Jerusalem: Magness, 1977.

———. *Studies in Jewish History.* 2 vols. Tel Aviv: Hakkibbutz Hameuchad, 1957 (Hebrew).

Alt, Albrecht. "Die Rolle Samarias bei der Entstehung des Judentums." In *Festschrift Otto Procksch zum 60. Geburtstag*, 5–28. Leipzig: Deichert, 1934.

Reprinted in idem, *Kleine Schriften zur Geschichte des Volkes Israel*. Vol. 2, 316–37. 3d ed. Münich: Beck, 1953.

Andersen, Francis I. "Who Built the Second Temple?" *ABR* 6 (1958): 1–35.

Anderson, H. "3 Maccabees." In *OTP* 2:509–30.

Andrews, H. T. "The Letter of Aristeas." In *APOT* 2.83–122.

Annandale-Potgieter, Joan. "The High Priests in I Maccabees and in the Writing of Josephus." In *VII Congress of the International Organization for Septuagint and Cognate Studies, Leuven 1989*, edited by C. E. Cox, 393–429. SBLSCS 31. Atlanta: Scholars, 1991.

Aptowitzer, Victor. *Parteipolitik der Hasmonäerzeit im rabbinischen und pseudoepigraphischen Schrifttum*. Veröffentlichungen der Alexander Kohut Memorial Foundation 5. Vienna: Kohut Foundation, 1927.

Ararat, Nisan. "Ezra and His Mission in the Biblical and Post-biblical Sources." *BM* 17 (1972): 451–92 (Hebrew).

Attridge, Harold W. *The Epistle to the Hebrews*. Hermeneia. Philadelphia: Fortress Press, 1989.

Avigad, Nahman. *Bullae and Seals from a Post-Exilic Judean Archive*. Qedem 4. Jerusalem: The Institute of Archaeology, the Hebrew Univ. of Jerusalem, 1976.

———. "A Bulla of Jonathan the High Priest." *IEJ* 25 (1975): 8–12.

———. "A Bulla of King Jonathan." *IEJ* 25 (1975): 245–46.

———. "Jerusalem: Burnt House (Area B)." In *NEAEHL* 2.734.

Bagnall, Roger S., and Peter Derow. *Greek Historical Documents: The Hellenistic Period*. SBLSBS 16. Chico, Calif.: Scholars, 1981.

Bailey, J. W. "The Usage in the Post Restoration Period of Terms Descriptive of the Priest and High Priest." *JBL* 70 (1951): 217–25.

Baldwin, Joyce G. *Haggai, Zechariah, Malachi. An Introduction and Commentary*. TOTC. Downers Grove, Ill.: InterVarsity Press, 1972.

Bammel, Ernst. "Die Bruderfolge im Hochpriestertum der herodianisch-römischen Zeit." In idem, *Judaica: Kleine Schriften I*, 21–27. WUNT 37. Tübingen: Mohr/Siebeck, 1986.

———. "Joasar." In idem, *Judaica: Kleine Schriften I*, 28–34. Reprint of *ZDPV* 90 (1974): 61–68.

———. "Pilatus' und Kaiphas' Absetzung." In idem, *Judaica: Kleine Schriften I*, 51–58.

———. "ΑΡΧΙΕΡΕΥΣ ΠΡΟΦΗΤΕΥΩΝ." In idem, *Judaica et Paulina: Kleine Schriften II*, 133–39. WUNT 91. Tübingen: Mohr/Siebeck, 1997. Reprint of *TLZ* 79 (1954): 351–56.

Barag, Dan. "The Effects of the Tennes Rebellion on Palestine." *BASOR* 183 (1966): 6–12.

————. "A Silver Coin of Yohanan the High Priest and the Coinage of Judea in the Fourth Century B.C." *Israel Numismatic Journal* 9 (1986–87): 4–21 with pl. 1.

————. "Some Notes on a Silver Coin of Johanan the High Priest." *BA* 48 (1985): 166–68.

Barag, Dan, and David Flusser. "The Ossuary of Yehoḥanah Granddaughter of the High Priest Theophilus." *IEJ* 36 (1986): 39–44.

Barclay, John M. G. *Jews in the Mediterranean Diaspora: From Alexander to Trajan (323 BCE–117 CE)*. Edinburgh: T. & T. Clark, 1996.

Bar-Kochva, Bezalel. *Pseudo-Hecataeus, "On the Jews": Legitimizing the Jewish Diaspora*. HCS 21. Berkeley: Univ. of California Press, 1996.

Bartlett, J. R. "Zadok and His Successors at Jerusalem." *JTS* 19 (1968): 1–18.

Batten, Loring W. *A Critical and Exegetical Commentary on the Books of Ezra and Nehemiah*. ICC. Edinburgh: T. & T. Clark, 1913.

Bauernfeind, O. "στρατεύομαι κτλ." In *TDNT* 7.704.

Baumann, Uwe. *Rom und die Juden: Die römisch-jüdischen Beziehungen von Pompeius bis zum Tode des Herodes (63 v. Chr.–4 v. Chr.)*. Studia Philosophica et Historica 4. Frankfurt: Lang, 1983.

Baumgarten, A. "Rabbinic Literature as a Source for the History of Jewish Sectarianism in the Second Temple Period." *DSD* 2 (1995): 14–57.

————. "Seekers After Smooth Things." *EDSS* 2.857–59.

Baumgarten, J. "On the Non-literal Use of maʿaser/dekate." *JBL* 103 (1984): 245–51.

————. *Qumran Cave 4 XIII: The Damascus Document (4Q266–273)*. DJD 18. Oxford: Clarendon, 1996.

Beavis, M. "Anti-Egyptian Polemic in the Letter of Aristeas 130–165 (The High Priest's Discourse)." *JSJ* 18 (1987): 145–51.

Béchard, D. P. "The Disputed Case against Paul: A Redaction-Critical Analysis of Acts 21:27—22:29." *CBQ* 65 (2003): 232–50.

Bedford, Peter Ross. *Temple Restoration in Early Achaemenid Judah*. JSJSup 65. Leiden: Brill, 2001.

Bengtsson, Håkan. "What's in a Name? A Study of the Sobriquets in the Pesharim." Dissertation, Uppsala Univ., 2000.

Berger, P.-R. "Zu den Namen ששבצר und שנאצר (Esr 1 8.11 5 14.16 bzw. 1 Chr 3 18)." *ZAW* 83 (1971): 98–100.

Betlyon, J. "The Provincial Government of Persian Period Judea and the Yehud Coins." *JBL* 105 (1986): 633–42.

Beuken, Wim. *Haggai-Sacharja 1–8. Studien zur Überlieferungsgeschichte der frühnachexilischen Prophetie*. SSN 10. Assen: van Gorcum, 1967.

Bevan, Edwyn Robert. *A History of Egypt under the Ptolemaic Dynasty.* London: Methuen, 1927.

———. *The House of Seleucus.* 2 vols. London: Arnold, 1902. Reprinted, New York: Barnes & Noble, 1966.

———. *Jerusalem under the High Priests: Five Lectures on the Period between Nehemiah and the New Testament.* London: Arnold, 1904; reprinted 1952.

Bi(c)kerman(n), E. J. "La charte séleucide de Jérusalem." *REJ* 100 (1935): 4–35. Reprinted in idem, *Studies in Jewish and Christian History,* 2.44–85. 3 vols. AGJU 9. Leiden: Brill, 1976–86.

———. *Chronology of the Ancient World.* 2d ed. Aspects of Greek and Roman Life. Ithaca, N.Y.: Cornell Univ. Press, 1980.

———. "The Edict of Cyrus in Ezra 1." *JBL* 65 (1946): 249–75. Reprinted in idem, *Studies in Jewish and Christian History,* 1.72–108.

———. *Der Gott der Makkabäer: Untersuchungen über Sinn und Ursprung der makkabäischen Erhebung.* Berlin: Schocken, 1937; English translation 1979.

———. "Héliodore au temple de Jérusalem." *AIPHOS* 7 (1939–44). Reprinted in idem, *Studies in Jewish and Christian History,* 2.159–91.

———. *Institutions des Séleucides.* Service des Antiquités, Bibliothèque archéologique et historique 26. Paris: Librairie orientaliste Paul Geuthner, 1938.

———. *The Jews in the Greek Age.* Cambridge: Harvard Univ. Press, 1988.

———. "Ein jüdischer Festbrief vom Jahre 124 v. Chr. (II Macc 1 1-9)." *ZNW* 32 (1933): 233–54.

———. "Makkabäerbücher." In *PW* 14.779–97.

———. "Une proclamation séleucide relative au temple de Jérusalem." *Syria* 25 (1946–48): 67–85.

———. "Zur Datierung des Pseudo-Aristeas." *ZNW* 29 (1930): 280–98.

Bilde, Per. *Flavius Josephus between Jerusalem and Rome: His Life, His Works, and Their Importance.* JSPSup 2. Sheffield: JSOT Press, 1988.

Black, Matthew. *The Book of Enoch or I Enoch.* SVTP 7. Leiden: Brill, 1985.

Blackman, Philip. *Mishnayot.* Vol. 2 of *Order Moed.* 2d ed. Gateshead: Judaica, 1983.

Blenkinsopp, Joseph. *Ezra-Nehemiah: A Commentary.* OTL. Philadelphia: Westminster, 1988.

———. "Prophecy and Priesthood in Josephus." *JJS* 25 (1974): 239–62.

Box, G. H., and W. O. E. Oesterley. "Sirach." In *APOT* 1.507–508.

Boyd, J. O. "The Composition of the Book of Ezra." *The Presbyterian and Reformed Review* 11 (1900): 261–97.

Bright, John. *A History of Israel.* 3d ed. Philadelphia: Westminster, 1981.

Bringmann, Klaus. *Hellenistische Reform und Religionsverfolgung in Judäa: Eine Untersuchung zur jüdisch-hellenistischen Geschichte (175–163 v. Chr.).* Abhandlungen der Akademie der Wissenschaften in Göttingen, Philologisch-historische Klasse, Dritte Folge 132. Göttingen: Vandenhoeck & Ruprecht, 1983.

Brody, R. "Caiaphas and Cantheras." Appendix IV in D. R. Schwartz, *Agrippa I: The Last King of Judaea,* 190–95. TSAJ 23. Tübingen: Mohr/Siebeck, 1990.

Brown, Raymond E. *The Gospel According to John I–XII.* AB 29. Garden City, N.Y.: Doubleday, 1966.

———. *The Gospel According to John XIII–XXI.* AB 29A. Garden City, N.Y.: Doubleday, 1970.

Bruce, F. F. *The Acts of the Apostles.* 3d ed. Grand Rapids: Eerdmans, 1990.

Büchler, Adolf. "La relation de Josèphe concernant Alexandre le grand." *REJ* 36 (1898): 1–26.

———. *Die Tobiaden und die Oniaden im II. Makkabäerbuche und in der verwandten jüdisch-hellenistischen Litteratur: Untersuchungen zur Geschichte der Juden von 220–160 und zur jüdisch-hellenistischen Litteratur.* Vienna: Hölder, 1899. Reprinted, Hildesheim: Olms, 1975.

Büchsel, Friedrich. "ἀλληγορέω." In *TDNT* 1.260–63.

Buehler, W. "The Pre-Herodian Civil War and Social Debate: Jewish Society in the Period 76–40 B.C. and the Social Factors Contributing to the Rise of the Pharisees and the Sadducees." Ph.D. diss., Basel, 1974.

Bull, Robert J. "Er-Ras, Tell." In *EAEHL* 4.1022.

———. "The Excavation of Tell er-Ras on Mt. Gerizim." *BA* 31 (1968): 58–72.

———. "Gerizim, Mount." In *IDBSup* 361.

Bultmann, Rudolf. *The Gospel of John: A Commentary.* Translated by G. R. Beasley-Murray. Philadelphia: Westminster, 1971.

Bunge, Jochen Gabriel. "Zur Geschichte und Chronologie des Untergangs der Oniaden und des Aufstiegs der Hasmonäer." *JSJ* 6 (1975): 1–46.

Burgmann, H. "Das umstrittene Intersacerdotium in Jerusalem 159–152 v. Chr." *JSJ* 11 (1980): 135–76.

Busink, T. A. *Der Tempel von Jerusalem von Salomo bis Herodes.* 2 vols. SFSMD. Leiden: Brill, 1970–80.

Cardauns, Burkhart. "Juden und Spartaner: Zur hellenistisch-judischen Literatur." *Hermes* 95 (1967): 317–24.

Cashdan, Eli. *Menaḥoth.* The Babylonian Talmud 5/2, edited by I. Epstein. London: Soncino, 1948.

Charles, R. H. "The Testaments of the XII Patriarchs." In *APOT* 2.282–367.

Chilton, Bruce. "Annas." In *ABD* 1.257–58.

Cody, Aelred. *A History of Old Testament Priesthood*. AnBib 35. Rome: Pontifical Biblical Institute, 1969.

Coggins, R. J. *Samaritans and Jews: The Origins of Samaritanism Reconsidered*. GPT. Atlanta: John Knox, 1975.

Cohen, Shaye J. D. "Alexander the Great and Jaddus the High Priest According to Josephus." *AJSR* 7-8 (1982–83): 41–68.

————. *The Beginnings of Jewishness: Boundaries, Varieties, Uncertainties*. HCS 31. Berkeley: Univ. of California Press, 1999.

————. *Josephus in Galilee and Rome: His Vita and Development as a Historian*. CSCT 8. Leiden: Brill, 1979; reprinted 2002.

————. "The Political and Social History of the Jews in Greco-Roman Antiquity: The State of the Question." In *Early Judaism and Its Modern Interpreters*, edited by Robert Kraft and George W. E. Nickelsburg, 33–56. The Bible and Its Modern Interpreters. Atlanta: Scholars; Philadelphia: Fortress Press, 1986.

Collins, John J. *Between Athens and Jerusalem: Jewish Identity in the Hellenistic Diaspora*. 2d ed. BRS. Grand Rapids: Eerdmans, 2000.

————. *Daniel*. Hermeneia. Minneapolis: Fortress Press, 1993.

————. "The Origin of the Qumran Community: A Review of the Evidence." In *To Touch the Text: Biblical and Related Studies in Honor of Joseph A. Fitzmyer, S.J.*, edited by M. P. Horgan and P. J. Kobelski, 159–78. New York: Crossroad, 1989.

————. *The Sibylline Oracles of Egyptian Judaism*. SBLDS 13. Missoula: SBL, 1974.

Collins, John J., and Peter W. Flint. "245. 4Qpseudo-Daniel^c ar." In *Qumran Cave 4 XVII Parabiblical Texts, Part 3*, consulting editor J. VanderKam, 153–64. DJD 22. Oxford: Clarendon, 1996.

Collins, Nina L. *The Library in Alexandria and the Bible in Greek*. VTSup 82. Leiden: Brill, 2000.

Colson, F. H. *Philo 8*. LCL. Cambridge: Harvard Univ. Press, 1939.

Cook, J. M. *The Persian Empire*. New York: Shocken, 1983. Reprinted, Barnes & Noble, 1993.

Cotton, Hannah M., and E. Larson. "4Q460/4Q350 and Tampering with Qumran Texts in Antiquity?" In *Emanuel: Studies in Hebrew Bible, Septuagint, and Dead Sea Scrolls in Honor of Emanuel Tov*, edited by S. M. Paul, R. A. Kraft, L. H. Schiffman, and W. W. Fields, 113–25. VTSup 94. Leiden: Brill, 2003.

Cotton, Hannah M., and Ada Yardeni, eds. *Aramaic, Hebrew, and Greek Documentary Texts from Naḥal Ḥever and Other Sites*. DJD 27. Oxford: Clarendon, 1997.

Cowley, A. E. *Aramaic Papyri of the Fifth Century B.C.* Oxford: Clarendon, 1923. Reprinted Osnabrück: Zeller, 1967.

Crenshaw, J. L. "The Contest of Darius' Guards." In *Images of Man and God*, edited by B. Long, 74–88, 119–20. Sheffield: Almond, 1981.

Cross, Frank Moore. *The Ancient Library of Qumran.* Revised 3d ed. Minneapolis: Fortress Press, 1995.

———. "Aspects of Samaritan and Jewish History in Late Persian and Hellenistic Times." *HTR* 59 (1966): 201–11.

———. "Daliyeh, Wadi ed-." In *ABD* 2.3–4.

———. "The Papyri and Their Historical Implications." In *Discoveries in the Wadi Ed-Daliyeh*, edited by P. W. Lapp and N. L. Lapp, 17–29. AASOR 41. Cambridge: ASOR, 1974.

———. "Papyri of the Fourth Century B.C. from Dâliyeh. A Preliminary Report on Their Discovery and Significance." In *New Directions in Biblical Archaeology.* Edited by D. N. Freedman and J. C. Greenfield, 45–69. Garden City, N.Y.: Doubleday, 1971.

———. "A Reconstruction of the Judean Restoration." *JBL* 94 (1975): 4–18. Reprinted in *Int* 29 (1975): 187–201.

———. "Samaria and Jerusalem: The Early History of the Samaritans and Their Relations with the Jews." In *The History of the People of Israel: The Return from the Babylonian Exile—The Period of Persian Rule,* edited by H. Tadmor, 89–94. Jerusalem: 'Am 'oved, 1983 (Hebrew).

Dahlberg, Bruce T. "Jehohanan." In *IDB* 2.810–11.

———. "Johanan." In *IDB* 2.929–30.

Danby, Herbert. *The Mishnah.* Oxford: Oxford Univ. Press, 1933.

Dancy, John Christopher. *A Commentary on I Maccabees.* BTT. Oxford: Blackwell, 1954.

Dandamaev, M. A. *A Political History of the Achaemenid Empire.* Leiden: Brill, 1989.

Daube, D. "Typology in Josephus." *JJS* 31 (1980): 18–36.

David, Ephraim. *Sparta between Empire and Revolution (404–243 B.C.): Internal Problems and Their Impact on Contemporary Greek Consciousness.* Monographs in Classical Studies. New York: Arno, 1981.

Davis, J. D. "The Reclothing and Coronation of Joshua." *Princeton Theological Review* 18 (1920): 256–68.

De Bruyne, D. "Le texte grec des deux premiers livres des Machabées." *RB* 31 (1922): 31–54.

Delcor, M. "Le temple d'Onias en Égypte: Réexamen d'un vieux problème." *RB* 75 (1968): 188–203.

Derenbourg, Joseph. *Essai sur l'histoire et la géographie de la Palestine d'après les Thalmuds et les autres sources rabbiniques.* Paris: Imprimerie impériale, 1867. Reprinted, Hildesheim: Gerstenberg, 1975.

Dinsmoor, W. B. *The Archons of Athens in the Hellenistic Age.* Amsterdam: Hakkert, 1966. Reprint of the 1931 edition.

Dion, Paul Eugène. "ששבצר und סנורי." *ZAW* 95 (1983): 111–12.

Dommershausen, Werner. "כהן." In *TDOT* 7.60–75.

Doran, Robert. "Pseudo-Hecataeus." In *OTP* 2.905–19.

———. *Temple Propaganda: The Purpose and Character of 2 Maccabees.* CBQMS 12. Washington, D.C.: Catholic Biblical Association, 1981.

Doudna, Gregory L. *4Q Pesher Nahum: A Critical Edition.* JSPSup 35. Sheffield: Sheffield Academic, 2001.

Downey, Glanville. *A History of Antioch in Syria from Seleucus to the Arab Conquest.* Princeton: Princeton Univ. Press, 1961.

Downey, Susan B. *Mesopotamian Religious Architecture: Alexander through the Parthians.* Princeton: Princeton Univ. Press, 1988.

Dyck, Jonathan E. *The Theocratic Ideology of the Chronicler.* BibIntSer 33. Leiden: Brill, 1998.

Efron, Joshua. "Simeon Ben Shataḥ and Alexander Jannaeus." In idem, *Studies on the Hasmonean Period,* 161–89. SJLA 39. Leiden: Brill, 1987.

Elliger, Karl. *Studien zum Habakuk-Kommentar vom Toten Meer.* BHT 15. Tübingen: Mohr/Siebeck, 1953.

Emmet, C. "III Maccabees." In *APOT* 1.164.

Epstein, I., ed. *The Babylonian Talmud.* 24 vols. London: Soncino, 1935–48.

Eshel, Esther, Hanan Eshel, and Ada Yardeni. *Qumran Cave 4 VI Poetical and Liturgical Texts, Part 1.* Consulting editors J. C. VanderKam and M. Brady. DJD 11. Oxford: Clarendon, 1998.

Eshel, Hanan. "The History of the Qumran Community and the Historical Details in the Dead Sea Scrolls." *Qad* 30 (1997): 86–93.

———. "4Q348, 4Q343, and 4Q345: Three Economic Documents from Qumran Cave 4?" *JJS* 52 (2001): 132–35.

Evans, Craig A. "Caiaphas Ossuary." In *Dictionary of New Testament Background,* edited by C. A. Evans and S. E. Porter, 179–80. Downers Grove, Ill.: InterVarsity, 2000.

Feldman, Louis H., trans. *Josephus.* Vols. 9–10: *Jewish Antiquities Books 18–20.* LCL. Cambridge: Harvard Univ. Press, 1965.

———. "Prophets and Prophecy in Josephus." *JTS* 41 (1990): 386–422.

Fensham, F. Charles. *The Books of Ezra and Nehemiah.* NICOT. Grand Rapids: Eerdmans, 1982.

Finkelstein, Louis H. "The Men of the Great Synagogue (*circa* 400–170 B.C.E.)." In *The Hellenistic Age*, edited by W. D. Davies and L. Finkelstein, 229–44. *CHJ* 2. Cambridge: Cambridge Univ. Press, 1990.

———. *The Pharisees: The Sociological Background of Their Faith*. Philadelphia: JPS, 1938.

Fitzmyer, Joseph A. "331. 4QpapHistorical Text C." In *Qumran Cave 4 XXVI Miscellanea, Part 1*, 275–80. DJD 36. Oxford: Clarendon, 2000.

———. *The Acts of the Apostles*. AB 31. Garden City, N.Y.: Doubleday, 1998.

———. *The Gospel According to Luke I-IX*. AB 28. Garden City, N.Y.: Doubleday, 1981.

Flint, Peter W. "4Qpseudo-Daniel ar^c (4Q245) and the Restoration of the Priesthood." *RevQ* 17 (1996): 137–50.

Flusser, David. "Caiaphas in the New Testament." '*Atiqot* 21 (1992): 81–87.

Forrest, W. G. G. *A History of Sparta 950–192 B.C.* Norton Library. New York: Norton, 1968.

Fraser, P. M. *Ptolemaic Alexandria*. 3 vols. Oxford: Clarendon, 1972.

Freyne, Sean. *Galilee from Alexander the Great to Hadrian, 323 BCE to 135 CE: A Study of Second Temple Judaism*. Edinburgh: T. & T. Clark, 1998. Paperback edition of 1980 volume.

Gafni, Y. "The Hasmoneans in Rabbinic Literature." In *The Hasmonean Period*, edited by D. Amit and H. Eshel, 261–76. Sederet 'Idan 19. Jerusalem: Yitzhak ben-Zvi, 1995 (Hebrew).

Gager, John G. *Moses in Greco-Roman Paganism*. SBLMS 16. Nashville: Abingdon, 1972.

Galling, Kurt. *Studien zur Geschichte Israels im persischen Zeitalter*. Tübingen: Mohr/Siebeck, 1964.

Gardner, A. E. "The Purpose and Date of 1 Esdras." *JJS* 37 (1986): 18–27.

Gauger, Jörg-Dieter. "Zitate in der jüdischen Apologetik und die Authentizität der Hekataios-Passagen bei Flavius Josephus und in Ps. Aristeas-Brief." *JSJ* 13 (1982): 6–46.

Geiger, J. "The Hasmonaeans and Hellenistic Succession." *JJS* 53 (2002): 1–17.

Geller, M. J. "Alexander Jannaeus and the Pharisee Rift." *JJS* 30 (1979): 202–11.

Gelston, A. "The Foundations of the Second Temple." *VT* 16 (1966): 232–35.

Gera, Dov. *Judaea and Mediterranean Politics 219 to 161 B.C.E.* BSJS 8. Leiden: Brill, 1998.

———. "On the Credibility of the History of the Tobiads (Josephus, *Antiquities* 12, 156–22, 228–236)." In *Greece and Rome in Eretz Israel*, edited by A. Kasher, U. Rappaport, and G. Fuks, 21–38. Jerusalem: Yitzhak ben-Zvi, IES, 1990.

Geva, Hillel. "Jerusalem, Tombs." In *NEAEHL* 2.756.

Ginsburg, Michael S. "Sparta and Judaea." *CP* 29 (1934): 117–22.

Gnuse, Robert. "The Temple Experience of Jaddus in the *Antiquities* of Josephus: A Report of Jewish Dream Incubation." *JQR* 83 (1993): 349–68.

Golan, David. "Josephus, Alexander's Visit to Jerusalem, and Modern Historiography." In *Josephus Flavius: Historian of Israel in the Hellenistic-Roman Period*, edited by U. Rappaport, 29–55. Jerusalem: Yitzhak ben-Zvi, 1982 (Hebrew).

Goldstein, Jonathan A. "Alexander and the Jews." *PAAJR* 59 (1993): 59–101.

———. *I Maccabees*. AB 41. Garden City, N.Y.: Doubleday, 1976.

———. *II Maccabees*. AB 41A. Garden City, N.Y.: Doubleday, 1983.

———. "The Tales of the Tobiads." In *Christianity, Judaism, and Other Greco-Roman Cults: Studies for Morton Smith at Sixty*. Part 3: *Judaism before 70*, edited by J. Neusner, 85–123. SJLA 12. Leiden: Brill, 1975.

Goodman, Martin. *The Ruling Class of Judaea: The Origins of the Jewish Revolt against Rome A.D. 66–70*. Cambridge: Cambridge Univ. Press, 1987.

Grabbe, Lester. *Judaism from Cyrus to Hadrian*. Vol. 1: *The Persian and Greek Periods*. Minneapolis: Fortress Press, 1992.

Graetz, Heinrich. "Die absetzbaren Hohenpriester während des zweiten Tempels." *MGWJ* 1 (1852–53): 585–96.

———. *History of the Jews*. Vol. 1: *From the Earliest Period to the Death of Simon the Maccabee (135 B.C.E.)*. Philadelphia: Jewish Publication Society, 1891.

———. "Zur Geschichte der nachexilischen Hohenpriester." *MGWJ* 30 (1881): 49–64, 97–112.

Gray, Rebecca. *Prophetic Figures in Late Second Temple Jewish Palestine: The Evidence from Josephus*. New York: Oxford Univ. Press, 1993.

Green, Peter. *Alexander to Actium: The Historical Evolution of the Hellenistic Age*. HCS 1. Berkeley: Univ. of California Press, 1990.

Greenhut, Zvi. *The Akeldama Tombs: Three Burial Caves in the Kidron Valley, Jerusalem*. IAA Reports 1. Jerusalem: Israel Antiquities Authority, 1996.

———. "The 'Caiaphas' Tomb in North Talpiyot, Jerusalem." *'Atiqot* 21 (1992): 63–71.

Greenwald, Y. *The History of the High Priests in its Relation to the General Political and Religious History of the Jewish People from the Earliest Times till the Destruction of the Second Temple*. New York: published privately, 1932 (Hebrew).

Greeven, H. "προσκυνέω, προσκυνητής." In *TDNT* 6.758–66.

Grelot, Pierre. *Documents araméens d'Égypte*. Littératures anciennes du Proche-Orient. Paris: Cerf, 1972.

Grintz, Yehoshua M. "Chapters in the History of the High Priesthood." *Zion* 23 (1958): 124–40 (Hebrew).

Gropp, Douglas Marvin. "Sanballat." In *EDSS*, 823–25.

———. *Wadi Daliyeh II. The Samaria Papyri from Wadi Daliyeh and Qumran Cave 4 XXVIII Miscellanea, Part 2*. Consulting editors J. VanderKam and M. Brady. DJD 28. Oxford: Clarendon, 2001.

Grosheide, H. H. "Ezra, de Schriftgeleerde." *Reformeerd Theologisch Tijdschrift* 56 (1956): 84–88.

———. "Twee Edikten van Cyrus ten Gunste van de Joden (Ezra 1:2-4 en 6:3-5)." *Gereformeerd Theologisch Tijdschrift* 54 (1954): 1–12.

Gruen, Erich S. *Heritage and Hellenism: The Reinvention of Jewish Tradition*. HCS 30. Berkeley: Univ. of California Press, 1998.

Gunneweg, A. H. J. "Zur Interpretation der Bücher Esra-Nehemia." In *Congress Volume. Vienna, 1980,* edited by J. A. Emerton, 146–61. VTSup 32. Leiden: Brill, 1981.

Gutman, Y. "Alexander of Macedon in the Land of Israel." *Tarbiz* 11 (1940): 271–94.

Habicht, Christian. *2. Makkabäerbuch*. JSHRZ 1.3. Gütersloh: Gütersloher, 1979.

———. "Royal Documents in Maccabees II." *HSCP* 80 (1976): 1–18.

Hadas, Moses. *Aristeas to Philocrates (Letter of Aristeas)*. Jewish Apocryphal Literature. New York: Harper, 1951.

———. *Hellenistic Culture: Fusion and Diffusion*. Morningside Heights, N.Y.: Columbia Univ. Press, 1959.

Hall, B. "Samaritan History: From John Hyrcanus to Baba Rabbah." In *The Samaritans*, edited by A. D. Crown, 32–54. Tübingen: Mohr/Siebeck, 1989.

Halpern, Baruch. "A Historiographic Commentary on Ezra 1–6: Achronological Narrative and Dual Chronology in Israelite Historiography." In *The Hebrew Bible and Its Interpreters*, edited by W. H. Propp, B. Halpern, and D. N. Freedman, 81–142. BJSUCSD 1. Winona Lake, Ind.: Eisenbrauns, 1990.

———. "The Ritual Background of Zechariah's Temple Song." *CBQ* 40 (1978): 167–90.

———. "Sacred History and Ideology: Chronicles' Thematic Structure—Indications of an Earlier Source." In *The Creation of Sacred Literature: Composition and Redaction of the Biblical Text*, edited by R. E. Friedman, 35–54. Univ. of California Publications: Near Eastern Studies 22. Berkeley: Univ. of California, 1981.

Hamp, Vinzenz, and G. Johannes Botterweck. "דין." In *TDOT* 3.187–94.

Haran, Menahem. "Book-Size and the Device of Catch-Lines in the Biblical Canon." *JJS* 37 (1986): 1–11.

———. "Priesthood, Priests." In *Encyclopaedia Miqra'it* 3.14–45. Jerusalem: Bialik, 1971 (Hebrew).

———. *Temples and Temple-Service in Ancient Israel: An Inquiry into Biblical Cult Phenomena and the Historical Setting of the Priestly School.* Oxford: Clarendon, 1978. Reprinted, Winona Lake, Ind.: Eisenbrauns, 1985.

Harrelson, Walter. "The Trial of the High Priest Joshua." *ErIsr* 16 (1982): 116–24.

Hayes, John H., and J. Maxwell Miller, eds. *Israelite and Judaean History.* OTL. Philadelphia: Westminster, 1977.

Hayward, Robert. "The Jewish Temple at Leontopolis: A Reconsideration." *JJS* 33 (1982): 429–43.

Hengel, Martin. *Jews, Greeks, and Barbarians: Aspects of the Hellenization of Judaism in the Pre-Christian Period.* Translated by J. Bowden. Philadelphia: Fortress Press, 1980.

———. *Judaism and Hellenism: Studies in Their Encounter in Palestine during the Early Hellenistic Period.* 2 vols. Translated by J. Bowden. Philadelphia: Fortress Press, 1974.

———. *The Zealots: Investigations into the Jewish Freedom Movement in the Period from Herod I until 70 A.D.* Edinburgh: T. & T. Clark, 1989.

Hensley, L. "The Official Persian Documents in the Book of Ezra." Ph.D. diss., Univ. of Liverpool, 1977.

Herford, R. Travers. *The Ethics of the Talmud: Sayings of the Fathers.* New York: Schocken, 1962.

———. *The Pharisees.* Boston: Beacon, 1962.

Herrmann, Siegfried. *A History of Israel in Old Testament Times.* 2d ed. Translated by J. Bowden. Philadelphia: Fortress Press, 1981.

Herzfeld, L. "Wann war die Eroberung Jerusalems durch Pompejus, und wann die durch Herodes?" *MGWJ* 4 (1855): 109–15.

Hoglund, Kenneth G. *Achaemenid Imperial Administration in Syria-Palestine and the Missions of Ezra and Nehemiah.* SBLDS 125. Atlanta: Scholars, 1992.

Holladay, Carl R. *Fragments from Hellenistic Jewish Authors.* Vol. 1: *Historians.* SBLTT 20. Chico, Calif.: Scholars, 1984.

Holleaux, M. "Sur un passage de Flavius Josèphe (Ant. xii.4)." *REJ* 39 (1899): 161–76.

Hölscher, Gustav. *Die Hohenpriesterliste bei Josephus und die evangelische Chronologie.* SHAW, 1939–40. 3. Abhandlung. Heidelberg: Winter, 1940.

Horbury, William. "The 'Caiaphas' Ossuaries and Joseph Caiaphas." *PEQ* 126 (1994): 32–48.

Horbury, William, and David Noy. *Jewish Inscriptions of Graeco-Roman Egypt.* Cambridge: Cambridge Univ. Press, 1992.

Horsley, Richard A. "High Priests and the Politics of Roman Palestine: A Contextual Analysis of the Evidence in Josephus." *JSJ* 17 (1986): 23–55.

Houtman, C. *Exodus.* HCOT 3. Leuven: Peeters, 2000.

Isaiah, Abraham ben, and Benjamin Sharfman. *The Pentateuch and Rashi's Commentary.* Vol. 3: *Leviticus.* Brooklyn: S. S. & R., 1950.

Japhet, Sara. *I & II Chronicles: A Commentary.* OTL. Louisville: Westminster John Knox, 1993.

———. "Sheshbazzar and Zerubbabel against the Background of the Historical and Religious Tendencies of Ezra-Nehemiah." *ZAW* 94 (1982): 66–98; 95 (1983): 218–29.

———. "The Supposed Common Authorship of Ezra-Nehemia Investigated Anew." *VT* 18 (1968): 330–71.

Jastrow, Marcus. *A Dictionary of the Targumim, the Talmud Babli and Yerushalmi, and the Midrashic Literature.* New York: Jastrow, 1903.

Jellicoe, Sidney. "The Occasion and Purpose of the Letter of Aristeas: A Reexamination." *NTS* 12 (1965–66): 144–50.

———. *The Septuagint and Modern Study.* Oxford: Clarendon, 1968. Reprinted, Winona Lake, Ind.: Eisenbrauns, 1993.

Jeremias, Christian. *Die Nachtgesichte des Sacharja.* FRLANT 117. Göttingen: Vandenhoeck & Ruprecht, 1977.

Jeremias, Joachim. *Jerusalem in the Time of Jesus: An Investigation into Economic and Social Conditions during the New Testament Period.* Translated by F. H. Cave and C. H. Cave. Philadelphia: Fortress Press, 1969.

Josephus. Translated by H. St. J. Thackeray et al. 10 vols. LCL. Cambridge: Harvard Univ. Press, 1926–1965.

Jung, L. *Yoma.* The Babylonian Talmud 2/5. Edited by I. Epstein. London: Soncino, 1938.

Kahana, Abraham. "מקבים ב." In הספרים החיצונים, 72–231. Vol. 2 of *The Non-Canonical Books.* Edited by A. Kahana. Reprint, Jerusalem: Maqor, 1970.

Kaiser, Otto. "Zwischen den Fronten: Palästina in den Auseinandersetzungen zwischen dem Perserreich und Ägypten in der ersten Hälfte des 4. Jahrhunderts." In *Wort, Lied und Gottesspruch: Beiträge zu Psalmen und Propheten. Festschrift für Joseph Ziegler,* edited by J. Schreiner, 2.197–206. FB 2. Würzburg: Echter; Katholisches Bibelwerk, 1972.

———. "חרב." In *TDOT* 5.150–54.

Kappler, Werner, ed. *Maccabaeorum liber I.* Septuaginta: Vetus Testamentum Graecum Auctoritate Societatis Litterarum Gottingensis editum IX, 1. Göttingen: Vandenhoeck & Ruprecht, 1936.

Kasher, Aryeh. "Alexander of Macedon's Campaign in Palestine." *BM* 20 (1975): 187–208 (Hebrew).

———. *The Jews in Hellenistic and Roman Egypt: The Struggle for Equal Rights.* TSAJ 7. Tübingen: Mohr/Siebeck, 1985.

Kehati, P. *Mishnayot. Moed* 2, vol. 4. Jerusalem: Hekhal Shelomoh, 1991 (Hebrew).

Keil, V. "Onias III.—Märtyrer oder Tempelgründer?" *ZAW* 97 (1985): 221–33.

Kim, Tae Hun. "The Dream of Alexander in Josephus *Ant.* 11.325–39." *JSJ* 34 (2003): 425–42.

Kindler, A. "Silver Coins Bearing the Name of Judea from the Early Hellenistic Period." *IEJ* 24 (1974): 73–76.

Klausner, Joseph. *The History of the Second Temple.* 5 vols. 6th ed. Jerusalem: Achiasaf, 1963.

Klein, R. "Sanballat." In *IDBSup* 781–82.

Knibb, Michael A. *The Ethiopic Book of Enoch.* 2 vols. Oxford: Clarendon, 1978.

Koch, Klaus. "Ezra and Meremoth: Remarks on the History of the High Priesthood." In *"Sha'arei Talmon": Studies in the Bible, Qumran, and the Ancient Near East Presented to Shemaryahu Talmon,* edited by M. Fishbane and E. Tov, 105–10. Winona Lake, Ind.: Eisenbrauns, 1992.

———. "Ezra and the Origins of Judaism." *JSS* 19 (1974): 173–97.

Koehler, L., W. Baumgartner, and J. J. Stamm. *The Hebrew and Aramaic Lexicon of the Old Testament.* Translated and edited under the supervision of M. E. J. Richardson. 4 vols. Leiden: Brill, 1994–99.

Kokkinos, Nikos. *The Herodian Dynasty: Origins, Role in Society, and Eclipse.* JSPSup 30. Sheffield: Sheffield Academic, 1998.

Koopmans, J. J. "Het eerste Aramese Gedeelte in Ezra." *Gereformeerd Theologisch Tijdschrift* 55 (1955): 142–60.

Kuhrt, Amélie. "The Cyrus Cylinder and Achaemenid Imperial Policy." *JSOT* 25 (1983): 83–97.

Lagrange, M.-J. "Où en est la question du recensement de Quirinius?" *RB* 8 (1911): 60–84.

Lake, Kirsopp. "The Chronology of Acts." In *The Beginnings of Christianity. Part 1: The Acts of the Apostles.* 5 vols. Edited by F. Foakes-Jackson and K. Lake, 5.445–74. London: Macmillan, 1920–33. Reprinted, Grand Rapids: Baker, 1979.

Lee, Thomas R. *Studies in the Form of Sirach 44–50.* SBLDS 75. Atlanta: Scholars Press, 1986.

Leith, Mary Joan Winn. *Wadi Daliyeh I. The Wadi Daliyeh Seal Impressions.* Edited by M. D. Coogan. DJD 24. Oxford: Clarendon Press, 1997.

Lemaire, André. "Le roi Jonathan à Qoumrân (4Q448 B–C)." In *Qoumrân et les manuscrits de la mer Morte,* edited by E.-M. Laperrousaz, 57–70. Paris: Cerf, 1997.

Levine, Lee I. "The Political Struggle between Pharisees and Sadducees in the Hasmonean Period." In *Jerusalem in the Second Temple Period: Abraham Schalit Memorial Volume,* edited by A. Oppenheimer, U. Rappaport, and M. Stern, 61–83. Jerusalem: Yitzhak ben-Zvi, Ministry of Defence, 1980 (Hebrew).

Lichtenstein, H. "Die Fastenrolle. Eine Untersuchung zur jüdisch-hellenistischen Geschichte." *HUCA* 8-9 (1931–1932): 257–317.

Lieberman, Saul. *Hellenism in Jewish Palestine: Studies in the Literary Transmission, Beliefs and Manners of Palestine in the I Century B.C.E.–IV Century, C.E.* Texts and Studies of the Jewish Theological Seminary of America 18. New York: Jewish Theological Seminary of America, 1962.

Liver, Jacob. *Chapters in the History of the Priests and Levites: Studies on the Lists in Chronicles, Ezra, and Nehemiah.* Publications of the Perry Foundation for Biblical Research in the Hebrew Univ. of Jerusalem. Jerusalem: Magnes, 1968 (Hebrew).

———. *The House of David from the Fall of the Kingdom of Judah to the Fall of the Second Commonwealth and After.* Jerusalem: Magnes, 1959 (Hebrew).

———. "יוחנן." In *Encyclopaedia Miqraʾit,* 3.590–91. Jerusalem: Bialik, 1971.

———. "עם."In *Encyclopaedia Miqraʾit,* 6.237–38. Jerusalem: Bialik, 1971.

Magen, I. "Gerizim, Mount." In *NEAEHL* 2.489.

———. "Mt. Gerizim—Temple City." *Qad* 33 (2000): 74–118 (Hebrew).

Main, E. "For King Jonathan or Against? The Use of the Bible in 4Q448." In *Biblical Perspectives: Early Use and Interpretation of the Bible in Light of the Dead Sea Scrolls,* edited by M. E. Stone and E. G. Chazon, 113–35. STDJ 28. Leiden: Brill, 1998.

Mandell, Sara R. "Did the Maccabees Believe That They Had a Valid Treaty with Rome?" *CBQ* 53 (1991): 202–20.

Mantel, Hugo. *Studies in the History of the Sanhedrin.* HSS 17. Cambridge: Harvard Univ. Press, 1965.

Marcus, Ralph, trans. *Josephus.* Vols. 6–8: *Jewish Antiquities, Books 9–17.* LCL. Cambridge: Harvard Univ. Press, 1937–63.

Martin, C. H. R. "Alexander and the High Priest." *TGUOS* 23 (1969–70): 102–14.

Mason, Steve. *Flavius Josephus on the Pharisees: A Composition-Critical Study.* StPB 39. Leiden: Brill, 1991.

Mazar, Benjamin. "The Tobiads." *IEJ* 7 (1957): 137–45, 229–38.

McCollough, W. Stewart. *The History and Literature of the Palestinian Jews from Cyrus to Herod, 550 BC to 4 BC.* Toronto: Univ. of Toronto, 1975.

McEvenue, Sean E. "The Political Structure in Judah from Cyrus to Nehemiah." *CBQ* 43 (1981): 353–64.

McGing, B. C. "Pontius Pilate and the Sources." *CBQ* 53 (1991): 416–38.

McKenzie, Steven L., and John M. Berridge. "Johanan." *ABD* 3.880–82.

McLaren, James S. *Power and Politics in Palestine: The Jews and the Governing of their Land 100 BC –AD 70.* JSNTSup 63. Sheffield: JSOT Press, 1991.

Meier, John P. *Companions and Competitors.* Vol. 3 of *A Marginal Jew: Rethinking the Historical Jesus.* ABRL. New York: Doubleday, 2001.

Mendels, Doron. "Hecataeus of Abdera and a Jewish 'patrios politeia' of the Perisan Period (Diodorus Siculus XL, 3)." *ZAW* 95 (1983): 96–110. Reprinted in idem, *Identity, Religion, and Historiography: Studies in Hellenistic History.* JSPSup 24. Sheffield: Sheffield Academic, 1998.

Meshorer, Yaᶜakov. *Ancient Jewish Coinage.* 2 vols. Dix Hills, N.Y.: Amphora, 1982.

———. *A Treasury of Jewish Coins from the Persian Period to Bar-Kochba.* Jerusalem: Yizthak ben-Zvi, 1997 (Hebrew).

Meyer, Eduard. *Die Entstehung des Judentums: Eine historische Untersuchung.* Halle: Niemeyer, 1896.

———. *Ursprung und Anfänge des Christentums.* 3 vols. Stuttgart: Cotta, 1921.

Meyers, Carol L. "Veil of the Temple." In *ABD* 6.785–86.

Meyers, Carol L., and Eric M. Meyers. *Haggai, Zechariah 1–8.* AB 25B. Garden City, N.Y.: Doubleday, 1987.

Meyers, Eric M. "The Persian Period and the Judean Restoration: From Zerubbabel to Nehemiah." In *Ancient Israelite Religion: Essays in Honor of Frank Moore Cross* edited by P. D. Miller, P. D. Hanson, and S. D. McBride, 509–21. Philadelphia: Fortress Press, 1987.

———. "The Shelomith Seal and the Judean Restoration: Some Additional Considerations." *ErIsr* 18 (1985): 33*–38*.

Michaelis, W. "συγγενής συγγένεια." In *TDNT* 7.736–42.

Mildenberg, L. "Yehud: A Preliminary Study of the Provincial Coinage of Judaea." In *Greek Numismatics and Archaeology: Essays in Honor of Margaret Thompson,* edited by O. Mørkholm and N. M. Waggoner, 183–96. Wetteren: NR, 1979.

Milgrom, Jacob. *Leviticus 17–22.* AB 3A. New York: Doubleday, 2000.

Milik, J. T. *Ten Years of Discovery in the Wilderness of Judaea*. SBT 26. London: SCM, 1959.

Millar, Fergus. "Reflections on the Trial of Jesus." In *A Tribute to Geza Vermes: Essays on Jewish and Christian Literature and History*, edited by P. Davies and R. White, 355–81. JSOTSup 100. Sheffield: JSOT Press, 1990.

———. *The Roman Near East 31 BC–AD 337*. Cambridge: Harvard Univ. Press, 1993.

Miller, J. Maxwell, and John H. Hayes. *A History of Ancient Israel and Judah*. Philadelphia: Westminster, 1986.

Mitchell, Hinckley G. *A Critical and Exegetical Commentary on Haggai, Zechariah, Malachi, and Jonah*. ICC. Edinburgh: T. & T. Clark, 1912.

Mölleken, W. "Geschichtsklitterung im I. Makkabäerbuch (Wann wurde Alkimus Hoherpriester?)." *ZAW* 65 (1953): 205–28.

Momigliano, Arnaldo. "Flavius Josephus and Alexander's Visit to Jerusalem." *Athenaeum* 57 (1979): 442–48.

Montgomery, James A. *A Critical and Exegetical Commentary on the Book of Daniel*. ICC. Edinburgh: T. & T. Clark, 1927.

Moore, Carey A. *Daniel, Esther, and Jeremiah: The Additions*. AB 44. Garden City, N.Y.: Doubleday, 1977.

———. *Judith*. AB 40. Garden City, N.Y.: Doubleday, 1985.

Moore, George F. *Judaism in the First Centuries of the Christian Era*. 2 vols. New York: Schocken Books, 1927. Reprinted 1930, 1971.

———. "Simeon the Righteous." In *Jewish Studies in Memory of Israel Abrahams*, edited by G. A. Kohut, 348–64. New York: Jewish Institute of Religion, 1927.

Mor, Menahem. "The High Priests in Judah in the Persian Period." *BM* 23 (1977): 57–67 (Hebrew).

———. "Samaritan History: The Persian, Hellenistic and Hasmonaean Period." In *The Samaritans*, edited by A. D. Crown, 1–18. Tübingen: Mohr/Siebeck, 1989.

Morgenstern, Julius. "Jerusalem—485 B.C." *HUCA* 27 (1956): 101–79.

———. "Jerusalem—485 B.C. (continued)." *HUCA* 28 (1957): 15–47.

———. "Jerusalem—485 B.C. (concluded)." *HUCA* 31 (1960): 11–29.

———. "Supplementary Studies in the Calendars of Ancient Israel." *HUCA* 10 (1935): 1–148.

Mørkholm, O. *Antiochus IV of Syria*. Classica et mediaevalia, dissertationes 8. Copenhagen: Gyldendalske, 1966.

Mosis, Rudolf. "יסד." In *TDOT* 6.109–21.

Mowinckel, Sigmund. *Studien zu dem Buche Ezra-Nehemia, 1; Die nachchronische Redaktion des Buches. Die Listen*. Oslo: Universitetsforlaget, 1964.

Murphy-O'Connor, Jerome. "Demetrius I and the Teacher of Righteousness (*I Macc.*, x, 25-45)." *RB* 83 (1976): 400–420.

Myers, Jacob M. *Ezra-Nehemiah*. AB 14. Garden City, N.Y.: Doubleday, 1965.

———. *I & II Esdras*. AB 42. Garden City, N.Y.: Doubleday, 1974.

———. "Turban." In *IDB* 4.718.

Netzer, Ehud. *Hasmonean and Herodian Palaces at Jericho*. Vol. 1. Jerusalem: IES, 2001.

———. "Jericho: Tulul Abu el-'alayiq." In *NEAEHL* 2.682–91.

———. "The Winter Palaces of the Judean Kings at Jericho at the End of the Second Temple Period." *BASOR* 228 (1977): 1–13.

Neusner, Jacob. *From Politics to Piety: The Emergence of Pharisaic Judaism*. Englewood Cliffs, N.J.: Prentice-Hall, 1973.

———. *Genesis Rabbah: The Judaic Commentary to the Book of Genesis: A New American Translation*. 3 vols. BJS 104–106. Atlanta: Scholars, 1985.

———. "Josephus' Pharisees: A Complete Repertoire." In *Josephus, Judaism, and Christianity*, edited by L. H. Feldman and G. Hata, 274–92. Detroit: Wayne State Univ. Press, 1987.

———. *The Rabbinic Traditions about the Pharisees before 70*. 3 vols. Leiden: Brill, 1971. Reprinted, Atlanta: Scholars, 1999.

———. *The Tosefta: Translated from the Hebrew with a New Introduction*. 2 vols. Peabody, Mass.: Hendrickson, 2002.

Newman, Judith H. *Praying by the Book: The Scripturalization of Prayer in Second Temple Judaism*. SBLEJL 14. Atlanta: Scholars, 1999.

Nickelsburg, George W. E. *Jewish Literature between the Bible and the Mishnah: A Historical and Literary Introduction*. Philadelphia: Fortress Press, 1981.

Niditch, Susan. "Father-Son Folktale Patterns and Tyrant Typologies in Josephus' Ant. 12.160–222." *JJS* 32 (1981): 47–55.

Noethlichs, K. *Das Judentum und der römische Staat: Minderheitenpolitik im antiken Rom*. Darmstadt: Wissenschaftliche Buchgesellschaft, 1996.

Noth, Martin. *The History of Israel*. 2d ed. Translated by P. R. Ackroyd. New York: Harper & Row, 1960.

Ó Fearghail, F. "Sir 50, 5-21: Yom Kippur or the Daily Whole-Offering?" *Bib* 59 (1978): 301–16.

Olmstead, A. T. *History of the Persian Empire*. Chicago: Univ. of Chicago Press, 1948.

———. "Tattenai, Governor of 'Across the River.'" *JNES* 3 (1944): 46.

Otto, Walter Friedrich. *Herodes: Beiträge zur Geschichte des letzten jüdischen Königshauses*. Stuttgart: Metzlersche Buchhandlung, 1913.

Parente, Fausto. "Onias III' [*sic*] Death and the Founding of the Temple of Leontopolis." In *Josephus and the History of the Greco-Roman Period:*

Essays in Memory of Morton Smith, edited by F. Parente and J. Sievers, 69–98. StPB 41. Leiden: Brill, 1994.

————. "The Third Book of Maccabees as Ideological Document and Historical Source." *Hen* 10 (1988): 143–82.

Pelletier, A. *Lettre d'Aristée à Philocrate: Introduction, texte critique, traduction et notes, index complet des mots grecs.* SC 89. Paris: Cerf, 1962.

Petersen, David L. *Haggai and Zechariah 1–8.* OTL. Philadelphia: Westminster, 1984.

————. "Zerubbabel and Jerusalem Temple Reconstruction." *CBQ* 36 (1974): 366–72.

Petitjean, Albert. "La mission de Zorobabel et la reconstruction du Temple: Zach., III, 8-10." *ETL* 42 (1966): 40–71.

————. *Les oracles du Proto-Zacharie: Un programme de restauration pour la communauté juive après l'exil.* EBib. Paris: Gabalda, 1969.

Poehlmann, W. "The Sadducees as Josephus Presents Them, or the Curious Case of Ananus." In *All Things New: Essays in Honor of Roy A. Harrisville,* edited by A. J. Hultgren, D. H. Juel, J. D. Kingsbury, 87–100. WWSS 1. St. Paul: Luther Northwestern Theological Seminary, 1992.

Pohlmann, Karl-Friedrich. *Studien zum dritten Esra.* FRLANT 104. Göttingen: Vandenhoeck & Ruprecht, 1970.

Pomykala, Kenneth E. *The Davidic Dynasty Tradition in Early Judaism: Its History and Significance for Messianism.* SBLEJL 7. Atlanta: Scholars, 1995.

Porten, Bezalel. *Archives from Elephantine: The Life of an Ancient Jewish Military Colony.* Berkeley: Univ. of California Press, 1968.

————. "The Documents in the Book of Ezra and the Mission of Ezra." *Shenaton* 4 (1978–79): 174–96 (Hebrew).

————. *The Elephantine Papyri in English.* Documenta et Monumenta Orientis Antiqui 22. Leiden: Brill, 1996.

————. "The Return to Zion in Light of the Elephantine Papyri." *BM* 16 (1963): 66–79 (Hebrew).

Porten, Bezalel, and Ada Yardeni. *Textbook of Aramaic Documents from Ancient Egypt.* 4 vols. Jerusalem: Hebrew Univ., 1986–99.

Porter, J. R. "Son or Grandson (Ezra X.6)?" *JTS* 17 (1966): 54–67.

Pritchard, James B., ed. *Ancient Near Eastern Texts Relating to the Old Testament.* 3d ed. Princeton: Princeton Univ. Press, 1969.

Pucci Ben Zeev, M. "Caesar and Jewish Law." *RB* 102 (1995): 28–37.

————. "Caesar's Decrees in the Antiquities: Josephus' Forgeries or Authentic Roman *Senatus Consulta*?" *Athenaeum* 84 (1996): 71–91.

————. "Greek and Roman Documents from Republican Times in the Antiquities: What Was Josephus' Source?" *Scripta Classica Israelica* 13 (1994): 46–59.

————. "The Reliability of Josephus Flavius: The Case of Hecataeus' and Manetho's Accounts of Jews and Judaism: Fifteen Years of Contemporary Research (1974–1990)." *JSJ* 24 (1993): 217–24.

————. "Seleukos of Rhosos and Hyrcanus II." *JSJ* 26 (1995): 113–21.

Puech, Émil. "523. 4QJonathan." In *Qumrân Grotte 4 XVIII. Textes Hébreux (4Q521–4Q528, 4Q576–4Q579)*, 75–83. DJD 25. Oxford: Clarendon, 1998.

————. *La croyance des Esséniens en la vie future: Immortalité, résurrection, vie éternelle?* 2 vols. EBib 21-22. Paris: LeCoffre, 1993.

————. "Le grand prêtre Simon (III) fils d'Onias III, le Maître de Justice?" In *Antikes Judentum und Frühes Christentum: Festschrift für Hartmut Stegemann zum 65. Geburtstag*, edited by B. Kollmann, W. Reinbold, and A. Steudel, 137–58. BZNW 97. Berlin: de Gruyter, 1999.

————. "Jonathan le Prêtre Impie et les débuts de la Communauté de Qumrân. 4QJonathan (4Q523) et 4QPsAp (4Q448)." *RevQ* 17 (1996): 241–70.

Pummer, Richard. "Antisamaritanische Polemik in judischen Schriften aus der intertestamentarischen Zeit." *Biblische Zeitschrift* 26 (1982): 224–42.

————. "Samaritan Material Remains and Archaeology." In *The Samaritans*, edited by A. D. Crown, 135–77. Tübingen: Mohr/Siebeck, 1989.

Purvis, James D. *The Samaritan Pentateuch and the Origin of the Samaritan Sect*. HSM 2. Cambridge: Harvard Univ. Press, 1968.

————. "The Samaritans and Judaism." In *Early Judaism and Its Modern Interpreters. The Bible and Its Modern Interpreters*, edited by R. A. Kraft and G. W. E. Nickelsburg, 81–98. Atlanta: Scholars, 1986.

Qimron, Elisha. *The Temple Scroll: A Critical Edition with Extensive Reconstructions*. JDS. Beer Sheva: Ben-Gurion Univ. of the Negev, 1996.

Rabin, Chaim. "Alexander Jannaeus and the Pharisees." *JJS* 7 (1956): 3–11.

Rahmani, L. Y. "Jason's Tomb." *IEJ* 17 (1967): 61–100.

————. "Silver Coins of the Fourth Century B.C. from Tel Gamma." *IEJ* 21 (1971): 158–60.

Rainey, Anson F. "The Satrapy 'Beyond the River.'" *AJBA* 1 (1969): 51–78.

Rajak, Tessa. *Josephus: The Historian and His Society*. Philadelphia: Fortress Press, 1984.

Rappaport, Uriel. "The Coins of Judea at the End of the Persian Rule and the Beginning of the Hellenistic Period." In *Jerusalem in the Second Temple Period: Abraham Schalit Memorial Volume*, edited by O. Oppenheimer, U. Rappaport, and M. Stern, 7–21. Jerusalem: Yitzhak ben-Zvi, Ministry of Defence, 1980 (Hebrew).

————. "The History of the Hasmonean State—From Jonathan to Mattathias Antigonus." In *The Hasmonean Period*, edited by D. Amit and H. Eshel, 61–76. Sideret 'Idan 19. Jerusalem: Yitzhak ben-Zvi, 1995 (Hebrew).

————. "The Jewish Leadership in Jerusalem in the First Part of the Great Revolt (66–68 CE)." In *The Ancient Period,* edited by I. Gafni, 75–83. Vol. 1 of *The Congregation of Israel: Jewish Independent Rule in Its Generations.* Jerusalem: Zalman Shazar Center for Jewish History, 2001 (Hebrew).

Redditt, Paul L. "Zerubbabel, Joshua, and the Night Visions of Zechariah." *CBQ* 54 (1992): 249–59.

Reich, Ronnie. "Ossuary Inscriptions from the 'Caiaphas' Tomb." *'Atiqot* 21 (1992): 72–77.

Richardson, Peter. *Herod: King of the Jews and Friend of the Romans.* SPNT. Columbia: Univ. of South Carolina, 1996.

Ritmeyer, Leen and Kathleen Ritmeyer. "Akeldama: Potter's Field or High Priest's Tomb?" *BAR* 20.6 (1994): 22–35.

Rivkin, Ellis. *A Hidden Revolution: The Pharisees' Search for the Kingdom of God Within.* Nashville: Abingdon, 1978.

Ronen, Yigal. "The Weight Standards of the Judean Coinage in the Late Persian and Early Ptolemaic Period." *NEA* 61 (1998): 122–26.

Rooke, Deborah W. "Kingship as Priesthood: The Relationship between the High Priesthood and the Monarchy." In *King and Messiah in Israel and the Ancient Near East: Proceedings of the Oxford Old Testament Seminar,* edited by J. Day, 187–208. JSOTSup 70. Sheffield: Sheffield Academic Press, 1998.

————. *Zadok's Heirs: The Role and Development of the High Priesthood in Ancient Israel.* OTM. Oxford: Oxford Univ. Press, 2000.

Rowley, H. H. "Nehemiah's Mission and its Background." *BJRL* 37 (1954–55): 528–61. Reprinted in idem, *Men of God: Studies in Old Testament History and Prophecy,* 211–45. London: Nelson, 1963.

————. "The Samaritan Schism in Legend and History." In *Israel's Prophetic Heritage: Essays in Honor of James Muilenburg,* edited by B. Anderson and W. Harrelson, 208–22. New York: Harper & Brothers, 1962.

————. "Sanballat and the Samaritan Temple." In idem, *Men of God: Studies in Old Testament History and Prophecy,* 246–76. London: Nelson, 1963. Originally published in *BJRL* 38 (1955–56): 166–98.

Rubenstein, Jeffrey L. *The History of Sukkot in the Second Temple and Rabbinic Periods.* BJS 302. Atlanta: Scholars, 1995.

————. "The Sadducees and the Water Libation." *JQR* 84 (1994): 417–44.

Rudolph, Wilhelm. *Chronikbücher.* HAT 21. Tübingen: Mohr/Siebeck, 1955.

————. *Esra und Nehemia samt 3. Esra.* HAT 20. Tübingen: Mohr/Siebeck, 1949.

Sacchi, Paolo. *The History of the Second Temple Period.* JSOTSup 285. Sheffield: Sheffield Academic, 2000.

Saldarini, Anthony J. *Pharisees, Scribes, and Sadducees in Palestinian Society: A Sociological Approach.* Wilmington, Del.: Glazier, 1988. Reissued BRS, Grand Rapids: Eerdmans, 2001.

———. "Sanhedrin." In *ABD* 5.975–80.

Sanders, E. P. *Judaism: Practice and Belief 63 BCE–66 CE.* Philadelphia: Trinity, 1992.

Sauer, Georg. *Jesus Sirach/Ben Sira.* ATD Apokryphen 1. Göttingen: Vandenhoeck & Ruprecht, 2000.

Schalit, Abraham. *King Herod: Portrait of a Ruler.* Jerusalem: Bialik, 1962 (Hebrew) = *König Herodes: Der Mann und sein Werk.* 2d ed. Berlin: de Gruyter, 2001.

Schechter, S., and C. Taylor. *The Wisdom of Ben Sira.* Cambridge: Cambridge Univ. Press, 1899.

Schmitt, Hatto H., ed. *Die Staatsverträge des Altertums.* Vol. 3: *Die Verträge der griechisch-römischen Welt von 338 bis 200 v. Chr.* Munich: Beck, 1969.

Schrenk, Gottlob. "ἱερός, etc." *TDNT* 3.221–83.

Schüller, S. "Some Problems Connected with the Supposed Common Ancestry of Jews and Spartans and Their Relations during the Last Three Centuries B.C." *JSS* 1 (1956): 257–68.

Schunck, Klaus-Dietrich. "'Hoherpriester und Politiker? Die Stellung der Hohenpriester von Jaddua bis Jonatan zur jüdischen Gemeinde und zum hellenistischen Staat." *VT* 44 (1994): 498–512.

Schürer, Emil. *The History of the Jewish People in the Age of Jesus Christ 175 B.C.—A.D. 135.* 3 vols. Revised and edited by G. Vermes and F. Millar with M. Black. Edinburgh: T. & T. Clark, 1973–87.

Schwartz, Daniel R. *Agrippa I: The Last King of Judaea.* TSAJ 23. Tübingen: Mohr/Siebeck, 1990.

———. "Ishmael ben Phiabi and the Chronology of Provincia Judaea." In idem, *Studies in the Jewish Background of Christianity,* 218–42. WUNT 60. Tübingen: Mohr/Siebeck, 1992. First published as "Ishmael ben Phiabi and the Chronology of the Province Judaea." *Tarbiz* 52 (1983): 177–200 (Hebrew).

———. "Joseph ben Illem and the Date of Herod's Death." In idem, *Studies in the Jewish Background of Christianity,* 157–66. Parallel publication in *Jews and Judaism in the Second Temple, Mishna and Talmud Period. Essays in Honor of Shmuel Safrai.* Edited by A. Oppenheimer, I. Gafni, and M. Stern. Jerusalem: Yitzhak ben-Zvi, 1993 (Hebrew).

———. "Josephus and Nicolaus on the Pharisees." *JSJ* 14 (1983): 157–71.

———. "Josephus on Hyrcanus II." In *Josephus and the History of the Greco-Roman Period: Essays in Memory of Morton Smith,* edited by F. Parente and J. Sievers, 210–32. StPB 41. Leiden: Brill, 1994.

————. "Josephus' Tobiads: Back to the Second Century?" In *Jews in a Graeco-Roman World*. Edited by M. Goodman, 47–61. Oxford: Clarendon, 1998.

————. "KATA TOYTON TON KAIPON: Josephus' Source on Agrippa II." *JQR* 72 (1982): 241–68.

————. "On Some Papyri and Josephus' Sources and Chronology for the Persian Period." *JSJ* 21 (1991): 175–99.

————. "Pontius Pilate's Appointment to Office and the Chronology of Josephus' *Antiquities*, Books 18–20." In idem, *Studies in the Jewish Background of Christianity*, 182–201. WUNT 60. Tübingen: Mohr/Siebeck, 1992. First published in Hebrew in *Zion* 48 (1982/83): 325–45.

————. "Pontius Pilate's Suspension from Office: Chronology and Sources." In idem, *Studies in the Jewish Background of Christianity*, 202–17. First published in *Tarbiz* 51 (1981–82): 383–98 (Hebrew).

Schwartz, Seth. "The Hellenization of Jerusalem and Shechem." In *Jews in a Graeco-Roman World*, edited by M. Goodman, 37–46. Oxford: Clarendon, 1998.

————. *Imperialism and Jewish Society, 200 B.C.E. to 640 C.E.* JCMAMW. Princeton: Princeton Univ. Press, 2001.

————. *Josephus and Judaean Politics*. CSCT 18. Leiden: Brill, 1990.

Scolnic, Benjamin E. *Chronology and Papponymy: A List of the Judean High Priests of the Persian Period*. SFSHJ 206. Atlanta: Scholars, 1999.

Segal, M. S. *The Complete Book of Ben Sira*. 2d ed. Jerusalem: Bialik, 1972 (Hebrew).

Sellers, Ovid R. *The Citadel of Beth Zur*. Philadelphia: Westminster, 1933.

Sherk, Robert K. *Roman Documents from the Greek East*: Senatus Consulta *and* Epistulae *to the Age of Augustus*. Baltimore: Johns Hopkins, 1969.

Sherman, Charles L. *Diodorus of Sicily*. Vol. 7. LCL. Cambridge: Harvard Univ. Press, 1952.

Shutt, R. J. H. "Letter of Aristeas." *OTP* 2.7–34.

Sievers, Joseph. *The Hasmoneans and Their Supporters: From Mattathias to the Death of John Hyrcanus I*. SFSHJ 6. Atlanta: Scholars, 1990.

————. "The Role of Women in the Hasmonean Dynasty." In *Josephus, the Bible, and History*. Edited by L. H. Feldman and G. Hata, 132–46. Leiden: Brill, 1989.

Skehan, Patrick W., and Alexander Di Lella. *The Wisdom of Ben Sira*. AB 39. Garden City, N.Y.: Doubleday, 1987.

Smallwood, E. Mary. "The Date of the Dismissal of Pontius Pilate from Judaea." *JJS* 5 (1954): 12–21.

————. "High Priests and Politics in Roman Palestine." *JTS* 13 (1962): 14–34.

————. *The Jews under Roman Rule: From Pompey to Diocletian: A Study in Political Relations*. SJLA 20. Reissued, Boston: Brill, 2001.

Smith, Morton. "Palestinian Judaism in the First Century." In *Israel: Its Role in Civilization*, edited by M. Davis, 67–81. New York: Jewish Theological Seminary of America, 1956.

———. *Palestinian Parties and Politics That Shaped the Old Testament*. Lectures on the History of Religions 9. New York: Columbia Univ. Press, 1971.

Smith, S. "Foundations: Ezra iv, 12; v, 16; vi, 3." In *Essays in Honour of the Very Rev. Dr. J. H. Hertz*, edited by I. Epstein, E. Levine, and C. Roth, 385–96. London: Goldston, 1942.

Smith, Walter Franklin. "A Study of the Zadokite High Priesthood within the Graeco-Roman Age: From Simeon the Just to the High Priests Appointed by Herod the Great." Ph.D. diss., Harvard Univ., 1961.

Smitten, W. T. in der. "Historische Probleme zum Kyrosedikt und zum jerusalemer Tempelbau von 515." *Persica* 6 (1974): 167–78.

Spaer, A. "Jaddua the High Priest?" *Israel Numismatic Journal* 9 (1986–87): 1–3.

Steck, Odil Hannes. "Das Buch Baruch." In *Das Buch Baruch, Der Brief des Jeremia. Zusätze zu Ester und Daniel*, edited by O. H. Steck, R. G. Kratz, and I. Kottsieper, 11–68. ATD Apokryphen 5. Göttingen: Vandenhoeck & Ruprecht, 1998.

Stegemann, Hartmut. *Die Entstehung der Qumrangemeinde*. Bonn: privately printed, 1971.

———. *The Library of Qumran: On the Essenes, Qumran, John the Baptist, and Jesus*. Grand Rapids: Eerdmans, 1998.

Sterling, Gregory L. *Historiography and Self-Definition: Josephos, Luke-Acts, and Apologetic Historiography*. NovTSup 64. Leiden: Brill, 1991.

Stern, Ephraim. *Material Culture of the Land of the Bible in the Persian Period 538–332 B.C.* Warminster: Aris & Phillips, 1982.

———. "The Persian Empire and the Political and Social History of Palestine in the Persian Period." In *Introduction; The Persian Period*, edited by W. D. Davies and L. Finkelstein, 70–87. *CHJ* 1. Cambridge: Cambridge Univ. Press, 1984.

Stern, Menahem. "Aspects of Jewish Society: The Priesthood and Other Classes." In *The Jewish People in the First Century*, edited by S. Safrai and M. Stern, 561–630. CRINT I/1. Philadelphia: Fortress Press, 1974.

———. "The Days of Jonathan and Demetrius II." In *Hasmonaean Judaea in the Hellenistic World*, 47–70.

———. "The Death of Onias III." *Zion* 25 (1959–60): 1–16 (Hebrew).

———. *The Documents on the History of the Hasmonaean Revolt with a Commentary and Introductions*. Tel Aviv: Hakkibbutz Hameuchad, 1965 (Hebrew). Reprinted 1972.

————. *Greek and Latin Authors on Jews and Judaism*. 3 vols. Jerusalem: Israel Academy of Sciences and Humanities, 1974–84.

————. "Notes on the Story of Joseph, Son of Tobiah (*Ant.* 12.154ff.)." *Tarbiz* 32 (1962): 35–47 (Hebrew).

————. "The Reign of Herod and the Herodian Dynasty." In *The Jewish People in the First Century*, 216–307.

————. "The Relations between Judea and Rome during the Reign of John Hyrcanus." *Zion* 26 (1961): 1–22 (Hebrew).

————. "Relations between Sparta and the Jews in the Hellenistic Period." In *Hasmonaean Judaea in the Hellenistic World: Chapters in Political History*, edited by D. R. Schwartz, 63–70. Jerusalem: Zalman Shazar Center for Jewish History, 1995 (Hebrew).

————. "The Seleucid Kings, 104–83 BCE." In *Hasmonaean Judaea in the Hellenistic World*, 108–17.

————. "Simon: An Independent Judaea." In *Hasmonaean Judaea in the Hellenistic World*, 71–87.

————. "Social and Political Realignments in Herodian Judaea." *The Jerusalem Cathedra* 2 (1982): 40–62.

Stokholm, N. "Zur Überlieferung von Heliodor, Katurnaḫḫunte und anderen missglückten Tempelräubern." *ST* 22 (1968): 1–28.

Strack, H. L., and G. Stemberger. *Introduction to the Talmud and Midrash*. 2d ed. Translated and edited by Marcus Bockmuehl. Minneapolis: Fortress Press, 1996.

Strathmann, Hermann, with R. Meyer. "λαός." In *TDNT* 4.29–57.

————. "λειτουργέω." In *TDNT* 4.215–31.

Strugnell, John. "The Historical Background to 4Q468g [= 4Qhistorical B]." *RevQ* 73 (1999): 137–38.

Sullivan, Richard D. *Near Eastern Royalty and Rome, 100–30 BC*. Phoenix Supplementary Volume 24. Toronto: Univ. of Toronto Press, 1990.

Tadmor, Hayim. "כרונולוגיה." 3.245–309 of *Encyclopaedia Miqraʾit*. Jerusalem: Bialik, 1971 (Hebrew).

Talshir, Zipora. *1 Esdras: From Origin to Translation*. SBLSCS 47. Atlanta: SBL, 1999.

Taylor, J. "A Second Temple in Egypt: The Evidence for the Zadokite Temple of Onias." *JSJ* 29 (1998): 297–310.

Tcherikover, Victor. *Hellenistic Civilization and the Jews*. New York: Atheneum, 1970.

————. "Palestine under the Ptolemies (A Contribution to the Study of the Zenon Papyri)." *Mizraim* 4-5 (1937): 9–90.

————. "War 1.1, 1 as a Historical Source." *Madaʿe-Hay-yahadut* 1 (1926): 179–86 (Hebrew).

Tcherikover, Victor, and Alexander Fuks. *Corpus Papyrorum Judaicarum*. 3 vols. Cambridge: Harvard Univ. Press, 1957–63.

Tedesche, Sidney, trans. *The Second Book of Maccabees*. Edited by S. Zeitlin. Jewish Apocryphal Literature. New York: Harper and Brothers, 1954.

Thackeray, H. St. J., trans. *Josephus*. Vols. 1–5: *The Life, Against Apion, The Jewish War, Jewish Antiquities Books 1–8*. LCL. Cambridge: Harvard Univ. Press, 1926–34.

———. *Josephus: The Man and the Historian*. The Hilda Stich Stroock Lectures. New York: Jewish Institute of Religion, 1929.

Thoma, Clemens. "The High Priesthood in the Judgment of Josephus." In *Josephus, the Bible, and History*, edited by L. H. Feldman and G. Hata, 196–215. Leiden: Brill, 1989.

———. "John Hyrcanus I as Seen by Josephus and Other Early Jewish Sources." In *Josephus and the History of the Greco-Roman Period: Essays in Memory of Morton Smith*, edited by F. Parente and J. Sievers, 127–40. StPB 41. Leiden: Brill, 1994.

Thomas, D. W. "A Note on *mḥlṣwt* in Zechariah 3:4." *JTS* 33 (1931–32): 279–80.

Throntveit, M.A. "Linguistic Analysis and the Question of Authorship in Chronicles, Ezra and Nehemiah." *VT* 32 (1982): 201–16.

Tiller, Patrick A. *A Commentary on the Animal Apocalypse of* I Enoch. SBLEJL 4. Atlanta: Scholars, 1993.

Tollington, Janet E. *Tradition and Innovation in Haggai and Zechariah 1–8*. JSOTSup 150. Sheffield: JSOT Press, 1993.

Torrey, C. C. *Ezra Studies*. Reprinted, New York: Ktav, 1970; originally published in 1910.

Tov, Emanuel. *Textual Criticism of the Hebrew Bible*. 2d rev. ed. Minneapolis: Fortress Press, 2001.

Tropper, D. "The Internal Administration of the Second Temple at Jerusalem." Ph.D. diss., Yeshiva Univ., New York, 1970.

Tuland, C. G. "ᵓUŠŠAYĀᵓ and ᵓUŠŠARNAᵓ: A Clarification of Terms, Date, and Text." *JNES* 17 (1958): 269–75.

———. "Josephus, *Antiquities*, Book XI: Correction or Confirmation of Biblical Post-Exilic Records?" *AUSS* 4 (1966): 176–92.

Uffenheimer, Benjamin. *The Visions of Zechariah: From Prophecy to Apocalyptic*. Jerusalem: Kiryat Sepher, 1961 (Hebrew).

VanderKam, James C. "Ezra-Nehemiah or Ezra and Nehemiah?" In *Priests, Prophets, and Scribes: Essays on the Formation and Heritage of Second Temple Judaism in Honour of Joseph Blenkinsopp*, edited by E. C. Ulrich, J. Wright, R. Carroll, and P. R. Davies, 55–75. JSOTSup 149. Sheffield:

Sheffield Academic, 1992. Reprinted in VanderKam, *From Revelation to Canon,* 2000.

———. *From Revelation to Canon: Studies in the Hebrew Bible and the Second Temple Literature.* JSJSup 62. Leiden: Brill, 2000.

———. "Jewish High Priests of the Persian Period: Is the List Complete?" In *Priesthood and Cult in Ancient Israel,* edited by G. A. Anderson and S. M. Olyan, 67–91. JSOTSup 125. Sheffield: Sheffield Academic, 1991. Reprinted in VanderKam, *From Revelation to Canon,* 2000.

———. "Joshua the High Priest and the Interpretation of Zechariah 3." *CBQ* 53 (1991): 553–70. Reprinted in VanderKam, *From Revelation to Canon,* 2000.

———. "People and High Priesthood in Early Maccabean Times." In *The Hebrew Bible and Its Interpreters,* edited by W. H. Propp, B. Halpern, and D. N. Freedman, 205–25. BJS 1. Winona Lake, Ind.: Eisenbrauns, 1990. Reprinted in VanderKam, *From Revelation to Canon,* 2000.

———. "Pesher Nahum and Josephus." In *When Judaism and Christianity Began: Essays in Memory of Anthony J. Saldarini,* edited by A. Avery-Peck, D. Harrington, and J. Neusner, 1. 299–311. Boston: Brill, 2004.

———. "Simon the Just: Simon I or Simon II?" In *Pomegranates and Golden Bells: Studies in Biblical, Jewish, and Near Eastern Ritual, Law, and Literature in Honor of Jacob Milgrom,* edited by D. Wright, D. N. Freedman, and A. Hurvitz, 303–18. Winona Lake, Ind.: Eisenbrauns, 1995.

———. "Those Who Look for Smooth Things, Pharisees, and Oral Law." In *Emanuel: Studies in Hebrew Bible, Septuagint, and Dead Sea Scrolls in Honor of Emanuel Tov,* edited by R. Kraft, S. Paul, L. Schiffman, and W. Fields, 465–77. VTSup 94. Leiden: Brill, 2003.

Vattioni, Francesco. *Ecclesiastico: Testo ebraico con apparato critico e versioni greca, latina e siriaca.* Pubblicazioni del Seminario de semitistica, Testi 1. Naples: Instituto orientale di Napoli, 1968.

Vaux, Roland de. "Les décrets de Cyrus et de Darius sur la reconstruction du Temple." *RB* 46 (1937): 29–57.

Vermes, Geza. *The Complete Dead Sea Scrolls in English.* New York: Penguin, 1997.

———. *Les manuscrits du désert de Juda.* Paris-Tournai: Desclée, 1953; 2d edition, 1954.

Wachholder, Ben Zion. "The Calendar of Sabbatical Cycles during the Second Temple and the Early Rabbinic Period." *HUCA* 44 (1973): 153–96. Reprinted in idem, *Essays on Jewish Chronology and Chronography.* New York: Ktav, 1976.

Walbank, F. W. *The Hellenistic World*. Rev. ed. Cambridge: Harvard Univ. Press, 1981.

Walton, Francis R. *Diodorus of Sicily*. Vols. 11–12. LCL. Cambridge: Harvard Univ. Press, 1957, 1967.

———. "The Messenger of God in Hecataeus of Abdera." *HTR* 48 (1955): 255–57.

Ward, James M. "Eliashib." In *IDB* 2.87.

Wellhausen, Julius. *Israelitische und jüdische Geschichte*. 2d ed. Berlin: Reimer, 1895.

Werner, Crossman. *Johann Hyrkan: Ein Beitrag zur Geschichte Judäas im zweiten vorchristlichen Jahrhundert*. Wernigerode: Angersteins, 1877.

Widengren, Geo. "The Persian Period." In *Israelite and Judaean History*, edited by John H. Hayes and J. Maxwell Miller, 489–538. OTL. Philadelphia: Westminster, 1977.

Williams, D. "*3 Maccabees*: A Defense of Diaspora Judaism?" *JSP* 13 (1995): 17–29.

Williamson, H. G. M. *1 and 2 Chronicles*. NCB. Grand Rapids: Eerdmans, 1982.

———. "The Composition of Ezra i–vi." *JTS* 28 (1977): 48–67.

———. *Ezra, Nehemiah*. WBC 16. Waco, Tex.: Word, 1985.

———. "The Governors of Judah under the Persians." *TynBul* 39 (1988): 59–82.

———. "The Historical Value of Josephus' *Jewish Antiquities* XI.297–301." *JTS* 28 (1977): 48–67.

———. *Israel in the Books of Chronicles*. SOTSMS. Cambridge: Cambridge Univ., 1977.

Willrich, Hugo. *Juden und Griechen vor der makkabäischen Erhebung*. Göttingen: Vandenhoeck & Ruprecht, 1895.

Wirgin, Wolf. "Judah Maccabee's Embassy to Rome and the Jewish-Roman Treaty." *PEQ* 101 (1969): 15–20.

Wise, Michael. *A Critical Study of the Temple Scroll from Qumran Cave 11*. SAOC 49. Chicago: Univ. of Chicago, 1990.

———. "The Life and Times of Ananias Bar Nedebaeus and His Family." In idem, *Thunder in Gemini and Other Essays on the History, Language, and Literature of Second Temple Palestine*, 51–102. JSPSup 15. Sheffield: Sheffield Academic, 1994.

———. "The Teacher of Righteousness and the High Priest of the Intersacerdotium: Two Approaches." *RevQ* 14 (1990): 587–614.

Woude, A. S. van der. "Wicked Priest or Wicked Priests? Reflections on the Identification of the Wicked Priest in the Habakkuk Commentary." *JJS* 33 (1982): 349–59.

Wright, G. Ernest. *Shechem: Biography of a Biblical City*. New York: McGraw-Hill, 1965.

Wright, J. W. "Eliashib." In *ABD* 2.460–61.

Wright, R. B. "Psalms of Solomon." In *OTP* 2.639–70.

Yadin, Yigael, "Pesher Nahum (4Q pNahum) Reconsidered." *IEJ* 21 (1971): 1–12.

———. *The Temple Scroll*. 3 vols. with supplement. Jerusalem: IES, the Institute of Archaeology of the Hebrew Univ. of Jerusalem, and the Shrine of the Book, 1983.

Yadin, Yigael, and Joseph Naveh. *The Aramaic and Hebrew Ostraca and Jar Inscriptions*. Masada I: The Yigael Yadin Excavations 1963–1965: Final Reports. Jerusalem: IES, The Hebrew Univ. of Jerusalem, 1989.

Zeitlin, Solomon. "שמעון הצדיק וכנסת הגדולה." *Ner maʿaravi* 2 (1924): 137–42.

———, ed. *The Second Book of Maccabees*. Translated by S. Tedesche. Jewish Apocryphal Literature. New York: Harper & Brothers, 1954.

Zer-Kavod, M. "Studies in the Book of Zechariah, 3." In *Publications of the IES 2: Biram Volume*, edited by H. Gevaryahu, B. Z. Luria, and J. Mahlman, 117–21. Jerusalem: Kiryat Sefer, 1956 (Hebrew).

Zias, Joe. "Human Skeletal Remains from the 'Caiaphas' Tomb." *ʿAtiqot* 21 (1992): 78–80.

Index of Ancient People

Aaron, 26, 27n87, 33–34, 45–46, 52, 84, 149–50, 154, 228, 266, 296, 302, 337, 369n346, 427n90

Abiathar, 265

Abraham, 125–26, 130, 134–36

Abtalion, 145

Acrotatus, 133

Agrippa I, 434n104, 435, 437, 439–43, 447, 448, 452, 470n199, 478

Agrippa II, 443n126, 452, 456, 460, 463, 465, 466, 470–77, 482–85

Albinus, 458, 459, 476, 482, 483

Alcimus, 48, 145, 152, 216, 226–45, 251–52, 256n51, 258, 279

Alexander Son of Aristobulus II, 347, 348–50, 362, 365, 386

Alexander the Great, 9, 43, 49, 61, 64–81, 83–84, 86, 88, 93, 96n114, 97–98, 113, 115, 117–18, 123, 128, 134, 139–40, 145–46, 148–49, 151–52, 160, 427

Alexander Balas, 244, 247, 252–56, 258–62, 266, 270

Alexander Jannaeus, 145, 267n81, 299–304, 312n199, 314–15, 318–37, 341n261, 360n322, 375, 394, 399, 401, 403n20, 417, 485

Alexander Zebinas, 292n140, 294–95

Alexandra, 371–72, 374–75, 378, 394, 398–404

Alexandra (see Salome Alexandra)

Ananel, 394–400, 402, 405–406, 408, 451, 489n232

Anani, 56

Ananias, 438n115, 472, 473, 475

Ananias Son of Nedebaeus, 417, 439n116, 453n157, 455–63, 465, 471, 482–83

Ananus, 418, 428, 438, 447, 455n162, 459n173

Ananus Son of Ananus, 422, 430n94, 476–82, 484

Ananus Son of Seth (see Ananus), 420–24

Andromachus, 78

Andronicus, 196, 204–206, 208, 211

Annas (see Ananus)

Antigonus (Mattityah), 296, 307, 312, 315–17, 348, 349n288, 353–54, 356n306, 365, 367–69, 374, 378n363, 385–94, 398, 404n22, 408n34

Antigonus Gonatas, 132–34, 163

Antiochus (prince), 206

Antiochus I, 164

Antiochus III (the Great), 49, 113, 128–29, 139, 142, 144–46, 149–51, 153, 169, 173–76, 183, 185–89, 200, 202

Antiochus IV (Epiphanes) , 113, 146, 148, 173–74, 182, 188–89, 192, 197–216, 218–24, 226–27, 230, 232, 252, 273, 288, 290n134, 302, 326, 340, 470n199

Antiochus V (Eupator), 152, 223–27, 229, 232–33, 236–37, 243, 253, 263n69, 288n130

Antiochus VI, 262–63, 271–72

Antiochus VII (Sidetes), 283, 285–86, 288–93, 333

Antiochus VIII (Grypus), 292n140, 295–96, 323–24, 326

Antiochus IX (Cyzicenus), 294–96

Antipater, 340–43, 347–54, 356–59, 361–65, 368n343, 373, 385–86, 397n9, 408–409, 414

Antony (see Mark Antony)

Apollonius (of Tarsus?), 193–195

Apollonius (Mysian?), 212

Archelaus, 414–16, 418–20

Archidamus, 131, 135

Index of Ancient Sources

27:9-10	168	5–7	5
31:21-24	121	5:1-12	13
31:48-54	46	7:49	36
		8:33-34	184
Deuteronomy		8:48-50	184
14:22-23	310n194	10:15	109
14:22-27	465	22:19-23	29
17:8-9	427		
17:9-11	28	**2 Kings**	
21:5	28	12:1-3	23
25:5-10	416	12:10 LXX	153
26:12-13	310n194	12:11 Eng	153
27:9-10	121	20:20	154
28:56	486	22–23	48n10
31:9-13	121	22:4	153
33:10	121	22:8	153
		23:4	153
Joshua		24:8	106
6:3-5	280	24:13	5
6:7	280	25:7	7
6:8	280	25:14-15	5
6:10	280	25:18	18, 38
6:20	280	25:21	38
8:1	280		
8:5	280	**Isaiah**	
8:10-11	280	3:18-23	27
8:14	280	4:2	31
8:16	280	6	29
8:20	280	8:18	30
10:21	280	34:10	17
10:33	280	44:28	1
20:6 (A; LXX)	153	62:3	27
Judges		**Jeremiah**	
14:9	26n81	20:1	191n220
		21:11-12	28
1 Samuel		22:1-4	28
8:20	252	23:5-6	31, 39n149
30:21	280	23:18	29
		26:9	17
2 Samuel		28:3	5
1:4	280	32	397
12:30	39	33	39-41
15:1-4	28	33:10	17
		33:12	17
1 Kings		33:14-15	31
3	74n66	40:6 LXX	40
3:16-28	28	52:13	18